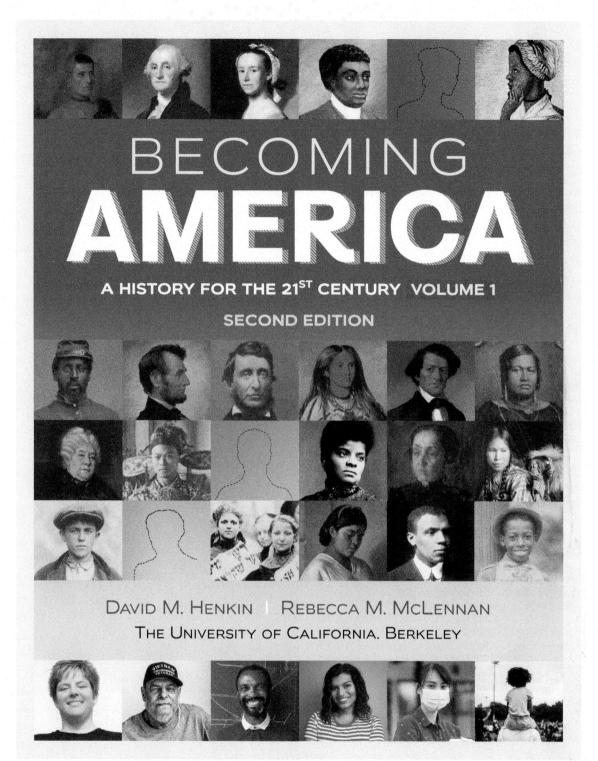

BECOMING AMERICA

A HISTORY FOR THE 21ST CENTURY   VOLUME 1

SECOND EDITION

DAVID M. HENKIN | REBECCA M. McLENNAN

THE UNIVERSITY OF CALIFORNIA. BERKELEY

Mc
Graw
Hill

BECOMING AMERICA: A HISTORY FOR THE 21ST CENTURY, SECOND EDITION

Published by McGraw Hill LLC, 1325 Avenue of the Americas, New York, NY 10019. Copyright ©2022 by McGraw Hill LLC. All rights reserved. Printed in the United States of America. Previous edition ©2015. No part of this publication may be reproduced or distributed in any form or by any means, or stored in a database or retrieval system, without the prior written consent of McGraw Hill LLC, including, but not limited to, in any network or other electronic storage or transmission, or broadcast for distance learning.

Some ancillaries, including electronic and print components, may not be available to customers outside the United States.

This book is printed on acid-free paper.

2 3 4 5 6 7 8 9 LKV 26 25 24 23 22

ISBN 978-1-260-06979-2 (bound edition)   ISBN 978-1-264-08818-8 (volume 1 bound edition)   ISBN 978-1-264-08822-5 (volume 2 bound edition)
MHID 1-260-06979-6 (bound edition)   MHID 1-264-08818-3 (volume 1 bound edition)   MHID 1-264-08822-1 (volume 2 bound edition)
ISBN 978-1-264-08827-0 (loose-leaf edition) ISBN 978-1-264-08820-1 (volume 1 loose-leaf edition) ISBN 978-1-264-08823-2 (volume 2 loose-leaf edition)
MHID 1-264-08827-2 (loose-leaf edition)   MHID 1-264-08820-5 (volume 1 loose-leaf edition)   MHID 1-264-08823-X (volume 2 loose-leaf edition)

Senior Portfolio Manager: *Jason Seitz*
Senior Product Developer: *Lauren A. Finn*
Marketing Manager: *Michael Gedatus*
Content Project Managers: *Sandy Wille; Vanessa McClune*
Senior Buyer: *Sandy Ludovissy*
Lead Designer: *David W. Hash*
Content Licensing Specialist: *Sarah Flynn*
Cover Images: *see page viii*
Compositor: *Aptara®, Inc*

All credits appearing on page or at the end of the book are considered to be an extension of the copyright page.

Library of Congress Cataloging-in-Publication Data

Names: Henkin, David M., author. | McLennan, Rebecca M., 1967- author.
Title: Becoming America: a history for the 21st century / David M. Henkin,
    Rebecca M. McLennan.
Description: Second edition. | New York, NY : McGraw Hill Education, [2022]
    | Includes bibliographical references and index.
Identifiers: LCCN 2021005126 (print) | LCCN 2021005127 (ebook) | ISBN
    9781264088188 (v. 1 ; hardcover) | ISBN 9781264088201 (v. 1 ; spiral
    bound) | ISBN 9781264088225 (v. 2 ; hardcover) | ISBN 9781264088232
    (v. 2 ; spiral bound) | ISBN 9781260069792 (hardcover) | ISBN 9781264088270
    (spiral bound) | ISBN 9781264088249 (ebook) | ISBN 9781264088256
    (ebook other) | ISBN 9781264088195 (v. 1 ; ebook)
Subjects: LCSH: United States—History—Textbooks.
Classification: LCC E178.1 .H485 2022 (print) | LCC E178.1 (ebook) | DDC
    973—dc23
LC record available at https://lccn.loc.gov/2021005126
LC ebook record available at https://lccn.loc.gov/2021005127

The Internet addresses listed in the text were accurate at the time of publication. The inclusion of a website does not indicate an endorsement by the authors or McGraw Hill LLC, and McGraw Hill LLC does not guarantee the accuracy of the information presented at these sites.

mheducation.com/highered

CONTENTS

1862–1883

Contents photos: *ch 1: Martha Smith/National Park Service; ch 2: North Wind Picture Archives/Alamy Stock Photo; ch 3: World History Archive/Alamy Stock Photo; ch 4: Everett Collection/Newscom; ch 5: Private Collection/The Bridgeman Art Library; ch 6: Private Collection/Picture Research Consultants & Archives; ch 7: Jon Helgason/Alamy Stock Photo; ch 8: Francis G. Mayer/Corbis/Getty Images; ch 9: Lebrecht Music & Arts/Alamy Stock Photo; ch 10: Library of Congress Rare Book and Special Collections Division [LC-USZ61-1448]; ch 11: Universal History Archive/Universal Images Group/Getty Images; ch 12: Heritage Images/Hulton Archive/Getty Images; ch 13: Free Library of Philadelphia/Bridgeman Images; ch 14: PAINTING/Alamy Stock Photo; ch 15: North Wind Picture Archives/Alamy Stock Photo; ch 16: Library of Congress Geography and Map Division*

Cover photos: *Pes-Ke-Le-Cha-Co, Chief of the Pawnees: The Metropolitan Museum of Art, New York, Gift of Gerald and Kathleen Peters, in celebration of the Museum's 150th Anniversary; George Washington: The Minneapolis Institute of Art, The William Hood Dunwoody Fund; Mrs. James Warren: John Singleton Copley/Art Reserve/Alamy Stock Photo; Benjamin Banneker: North Wind Picture Archives/Alamy Stock Photo; Phillis Wheatley: Lebrecht Music & Arts/Alamy Stock Photo; Unidentified African American soldier in Union cavalry uniform: Library of Congress Prints & Photographs Division [LC-DIG-ppmsca-37027]; Abraham Lincoln: National Portrait Gallery, Smithsonian Institution; Henry David Thoreau: Everett Historical/Shutterstock; Sha-kó-ka, a Mandan girl: Smithsonian American Art Museum; Frederick Douglass: National Portrait Gallery, Smithsonian Institution; Queen Kalama Hakaleleponi Kapakuhaili: Digital image courtesy of the Getty's Open Content Program; Elizabeth Cady Stanton: National Portrait Gallery, Smithsonian Institution; transfer from the National Museum of American History; Chinese actor: Digital image courtesy of the Getty's Open Content Program; Ida B. Wells: Alpha Historical/Alamy Stock Photo; mother of Henry O. Tanner: Smithsonian American Art Museum, Gift of Dr. Nicholas Zervas; Inuit woman with papoose on back: Library of Congress Prints and Photographs Division [LC-USZ62-101165]; James Donovan, Irish sweeper: Library of Congress, Prints & Photographs Division [LC-DIG-nclc-05054]; Two girls wearing "ABOLISH CH[ILD] SLAVERY!!" banners: Library of Congress, Prints and Photographs Division (LC-DIG-ppmsca-06591); Indian Woman with Marigold (Mujer indígena con cempasúchil): LACMA-Los Angeles County Museum of Art; John Baxter Taylor: The History Collection/Alamy Stock Photo; Roland, newsboy: Everett Historical/Shutterstock; Woman: Glow Images; U.S. Navy Vietnam War Veteran: Willowpix/Getty Images; Businessman: Klaus Vedfelt/Getty Images; Woman: Krakenimages.com/Shutterstock; Student: pang_oasis/Shutterstock; Man carrying a child on his shoulders: Red Marker/Shutterstock*

MAPS

Maps help students develop their understanding of how geography and history intersect. They also encourage students to think analytically about the relationships between people and natural resources, the relationships among different peoples, movements of people across borders, changing demographics and political associations, and other factors that impact historical actions. The second edition of *Becoming America: A History for the 21st Century* provides several ways to use primary source documents in your course.

MAPS SUPPORT GEOGRAPHICAL AND HISTORICAL THINKING

Maps in the text reinforce narrative discussions of borders, resources, trade routes, migrations, battles, elections, and more with visual presentations of the same material, buttressing student learning by providing complex information in multiple formats for different learning styles.

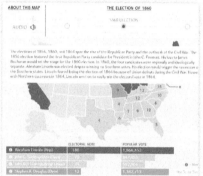

Maps in Context in Connect History provide opportunities for hands-on learning. For some interactive maps, students click on the boxes in the map legend to see changing boundaries, visualize migration routes, or analyze war battles and election results. With others, students manipulate a slider to help them better understand change over time. New interactive maps integrate advanced navigation features, including zoom, as well as audio and textual animation.

INTERPRETING THE SOURCES

FRAMEWORK FOR VISUAL ANALYSIS

WHERE IN THE ARCHIVES?

CHAPTER-BY-CHAPTER CHANGES

Chapter 1

- Updated language on the earliest migrations from Asia to align with recent archaeological evidence
- Integrated disparate material about Cahokia into the account of Mississippian civilization
- Streamlined the history of religious conflicts in western Europe to highlight their role in sparking exploration and colonization in the Americas
- Clarified the importance of Mali and West Africa polities in the period before the Atlantic slave trade
- Translated the value of the Potosi silver mine extractions into 2020 U.S. dollars
- Emphasized that contemporary concerns are rooted in the past by highlighting
  - that descendants of Beringia migrants became the indigenous population of the Western Hemisphere;
  - changing climate during the Warming Period and the Little Ice Age and their impacts on agriculture, diet, and social and political stability in pre-contact North America;
  - that Cahokian chunkey was both entertaining sport and an instrument of politics and diplomacy;
  - Europe's bubonic plague of 1347–1351 and its social impacts;
  - the model for expanding Christianity to distant lands provided by the Crusades;
  - the Columbian Exchange in North America (including the immigration of three hundred thousand Spaniards, the resulting mestizos, and the influx of two hundred thousand enslaved West Africans);
  - that influenza and smallpox devastated Tainos and Aztecs as much as did European military advantages;
  - the impact of new printing techniques on the circulation of Luther's *Ninety-five Theses*;
  - religious conflict of the Reformation and how it widened the northern/southern Europe divide; and
  - the migration of Europeans and Africans to North America in the sixteenth century and subsequent massive epidemics
- Updated bibliographic recommendations to include Toby Green's *A Fistful of Shells* (2019) on West Africa and early economic globalization, David Madsen's *Entering America* (2004) on the environmental history of Beringia, and Heather Martel's *Deadly Virtue* (2019) on French Protestants in Florida

Chapter 2

- Integrated the 1680 Pueblo Revolt into the main narrative of Spanish colonization in New Mexico
- Eliminated material on Dutch colonization that obscured the main comparisons to other colonial projects
- Condensed and simplified the account of theological disputes in New England
- Translated the value of the purchase of Manhattan Island into 2020 U.S. dollars
- Emphasized that contemporary concerns are rooted in the past by highlighting
  - theatrical performances staged by Oñate for political purposes—to encourage indigenous Pueblos to submit to Spanish rule;
  - religious conflict between Spanish Catholics and indigenous Pueblos in New Mexico;
  - disease outbreaks (of measles, whooping cough, and smallpox) brought by Europeans to the Iroquois of the Great Lakes;
  - conflict between centralized religious authority and proliferating sects and denominations;
  - the impact of climate differences between New England and Virginia on population growth, demographics, agriculture, labor, and social organization;
  - the migration of English Puritans to New England; and
  - disease outbreaks brought by Europeans to indigenous inhabitants in New England
- Updated bibliographic recommendations to include Jorge Cañizares-Esguerra's *Puritan Conquistadors* (2006) on colonizers' preoccupations with demonic forces and Sam White's *A Cold Welcome* (2017) on the challenges and implications of climate change for European colonization

Chapter 3

- Integrated the 1739 Stono Rebellion into the larger account of slavery in colonial Lowcountry
- Reassessed and modified language dehumanizing to those who lived under slavery
- Edited the study questions on the *Curse of Ham* to clarify the document's historical significance
- Added an image of Charleston to foreground the city's significance as an economic hub and a port of entry for enslaved people

- Compared the cost of an indentured servant's ocean voyage to the value of labor and translated that into 2020 U.S. dollars
- Emphasized that contemporary concerns are rooted in the past by highlighting
  - the relationship between religious differences (among Christians, Muslims, and others) and slavery;
  - the enslavement and forced migration of 12 million Africans across the Atlantic to British North America and the West Indies; and
  - the impact of tropical diseases in the colonies on enslaved Africans who lacked immunities
- Updated bibliographic recommendations to include Sharon Block's *Colonial Complexions* (2018) on runaway advertisements and racial difference, Jennifer L. Morgan's *Laboring Women* (2004) on the sexual exploitation of enslaved women, Gregory O'Malley's *Final Passages* (2014) on the trafficking of enslaved Africans among British colonies, and Lorena S. Walsh's *Motives of Honor, Pleasure, & Profit* (2010) on Chesapeake slaveholder strategies

Chapter 4
- Removed a description of elite homes in Chesapeake
- Radically reduced the discussion of cultural refinement and social hierarchy in the eighteenth century
- Focused the study questions on Benjamin Franklin's discussion of colonial demography to highlight his distinctive vocabulary of racial difference
- Condensed and simplified the account of political disputes in Restoration England to highlight their relevance for the colonial experience
- Eliminated a map of northwestern European sources of voluntary immigration to British America
- Translated the cost of cattle in eighteenth-century British American colonies into 2020 U.S. dollars
- Emphasized that contemporary concerns are rooted in the past by highlighting
  - the migration of English Quakers to the Delaware Valley;
  - New England's cold climate and colonists' life expectancies;
  - the migration of Scots-Irish to Carolina, Virginia, and the middle colonies;
  - the privileging of Protestants over Catholics in British imperial immigration policy;
  - taverns as places of entertainment and expression of political views and dissent;
  - the emphasis of colonial newspapers on news from abroad, which impacted trade, ship arrivals, commodity prices, and diplomacy; and
  - religious conflict between the Old Lights and the New Lights of the Great Awakening

- Updated bibliographic recommendations to include Michelle Morris's *Under Household Government* (2013) on family and sexuality in the Puritan colonies and Douglas Winiarski's *Darkness Falls on the Land of Light* (2017) on the enthusiasm for the Great Awakening in New England

Chapter 5
- Revised the chapter opening to compare the geographical perspectives of two prominent American women, one an Illini and the other a British colonist
- Deemphasized the British line of forts built along the Connecticut River
- Simplified and condensed the account of diplomatic relations between the British colonies and the Iroquois League
- Added an image of indigenous women wearing European clothing in Spanish California
- Cut a redundant map of colonial settlements in North America in 1700
- Narrowed and clarified the table of imperial wars in North America 1689–1748
- Deleted a map of the battle sites of Pontiac's Rebellion
- Focused the discussion of Anglicization in the colonies to emphasize the role of consumer goods in forging connections among dispersed colonists
- Translated Britain's 1763 national debt into 2020 U.S. dollars
- Emphasized that contemporary concerns are rooted in the past by highlighting
  - the religious motivations and character of political conflict between European colonial powers;
  - the development of new communications infrastructure in the British colonies;
  - the impacts of yellow fever, gastric illness, and other diseases on Britain's regular army in the Caribbean;
  - the migration of French Acadians to French Louisiana and the growth of a new, Cajun, culture; and
  - the use of communicable disease (smallpox) as a military weapon against indigenous people
- Updated bibliographic recommendations to include Susan Sleeper-Smith's *Indigenous Prosperity and American Conquest* (2018) on native women in the Ohio River valley and Sophie White's *Wild Frenchmen and Frenchified Indians* (2014) on culture and racial identity in colonial Louisiana

Chapter 6
- Condensed the discussion of the Boston Liberty Tree and illustrated the distinction between liberty trees and poles with an additional image
- Removed the discussion of the sack of St. Eustatius during the Revolutionary War

- Diminished the number and length of quotations from revolutionary pamphleteers
- Translated the value of the tea dumped into Boston Harbor in 1773 into 2020 U.S. dollars
- Emphasized that contemporary concerns are rooted in the past by highlighting
  - how tarring and feathering functioned as entertaining and political public-shaming ritual;
  - how information—and misinformation—about the start of war spread from one community to the next;
  - the use of print media and anonymous authorship to spread information and revolutionary ideas;
  - that pandemic (smallpox) during the Revolutionary War affected wartime slave rebellion;
  - the religious character of the colonists' political revolution;
  - the popularization of a political event through a dance craze ("General Burgoyne's Surrender"); and
  - the migration out of the colonies after the Revolutionary War of free Black and formerly enslaved people who had joined the British cause—and of those who continued to live in slavery at the hands of Loyalist slaveholders
- Updated bibliographic recommendations to include Joseph Adelman's *Revolutionary Networks* (2019) on the impact of printers on the independence movement and Kathleen DuVal's *Independence Lost* (2016), which narrates the Revolution from the perspective of the Gulf Coast

Chapter 7
- Simplified the explanation of written authority in the U.S. Constitution
- Focused the discussion of early U.S. literature and pared the information on copyright law
- Removed descriptions of Baltimore's post office buildings
- Translated the cost of 1792 newspaper postage into 2020 U.S. dollars
- Emphasized that contemporary concerns are rooted in the past by highlighting
  - the congressional resolution to have the Declaration of Independence printed for distribution to assemblies, conventions, militias, courthouses, churches, and public squares in every state;
  - the use of street theater to celebrate and build unity among the thirteen new free and independent states;
  - disputes over land and borders between the Iroquois League and the new United States;
  - religious disagreement among the framers at the Constitutional Convention;

- romantic storylines about virtue and corruption in popular literature that mimic or dramatize political concerns; and
- how subsidies to the U.S. Post Office guaranteed newspapers wide distribution and created a national broadcast medium
- Updated bibliographic recommendations to include Trish Loughran's *The Republic in Print* (2007), which challenges the idea that the new nation formed a single reading public; William Warner's *Protocols of Liberty* (2013) on the importance of media and communications to the revolutionary era; and Will Slauter's *Who Owns the News* (2019), which contextualizes copyright in the new republic within a broader story of property and information

Chapter 8
- Condensed coverage of yellow fever in 1793 Philadelphia
- Added coverage about the implications of the arrival of refugee slaveholders from Cuba to New Orleans after the abolition of the international slave trade
- Replaced an image of Detroit in 1811 with one more easily discernible
- Removed a lengthy account of the Yazoo lands controversy
- Compared the value of the Louisiana Purchase with 2020 U.S. dollars
- Emphasized that contemporary concerns are rooted in the past by highlighting
  - the movement after the Haitian Revolution of white slaveholding refugees and enslaved people into the United States;
  - Methodist preachers' recruitment of converts across race and class lines;
  - the epidemiology of the yellow fever epidemic in Philadelphia, the nation's capital;
  - the division of news into partisan, contradictory, and mutually unintelligible versions of current events after the Sedition Act;
  - the Haitian refugee crisis and its impact on the demography of 1790s Philadelphia and New Orleans a decade later; and
  - the prominence of anti-Muslim themes in U.S. popular culture during the Barbary conflict
- Updated bibliographic recommendations to include Susan E. Klepp's *Revolutionary Conceptions* (2009) on women's role in limiting family size, Amanda Porterfield's *Conceived in Doubt* (2012) on the efforts of religious institutions at containing skepticism, and Catherine E. Kelly's *Republic of Taste* (2016) on the contributions of the arts to politics and national identity

Chapter 9

- Reorganized coverage of the 1811–1812 New Madrid earthquakes and emphasized their ecological disruption
- Developed the connection between westward expansion and the Panic of 1819
- Edited language about the representation of native peoples
- Updated the account of Denmark Vesey's alleged slave rebellion to align with recent scholarship
- Simplified and condensed the account of the Missouri Compromise
- Compared Denmark Vesey's lottery winnings with 2020 U.S. dollars
- Emphasized that contemporary concerns are rooted in the past by highlighting
  - the religious dimension of the Pan-Indian revolt that helped trigger the War of 1812;
  - the migration of fugitives from slavery to live among Seminoles in Spanish Florida;
  - the complex time line by which news of the final events of the War of 1812 reached different Americans;
  - the competitive market of religious denominations and unofficial national religious establishment that emerged as an alternative to a government-sponsored religion;
  - the information network of Methodist circuit riders and classes;
  - Cherokee expulsion and resettlement in Oklahoma via the Trail of Tears; and
  - the role of dramatizing indigenous characters in the politics of entertainment during the Removal era
- Updated bibliographic recommendations to include Claudio Saunt's *Unworthy Republic* (2020) on the expulsion and dispossession of Native Americans in the 1830s and Conevery Bolton Valencius's *The Lost History of the New Madrid Earthquakes* (2013), which reconstructs and reinterprets the seismic events that shook most of the United States at the beginning of the war era

Chapter 10

- Reduced the coverage of Nauvoo, Illinois, and relocated it to the account of early Mormonism
- Eliminated a detailed discussion of volunteer fire companies and saloons in relation to party politics
- Condensed the discussion of European perceptions of American economic equality
- Compared textile factory pay in 1830 with 2020 U.S. dollars
- Emphasized that contemporary concerns are rooted in the past by highlighting
  - the influence of popular theater on the career of Congressman Davy Crockett;
  - the convergence of campaigning and entertainment in the form of rallies, demonstrations, parades, emotional appeals, and songs that spread mass democracy;
  - the relationship between ecological and economic change during the canal-building era;
  - the relationship between improved communications speed and improved transportation during market expansion and urbanization;
  - the movement of rural Northeasterners and immigrants into New York, resulting in a Manhattan population exceeding that of twenty of the thirty-three states;
  - theological controversies stirred up by the Second Great Awakening; and
  - religious conflicts that sparked the Mormon Exodus
- Updated bibliographic recommendations to include Vincent DiGirolamo's *Crying the News* (2019) on the rise of the American newsboy, Alexander Keyssar's *The Right to Vote* (2000) on suffrage extension, Jeffrey Sklansky's *Sovereign of the Market* (2017) on Jacksonian era banking, Andrew Robichaud's *Animal City* (2019) on animal life in nineteenth-century cities, and Laurel Thatcher Ulrich's *House Full of Females* (2017) on women in early Mormonism

Chapter 11

- Removed coverage of the New Orleans Slave Market.
- Condensed and sharpened the discussion of sexual coercion on plantations
- Emphasized the impact of slave patrols on the enslaved population
- Reassessed and modified language dehumanizing to those who lived under slavery
- Clarified the account of the exaggerated impact of Whitney's cotton gin
- Emphasized that contemporary concerns are rooted in the past by highlighting
  - climate impact on the geography and economics of cotton production in the antebellum era;
  - the movement of 1 million enslaved people from the East into the country's interior—a number exceeding those Africans brought into the colonies or the United States during the international slave trade;
  - the link between entertainments in the South and slaveholding culture;
  - religious education and practices of enslaved African Americans;
  - new media use by abolitionists to dominate news transmission in the South; and

- the migration of white slaveholders and enslaved Black people to the Mexican state of Texas, eventually outnumbering Mexicans ten to one
- Updated bibliographic recommendations to include Daina Ramey Berry's *The Price for Their Pound of Flesh* (2017) on the conflict between enslaved people's personhood and status as property, Stephanie E. Jones-Rogers's *They Were Her Property* (2019) on female slaveholders' economic power, Manisha Sinha's *The Slave's Cause* (2016) on the history of radical abolitionism, and Andrew J. Torget's *Seeds of Empire* (2015) chronicling political revolution in Texas borderlands

Chapter 12

- Integrated coverage of Elijah Lovejoy's 1837 murder within the main narrative on anti-abolitionist violence
- Explicated the relationship between middle-class formation and antebellum reform movements
- Focused the explanation of the connection between reform and Catholicism before and after the influx of Catholic immigrants
- Provided the value of the bounty set by Georgia for the apprehension of William Lloyd Garrison in 2020 U.S. dollars
- Emphasized that contemporary concerns are rooted in the past by highlighting
  - an alternative popular musical culture committed to abolition and temperance;
  - religious conflicts between immigrants and reformers;
  - ecological triggers of the Irish potato famine starting in 1845;
  - the rise of Catholicism as the largest religious denomination in America after the immigration of 1.5 million Irish between 1845 and 1854;
  - the rise of magazines for women as sources of authority; and
  - conflict between Protestants and Catholics over religion in public schools
- Updated bibliographic recommendations to include Amy E. Hughes's *Spectacles of Reform* (2012) on abolitionist drama and performance, Lisa Tetrault's *The Myth of Seneca Falls* (2014) on the legacy of the 1848 convention, and April Haynes's *Riotous Flesh* (2015) on the reform campaign against female masturbation

Chapter 13

- Removed coverage of the Astor Place Riot of 1849
- Tightened the narrative of the U.S. invasion of Mexico
- Expanded coverage of state-sponsored militia campaigns to exterminate Native Americans in California in the 1850s

- Deemphasized the role of the French in gold rush California
- Compared the monies Mexico received for lands ceded to the United States with 2020 U.S. dollars
- Emphasized that contemporary concerns are rooted in the past by highlighting
  - the impact of telegraphy on how Americans followed spectator sports and news of the Mexican War;
  - how Protestant-Catholic conflict factored into war with predominantly Catholic Mexico;
  - mass annual migration from the Missouri River to the Pacific coast via the Overland Trail;
  - cholera epidemics on the Overland Trail;
  - the migration of Mormons led by Brigham Young to the Great Salt Lake in Mexican territory;
  - the complex and shifting political borders crossed by masses of overland migrants;
  - theaters as sites of political expression and conflict; and
  - blackface entertainment's intimate connection with the Democratic Party
- Updated bibliographic recommendations to include Michel Gobat's *Empire by Invitation* (2018) on U.S. filibusters in Central America, Benjamin Reiss's *The Showman and the Slave* (2001) on P. T. Barnum's early career, Alberto Varon's *Before Chicano* (2018) on the ways Mexican American thinkers imagined citizenship after 1848, Darcy Grigsby's *Enduring Truths* (2015) on the relationship between photography and abolitionism in the life of Sojourner Truth, and Amy K. D. Lippert's *Consuming Identities* (2018) on images in gold rush California

Chapter 14

- Removed coverage of Mount Vernon
- Condensed the coverage of the rise of Chicago and clarified its relationship to national politics, long-distance commerce, and the fate of the union
- Compared the capital invested in 1850s railroad construction with more recent infrastructure projects in 2020 U.S. dollars
- Emphasized that contemporary concerns are rooted in the past by highlighting
  - the complex role of stage versions of *Uncle Tom's Cabin* in the political debate over slavery;
  - how the railroad mobilized labor, altered perceptions of proximity, and impacted the map of slavery politics;
  - how rail transportation and urban growth shaped Midwestern ecology and a new prairie landscape west of the Great Lakes;
  - the anti-Catholic foundation of nativist hostility toward Irish immigrants;

- the migration of partisans in the slavery conflict to Kansas for the purpose of influencing the fate of slavery in the territory; and
- the use of print media by Senator Charles Sumner to deliver his speech on slavery in Kansas to the antislavery public
- Updated bibliographic recommendations to include Andrew Delbanco's *The War Before the War* (2018) on the conflicts over fugitives from slavery, Hidetaka Hirota's *Expelling the Poor* (2016) on the deportation of Irish immigrants, Amy G. Richter's *Home on the Rails* (2005) on domestic ideals and rail travel, and Ariel Ron's *Grassroots Leviathan* (2020) on agricultural reform and the Republican Party

Chapter 15

- Incorporated coverage of the 1863 New York Draft Riots within the main narrative of the war
- Sharpened and trimmed the discussion of guerilla warfare in Missouri
- Provided more examples of actions taken by enslaved people to emancipate themselves and to shape the course and outcome of the war
- Reduced the discussion of attitudes toward death in America culture
- Augmented the coverage of social conditions in the South to include the Richmond bread riot and other women-organized acts of political protest under the Confederacy
- Emphasized short-term and long-term impacts of Sherman's March to the Sea
- Compared Union army wages paid to soldiers, Black and white, with 2020 U.S. dollars
- Emphasized that contemporary concerns are rooted in the past by highlighting
  - the flight of enslaved people across Union lines in order to secure their own freedom;
  - how news of the Emancipation Proclamation spread via a "grapevine telegraph" among enslaved people and across plantations;
  - that diseases (measles, mumps, smallpox, malaria, typhoid, and dysentery) spread in military camps, hospitals, and prisons and that twice as many soldiers died from disease than from battle injuries;
  - the newspaper publication of casualty lists and telegraph postings during major battles that fostered real-time public gatherings;

- readers' questioning of the veracity of newspaper reporting that did not already reflect their points of view; and
- a president enlisting a famous photographer to craft his image for the public
- Updated bibliographic recommendations to include Brian P. Luskey's *Men Is Cheap* (2020) on the labor market that shadowed Union soldier recruitment, Stephanie McCurry's *Confederate Reckoning* (2010) on the political agency of white women and enslaved African Americans, and David Williams's *I Freed Myself* (2014), which argues that enslaved people initiated their own emancipation

Chapter 16

- Explained the significance and limitations of the constitutional amendment protecting Black suffrage
- Added a photograph of a freed persons's use of clothing to assert her freedom
- Compared the Freedmen's Bureau's first annual budget with 2020 U.S. dollars
- Deemphasized coverage of the Crescent City Slaughterhouse
- Emphasized that contemporary concerns are rooted in the past by highlighting
  - that a smallpox epidemic spread by mass mobilization of soldiers and refugees claimed the lives of tens of thousands formerly enslaved people;
  - the way rumors and news about Reconstruction circulated among freed persons;
  - the migration of Northerners to the postwar South in search of land, an agrarian way of life, or small business opportunities;
  - disagreements about monoculture versus crop diversification; and
  - the use of entertainers (musicians, actors, and other performers) to popularize and advance sociopolitical agendas, including that of the Klan
- Updated bibliographic recommendations to include Joseph P. Reidy's *Illusions of Emancipation* (2019) on the transition from slavery to freedom and Nicole Myers Turner's *Soul Liberty* (2020) on the religious organizing of Black Virginians

PREFACE

The story of American history is a story of interconnection, reinvention, and change over time, through generations and across populations. Our past and present are not separate arcs but rather one shared story with many subplots, characters, and themes. Even in times of deep division, Americans' lives and aspirations have been linked. In *Becoming America,* we strive to help students recognize themselves, their interconnections, and our own time in the great sweep of history, highlighting both the resonances and the disjunctions between past and present and exploring the multitude of ways in which the nation remains a work in progress.

Respecting the necessity of canonical coverage while incorporating the insights of more recent scholarship, *Becoming America* seamlessly weaves political, social, economic, environmental, and cultural perspectives into a unified narrative of American history. In an effort to connect students with the American past, we highlight the deep roots of certain contemporary concerns and phenomena. Innovative new features teach students how to analyze and interpret written and visual evidence, equipping them with powerful tools with which to understand the deep connections that bind not only culture, politics, and economics but also past and present.

Our approach extends through all of the program's components, including the adaptive SmartBook, comprehensive learning activities aligned with the book's in-depth features, reading quizzes, map activities, podcasts, lecture slides, test bank, and more.

Students should come away with a contextualized understanding of the deep changes that have characterized the American past; an appreciation for the interconnections among people, perspectives, issues, and events; and the analytical skills with which to rigorously interpret diverse sources and media. *Becoming America* encourages students to develop critical thinking habits and to look with different eyes at their own communities and society. Above all, *Becoming America* empowers students to think in a historically informed way about the urgent questions of our times and to participate fully and creatively in America's diverse and vital democracy.

HISTORY THROUGH A TWENTY-FIRST-CENTURY LENS

The story of America's becoming the nation and the society that students encounter today requires us to reassess our understanding of the past and refocus on areas often underemphasized. *Becoming America* incorporates recent scholarship while addressing contemporary cultural and political concerns. In doing so, the project improves on traditional history books in several important ways:

- **Two chapters on slavery.** Many books devote a single chapter to the institution of chattel slavery and identify its development with the American South. In contrast, we devote two chapters to this subject—one (Chapter 3) on the importance of the Atlantic slave trade and the experience of enslaved Africans in the larger history of the colonization of North America, then another (Chapter 11) on slavery in the antebellum South. Twenty-first-century scholarship and perspectives warrant renewed focus on slavery's *centrality* to the development of American societies and cultures, and this presentation will help students understand the longer history of chattel slavery, the wider impacts of chattel slavery beyond the American South, and the process by which slavery expanded and changed in the nineteenth century—ensuring an accurate foundation for subsequent political history.

- **Two chapters on the Revolutionary era.** Traditional approaches compress into a single story two *distinct but overlapping* developments that we have chosen to narrate separately to emphasize their significance. Chapter 6 describes a violent rupture between Britain and thirteen of its mainland colonies; Chapter 7 tells how those thirteen colonies, as they secured their independence, came together to form a new nation through the process of long-distance communication, intense debate, and the creation of founding documents.

- **A chapter on antebellum reform.** Traditional texts frame the forward-looking ideas (about slavery, prisons, public education, feminism, or collective living) that emerged during the 1830s and 1840s as an eclectic set of Northern reform causes and leaders. In contrast, we argue in Chapter 12 for the existence of a *broad culture of reform* among the Northern middle class that students will be able to recognize as both controversial and transformative of everyday life. We emphasize different and more important movements, linked not by their affinity to modern progressive sensibilities but by their shared ideologies.

- **A broader framing of Reconstruction.** Contemporary political developments have fueled popular interest in the much-studied Reconstruction Era. Whereas most narratives bracket Reconstruction as an anomalous episode between 1865 and 1876, we begin Chapter 16 during the Civil War and take it beyond the settlement of the 1876 election. Following the cues of recent scholarship, we help students see not only the well-documented political defeat of Reconstruction but also the complex legal and cultural battles over the South's racially inclusive democracy and the vital role that Reconstruction-era Black churches and press played in the Black freedom movement long after Reconstruction.

CONTEMPORARY CONCERNS ENGAGE LEARNERS BY CONNECTING URGENT ISSUES OF TODAY TO EXAMPLES THROUGHOUT HISTORY

A new Contemporary Concerns feature highlights the following issues throughout the text and as they have played out in specific historical contexts. These features mobilize students' interests in the urgent issues and debates of our time in order to open up the American past and highlight its relevance.

- **Crossing Borders:** How were American borders drawn, how have they changed, and how have migration patterns made and remade people, political power, regions, and nations?
- **Media and Information:** How have people living in America received information and assessed its validity?

> measure in the history of guilty man." ● Throughout the South, even in areas not covered by the Proclamation, those who had lived under the slavery regime rejoiced. News passed quickly through word of mouth along what contemporaries called a "grapevine telegraph" linking enslaved people across plantations, and several slaveholders reported first hearing about the Proclamation from them. In Northern cities and in occupied areas of the Confederacy, Black men and women ushered in January 1 as the dawn of a Jubilee, the biblical year of freedom for all enslaved people. ●

- **Climates and Ecologies:** How have ecological interdependence and shifting climate patterns shaped, or been shaped, by politics, economics, and society?
- **Disease and Epidemic:** How has the transmission of pathogens or the experience of mass illness shaped major events and developments in the American past?

> As it ended slavery, the Civil War wreaked havoc in the lives of 4 million people previously enslaved in the South. ● Approximately half a million of them escaped during the course of the conflict, and they were especially vulnerable to diseases that came with the mass mobilization of soldiers and refugees. Tens of thousands of formerly enslaved people died in a smallpox epidemic that erupted in Washington, D.C., in 1862 and spread to the Upper South over the next two years. ● Those who remained on plantations during

- **Conflicting Faiths:** How have differences and disputes over religious belief and practice fueled political movements, shaped social divisions, and influenced the formation of cultures and states?
- **Politics and Entertainment:** How have visual and performing arts, entertainment, and celebrity shaped, reflected, or intersected with contests for political power?

STREAMLINED CONTENT IMPROVES READABILITY

Streamlined for today's learners, the second edition is briefer by 20 percent without sacrificing coverage or breadth. Language is tightened and details are clarified in narratives, boxes, and references, and the image program is trimmed; this presents critical information in a more manageable and smaller format.

PRIMARY SOURCES

INTERPRETING THE SOURCES
Mississippi's Black Code, 1865

Though they varied from state to state, planter-dominated governments throughout most of the South passed restrictive laws, called Black Codes, designed to re-establish their authority in the aftermath of the legal emancipation of people from slavery. Following is an example from Mississippi.

1. Civil Rights of Freedmen in Mississippi

Sec. 1. *Be it enacted* . . . That all freedmen, free negroes, and mulattoes may sue and be sued, implead and be impleaded, in all the courts of law and equity of this State, and may acquire personal property, and choses in action, by descent or purchase, and may dispose of the same in the same manner and to the same extent that white persons may: *Provided,* That the provisions of this section shall not be so construed as to allow any freedman, free negro, or mulatto to rent or lease any lands or tenements except in incorporated cities or towns, in which places the corporate authorities shall control the same. . . .

2. Mississippi Vagrant Law

Sec. 1. *Be it enacted,* etc. . . . That all rogues and vagabonds, idle and dissipated persons, beggars, jugglers, or persons practicing unlawful games or plays, runaways, common drunkards, common night-walkers, pilferers, lewd, wanton, or lascivious persons, in speech or behavior, common railers and brawlers, persons who neglect their calling or employment, misspend what they earn, or do not provide for the support of themselves or their families, or dependents, and all other idle and disorderly persons, including all who neglect all lawful business, habitually misspend their time by frequenting houses of ill-fame, gaming-houses, or tippling shops, shall be deemed and considered vagrants . . . and upon conviction thereof shall be fined not exceeding one hundred dollars, with all accruing costs, and be imprisoned at the discretion of the court, not exceeding ten days.

Sec. 2. . . . All freedmen, free negroes and mulattoes in this State, over the age of eighteen years, found on the second Monday in January, 1866, or thereafter, with no lawful employment or business, or found unlawfully assembling themselves together, either in the day or night time, and all white persons so assembling themselves with freedmen, free negroes or mulattoes, or usually associating with freedmen, free negroes or mulattoes, on terms of equality, or living in adultery or fornication with a freed woman, free negro or mulatto, shall be deemed vagrants, and on conviction thereof shall be fined in a sum not exceeding, in the case of a freedman, free negro or mulatto, fifty dollars, and a white man two hundred dollars, and imprisoned at the discretion of the court, the free negro not exceeding ten days, and the white man not exceeding six months. . . .

3. Penal Laws of Mississippi

Sec. 1. *Be it enacted* . . . That no freedman, free negro or mulatto, not in the military service of the United States government, and not licensed so to do by the board of police of his or her county, shall keep or carry fire-arms of any kind, or any ammunition, dirk or bowie knife, and on conviction thereof in the county court shall be punished by fine, not exceeding ten dollars, and pay the costs of such proceedings, and all

"Free to Work." Under the Black Codes, planter-dominated legislatures tried to force freed people, including children, to enter into year-long labor contracts for work they once performed when enslaved. Papers, 1865, Accession 10060, University of Virginia Library Charlottesville, VA.

such arms or ammunition shall be forfeited to the informer; and it shall be the duty of every civil and military officer to arrest any freedman, free negro, or mulatto found with any such arms or ammunition, and cause him or her to be committed to trial in default of bail.

Source: Mississippi Slave Code, 1865. Historians, Code of Mississippi, 1798-1871, H.O.B. Vagrancy Act of Mississippi, 1865, Kermit L. Hall, Paul Finkleman, and James W. Ely, Jr., American Legal History: Cases and Materials (Oxford: Oxford University Press, 2005), 251-255.

Explore the Source

1. Why might white lawmakers have seized upon vagrancy as the focus of a Black Code?

2. What role do the authors of this code envision for people of color in the post-slavery South?

3. Why might lawmakers have banned marriage between Black people and white people?

War and Disability. Bowman, W. E. (William Emory/Library Of Congress)

BEHIND THE IMAGE

John W. January, a Union army soldier from Illinois, ordered this cabinet card, a new, larger type of carte de visite (see Chapter 13) that was becoming popular in the years after the Civil War. Cabinet cards featured photographs of the individuals or companies who had commissioned them mounted onto thick card stock measuring 6.5 × 4.25 inches, and some included text on the reverse. January had lost his feet due to scurvy and gangrene while imprisoned in the South. Even before this card appeared, January had become a symbol of the suffering of Union soldiers in the mass media. In its June 17, 1865, issue, *Harper's Weekly* printed an article titled "Rebel Cruelties" that featured a drawing of January, lying emaciated and footless in a hospital bed.

WITHIN THE IMAGE

January displays ❶ both his amputated and prosthetic limbs, placing them side by side to expose the violence of his wartime wound. ❷ Though his dress and elegant furniture mark him as genteel, the prominent placement of the prosthetics and stumps announces his primary identity as a wounded warrior. ❸ January wears what appears to be a medal of the Grand Army of the Republic,

a fraternal organization of Northern veterans, though such cabinet cards were popular among Confederate amputees as well. ❹ What made this card distinctive was the "Autobiography" on the other side, which provides a detail not implied by the photograph. In the text, January claims to have amputated his own feet, giving his common disability a special, heroic dimension.

BEYOND THE IMAGE

January's cabinet card was part of a larger campaign to publicize the conditions experienced by Union prisoners of war. Lecturing to Northern audiences (to whom these cards were sold), he re-enacted his self-amputation by detaching his prosthetics and exhibiting the pocketknife he had used to perform the surgery. January's account was disputed by a fellow soldier, who claimed to have performed the amputation and even published an alleged confession from January that he had made up the story to profit from lecturing. Quite apart from the controversy, the spectacle of lost limbs was a prominent part of public life in the postwar years. Injured and disabled men filled American towns and cities, prompting several municipalities to enact "unsightly beggar ordinances," prohibiting the exhibition of maimed or unsightly bodies in public space.

Primary sources illuminate historical context and give students of history a lens into the thinking and expression of historical figures. These sources also help students think critically about history and expose them to contrasting perspectives on key events. The second edition of *Becoming America: A History for the 21st Century* provides several ways to use primary source documents in your course.

PRIMARY SOURCES PROMOTE THINKING CRITICALLY ABOUT HISTORY

An **INTERPRETING THE SOURCES** box in every chapter examines historical evidence through a showcased primary source, such as a document, a speech transcript, a map, or an artifact. A headnote contextualizes the selection, and Explore the Source questions challenge students to analyze its significance.

New visual analysis emphasis in each chapter models a framework that students can use to analyze visual documents by considering their historical context, the artist's decisions, and a work's social impact:

- **Behind the Image** explores the historical context (such as the social or political issues of a place or time) or the artist's goals (whether political, ideological, commercial), so that students learn to see images not as illustrations of text narrative but as historical artifacts in their own right.

- **Within the Image** calls attention to the artist's decisions regarding elements (such as subject, composition, color, or symbol) to help students recognize that these choices are intentional and understand how their sum reveals the artist's message.

- **Beyond the Image** discusses the reception and impact of the image to remind students that images have always had power and resonance, both during and beyond their initial circulation.

A **SINGULAR LIVES** box in each chapter spotlights individuals whose experiences, perspectives, or status might have represented a larger group experience, defied dominant stereotypes, altered the course of a major development, or embodied a particular predicament.

- **New Where in the Archives?** assignment asks, "How do we know what we know about this person's life?" Primary sources are listed; the institution housing the sources is named; and URLs are provided. The assignment develops analytical skills and reveals the interpretive nature of the past.

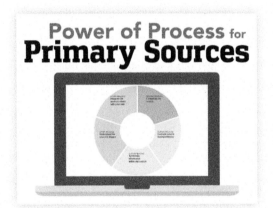

Power of Process for Primary Sources is a guided reading and critical thinking tool that aids historians teaching students about primary sources. As part of Connect U.S. History, McGraw Hill Education's learning platform, Power of Process contains a database of over four hundred searchable primary sources in addition to the capability for instructors to upload their own sources. Instructors can then select a series of strategies for students to use to analyze and comment on a source. The Power of Process framework helps students develop essential academic skills such as understanding, analyzing, and synthesizing readings and visuals such as maps, leading students toward higher-order thinking and writing.

MCGRAW HILL CONNECT

PODCASTS CONTEXTUALIZE HISTORY THROUGH THEIR STORYTELLING POWER

New podcast assignments help students experience history in a whole new way. We've gathered some of the most interesting and popular history podcasts currently available and built assignable questions around them. These assignments allow instructors to bring greater context and nuance to their courses while engaging students through the storytelling power of podcasts.

SMARTBOOK 2.0 TAILORS CONTENT TO EACH INDIVIDUAL STUDENT

New SmartBook 2.0, available within Connect U.S. History, has been updated with improved learning objectives to ensure that students gain foundational knowledge while learning to make connections to help them formulate a broader understanding of historical events. SmartBook 2.0 personalizes learning to individual student needs, continually adapting to pinpoint knowledge gaps and focus learning on topics that need the most attention. Study time is more productive, and as a result, students are better prepared for class and coursework. For instructors, SmartBook 2.0 tracks student progress and provides insights that can help guide teaching strategies.

WRITING ASSIGNMENT TOOL IMPROVES WRITTEN COMMUNICATION SKILLS

New Writing Assignment Plus tool delivers a learning experience that improves students' written communication skills and conceptual understanding with every assignment. Assign, monitor, and provide feedback on writing more efficiently and grade assignments within McGraw Hill Connect® and McGraw Hill Connect Master® 2.0. Writing Assignment Plus gives you time-saving tools with a just-in-time basic writing and originality checker. Features include

- Grammar/writing checking with McGraw Hill learning resources
- Originality checker with McGraw Hill learning resources
- Writing statistics
- Rubric building and scoring
- Ability to assign draft and final deadline milestones
- Tablet ready and tools for all learners

APPLICATION-BASED ACTIVITIES PROVIDE OPPORTUNITIES TO APPLY KNOWLEDGE

New application-based activities are highly interactive, automatically graded, online, learn-by-doing exercises that provide students a safe space to apply their knowledge and problem-solving skills in class and in everyday life. Skill-based activities focus on topics such as "How to Read Primary Sources" and "Analyzing Audience."

CREATE FACILITATES THE CUSTOMIZATION OF COURSE MATERIALS

 **Create** allows you to quickly and easily create custom course materials with cross-disciplinary content and other third-party sources. Select primary source documents that meet the unique

needs of your course: No two history courses are the same!

- Choose your own content: Create a book that contains only the chapters you want, in the order you want. Create will even renumber the pages for you!
- Add readings: Use our American History Collections to include primary sources, or *Taking Sides: Annual Editions*. Add your own original content, such as syllabus or history major requirements!
- Choose your format: Print or eBook? Softcover, spiral-bound, or loose-leaf? Black-and-white or color? Perforated, three-hole-punched, or regular paper?
- Customize your cover: Pick your own cover image and include your name and course information right on the cover. Students will know they're purchasing the right book—and using everything they purchase!
- Review your creation: When you are all done, you'll receive a free PDF review copy in just minutes! To get started, go to create.mheducation.com and register today.

INSTRUCTOR RESOURCES

Becoming America offers an array of instructor resources to support in-person and online U.S. History courses.

TEST BANK

By increasing the rigor of the test bank development process, McGraw Hill has raised the bar for student assessment. Each question has been tagged for level of difficulty, Bloom's taxonomy, and topic coverage. Organized by chapter, the questions are designed to test factual, conceptual, and higher-order thinking.

TEST BUILDER

Test Builder is a cloud-based tool that enables instructors to format tests that can be printed and administered within a Learning Management System. Available within Connect, Test Builder offers a modern, streamlined interface for easy content configuration that matches course needs without requiring a download.

Test Builder enables instructors to

- Access all test bank content from a particular title
- Easily pinpoint the most relevant content through robust filtering options
- Manipulate the order of questions or scramble questions and/or answers
- Pin questions to a specific location within a test
- Determine their preferred treatment of algorithmic questions
- Choose the layout and spacing
- Add instructions and configure default settings

POWERPOINT

The PowerPoint presentations highlight the key points of the chapter and include supporting visuals. New to this edition, all slides are WCAG compliant.

INSTRUCTOR'S MANUAL

The instructor's manual provides a wide variety of tools and resources for presenting the course, including learning objectives and ideas for lectures and discussions.

REMOTE PROCTORING

New remote proctoring and browser-locking capabilities from Proctorio are seamlessly integrated within Connect to offer more control over the integrity of online assessments. Instructors can enable security options that restrict browser activity, monitor student behavior, and verify the identity of each student. Instant and detailed reporting gives instructors an at-a-glance view of potential concerns, thereby avoiding personal bias and supporting evidence-based claims.

Instructors: Student Success Starts with You

Tools to enhance your unique voice

Want to build your own course? No problem. Prefer to use an OLC-aligned, prebuilt course? Easy. Want to make changes throughout the semester? Sure. And you'll save time with Connect's auto-grading too.

65%
Less Time Grading

Laptop: McGraw Hill; Woman/dog: George Doyle/Getty Images

Study made personal

Incorporate adaptive study resources like SmartBook® 2.0 into your course and help your students be better prepared in less time. Learn more about the powerful personalized learning experience available in SmartBook 2.0 at **www.mheducation.com/highered/connect/smartbook**

Affordable solutions, added value

Make technology work for you with LMS integration for single sign-on access, mobile access to the digital textbook, and reports to quickly show you how each of your students is doing. And with our Inclusive Access program you can provide all these tools at a discount to your students. Ask your McGraw Hill representative for more information.

Padlock: Jobalou/Getty Images

Solutions for your challenges

A product isn't a solution. Real solutions are affordable, reliable, and come with training and ongoing support when you need it and how you want it. Visit **www.supportateverystep.com** for videos and resources both you and your students can use throughout the semester.

Checkmark: Jobalou/Getty Images

Students: Get Learning That Fits You

Effective tools for efficient studying

Connect is designed to help you be more productive with simple, flexible, intuitive tools that maximize your study time and meet your individual learning needs. Get learning that works for you with Connect.

Study anytime, anywhere

Download the free ReadAnywhere app and access your online eBook, SmartBook 2.0, or Adaptive Learning Assignments when it's convenient, even if you're offline. And since the app automatically syncs with your Connect account, all of your work is available every time you open it. Find out more at **www.mheducation.com/readanywhere**

"I really liked this app—it made it easy to study when you don't have your text-book in front of you."

- Jordan Cunningham,
Eastern Washington University

Everything you need in one place

Your Connect course has everything you need—whether reading on your digital eBook or completing assignments for class, Connect makes it easy to get your work done.

Learning for everyone

McGraw Hill works directly with Accessibility Services Departments and faculty to meet the learning needs of all students. Please contact your Accessibility Services Office and ask them to email accessibility@mheducation.com, or visit **www.mheducation.com/about/accessibility** for more information.

ACADEMIC SKILLS

Students, use this overview to develop fundamental academic skills such as the ability to contextualize historical facts, the ability to recognize the interpretive nature of the past, the ability to analyze historical visual documents, and the ability to use the pedagogical tools in your book to study smarter.

THE ABILITY TO CONTEXTUALIZE HISTORICAL INFORMATION DEEPENS HISTORICAL THINKING

Learning historical information—such as names, dates, places, and events—is an important part of studying history. But it is only a beginning. In order to work with historical information—to explain, to analyze, and to interpret—historical reasoning skills are needed. One such skill is that of historical contextualization, or the ability to contextualize historical facts.

1. **Be aware that people often assign values**, attitudes, and intentions from our contemporary world to people or events in the past.
   - Mitigate such a present-oriented perspective by writing a list of your current assumptions—and a second list of your prior knowledge.

2. **Construct a historical context** for the people or events you are investigating and ensure it is multifaceted.
   - List key events that preceded the issue you are exploring and may have informed contemporaneous attitudes.
   - Create a mental map of the location in its time, whether a building, a neighborhood, or a battlefield.
   - Consider the mobility and communication technologies available at the time. (Did most people move on foot, by horse, or in trains? Did they get information quickly—or days or weeks after events had passed?)
   - Reflect on how people ensured they had necessities such as food and shelter: If people needed money, who could earn it and how?
   - Consider other systems that impacted the people or events you are investigating, such as political, religious, and cultural norms, standards, or influences.

3. **Apply the historical context** you have built to the specific historical issue you are investigating.
   - Write one sentence each in which you apply what you know—about key preceding events, location, mobility technologies, communication technologies, economic considerations, political influences, religious influences, and others—to the people or events you are investigating.

4. **Develop historical empathy.** Use what you know about the context, the circumstances, that impacted and influenced people's actions and their intentions.

THE ABILITY TO RECOGNIZE THE INTERPRETIVE NATURE OF THE PAST STRENGTHENS CRITICAL THINKING

Think of historians as detectives, trying to uncover the secrets of the past. In order to learn what happened in earlier times, they need to collect evidence. Some evidence will have been created in the time historians are studying, and some evidence will have been generated afterward, often in an attempt to analyze or to interpret. Learn to understand the differences between these types of evidence. Recognize that both have value and provide insight into the past. The process of analyzing such historical evidence reveals the interpretive nature of the past.

A **primary source** is a firsthand account that dates to the time of the subject matter. Primary sources provide insight into historical actors' values, priorities, communication styles, technologies, and more. Examples of primary sources include written texts such as the following:

- Those written contemporaneously to interpret events for people living at the time or for future generations, such as articles in newspapers or magazines, literature, speeches, and autobiographies

Framework adapted from Tim Huijgen, Wim van de Grift, Carla van Boxtel & Paul Holthuis (2018), *Promoting historical contextualization: the development and testing of a pedagogy*, Journal of Curriculum Studies, 50:3, 410-434, DOI: 10.1080/00220272.2018.1435724.

- Those never meant to be read by historians, such as diaries, advertisements, lyrics, private correspondence (including letters, e-mails, and memos), and informal writing (including shopping lists and graffiti)

- Those produced by the bureaucracies of governments, churches, private organizations, and businesses: birth

Library of Congress, Prints & Photographs Division

and marriage records, town records, property deeds, maps, laws, the census, and church chronicles

Examples of primary sources can also be non-text based, such as artifacts (including cave paintings, ceramic vessels, and textiles), architectural ruins, cemeteries, sculptures, paintings, daguerreotypes, photographs, and recordings (including songs, interviews, and speeches).

A secondary source is created by someone who did not experience a time period or an event firsthand. A secondary source is a valuable interpretation of history using the passage of time to better understand the historic past.

Examples of secondary sources include scholarly articles, books of historical research, textbooks, and encyclopedias.

Analyze a primary or secondary source by asking questions about its authorship, bias, audience, purpose, and context:

1. **Who** wrote or created the source?
   - What biases may have informed the creator's point of view?

2. **For what audience** was the source produced? We usually tailor our communication to our audience.
   - Was it meant to be public or private?
   - Is the language formal or informal?
   - Are facts and explanations written for informed experts or common people?
   - Was the audience friendly or hostile?
   - What social and economic relationships connected the author with the audience?

3. **Why** was the source created?
   - What was the creator's motivation?
   - What was the source's purpose?

4. **When and where** was the source created?

5. **How do we evaluate the accuracy** of the source? Can we detect a bias in the source?

THE ABILITY TO ANALYZE VISUAL DOCUMENTS EXTENDS HISTORICAL THINKING

We know that primary sources and secondary sources are evidence historians use to make sense of the past. But visual sources require additional analytical skills from text-based sources. Consider the three-step framework below for analyzing visual documents as a strategy you can use in your own academic work.

Winslow Homer, "News from the War," from *Harper's Weekly*, June 14, 1862. *The Picture Art Collection/Alamy Stock Photo*

BEHIND THE IMAGE

Massachusetts-born artist Winslow Homer (1836–1910) was around twenty-five years old when the U.S. Provost Marshal's Office granted him approval to visit Union military camps at the front. Based on his observations there, Homer produced dozens of images for *Harper's Weekly*, a pictorial magazine founded in New York City in 1857. Homer spent about ten weeks in Virginia war zones in 1861 and 1862 and drew this illustration on his return to New York.

BEHIND THE IMAGE

- **Understand** visual images as historical artifacts and evidence.

- **Identify the historical context**, such as the social or political issues of a place or a time.

- **Summarize the artist's goals**, whether political, ideological, commercial, or other.

WITHIN THE IMAGE

Homer's illustration surveys the many media that pro-vided war news. ① In the central scene, a woman slumps over a parlor table, clutching a piece of paper. ② The wires bordering the top of the image suggest that the paper in her hand is a telegraph; below the woman, the word *wounded* signals that she has received distressing news. Despite the insularity and serenity often associated with middle-class parlors (symbolized by the vined plant, caged songbird, and decorated folding screen), telegraphic communication exposes the home to the rav-ages of war. Other scenes focus on the mail. ③ At top

BEYOND THE IMAGE

"News from the War" appeared as a prominent, two-page spread in a mass-circulated magazine (*Harper's* had over two hundred thousand subscribers during the war era), and thousands more saw it second-hand. At a time when technological constraints made it unfeasible to publish photographs in newspapers, illustrations like this shaped the visual imagination of war throughout the North. ⑧ By including both his profession and the publication in which the drawing appeared, Homer highlighted his own place within the media landscape he was portray-ing, and he would go on to become one of the leading American painters of the nineteenth century.

WITHIN THE IMAGE

- **Recount the artist's decisions** regarding elements such as subject, compo-sition, color, and symbol.

- **Recognize the intentionality** of these choices.

- **Assess how the artist reveals the message** through the sum total of these choices.

BEYOND THE IMAGE

- **Describe the contemporaneous reception** of the image.

- **Explain the impact**, both short- and long-term, of the image.

- **Underscore the power and resonance** of the image, both during its initial circulation and beyond.

LEARNING TOOLS HELP YOU FIND INFORMATION, RECOGNIZE WHAT'S IMPORTANT, AND MAKE CONNECTIONS

Textbooks differ from materials read for pleasure in two fundamental ways: They are longer, and they deliver information that is likely new to readers. For these reasons, they are structured purposefully and include learning tools. Analyze the organizational structure to recognize how concepts are related. Use the learning tools to recognize when key concepts surface and to find them quickly when studying. See the following examples from *Becoming America*.

The table of contents organizes information both chronologically *and* themat-ically: Although each chapter indicates the years covered, the years may overlap those of adjacent chapters for thematic reasons.

Chapter titles, major headings, and subheadings organize information by theme. Before you read, use them to preview information. As you read, con-tinue to use them to help you understand how the details (names, dates, places) aggregate to tell a story about American history.

In-depth features take a closer look at four aspects of history:

- **Interpreting the Sources** introduces and reprints one or two primary sources. Learn about a topic in depth not only from historical actors' points of view but also in their own words and images.
- **Hot Commodities** explores economic forces (demand, supply, cost, con-text) and cultural or political significance of one commodity in its day.
- **Singular Lives** profiles an ordinary person, states how we know what we know about them, and includes an assignment to help you practice the skill of analyzing historical documents.
- **Visual Analysis** models a three-step framework for analyzing visual sources that you can pick up and deploy in your own coursework.

most of the original constitutions explicitly embraced the idea that legitimate governments drew their power from the consent of the people they governed and were obliged to respect certain **natural rights.** A majority of state constitutions explicitly listed these rights and their derivatives, which typically included civil liberties such as free speech, protection from unjustified searches and seizures, right to trial by jury, and the right to practice one's religious conscience (several states did, however,

Bold type within the chapter indicates the first use of each Study Term or the first use where it is defined. As you read, notice these visual cues and recognize they are signaling a particularly important concept.

Study Terms at the end of each chapter highlight important concepts from the chapter. These are organized in the order they appear. After you have finished reading a section, look at the Study Terms list and confirm that you can remember their definitions.

natural rights   Basic individual rights that many eighteenth-century pamphleteers, orators, and theorists believed to emanate from nature or God rather than from tradition or government.

The glossary at the end of the book collects the study terms, includes their definitions, and is organized alphabetically. Use it to refresh your memory about a term's meaning when you can't remember in what chapter you'd read it.

A pop-up of the glossary definition can be generated in the eBook by mousing over boldface study terms within the chapter.

The index at the end of the book organizes subjects and people alphabetically.

- Complex topics are subdivided into narrower categories.
- Page references indicate where topics are covered in the text. Page numbers that include an italicized *m* indicate that the information is found in a map; an italicized *t* indicates information presented in a table; an italicized *f* indicates the information presented in a figure.

The search function in the eBook is aligned with the index. Rather than list page references, search results include surrounding words for context.

ACKNOWLEDGMENTS

The authors take great pleasure in thanking the many students, colleagues, friends, family members, teachers, reviewers, and collaborators who have participated in this project since its inception some fifteen years ago. Over that long haul, a number of highly talented U.C. Berkeley doctoral students contributed significant research to *Becoming America*, and we are proud to list them here. J. T. Jamieson, Amy O'Hearn, and Drs. Corey Brooks, Adrianne Francisco, Anthony Gregory, Bobby Lee, Erica Lee, Sarah Gold McBride, Giuliana Perrone, and Jacqui Shine have left a powerful imprint on the current edition, which justifies our pride in thinking of this as a Berkeley book. So, too, have the contributions and support of our departmental colleagues, past and current, especially Robin Einhorn, Mark Peterson, James Vernon, and Peter Zinoman.

We are extremely grateful to the team at McGraw Hill, led by Jason Seitz and Lauren Finn, for laboring so hard to make this new edition a reality. Thank you to Deb DeBord and Martha Ghent for expert copyediting and proofreding respectively, Sarah Flynn for her creativity and enthusiasm, and Michael Gedatus, Dawn Groundwater, Sandy Wille, and Lauren McFalls for their help and patience.

A few longer-term debts remain fresh in our minds. *Becoming America*'s visual program owes much to the expertise and aesthetic flare of Rebecca Groves. Jon-David Hague can still claim credit for helping conceive this reframing of U.S. history. And the same might be said of our mentors at various institutions and stages along the way. Thank you to the late David Brion Davis and to Barbara J. Fields, Eric Foner, Jennifer Jones, and Mary P. Ryan.

Finally, we owe a debt of gratitude to the McGraw Hill Academic Integrity Board of Advisors who reviewed and commented on chapter content, the illustration program, and language and conventions.

Susan Bragg, *Georgia Southwestern State University*
Eileen Ford, *California State University, Los Angeles*
Nicholas Fox, *Houston College*
Rudy Jean-Bart, *Broward Community College*
Darnell Morehand-Olufade, *University of Bridgeport*
Sharon Navarro, *University of Texas at San Antonio*
Jeffrey Ogbar, *University of Connecticut*
Andrea A. Oliver, *Tallahassee Community College*
Birte Pfleger, *California State University, Los Angeles*
Linda Reed, *University of Houston*
Jennifer Epley Sanders, *Texas A&M University*

Our heartfelt appreciation goes to those reviewers who participated in the second edition. Your assessments, arguments, and suggestions informed our own debates and strengthened our project.

J. Brett Adams, *Collin College*
Jennifer Hudson Allen, *Dallas College*
Guy Aronoff, *Humboldt State University*
Patrick Ashwood, *Hawkeye Community College*
Shelly Bailess, *Liberty University*
Alexander Bielakowski, *University of Houston-Downtown*
Edward J. Blum, *San Diego State University*
Beau Bowers, *Central Piedmont Community College*
Kevin Brady, *Tidewater Community College*
Jeff Bremer, *Iowa State University*
Matthew Cain, *College of Southern Maryland*
Robert J. Caputi, *Erie Community College*
Alton Carroll, *Northern Virginia Community College*
Annette Chamberlin, *Virginia Western Community College*
Sharon Michelle Courmier, *Lamar Institute of Technology*
Thomas Crupi, *The University of North Carolina*
Leilah Danielson, *Northern Arizona University*
Cory Davis, *University of Illinois at Chicago*
Laura Dunn, *Eastern Florida State College*
Ilan Ehrlich, *Bergen Community College*
Joseph Faykosh, *Central Arizona College*
Elizabeth Fickling, *Coastal Carolina Community College*
Andrew Frank, *Florida State University*
Michael Gabriel, *Kutztown University*
David Gaines, *Sinclair Community College*
Robert Genter, *Nassau Community College*
Vincent Gill, *Middle Georgia State University*
Noah Goode, *Central Piedmont Community College*
Sharelle Grim, *Mississippi Delta Community College*
William J. Hansard, *University of Texas at Arlington*
Sandra Harvey, *Lone Star College-CyFair*

Pat Herb, *North Central State College*

David P. Hopkins, Jr., *Midland College*

Rebecca Jacobs-Pollez, *Murray State College*

Duncan Jamieson, *Ashland University*

Lesley Kauffman, *San Jacinto College*

Jennifer Koslow, *Florida State University*

Timothy Lay, *Cleveland State Community College*

J. Michael Long, *Front Range Community College*

Stephen Lopez, *San Jacinto College*

Mary Lyons-Carmona, *Metropolitan Community College*

David Mason, *Georgia Gwinnett College*

John Mohr, *The University of Alabama in Huntsville*

Brandon Morgan, *Central New Mexico Community College*

William Morgan, *Lone Star College Montgomery*

Joshua Moser, *Sussex County Community College*

Gwen Noble-Wold, *Everett Community College*

Chloe Northrop, *Tarrant County College*

Robert O'Brien, *Lone Star College-CyFair*

Andrea L. Oliver, *Tallahassee Community College*

Kayla Pina, *Cleveland State Community College*

Daniel Ponce, *Enterprise State Community College*

George Reklaitis, *Brookdale Community College*

Mark Roehrs, *Lincoln Land Community College*

Jim Rogers, *Louisiana State University at Alexandria*

Justin Rogers, *University of Mississippi*

Michael Rubinoff, *Arizona State University*

Donald Seals, *Kilgore College*

Joy Schulz, *Metropolitan Community College*

Scott Seagle, *Iowa Wesleyan University*

Steven Showalter, *Lee College*

David Simonelli, *Youngstown State University*

Anthony N. Stranges, *Texas A&M University*

Bianka Stumpf, *Central Carolina Community College*

JoAnne Sundell, *Erie Community College*

Chris Thomas, *Reynolds Community College*

Scott Wade, *Tidewater Community College*

Lawrence Wallis, *Mercer County Community College*

Scott Williams, *Weatherford College*

Mary Montgomery Wolf, *University of Georgia*

Dirk Yarker, *Texas Southmost College*

Adam Zucconi, *Richard Bland College*

Barbara Zanger Zuniga, *California State University, Monterey Bay*

ABOUT THE AUTHORS

David M. Henkin

Since David Henkin joined the history faculty at the University of California, Berkeley, in 1997, he has taught and written about subjects that rarely make it into traditional textbooks. He has offered entire courses on baseball, Broadway, time, leisure, the road, family life, news, and urban literature while publishing books and essays about street signs, paper money, junk mail, intimate correspondence, calendars, and temporal rhythms in the nineteenth century. The task of integrating that kind of material into the traditional narrative of the American past has been the singular challenge of his professional life. David holds a BA from Yale University and a PhD from U.C. Berkeley, and he was awarded Berkeley's Distinguished Teaching Award in the Social Sciences. Beyond the Berkeley campus, David teaches classes on the Talmud, plays cards, eats lots of fish and berries, and roots passionately for the St. Louis Cardinals. Raised in New York, he makes his home with friends and community in San Francisco.

Rebecca M. McLennan

Rebecca M. McLennan is Preston Hotchkis Professor of History at the University of California, Berkeley. Passionately dedicated to making U.S. history exciting and relevant for today's students, she has taught courses on American and global food history, consumer culture, the New Deal, and the history of American crime and punishment. She also regularly teaches her department's gateway U.S. history survey course. Rebecca's publications include *The Crisis of Imprisonment: Protest, Politics, and the Making of the American Penal State, 1776-1941* (Cambridge University Press, 2008), which won several major book awards, and she is currently completing a history of the origin and legacies of the Bering Sea crisis at the turn of the twentieth century. Born and raised in Aotearoa New Zealand, Rebecca completed her BA at Otago University in Dunedin and her PhD at Columbia University. In her spare time, conditions permitting, she swims in San Francisco Bay, cooks for family and friends, and listens to John Coltrane.

1 | CONVERGENCE OF MANY PEOPLES: AMERICA BEFORE 1600

Chapter Questions

1. How and over what time frame did human life develop in North America?

2. What crucial changes occurred in several North American societies during the warming period?

3. How relevant was religion to European exploration of the Atlantic, and in what specific ways?

4. What role did Africa play in the early history of European exploration?

5. What was the Columbian exchange, and how did it influence the Americas and Europe?

Early American Artifacts. Objects like the water jugs, beads, cat carving, and stone ax pictured here help historians reconstruct some strands of the diverse history of life in North America in the centuries preceding the arrival of Europeans and Africans. *Aldo Tutino/Art Resource*

From some perspectives, U.S. history is a short story. The United States of America was not founded until the last quarter of the eighteenth century, and the ancestors of most of its current citizens arrived in the country far more recently. But the lands that now form the United States have a long history, spanning tens of thousands of years of human habitation. As in every other part of the globe, life in the United States today is built atop layers of past events and culture, and U.S. history includes everything we know about that past.

For all but the last few centuries, we find only scattered and obscure clues about the way ordinary people led their lives—whether in America, Africa, Asia, Europe, or any other part of the globe. Much of what historians know about work, play, and worship in the distant past has been reconstructed from artifacts

Time Line

15,000–14,000 Before Present
First migrants cross into North America

5000 BCE
Maize cultivation begins in Mexico

1600 BCE
Moundbuilding appears in Louisiana

900–1300 CE
Warmer temperatures lead to agricultural expansion in North America and northern Europe

900–1150
Ancestral Puebloan (Anasazi) civilization flourishes near Chaco Canyon

1050
Rise of Cahokia

1076
Latin Christendom embarks on Crusades and Reconquista

1300
Little Ice Age begins in North America

1300–1350
Fall of Cahokia

1433
Fall of Timbuktu

1472
Spain authorizes conquest of the Canary Islands

1482–1485
Portuguese establish trading posts off the African coast

1492
Christopher Columbus arrives in San Salvador

1507
Martin Waldseemüller names the American continent

1517
Martin Luther begins Protestant Reformation

1521
Hernán Cortés conquers Tenochtitlán

1532
Francisco Pizarro invades Inca Empire

1534
Henry VIII breaks from Catholic Church

1564
French settle La Caroline

1565
Spanish found St. Augustine

1585
English establish settlement on Roanoke Island

1588
English navy defeats Spanish Armada

buried in the earth, changes wrought in the landscape, skeletal remains of people and animals, soil samples, seed deposits, tree rings, glacial ridges, religious rites, folklore, and language. This is especially true in the case of North America, where our knowledge of the past is restricted further by the fact that rulers did not maintain written records and religious insights were not passed down on parchment or paper. For this reason, historians have depended on the methods and findings of archaeologists, anthropologists, paleontologists, linguists, and biologists to discover basic facts about the politics, religion, and social order in North America until the seventeenth century.

Scholars have uncovered a tumultuous history of diverse societies, cultures, and city-states spread across the North American continent in the thousand years before the arrival of significant numbers of Europeans and Africans in the 1600s. Over the course of that millennium, new North American centers of political power and cultural influence emerged and then dispersed. Meanwhile, religious and political conflicts spurred monarchs in Europe to sponsor expeditions to the Americas, bringing into contact peoples from the two sides of the Atlantic Ocean. The initial exchanges of people, animals, plants, and germs from three continents would ultimately trigger profound changes in American life— and in the land itself. In the hundred years after the voyages of Christopher Columbus, the contacts between indigenous North Americans and the newcomers from across the ocean multiplied and extended. Still, this contact was limited to a few parts of the continent, and its historical significance remained to be seen.

NORTH AMERICA BEFORE CONTACT

The peoples living in North America prior to Columbus's arrival in 1492 were the descendants of migrants from Asia who had arrived approximately fourteen or fifteen thousand years earlier, when those two continents were connected. From the time of these initial migrations, the population of the Americas (a term invented by Europeans) grew to tens of millions as people made their way across and down the landmass. As they migrated, they developed ways of living specific to the climate and landscapes of the regions they settled. They belonged to innumerable groups and spoke hundreds of quite different languages. Yet several centuries before Columbus, major environmental changes and political innovations forged new links among the diverse societies of North America.

EARLY SOCIETIES OF NORTH AMERICA

Early humans, who had migrated out of Africa over thousands of years, finally reached North America from Asia around 15,000–14,000 BP (before present).

- They crossed from Siberia into Alaska via a land bridge across what is now the Bering Sea (see Map 1.1) and made their first homes on the continent in **Beringia,** a vast, unglaciated region that included the land bridge as well as hundreds of miles of land on both sides, from Siberia to the Yukon. Scholars debate the number and timing of migrations into and across Beringia (and some of the migrants may have traveled along the coast rather than overland), but these journeys had ended by the year 10,000 BP, when rising global temperatures melted glaciers and the land bridge was submerged. The descendants of the Beringia migrants became the indigenous population of a Western Hemisphere that was now separated from the rest of the human family.

CROSSING BORDERS

The earliest indigenous Americans, whom archaeologists call **Paleo-Indians** (ancient Indians), migrated throughout North America, and their descendants adapted to varying local climates and ecologies. Some general patterns linked the whole continent: Major protein sources were hunted and gathered rather than harvested, and unlike in Europe, large domesticated animals like pigs and cows were not available as food sources. Still, the lives of North American peoples varied from region to region. In the Great Basin region between the Rocky Mountains and the Sierra Nevada, native groups subsisted largely on fish, as did those along the coastline of what we now call California. Farther east, they hunted deer and gathered acorns. In all of these regions, settlers developed distinct languages, religions, and cultures in the places that now compose the United States.

Paleo-Indians also ventured farther south in the hemisphere, forming indigenous groups and cultures in **Mesoamerica** (the name scholars use for the region comprising central Mexico and Central America prior to European settlement) and South America. In these warmer climates, the cultivation of **maize** (Indian corn) supported much larger, denser settlements than in the north. Maize was first grown in Mexico around 5000 BCE (before the Common Era; or BC, before Christ), and over the next several millennia the crop became the foundation of agricultural societies throughout Mesoamerica, as well as along the slopes and valleys of the Andes. Mesoamerican cultures like the Olmecs, the Maya, and the Zapotecs all depended on corn and legumes and sustained the greatest population centers in the hemisphere. By the year 1000 CE (of the Common Era), the vast majority of people living in the Americas were clustered in and around this region.

Corncob Evolution. Corncobs have grown progressively larger over centuries of domestication. The earliest corncobs were small—about the size of a person's thumbnail. Maize cultivation fueled the growth of the earliest-known North American civilizations and continues to sustain life on the continent. Over 125,000 square miles of land in the United States are now devoted to growing corn, which is the dominant ingredient in the modern American diet. *Courtesy of John Doebley*

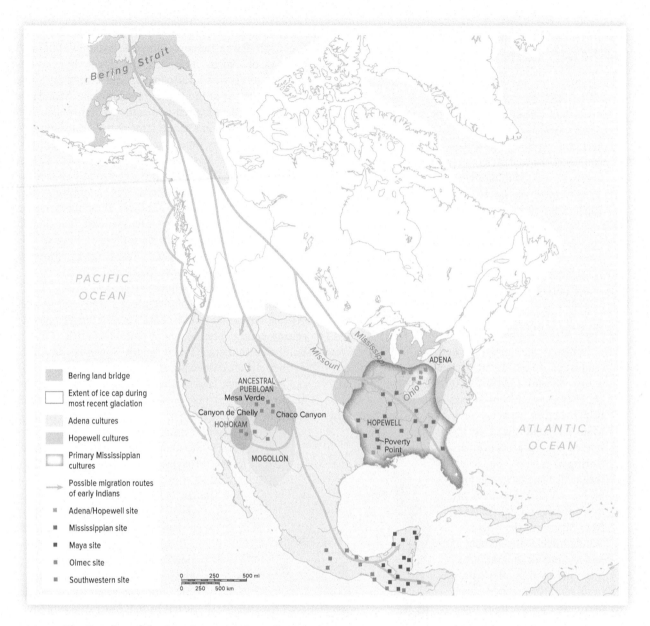

Map 1.1 The Peopling of the Americas. Scholars and scientists continue to uncover evidence about the migration patterns of the earliest Americans. This map indicates possible routes of those migrations, along with the earliest-known centers of American civilization. Recent research on fossils and genomes suggests that migrants settled the Pacific coast before creating the inland cultures named on this map.

Throughout North America, the predominance of hunting, fishing, and gathering meant that populations were smaller and more dispersed than those to the south. Nonetheless, archaeologists have uncovered evidence of centralized communities, including the earliest-known examples of monumental architecture in the Western Hemisphere. **Poverty Point** in northeastern Louisiana, the site of one of the Americas' first cities, boasted a massive earthwork mound that people from the region used for religious exhibitions and gatherings as early as 1600 BCE. A **moundbuilding** project of this scale, which would have required a large and well-organized workforce, offers a glimpse of the kinds of cultural and political power that might have developed in ancient North America.

THE AGRICULTURAL REVOLUTION AND THE CITIES OF THE SOUTHWEST

Around the tenth century CE, life in much of North America began to shift dramatically. In disparate parts of the continent, Native American groups altered their diets and social arrangements and became more dependent on agriculture. North Americans had planted food sources for centuries, but not until the end of the first millennium did agriculture become the dominant means of subsistence in the lands that would become the United States. We have no written records of the wars, political struggles, internal debates, or religious visions that precipitated or accompanied this major change in daily life. ● But we do know one crucial factor: It got warmer. From about 900 to 1300, in what climatologists call the North Atlantic Warm Period, significantly higher average temperatures increased the number of frost-free days on much of the continent. As growing seasons became longer and more dependable, it was possible to breed new variants of food crops that had grown originally in

CLIMATES AND ECOLOGIES

Mesoamerica. North Americans cultivated a distinctive kind of maize (with eight rows of kernels) that could be harvested sooner than Mexican maize and could therefore thrive in northern climates. ● Together with locally adapted squashes, gourds, and beans, the maize harvests supported a nutritious, plant-based diet. A new agricultural order took hold so firmly that native religions would soon put beans, squashes, and especially maize at the center of their origin stories and religious rituals, which featured corn priests and honored the corn mothers who bestowed the gift of life in the form of corn. Some Native American groups later paid homage to the trio of beans, squashes, and corn in festivals to the "three sisters."

CLIMATES AND ECOLOGIES

The **agricultural revolution** transformed societies through much of North America. First, it led to denser living patterns, because raising crops required less territory than hunting and gathering. People in the Southwest, for example, developed small farming villages, where large groups of relatives shared multiunit dwellings. Communities often invested in more substantial building projects than before. The Hohokam people in southern Arizona built canals to irrigate their farmland, as well as subterranean ball courts and storage facilities. In New Mexico, the

Mesa Verde.   This Ancestral Puebloan city in southwestern Colorado featured multistory cliff dwellings, whose ruins can be visited today.
Martha Smith/National Park Service

Mogollon culture designed terraces to help retain soil moisture and experimented with multistory houses made of stone, adobe, and timber.

More dramatically, the Southwestern Native Americans formerly known as the Anasazi but now called Ancestral Puebloans built several major cities during this period. In the largest of these, **Chaco Canyon** in the Four Corners area of northwestern New Mexico, a population of several thousand lived in stone housing blocks, some of them quite elaborate. One of these blocks, built in the eleventh century and later called Pueblo Bonito, contained seven hundred rooms, each of which required cutting and transporting more than 40 tons of sandstone. Even more impressive than the physical grandeur of Chaco Canyon was its role as the metropolitan center of a region where tens of thousands of people made their homes. Over 250 miles of roads flowed into and out of the city, attracting immigrants, political supporters, and religious pilgrims, many of whom came to make astronomical observations and celebrate rites and festivals that marked pivotal moments in the agricultural year.

With the transition toward agriculture and urbanization came a number of social and cultural changes, including greater stratification. Those who occupied the largest houses ate more protein, accumulated prestigious goods from distant locations, and were singled out for special honor when they died. Many archaeologists suspect that members of the subordinate classes were forced into labor on arduous construction projects. For women in the Southwest, the rising importance of agriculture could be empowering, since growing, gathering, and preparing food from the ground was traditionally women's work. Even when some farming labor shifted into men's hands, the foods they harvested were nonetheless identified with the world of women, as the stories about corn mothers and the three sisters suggest. Perhaps for this reason, households were organized around mothers (and other female relatives), and women maintained possession of the housing units.

The great centers of the Four Corners region began to decline and disperse around the middle of the twelfth century. Sustained droughts undermined the authority of

Chunkey Player Effigy Pipe, 1250–1350, Muskogee County, Oklahoma. The game of chunkey, a powerful symbol of Mississippian culture, remained popular among Eastern Native Americans until lacrosse supplanted it in the nineteenth century. *Ira Block/National Geographic Creative/Alamy Stock Photo*

the Chaco Canyon rulers, and large segments of the urban population relocated to smaller communities and more economically and ecologically sustainable living arrangements. Later groups of Southwestern Native Americans retained some aspects of their urban ancestors' culture but favored more participatory religious rites, less dense settlement patterns, and more modest architectural styles. Some scholars have interpreted these cultural patterns among the Pueblo in the late thirteenth and fourteenth centuries as deliberate rejections of the hierarchy and violence of the Chaco Canyon era.

THE RISE AND FALL OF MISSISSIPPIAN CIVILIZATION

As the Native Americans in the Southwest built a new culture around longer growing seasons and crop cultivation, similar transitions were taking place in very different environments in the eastern half of the continent. In the flood plains of the Mississippi River valley, along the Ohio and Arkansas Rivers, and as far away as the Southeast interior, Native Americans were exploiting the climate change to grow the same trio of maize, squashes, and beans. Though they spoke different languages and inhabited a vast stretch of land, the peoples who made this transition to agriculture were connected to a broad cultural complex called **Mississippian civilization** (see Map 1.2).

At the core of Mississippian civilization lay the metropolitan center later known as **Cahokia** (its original name has not survived), near present-day East St. Louis, Illinois. Along with rich soil for growing crops and dense, nearby woods for hunting, its location was ideal for a cultural hub: It stood just below the confluence of the Mississippi and Missouri Rivers, connected to much of the continent's interior through a vast water transportation network.

Cahokia had both a powerful pull and a broad reach. By the end of the twelfth century, the capital (not counting its

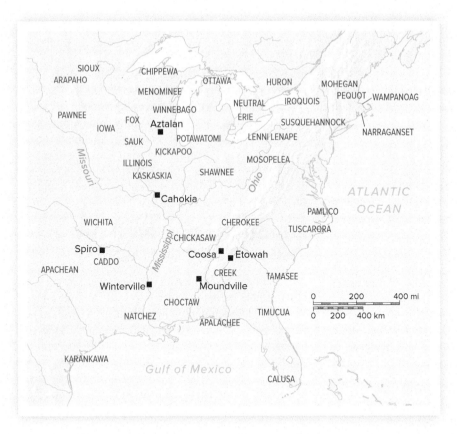

Map 1.2 The Vast Reach of Mississippian Civilization, ca. 800-1500 CE   Mississippian trade routes, cultural connections, and political ties spread through much of the Midwest and Southeast. By 1500, that civilization was thoroughly dispersed, and new nations rose in these territories.

Alabama, Etowah in Georgia, and Apalachee near Tallahassee, Florida. They shared with Cahokia a pattern of striking social inequality. As in many other stratified societies, differences between chiefs and commoners were made to seem natural through monumental architecture, the display of prestigious ceremonial goods, and the acquisition and cultivation of esoteric knowledge. All of these factors reinforced the idea that powerful leaders stood somewhere between ordinary human beings and the superhuman forces that controlled the universe. Mississippian chiefdoms also engaged in more organized and sustained warfare, and there is evidence of elaborate ceremonies involving the ritual sacrifice of women, who might have been captives. Physical anthropologists have determined that about one out of three male and one out of four female Mississippians died violent deaths.

several suburbs) held between ten and twenty thousand people—a population roughly the size of London in the same period. More people lived in Cahokia in the year 1200 than in any other city in the Americas north of the Rio Grande until the late eighteenth century. Some immigrants to Cahokia were probably attracted by rumors of the city's ambitious earthwork mounds.

POLITICS AND ENTERTAINMENT

• **Chunkey,** a Cahokian version of an older hoop-and-pole game that involved throwing a stone disk across a clay playing field, became an especially prominent feature of Mississippian culture. It served as a ritualized spectator sport, an object of high-stakes gambling, and even an instrument of diplomacy and politics. The ascent of chunkey as the major game of its era both reflected and reinforced the cultural dominance of the Cahokian capital, much as particular sports spread British culture in the nineteenth century and U.S. culture in the twentieth. •

Other moundbuilding chiefdoms that were part of the Mississippian culture included Moundville and Coosa in

Rather suddenly in the early 1300s, this grand civilization began to disintegrate. Cahokia's leadership and prestige were probably weakened by drought, an earthquake, and warfare. The larger economy of the city may also have been damaged by resource depletion, crop failures, and health hazards posed by overcrowding. There may also have been local power struggles, or crises of religious faith, though no traces of such developments have turned up in the soil. What we do know is that the demise of Cahokia was not a local phenomenon. • One by one, major Mississippian cities were abandoned during the early fourteenth century, a moment that also marked the beginning of a long cooling period known as the **Little Ice Age,** which lasted into the nineteenth century. As in the Southwest, changes in the weather appear to have undermined the new cities built by Americans around the rise of three-crop agriculture. The farming practices and diets introduced in the warming period survived, but the great urban centers did not. • Migrants from the cities created new, decentralized villages; relocated to

CLIMATES AND ECOLOGIES

new regions; forged new political alliances; and built new groups and nations. Most of the nations that Europeans later encountered in North America were creations of this post-Mississippian dispersal.

The end of the Cahokian regime shaped life in a large part of North America as dramatically as the regime itself had. From the Missouri River to the Atlantic Ocean, the fourteenth and fifteenth centuries were a time of population movement, shifting trade relations, and political transition. Both the spread of farming during the warming period and the dispersal of the urban chiefdoms after the weather cooled created instability and change. Scholars debate, for example, whether the formation of the powerful Iroquois and Huron confederacies in the Great Lakes region around the beginning of the fifteenth century was the result of the spread, or the fall, of Mississippian civilization. Whatever the case, by the time of Cahokia's decline, events in one part of the continent could affect people far away. Though the extraordinarily diverse array of people whom Europeans would lump together into a single group spoke different languages and belonged to discrete nations, they already lived in a connected world.

CULTURES OF THE PACIFIC COAST

The agricultural revolution of the warming period bypassed several sparsely populated parts of North America that were too cold (Canada and Alaska) or too arid (Utah and Nevada). Agriculture also made few inroads along the Pacific coast, which nonetheless was by far the most densely populated portion of the country in the era right before Columbus's voyages—about four times as dense as the Northeast or the Southeast. Indigenous Californians were a striking exception to the rule that dense settlement went hand in hand with agriculture.

More than anything else, the abundance of marine life in California and the Pacific Northwest made agriculture unnecessary. Salmon, rather than maize, was the backbone of the economy. But while the Native Americans in the far West did not farm, they did not live effortlessly off the Earth's bounty. Native Californians developed sophisticated techniques for collecting and preparing seeds, roots, and nuts. They also set fires strategically to stimulate the growth of particular plant life, diversify their food sources, facilitate hunting, and adjust to changing climate conditions. Recent research supports the view that native Californians enjoyed more nutritious, varied diets and greater labor efficiency than their agricultural counterparts in the Eastern half of the continent.

The diverse ecology of the Pacific coast supported hundreds of different groups and language communities. West

Coast Native Americans did not develop large chiefdoms. Nonetheless, many California communities underwent some of the same social changes from the eleventh century onward that took place in the urban centers of the Southwest, Midwest, and Southeast. Among the Chumash who lived in the Channel Islands and around the present-day city of Santa Barbara, some of the Pomo groups along the North Central Coast, and the small Shellmound chiefdoms of the San Francisco Bay Area, the scale of specialized economic activities (storing salmon and acorns and directing fires) produced economic inequality and the accumulation of private property.

EUROPE AND AFRICA ON THE EVE OF CONTACT

On the other side of the Atlantic, a parallel climatic cycle of a warming period followed by a Little Ice Age affected Western European communities as well. A series of economic, political, and intellectual changes put into motion by these trends and others set the stage for explorations that would lead to contact with the Americas. At the same time, kingdoms in West Africa became more deeply enmeshed in Eurasian trade networks. Eventually, the Portuguese set up trading posts there, where enslaved Africans would be purchased for plantation work. Religious affiliations and rivalries also shaped the course of events in Europe and Africa and provided an important context for subsequent encounters.

CHANGE AND CONFLICT IN NORTHWESTERN EUROPE

Western Europe from the tenth through the thirteenth century (the Late Middle Ages or late medieval period) experienced rising temperatures associated with the North Atlantic Warm Period. This climatic change enabled farmers north of the Alps and Pyrenees (especially in France, the German States, The Netherlands, and England; see Map 1.3) to extend the growing season and breed new varieties of food crops, including nutrient-rich legumes. Since Western Europe was already a farming society, the change was less dramatic than the advent of agriculture in parts of North America. Nonetheless, the impact was significant. With the rise in productivity and nutrition, the population of northwestern Europe soared.

● Then, as in North America, the beginning of the Little Ice Age brought suffering and instability. In Europe, colder temperatures in the early fourteenth century destroyed crops and bred famine, after which devastating diseases swept the continent. ●

CLIMATES AND ECOLOGIES

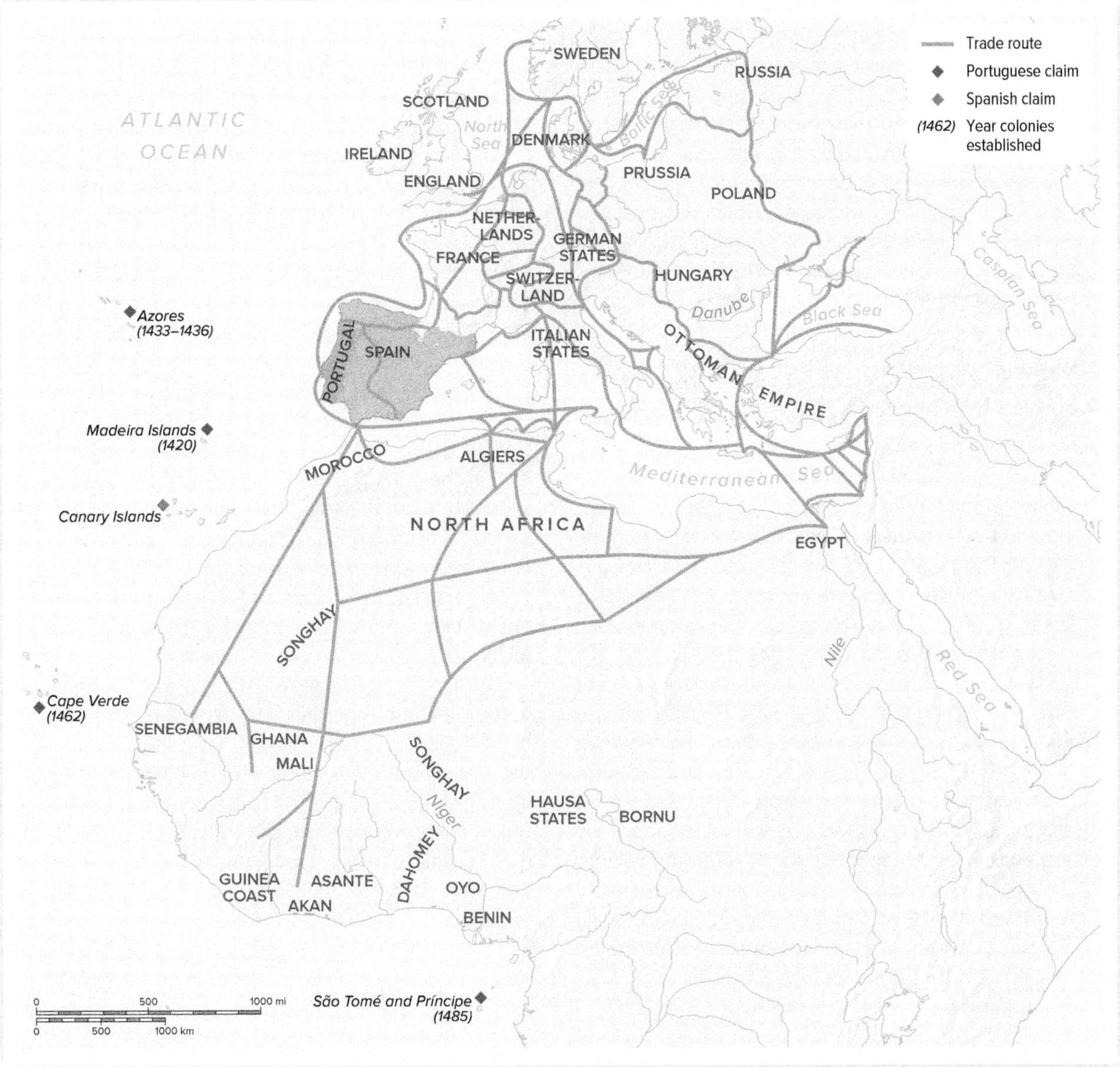

Map 1.3 Western Europe and West Africa on the Eve of Contact, ca. 1400–1500. Networks of long-distance commerce connected Europe and Africa. Along with religious crusades, this web of trade laid the groundwork for future patterns of colonization, conquest, and slave trading. Long before the Atlantic slave trade, West African gold production financed the economic expansion of Mediterranean Europe.

● Most dramatic was the bubonic plague of 1347–1351, known as the Black Death. Increased warfare had combined with famine and disease to create a demographic catastrophe. By century's end, France had lost approximately 40 percent of its population, and in some areas as much as 90 percent, while almost half of England's people had died. The consequences were far reaching. Previously landless survivors gained new access to property in ravaged areas, and labor shortages triggered population movements and unrest. The traditional social order in which all men and women knew their proper places loosened. ●

Unlike in North America, instability in England and France during the fourteenth and fifteenth centuries drew people toward big cities rather than away from them. Thus, while Native American chiefdoms decentralized, those in

Europe began to consolidate into **nation-states** under the control of more powerful monarchs. The kings (and occasionally queens) of Western Europe marshaled staggering financial resources to mobilize and equip massive armies for the international wars that consumed the region during this period. European monarchs were also religious figures with a status, like Native American chiefs, somewhere between the human beings who revered them and the divine forces said to authorize their rule. By the end of the fifteenth century, on the eve of the convergence of European, African, and American cultures, northern Europe was itself a world in transition.

CRUSADES, RECONQUISTA, AND THE BEGINNINGS OF EXPLORATION

● During the Middle Ages, Western European kingdoms claimed allegiance to **Latin Christendom,** a religious community unified under the authority of the pope in Rome. Latin Christendom saw itself as a universal faith that applied to all countries and lands. Its Catholic Church (the word *catholic* means comprehensive, inclusive, or broad) was able to absorb or subsume older, varied religious traditions throughout the continent. The unity of Latin Christendom was reinforced by a series of wars against non-believers (primarily Muslims but also Jews and heretics), known as the **Crusades.** Between 1095 and 1291, men from across Europe enlisted in these wars, drawn in part by assurances from the pope that their sins would be forgiven, and joined armed pilgrimages to wrest control of Jerusalem from Muslims. Though they secured no lasting Catholic presence in Southwest Asia, the Crusades fostered a kind of broad European identity at home and provided a model for expanding Latin Christendom to distant lands. ●

By the fifteenth century, increasingly powerful European monarchs had tapped into the crusading spirit. In the Iberian Peninsula (modern Spain and Portugal), armies from Aragon, Castile, Catalonia, and Portugal had waged a prolonged holy war from the eighth century onward to "reconquer" the peninsula from Muslims. These Iberian crusades, known as the **Reconquista** (the Spanish and Portuguese word for reconquest), were generally more successful than those in Southwest Asia. By 1252, Muslim rule survived only in the southern part of the peninsula. Two centuries later, Spanish and Portuguese governments reinvigorated the struggle to purify the land of non-Christians. In 1848, Spain initiated an Inquisition to weed out heretic and closet Jews. In 1492, they expelled Muslims from their last stronghold in Grenada.

As part of this ongoing campaign of Reconquista, Christian rulers on the Iberian Peninsula also explored the islands in what they called the Western Ocean (the Atlantic). In 1402, King Enrique III of the Spanish kingdom of Castile authorized conquerors, called **adelantados** (advance men), to organize and fund raids on the **Canary Islands** (see Map 1.3). In 1472, Ferdinand and Isabella ordered the invasion of the remaining three islands not yet under Spanish control. The conquest followed a model with roots in earlier raids on Muslim areas in Europe and the Mediterranean: Adelantados agreed to pay the monarch a one-fifth cut of any spoils, taxes, or natural resources extracted from the areas they conquered. In addition to gaining property to exploit, they received a noble title and the promise that God would forgive their sins. The final Canary island of Tenerife fell into Spanish hands in 1496. The islands' indigenous population, the Guanches, had been divided among many small chiefdoms, and the invaders were able to exploit the animosities among rival chiefdoms over a long and bloody century of war. An estimated thirty thousand Guanches died as a result of the conflict; others were enslaved on the islands or enslaved and sent to Europe.

During the same period, Portugal was even more successful in colonizing islands in the Atlantic. In 1415, Portuguese forces captured the Muslim port city of Ceuta on the African side of the Strait of Gibraltar, thereby opening up the Atlantic coast of Africa to Christian ships. In the wake of this victory, Portugal's Prince Henry "the Navigator" became Europe's leading promoter of maritime exploration. Drawing on his political power, his financial resources and connections, his access to scholarly books and maps, and recent innovations in navigational instrument development, Prince Henry set up a school of navigation and sponsored expeditions. Ship captains who trained under him set out to explore the Atlantic, conquer new territory for Portugal, and discover potential water routes to Asia. Many of Henry's backers were Italian merchant houses interested in Asian goods, but Henry and his ship captains saw these seafaring projects in more religious terms, as did the pope. A water route to China or Japan—places that educated Europeans had read about in the travel tales of Marco Polo, who had journeyed to Asia in the late thirteenth century—could open up new territories to Christendom and give the Catholic Church a new line of attack in its war against Islam.

In contrast to the Spanish-controlled Canaries, most of the Atlantic islands taken by Portugal were uninhabited. Henry's first target was the Madeira Islands, which he claimed in 1420 on behalf of the Order of Christ, a

Malian Emperor Mansa Musa as Depicted in the Catalan Atlas, 1375. *Library of Congress Geography and Map Division [G1001 .C7 1959 Vault]*

BEHIND THE IMAGE

The Catalan Atlas was a massive map produced over two years by Abraham and Jehuda Cresques, a father-and-son team of Jewish cartographers from the island of Majorca, for the king of Aragon. Majorca, a Spanish-controlled island between Barcelona and Algiers, was a center of geographical expertise in the fourteenth century, and its Jewish community (part of a dispersed religious community with connections to both Christian and Muslim lands in much of the Mediterranean world) included many accomplished mapmakers. In keeping with medieval map conventions, it presented the world comprised of three continents. Compared to other world maps produced in medieval Europe, the Catalan Atlas reflected its producers' greater familiarity with Africa.

WITHIN THE IMAGE

1 Malian emperor Mansa Musa, the dominant figure in this section of a much larger map, is shown wearing a gold crown, holding a gold nugget and gold scepter, and seated on a gold throne with plush cushions. These items not only display royalty and wealth but also allude to the importance of African gold to the larger system of economic exchange. **2** Facing a Saharan terrain marked by tent dwellings, he extends the nugget toward **3** a trader from the western Sahara, who travels along a grid of travel routes that extend in all directions. The artist's point that Mansa Musa commands the attention of a wide world is emphasized by **4** text on the map calling the Malian emperor "the richest and most distinguished ruler of this whole region, on account of the great quantity of gold that is found in his land."

BEYOND THE IMAGE

King Pedro III of Aragon paid the father-and-son mapmakers handsomely for their work, which he presented as a gift to King Charles V of France several years later. The gift was stored in the French national library, both as a luxurious artistic treasure and as a symbol of the geographical knowledge and ambition that rulers in Latin Christendom valued during this era of exploration and expansion. Since the nineteenth century, this panel of the Catalan Atlas has been studied as evidence of medieval European interest and curiosity in the powerful civilizations of Africa before the rise of the Atlantic slave trade.

community of knights to which he belonged. Then, in the 1430s, one of his ship captains found more unpopulated territory farther west, in the Azores. By the middle of the century, Portuguese adventurers had established agricultural colonies in both island chains, relying on the labor of a mix of mostly free settlers and some captives. Henry also sponsored expeditions along the Atlantic coast of Africa. These voyages established trade contacts with the powerful kingdom of **Mali,** introduced Christianity to West Africa, and in the 1460s added the uninhabited islands of Cape Verde to Portugal's growing Atlantic empire.

Closer to the African mainland, the Portuguese claimed two islands in the Gulf of Guinea in 1471, which they colonized in 1485 and named **São Tomé and Príncipe.** Among the original colonists of São Tomé was a large group of Jewish children who had been taken from their parents in Portugal to the South Atlantic to be brought up as Christians. Quickly, however, the Portuguese began introducing enslaved Africans to work on sugar plantations. This colony represented the beginning of large-scale African slavery in the Atlantic.

After establishing their Atlantic island empire and trading posts along the African coast, the Portuguese-sponsored captains turned their attention to finding the sea route to Asia. In 1488, Bartholomeu Dias established the possibility of such a journey when he sailed around the Cape of Good Hope at Africa's southern tip. Ten years later, a Portuguese fleet under the command of Vasco de Gama sailed to India. Portugal would build a vast commercial empire in South Asia, Indonesia, and China over the next centuries, and Catholic missionaries would try to spread Christianity to those lands. But for the history of the Americas, by far the more important consequence of the explorations sponsored by Prince Henry lay in the eastern Atlantic. In the Azores, Madeira, and especially the sugar plantations of São Tomé, Portugal laid the groundwork for the vast and notorious Atlantic slave system.

WEST AFRICA AND ISLAM

Far closer to the Americas lay another major region that would contribute to the formation of what came to be called the New World. West Africa south of the Sahara covered a large terrain and included many states and smaller chiefdoms (see Map 1.3). It was home to a wide range of ethnicities and cultures, hundreds of distinct language communities, and several different religious traditions. Most West Africans were farming people, clustered in small villages and bound by powerful ties to large kin networks, though several important urban centers flourished as well.

A number of states and chiefdoms wielded political power in various parts of the region, but medieval West Africa can be divided into two periods, corresponding with powerful political regimes that dominated much of the region. From the eighth century onward, the kingdom of **Ghana** controlled a significant empire, centered several hundred miles northwest of the country that bears that name today. Ghana leveraged its extensive gold deposits to establish far-flung trade routes, but attacks from Muslim Berbers in the year 1076 precipitated the decline of its empire during the following century. Ghana's successor, the kingdom of Mali, controlled an even vaster territory and emerged as the imperial superpower and trading center in the thirteenth century.

During the same period when Christians were expelling Muslims from Iberia and organizing Crusades to the Holy Lands, Muslim traders from North Africa and Southwest Asia were spreading Islam into the interior of the African continent. Traders introduced Muslim ideas and influences to Mali, along with precious metals, spices, horses, and a range of manufactured goods. Mali's rulers adopted Islam, and the city of Timbuktu became a significant center of Islamic learning, with a university whose faculty was as distinguished and renowned as any in Europe at the time. Islam, a scriptural religion (a faith organized around the reading of sacred texts), flourished along the coasts of the continent and in commercial cities where literacy was more common. In the more rural areas, where most West Africans lived, Islam made fewer inroads, though many illiterate peasants learned about the religion through mystic poems composed in vernacular languages (the spoken and written languages of particular regions) rather than in the sacred Arabic.

The main commodities that traders wanted from West Africans were gold and human beings. Slavery thrived in much of the world at this time, and the demand for enslaved labor in Muslim states in North Africa and Southwest Asia had soared. In the **African slave trade,** the fact that Islam had spread to Mali without becoming the majority religion of the area probably made a big difference. Muslims preferred to enslave religious outsiders, so non-Muslims obtained from Africa south of the Sahara were valued as laborers, while Muslims from the same region became trusted trading partners. By around 1500, enslaved people from Africa had replaced those from southeastern Europe (mostly from the Black Sea region) as the primary bound labor force in much of the Muslim heartland. Unlike the men and women sold into slavery in the Americas in subsequent centuries, enslaved persons bound for the Muslim world were mostly employed as domestic servants or concubines, not as agricultural fieldworkers. Two-thirds of them were women.

Over the course of the fifteenth century, Malian rule faced rebellions on several fronts. Timbuktu fell to nomadic invaders in 1433, and by 1500 the empire had collapsed as much of its territory came under the control of Songhay, a rival state to the east. During the same period, Portuguese explorers, traders, and missionaries began arriving in West Africa. Mali's authorities resisted the European visitors and forced them to remain on the coast—a ban that unintentionally protected Europeans from diseases that had spread in the African interior. But even confined to the edge of the continent and reliant on networks of African merchants to supply the commodities they sought, the Portuguese would have a powerful impact on life in the region.

Farther south along the Gold Coast, in the Kingdom of the Kongo, Portuguese commercial interests established a trading center in 1482 that came to be known as Elmina Castle. The Portuguese used the castle, now the oldest European building in Africa south of the Sahara, to trade for gold, triggering competition for the precious metal within African societies. A century later, as enslaved people began to displace gold as West Africa's major export, Elmina Castle became a major stop on the passage of Africans to the Americas.

CONVERGENCE AND CONTACT

Early Portuguese and Spanish ventures in the eastern Atlantic initiated a larger process of exploration, which would ultimately drive sailors across the ocean to the shores of the Caribbean and the massive continent just beyond. Spain took the lead in this next phase of the age of exploration, first through Columbus and then through the many conquerors who followed in his wake. As in earlier European expeditions to the Azores and São Tomé, Spain expected lands on the other side of the ocean to yield wealth through the labor of indigenous pagan populations or other enslaved non-Christians. Spanish adelantados quickly established colonies in the Americas.

COLUMBUS'S FIRST AND SECOND VOYAGES

After several unsuccessful overtures to a number of European monarchs, including the Spanish rulers who would ultimately sponsor his voyage, an Italian sailor from Genoa named Christopher Columbus was finally appointed as an adelantado for Spain's Queen Isabella in 1492. That January, Spanish forces had captured the stronghold of Granada, ending eight centuries of Islamic rule on the Iberian Peninsula. Later in 1492, Spanish Jews who refused to convert to Christianity were expelled from the country. All three events—Granada's capture, the Jews' expulsion, and Columbus's voyage—were connected. All were efforts of a rising nation-state to expand its power while spreading the rule of Latin Christendom.

Contrary to popular myth, Christopher Columbus was no visionary geographer. What separated Columbus from the geographical authorities of his day was not his faith that the Earth was round (a view they shared) but his erroneous belief that Japan lay close to Europe, just beyond the Canary Islands. Nonetheless, Columbus had on his side a great deal of seafaring experience and an intuitive grasp of the Atlantic's circular wind patterns. Columbus headed south from the Canaries, where he knew that autumn winds blew in an easterly direction. He guessed, correctly, that powerful westerly winds farther north would secure his safe passage home.

Six weeks out from the Canary Islands, Columbus and his three ships dropped anchor at a small island 300 miles north of Cuba, in part of the present-day Bahamas. Naming the island San Salvador (after the Savior, Jesus Christ), Columbus spent the next three months surveying the other islands in the area and hoping to find a connection to the grand khan of China. The Arawak-speaking **Tainos,** who lived in these islands, fulfilled few of the visitors' expectations of inhabitants of Asia or the East Indies. But Columbus still called them "Indians"—and that name stuck well past the point when it became clear that his ships had not reached Asia.

Columbus returned to Europe with evidence of the promising islands he had discovered. At the Spanish court in Barcelona, he displayed parrots and colorful masks that his audience had never seen before. He also produced some gold, which he had found on the large island Hispaniola (present-day Haiti and the Dominican Republic). Finally, he presented seven men, the survivors among the twenty Tainos he had taken aboard his ship for the return voyage. To the Spanish court in 1493, these were men in need of baptism and salvation.

Excited by Columbus's presentation, the Spanish monarchy made him a nobleman and outfitted him for a return trip to Hispaniola. For this second voyage, he commanded seventeen ships carrying over twelve hundred men, including priests, miners, artisans, and soldiers.

Importantly, this was a colonization party, not an exploration party. When Columbus arrived in Hispaniola, he discovered that the thirty-nine sailors he had left behind on the first journey had committed acts of violence and been killed by the Tainos in response. Undaunted, Columbus and his men began the business of making the new colony profitable. First through diplomatic gift exchanges and then through a heavy tax on the Tainos, the Spanish authorities extracted large quantities of gold from the island. When the local population proved unable to meet the arduous gold tax, the Spanish declared war. By 1496, about one hundred thousand Tainos in Hispaniola (roughly a third of the island's 1492 population) had been killed. By 1499, the surviving inhabitants had been subjected to a regime of forced labor.

THE SPANISH CONQUEST

Using Hispaniola as a base, other Spanish adelantados conquered neighboring islands in the Caribbean, including Puerto Rico (1508), Jamaica (1509), and Cuba (1511). In each case, the invaders proclaimed the sovereignty of the pope and the Spanish monarchy over the island and forced the local population to work for them (see Interpreting the Sources: The Requerimiento). Spain soon boasted an empire in the western Atlantic that rivaled Portugal's imperial domain farther east. Pope Alexander VI had given his blessing to these empires in 1493 and approved the geographical division. Drawing a line on a map of the ocean that southern Europeans were exploring (see Map 1.4), the pope granted all heathen land on one side to Spain and that on the other side to Portugal.

Following Columbus's initial voyage, Europeans would learn a great deal about the ocean he had crossed. On his third trip, in 1498, Columbus ventured south of the Caribbean islands and sailed along rivers in the South American mainland, which he speculated might be attached to China. A different Spanish expedition, a year later, landed in what is now Venezuela. In 1500, Portuguese ships under the command of Pedro Ýlvars Cabral stumbled upon what appeared to be an enormous island, which he dubbed Terra Santa Cruz. A subsequent Portuguese exploration concluded that this territory, which is in northern Brazil, was not an island at all but part of a massive continental landmass.

By the early 1500s, European mapmakers and geographers had become convinced that a large continent, separate from Asia, lay on the western edge of the ocean.

A German cartographer named Martin Waldseemüller depicted this continent on a map he published in 1507. Instead of honoring Columbus, Waldseemüller named the continent after Florentine businessman Amerigo Vespucci, who served first as an observer and then a navigational expert on the expeditions that reached Venezuela and Brazil. Feminizing Vespucci's first name to suit the imagined gender of a continent, Waldseemüller's map identified the landmass on the other side of the waters as *America*. Support for Waldseemüller's picture of the world came in 1513, when Vasco Núñez de Balboa landed at Panama, crossed the isthmus, and returned to Europe with reports of a large sea on the other side. In 1519, Ferdinand Magellan of Spain used this knowledge to attempt to sail around the world. The following year, he rounded the southern tip of South America, crossing from the Atlantic into the Pacific. Magellan was killed in the Philippines, but part of his original expedition succeeded in circumnavigating the globe in three years.

A much clearer view of the Western Hemisphere then came into focus in Europe. An enormous continent lay between Europe and Asia, and it would be called **America.** In 1519, the same year that Magellan set out on his round-the-world voyage, a military force led by Spanish conquistador (conqueror) Hernán Cortés invaded the mighty Aztec Empire in Mexico. Enlisting the support of other native peoples who resented Aztec rule, Cortés and his allies besieged the populous capital of Tenochtitlán in 1521 and forced its surrender, killing over fifty thousand Aztec. Cortés ordered the destruction of the city and rebuilt on its ruins a new capital of Spain's American empire.

Another expedition, led by conquistador Francisco Pizarro, invaded the land of the Inca, a region of more than nine million inhabitants centered in what is now Peru. In 1532, as the Inca Empire was reeling from civil war and from diseases introduced to the continent by earlier European explorers, Pizarro's small force captured the emperor, Atahualpa, and held him for a huge ransom in precious metals. The Spanish executed Atahualpa a year later and established the city of Lima. Fighting between the Spaniards and Inca continued for years, but another powerful civilization had been subdued.

In Mexico and Peru, as in the Caribbean, Spain established a colonial empire based on the exploitation of indigenous labor. Legally speaking, the native people were allowed to remain on their land, but the Spanish Crown granted their labor to individual conquerors in a labor regime known as the **encomienda.** The native

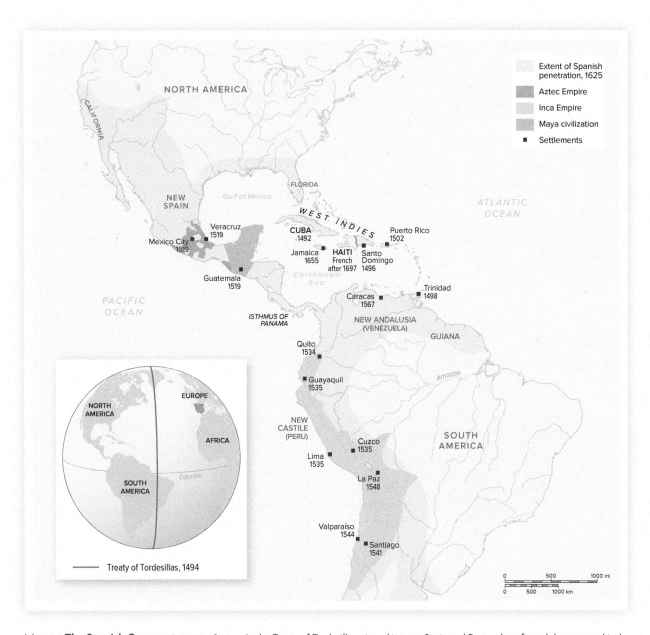

Map 1.4 The Spanish Conquest, 1492–1600.   In the Treaty of Tordesillas, signed in 1494, Spain and Portugal confirmed the geographical boundary set a year earlier by the pope. The line would have important implications for the settlement of South America, but the pope was not concerned with the geography of the American continents, about which Europeans still knew almost nothing. The line was intended to recognize the colonies that Spain and Portugal had already claimed.

people did not technically belong to the Spanish under the encomienda system, but they were forced to produce export goods and to labor in mines, sugar mills, and public construction projects. Because Mexico and Peru turned out to hold vast deposits of gold and (especially) silver, the system yielded enormous tangible riches for the Spanish Empire. The silver-mining town of **Potosí,** in present-day Bolivia, quickly attained a population of one hundred sixty thousand by 1600 (surpassing any city on the European continent at the time) and produced 45,000 tons of silver over the next two centuries. Within a few generations of Columbus's arrival, Spanish conquests had radically reorganized the political and economic conditions of the most populous parts of the hemisphere.

INTERPRETING THE SOURCES

The Requerimiento

As Spanish conquerors arrived on islands in the western Atlantic during the early sixteenth century, they issued the following proclamation, asserting their rights to rule over the local population. A version of the Requerimiento (requirement) had been used earlier by the Spanish in the Canary Islands, but by 1513 the Spanish were following a standard text composed by a lawyer named Palacios Rubios. Although the text was written (and typically proclaimed) in Castilian Spanish, which presumably no indigenous person could understand, the invaders made a point of reading it in the presence of the people to whom it was addressed. When Pedrarias Dávila arrived on the Caribbean island of Dominica in 1513, he had his notary read the Requerimiento and instructed a young native girl (who had been kidnapped, taken to Spain, and then brought back) to help explain its meaning. His audience responded by firing poisoned arrows. On other occasions, the text was read to empty villages or shouted from a ship. One of Dávila's commanders had the Requerimiento read to indigenous people who already had ropes around their necks.

It is impossible to say what this proclamation communicated to the indigenous people of Central America and the Caribbean in the sixteenth century, but the text offers insight into what the Spanish took to be the justification for their actions.

We ask and require . . . that you consider what we have said to you, and that you take the time that shall be necessary to understand and deliberate upon it, and that you acknowledge the Church as the ruler and superior of the whole world, and the high priest called Pope, and in his name the king and queen . . . our lords, in his place, as superiors and lords and kings of these islands and this mainland. . . .

If you do so [acknowledge the Church as ruler] you will do well, and that which you are obliged to do to their highnesses, and we in their name shall receive you in all love and charity, and shall leave you your wives and your children and your lands free without servitude, that you may do with them and with yourselves freely what you like and think best, and they shall not compel you to turn Christians unless you yourselves, when informed of the truth, should wish to be converted to our holy Catholic faith . . . as almost all the inhabitants of the rest of the islands have done. . . .

But if you do not do this or if you maliciously delay in doing it, I certify to you that with the help of God we shall forcefully enter into your country and shall make war against you in all ways and manners that we can, and shall subject you to the yoke and obedience of the Church and their highnesses; we shall take you and your wives and your children and shall make slaves of them, and as such sell and dispose of them as their highnesses may command; and we shall take away your goods and shall do to you all the harm and damage that we can, as to vassals who do not obey and refuse to receive their lord and resist and contradict him; and we protest that the deaths and losses which shall accrue from this are your fault, and not that of their highnesses, or ours, or of these soldiers who come with us. And that we have said this to you and made this Requerimiento we request the notary here present to give us his testimony in writing, and we ask the rest who are present that they should be witnesses of this Requerimiento.

Explore the Source

1. According to the Requerimiento, were indigenous people forced to convert to Christianity? What were their options?

2. Why do you think it was important to the Spanish to have a document like the Requerimiento?

THE COLUMBIAN EXCHANGE

As Spaniards imposed new regimes in the Caribbean and warred against powerful empires in Mexico and South America, they precipitated new flows of people, information, goods, flora, fauna, and microbes between the two sides of the Atlantic Ocean. Scholars refer to this widespread, complex process as the **Columbian exchange.** From one perspective, the most obvious component of the exchange was the influx of people from Europe and Africa to the Americas. Indeed, approximately three hundred thousand Spaniards immigrated to mainland New Spain during the sixteenth century. The overwhelming majority were male, and most Spanish immigrants married indigenous women and fathered children with them. By the end of the century, towns and cities throughout Mexico and Central America held large numbers of **mestizos** (Spanish-Indians). More than two hundred thousand enslaved West Africans were brought to Spain's colonies as well in this period, mostly to the West Indies but also to the mainland.

CROSSING BORDERS

CROSSING BORDERS

DISEASE AND EPIDEMIC

● The most striking demographic change, however, was mass death. Spanish conquerors brought guns to the Americas and used lethal force to secure the obedience of local populations. But what they did not know was that they came bearing a far deadlier weapon: disease. Europeans who survived childhood had acquired immunities to smallpox, measles, typhoid fever, and other diseases endemic to their part of the world, but they carried those pathogens in their systems. Because indigenous Americans had been isolated from such pathogens for millennia, they lacked immunological defenses against germs introduced by the newcomers, beginning with Columbus's first voyage. The total devastation of the Tainos in the Caribbean and the defeat of the Aztec Empire were as much the consequences of influenza and smallpox as they were of European military advantages. ● Population estimates for pre-Columbian America range widely, but even if we accept the most conservative figures, the population of Mexico dropped from eight million to two million during the 1500s. Estimates at the higher end of the scale raise the population loss to twenty-three million.

Potosí Mines, Engraving by Theodor de Bry, 1596. Domingo de Santo Tomás, a Spanish priest who arrived in Peru in 1540, described Potosí as "a mouth of hell, into which a great mass of people enter every year and are sacrificed by the greed of the Spaniards to their 'god.'" *North Wind Picture Archives/Alamy Stock Photo*

Like many other elements of the Columbian exchange, diseases traveled mostly in one direction—toward the Americas. With the exception of syphilis, no deadly American diseases made their way back to Europe. Along with the diseases, humans, animals, and plants moved west rather than east across the ocean. Horses may have been especially startling to indigenous Mesoamericans, since they were instrumental to the conquest, but other animals, including cattle, sheep, and goats, multiplied even more rapidly than horses. By the early seventeenth century, there were already nine times as many European animals as American animals in Mexico. Rats and European weeds also made the journey west, allowing what some scholars have described as a wholesale transplanting of European ecosystems.

Other objects flowed in the opposite direction—from west to east. Some, like gold and silver, involved the extraction of resources from one hemisphere to enrich and ennoble the people and nations in the other. But other American goods, including tobacco and cacao (the plant from which chocolate is derived), built cultural bridges across the Atlantic. Two products cultivated originally in Mesoamerica, tobacco and cacao were special objects of both social exchange and religious ritual among the Aztec. After they crossed the ocean, tobacco and chocolate came to assume special significance in European culture as well—for their healing properties and their ceremonial role in forging social relationships or marking class distinction. Other American foods would completely transform diets

How Much Is That?

Annual Mining Yields from Potosí

By the end of the sixteenth century, Spanish conquerors were overseeing the extraction of about 250 tons of silver every year, valued at approximately 8 million pesos. According to one common historical currency conversion, this would correspond to an annual yield of about 519 million dollars in 2020.

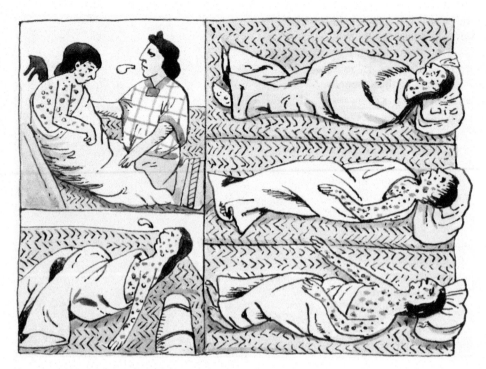

Aztec Suffering from Smallpox in the Wake of European Contact. This illustration is from *La Historia General de las Cosas de Nueva España*, now known as the *Florentine Codex*, a sixteenth-century ethnography (cultural study) by Spanish Franciscan missionary Bernardino de Sahagún. *Dorling Kindersley/Getty Images*

in far-flung parts of the globe. Maize was quickly introduced in West Africa and Europe and from there to Southwest Asia, India, and China. Potatoes, which had thrived originally in the Andes, went first to Spain in the sixteenth century and later found a home in the cooler and wetter climates of northern Europe. Red tomatoes from the Americas entered Italy in the sixteenth century and became a core ingredient in Italian cuisine. The encounter between the Iberian Peninsula and Mesoamerica brought a wide range of new plants—sweet potatoes, pumpkins, pineapples, avocados, peanuts—to the tables of men and women who had little other connection to either of those places.

NORTH AMERICA IN THE ERA OF EUROPEAN CONTACT

Northern Europeans were largely uninvolved in the fifteenth-century Atlantic explorations and the colonization that followed in Columbus's wake. Indeed, the first chapter of European expansion was dominated by southern Europe (Italian and Iberian seafarers and

Iberian monarchs) and focused mostly on the Atlantic islands, the Caribbean, Central America, and the African coast. But northern European countries with access to the Atlantic Ocean, including England and France, were interested in western lands and eager to follow the Spanish and Portuguese examples. Impelled in part by new religious crises and conflicts, northerners joined the world of Atlantic exploration and conquest and brought North America into the orbit of the Columbian exchange.

EARLY NORTHERN EXPLORATION

Northern Europeans had, in fact, preceded Columbus across the waters by five centuries. The first recorded contacts between Americans and Europeans had taken place around 980, when Norse settlers from Scandinavia colonized the island of Greenland and briefly tried to settle in Newfoundland. By the fifteenth century, however, this encounter was a distant memory in European culture, preserved only in Icelandic sagas. Northern Europeans were not tempted to sea by stories of icy and inhospitable lands.

Northern countries had trouble competing with Spain and Portugal in the business of western exploration and colonization, in part because they lacked comparable financial resources and technical sophistication but also because the areas of the Atlantic world that were closest to them were less inviting. Following Columbus's voyages to the West Indies, King Henry VII of England hired his own Italian navigator, John Cabot (Giovanni Caboto), to sail across the Atlantic from England in 1497. But Cabot did not find in Newfoundland any of the resources that Columbus had found in Hispaniola, nor did he discover a northern route to Asia. Cabot, in fact, never returned from his second voyage. Other aspiring English conquerors survived to tell their stories but were no more encouraged by what they had found along the shores of Canada during the Little Ice Age. Though Cabot and his successors had seen vast fisheries in Canada's Grand Banks, these were not enough to interest King Henry or any other European monarch.

France also hired an Italian explorer, Giovanni da Verrazano, who surveyed the coast from Maine to North Carolina in 1524, but he found nothing to inspire colonization. A decade later, Jacques Cartier embarked on the first of another set of French expeditions, this time following the St. Lawrence River through Quebec. Cartier returned with stories of large river towns but without news of a passage to China or Japan. And the cache of diamonds and gold he presented to the French court in 1542 turned out to be quartz crystals and pyrite ("fool's gold").

By the time of these French and English expeditions, Spain had ventured northward from the Caribbean and Mexico into Florida, the Southwest, and the Great Plains. These forays, between 1513 and 1546, proved temporary and led only to the conclusion that the land north of Mexico was not worth the trouble. For more than seven decades after Columbus, no significant European colonization projects targeted the areas that became the United States.

PROTESTANT EXPLORERS AND CONQUERORS

While Christians in Spain and Portugal looked to spread their faith to new frontiers in the early sixteenth century, religious life in northern Europe was disrupted by the challenge of the **Protestant Reformation.** In 1517, a monk named Martin Luther in the German town of

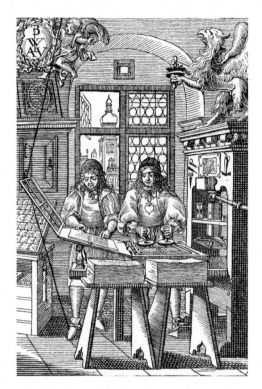

Sixteenth-Century Print Technology Depicted in a Woodcut Illustration from *The Book of Trades*, 1568. Martin Luther's scholarly disquisition might not have been intended for general consumption, but once translated from Latin to German and set in type, it reached a wide readership. By one count, one out of three books published in German between 1518 and 1525 was authored by Luther. *FALKENSTEINFOTO/Alamy Stock Photo*

Wittenberg began calling for reforms in the governance of the Catholic Church. Luther's *Ninety-five Theses* was a detailed scholarly critique of the authority of the Church to grant pardon and absolution from sin. ● It reached a wide audience, because it was reproduced with the new printing techniques that had become available in Europe several decades earlier, and it quickly inspired broader critique of papal infallibility and Church corruption. Within a decade of the publication of the *Theses*, the Protestant religious movement was born. ● Protestants stressed the view that only God can grant salvation and that human beings can hope to achieve this salvation only through faith. In effect, the Reformation rejected centuries of accumulated religious tradition, ritual, and authority. It also severed the connective tissue that had united Western Europe, at least symbolically, during the Middle Ages.

MEDIA AND INFORMATION

CONFLICTING FAITHS

● The Protestant-Catholic split led to bitter and violent internal strife through much of Europe. Because the reformers attracted more followers in the upper part of the continent (in Switzerland and north of the Alps), the Reformation also widened and emphasized the divide between northern and southern countries. In 1534, a major northern power officially broke with Rome when England's King Henry VIII declared himself supreme head of the Church of England and began confiscating and redistributing the lands that had belonged to the Catholic Church. ● Henry had not been swayed by Luther's ideas; he simply wanted to dissolve his marriage to Catherine of Aragon (who was past childbearing age) in order to produce a male heir with Anne Boleyn, and the pope refused to grant an annulment. The **English Reformation** that Henry initiated preserved many features of Catholic hierarchy, liturgy, and sacrament, but his monarchy was deeply invested in the Protestant rejection of the Roman Church, for if papal authority represented God's will, the king of England was an adulterer and his eventual heir to the throne an illegitimate pretender. Anne Boleyn did not bear him a male heir, but her daughter, Elizabeth, took the throne in 1558. Elizabeth's claim to legitimacy also depended on a rejection of the pope's authority.

Under Queen Elizabeth I, who ruled until 1603, English naval adventurers, known as sea dogs, preyed on Spanish ships. Active from the 1560s until 1605, they defended their piracy as an assault against Catholicism. At this time, England also re-embarked on its own discovery of the Americas. Sea dog Humphrey Gilbert secured a charter from Queen Elizabeth to spread the Christian faith to "remote heathen and barbarous lands" and made two unsuccessful efforts to establish a large colonial estate in Newfoundland. Gilbert died at sea following the second venture in 1583, and the charter was reassigned to his half-brother, Walter Raleigh. Meanwhile, the English navy's defeat of the supposedly invincible Spanish Armada in 1588 signaled a major shift in

Algonquian Chief, Watercolor by John White, ca. 1585. The painting recalls artist-colonist White's encounters with Indians in the Outer Banks region. The inscription reads, "The manner of their attire and painting them selves when they goe to their generall huntings, or at theire Solemne feasts." *New York Public Library/Science Source*

the balance of power between Catholic and Protestant states.

England's Protestant adventurers also took the fight to Ireland. English settlers had been in Ireland since the eleventh century, but in 1565, Queen Elizabeth's government announced a new policy of subjecting all of Ireland to English rule. Because Ireland was Catholic, men like Raleigh and Gilbert financed and directed the conquest of Ireland as part of their wider religious crusade. The English saw their Irish Catholic enemies as quite different from their Spanish ones, however. The Gaelic Irish, living in a world that had not been swept up in Europe's agricultural revolution, appeared to the English as savages, "more uncivill, more uncleanly, more barbarous and more brutish . . . then in any part of the world that is known." Indeed, the English saw Ireland's indigenous population as savages, much as Columbus had viewed the native people of Hispaniola. During two long campaigns of brutal suppression, from 1568 to 1583 and from 1594 to 1603, English conquerors undertook the process of subjugating the region in order to "civilize" it. Ireland continued to serve as both a parallel theater and a training ground for the Atlantic adventures of the sea dogs and for early English expeditions to the Americas.

The first Protestant crusaders to build colonies in the lands that would later become the United States did not come from England, however. Rather, they were Huguenots—Protestants from Catholic France—seeking both a refuge from persecution in Europe and a beachhead in the Americas against the advances of the Catholic armies of King Felipe II of Spain. In 1562, the

Map 1.5 European Explorations in North America, 1500–1600.   Although they established no lasting settlements in North America during the sixteenth century, French and English expeditions explored many parts of the land that became the United States and contested Spanish efforts at colonizing the mainland.

French pirate and explorer Jean Ribault placed a stone column near the mouth of the St. John's River in the vicinity of present-day Jacksonville, Florida, proclaiming the creation of New France. Two years later, about three hundred French Huguenots settled near Ribault's spot, where they established the colony of **La Caroline** (see Map 1.5). The Spanish understood the Huguenot settlement for what it was—a Protestant fortress that might later be used to attack Spanish colonies of the Caribbean. In 1565, Spain dispatched a thousand soldiers under the command of Pedro Menéndez de Avilés to destroy La Caroline. Menéndez captured the fort and executed most of the survivors. The Spanish also decided to colonize Florida in order to keep the Protestants out of the region. In 1565, just days before the attack on La Caroline, Menéndez founded **St. Augustine,** the oldest city still in existence in the United States.

The La Caroline massacre did not deter England's Protestant queen from granting Walter Raleigh a charter to establish a colony in the Americas. Observing the failures of Humphrey Gilbert in Newfoundland, Raleigh selected a far more temperate location and named it Virginia in honor of Elizabeth I, the "Virgin Queen." In 1584, Raleigh sent an exploratory party to the region, and they selected for settlement **Roanoke Island** on the Outer Banks of what is now North Carolina. Raleigh's explorers returned to London with two North American men from the vicinity of Roanoke Island in present-day North Carolina (see Map 1.5), who shared details of the area's geography and politics. (One of these men, Manteo, would become the first Native American to convert to Anglicanism; see Singular Lives: Manteo, Cultural Broker.) Five hundred Englishmen sailed for the new colony the following year, led by veterans of the Irish campaigns. Mishaps and diversions along the way delayed their arrival and thinned their numbers. One group returned to Europe for supplies and reinforcements, and the remaining men abandoned the settlement nine months later after provoking the local Roanokes and killing their chief.

A persistent Raleigh sent another expedition to the region in 1587, this time with a party of 110 colonists that included families. Facing a severe drought and mindful of their previous experiences with English settlers, no native groups would help the colonists secure food. Attempts to get supplies to the colony were frustrated by England's war with Spain, which commanded all of England's naval resources. When English ships finally reached Roanoke in 1590, the only trace of English settlement was the word *Croatoan* carved in English letters on a tree. Another Protestant colony had failed.

EARLY CONTACTS IN THE NORTH

Although by 1550 the Columbian exchange was transforming life in Mesoamerica and South America, its

SINGULAR LIVES

Manteo, Cultural Broker

Of the millions of men and women who lived in North America in the sixteenth century, few imprinted their names on the historical record. But the European visitors who explored various parts of the Atlantic coast learned some of these names and recorded valuable details about the lives they represented. When Walter Raleigh's explorers returned to London in 1584 from their initial voyage to the Carolina coast, they took with them two North American men. One of them, Wanchese, was a commoner from Roanoke, where Raleigh hoped to build his colony. The other, Manteo, was a minor chief from a nearby island. When the two men returned to North America the following year, Wanchese bore a dire message to his fellow Algonquians: The English were powerful, ambitious men who should not be trusted or helped. Manteo, on the other hand, embraced his new role as a kind of cultural intermediary between the English and the Algonquians, translating one society's words and rituals for the other.

How Manteo felt about the escalating hostilities between the newcomers and the indigenous people is hard to tell from the sources. Although he never changed his name, his trip to England had clearly transformed his identity. Manteo wore English clothing and never returned to the community in which he had grown up, and he advised Sir Richard Grenville (the English commander of the fleet that sailed with Manteo back to Roanoke) on diplomatic matters, earning his trust. Yet he strategically withheld information from the colonists when he needed to and remained an enigmatic figure in the treacherous world of Roanoke politics.

Historians often cite Manteo as a promising example of white–Native American cooperation in the early years of American colonization, but the historical significance of that example is as elusive as the fate of Raleigh's colony. From an English perspective in the 1580s, however, Manteo represented the bright prospects of England's North American crusade. Baptized in 1587 on Roanoke Island, Manteo became the first Native American to convert to Anglicanism.

Where in the Archives?

Though he was a chief in Carolina and a celebrity in Elizabethan England, much of what is known today about Manteo comes from a small number of written accounts penned by Englishmen who were invested in promoting the value of the Roanoke colony and the prospects of English settlement in North America.

One such account was produced by John White, an artist and mapmaker who joined the original expedition and became governor of the short-lived colonial expedition. His report on the return trip with Manteo and Wanchese offers some evidence regarding their actions and perspectives. John White's "The Fourth Voyage Made to Virginia in the Yere 1587" was published in the collection *Early English and French Voyages, Chiefly from Hakluyt, 1534-1608*, edited by Henry S. Burrage (New York: Charles Scribner's Sons, 1906). The article (on pages 279–300) can be found through HathiTrust (https://catalog.hathitrust.org/).

Assignment

Locate and read White's report. Write a short response (300 words) reflecting on the following two questions:

1. Which details from the narrative does White attest?

2. How does White perceive Manteo's identity and character?

---

impact on North America was slight. In most of the land that would become the United States, native groups experienced little fallout from the conquest in the south or the passage of people, goods, and microbes across the Atlantic Ocean. But over the second half of the sixteenth century, increasing numbers of North Americans had some indirect contact with Europe (see Hot Commodities: Cod).

Most North Americans encountered European goods brought by explorers and traders long before they met Europeans. The European goods that North Americans valued, such as ax heads, brass kettles, and glass beads, traveled deep into the interior as they passed from one chief to another along the same routes that had carried other prestigious objects long before European contact.

In a few parts of North America, however, live contact between Europeans and Americans was becoming more common. Spain sent an expedition to the upper Rio Grande valley in 1598 and claimed a new colony, which the party called New Mexico. Catholic missionaries traveled along the Florida peninsula and established missions up the coast as far north as the Chesapeake Bay. Along with Raleigh's various unsuccessful attempts to establish Virginia, the abortive ventures in Newfoundland, and the Huguenot colony at La Caroline, the Spanish outposts contributed to a series of mini-exchanges that had brought select native

HOT COMMODITIES
Cod

Well before Europeans began migrating to North America, they ate American cod. The Atlantic cod fish, *Gadhus morhua*, is an unusually prolific and durable species: omnivorous, resistant to parasites, and highly fecund. From a human perspective, it is also a remarkable food source. Low in fat and high in protein, cod is well suited to drying and salting and can last a long time. It is also easy to catch. For centuries, the North American banks between Newfoundland and southern New England have been home to the densest concentration of cod in the world.

Basque fishermen from northern Spain and southwestern France harvested the North Atlantic cod bounty as early as the fourteenth century and began importing vast quantities to Europe. By the end of the fifteenth century, French, Portuguese, English, and Spanish ships had discovered the source of the Basque supply and joined the cod rush. Quickly, cod became a staple of the European diet, accounting for more than half of the fish consumed on the continent by 1550.

European navies and seafaring expeditions valued dried cod, because it could sustain a crew over long journeys. But landlocked consumers in Catholic Europe had other reasons to buy fish. Since the fourth century, the Catholic Church had condemned eating meat on certain days, and over the subsequent centuries an elaborate calendar of fast days and lean days emerged. Catholics did not eat meat or other "hot" foods on Friday (the day linked to Jesus' crucifixion), during

Cod Fish. European demand for this prolific food source helped stimulate early contact between Western Europe and North America. *Grafissimo/Getty Images*

Lent, or on specified holy days. In all, fasts and food taboos (which in some cases forbade dairy, eggs, and wine as well) covered over one hundred days per year. Fish was allowed on fast days, however, and dried cod from the North American banks became popular. Western Europeans often ate dried cod with mustard or fatty, dairy-based sauces.

Cod became big business in the sixteenth century and contributed to a shipbuilding boom as European merchants competed for the North Atlantic fish trade. The cod trade also habituated European sailors to sailing across the Atlantic. Unlike the gold and silver that Spain extracted from its southern colonies, cod was not a valued currency. And unlike American tobacco, chocolate, or sugar, cod was not really a novel delicacy on the European consumer market. But it was one part of the transatlantic commodity exchange that drew

Europe's attention to the northern part of the Americas, encouraging the idea that the region's cold and inhospitable climate might nonetheless hold valuable natural resources.

As fishing crews set up camps to dry their cod haul, they interacted with native populations. Thus, through the sixteenth century, fishermen—rather than colonial explorers or priests—initiated the most regular and significant contacts between Europeans and Native Americans.

Think About It

1. Why might cod have been more valuable to Europeans than to North Americans?

2. How might cod have contributed to the eventual colonization of the lands that became the United States and Canada?

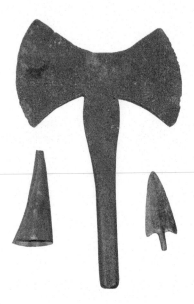

Native American Women Planting Corn. Theodor de Bry's 1590 depiction struck the European newcomers as an odd division of labor. In Europe, fieldwork was considered manly. *North Wind Picture Archives/Alamy Stock Photo*

Susquehannock Tools and Ornaments. These articles were fashioned out of brass stripped from European trade kettles. Before the seventeenth century, indigenous people tended to value the few European goods in circulation mostly for their raw materials or their symbolic associations rather than for their intended uses. *©Matson Museum of Anthropology, Pennsylvania State University*

populations of North America into an Atlantic world. Wherever these exchanges occurred, disease and death followed. An Englishman in Roanoke in 1585 noted that in the Native American villages he visited, "people began to die very fast, and many in short space." Franciscan missionaries claimed to have brought sixteen thousand Florida inhabitants into the Catholic fold in the early 1600s, but within a few years half of them had died, presumably by contagions borne by the Franciscans. As more European settlements—English, French, Dutch, and Spanish—took hold in the early 1600s, the same diseases that had swept Mexico visited the northern part of the continent.

CONCLUSION

Several decades ago, scholars and writers who were uncomfortable with the conventional notion that Columbus had *discovered* the Americas began speaking of European exploration and settlement as a *conquest* or an *invasion* rather than a discovery. Such terms apply well to Mexico, Central America, and the Caribbean, where colonization led to the rapid, wholesale destruction of native communities in the sixteenth century. But they are potentially misleading descriptions of what happened north of the Rio Grande before the seventeenth century. The sporadic arrivals of Europeans on the eastern shores of the vast territory that would become the United States did not instantly usher in a new era. Compared to the original Beringian migrations that had populated the continent, the agricultural changes of the warming period that had revolutionized settlement patterns, or the dispersals of peoples that had reshaped national and tribal boundaries in the thirteenth and fourteenth centuries, the events of the 1500s seem less dramatic. After all, much of North America was *already* in flux in 1492.

In retrospect, however, events in Mesoamerica already showed the possible stakes of European migration to North America. Inspired by their universalistic religion, motivated by international competition, and unknowingly harboring deadly germs, the migrants were capable of turning life in the Americas upside down. Equally ominous, in retrospect, was the emerging large trade in enslaved West Africans, which removed them from established homelands and brought them to the Americas.

STUDY TERMS

Beringia	Cahokia	Mali	mestizo
Paleo-Indians	chunkey	São Tomé and Príncipe	Protestant Reformation
Mesoamerica	Little Ice Age	Ghana	English Reformation
maize	nation-state	African slave trade	La Caroline
Poverty Point	Latin Christendom	Tainos	St. Augustine
moundbuilding	Crusades	America	Roanoke Island
agricultural revolution	Reconquista	encomienda	
Chaco Canyon	adelantado	Potosí	
Mississippian civilization	Canary Islands	Columbian exchange	

FURTHER READING

A database of additional full-text readings is available through Power of Process for Primary Sources in Connect.

Robert Bettinger, *Orderly Anarchy* (2015), argues that California's populous aboriginal societies were organized around small, autonomous groups.

Alfred Crosby, *Ecological Imperialism* (1986), provides a classic account of the damage caused by European pathogens.

Toby Green, *A Fistful of Shells* (2019), offers an account of the contributions of West Africa to early economic globalization.

Mark Kurlansky, *Cod* (1997), describes the far-reaching historical impact of a transatlantic fish trade that preceded European colonization.

David Madsen, ed., *Entering America* (2004), presents current research in the environmental history of Beringia.

Charles C. Mann, *1491* (2006), opens a wide-angle lens on America before Columbus.

Heather Martel, *Deadly Virtue* (2019), argues for the significance of the failed colonial ventures of French Protestants in Florida.

Marcy Norton, *Sacred Gifts, Profane Pleasures* (2008), examines the cultural significance of chocolate and tobacco in the Columbian exchange.

Michael Oberg, *The Head in Edward Nugent's Hand* (2008), reinterprets the course and significance of the abortive English colony at Roanoke.

Timothy Pauketat, *Cahokia* (2009), relates the remarkable archaeological rediscovery of an ancient city along the Mississippi River.

Daniel K. Richter, *Before the Revolution* (2011), draws powerful parallels between Europe and North America in the periods prior to their contact.

Christina Snyder, *Slavery in Indian Country* (2010), emphasizes the importance of captivity to the history of Native American politics before the arrival of the Europeans.

2 | EARLY COLONIES

Chapter Questions

1. What different colonial projects did Spain, England, France, and The Netherlands initiate in North America, and why?

2. In what crucial ways did the New England and Chesapeake colonies differ?

3. Why did tensions arise between colonists and native people in the various lands Europeans settled in the first half of the seventeenth century, and how did those tensions explode after 1675?

Visions of a New World. Martin Pringe, who explored the coast around present-day Massachusetts in 1603 as an agent of English merchants, produced this image of what he called "North Virginia." *Virginia Historical Society, Richmond, Virginia, USA/The Bridgeman Art Library*

In February 1675, the body of John Sassamon was found under the ice at Assawompset Pond in what is now southeastern Massachusetts. Born a Wampanoag early in the century, Sassamon had been orphaned at a young age and raised by English immigrants as a Christian. Eloquent and literate in both the Massachusett language and English, Sassamon served for several decades as a mediator between the Algonquian people and English colonists on the North Atlantic Coast, in a world the colonists called New England. Sassamon had also advised the Wampanoag leader Metacom, whom the English dubbed King Philip.

Relations between Metacom and the English colony of Plymouth deteriorated in the early 1670s, and in January 1675, Sassamon informed the Plymouth authorities that King Philip was planning to attack them. A week later, Sassamon disappeared, and soon after, his body was discovered. In due course, a witness stepped forward to testify that three of Metacom's advisers were responsible for the killing. After a jury of

1598
Juan de Oñate leads expedition to settle New Mexico

1607
Jamestown founded

1608
Samuel Champlain settles Québec

1610
Santa Fe established

1612
Tobacco successfully cultivated in Virginia

1620
Mayflower lands in Plymouth

1624
First Dutch settlers arrive in New Netherland

1629
Massachusetts Bay Colony founded

1637
Pequot War

1664
England's first conquest of New Netherland

1675
King Philip's War begins

1676
Nathaniel Bacon leads rebellion against Virginia

1680
Pueblo Revolt

Englishmen and Christian Native Americans convicted the men of murder, a Plymouth court ordered their execution. A protracted and bloody war followed.

The career of the man at the center of this drama epitomized how intertwined the lives of European settlers and Native Americans had become over the course of the seventeenth century. By 1614, English, Dutch, French, and Spanish colonizers had secured settlements on North America's Atlantic Coast, and in 1638 Sweden established a fur-trading colony in the lower Delaware Valley. These colonies encountered many of the same problems that had plagued earlier ventures,

but at midcentury their settlements were still standing. Although the new colonies remained small outposts on the periphery of a region dominated by Native American nations, they had a profound impact on the lands that would become the United States. In addition to the diseases that followed in the colonists' wake, Europeans introduced deadly weapons, ecologically disruptive animals, and unfamiliar ways of using and thinking about land. By the second half of the seventeenth century, European colonization was changing the face of the continent.

The new colonies varied markedly. French, Dutch, and Swedish settlements were organized around fur trading, whereas English settlements focused on farming. In the Chesapeake Bay region, English colonists grew tobacco on relatively isolated plantations, whereas those in New England worked smaller farms and clustered in towns. In Florida and in the Southwest, the Spanish established a mission system to convert Native Americans and control their labor, whereas English Protestants sought other strategies for spreading the gospel. Religious differences and national rivalries shaped colonial enterprises during this period.

Geography, demography, and economics mattered as well. The very different European colonies established in Virginia, New England, New Netherland, New France, and New Mexico reflected these variables and eventually shaped settlement patterns for many of the societies that would become the United States.

Despite their differences, these colonial experiments shared a fragile quality, and by the 1670s, most were facing possible extinction. The violence that erupted in Sassamon's New England was just one of three major wars in the continent's largest European colonies between 1675 and 1680, ending the period of tense coexistence that had allowed those colonies to take root.

NEW SPAIN IN NORTH AMERICA

As the seventeenth century opened, Spain was the leading European colonial power in the Americas. Spain's dominion was located primarily in Central and South America, where colonial authorities exploited the labor of an indigenous population that they supplemented with enslaved Africans. As the Spanish continued their quest for gold, a passage to Asia, and the conversion of the Americas to the Catholic faith, they also sent expeditions northward, where they established smaller colonies in present-day Florida and New Mexico.

Multistory Adobe Housing of the Southwestern Pueblos, Taos, New Mexico. From the Spanish word for town, the term *pueblo* (lowercase) now refers to the adobe-constructed villages. Pueblo (capitalized) Native Americans are peoples from the Rio Grande Valley, as well as Zuni and Hopi. *Chon Kit Leong/Alamy Stock Photo*

THE ESTABLISHMENT OF NEW MEXICO

By the last quarter of the sixteenth century, Spanish colonization in the Americas had taken a turn. After several decades of destructive conquest (see Chapter 1), the Spanish reconsidered their policies in the Americas. Facing severe internal criticism for the brutality of Spanish conduct in Mexico and a powerful external challenge from the Protestant Reformation, King Philip II of Spain issued the **Ordinances of Discovery** in 1573, which renounced and prohibited the wanton massacre of native people. "Discoveries are not to be called Conquests," the law declared, and should be "carried out peacefully and charitably." On this new model, missionaries would direct the pace of all future settlement. **Franciscan** priests, members of a medieval religious order who had been laboring to convert native Mexicans since 1524, now sought new territory in which to save souls. Accordingly, in 1581, the Franciscans dispatched an expedition to learn more about the people and the terrain north of the Rio Grande.

On the basis of the Franciscan reports, King Philip authorized a prosperous miner named Juan de Oñate, who had been born in New Spain, to establish the colony of **New Mexico.** In the spirit of the 1573 Ordinances, the king instructed Oñate that his "main purpose shall be the service of God Our Lord [and] the spreading of His holy Catholic faith," but he added that it would also be necessary to "reduce" and "pacify" the local population. Oñate set out from the Mexican city of Zacatecas in January 1598 with 129 soldiers, 7 missionaries, more than 300 other colonists, and lots of sheep, goats, and cattle. He journeyed past long stretches of sparsely inhabited desert into the world of the **Pueblos,** the name that Spanish colonists coined to designate the diverse indigenous peoples they encountered in the Southwest.

Imperial Graffiti. Juan de Oñate left his mark in the sandstone of what is now known as Inscription Rock, El Morrow National Monument, New Mexico. The translation is "Passed by here adelantado Juan de Oñate to the discovery of the sea of the south on the 16 April the year 1605." The rock also bears much earlier petroglyphs (carvings on rock) done by Pueblo people. *Witold Skrypczak/Lonely Planet Images/Getty Images*

POLITICS AND ENTERTAINMENT

● Eager to secure the peaceful submission of the Native Americans he encountered, Oñate staged a series of theatrical ceremonies. His intent was to remind his audiences of the Spanish conquest of Mexico some seventy-five years earlier and to trumpet the benefits of Spanish Catholic rule. Everywhere he went, Oñate marched under a banner bearing the same religious image that Hernán Cortés had carried on entering Tenochtitlán in 1519. As part of the ceremony establishing a new colonial capital in a town renamed San Juan de los Caballeros, Oñate gathered the local chiefs for a performance of a medieval play, *The Christians and the Moors*, set during the Spanish Reconquista (see Chapter 1). The play ends with the infidel Moors accepting Christ and submitting to Spanish rule. Oñate expected the Pueblos to get the not-so-subtle message. ●

Though a number of chiefs pledged fealty to the invaders, tensions between the Spanish and the indigenous people surfaced quickly. In December 1598, Oñate's nephew Juan de Zaldívar visited the pueblo of Acoma to trade for food. Told that it would take several days to grind the quantity of corn he demanded, Zaldívar withdrew and returned three days later with a heavily armed entourage. Acoma residents killed Zaldívar and some of his party, to which the Spanish responded by razing the Acoma pueblo, killing eight hundred people, and dealing harshly with the survivors. All men and women between the ages of twelve and twenty-five were sentenced to twenty years of servitude. Two Native Americans from other pueblos who had been visiting Acoma were sent back to their communities with their right hands cut off to warn neighboring peoples against resisting the Spanish. Clearly, peaceful missionaries were not calling the shots in New Mexico.

Oñate's violent regime alarmed the Spanish viceroy and alienated some of the colonists, who had grown disenchanted with the harsh terrain and disappointed by the absence of gold. Spain ordered an end to the exploration of the region, rescinded Oñate's license, and in 1608 threatened to dissolve the colony altogether. After Franciscan missionaries appealed to the Spanish monarchy on behalf of the indigenous people they claimed to have converted already, Spanish authorities turned New Mexico into a royal colony and by 1610 had relocated the Spanish-speaking population to a new capital in Santa Fe, built largely by Native American laborers. Henceforth, New Mexico would be a marginal missionary outpost.

THE MISSIONARY REGIME IN THE SOUTHWEST

After 1610, New Mexico became a theocracy run by Franciscan priests who had been instrumental to the missionary effort in central Mexico in the previous century. Moving north from Mexico, Franciscans established mission towns, with large churches in the center, throughout the Rio Grande Valley in what is now north central New Mexico. By 1626, twenty-six missions had been built, and half a century later, more than two thousand colonists occupied these towns. Pueblos visited the missions, often receiving gifts in return for submission to baptism rituals and promises of Christian living.

● From this base of operations, the Franciscans launched an attack on traditional Pueblo rites, which revolved around a culture of worship known as the *katsina*. Missionaries outlawed katsina dances and masks and imposed strict penalties for violations of the prohibition. More effectively, they superimposed Christian symbols and rituals onto established patterns of native worship and theology. Pueblo prayer-sticks, for example, became associated with the Christian cross, and landmarks in the Pueblo calendar, such as the winter solstice, acquired links with events in Jesus' life. Although indigenous people adopted many of these Catholic practices, they resented and resisted Spanish attacks on their religious faith, which they continued to practice in underground structures called *kivas*. ●

CONFLICTING FAITHS

Franciscans also sought to subvert Pueblo gender roles and suppress Pueblo sexual culture. In Pueblo tradition, for example, weaving was men's work, whereas housing construction belonged in the feminine domain. When the missionaries tried to impose a new division of labor, they encountered resistance. "If we compel any man to

Ansel Adams's Photograph of the San Estevan Del Rey Mission Church, Acoma, New Mexico. This Spanish colonial mission church was founded by Franciscans in 1629. *National Archives and Records Administration [NWDNS-79-AAA-3]*

work on building a house," one missionary noted, "the women laugh at him . . . and he runs away." Spanish missionaries were even more shocked by the sexual practices of the Pueblos, which allegedly included polygamy, extramarital relations, homoeroticism, and the performance of sex acts in sacred rituals. Indeed, indigenous attitudes toward sexuality posed major obstacles to the spread of Catholicism, which held out a model of spiritual life among priests devoid of sexual relations altogether.

The encounter between Spanish missionaries and Pueblo peoples in New Mexico bred conflict and animosity. The Native Americans resented the onerous demands for corn and labor on which the colony depended and chafed against restrictions on their religious worship. Although Spanish policies varied between more and less aggressive enforcement of laws that suppressed Pueblo culture, a general climate of hostility prevailed, punctuated by periodic local rebellions, executions of missionaries by Pueblos, and bloody reprisals by the Spanish. All of these conflicts took place against the larger backdrop of population loss. When Oñate arrived in 1581, more than eighty thousand Pueblo people lived in about one hundred villages. Fifty years later, the native population had been cut in half. Fifty years after that, only thirty villages remained. As elsewhere in the Americas, smallpox and other European diseases accounted for most of the loss of life, but drought, crop failure, and Spanish rule contributed

as well. Though many Pueblos had embraced the trappings of Christianity as a strategy for survival, by 1680 the strategy did not seem to be working. That year, about seventeen thousand Pueblos from more than twenty-five independent villages across the Rio Grande Valley rose up in armed rebellion against Spanish rule, the first successful war of independence against a European colonial power. Rebel forces divided New Mexico in half, blocked the roads to Santa Fe, and besieged the capital for nine days. They also dismantled the mission system, mutilating the bodies of priests, defacing Catholic icons, and razing settlements. The **Pueblo Revolt** drove the Spanish governor south to El Paso and restored Pueblo autonomy in the Southwest for twelve years.

MISSIONS IN FLORIDA

As in New Mexico, relatively few Spanish settlers lived in the colony of La Florida in the seventeenth century. Because of its strategic importance in battles with pirates and rival European colonies, Florida held many more Spanish soldiers than New Mexico did, but the colony's main business was still the spread of Catholicism. Franciscans established forty-four mission towns over a wide swath of land from Savannah all the way west past Tallahassee (see Map 2.1). By many measures, their campaign was a great success. Some thirty-five thousand Native

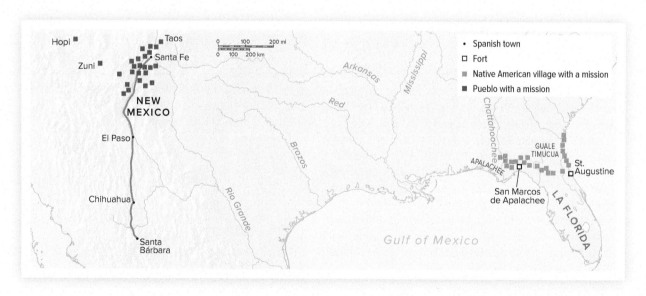

Map 2.1 Spanish Settlements North of Mexico, ca. 1675. Although they were marginal components of Spain's vast American empire, small Spanish settlements in New Mexico and La Florida stood at the vanguard of a century of European colonization efforts in the lands that became the United States.

Americans from a range of nations and language groups entered the orbit of these missions, at least nominally embracing the Christian faith. How deeply the new religion entered native cultures and lives is harder to know. Missionaries sought to stamp out both private sexual acts and public ceremonial sports, for example, but with few priests administering confessions to many Indians, the system probably had limited reach.

Florida's indigenous people continued their hunting and farming practices, but the Spanish exacted heavy food and labor taxes to supply the colony's garrisons and missions. These burdens, along with the expansion of Spanish cattle farming, put severe pressures on a population already diminished by European diseases. The Native Americans rebelled against Spanish rule in 1645, 1647, and 1656, but Florida had the military resources to suppress them brutally and decisively. Nothing comparable to the Pueblo Revolt shook Spain's rule in the Southeast.

NEW FRANCE AND NEW NETHERLAND IN THE IROQUOIS WORLD

Within a short time span, other European powers joined Spain in the competition to colonize North America. French Catholics established their own missions for spreading the faith in the northern part of the continent, primarily around the Great Lakes and in what is now Québec in Canada. But unlike the Spanish colonies, New France in the seventeenth century was organized primarily around trade relationships with the original inhabitants. The same was true for the new Protestant outposts the Dutch established farther south. Located in areas where Native Americans were numerous, small settlements of French and Dutch colonists sought initially to collaborate with local powers rather than to subjugate them or exploit native laborers. Nonetheless, these modest trading posts exerted a significant impact. They transformed indigenous communities from the Atlantic Ocean to the Great Lakes—in ways Europeans could not have anticipated, let alone intended. For indigenous North Americans as much as for northern European migrants, the seventeenth century saw the making of a new world.

THE IROQUOIS LEAGUE AND EUROPEAN TRADE

In the northeastern part of the continent, Europeans entered a region dominated by a powerful bloc of nations known as the Haudenosaunee, the "People of the Longhouse." This **Iroquois League** was a political alliance among five native groups located south of Lake Ontario: Mohawk, Seneca, Cayuga, Oneida, and Onondaga. The League was governed by a council of chiefs appointed by clan matrons in each of the five nations and was designed to accommodate the addition of new members. Native peoples in other parts of North America had been dispersing on the eve of European contact, but the Great Lakes region was an exception. Both the Hurons (who lived on the Canadian side of Lake Ontario) and the Iroquois were consolidating. When northern Europeans arrived in the area, the Iroquois described their League as ancient, but most scholars believe it had formed in the era immediately preceding European contact as a mechanism for ending a period of constant, small-scale warfare. Internal peace also enabled League members to wage much wider and more destructive battles with external enemies.

• As the number of French, Dutch, and English colonists arriving in the Great Lakes region grew in the early 1600s, microbes that had been introduced to the coastal areas a century before spread into Iroquois country. Furthermore, because the settlers now included more children, who had acquired fewer immunities than their parents, so-called childhood diseases such as measles and whooping cough wreaked havoc among adults in the nations of the Iroquois League. A deadly smallpox outbreak wiped out more than half of the League's population in the early 1630s. Iroquois nations responded to such catastrophic losses by raiding other groups and villages. • Scholars refer to these raids as *mourning wars*, since they were intended to bring comfort to the bereaved. But the ultimate goal of Iroquois warfare was to obtain captives, adopt new warriors, and preserve the League's power. During the middle of the seventeenth century, Iroquois nations fought battles with old and new enemies throughout the region. By midcentury, a series of mourning wars with the Huron Confederacy had utterly destroyed that nation.

As European germs depopulated Iroquois villages and impelled the survivors to go to war, European trade goods also strengthened the hand of the Iroquois League. Iron blades made traditional native weapons far more lethal, and firearms rewrote the rules of native warfare. The Iroquois used guns acquired largely from the Dutch to defeat the neighboring Mahican and corner more of the Dutch market, then exploited that advantage in their mourning wars. Iron tools such as axes, chisels, and awls also changed their daily work habits and artistic practices, and European copper and glass found new practical

DISEASE AND EPIDEMIC

and aesthetic applications. All signaled the power and prestige of the native groups that dominated trade.

Ironically, one of the new trade goods that northern Native Americans valued most was not imported from Europe at all. **Wampum,** small beads made from the white shells of whelks or the purple shells of quahog clams, was both a local resource and an artifact of European contact. In earlier periods, North Americans had prized the shells and occasionally used them in beaded jewelry. However, it was not until European traders brought the iron tools that made it possible to drill holes in the tiny shells and string them together that Native Americans could create what counted as true wampum. In the early 1600s, tens of thousands of wampum beads were being produced and traded, in both directions, between colonists and indigenous people. Wampum became especially important to the public ceremonial life of the Iroquois nations, where an estimated three million wampum beads were in circulation by midcentury. For European settlers, wampum functioned as the dominant currency, at least until significant quantities of silver came in from Europe after 1650. Native peoples did not typically use wampum as a medium of economic exchange in their own communities, but they prized it for its aesthetic and spiritual value. Iroquoian peoples benefited from the fact that there was a single good that could be traded both to Dutch settlers and to fur-trading Native Americans in the north, who supplied the Iroquois with the thick animal pelts that most interested the European newcomers (see Hot Commodities: Beaver).

THE FRENCH IN CANADA

French explorers, traders, and fishing ships had operated along the Atlantic Coast of North America during the sixteenth century, and French colonists had tried unsuccessfully to establish footholds along the St. Lawrence River, in Florida, and in Nova Scotia. The first permanent French settlement in the Americas began in 1608, when Samuel Champlain led an expedition to find an advantageous spot in the interior of the continent for trading with native inhabitants. Champlain settled on a cliff site along the St. Lawrence River where it was narrow enough to be easily defended, and he called it **Québec** based on the Algonquian word for a narrow passage. Québec's founding launched the Canadian colony New France.

Unlike in other European colonies, where trading with Native Americans supplemented a larger goal of conquest or resource extraction, the French authorities in Canada saw commerce as a goal in itself. Fur trading

was a lucrative business, but the Québec colony was vulnerable to English piracy. France licensed a new investment consortium to run New France in 1628, and these investors reinvigorated the colony by bringing on board Jesuit priests and making missionary activity a fundamental part of French colonization. In the town of Québec, Ursuline nuns offered religious instruction and medical care to local indigenous women, whereas the black-robed Jesuits traveled to Algonquin, Innu, and Wendat camps and villages to establish diplomatic inroads. As an inducement to conversion, the Jesuits offered lower prices on trade goods to Native Americans who embraced Christianity and granted them the exclusive right to buy guns.

Few settlers came to New France, and hardly any paid their own way. By 1640, more than three decades after Québec's founding, the French population of North America was less than three hundred. Badly outnumbered by the indigenous population and completely dependent on native peoples for trade, French colonists pursued much more peaceful relations with Native Americans than did other Europeans. For example, Catholic missionaries in New France tended to be more tolerant than their counterparts in New Spain of traditional native religious practices and beliefs, which they hoped to supplant gradually rather than immediately. Those Frenchmen who were not in the clergy intermarried frequently with native women, a practice endorsed in the 1660s by official French policy. However, despite New France's more benign colonial practices, the arrival of the French was not a positive development for the region's Huron population. The newcomers spread the same diseases as other Europeans, and competition over the fur trade intensified the military conflicts among indigenous nations. New France's Huron allies bore the brunt of these wars.

NEW NETHERLAND

A new European superpower emerged around 1600. Through most of the previous century, the seventeen provinces that made up **The Netherlands** remained under Spanish rule, but in 1579 the seven Protestant provinces in the north united to declare themselves a sovereign nation. Over the next thirty years, this coalition of republics, led by Holland, waged war against Spain, finally winning independence in 1609. As part of this conflict, The Netherlands embarked on an ambitious program of maritime expansion and became the world's commercial powerhouse in the seventeenth century. The Dutch (the name for both the people and the language of The Netherlands)

HOT COMMODITIES

Beaver

The harsh climate of the northern parts of the continent discouraged early European settlers from trying to grow staple crops or build agricultural colonies, but cold weather presented a particular commercial opportunity. To adapt to their environment, several species of Canadian animals had grown long, luscious pelts. Humans discovered that they could wear these pelts for comfort or prestige. Of all these fur-bearing animals, the most important to the course of North American history was the beaver.

In the early seventeenth century, broad-brimmed beaver-felt hats became fashionable in Europe. Before 1600, Dutch traders had imported beaver pelts from Russia, but with the growing demand, Russian beavers had been hunted to the point of extinction. In North America, beavers were abundant in 1600, and unlike timber, ice, and other export items in demand in Western Europe and its colonies, pelts were relatively light and easy to transport. Indigenous people had hunted beavers for centuries, but because native people sought pelts strictly for immediate use, animal populations had remained high, and they expanded their hunting practices only after developing a need for European goods. After all, as one native leader pointed out to a French missionary, the beaver served many purposes well—"it makes kettles, hatchets, swords, knives, bread." And as the Iroquois learned quickly, beavers could also be exchanged for firearms. Consequently, whole villages devoted their entire hunting seasons to tracking beavers, neglecting other economic activities and becoming even more dependent on

American Beavers. This small, furry rodent, depicted here in John James Audubon's *The Viviparous Quadrupeds of North America* (1840s), played a powerful role in the ecology of the Northeast. Overhunting in the 1600s remade the American landscape. *Artmedia/Alamy Stock Photo*

European trade and the political alliances necessary to sustain it.

Because beavers reproduce slowly and lead relatively sedentary lives, they disappeared rapidly from several regions. Areas closer to the coast were stripped of their beaver populations by the middle of the seventeenth century. The species as a whole proved resilient, but local extinctions altered the landscape in complex ways. Beaver dams played a powerful role in many ecosystems by trapping soil runoff and controlling the water flow. Damming typically had the effect of raising water temperatures and supporting more insects, fish, and waterfowl. The trees that beavers felled, moreover, also supported life forms that nourished larger animals. But once the beavers were removed from the picture, everything changed. Dams disappeared, water flowed freely, soil eroded, and animal protein sources vanished. In their place grew rich fields of tall grass, which would become perfect grazing grounds for cattle. Overhunting beavers, in other words, had the remarkable and unintended ecological consequence of creating a landscape that was better suited to cows, pigs, and sheep than to deer, moose, and bears—and thus more hospitable and attractive to European farmers.

Think About It

1. What distinguished European and native people's uses of beaver pelts?

2. Why were Europeans unable to supply their own beaver needs?

cut into Spanish trade routes in the Atlantic, replaced the Portuguese as the dominant player in the African slave trade and the Brazilian sugar trade, built a fortress city in what is now Indonesia, captured several small islands in the Caribbean, and eventually contested Portugal's control of Brazil itself. The **United Dutch East India Company,** a commercial enterprise that oversaw many of these adventures, was less interested in acquiring territory and building colonial plantations than in commanding the seas and dominating global trade.

In pursuit of this goal, the East India Company hired the English ship captain Henry Hudson to explore a northwestern passage to Asia in 1609. Though he did not find such a passage, Hudson sailed into North America along the river that now bears his name. He found willing trade partners near present-day Albany among the Mahican. Hudson returned to Europe, and his reports encouraged a wave of Dutch commercial expeditions to the region, which the Dutch began calling **New Netherland,** several years before it became an official colony.

In 1621, when a twelve-year truce between Spain and The Netherlands ended, the Dutch expanded their operations in the Americas and chartered the **West India Company.** This new corporation focused on pillaging Spanish trading activities in the Atlantic world. To support its war on Spanish commerce, the company also established permanent trading settlements in the area explored by Hudson and recruited migrants to help defend their project against European rivals.

The first permanent Dutch settlers arrived in small groups in 1624 (see Singular Lives: Catalina Trico, Founding Mother), mostly setting up shop at the northern end of the Hudson River in Fort Orange (Albany). Several of the newcomers, however, remained at the harbor on what is now Governor's Island just south of Manhattan. In 1626, the course of Dutch colonization in the Hudson River area took a sharp turn. The Fort Orange settlers allied themselves with the Mahican, on whose territory they were living. Mohawk from the Iroquois League attacked the Mahican and killed the commander of the Dutch fort. A new leader, named Peter Minuit, created a center of operations on the southern tip of Manhattan, which he famously bought from a group of Lenni Lenape for trade goods valued at 60 guilders (see How Much Is That? Manhattan Island). It is hard to know what the indigenous people thought they were selling Minuit, but it is clear that they remained on the island for years thereafter. Most likely, they were agreeing to welcome the Dutch onto the island in exchange for the gifts. Minuit set up camp in lower Manhattan, built thirty wooden houses and an earthen

Advertising America. This Dutch publication from 1671 promoted colonization and celebrated the wonders of a distant world. *INTERFOTO/Alamy Stock Photo*

fort, and brought the Fort Orange settlers south to the colony's new headquarters. New Amsterdam, as it was called, became a multicultural port town and the center of Dutch colonial government in North America.

Relations between Native Americans and New Netherland colonists varied. Like their French counterparts in the north, Dutch participants in the beaver trade depended on the cooperation of their commercial partners. Small communities of Dutch settlers in the upper Hudson cultivated close ties with the Iroquois nations, and Dutch firearms enabled the Mohawk, in particular, to become a dominant force in the region. Farther south, however, where the beaver population was scarce, colonists were more interested in farming and depended less on the indigenous population. As Dutch farmers' cattle ate the native people's corn and as the native people hunted on grounds the Dutch thought they owned outright because of a sale, conflicts over land spiraled. Frequent skirmishes erupted, and Dutch officials imposed their authority over the native nations in Manhattan, Long Island, and the lower Hudson Valley with brutal severity. Dutch colonial leaders, unlike those in New France, did not have to worry that such treatment might jeopardize efforts to attract Native Americans to Christianity. The Dutch did not engage in significant missionary activity.

New Netherland was a small component of a far-flung Dutch Empire, and the colony attracted few emigrants from the home country. Of the approximately nine thousand Europeans who lived in the area claimed by the colony, about half came from places other than The Netherlands. Many were French-speaking refugees to Holland from what is now Belgium. Others were Sephardi Jews fleeing Brazil and the Caribbean, who were tolerated in New Netherland despite the West India Company's official policy of admitting only adherents of the Dutch Reformed Church. Others were Swedes who established a colony along the Delaware River under Dutch auspices in 1638. The town of **New Amsterdam** included Italians, Bavarians, English, and Spaniards as well as Africans

For more than two centuries, New York has been the leading urban center in the United States, but the city's history is even older than that of the nation. Since the 1620s, a settlement on Manhattan has been drawing immigrants, visitors, and traders from diverse societies and distant continents. Who exactly founded this remarkable polyglot metropolis?

Originally the project of an investment company chartered by the government of The Netherlands, the city that became New York is identified in popular consciousness with a few illustrious individuals. Explorer Henry Hudson became a household name among New Yorkers, but only after the English renamed the river for him in 1664. Peter Minuit, the Dutch West India Company official who ran the New Netherland colony in its early years, gets credit for acquiring land from local inhabitants. But in many ways the founding New Yorkers were ordinary men and women who chose, for various personal reasons, to make their homes in the New Netherland colony.

Historians have reconstructed some of the calculations and deliberations of a French-speaking Protestant teenager named Catalina Trico, who sailed to the Americas from Amsterdam in 1624 as part of the first group of Dutch colonists in Manhattan. Like many newcomers in the Dutch city of Amsterdam, Trico had migrated from Catholic-controlled regions in other parts of the Low Countries, but unlike most of them she decided not to remain in Europe. Four days before embarking on her transatlantic voyage, Trico married Joris Rapalje, a Flemish textile worker. The two of them, along with a small number of adventurous travelers, signed up for six years of labor and service with the Dutch West India Company in return for a promise of land on the other side of the ocean.

One of Trico's distinctions as a pioneering figure in New Amsterdam's early history was the fact that she and Rapalje were among the first to buy land in Manhattan. Not long after arriving, they built two houses on this land, on what is now Pearl Street and was then near the eastern shoreline of the island. Trico and her husband subsequently moved across the river to a new village called Breuckelen, where they raised eleven children. Sarah, their oldest daughter, was probably the first child of European descent born in what would become New York City. But Sarah was just the first of Trico's contributions to New York's growing population. Descendants of the Trico-Rapalje union have been estimated at more than one million.

Where in the Archives?

In 1688, at the age of eighty-three, Catalina Trico recounted a very brief summary of her life, under oath, before a Long Island justice of the peace. Many of the details in her narrative are attested in other kinds of sources as well, including Dutch marriage archives, New York land deeds, and genealogical records now housed at the New York Public Library.

Her life narrative was summarized in an 1850 collection of historical documents of early life in New York: "Catalina Trico to William Morris" appears in *The Documentary History of the State of New-York,* Vol. 111, ed. E. B. O'Callaghan (Albany: Weed, Parsons & Co., 1850). It can be found in the Women & the American Story collection of the New-York Historical Society Library (https://wams.nyhistory.org/early-encounters/).

Assignment

Read Trico's short autobiographical statement. In a single paragraph, explain what you learn about her experience and perspective that might not be found in the kinds of legal documents and records listed here.

who had been enslaved and brought to the Dutch colony. By 1664, one-fifth of the town's two thousand residents had been born in Africa.

In 1664, Dutch rule formally came to an abrupt end when the English invaded and seized control (see Chapter 4). The overall makeup of the colony changed little during this transition, but the economic and political affairs of the region were now subject to the English monarchy. One consequence was official religious toleration. Rather than try to replace the established Dutch church with an official Anglican one, England decided to grant legal recognition to the colony's religious diversity.

STUART ENGLAND AND THE SETTLEMENT OF THE CHESAPEAKE

Well before the English conquest of New Netherland, English settlers also built colonies in North America. Although these colonial societies would eventually play dominant roles in the formation of the United States, they did not begin as powerhouses. Having lagged behind other European empires in exploring the Americas, the English were seeking to colonize regions that others had considered and rejected. England was still a minor player

How Much Is That?

Manhattan Island

Legend has it that the Dutch bought New York for 24 dollars, a figure concocted over two hundred years later using the mid-nineteenth-century exchange rate for 60 guilders. Although greater than six months' salary of a West India Company soldier, 60 guilders in the 1620s was roughly equivalent to other exchanges of goods for land between Dutch traders and native people. Adjusted for inflation, it would have the purchasing power of 1,200 dollars in 2020, which sounds like a great bargain for Manhattan real estate. Of course, neither the buyers nor the sellers believed they were exchanging a commodity in a real estate market—no such market existed.

in the settlement of the Americas when a new colony called Virginia was established in 1607 in what seemed like an inauspicious location. But while French, Dutch, and Spanish colonies continued to attract mostly missionaries and traders, England was the one European country that saw significant emigration to the continent in the seventeenth century. Large numbers of English men and women left their homeland owing to economic crisis, political turmoil, and religious conflict. Many of those emigrants crossed the Atlantic and some settled in the Chesapeake Bay region, where the first enduring English colony in North America took root.

CRISIS IN ENGLAND

Between 1535 and 1635, the population of England doubled, almost fully recovering from the massive demographic losses of the bubonic plague era (see Chapter 1). England's population growth occurred at a time when colder temperatures yielded smaller harvests and caused economic strain. Compounding the crisis was a change in land use. In the medieval era, English landowners typically saw themselves as lords with responsibilities to the peasants whose lives they dominated and whose labor they exploited. But as the larger system of feudal obligation loosened after the plague, landowners increasingly saw their land simply as private estates to be managed for profit. During the late sixteenth and early seventeenth centuries, they raised rents, evicted long-standing tenants, converted cultivated fields to pastures for sheep, and built

fences around those pastures. Fences—or "enclosures," as they were called—turned land that had been traditionally considered the common possession of a community into a new kind of private property. This **enclosure movement** became both a cause and a symbol of widespread discontentment among England's rural populace.

These economic developments uprooted people all over the English countryside. As many as two hundred fifty thousand people moved from farms and villages to growing cities during this period. London's population more than doubled between 1550 and 1600, then roughly doubled again between 1600 and 1650. By 1635, approximately three hundred fifty thousand people lived there, making London the largest city in Europe—and possibly in the world. Some of those on the move sought to leave the country altogether. Emigration was expensive and sometimes illegal, but the lure of starting over in a new land could be great, especially in times of political turmoil.

The reigns of James I (1603-1625) and his son Charles I (1625-1649) stirred up intense conflict over the policies and prerogatives of the monarchy. In 1629, their campaign to expand their power reached a new height when Charles decided to rule without Parliament. When Charles reconvened Parliament in 1640, it refused to authorize his military ventures, and by 1642, Royalists (supporters of the king) and Parliamentarians were raising competing armies. The political instability of Charles's reign and the violence that ensued during the **English Civil War** of the 1640s fueled emigration further.

● But the greatest impetus for leaving England was religious strife, which deeply colored and shaped the period's political divisions. Two overlapping lines of religious conflict emerged in England under Stuart rule. The first was about uniformity. In an attempt to centralize authority in a time when sects and denominations were proliferating, James I imposed restrictions on Catholics, Presbyterians, and others who did not conform to the Church of England. His most enduring legacy, the famous **King James Bible** (1611), was part of a campaign to create a distinctively English holy book and to standardize Bible-reading practices. The King James version of Scripture was designed to be read in churches, not in private homes or at informal gatherings. ●

The fight over centralized worship exposed a larger theological split. On one side stood the Stuart monarchy and officials of the Anglican Church, who believed that orderly church services supervised by authorized clergymen were necessary to guide ordinary

CONFLICTING FAITHS

Christians to salvation. On the other side stood a growing number of radical Protestants who stressed the idea that salvation was predestined (in other words, nothing human beings did could bring it about). Further, they objected to the lingering ritualism and worldliness of England's established church. Known as **Puritans** (though they often referred to themselves simply as the "godly"), these dissenters were strict Calvinist Protestants who charged that the English Reformation had not fully purged itself of Catholic heresy. Puritans clashed bitterly with their opponents over such questions as whether ministers should wear special garments, whether December 25 should be celebrated as a holiday, whether it was appropriate to make the sign of the cross during a baptism, and whether it was permissible to dance on the Sabbath. In all cases, the Puritan answer was a resounding no.

Once Charles I assumed the throne, the government took a harder line and began requiring the practices and rituals to which Puritans objected. By the 1630s, many Puritans felt persecuted and despaired of achieving salvation if they remained in England. Subsequently, when Charles's political opponents gained the upper hand, it was the Anglicans' turn to consider emigration. Throughout the mid-seventeenth century, religious wars helped recruit settlers for England's overseas colonies.

Whether Puritans or Anglicans, Royalists or Parliamentarians, English emigrants looked to the Americas for relief from strife and overpopulation at home. They imagined North America as an underinhabited and undercultivated wilderness where they could live without constraint or conflict. Although the men and women who left England to settle across the ocean in the first half of the seventeenth century hoped for a world that differed from the one they were leaving behind, they also saw themselves as spreading the benefits of their English Protestant civilization. Early English colonists set out to distinguish themselves not only from the Native Americans they might convert but also from their Spanish Catholic counterparts, whom they regarded as brutal conquerors.

JAMESTOWN AND POWHATAN

In 1607, seventeen years after the failure of the Roanoke project (see Chapter 1), English colonists made a second attempt at settling the Chesapeake Bay region. Like Walter Raleigh before them, the investors who received a royal charter to establish such a settlement called it Virginia. They also shared many of the aspirations of the adventurers who had tried to build earlier colonies in Newfoundland and Roanoke: They hoped to spread the Protestant faith to the heathen population, thwart the expansion of Catholic Spain, discover gold (or some other valuable good), and find a passage to the Pacific Ocean. To sustain the settlement, Virginia's designers also expected to subdue the local inhabitants, who might then be made to provide the colonists with food.

The first ships dropped anchor on April 26, 1607, on marshlands along the James River (named for the new king), close to 50 miles upstream from Chesapeake Bay. The English settlers selected this swampy site, which they called **Jamestown,** for its utility as a fort to protect against possible attack by the Spanish, who also claimed the Chesapeake region on maps of their domain. Prospects for a thriving colony on the James River were dismal. Jamestown sat in the tidewater region of **Tsenacommacah,** dominated by a powerful confederacy of thirty Algonquian chiefdoms under the leadership of the paramount chief, Powhatan. The European strategy of dividing and conquering small native groups would thus be harder to pursue. In any case, Powhatan's men were wary from their previous encounters with white visitors and initially refused to barter food with the newcomers.

To make matters worse, most of the first English residents of Virginia were gentlemen or their servants, not farmers accustomed to feeding themselves by raising crops. Compounding this challenge, the English were susceptible to diseases that incubated easily in a warm climate, a malarial swampland, and an unfamiliar ecosystem. Within a few months, half of the original colonists died of illness or starvation. The new settlers who continued to arrive also perished at staggering rates. After the especially brutal winter of 1609–1610, only about sixty English colonists out of five hundred who had made the voyage remained alive in North America, some of them having subsisted on frogs, snakes, or their starved neighbors' corpses. Overall, about four out of five Virginia settlers died within the colony's first decade. In its early history, Jamestown was as devastating a failure as Roanoke.

Jamestown enjoyed a few advantages over Roanoke that enabled Virginia to weather these early setbacks and become the first enduring English colony in North America. First, the Virginia Company investors stubbornly refused to pull the plug on the colony, continuing to raise money and recruit migrants even as the project failed to turn a profit. Second, Captain John Smith, a veteran of religious wars against Catholics and Muslims, imposed strict military discipline by which he forced all Jamestown settlers to work the land. Third, Jamestown found a profitable crop. Englishman John Rolfe introduced seeds of the tobacco plant from the West Indies to Virginia soil and in 1612 enjoyed an impressive harvest, which was sampled enthusiastically back in England. In 1617, ten years after the first settlers arrived, colonists dispatched the first commercial shipment of tobacco leaves across the Atlantic. The successful cultivation of tobacco boosted the colony's financial prospects, and the Virginia Company began offering land incentives to encourage migration. Over the next five years, Virginia's English population soared from under 400 to 1,240.

Perhaps even more important to the colony's initial survival, however, was the decision by Powhatan's people to trade their corn surplus. Virginians' lives depended on the native people's grain, and this dependence produced tense relations between the native inhabitants and immigrants. Periodically, Powhatan would forbid trade with the English, who would then retaliate by attacking villages and raiding their corn stocks. For the first several years of the Jamestown experiment, demanding Englishmen and wary Native Americans regularly skirmished over the corn trade.

From the beginning, Powhatan had not been sure what to make of the Virginians. From his perspective, the well-armed migrants held some attraction as potential allies, and he was pleased to receive gifts from a faraway land. Perhaps to cement an alliance, Powhatan's men captured John Smith in late 1607 and threatened to execute him, only to release him at the last moment. In Smith's retelling of the event, Powhatan stayed the execution because Pocahontas, one of his many daughters, interceded on Smith's behalf. If Smith's story is accurate, Pocahontas was likely participating in a ceremony in which Powhatan ritually adopted Smith and incorporated the English visitors as a subordinate people. The meaning of such a ritual was probably lost on the English, however, who continued to see themselves as conquerors and the native people as their future subjects.

Smith left Virginia soon thereafter as a result of a rebellion against his autocratic leadership, but Pocahontas remained an influential player in the diplomatic relations with the colonists. In 1613, during a period of escalating warfare, the colonists captured Pocahontas and held her as a prisoner in Jamestown. During her year-long incarceration, she converted to Christianity and attracted the attention of John Rolfe. In 1614, Rolfe proposed to Powhatan a marriage with Pocahontas, and the paramount chief accepted eagerly. The marriage between Pocahontas and Rolfe sealed a diplomatic alliance between their peoples and ushered in a brief era of peace for the fledgling

Virginia colony. Two years later, Pocahontas sailed across the ocean as part of a delegation of Native Americans and was received by King James I of England as a high-profile Protestant convert. Pocahontas, who may have seen the mission as part of her own quest to incorporate the English into her father's kingdom, became fatally ill and never returned to her home in Tsenacommacah.

Back in Virginia, the peace unraveled. Powhatan died in 1618, and political power fell to a chief named Opechancanough, who considered the English more trouble than they were worth. In March 1622, Opechancanough launched a series of assaults on the colonists, killing over three hundred people—more than one-quarter of Virginia's population—in one day. The English settlers responded with a long campaign designed to kill the native people they had once hoped to convert. The governor of Virginia now considered it "infinitely better to have no heathen among us . . . than to be at peace and league with them." After several years of fighting, the English drove their enemies out of their settlement region and dictated peace terms to Opechancanough's people.

Opechancanough's Uprising marked a turning point—not only in Virginia's relations with the indigenous

POWHATAN
Held this state & fashion when Capt. Smith was delivered to him prisoner 1607

Powhatan. This image of the Algonquians' paramount chief is a detail from John Smith's 1612 Map of Virginia. *North Wind Picture Archives/Alamy Stock Photo*

population but also in the governing structure of the colony. Alarmed by reports of violence, high death rates, and slow progress on the campaign to spread Christianity, King James I ordered an investigation. Based on the results of the probe, which confirmed suspicions that the colony was badly managed but also encouraged optimism about the value of the tobacco trade, the king revoked the merchant investors' charter in 1624. Henceforth, Virginia would be a royal colony, controlled directly by the English monarch, who would appoint colonial governors and could invalidate any law passed by Virginia's representative assembly. Although Virginia, with a population of only 1,200, remained a fragile enterprise in 1624, the English government was now taking a direct interest in the colony's affairs and prospects.

Rebecca, the Woman Better Known as Pocahontas. This daughter of Powhatan was originally given the names Amonute and Matoaka. The nickname Pocahontas connoted a playful or mischievous character. Engraved in England in 1616, this is the only portrait of Pocahontas made during her lifetime. *VCG Wilson/Fine Art/Corbis/Getty Images*

Ætatis suæ 21. Aᵒ. 1616.

MIGRATION AND GROWTH

Buoyed by thriving tobacco production and better protected against the Native Americans, the new royal colony grew. By 1624, Virginia was shipping 200,000 pounds of tobacco to England. Fourteen years later, that figure had risen to 3 million. The population climbed steadily as well. By 1619, Virginia landowners were already importing Africans to work their lands (see Chapter 3), but most migrants to the colony at this time were poor young Englishmen who arrived as indentured servants obligated to a master for a specified term. By 1640, eight thousand people lived in the scattered farms and villages of Virginia (see Map 2.2). It was still a small settlement, even compared to other English colonies at the time, such as Barbados and Massachusetts, but the continued flow of immigrants and the declining mortality rates made Virginia seem viable.

Over the next twenty-five years, however, a much larger society emerged in the Chesapeake region. Massive migrations from England fueled this growth: Between 1645 and 1665, the number of English settlers in Virginia more than tripled. The new Virginians came in two main varieties. Most were indentured servants from the lower ranks of English society, men between the ages of fifteen and

twenty-four from the rural southwestern parts of the country who signed up to labor in Virginia in exchange for their transportation costs. In a minority of cases, servants were sent against their will (see Interpreting the Sources: Ballads About Virginia). Descendants of these immigrants would compose a majority of the Virginia Colony for the rest of the century.

A second large group of migrants hailed from more prosperous backgrounds. These were elite men and women recruited by the colony's aristocratic governor, Sir William Berkeley, who presided over Virginia from 1642 to 1676. In particular, Berkeley attracted well-to-do younger sons of elite English families who did not stand to inherit estates. Governor Berkeley offered them large tracts of land in Virginia and vested them with political power. Most of the colony's elite immigrants were adherents of the Anglican Church and supporters of King Charles I in his clashes with Parliament during the English Civil War of the 1640s. After the king was beheaded in 1649 and the Royalists were defeated in battle in 1651, some partisans of the losing side, often referred to as Cavaliers, sought refuge in the Americas. The migration of English Cavaliers during the first half of Berkeley's long term in office helped create Virginia's ruling class, and their values shaped laws and social hierarchies in the growing colony.

The other development contributing to the growth of English settlement in the Chesapeake was the establishment of the neighboring colony of Maryland in 1632. Unlike Virginia, Maryland was a **proprietary colony,** which meant that the king granted land and legal authority over that land to an individual (or a group). In the case of Maryland, the proprietor was Cecil Calvert, a Catholic whose father was close to King Charles I. Maryland expanded along a similar time line as its large neighbor to the south. Like Virginia,

Maryland was a tobacco colony dominated by plantation owners and populated by a steady supply of male indentured servants from southwestern England.

Maryland extended religious toleration to all Christians who believed in the Trinity. English Catholics occupied many prominent positions in the early colony's government and built a prosperous minority community, which remains thriving and influential in Maryland to this day. Most immigrants to Maryland were not Catholic, however, and the colony's Catholic priests and leaders were careful not to proselytize among Protestant settlers, lest they incur the wrath of the English government. Instead, they encouraged their followers to keep a low public profile.

BACON'S REBELLION

The English Chesapeake was a highly stratified society, divided sharply according to wealth, power, and status.

The success of the tobacco economy masked conflicts over access to land and resources. As immigrants streamed in, two of those conflicts hardened. The first was between poorer and wealthier English colonists. By midcentury, a fall in mortality rates meant that more servants were outliving the terms of their indenture and expecting to acquire their own land. And with high land prices propped up by the tobacco trade, freed servants were increasingly unable to find suitable farmland. By the 1670s, a majority of the colony was landless, angry, and heavily armed.

The other line of conflict pitted colonists against Native Americans. An aging Opechancanough mounted a final, deadly, and ultimately unsuccessful attack on Virginians in 1644, and two years later the native inhabitants of the Tsenacommacah region signed a treaty confining their settlement to the north side of the York River. The treaty did little to prevent Virginia's settlers from encroaching on Native American territory, however, especially as English migration increased. Virginia's aspiring landowners coveted native lands for tobacco planting, and the colony's growing population of servant animals—cows, pigs, horses, sheep, and goats—routinely grazed beyond the borders of the settlers' farms, destroying Native Americans' cornfields. Native Americans often directed their anger about English colonization against the encroaching settlers' four-legged vanguard. Pigs appear to have been special targets, and colonists regularly accused the native inhabitants of stealing, butchering, or encouraging their dogs to kill English hogs.

Periodic pig-killings and other acts of frontier violence between local Native Americans and Virginians reinforced a larger development in the Chesapeake. As colonists expanded north and west into Tsenacommacah country after the 1646 treaty, they came into more frequent contact with indigenous groups beyond the boundaries of the old Powhatan confederation. Through this contact, the English learned about far-reaching networks of trade

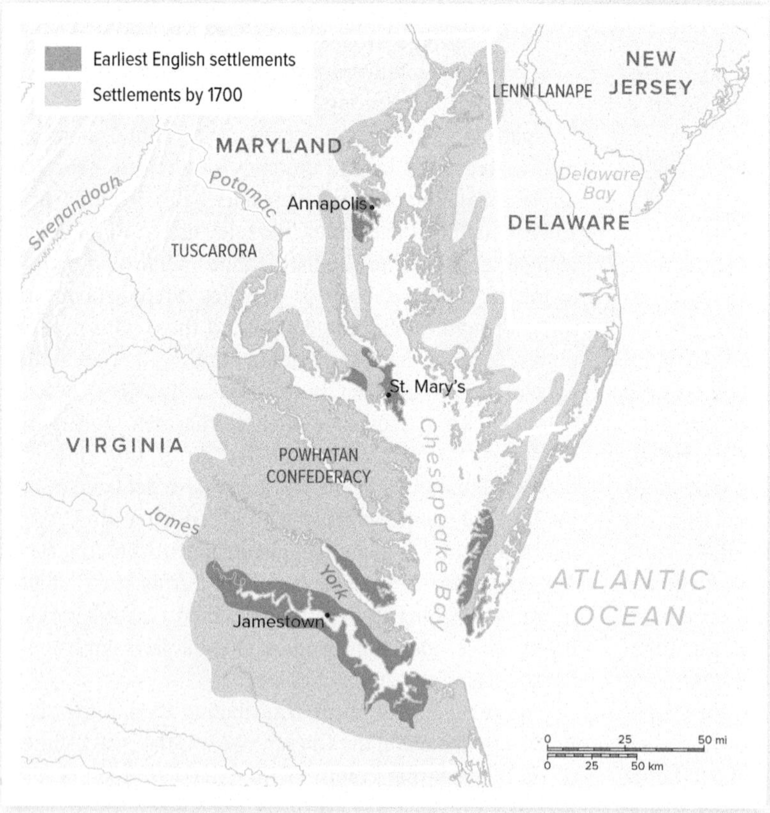

Map 2.2 English Settlements in the Chesapeake, ca. 1607–1660. As in other parts of the American South, the navigable rivers of eastern Virginia enabled farmers to load their crops directly onto ships rather than having to send them by wagon to a market town or port city. The Chesapeake Bay region featured 6,000 miles of shoreline; thus, the English colonists felt little need to develop cities there in the seventeenth century.

INTERPRETING THE SOURCES

Ballads About Virginia

Most of the English migrants to Virginia in the middle of the seventeenth century were unskilled laborers or tenant farmers hoping to escape a life of poverty. Since many of them were illiterate, historians have relatively few sources that document their aspirations, expectations, and disappointments. Several folk songs composed during the period, however, offer glimpses into the world of these migrants, often filtered through humor and mockery. One popular ballad, originally published in 1650, tells the story of a weaver who punishes his unfaithful wife by selling her to a ship captain for 10 pounds and tricking her into boarding a boat bound for Virginia. The following text is from another seventeenth-century ballad, which chronicles the ordeals of women who were duped into sailing to America. Strong evidence supports the view that such practices were not simply the fabrications of balladeers.

Give ear unto a Maid, that lately was betray'd,

And sent into Virginny, O:
In brief I shall declare, what I have suffer'd there,
When that I was weary, weary, weary, weary, O.
[Since] that first I came to the Land of Fame,
Which is called Virginny, O.
The Axe and the Hoe wrought my overthrow.
When that I was weary, weary, weary, weary, O.
Five years served I, under Master Guy,
In the land of Virginny, O;
When she sits at Meat, then I have none to eat,
When that I was weary, weary, weary, weary, O.
. . .
Instead of Beds of Ease, to lye down when I please,
In the Land of Virginny, O;
Upon a bed of straw, I lye down full of woe,
When that I was weary, weary, weary, weary, O.
. . .
Instead of drinking Beer, I drink the water clear,
In the Land of Virginny, O;
Which makes me pale and wan, do all that e'er I can,

When that I was weary, weary, weary, weary, O.
. . .
Then let Maids beware, all by my ill-fare,
In the Land of Virginny, O;
Be sure to stay at home, for if you do here come
You all will be weary, weary, weary, weary, O.

"The Trappan'd Maiden," written in the seventeenth century, reprinted in C. H. Firth, An American Garland: Being a Collection of Ballads Relating to America, 1563–1759 (Oxford: Blackwell, 1915), pp. 51–53.

Explore the Source

1. What makes Virginia so unpleasant, according to the song?

2. What had been the speaker's expectations before sailing across the ocean?

3. Who exactly might have "betray'd" the maiden?

4. Why might Virginia have been especially eager to attract female migrants, and why might English-women have been especially reluctant to emigrate there?

---

in Eastern North America, involving numerous native peoples as well as Spanish and Swedish outposts. At the same time, English settlers also became exposed to raiding Iroquois war parties from the distant north. Not fully understanding this wider geopolitical context, anxious colonists conflated the various threats posed by very different groups of indigenous people.

All these conflicts converged in 1675 around an Englishman named Nathaniel Bacon, who had arrived in Virginia the previous year. In July, a group of Doeg Native Americans living on the Maryland side of the Potomac River seized some pigs belonging to a Virginia planter colonist whom they accused of not paying a debt. A series of reprisals followed, involving more parties. When the Susquehannocks, an Iroquoian-speaking people from the North who had moved to Maryland, attacked colonists in the westernmost reaches of Virginia and Maryland settlement, a wave of fear rippled through the colonies.

Bacon, an aristocratic relative of Governor William Berkeley's wife, seized the opportunity to lead land-hungry English settlers—mostly current or recent indentured servants—on a series of attacks against what he called "foreign Indians." This campaign drew many followers and supporters, but once Bacon sought authorization for a broader war "against all Indians in general," Berkeley declared Bacon a rebel. As landless settlers flouted the governor's orders and refused to abandon their campaign, Virginia descended into political and military chaos. Bacon's supporters elected him to the House

BEHIND THE IMAGE

Cecil Calvert became the first proprietor of Maryland when his father, who had requested the charter from King Charles I, died before it was sealed in 1632. Calvert stayed in London to protect his claims—there were concerns that, as Catholics, the Calverts should not be entrusted with such a proprietorship—and instead sent his brother, Leonard, to America to help establish the new colony. Calvert never managed to visit Maryland in his lifetime and commissioned this portrait in part to assert his connection to the colony he ruled on paper. The artist, Gerard Soest, made a career of painting members of the English nobility. Because most of his paintings devote the entire canvas to a single subject, the decision to add two figures to this portrait was probably Calvert's.

WITHIN THE IMAGE

Calvert poses with ① his young grandson, also Cecil, when the grandson was back on a visit. ② Extending a map of the colony, bearing the family seal of arms, to his namesake and future heir, Calvert asserts his ability to extend his power across time and space. ③ The painting's rich colors, highlighted by the clothing and carpet at the center of the image, capture the splendor of Calvert's possessions. ④ Calvert's Persian-style vest, a fashion item introduced by King Charles II a couple years before the painting, also expresses English national pride and a rejection of the French styles that had dominated court life. ⑤ The figure of the Black servant, cast in the shadows, directs the viewer's gaze toward the child and the map but also stands for the growing system of African slavery in the Chesapeake.

BEYOND THE IMAGE

Soest's painting remained in the private possession of the family for centuries until it was sold at auction in 1933, along with several other family portraits. Even

Gerard Soest, 2nd Lord Baltimore, Cecil Calvert (1606–1675).   *Peter Newark American Pictures/The Bridgeman Art Library*

then, it would take scholars some time to date the painting and identify the young child as the grandson. Although the painting's exhibition was limited, it offered a model for how Calvert patriarchs would present themselves on canvas in Maryland. Whereas George Calvert, Cecil's father, had sat for a more austere painting in 1621, displaying only himself and his hat, surviving portraits of Cecil's children, nephews, and other male descendants echo details from the Soest model, including the young African attendant in the shadows.

of Burgesses, but when he arrived in Jamestown to take his seat, Berkeley had him placed in chains. After a series of blustery maneuvers on both sides, Bacon's men turned their guns on the legislature, extorted a written authorization to lead more raids against Native Americans, and proceeded to march through the colony. Two armies of Virginians—each comprising English servants, enslaved Africans, and tobacco planters—pillaged the countryside in 1676 and took turns capturing Jamestown, which Bacon ultimately burned to the ground, forcing Berkeley to flee the colony. A few weeks later, however, Bacon contracted dysentery and died, ending the military threat to Berkeley's rule. With the execution of twenty-three of Bacon's followers, order was restored.

Bacon's Rebellion meant different things to different participants. Many Virginians on both sides of this civil war took seriously Bacon's calls for lower taxes and a wider distribution of land and political power in the expanding colony. Others probably saw the battle between Bacon and Berkeley as an internal economic contest pitting those elites who coveted Native American lands against those who valued trade relations. For its part, Virginia's new leadership, which took the reins after Berkeley was recalled to England in 1677, saw one clear lesson in the bloodshed and chaos: A large population of landless settlers posed a grave threat to the political hierarchy. To quell this danger, colonial authorities endorsed Bacon's policy of aggressive expansion into Native American territory to open up more land to former indentured servants. They also began encouraging the importation of enslaved Africans, who, because they would be kept in perpetual servitude, would defuse the class struggle within the white population (see Chapter 3).

From a Native American perspective, Bacon's Rebellion had landed a devastating blow. Settler attacks scattered the Susquehannocks, forcing them northward to face the violence of their old enemies in the Iroquois League. But Bacon's militia also inflicted heavy casualties on those Tsenacommacah groups that had been Virginia's allies and trading partners. In 1677, these native peoples met with the colony's new governor to sign the Treaty of Middle Plantation, which acknowledged their subjection to English rule and promised them protection from settlers' attacks only if they remained within a 3-mile buffer zone of the latter's villages. Effectively, the treaty created the first reservations in the lands that would become the United States.

THE FOUNDING OF NEW ENGLAND

England's other major colonial project during the early seventeenth century—dubbed New England by a royal charter—contrasted sharply with its enterprise in the Chesapeake. Not only were the backgrounds and motives of the New England and Chesapeake colonists quite different, but the physical environments they settled also shaped contrasting societies.

New England's settlers arrived as families and included very few enslaved or indentured people. Moreover, unlike the elites who flocked to the Chesapeake, the leading families in these Northern Colonies were critical of the Anglican Church and supported Parliament, not King

The Old Brick Church in Smithfield, Virginia. Now known as St. Luke's, the church is the nation's oldest surviving Gothic building. Construction began in 1632 and took about five years to complete. The interior fittings were not fully installed until over two decades later. As the English colony grew and settlers moved farther inland, church construction did not keep pace. Many colonists lived more than 5 miles away from the nearest house of worship. *Courtesy of Historic St. Luke's Church, photo by Kevin Lanpher*

Charles I, in the English Civil War of the 1640s. Indeed, the political and religious situation under Charles, along with widespread economic depression and disease, had powerfully influenced their decision to emigrate.

• New England was even colder at that time than it is today, and much colder than the Chesapeake. This fact had profound consequences. For one thing, New England's shorter planting season made it less likely to produce a staple crop on a large scale or to enslave a massive workforce to labor on plantations. For another, New England's climate made it a healthier place for English migrants than Virginia, where deadly organisms flourished in the hot summers. Whereas Virginia needed a constant supply of new migrants simply to maintain its population levels in the first half of the century, New England's original settler group multiplied quickly, doubling every generation throughout the colonial period. • Indeed, though founded after the settlement of Jamestown, the colonies of Plymouth, Massachusetts Bay, New Haven, Rhode Island, and Connecticut developed earlier than Virginia. With that growth came clashes with Native Americans and discord within the immigrant community itself.

CLIMATES AND ECOLOGIES

PILGRIMS AND PURITANS

The earliest English colonists to settle the cold northeastern region of North America were not stirred by visions of a fur-trading empire or a northern route to Asia. They were religious dissenters. Two groups of English Protestants immigrated to North America starting in the 1620s. The first, called Separatists, had so despaired of the possibility of achieving salvation within what they saw as the insufficiently reformed Church of England that they sought to remove themselves from its corrupting influence. A congregation of Separatists, later known as **Pilgrims,** immigrated illegally to Holland in 1608–1609. But after a few years there, some of the transplants worried about the influence of Dutch culture on their children and began casting their sights toward America. Rather than settle in Dutch colonies on the Hudson River, the Pilgrim community, which still saw themselves as English, struck a deal with some English investors to help settle Virginia. The first Pilgrim immigrant party set sail for the Chesapeake Bay in 1620 on board the *Mayflower*, but upon stopping in Cape Cod after a storm, they changed their plans. Since they had no legal claim to the land where they were about to disembark, they needed some other basis for forming a colony. Forty-one men aboard the ship signed the famous **Mayflower Compact,** binding themselves to one another as a single political body and agreeing to build a society on shore based on "just and equal laws."

The *Mayflower* passengers had exhausted most of their food supplies en route and could find no trade partners among the native population near their new settlement, which they named **Plymouth.** Almost half of the original settlers died during the first winter, much like their counterparts in Jamestown. The following year, however, the Pokanoket Tribe, under the leadership of Massasoit, decided to open commercial and diplomatic relations with the English to strengthen themselves against rivals and enemies. An ambitious and entrepreneurial Pawtuxet named Squanto aided the colonists in these negotiations. Squanto had risen to prominence in a region recently turned upside down by diseases introduced to North America by earlier European traders and explorers. One of those explorers had kidnapped Squanto in 1614 and taken him to Europe, where he learned some English. After returning to Massachusetts to discover that he was the sole survivor of a village devastated by an epidemic, Squanto acted as translator and guide for Plymouth and helped broker a treaty between the two peoples. Plymouth became an economically viable colony in a short period, though it remained small, containing no more than a couple hundred settlers for much of the 1620s.

Landing of John Alden and Mary Chilton.

Hand-Colored Woodcut of the Landing at Plymouth from the Mayflower. This interpretation of the Pilgrims' landing highlights the role of women in the original settlement of Plymouth. In fact, the first landing party of the *Mayflower* was entirely male. *North Wind Picture Archives/Alamy Stock Photo*

A decade after the *Mayflower* docked at Plymouth, a much bigger exodus began arriving on New England's shores. Like the Separatist Pilgrims, these Puritan immigrants were hardline Protestants who had long decried the lingering Catholicism of the Anglican Church, but unlike the Separatists they had hoped to reform the established religion from within. By the late 1620s, however, Puritans had found their place within that religion increasingly untenable and begun sailing toward North America in unprecedented numbers.
● During the eleven years when King Charles I ruled without Parliament (1629–1640), fifteen to twenty thousand English Puritans moved to New England. Though many more English emigrants moved to the West Indies and the Chesapeake than to New England during the 1630s, the cultural impact of the New England arrivals exceeded their initial numbers. Because they came in family units, with balanced sex ratios, and because of the healthier climate, the English settlers in Massachusetts multiplied much faster than did their counterparts elsewhere in the Americas. By century's end, approximately ninety thousand descendants of this **Great Puritan Migration** lived in New England. More than eight million Americans today can trace their ancestry to this migration. ●

CROSSING BORDERS

The largest of the New England settlements was called the **Massachusetts Bay Colony,** founded in 1629 by a consortium of London merchants. Unlike other recipients of royal colonial charters, the Massachusetts Bay Company had been authorized to hold its meetings wherever it pleased. Noting this loophole, the company's Puritan investors decided to immigrate to New England, where the colonists would be able to govern themselves locally, with less interference from London. Although they were a persecuted religious minority in England, Puritan leaders in Massachusetts Bay enjoyed a great deal of power and autonomy. They wished to use that power to do more than convert heathens, engage in lucrative trade, better their economic circumstances, and strike a blow in the ongoing struggle against the Catholic powers. They also aspired to create a new kind of godly society, made up of saintly individuals whose personal piety and commitment to communal living would serve as a model throughout Christendom. In the famous words of John Winthrop, the colony's first governor, "We must consider that we shall be as a city upon a hill" and that "the eyes of all people shall be upon us." They named the actual city they founded in 1630 Boston, and it would remain the major seat of government in colonial New England.

PURITAN SOCIETY, TOWNS, AND RELIGIOUS PRACTICE

Most Puritan immigrants who settled in Massachusetts Bay or its smaller neighbor Plymouth (the two colonies would formally unite as Massachusetts in 1691) arrived in families, and family life remained at the core of colonial society in New England. As in other English colonies at the time, each household was organized around the authority of a patriarch, who commanded the obedience of his wife, his children, the servants, and an assortment of others

Seal of the Massachusetts Bay Colony. The words put in the mouth of the Native American figure, "Come over and help us," are drawn from the Bible, from Paul's Epistle to the Philippians. *Della Huff/Alamy Stock Photo*

who lived under his roof. New England households often included multiple generations of kin, as well as individuals who were not related by blood or marriage.

Puritan women had significant opportunities to wield moral authority, especially in church, but family life was not the domain of female influence that it would become in New England two centuries later (see Chapter 12). The Puritan family was a male-dominated institution, and Puritan society relied on strict patriarchal discipline to maintain social order. New England laws penalized or prohibited the practice of single adults living alone.

In many ways, however, the most distinctive and fundamental building block of Puritan society in North America was not the family but the town. Unlike settlers in Virginia, who spread out on farms, New Englanders clustered in small, tight-knit communities near the coast or along major rivers.

These communities were religious congregations, bound together by covenants in which town members agreed to build a godly community. Every town included a church, though it might be more accurate to say that every town *was* a church. Not everyone in the town was technically a church member, since membership was available only to those who could convince the community that they had been elected for salvation by divine grace. But everyone was expected (and after 1635, required) to attend services and hear preaching at the local church building, the **meetinghouse.** Church meetings dominated the public life of Puritan towns.

Scholars often refer to the brand of Calvinist Protestantism practiced in Puritan New England as Congregationalism, since it refused to subordinate local congregations to a central denominational hierarchy. The congregation, in other words, was the only unit of church authority. Congregationalists also sought to maintain a strict division between church and government—not to protect civic life from religious interference but to protect church life from being tainted by profane affairs and considerations. The separation between civil and religious authority did not mean religious freedom, however. Violations of religious laws were punishable

Elizabeth Clarke Freake and Baby Mary, unknown artist, ca. 1670. Contrary to the popular image of Puritans dressed in black, colonial New Englanders tended to wear red, blue, and what they called "sad colors," such as russet. Wearing black was considered flashy and pretentious. *Barney Burstein/Corbis/VCG/Getty Images*

offenses, and criminal penalties were often based on Scripture. Those who dissented from a town's religious orthodoxy were not free to start their own church.

The shared religious values of New England's Puritans exerted a wide-ranging impact on the Massachusetts Bay and Plymouth Colonies. New England towns stripped the traditional English calendar of its saints' days and banned annual holiday observances such as Christmas, Easter, and April Fools' Day. The only holy day on the New England calendar was the Lord's Day, which came once a week and required a complete cessation of work, travel, and amusement. Musical instruments, pipe smoking, and fruit picking were all forbidden on the Sabbath, as was sexual intercourse. New England colonists often gave their children distinctive biblical names that reflected the high value they placed on reading Scripture. Johns, Sarahs, Marys, and Josephs abounded, but New Englanders also honored more obscure characters like Mehetabel, Abijah, and Mahershalalhashbaz. Some parents even drew on ordinary words from the English translation of the Bible,

which may account for children named Notwithstanding Griswold and Maybe Barnes.

The Puritan emphasis on reading Scripture also produced a society with broad literacy and a robust culture of reading, writing, and printing. Puritans believed that personal reading of Scripture was a requirement for salvation. Colonial laws therefore obligated parents to teach their children how to read and required towns with fifty or more families to establish a school, though attendance at the school was not mandated. By midcentury, New England colonies were probably the most literate societies in the Americas. In 1660, two out of three men and more than one out of three women were able to sign legal documents, and a great number of those who could not write could still read.

New England ministers used the printing press as well as the schoolhouse for spreading literacy. The colony's first press (the first anywhere in the Americas north of Mexico) was shipped from England in 1638 and established in Cambridge. At first, the colonists used it sparingly, since most of their reading needs were easily supplied from England. But by midcentury, a minister named John Eliot had embarked on a massive publishing project in order to spread Bible literacy—not to the Puritan settlers in New England towns but to the region's native inhabitants. Eliot learned the Massachusett language and, along with several Christian Native American collaborators, developed a system for rendering Massachusett in the Latin alphabet. Between 1647 and 1689, Eliot published a series of books of Scripture, catechism, and religious instruction for readers of Massachusett. The amount of paper used to produce two Massachusett versions of the Bible exceeded the entire English-language output of the Cambridge printing press in the decade before Eliot began his project. Eliot flooded the Christian Native American population with Massachusett Scriptures, even though only a small portion of that population was literate. Printing in New England did not necessarily reflect demand but rather a religious and cultural ideal.

INTERNAL DIVISIONS

Despite their sense of shared purpose, early New England colonists did not live in a world of peace and harmony. Small towns in which a few founding patriarchs controlled the distribution of land tended to breed resentments. Moreover, close-knit communities where everyone was bound together by a religious covenant inevitably presented ample opportunities for neighbors to scrutinize and criticize one another's godliness. Such conflicts contributed to a rising tide of **witchcraft accusations,** which washed over New England during the seventeenth century. Belief in the power of witches was common in England and in other English colonies at the time, but prosecution for witchcraft occurred far more frequently in Massachusetts Bay and Connecticut, especially in the second generation of settlement. Seventy-nine people, mostly but not exclusively women, were accused of being witches in New England between 1647 and 1663, and fifteen were convicted and executed. (Later in the century, the Massachusetts town of Salem would become the site of the most infamous witch trials in the English colonies.) The targets of these prosecutions were often women who had accumulated property and thereby acquired a measure of independence in a society run by men. But the fear that one's neighbors might be using supernatural powers to cause misfortune reflected more general tensions that plagued small, religious utopias.

Most colonists feared the damages that witches might wreak, but Puritan clergymen also saw witchcraft as a form of heresy, in which the accused stole away from the religious covenant of a community and made a side deal with the devil. New England society was continually haunted by the prospect of broken covenants. Such prospects were woven into the tense fabric of the colonists' religious world view. On the one hand, Puritanism valued individual conscience as the ultimate source of religious authority. But on the other hand, Puritan communities demanded strict conformity to what they regarded as religious truths. Theological dissent constituted grounds for excommunication and exile.

Religious exiles led to the formation of new colonies on the western edges of New England settlement. Roger Williams, a Separatist who arrived in Massachusetts in 1631, took the individualist implications of Puritan theology to a radical extreme. Objecting to mandatory church attendance and to any connection between religious worship and ungodly people, Williams moved toward a larger rejection of state authority. Once he began questioning the rights of the colony to claim land that belonged traditionally to Native Americans, the Massachusetts General Court ordered him banished. Williams and his followers fled in 1636, first toward Plymouth and then farther south and west to a place he called Providence, on land given to him by the Narragansett people. The new settlement, chartered by Parliament in 1644 as **Rhode Island,** became a colony in its own right. By the law of this colony, individuals could practice whatever religion they chose, though even there a heretical preacher could be flogged or exiled.

Around the same time that Williams fled Massachusetts, a new arrival in Boston named Anne Hutchinson triggered controversy by taking another Protestant principle to its subversive conclusion. Since human beings could be saved only by divine grace and not by their deeds, Hutchinson preached that nothing her New England neighbors did to prepare themselves for salvation—prayer, church attendance, or Sabbath observance—had any effect. Governor Winthrop brought Hutchinson up on charges of "traducing the ministers," and his supporters branded Hutchinson's followers as antinomians (those who reject the law). The Massachusetts establishment was especially outraged by Hutchinson's claims to have received direct revelation from God, not through Scripture, and by the fact that she was overstepping the social roles prescribed for women. "You have rather bine a Husband than a Wife and a preacher than a Hearer," one clergyman charged. In 1638, authorities banished Hutchinson from the colony, and she took refuge in Rhode Island.

Another dissenting Puritan minister, Thomas Hooker, left Massachusetts in 1636 to establish a new home in Hartford, in the Connecticut River valley (see Map 2.3). Hundreds of colonists followed Hooker southward, drawn by opportunities to own land, Hooker's considerable talents as a preacher, and his more inclusive approach to religious communal life. Two years later, a different group of New England settlers established New Haven. The New Haven Colony set stricter standards for church membership to combat what church authorities saw as increasing laxity in Massachusetts. In 1662, New Haven and Connecticut were joined under a single royal charter, and Hooker's followers dominated the new, united colony.

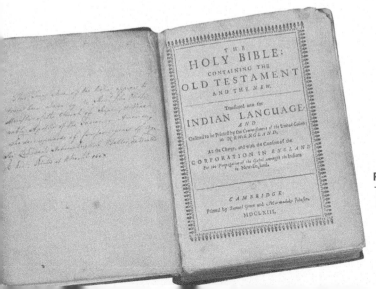

Frontispiece and Title Page of the Massachuset Bible, 1663. The earliest printed publications in the lands that became the United States were mostly in the Massachusett language. *SuperStock/Alamy Stock Photo*

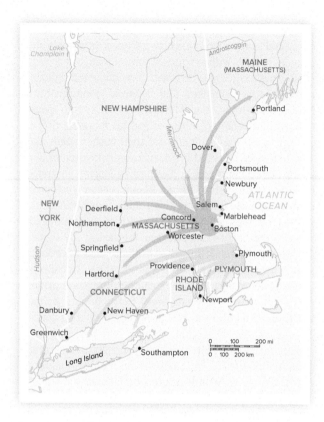

Map 2.3 English Settlements in New England, ca. 1620–1660. From two small settlements in 1620 and 1630, Puritan colonists spread out into numerous new townships and colonies throughout the region.

Doctrinal differences and competing visions of church governance separated the various New England colonies during the 1630s and 1640s, but social tensions pulsed throughout the region. As the colonies grew, new commercial opportunities arose. In addition to the fur trade, colonists began clearing forests and exporting timber for use as wine barrels and ship masts. Salted codfish became an even larger export. In smaller towns, most colonists were affected only indirectly by commercial expansion and continued to farm for subsistence. But for those living in larger seaport towns such as Boston, Salem, and Plymouth or in river settlements such as Springfield and Hartford, political and religious disputes often pitted landowning families trying to defend an older social order against newly wealthy families reaping the benefits of long-distance trade and embracing a more materialistic lifestyle.

Commercial opportunities may also have contributed to the perception among New England ministers that religious piety and devotion were diminishing. Indeed, after midcentury, rates of church membership began to decline sharply.

A big factor in the weakening of Puritan zeal in the colonies was the success of the Puritan Revolution in England, which significantly reduced the number of religiously minded migrants. Fewer new settlers arrived in New England after 1650, and those who came more nearly resembled the young men who moved to the Chesapeake during this period. Many of them farm laborers in the western countryside or servants in the seaport towns, these immigrants joined churches much less commonly than their predecessors had.

After 1650, the founding generation of colonists was in the minority. Facing lower rates of church membership, New England town leaders also worried about losing the offspring of members and argued that this second generation should be generally presumed to be godly even if they had not yet undergone a conversion experience. Most ministers accepted this presumption for the children of church members, but once they also had children, the system ran into trouble. Allowing the third generation to be baptized without evidence of being seized by the Holy Spirit appeared to undermine the Puritan conviction that salvation was bestowed by divine grace, not by birth or upbringing. As a compromise, New England's Congregational Churches introduced the idea of a Half-Way Covenant in 1662, under which the baptized children of full church members occupied a middle status. They could baptize their children, but they could not vote or take communion. Now with multiple grades of membership, and with many more colonists not belonging to the church at all, the older model of a homogeneous religious community crumbled.

CONFLICTS WITH NATIVE AMERICANS

Ultimately, the most devastating conflicts in seventeenth-century New England occurred between settlers and the region's indigenous residents. Colonists expanded westward and southward from the original colonial outposts into areas that were being quickly depopulated by disease. The Massachusett people, who had earlier numbered 20,000, were reduced to 750 by 1631. And the worst was yet to come. A smallpox outbreak in 1633 killed as many as 95 percent of the inhabitants of some villages and ravaged parts of the interior that had been spared in earlier epidemics. These calamities facilitated the growth of the New England colonies by allowing settlers to take over abandoned village sites.

At the same time, the depopulation of native villages created problems for the colonists. Diseases disrupted power relations among the Algonquian peoples (the language group that linked most native villages in New England) and unsettled political alliances. Some ravaged native villages sought to replenish their military ranks by raiding their neighbors and taking captives. Others could no longer resist the incursions of the Iroquois League, who were seeking to replenish their own thinned ranks. As they expanded in the mid-1630s toward the Connecticut River valley, New England settlers thus entered an unstable political environment.

They also clashed with the Pequot people, the regional power that had dominated the area's wampum trade. Spared the wrath of the earlier wave of diseases that swept through the coastal villages in 1616–1619, the Pequot people were hit hard by the 1633 epidemic. From a population of about sixteen thousand at the beginning of the decade, only three thousand remained in 1636. Trying to preserve their position against Dutch, English, and other Native American traders, the Pequots got embroiled in a complicated conflict in 1636–1637. The Puritan colonies turned this conflict, which would become known as the **Pequot War,** into a test of their own resolve to subjugate native people. After a series of attacks and reprisals between Pequots and colonists, Massachusetts and Connecticut overlooked their theological differences and raised a large joint army. Together with the Narragansett and Mohegan peoples, they surrounded the principal Pequot village on the Mystic River in Connecticut and set it ablaze, burning more than three hundred Pequots to death. Survivors were executed, sold into slavery, or delivered by the English as captives to their Native American allies.

DISEASE AND EPIDEMIC

● Beyond sparking political crises in the region, epidemics also strengthened the hand of Puritan missionaries in their quest to convert native inhabitants. As in other parts of North America, European plagues undermined the authority of native leaders and medicine men while appearing to demonstrate the power of the invaders' gods. ● On their deathbeds, many Algonquians accepted Christianity in 1633 and entrusted their children to Puritan families and ministers. The New England colonies were interested primarily in their own godly settlements rather than their heathen neighbors, but a number of Congregationalist ministers devoted themselves to the task of converting the native people. These converts were not integrated into New England communities but were gathered into so-called **praying towns.** John Eliot founded Natick, the first of these towns, in 1650. Six more were established in Massachusetts Bay over the next few years, and another seven farther inland by 1674. For residents, these Christian communities appeared to offer a viable refuge from the violence, disease, and instability that were increasingly engulfing the region. Only a small minority of native inhabitants in New England as a whole embraced Christianity or moved to the praying towns, but

English Depiction of the Mystic River Massacre, Engraving by John Underhill, *News from America,* **1638.** Pilgrim leader William Bradford described the attack in language reminiscent of the biblical book of Lamentations: "Those that escaped from the fire were slain with the sword; some hewed to pieces, others run threw with their rapiers. . . . It was a fearful sight to see them thus frying in the fier, and the streams of blood quenching the same." *Mashantucket Pequot Museum and Research Center, Archives & Special Collections*

in eastern Massachusetts and around Plymouth, the figure neared 25 percent.

KING PHILIP'S WAR

Despite the bloody conflict with the Pequots, the New England colonies managed to avoid major violence with the Wampanoag people, who lived closer to most of the English settlers along the seaboard in southern Massachusetts and Rhode Island. Wampanoag chief Massasoit had made a peace treaty with the Plymouth Colony in 1621, and the arrangement prevailed until Massasoit's death forty years later. Indeed, Massasoit's family and his people prospered during New England's expansion, because the Wampanoag had become crucial trading partners with the English colonists and powerful diplomatic intermediaries between New England and other native groups. But by the time Massasoit died in 1661, the English wanted the Wampanoag people's land more than they needed their wampum or political support.

Wamsutta, Massasoit's son and successor as chief, made the colonial authorities nervous, and they forced him to appear in Plymouth for questioning. When Wamsutta died soon after, many Wampanoag suspected the English of having poisoned him. His younger brother Metacom assumed power under the cloud of deteriorating English–Native American relations. Settlers and their cattle had been encroaching on Wampanoag villages and disrupting their subsistence pattern for decades, but by the 1660s the native people's predicament seemed bleaker. Colonists now outnumbered indigenous people in southern New

England by almost three to one, and English courts were asserting their jurisdiction over conflicts between whites and Native Americans.

Metacom, whom the colonists called Philip, was summoned to Plymouth a decade later over his refusal of the colonists' demand that he surrender his arms. There, he was forced to put his mark on a treaty acknowledging the supremacy of royal authority and Plymouth's government. Metacom began considering his options.

When John Sassamon, Metacom's former trusted aide and translator, informed Plymouth authorities in 1674 that the chief was preparing a revolt, such a plan may only have been in the initial stage. But by the following year, when two of Metacom's advisers were executed for Sassamon's murder, the chief had assembled a multinational coalition for a war against the colonists. Metacom attacked the Plymouth town of Swansea in June 1675. More than fifty New England towns would face such assaults over the next fourteen months, and nearly half of them were destroyed.

Although colonists would call this conflict **King Philip's War,** it involved many more Algonquian than just Metacom and the Wampanoag. The war was, in fact, a massive uprising involving several indigenous groups and many native warriors who had previously embraced Christianity. Nipmucs in central Massachusetts joined the attack, as did the Pocumtucks farther west and many Pocasset warriors from the east. The Narragansett initially sought to remain neutral but were swept into the war once the English colonies attacked their fortified encampment in Rhode Island for harboring the wives and children of warriors who sided with Metacom. Other native groups allied with the colonists, and many Christian Native Americans from the praying towns aided the English war effort. Still, to most participants the conflict appeared to be an all-out Native American assault on New England and its way of life. Metacom's men waged their defiant assault in the name of Native Americans, not just their various groups or villages. A note tacked to a tree near the burning town of Medfield, Massachusetts, in 1676 warned, "Thou English man hath provoked us to anger & wrat & we care not though we have war with you this 21 years. . . ." While destroying more than twenty-five New England towns, Native Americans targeted symbols of the English way of life, including cattle, fences, and Bibles. According to English reports, Metacom's followers dismembered cows rather than simply killing them and on one occasion buried a Bible inside the stomach of a slain colonist.

At the end of 1675, New England society appeared to be on the brink of collapse. Rhode Island and Connecticut united with the older colonies, but the attacks

PHILIP. *KING* of Mount Hope.

Paul Revere's Unflattering Portrait of Metacom, from ***The Entertaining History of King Philip's War* (1772).** This propaganda tract was a reprint of the *Diary of King Philip's War* (1716) by Benjamin Church, a military captain involved in Metacom's assassination. *The Granger Collection, New York*

continued. After a series of assaults in February 1676, the Massachusetts Bay council, anticipating the worst, considered building a wall around Boston. The tide had already begun to turn in the colonists' favor, however, as Metacom's supporters began to suffer from food shortages and disease. The native coalition started to fray, and by summertime, English troops were sweeping through Rhode Island and Connecticut, rounding up rebellious Native Americans and selling them, enslaved, out of the colonies. On August 12, a Christian Native American fighting under the English shot Metacom to death.

King Philip's War took more lives in proportion to the population than any subsequent military conflict in American history. Nearly one thousand colonists and more than two thousand Native Americans died during the attacks. Three thousand other Native Americans perished of disease or starvation, and another three thousand were exiled or sold into slavery. English settlement was pushed back, at least temporarily, almost to the seaboard, and all four New England colonies were economically depleted—and thoroughly dependent on England for survival.

CONCLUSION

Despite their crucial differences and bitter rivalries, the European colonies established in North America during the first half of the seventeenth century had much in common. Whether they came to trade, preach, mine, conquer, or farm, European migrants precipitated many of the same devastating changes and conflicts. Strikingly, three large, far-flung colonies all suffered violent upheavals in the few years between 1675 and 1680. King Philip's War, Bacon's Rebellion, and the Pueblo Revolt originated in separate circumstances and produced very different consequences, but all three events were climactic explosions in the tense relations between colonists and original inhabitants. These wars culminated decades of accumulated resentment and misunderstanding and reflected powerful processes of economic, ecological, and biological havoc. For indigenous people and newcomers alike, those processes had created a new world, increasingly oriented toward large patterns of global commerce.

Even by 1680, however, Europeans occupied only a small place in North America. Native inhabitants controlled most of the continent, and native religions and cultures continued to dominate. In retrospect, the steady growth of England's colonies, which now included the former New Netherland, may appear portentous. As the dust from the conflicts of the 1670s settled, English colonists outnumbered all other Europeans in North America, and their offspring and animals were moving westward and forming new communities on Native American lands. England's colonies did not form a shared world in the seventeenth century, however. The Chesapeake region and New England were, in some respects, as culturally and economically distinct in 1680 as Catholic New France and Protestant New Netherland had been in 1650. And one of the greatest divisions between those two English colonies was just beginning to emerge.

STUDY TERMS

Ordinances of Discovery	King James Bible
Franciscans	Puritans
New Mexico	Jamestown
Pueblos	Tsenacommacah
Pueblo Revolt	proprietary colony
Iroquois League	Bacon's Rebellion
wampum	Pilgrims
Québec	Mayflower Compact
The Netherlands	Plymouth
United Dutch East India Company	Great Puritan Migration
New Netherland	Massachusetts Bay Colony
West India Company	meetinghouse
New Amsterdam	witchcraft accusations
enclosure movement	Pequot War
English Civil War	praying towns
	King Philip's War

FURTHER READING

A database of additional full-text readings is available through Power of Process for Primary Sources in Connect.

Virginia DeJohn Anderson, *Creatures of Empire* (2004), highlights the role of domestic animals in the colonization of the Chesapeake and New England.

Jorge Cañizares-Esguerra, *Puritan Conquistadors* (2006), emphasizes the similar preoccupations of English and Spanish colonizers with fighting demonic and satanic forces.

William Cronon, *Changes in the Land* (1983), explores the environmental impact of European land uses in colonial New England.

David Hackett Fischer, *Albion's Seed* (1989), traces four distinct colonial settlements in English North America to four different regions and cultures in England.

Ramon Gutiérrez, *When Jesus Came, the Corn Mothers Went Away* (1991), shows the centrality of disputes about marriage, gender, and sexuality to the history of Spanish–Native American relations in New Mexico.

Carol Karlsen, *The Devil in the Shape of a Woman* (1987), grounds the history of New England witchcraft accusations in the social history of gender relations.

Andrew Knaut, *The Pueblo Revolt of 1680* (1995), covers the dramatic uprising against Spanish authority in New Mexico.

Jill Lepore, *The Name of War* (1998), stresses the role of language and writing in the history of King Philip's War.

Andrés Reséndez, The *Other Slavery* (2016), surveys the long and complex history of Native American enslavement in Spanish America.

Sam White, *A Cold Welcome* (2017), considers the implications of climate change for European colonization efforts.

1660–1750

3 | SLAVERY & RACE

Chapter Questions

1. When and why did African slavery take hold in the American colonies?

2. What was the course of development of the attitudes and laws that allowed slavery to expand?

3. What were the experiences of the first generations of African Americans, from enslavement and the Middle Passage to the creation of slave communities with African identities?

4. How did slavery differ across the various regions of colonial North America?

Bound in America. Small numbers of African captives first came to the Chesapeake Bay as enslaved laborers around the beginning of the 1600s. By the nineteenth century, iron shackles such as these represented a vast system of long-established slave societies in the Americas. *oliver leedham/ Alamy Stock Photo; Hemera Technologies/Jupiterimages*

O n May 13, 1643, a man named Francis Payne and a woman named Jane Eltonhead entered into two contracts in Northampton County, Virginia. In the first document, Eltonhead agreed to lease farmland to Payne for the year. Payne would have full control over the planting and would own all of its produce, after paying the rent of 1,500 pounds of tobacco and six bushels of corn. The second contract was more momentous. Payne agreed to use the proceeds of the farm to acquire three male servants, aged fifteen to twenty-four, each of whom would serve Eltonhead for at least six years. In return, Payne would become a free man.

Francis Payne was enslaved and Jane Eltonhead's legal property. But by 1649, he had accumulated enough wealth to buy the three servants stipulated in the contract and to secure his own freedom. Seven years later, Payne succeeded in purchasing the freedom of his wife and children, who had

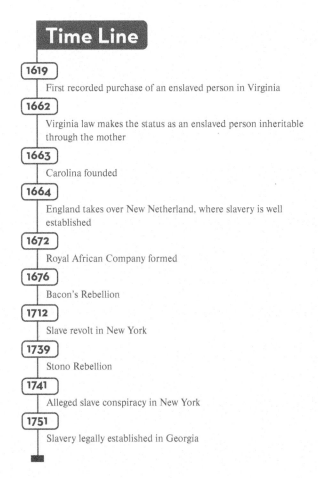

Time Line

1619
First recorded purchase of an enslaved person in Virginia

1662
Virginia law makes the status as an enslaved person inheritable through the mother

1663
Carolina founded

1664
England takes over New Netherland, where slavery is well established

1672
Royal African Company formed

1676
Bacon's Rebellion

1712
Slave revolt in New York

1739
Stono Rebellion

1741
Alleged slave conspiracy in New York

1751
Slavery legally established in Georgia

remained in slavery throughout this period. Enslaved people in Virginia, like Francis Payne and his family, were Africans in origin or descent, and they found themselves in North America as a result of the transatlantic slave trade. The first recorded slave purchase in Virginia dates to 1619, and enslaved Africans had been in the colony even earlier. By the time the English, Spanish, Dutch, and French had established permanent colonies on the North American mainland, a massive system of slavery was firmly entrenched elsewhere in the Americas. But on the mainland, in those colonies that would later become the United States, slavery emerged slowly. In English Virginia during the first half of the seventeenth century, an enslaved man like Francis

Payne could accumulate wealth, acquire servants, and buy his freedom without alarming the white community. Over the next fifty years, however, the American colonies would build a rigid slave regime, under which stories like Payne's would become practically impossible.

As slavery became solidly established in England's American colonies, regional variations took shape. Some colonies in the South became **slave societies,** depending largely on forced African labor for their economic survival. Colonies farther north became what historians call **societies with slaves,** where enslaved African Americans made up only a small part of the labor force and family farming predominated. North American slavery differed fundamentally from larger plantation systems that thrived in the Caribbean and South America. But as in other colonies from Canada to Chile, the demand for agricultural labor stimulated a massive forced migration of Africans across the Atlantic that would shape all of colonial America's cultures.

THE TRANSITION TO SLAVE LABOR

In the first half of the seventeenth century, colonial North America was not a slave society. However, this does not mean that the men, women, and children who tilled the soil did so voluntarily, cheerfully, or without restraint. Most of them labored under the authority of masters, parents, or husbands. But few of them were defined as someone else's permanent legal property. And before the 1660s, serving a master was not associated with a particular racial or ethnic identity. Enslaved Africans appeared in Spanish Florida as early as the 1560s and in Virginia soon after the founding of Jamestown. But these Africans were few in number and did not initially dominate the agricultural workforce in any North American colony. Whereas thousands of Africans were brought every year in shackles to work on sugar plantations in Brazil and the Caribbean, English colonists on the eastern seaboard relied primarily on European labor. Between 1660 and 1750, however, a crucial transformation took place. Colonists on the American mainland began purchasing more Africans, exploiting their labor on a grander scale, and creating stark legal distinctions between races.

BEFORE THE SPREAD OF SLAVERY

The English colonies in North America were agricultural enterprises that depended for their survival and success on a great deal of hard work. Colonists cleared land for farming, worked the fields, grew their own food, cultivated crops or extracted other resources for export, and made much of their own clothing, cleaning products, and household goods. In New England, new immigrants provided much of this labor, working under the supervision of patriarchs or close-knit religious communities. Colonists in the tobacco-growing Chesapeake depended even more heavily on migrant labor, since Virginians died more quickly than they reproduced during the first half of the century (see Chapter 2). Unlike the New England colonies, however, the Chesapeake could not draw on a stream of religious dissenters from Europe. Instead, they recruited farm laborers, landless artisans, and restless teenagers from England with promises of wealth and independence. To pay the high costs of travel, the new recruits, who were overwhelmingly male, contracted to work with employers in Virginia, typically for five to seven years. From the 1620s through the 1670s, approximately 80 percent of all British immigrants to the Chesapeake region paid their passage by becoming indentured servants.

Indentured servants were at the mercy of their masters, who could beat them if they did not perform satisfactory labor in the tobacco fields—or sell them to other employers for the duration of the contract. Once the period of indenture was over, servants who survived typically received a small cash payment or a plot of land with which to begin their lives as free people. About half the time, however, indentured servants died before their contracts expired. Despite these odds, indentured servitude continued to lure English migrants to Virginia in significant numbers through the 1650s. Working alongside these servants were smaller numbers of involuntary migrants, including petty criminals, political prisoners from Scotland and Ireland, and West Africans sold into slavery and transported across the Atlantic Ocean by European traders.

The West Africans brought to the Chesapeake region between 1620 and 1660 represented a negligible fraction of the enormous slave trade that was supplying the sugar plantations of the Caribbean and Brazil during this period. They also accounted for a very small part of the colony's workforce. Only 23 Africans lived in Virginia in 1625, and just 300 in 1650. As late as 1660, Virginians with African ancestry composed less than 4 percent of the population. This first generation of enslaved Africans in the Chesapeake formed a diverse and cosmopolitan group. Most had come by way of other colonies, such as the English colony of Barbados and the Dutch colony of New Netherland, and were familiar with multiple African and European languages.

Africans brought to the Chesapeake before the 1660s came as enslaved people, not indentured servants. But they performed the same kinds of labor as indentured servants, and not all of them remained enslaved for life. Though their prospects of achieving freedom were limited, a number of enterprising, industrious, and relatively fortunate men and women managed to purchase their freedom by producing tobacco in excess of what their slaveholders required. In other words, slaveholders were often willing to part with an enslaved laborer as long as they received financial compensation for their investment. Some of those formerly enslaved became landowners and even slaveholders. In Northampton County, Virginia, where Francis Payne lived, about 30 percent of that county's African-descended population was free. The majority remained in bondage, but colonial laws had not yet established the rule that slave status was both permanent and inherited. The lines between servants and enslaved people were just beginning to harden in the Chesapeake during the 1660s. White servants were different from enslaved Black people, because the former came to America voluntarily but the latter were brought against their will. Nonetheless, the two groups worked side by side in the tobacco fields, socialized together, and sometimes collaborated in their attempts to escape.

In other parts of colonial North America, a similar pattern persisted for most of the seventeenth century. From Puritan Massachusetts to Dutch New Netherland to the Chesapeake, slavery was accepted and legal, but relatively few people were held in bondage. Most of the enslaved were Africans, and most Africans were enslaved, but some Africans were free men and women who owned land, testified in courts, and even controlled the labor of others. Native Americans were also enslaved, usually after being captured in war. Until the last quarter of the century, no colony on the continent depended primarily on slave labor.

SERVITUDE AND SLAVERY IN THE CHESAPEAKE

During the 1660s, Chesapeake landowners began to turn from indentured servitude and toward race-based **chattel slavery,** a system that treats individuals as personal property that can be bought and sold. Several related developments contributed to this momentous change. In England, a declining birthrate during the civil war of the 1640s and a rise in employment and wages after the restoration of the monarchy reduced some of the pressures that made migrating to the Americas attractive. At the same time, English men and women who wanted to emigrate were lured by the promise of a better life in the newer colonies of Pennsylvania, New Jersey, Delaware, and New York (see Chapter 4). All of these factors lessened the supply of indentured servants to the Chesapeake at a time when the tobacco trade was booming and the demand for field labor was growing.

Meanwhile, enslaved Africans were becoming more available in the Chesapeake. After their victory in the Anglo-Dutch War (see Chapter 4), England began playing a larger role in a slave trade that had been dominated up to that point by Holland and Portugal. The **Royal African Company** was chartered by the English Crown in 1672 to run a slave-buying operation in West Africa, and by the 1680s it was abducting and transporting thousands of Africans every year to the Americas, mostly to the Caribbean but also to English mainland colonies. Earlier in the century, people in slavery had been much more expensive than servants, but by the 1680s, the price difference between the two had narrowed considerably (see How Much Is That? Indentured Servants in the Chesapeake). As mortality rates declined, an African laborer who could be kept for life became far more valuable than a European on a six-year contract.

These changes in the labor market came at a time when Virginia's planters were growing anxious about the social order of the colony. Bacon's Rebellion alerted large landowners to the dangers of depending on servants, who were now more likely to survive their indentures and demand land. Poor ex-servants allied with enslaved and freed people during the rebellion, and planters began to see how the indenture system could lead to class conflict. If they turned to enslaved Africans instead and assigned them a more clearly inferior status, planters could drive a wedge between poor whites and Blacks and preempt this conflict. As the demand for African workers rose, slave ships made more frequent trips to the Chesapeake, and the transition to a slave labor system accelerated. At the time of Bacon's Rebellion, white servants outnumbered enslaved Black

people in the Chesapeake by about four to one, but by the early 1690s, the ratio had inverted completely. In the last thirty years of the century, the Black population increased fivefold. The tobacco region was becoming a slave society.

CODIFYING BLACK SLAVERY

The transition to slave labor was not simply the result of individual planters' decisions to purchase enslaved workers. Instead, beginning in the 1660s, the Chesapeake colonial governments enacted new laws that supported slaveholding.

Slavery had not been practiced in England for centuries, and English law provided no clear precedents for holding bound laborers permanently or for determining the legal status of their children. Drawing on Caribbean models, the Virginia legislature in 1662 broke new ground in North America, declaring that slave status was inherited through the mother. This meant that sexual relations between a white man (including a slaveholder) and an enslaved woman could increase the numbers of people enslaved to the owner. This one legal innovation raised the value of enslaved women—and created enormous incentives for rape and coerced reproduction. Then, five years later, Virginia law reassured slaveholders that slave property would not be undermined if an enslaved person converted to Christianity. Maryland offered slaveholders the same protection in 1671. Other laws placed bounties on runaways and shielded slaveholders from prosecution for violence against their enslaved laborers. All of these laws encouraged tobacco planters to buy African labor as a long-term investment.

Colonial laws from this period made clear that the white society as a whole had an interest in differentiating

Manufacturing Molasses in Barbados. By the time Virginia tobacco planters turned to slave labor, a much larger slave system was emerging in the Caribbean, fueled by a rising European demand for sugar. *Fotosearch/Archive Photos/Getty Images*

enslaved people from servants and regulating relations between Africans and Europeans. Virginia's slave code of 1682, which would be copied in Maryland, Delaware, and North Carolina, prohibited people in slavery from owning weapons, leaving their owners' plantations without permission, or striking any white person, even in self-defense. Both Maryland and Virginia banned marriages between Black men and white women—as did Massachusetts (in 1705) and eventually every other colony—thus outlawing a practice that had been tolerated and even recognized earlier in the seventeenth century. Finally, in 1691, Virginia made it illegal for slaveholders to free people without paying to have them expelled from the colony. Colonial lawmakers were not simply seeking to protect a form of property; they were creating a racially divided slave society where free Black people would not be welcome.

Virginia was the most populous English colony in North America in the 1660s, and more enslaved Africans lived in tobacco country than anywhere else on the mainland. But by century's end, a larger pattern of slaveholding was emerging in nearby colonies. When New Netherland fell into English hands in 1664, the empire acquired a territory where slavery had been established for decades. And one year earlier, the chartering of **South Carolina** created the first English colony on the mainland designed from the outset around slavery.

In South Carolina's early years, settlers bought or captured Native Americans, some of whom they then removed to the West Indies out of fear that the local native inhabitants would be more likely to run away and better positioned

to organize slave revolts. A third of the colony's enslaved labor force was Native American at the beginning of the century. But South Carolina's founding planters and proprietors had always intended to introduce enslaved Africans. In an effort to lure planters from Barbados, they instituted **slave codes** that secured the legal status of slavery. South Carolina laws encouraged further growth of the slave system by granting land to any white settler who brought enslaved Africans into the colony. By 1680, South Carolina had a higher proportion of enslaved persons in its total population than any other mainland colony, a distinction it would hold throughout the colonial period.

The final major piece of the colonial slavery picture fell into place in 1750. That year, Georgia, founded seventeen years earlier as a refuge colony for debtors and a buffer between South Carolina and Spanish Florida (see Chapter 4), decided to legalize slavery, which a royal decree confirmed in 1751. The legal foundation of slavery throughout British America was now laid.

ATTITUDES TOWARD RACE

With few exceptions, the men, women, and children who were held as chattel in the colonies that would become the United States were Africans or the descendants of Africans. Many factors contributed to the colonists' decision to enslave Africans rather than Europeans or Native Americans. Most important was the fact that a thriving traffic in humans from Africa to the Americas had already existed before the mainland English colonies formed. Since a growing global demand for sugar had fueled a steady flow of enslaved African laborers to sugar-producing plantations farther south, mainland planters were participating in an established trade, and captives far from their homelands were deemed easier to control than indigenous enslaved people. But the flourishing of the transatlantic slave trade was itself a reflection of European beliefs about race and religion. Europeans saw Africans from south of the Sahara as fair game for certain kinds of exploitation that were otherwise taboo.

People throughout the world had practiced slavery, in various forms, for millennia. Often, human beings enslaved people they defined as outsiders, such as members of enemy groups as an act or consequence of warfare. The very word *slave*, for example, comes from a

INTERPRETING THE SOURCES
The Curse of Ham

In the history of racial prejudice against Africans from south of the Sahara, no text has been as widely discussed and quoted as the so-called curse of Ham from the book of Genesis in the Hebrew Bible. Neither the Hebrew nor the Christian Bible (nor the Quran) speaks of racial differences or links slavery with skin color. But as Muslims, Christians, and Jews (a small number of Jewish merchants and planters played a minor role in American slavery, mostly in the Dutch colonies of Curacao and Suriname) entered the Atlantic slave trade, they found new meaning in an ancient curse that Noah had placed on his son Ham after the great flood.

Before the rise of the African slave trade, the character of Ham had not been identified with the African continent and was rarely associated with Blackness. In the eighteenth century, however, the idea that Ham represented Africa south of the Sahara became commonplace. By the nineteenth century, Christian commentators were routinely citing the so-called curse of Ham to justify the enslavement of Black people.

The story of the curse appears as Noah's family is about to repopulate the Earth. The biblical passage itself is somewhat enigmatic; in fact, Noah's curse seems to be directed not to Ham but to Ham's son, Canaan.

Genesis 9: 18–26:
The sons of Noah, exiting the ark, were Shem, Ham, and Japheth; Ham was the father of Canaan. These three were the sons of Noah, and from them the whole world spread out.

Noah started tilling the soil and planted a vineyard. He drank of the wine and got drunk, and exposed himself inside his tent. Ham, the father of Canaan, saw his father's nakedness and told his two brothers outside. So

Shem and Japheth took the garment, placed it on both their shoulders, walked backwards, and covered their father's nakedness; facing backwards, they never saw their father's nakedness. When Noah awakened from his wine, he knew what his youngest son had done. He said: "Cursed be Canaan, a slave of slaves shall he be to his brothers." And he said: "Blessed be the Lord, God of Shem, let Canaan be a slave to him. May God enlarge Japheth, and may he dwell in the tents of Shem, and let Canaan be a slave to him."

Explore the Source

1. In this story, how do some members of the same human family come to be enslaved to other members of that family?

2. What is the nature of the crime or sin for which Canaan's slavery is a punishment?

3. Why do you suppose American colonists in 1700 might have read this text as a justification of their slave system?

Latin word designating a person whose Slavic descent marked him or her as an ethnic outsider. • By the twelfth and thirteenth centuries, religious faith played a major role in establishing boundaries. Both Muslim Arabs and Christian Europeans enslaved members of the other group in great numbers. Increasingly, though, they turned their attention to Africans from south of the Sahara, most of whom were not protected members of either faith. •

Religion would continue to be an important factor in European thinking about slavery in the Americas. The Spanish outlawed the enslavement of Native Americans in 1542 (though the practice continued), in part because they saw their mission as that of spreading Christianity to the native inhabitants. And when English settlers began introducing enslaved Africans to the Chesapeake in the seventeenth century, the question of whether a Christian African could be enslaved remained open.

Virginia's 1670 law stipulated that an enslaved person who converted could remain enslaved; however, not for another twelve years would Virginia allow the perpetual enslavement of an African who had been baptized *before* entering the colony.

The transition from servitude to slavery in the Chesapeake involved a shift toward a greater emphasis on race, rather than just religion, as a mark of slave status. The word *racism* would not enter the English language until the 1930s, and the theories of racial difference on which modern racism rests did not become popular until the nineteenth century. But English colonists inherited a powerful tradition of anti-African prejudice and racial thinking, from both European and Arab sources. By the fifteenth century, the idea that human beings belonged to different families and that some people were condemned by their bloodlines to servitude and persecution (see Interpreting the Sources: The Curse of Ham) was

CONFLICTING FAITHS

57

commonplace, especially in Spain and Portugal, where Christians developed new theories of blood purity, initially to express concerns about people suspected of having secret Jewish ancestry. The racial prejudice of Spanish and Portuguese Christians helped justify the African slave trade to the Americas.

But if racial prejudice encouraged slavery, slavery also bred racial prejudice. English colonists now viewed Africans less as heathens who might convert and more as Black people who were permanently distinct from them. The words *negro* and *slave* became increasingly interchangeable toward the end of the seventeenth century, a shift that reflected a major change in colonial life. Before white Virginians began buying large numbers of Africans, people of African and European descent had much closer social relations, and class was probably more important than ethnicity in determining social status. Free Blacks and free whites traded with one another, socialized, and formed friendships, as did enslaved Africans and indentured Europeans. For instance, when George Williams, a white seaman, died in 1667, he made his friend Emanuel Driggus, an African and a freed person, the executor of his will. But once tobacco planters shifted to slave labor, and once colonial law defined the boundaries of slavery in racial terms, white and Black Virginians fell on opposite sides of a great divide. Immigrants without African ancestry could exploit new opportunities to own land and achieve economic dependence. And even though class differences remained, poorer free farmers could draw some solace from the idea that their skin color kept them above the degraded status of people in slavery.

AFRICANS IN NORTH AMERICA

The transition to African slavery in England's southern mainland colonies would prove monumentally fateful for subsequent American history. But it was a small development in a larger Atlantic slave system that had been in place in South America and the Caribbean for more than a century. ● From 1500 to 1820, almost four times as many Africans as Europeans left for the Americas. Deported in chains from European trading posts along the shores of West Africa, more than twelve million men, women, and children made the harrowing journey across the Atlantic (see Table 3.1). The vast majority hailed from the western portion of the continent most accessible to European traders (see Map 3.1), but some came from as far east as what are now Mozambique,

CROSSING BORDERS

Tanzania, and the island of Madagascar. Only a small fraction—around 5 percent—of the captives disembarked in the North American colonies that became the United States (see Map 3.2). ● However, unlike enslaved people destined for a brutally shortened life toiling in West Indian sugar plantations or South American silver mines, Africans in British North America survived and reproduced. Their descendants, along with a steady stream of new arrivals, would eventually form the world's largest African **diaspora,** a community connected by a remembered or envisioned relationship to their distant homeland.

CROSSING BORDERS

CAPTURE AND THE MIDDLE PASSAGE

European slave traders did not typically seize free people in Africa and ship them across the Atlantic. Rather, they purchased human beings who were already enslaved in Africa, though under a system of slavery that was not always permanent. Often captives of war, these men and women were political prisoners or victims of kidnapping raids by predatory African states or enterprising African middlemen seeking to profit from the trade with Europe. All along the western coast of Africa, European traders purchased these enslaved people with such goods as textiles (often from Asia), metals, weapons, liquor, tobacco, and cowrie shells (see Hot Commodities: Cowrie Shells).

Africans were sold to slave merchants from several European nations, including Portugal, Holland, England, Denmark, and France, but the people in slavery represented a far wider array of nations, ethnicities, and

TABLE 3.1	THE ATLANTIC SLAVE TRADE, BY CENTURY
Century	Estimated Number of Enslaved Men, Women, and Children Departing from Africa
Fifteenth	81,000
Sixteenth	338,000
Seventeenth	1,876,000
Eighteenth	6,495,000
Nineteenth	4,027,000

Source: Paul E. Lovejoy, *Transformations in Slavery: A History of Slavery in Africa* (Cambridge: Cambridge University Press, 1983), 19.

languages. Captives came from regions that stretched along 3,500 miles of coastline and extended up to 1,000 miles inland. The men, women, and children shipped to the American colonies did not see themselves as *Africans* but rather as members of villages or language-based ethnic groups. As they gathered in coastal forts, where they awaited deportation, captives massed together with people who spoke unfamiliar languages, hailed from distant lands, or even belonged to enemy states.

The new world to which they were headed was even more alien. No enslaved Africans had returned from the Americas during the seventeenth century with reports of plantation life. Because Europeans were falsely reputed to be cannibals, many of the captives imagined that they were being shipped off to slaughter. What awaited them was, in some ways, just as horrific. The horrors began with the Atlantic crossing, which Europeans called the **Middle Passage** because the journey formed the second leg of a triangular trade itinerary that took slave ships from Europe to the African coast, then to the Americas, and then back to Europe. From the perspective of the human cargo, there was nothing triangular or intermediate about this trip. For them, the Middle Passage was an irreversible exile to a life of pain and degradation.

Packed into windowless ship holds and chained together in pairs, the captives lay on shelves for journeys that could last twenty weeks in the early years of the trade and that, even by the eighteenth century, rarely took less than five weeks. ● Ship holds stank of human waste, as the chained passengers stepped over one another and relieved themselves in uncovered tubs installed for that purpose. Once or twice a day, enslaved people were taken up to the deck, still in shackles, to eat, get hosed down, and engage in exercises that their captors mistakenly thought could prevent scurvy. They contracted various illnesses, including dysentery, yellow fever, dehydration, and wound infections from the brands that

had been burned onto their bodies, and death tolls were high, even though ship captains had every incentive to arrive in the Americas with as many living captives as possible. The Royal African Company's ships lost almost a quarter of their human cargo between 1680 and 1688, and even in the eighteenth century, when faster ships and sanitary improvements lowered mortality rates, it was common for 10 percent of the enslaved passengers to die en route. ● The dead were simply tossed overboard.

Because Africans sought to resist their captivity in various ways, slave ships were equipped with mouth openers, thumb screws, whips, and other devices designed to deter resistance. Historians estimate that **slave mutinies** took place on every eight to ten journeys, but most were brutally suppressed by heavily armed crews. These rebellions added to the death totals among the captives and offered some clues as to the kind of disciplinary treatment they could expect from European slaveholders. The crew of a Danish

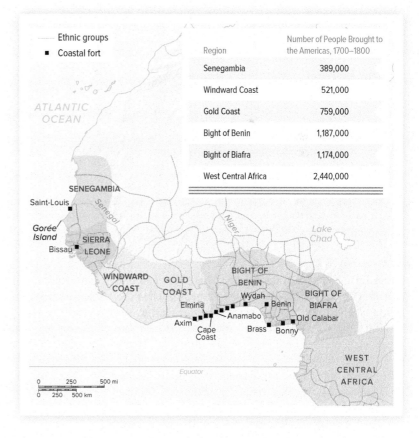

Region	Number of People Brought to the Americas, 1700–1800
Senegambia	389,000
Windward Coast	521,000
Gold Coast	759,000
Bight of Benin	1,187,000
Bight of Biafra	1,174,000
West Central Africa	2,440,000

Map 3.1 West African Sources of the Atlantic Slave Trade. Enslaved Africans hailed from very different societies and regions. In the Americas, many maintained distinctive regional identities while coming to see themselves as Africans.

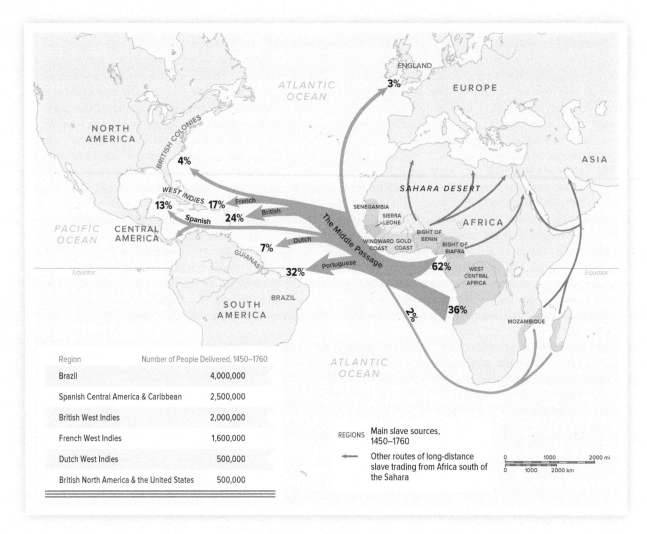

Region	Number of People Delivered, 1450–1760
Brazil	4,000,000
Spanish Central America & Caribbean	2,500,000
British West Indies	2,000,000
French West Indies	1,600,000
Dutch West Indies	500,000
British North America & the United States	500,000

REGIONS — Main slave sources, 1450–1760

⟵ Other routes of long-distance slave trading from Africa south of the Sahara

• Map 3.2 American Destinations of the Atlantic Slave Trade, ca. 1450–1760. Though enslaved Africans arrived at colonies throughout the hemisphere, a few colonies dominated the trade. Recent studies estimate that sugar-producing colonies in Brazil and the Caribbean absorbed approximately 90 percent of the Atlantic slave trade. More people were brought in slavery to the tiny island of Jamaica than to all the mainland North American colonies combined. •

slave ship in 1709, for example, cut off the right hand of a captive who had led an abortive revolt and exhibited the hand to the rest of the ship. On the following day, his left hand met the same fate. The day after that, the man was decapitated, and his headless torso was displayed. In the face of such brutality, some captives sought to take their own lives by refusing to eat, banging their heads against iron bars, or managing to get to the side of the ship. Thomas Phillips, captain of an English slave ship during the 1690s, described Africans leaping out of boats, "having a more dreadful apprehension of Barbadoes than we have of hell."

The great majority of captives, however, struggled to survive, formed close bonds with their fellow passengers,

and tried to prepare themselves for whatever lay at the end of the journey. On arrival, the captives were resold, either at fixed prices to eager purchasers who boarded the docked ships or at auctions in the streets, taverns, merchant houses, and public squares of port towns. Most of the arrivals were then transported to farms and plantations to perform backbreaking agricultural labor. They had survived one ordeal, but another was just beginning.

BORN INTO SLAVERY

The roughly four hundred thousand Africans brought to North America between 1675 and the American

HOT COMMODITIES
Cowrie Shells

Historians often speak of a triangular trade circuit that connected Western Europe, the American colonies, and West Africa. In the basic model, European nations exported textiles, metals, and manufactured goods to Africa, where they were exchanged for enslaved persons, who were then brought to the colonies, which in turn produced sugar and other raw materials for European consumption. But transatlantic trade in the seventeenth and eighteenth centuries was never a simple triangle. Some ships sailed back and forth directly between Europe and America, whereas others made several intermediate stops along the way. The triangle model also ignores the important role of Asia in the trade to the Americas. Rather than picturing a closed triangle across the Atlantic Ocean, historians are now more likely to describe a complex web of global exchange, involving numerous commodities and disparate economies across the planet.

One crucial player in the new global commerce of goods and labor was the cowrie, a snail-like, aquatic creature that lives in the tropical parts of the Indian and Pacific Oceans. Because of their beauty, durability, and distinctiveness, cowrie shells had long been valued, both as prestigious ornaments and as money, in many regions

Cowrie Shell Dug out of the Ground near Slave Quarters, Monticello, Virginia. Because of their shape, cowrie shells were often associated with fertility. Their widespread use as money, however, explains the cowrie's Latin name, *Cypraea moneta*. ©*Thomas Jefferson Foundation at Monticello*

Modern Cowrie Shells. People today still prize the shells for their beauty. *xiao zhou/Getty Images*

of the world, including Africa. European traders also prized cowrie shells as packing materials that could protect fragile Asian porcelain wares as they traveled in ship holds. But the real value of these early versions of packing peanuts was set by African slave traders along that continent's western coast, where cowrie shells were the leading currency during the seventeenth and early eighteenth centuries. Merchants returning to Europe from China or India would stop in places like the Maldive Islands to purchase the shells, then export them to Africa in exchange for human beings.

Because of this global commerce, cowrie shells from the other side of the world have turned up in archaeological excavations in the Chesapeake region. In Thomas Jefferson's Monticello, researchers unearthed a cowrie shell in the area where enslaved workers had lived. This

shell appears to have been worn as jewelry by an enslaved African brought to Virginia but whose name has been lost to us. Buried cowrie testifies to the economic links that bound places like China, the Maldives, France, Benin, Barbados, and Virginia into a single global economy. The Monticello shell also tells a different story: Men and women, captured and brought to a distant land, wore beautiful shells to retain some connection to a world they would never see again.

Think About It

1. What commodities in European society at the time might be compared to cowrie shells for their beauty, durability, or commercial usefulness?

2. How does the cowrie shell complicate the idea that Africans were part of a triangular trade?

Revolution did not differ fundamentally from the millions transported to sugar-producing colonies in the West Indies or Brazil during the same period. But unlike their kin and compatriots in more tropical climates, the people enslaved in North America lived longer on average and had much higher birthrates. This trend exerted a powerful impact on slavery in the mainland colonies.

• In most North American slave societies, life expectancy was very low. Africans lacked immunities to many tropical diseases in the colonies (though Europeans were even more susceptible), and the debilitating gang labor involved in growing and milling sugar took a devastating toll, especially in Cuba and Brazil but also in the British Caribbean. And because slaveholders were constantly replenishing their labor supply by importing African men to replace those who died (slave purchasers consistently preferred male laborers), sex ratios among slave communities were imbalanced and fewer children were born. • The high proportion of African-born people enslaved in most colonies thus produced a vicious cycle of high mortality, low birthrates, and the continued resupply of African captives. From their formation in the sixteenth and seventeenth centuries until well after the abolition of the slave trade in the early nineteenth century, slave societies throughout Latin America and the West Indies relied on a labor force that was mostly African born.

The one major exception to this rule was mainland North America. Several factors contributed to the higher birthrates and lower death rates in Britain's mainland colonies, including climate, diet, work pace, slaveholder practices, and the geographical distribution of people in slavery. But the crucial point is that the trend was self-perpetuating. Once slave populations began to grow due to human reproduction and not exclusively through the introduction of enslaved people from overseas, sex ratios evened out and birthrates grew even higher. And since more of the population was **creole** (born in the colonies), more enslaved people had acquired immunities to local disease. American-born mothers' tendency to wean children at an earlier age than African-born mothers further raised birthrates by reducing the time between pregnancies.

The shift to a mostly creole enslaved population occurred earlier in the Chesapeake and the North than in South Carolina. By 1740, only a third of the colony's enslaved people had been born in Africa. In South Carolina, by contrast, where slave men and women reproduced more slowly and slaveholders relied more on the introduction of enslaved people from overseas, Africans dominated the enslaved population until about midcentury. But even in that colony, human reproduction became the primary contributor to the growth of the slave system. By 1750, the distinctive demographics of North American slavery were clear. The enslaved labor force in the colonies that would become the United States was self-reproducing and mostly born in North America.

AFRICAN DIASPORA

Creole descendants of Africans in North America undoubtedly experienced slavery differently than those born in Africa and living farther south, if for no other reason than they had not been kidnapped from their homes and subjected to the Atlantic crossing. And because they labored on smaller slaveholding units and lived in colonies with larger white populations, enslaved North Americans were in some ways quicker to acculturate to their new surroundings. Nonetheless, African customs, beliefs, memories, and practices survived in the mainland colonies and infused the lives of enslaved Americans.

Even as slave populations became native born, the memory of the old country remained strong during

Human Cargo.   This image, from Chambon's *Le Commerce de l'Amerique par Marseille* (ca. 1764), depicts "an Englishman licking a Negro's chin to ascertain his age, and to determine from the taste of his sweat if he is sick" and Africans weeping as their loved ones are forced onto a slave ship. *Everett Collection/Shutterstock*

the colonial era. By the time slavery was abolished in the United States, most African Americans claimed several generations of ancestors born on American soil. But in the first half of the eighteenth century, most of the enslaved had either survived the Middle Passage or were the children of survivors. Survivors and their children may have lived in Virginia, New York, or South Carolina, but they understood that they had come from very different places across the water. As with voluntary immigrants in other periods of American history, African captives tried to transmit their heritage to their offspring.

Although the slave trade routinely broke up African families, and no colony granted legal recognition to the marriage or parenthood of enslaved people, Africans in America still managed to form, maintain, and rebuild family relationships. Slaveholders often encouraged conjugal relations between men and women on the same plantation (or nearby), both to increase the labor force and to prevent them from absconding to visit partners elsewhere. Enslaved parents could not protect offspring from the brutal authority of slaveholders, but they waged a constant struggle to influence their children's development. The naming of slave children presented an early opportunity to remind them of their roots. Slaveholders typically sought to impose English names on newly acquired Africans, but parents generally assumed the right to bestow names on sons and daughters born into bondage. Often observing the West African custom of naming children in accordance with the day of the week on which they were born, parents might name a boy born on Friday Kofi or Cuffee, whereas a girl born on Tuesday would be named some variant of Abena. Other African-language names referred to birth order or preserved the memory of relatives still living in the old country.

Outside the bonds of parents and children, African cultures and identities were sustained by growing **slave communities.** Although the enslaved did not form a majority in any mainland colony other than South Carolina, they were clustered in areas where Africans and their children predominated. Whether or not they labored on large plantations, people in slavery conducted most of their social relations with one another during the mid-eighteenth century, and some lived in what essentially was an all-Black world. Even in New England, where enslaved people made up only 3 percent of the population in 1750, Africans and their descendants were sufficiently concentrated in seaports, along rivers, and in particular farm regions where they were able to sustain distinctive cuisine, clothing fashions, festivals, and funeral rites, all of which drew on traditions from Africa.

In areas where enslaved people predominated, they were also able to preserve their linguistic heritage. Many, born in Africa, learned just enough English to recognize some basic work-related commands. In the slave quarters, they spoke in their native tongues or used a patois (mixed language) that integrated African syntax and pronunciation and may not have been understood by whites. Enslaved people in the coastal region of the South Carolina Lowcountry, where Blacks vastly outnumbered whites, spoke a patois known as **Gullah,** which became a more formal language of its own by the nineteenth century.

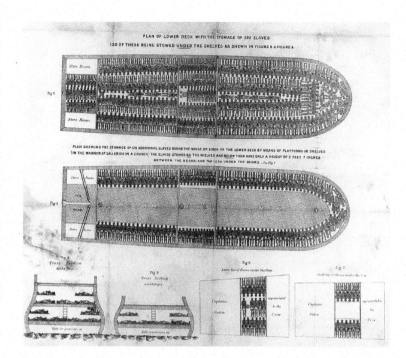

Diagram of the British Slave Ship *Brookes,* **ca. 1788.** Typically, the ships that carried enslaved Africans across the Atlantic held between two hundred and four hundred men, women, and children. Though children tended to be healthier than adults at the start of the voyage, they were subject to abuse and torture on board. It was common for girls as young as eight to be sexually assaulted by crew members. This iconic image, engraved by the English abolitionist Thomas Clarkson, was the first visual representation of slave suffering ever produced for a mass audience. *The Bridgeman Art Library/Getty Images*

Although the horrors of the Atlantic crossing may have tested the faith and shaken the world views of many captives, Africans did not abandon their ancestral religions when they arrived in the American colonies. Before 1750, Africans and their descendants maintained rituals, rites, taboos, and beliefs rooted in a variety of religious traditions. Some were adherents of Islam (see Singular Lives: Ayuba Suleiman Diallo, Redeemed Captive), which had made significant inroads in the Senegambian region from which many enslaved people came. But most had been raised in religions that were transmitted through oral tradition rather than scripture and that emphasized magic and the conjuring of the spirit world. Many of their beliefs and practices overlapped with those of white Christians at the time, who also sought contact with spirits, consulted sorcerers, and feared the power of witches and wizards. Other African religious traditions, such as marrying more than one woman and burying the dead with food and drink, stood out more conspicuously in colonial America. As the century wore on, more slaveholders and other whites began preaching to enslaved

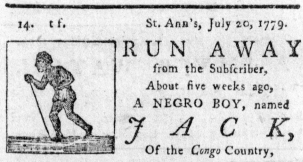

14.   t f.   St. Ann's, July 20, 1779.

RUN AWAY
from the Subfcriber,
About five weeks ago,
A NEGRO BOY, named
J A C K,
Of the *Congo* Country,
About 15 or 16 years of age, and has no Brand Mark.
—He fpeaks tolerable good Englifh, and it is fuppofed
that he has taken the Clarendon road, being well ac-
quainted in that parifh.

TWO POUNDS FIFTEEN SHILLINGS Reward
will be given for taking him up, and lodging him in
any of the Gaols of this Ifland, giving information
thereof.

ANDREW BYRNE.

Runaway Slave Advertisement, *Virginia* **Gazette,**
Williamsburg, 1770. Note the reference to the runaway's African
birth and moderate proficiency in English. *Royal Museums Greenwich*

ground as people who had once lived on the African continent and now were part of a diaspora.

VARIETIES OF COLONIAL SLAVERY

Unlike in later periods, slavery was not confined to a single region of North America during the colonial era. By the eighteenth century, Africans and their descendants were held in legal bondage in English colonies up and down the Atlantic Coast and in Spanish and French colonies along the Gulf of Mexico. Most of those in slavery labored in commercial agriculture, producing and processing staple crops for export. Others worked on family farms, in urban workshops, on construction projects, or as domestic servants. Enslaved people in disparate colonies typically came from different parts of Africa and had varying experiences of slavery. Under certain conditions, they were able to band together to resist their oppression and stage strategic attacks against the regimes under which they labored.

TOBACCO FARMING IN THE CHESAPEAKE

The largest slave system by far in colonial North America emerged in the Chesapeake Bay region. By 1750, three out of five people enslaved in the thirteen colonies that would become the United States lived in Virginia or Maryland. Most men, women, and children (usually beginning at around age ten or eleven) enslaved in those two colonies cultivated tobacco, which was exported in massive quantities to the British Isles and then sold all over Europe. By 1700, the Chesapeake colonies (including the northeastern corner of North Carolina) were shipping 38 million pounds of tobacco annually, and at various points in the next century, the figure rose to around 60 million. Later in the colonial period, many Virginia planters began growing wheat alongside or in place of tobacco, but before 1750, the tobacco leaf dominated the local economy.

Tobacco and slavery did not always go hand in hand. Tobacco had been the staple crop of the Chesapeake long before Virginia colonists began introducing large numbers of Africans into the area, and nonslaveholding family farms continued to grow tobacco during the eighteenth century. But tobacco production and slave labor were certainly compatible. Tobacco growing did not require vast acreage, expensive equipment, or large

people, and by the time of the American Revolution, a large portion of the African American population had adapted and adopted some form of Christianity. But before 1750, the religious lives of people in slavery reinforced links with their African heritage.

Africans in America also imported musical instruments, clothing styles, quilting patterns, basket-weaving techniques, medical expertise, tattoos, and other African cultural forms that would connect them to the old country and influence the larger societies in which they lived. African traditions would especially shape speech patterns and foodways now associated with traditional Southern culture. Spoonbread, for example, a pudding dish made from cornmeal, evolved from the cooking techniques of enslaved people seeking to re-create or approximate the traditional African dishes fufu and kenkey.

As enslaved people built new communities in the colonies, these African forms evolved, much as they had back in Africa in the centuries before the slave trade. But their culture continued to bear the stamp of the worlds from which they had been exiled. Far from losing their African identity in the Americas, enslaved people actually found that identity. Arriving in America as Igbos, Bambaras, Wolofs, or Yorubas, they found common

SINGULAR LIVES

Ayuba Suleiman Diallo, Redeemed Captive

Ayuba Suleiman Diallo, who also went by the name Job ben Solomon, was born around 1702 in the West African region of Bondou, between the Senegal and Gambian Rivers. Son of a prosperous Fula merchant, cattle herder, and high priest, Diallo was raised as a Muslim and distinguished himself by memorizing the entire Quran as a teenager. One day in 1731, while traveling far from home on business that involved the sale of two enslaved people owned by his family, Diallo was captured by some Mandingo men and sold to an English slaver, who brought him in chains to Maryland.

Other men and women aboard the slave ship may have come from equally distinguished backgrounds. Like Diallo, they could have been well off, important personages in their communities who were also slaveholders. Now they were all thrust together, heads shaven to indicate their status as prisoners and branded to mark them as property.

Like Diallo, those who survived the Middle Passage were brought ashore in Annapolis, Maryland, where strange men speaking a foreign language put them to work growing tobacco. Each one of them could have told a heart-wrenching story of loneliness and dislocation. Diallo's story entered the historical record as a result of an unusual set of circumstances that would wind up rescuing him, alone among his shipmates, from permanent exile.

Because Diallo resisted fieldwork, his slaveholder assigned him to cattle herding. This was a trade with which he was familiar and that allowed him to slip into the woods to fulfill his prayer requirements at prescribed times, though a white boy often followed him, mocking Diallo's devotions and throwing dirt in his face.

Like many newly arrived, Diallo hatched an escape plan, but the odds were stacked against him. Maryland's fugitive slave laws encouraged and empowered anyone (white or Native American) to apprehend Black men who could be runaways, and though Diallo made it across the county line, he was soon arrested and jailed in a local tavern. While in custody, he met a man who spoke his native language, and he learned how difficult it would be to escape, so he tried a different approach. Unlike most Africans in North America, Diallo was highly literate, and he wrote a letter in Arabic to his father, detailing his predicament and asking to be ransomed. He requested that the letter be delivered to the slave broker in Annapolis who had sold him to his current owner, hoping that it might travel back to Senegambia along the other two legs of the triangular trade route that had brought him to North America.

Perhaps because the Arabic letter was a curiosity or perhaps because Diallo's slave translator had intimated to the white Maryland colonists that Diallo's Fula family was rich and powerful, the letter was delivered to Annapolis. From there, it was routed to London, where it found its way into the hands of an Arabic professor at Oxford. Translated into English, Diallo's written account of his captivity interested officials of the Royal African Company, who arranged to buy Diallo from his Maryland owner and bring him to England. Diallo learned some English on his way to Europe and negotiated an agreement with the Royal African Company. In return for Diallo's help in securing greater access for British traders to gold, gum, and non-Muslims to enslave from the Senegambia, the company would return Diallo to his home and not buy any more Muslims. Late in 1734, Diallo was back in Africa, his horrible ordeal at an end. He soon learned, however, that his father had died, one of his wives had remarried, and wars had ravaged his native land and stripped it of its wealth.

Ayuba Suleiman Diallo. This engraving was published in the English monthly *The Gentleman's Magazine*, 1750. ©*Christie's Images/The Bridgeman Art Library*

Where in the Archives?

Much of what historians know of Diallo's enslavement comes from the perspective of two white men, Thomas Bluett and Francis Moore. Bluett, a Maryland judge who helped Diallo, relied mostly on conversations between the two men to write a biography of Diallo told from Bluett's vantage point. Moore traveled with Diallo and had firsthand knowledge of that part of his life.

Bluett's *Some Memoirs of the Life of Job, the Son of Solomon* was published in London in 1734, the year Diallo returned to his homeland, and can be found in the digital collections of the University of North Carolina (https://docsouth.unc.edu/neh/).

Information on Diallo's return to Africa appears in a chapter of Moore's *Travels into the Inland Parts of Africa* (1738), which can be found at HathiTrust (https://catalog.hathitrust.org/).

Assignment

Locate and read Bluett's text as well as the section on pages 202–208 of Moore's text.

1. List three interesting differences between the two perspectives on Diallo and his background.

2. In a single paragraph, compare how the two authors talk about the significance of Diallo's Muslim faith.

Parrish House, Louisa County, Virginia, and Tobacco Barn, Green Hill Plantation, Campbell County, Virginia.   The buildings of both Blacks and whites in eighteenth-century Virginia reflected construction patterns imported from West Africa as well as from England. West and Central African homes tended to be small, with few openings other than a doorway. African influence on colonial building also led to the use of thatched roofs. *From: Glassie, Henry H.* Folk Housing in Middle Virginia: A Structural Analysis of Historic Artifacts. *Knoxville: University of Tennessee Press, 1975; Library of Congress, Prints & Photographs Division [HABS VA,16-LONI.V,1D—1]*

workforces, so a farmer with only a few enslaved workers could profitably employ them on a tobacco field. And because soil conducive to tobacco abounded in much of the region, this staple crop encouraged the spread of small slaveholders rather than the amassing of large plantations in just one part of the colony.

Tobacco cultivation exhausted soil quickly, and small farmers and large plantation owners alike often let portions of their land lie fallow for years at a time rather than buying enough slave labor to till the entire acreage. Though a few wealthy planters built substantial operations, most slaveholders in the Chesapeake in the middle of the eighteenth century owned five people or fewer. Vast slaveholdings of this size, already common in the West Indies in this era, were rare in the Chesapeake.

Compared to other staple crops, tobacco farming required closer supervision, because the tobacco leaf was especially fragile, and planters generally operated on the **gang system,** under which small teams of enslaved laborers worked in tandem, straining to match the pace set by a foreman (also enslaved), all under the vigilant eye and lash of an overseer. This gang system epitomized not only the demanding nature of tobacco fieldwork but also the high degree of contact between whites and Blacks on the plantation. Slaveholders and overseers scrutinized and intervened in the lives of the enslaved to a greater degree in the Chesapeake than in most large American slave societies during this period.

Needless to say, more frequent contact did not necessarily lead to better treatment. Slaveholders on tobacco plantations may have taken a greater interest in the lives of their enslaved workers, but such interest could lead to whipping, torture, mutilation, or sexual assault. Still, the close bonds that occasionally formed across the color line in eighteenth-century Virginia reflected the distinctive features of the tobacco colonies: Enslaved people were relatively dispersed, worked in small groups, lived near their owners, and worked closely with white overseers. These circumstances made it more difficult for Africans in the Chesapeake to resist their enslavement. Not a single white person was killed in colonial Virginia by an organized slave revolt.

RICE IN THE LOWCOUNTRY

Colonial North America's second largest slave system lay farther south, in the Lowcountry of South Carolina and Georgia. Compared to the Chesapeake system, Lowcountry slavery more closely resembled slavery in the Caribbean. Here, absentee slaveholders commonly entrusted large plantations of more than a hundred enslaved people to managers and overseers. By 1708, less than forty years after its founding, South Carolina had become the only mainland colony with a slave majority.

Sketch of a Banjo. An African instrument introduced by enslaved people in the American South, the banjo originally had no frets and was made by stretching a skin over a hollow gourd. *World History Archive/Alamy Stock Photo*

A number of factors shaped the demographics of slavery in South Carolina. First, slavery was established there after indentured servitude had already declined as a viable means of attracting cheap European labor to the colonies. Second, South Carolina was the southernmost English mainland colony in the late seventeenth century, lying closer to the main routes of the transatlantic slave trade that brought Africans to the Caribbean. Third, the colony's first settlers were Barbadians who were already slaveholders and thus were familiar with the trade.

As much as any of those circumstances, however, it was a new crop that sustained the persistent differences between the Lowcountry and the Chesapeake. **Rice** was still unknown in much of Europe when it was imported to North America from Madagascar in the seventeenth century. Enslaved people from West Africa brought with them experience and expertise in rice cultivation, and South Carolina's planters put them to work clearing swamplands and planting what would become the colony's staple. Slaveholders in the Lowcountry relied particularly on men and women from the Senegambian region, who were familiar with planting, processing, winnowing, and cooking rice. Consequently, the standard South Carolina methods for planting rice—including the use of hoes and coiled baskets and a distinctive sowing technique that involved pressing into the ground with one's heel and covering the seed with one's foot—all closely matched Senegambian practices. African agricultural knowledge and technology made a brutal slave system economically profitable.

Unlike tobacco operations, rice plantations entailed significant start-up costs for draining swamps and building dams, dikes, and ditches. Simply to enter the rice-growing business required a substantial labor force. In addition, rice could be cultivated without close supervision, and the productivity of laborers on rice plantations could be measured more easily than with tobacco, since quantity mattered more than quality. So instead of the gang system of the Chesapeake, rice planters instituted a **task system,** in which enslaved laborers were assigned a certain volume and type of work and had to complete it by the end of the day. Typically, an enslaved adult in colonial South Carolina was required to plant a quarter-acre field in the course of a day. Though an onerous assignment that generally forced bondspeople to supply more of their own food than those in the gang system, the quarter-acre task gave people enslaved in the Lowcountry greater control over their time and introduced opportunities to spend their *own* time cultivating private plots for their own consumption.

Combined with the size and concentration of the slave population, the task system meant that Africans and their descendants in South Carolina had less contact with the culture of their slaveholders and were somewhat better positioned to engage in organized resistance. South Carolina was also the only colony before 1733 where slaveholders had to worry that enslaved people might flee to the territory of a hostile European power. Spanish Florida, with its capital in nearby St. Augustine, provided an asylum for Africans in South Carolina and inspired those in slavery to imagine that they might have allies in a showdown with their owners.

The **Stono Rebellion** of 1739 confirmed the fears of white South Carolinians. Encouraged by reports that a war had erupted between Spain and Britain, about twenty enslaved men, mostly Angolans, seized arms from a local store, raised a banner, and began beating drums and shouting "Liberty!" in the hope of recruiting more comrades for a march toward Spanish Florida. As they proceeded southward, the Stono rebels burned homes and killed about twenty white people, including women and

Pewter Slave Passport. This artifact shows a slaveholder's house with slave cabins in the background. Tags, badges, and tickets were part of a system of surveillance of enslaved people in Charleston, South Carolina. Though metal badges like this one were more common after 1800, tickets identifying an enslaved person's owner and destination were in use in Charleston as early as 1690. *©Virginia Historical Society*

Port of Arrival. Charlestown was not only the principal processing center for the staple crops—rice and, later, indigo—that were exported to England; it also dominated the trade in enslaved people by functioning as their primary place of entry. Forty percent of all Africans brought to North America before 1808 entered via Charlestown. For that reason, the port is sometimes called the Ellis Island of African America. *Hulton Archive/Stringer/Getty Images*

children (they spared a man known to be kind to his enslaved workers). Now a troop of between seventy and ninety, they traveled 10 miles unchecked and set up in an open field. But well-armed planters attacked, and a battle ensued, in which many of the rebels were killed. Over the next two days, white colonists, aided by Native Americans paid to catch enslaved people, hunted down Blacks who had participated in the rebellion, killed them, and placed their heads on poles as a warning to others.

The failed revolt, coming at the end of a decade of rebellions, violent clashes, and abortive conspiracies through much of the Caribbean, inaugurated an era of extraordinary vigilance about the security of the Lowcountry slave system. In 1740, South Carolina legislators passed the Negro Act, which required every member of a militia to serve in a slave patrol and prohibited slaveholders from manumitting (granting freedom to) their enslaved workers. The following year, the legislature tried to protect whites in the colony by imposing a tariff on slave imports, but the tariff failed to slow the arrival of Africans into the colony. Ultimately, despite fears of a race war, rice cultivation was too profitable for Lowcountry planters to resist the impulse to buy more enslaved workers.

The other major difference between the Chesapeake and the Lowcountry was the presence in South Carolina of an urban center. Because rice was bulkier than tobacco and needed more elaborate processing, the Lowcountry rice economy supported the growth of the region's major port. Charlestown (later renamed Charleston) was the fourth-largest city in British North America by the middle of the eighteenth century. In the Chesapeake, by contrast, tobacco farmers were able to ship their goods to market directly. Cities such as Norfolk, Alexandria, and Baltimore grew only once the Chesapeake turned to wheat cultivation after 1750.

SLAVERY IN THE NORTH

Although slavery would later become known as the "peculiar institution" of the South, the colonies north of the Chesapeake Bay also legalized slavery and imported Africans to labor in a variety of employments. Colonies such as Massachusetts, New York, and Pennsylvania were agricultural, and many of their farms produced and sold surplus crops, but without a major export staple, the scale of commercial agriculture in the North was much smaller and the demand for enslaved labor relatively low. In 1750, about thirty thousand Africans and their descendants were enslaved in the North, compared to two hundred seventeen thousand in the South.

Still, slavery was an entrenched institution in many parts of the North. The Northern colony with the highest

Savages of Several Nations, **by Alexandre de Batz, 1735.**   *The Picture Art Collection/Alamy Stock Photo*

BEHIND THE IMAGE

Alexandre de Batz, a French architect and military engineer, moved to the French colony of Louisiana in the late 1720s. While surveying colonial territories for the French Crown, he produced several images of native life, including this watercolor, set near New Orleans. He used his skills as a draftsman and his broad familiarity with Illinois life to present a study of the clothing, body art, and weaponry of the Illinois, one of the indigenous peoples who dominated the territories formally claimed by France during the eighteenth century.

WITHIN THE IMAGE

Although the image may have been designed to stoke colonial curiosity about animals, weapons, and clothing associated with Illinois culture, several striking details and numerous notations in French allow the painter to tell a set of stories about captive labor. **1** The woman seated at the far left is identified as an enslaved worker from the Fox Tribe, captured in war by the Illinois and put to work in the skilled crafts of preparing an animal hide, preserving sides of meat, and making tallow. **2** The

dead animal, probably a bison, links the Illinois to larger patterns of hunting and exchange, **3** while the lone African, notably unarmed, represents the presence of the Atlantic slave trade. De Batz names the painting *The Savages of Several Nations*, and he shows that what make Louisiana multinational are the close ties between long-distance trade and slavery.

BEYOND THE IMAGE

Although de Batz's pictures featured only native and African residents of Louisiana, his intended audience was actually French. The exhibition of his work caused a sensation among French viewers, who may have been especially interested in the display of native bodies. From a French perspective, the watercolor belonged to the inventory of colonial possessions, and the various people, animals, and commodities he illustrated belonged to the king of France, along with the other objects that de Batz surveyed, sketched, and recorded. But the display of racial diversity might also have sparked some anxiety back in Europe. Around the same time as this painting, King Louis IV banned intermarriage in the colony.

Execution of Accused Participants in a Plot to Burn New York in 1741. Two of the Black men hanged for their alleged role in a slave conspiracy were chained to posts, their corpses left to rot in public view as a warning. Others were burned alive. *North Wind Picture Archives/Alamy Stock Photo*

enslaved population was New York, where the Dutch had transported Africans as early as 1626. By the time England took over the colony in 1664, Black people in slavery made up a fifth of the population of the city of New Amsterdam, though the line between the enslaved and servants under Dutch rule was not as clear as it would become later in the century. By 1750, there were more than eleven thousand enslaved people in New York and more than five thousand in neighboring New Jersey. Slave labor played an important role on commercial wheat farms in the Hudson River Valley and on Long Island. The only Northern colony other than New York with at least 10 percent of its population enslaved was Rhode Island, where African laborers were concentrated in seaports and on dairy farms.

In the colonial North, Africans and African Americans built roads, herded cattle, and engaged in skilled artisanal work. Some enslaved people in New York and New Jersey were field hands or domestic servants, but others worked as carpenters, butchers, weavers, and blacksmiths. One key difference between the slave societies in the South and the societies with slaves in the North was that Northern slavery was disproportionately urban. There were few cities in colonial America, but slavery was prominent in all of them. By 1750, about one-fifth of Boston households and one-half of those in New York were slaveholders. Enslaved people themselves formed more than one-third of the population of Kings County (Brooklyn) and close to one-fifth of New York City. Although the overwhelming majority of Africans brought to the Americas were put to work on farms, those who wound up living in the North during the eighteenth century were more likely than any other ethnic group (other than Jews) to be living in cities.

Living in proximity to white people but not always under the supervision of their owners (who often hired them out to other employers), people enslaved in the North aroused white fears of revolts. Colonial authorities in the city of New York worried continually about revolutionary conspiracies. In 1712, over twenty enslaved men and women from the Gold Coast region, joined by some enslaved Native Americans, staged a violent uprising, setting fire to a building and killing nine white citizens who were trying to extinguish the flames. The militia eventually quashed the rebellion and tortured and executed its ringleaders. The following year, the city council passed a law prohibiting enslaved persons from being in the streets at night without a lantern or candle. In 1741, an outbreak of fires prompted fears of a more widespread plot, and authorities executed thirty-eight people, burning some of them alive. Eighty-four other Black New Yorkers were deported to the Caribbean.

SLAVERY ON THE GULF COAST

Between 1660 and 1750, the number of enslaved Africans held in North America outside the English-speaking colonies was small. Native Americans did not enslave Africans during this period, and the French and Spanish slave systems were concentrated in the Caribbean. The Spanish had introduced large numbers of enslaved Africans in Mexico during the 1500s, but this system had declined by the beginning of the following century. In the lands that would become the United States, Spanish and French colonies did not develop the kind of commercial agriculture that depended on large numbers of laborers. In 1750, only three hundred Africans were enslaved in Spanish Florida, which continued to provide a refuge for those escaping across the border from British colonies. French Louisiana, on the other hand, did establish plantation slavery, introducing close to six thousand enslaved people between 1719 and 1743. But these people lived short, difficult lives in Louisiana, and the colony's enslaved population was less than five thousand in 1750—smaller than that of New Jersey.

Still, half the population of French Louisiana at midcentury were Africans or their descendants. Enslaved workers from Senegambia introduced rice cultivation and laid the foundations for the construction of New Orleans by building levees along the Mississippi River and clearing forests. The high proportion of Africans from the same region and ethnicity helped maintain their original identities among Louisiana's enslaved population. It also raised the danger of rebellion. Two alleged plots were exposed in 1731, one of which was said to involve hundreds of Bambaras from Senegal. Slave insurrections, both real and imagined, impeded the growth of Louisiana under both French and (after 1763) Spanish rule. In the nineteenth century, after it was annexed by the United States, Louisiana would become a leading center of sugar and cotton cultivation and the site of an especially brutal and profitable slave system.

CONCLUSION

By 1750, the British colonial system in North America was closely tied to the Atlantic slave trade. Though Africans in exile had been part of the colonial world as long as Europeans, they were a small minority for much of the seventeenth century, and their labor was but a small element in a varied workforce. Over a short time span, however, the colonists' slave-buying spree had made African labor central to the production of staple crops and defined a hard line between slavery and freedom. During the same time period, the enslaved population shifted. African survivors of the Middle Passage were soon outnumbered by Americans of African descent. And throughout the continent—but especially in the South, where enslaved populations would continue to grow through the rest of the century—the line between Black and white calcified into a deep and fundamentally violent social divide.

STUDY TERMS

slave societies	slave mutinies
societies with slaves	creole
chattel slavery	slave communities
Royal African Company	Gullah
South Carolina	gang system
slave codes	rice
diaspora	task system
Middle Passage	Stono Rebellion

FURTHER READING

A database of additional full-text readings is available through Power of Process for Primary Sources in Connect.

Sharon Block, *Colonial Complexions* (2018), uses runaway advertisements to study changing understandings of racial difference in the late colonial period.

T. H. Breen and Stephen Innes, *"Myne Owne Ground"* (1980), studies the lives and prospects of Africans and their descendants in Virginia, before the entrenchment of chattel slavery.

David Brion Davis, *Inhuman Bondage* (2006), synthesizes decades of slavery scholarship, especially the evolution of Western attitudes about race and freedom.

Michael A. Gomez, *Exchanging Our Country Marks* (1998), emphasizes the retention of African religions, languages, and ethnic identities among enslaved North Americans.

Leslie Harris, *In the Shadow of Slavery* (2004), surveys the history of African Americans in colonial New York City.

Winthrop D. Jordan, *White over Black* (1968), uncovers deep patterns of anti-African prejudice in English thought prior to the entrenchment of North American slavery.

Edmund Morgan, *American Slavery, American Freedom* (1975), explains the decline of indentured servitude and the entrenchment of slavery in the Chesapeake after Bacon's Rebellion.

Jennifer L. Morgan, *Laboring Women* (2004), analyzes the exploitation of enslaved women as bearers of children.

Gregory O'Malley, *Final Passages* (2014), documents the trafficking of Africans from one British colony to another.

Stephanie Smallwood, *Saltwater Slavery* (2007), powerfully details the history of the Middle Passage.

Lorena S. Walsh, *Motives of Honor, Pleasure, & Profit* (2010), reconstructs the strategies of Chesapeake slaveholders.

1660–1750

4 | BRITISH COLONIES IN AN ATLANTIC ECONOMY

Chapter Questions

1. How did the settlement of the various Restoration colonies differ?

2. How did the British system of imperial regulation work?

3. What characterized the lifestyles of the farming majority and the urban minority in this period?

4. What were the Enlightenment and the Great Awakening, and how did they influence life in the colonies?

Middle Colonies. New York, viewed from the southwest in this painting from around 1730, became a bustling port town in the growing British Empire. *Everett Collection/Newscom*

As he recounted over thirty years later, William Moraley had been drinking beer at a London pub when he decided to immigrate to America in 1729. He had fallen on hard times, having been largely cut out of his father's will after abandoning both a legal education and then a career in the watchmaking trade. A recruiter had spotted him reading advertising posters for foreign lands at the London shipping docks and taken him to the pub to pitch the idea of signing up to be an indentured servant in the American colonies for five years. Thirty-year-old Moraley set sail, but not for the well-established Chesapeake Bay region, where tobacco planters were completing the momentous shift in labor from European servants to enslaved Africans. Instead, his destination was a new port city, called

Time Line

1660
Stuart Dynasty restored
Navigation Acts establish new commercial regime in English colonies

1664
England invades New Netherland, establishes New York

1674
Anglo-Dutch War ends

1675
Quaker migration to North America begins

1681
Pennsylvania founded

1688
William and Mary assume English throne in Glorious Revolution

1689
John Locke publishes *Two Treatises on Government*

1704
Boston News-Letter, first newspaper in the colonies, begins publication

1707
England and Scotland unite as Great Britain

1717
Scots-Irish migration to North America begins

1732
Georgia established

1735
John Peter Zenger tried for libel

1741
George Whitefield begins preaching tour in North America

Philadelphia, in the growing colony of Pennsylvania. On arrival, his indenture was purchased by a clockmaker in the nearby colony of New Jersey.

The world Moraley entered in 1729 was remarkably different from the early European outposts established on the North American mainland over a century earlier. English colonies now filled in the coastal lands between New England and the Chesapeake and stretched even farther south, all the way to the border with Spanish Florida. A more geographically diverse group of European Protestants was settling the colonies in this period, and most arrived with the goal of acquiring land and living in an agricultural society that was unlike the one emerging on slave plantations in the South. Moraley did not share that ambition. He had no interest in farming or in completing the term of his indenture. Instead, he wandered from one village to another, dodging creditors and scouring the growing countryside in vain for a wealthy widow who might support him. After five years in this new land, Moraley gave up his quest and returned penniless to England.

For the majority of European immigrants to the British colonies during the late seventeenth and early eighteenth centuries, however, the move to America was permanent. Most settled in rural areas that probably felt far removed from the worlds they had left behind. But even the most remote farm community was enmeshed in a complex system of commercial and cultural exchange that put people in contact with goods, information, and philosophical and religious ideas from within the colonies and across the world.

RESTORATION AND EXPANSION

In the 1660s, colonization in North America received a major jolt from political changes in England. Oliver Cromwell, the Puritan leader of the revolutionary movement that had ushered in a decade of Parliamentary rule, died in 1658. Two years later, conservative forces invited Charles II, son of the king whom Cromwell's supporters had executed during the civil war, to take the throne. The **Restoration** of the Stuart monarchy (1660), as the event was called, led to a new effort by the British Crown to expand its overseas empire and coordinate colonial affairs. A series of new colonies appeared in the Restoration era, mostly in the mid-Atlantic area between New England and the Chesapeake, attracting an overseas migration as great as any of the earlier ones. Charles II pursued aggressive policies to wrest trade from the Dutch, and Parliament enacted laws to wring more profits from North American colonies.

CHARLES II AND THE NEW IMPERIAL ORDER

After Charles II returned from exile in 1660 to assume the throne, a host of political and cultural changes swept over England. A new Parliament passed laws to enforce religious conformity, reintroducing the old liturgy, church hierarchy, and holidays that the Puritans had sought to abolish. The king, meanwhile, who had a Catholic mother and eventually converted to Catholicism himself, pulled England back from its role as a crusader for global Protestantism and turned his attention instead to a series of campaigns against the Protestant Netherlands.

Charles II moved quickly to seize Dutch wealth from the seas and from the lucrative Atlantic trade routes that Holland had dominated since early in the century. To compete with the Dutch in the trafficking of human beings, he chartered the Royal African Company (see Chapter 3), which he placed under the directorship of his brother James, the Duke of York. Within months of its official establishment in 1663, the Royal African Company captured Dutch slave-trading posts on Africa's Gold Coast. A year later, the English invaded the Dutch colony of New Netherland. Both of the towns of New Amsterdam (renamed New York) and Fort Orange (renamed Albany) promptly surrendered to the invaders, and the Dutch lost their commercial centers in North America. An inconclusive **Anglo-Dutch War** raged for three years. Though the Dutch recaptured most of their slaving forts in Africa and many of their commercial interests survived

the fight, England retained control of New York. One final time, in 1672, Dutch ships managed to retake their lost colony, but in a 1674 treaty, The Netherlands renounced claims on the American continent.

By virtue of this conquest, the Duke of York became the proprietor of a huge stretch of land that encircled the older New England colonies and ran southwest to the Chesapeake. Other members of King Charles's inner circle also received personal estates within this domain. Beyond enriching his friends and relatives, the king's plan was to enlarge his Empire in America. In the first decade of the Restoration, new colonies were carved out in Carolina, New York, East New Jersey, West New Jersey, and New Hampshire (see Map 4.1). In 1681, another colony was established, in Pennsylvania. English settlers now occupied a continuous chain of colonies between French Canada and Spanish Florida.

While authorizing new settlements, the English government also sought to impose a new order on its American seaboard empire. Rather than allow investor companies or individual proprietors to run independent colonies, both Parliament and the English Crown pushed for more centralized control starting in the 1660s. Royal commissioners sailed to America to investigate local affairs, scrutinize colonial charters, and assert royal authority. The main policy thrust behind this move was to make England's American settlements more commercially profitable for the home country.

To support that goal, Parliament passed a series of **Navigation Acts,** which restricted the way commodities produced in English colonies entered international markets and the way commodities produced elsewhere were brought into the colonies. These laws were intended to make sure that English ships and English ports handled the commercial traffic generated by English colonial activity. Such trade restrictions reflected a cluster of ideas (branded **mercantilism** a century later) about how colonization could make a nation rich and powerful by increasing exports, decreasing imports, encouraging shipbuilding and manufacturing, and raising revenues.

The first Navigation Act had been enacted in 1651 to prevent Dutch ships from bringing goods from America, Asia, and Africa into England. After the Restoration, Parliament expanded this campaign, establishing a new system of commercial regulation that would last until the American Revolution more than a century later. In addition to granting English ships a monopoly on trade out of the colonies, the Navigation Act of 1660 stipulated that certain articles produced in the colonies—tobacco, cotton, sugar, indigo, dyewoods, and ginger—had to be shipped

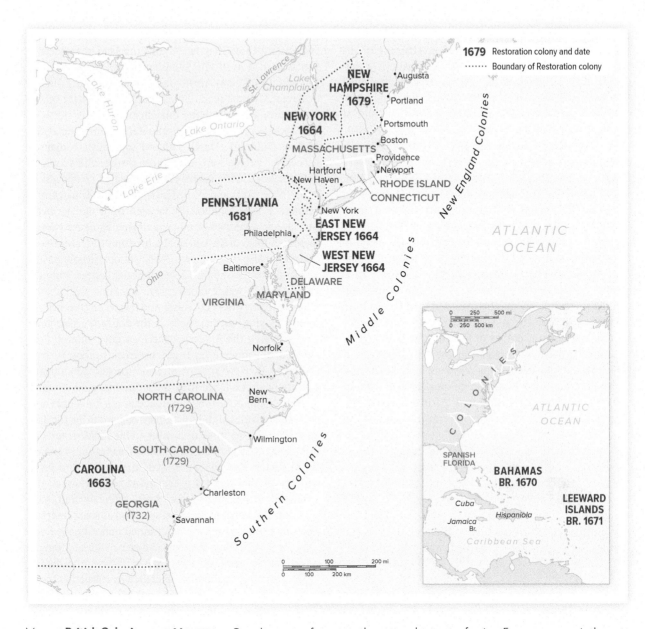

Map 4.1 British Colonies, ca. 1660–1750.   Over the course of a century, the scattered outposts of various European powers in the eastern part of North America were replaced by a continuous chain of seaboard colonies belonging to one empire.

directly to England (where they would be subject to import taxes) before they could be re-exported elsewhere. Three years later, the **Staple Act** granted England similar privileges for trade *into* the colonies. American colonists could only buy European goods that had passed first through England. Piracy, smuggling, and resistance made it impossible for authorities in London to achieve complete control over American trade, but the Navigation Acts brought significant profits to both English merchants

and to the royal treasury. Trade laws also formed the basis of England's attempts to govern its growing empire.

THE MIDDLE COLONIES

From a North American perspective, the most dramatic change associated with the English Restoration was the growth of England's **Middle Colonies**—New York, New Jersey, Pennsylvania, and Delaware—which were established on land that had been claimed and settled by the

Dutch and then granted by Charles II to the Duke of York. The duke entrusted New York to the care of his deputy, Richard Nicolls, who became the colony's governor. In the southwestern part of the territory, the duke also granted land parcels to two other aristocratic supporters of the Stuarts, and these became the colonies of East and West New Jersey.

In 1681, King Charles carved out a 45,000-square-mile colony just west of the Jerseys and the Delaware River as a gift to an aristocrat named William Penn, whose late father (of the same name) had lent money to the king. The younger Penn, recently released from prison for his heretical religious views, had been seeking a refuge for a new religious movement in mid-seventeenth-century England called the Society of Friends, or Quakers. The king's charter made him the proprietor of a colony called Pennsylvania. A year later, Penn augmented the colony by purchasing additional land on the Atlantic seaboard from the duke. This land would become the separate colony of Delaware in 1704.

Unlike English settlements in the Chesapeake and New England, the Middle Colonies were built, in part, on top of an established European colonial project with an ethnically diverse European and African population.

Late-Eighteenth-Century British Painting of a Quaker Meeting. The name *Quakers* began as a disparaging term used by their English detractors, but because it referred to those who "tremble at the word" of God (in the phrase of the biblical prophet Isaiah), members of the Society of Friends ultimately accepted the designation. ©*The Granger Collection, New York*

New York and New Jersey were superimposed onto New Netherland (see Chapter 2), and the land that became Delaware had been settled earlier by Swedes and Finns. In the city of New Amsterdam, enslaved and formerly enslaved Africans made up as much as a quarter of the population by the time the English arrived.

This complex history of prior settlement shaped the Middle Colonies. Dutch cultural influences remained especially strong well after New Netherland's official demise. The Dutch language continued to be spoken in many New York and New Jersey homes and in church settings. Foods traditionally favored by Dutch farmers, such as beets, endives, spinach, and parsley, figured prominently in local diets. Colonial Christmas observances in this region also bore a heavy Dutch stamp. Although New England Puritans banned celebrating such a holiday, December 25 was a more festive occasion west of the Hudson River, where colonists preserved Dutch practices such as leaving wooden shoes by the door to receive gifts. And although the modern American gift-giving mythology did not emerge until the nineteenth century (see Chapter 12), New York children in the late seventeenth century heard Dutch stories about *Sinter Claes*.

New communities and different cultural influences also took root in the Middle Colonies beginning in the last quarter of the seventeenth century. One major source of this change was **Quaker migration.** Quakerism preached the importance of an "inner light" that came from Jesus and lay at the core of every individual. Whereas the Church of England stressed social hierarchy and tradition and Puritans regarded salvation as a fate reserved by divine grace for a predestined minority, the Society of Friends attracted followers with a different, encouraging message: Salvation was available to all and required no deference to learned authorities. Quakers also challenged the government by refusing to pay church taxes or swear in court and by advancing ideas of human equality that threatened established divisions based on wealth, social rank, and gender. King Charles's decision to charter William Penn's colony may have reflected his desire to quell domestic dissent by shipping Quakers overseas. Quakers proved eager to escape persecution and join in what Penn called his "Holy Experiment."

● English Quakers migrated to various American colonies during the 1650s, but the larger stream began in 1675, when a party of the Society of Friends helped settle West Jersey, the first major American destination for Quaker refugees. Once Pennsylvania was established six years later, the stream became a tide. Close to

CROSSING BORDERS

twenty-three thousand migrants, mostly but not exclusively Quakers, moved to the Delaware Valley between 1675 and 1715. • Penn aggressively recruited the majority of these new arrivals from communities of Friends in England, Wales, and Ireland. He also sent promotional tracts and agents to lure Protestants from Holland and the German Rhineland with descriptions of Pennsylvania's fertile farmland and promises of religious freedom. Some new settlers arrived in family groups, whereas others came as individual servants, a social composition that lay somewhere between that of New England and that of the Chesapeake.

Compared to other English colonists, Pennsylvanians enjoyed far more peaceful relations with the continent's native inhabitants. Quaker founder George Fox had visited the Delaware Valley in 1672 and recommended the region to Penn on the grounds that the Lenni Lenape (whom settlers would later call the Delaware people) were "very loving." The Delaware, weakened by epidemics earlier in the century and fearful of the growing power of the Iroquois League, eagerly seized the opportunity to form bonds with the newcomers, who came bearing vast quantities of trade goods. Quaker colonists also brought more tolerant views of Native Americans, and many Quakers were pacifists. Penn was committed to preventing the unlawful confiscation of Delaware lands and took pains to make sure that no native inhabitants were dispossessed or evicted without fair negotiation and equitable compensation. Relations between Pennsylvania colonists and the Delaware grew tenser after 1710, when an aging Penn no longer exerted authority over colonial affairs. Still, a fragile peace would prevail in the colony until the middle of the eighteenth century.

THE GLORIOUS REVOLUTION IN NORTH AMERICA

While English settlements grew and proliferated, the Stuart monarchy stepped up its campaign to bring the colonial empire under tighter control. In 1684, England repealed the Massachusetts Bay charter. The following year, King Charles II died, and his brother James (then the Duke of York) assumed the throne as James II of England (and James VII of Scotland). The new king set about nullifying the charters of neighboring colonies, redrawing their boundary lines, and reorganizing the English Empire north of Maryland into a supercolony called the **Dominion of New England.** The dominion was to be ruled directly by the king's agent, Edmund Andros, who had previously served as governor of New York. Existing colonial legislatures were to be disbanded, and no new ones could be formed. Andros was instructed to guarantee religious freedom, encourage the importation of enslaved Africans, maintain peaceful relations with native peoples, enforce the Navigation Acts, collect taxes on all land sales, and exert absolute authority over the whole region from his headquarters in Boston.

The Andros government met resistance, especially in New England, but soon events in England changed the balance of power altogether. James's ascent in 1685 had been highly controversial, because he was a Catholic, but many opponents took comfort in the thought that the new king was elderly and would soon enough be succeeded by one of his Protestant daughters. Then in June 1688, James's second wife, Catholic Queen Mary of Modena, bore a son, who would be heir to the throne. Fearing a new Catholic dynasty with ties to France, the king's Protestant opponents united behind a plan to replace James with his Anglican daughter Mary and her Dutch husband, William of Orange. William wasted no time in accepting the invitation to rule England, leading an invasion party of forty thousand men across the North Sea. Facing such an overwhelming force, the king's supporters mounted no resistance. James escaped the royal palace and threw the Great Seal of England into the Thames River in the belief that William and Mary could not rule without it. Undeterred, supporters of the Dutch invasion maintained that James had vacated the thrones of England,

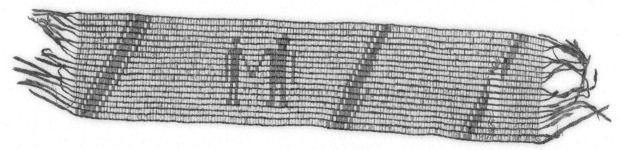

Wampum Belt Depicting a Treaty Between William Penn and the Delaware. Historians speak of a "long peace" between native people and Pennsylvania colonists, lasting between the colony's founding and the end of the French and Indian War. *FLHC A29/Alamy Stock Photo*

Scotland, and Ireland. In a bloodless regime change known as the **Glorious Revolution,** King William III and Queen Mary II took over England's growing empire.

When reports of the coup reached Boston, colonists there denounced the Dominion of New England, revived the Massachusetts Bay charter, and put Governor Andros in jail. In Maryland, Protestants took the revolution as a cue to depose the colony's Catholic proprietor. The most dramatic political fallout took place in New York, where a German-born merchant named Jacob Leisler staged his own revolution in support of the new Protestant monarchy in England. In 1689, Leisler organized a militia, seized the local fort, and established a Committee of Safety to rule the colony. **Leisler's Rebellion** ignited long-simmering political, economic, and ethnic conflicts in New York, and political chaos ensued for two years.

The larger significance of the Glorious Revolution in North America was a change in colonial policy. Beginning with William and Mary, English monarchs ruled their American possessions with a lighter touch, continuing to insist that the colonies contribute to the commercial growth of the empire but abandoning their predecessors' campaign to make the colonies submit to royal authority. The Protestants who ruled England after 1688 turned their attention to their Catholic rivals and needed colonists' support for a series of wars against the French in North America (see Chapter 5). From 1688 to 1763, a new political order took shape in England's North American colonies, which became "British" when England and Scotland united as Great Britain in 1707. Parliament continued to administer trade policy within the framework of the Navigation Acts, and colonial governors were still appointed by the British Crown or proprietors, but colonial assemblies gained increasing autonomy.

A GROWING WORLD OF MIGRANTS

While events in English politics determined the shape and structure of its colonies, life in those colonies was more fundamentally changed by massive population growth. In 1650, fewer than fifty thousand English settlers occupied the lands that later became the United States. Fifty years later, England's mainland colonies held more than two hundred fifty thousand colonists. Fifty years after that, close to a million Europeans and about two hundred fifty thousand Africans lived in British America. Some of this rise stemmed from high birthrates and increasing life spans, but much of the growth reflected migration from across the Atlantic. By the eighteenth century, both free and bound newcomers tended to come from lands other than England. As they settled in different regions along the eastern seaboard, they contributed to the development of a range of colonial societies, some of them ethnically heterogeneous.

NATURAL INCREASE IN NEW ENGLAND

More so than the rest of British North America in 1700, the four New England colonies (Connecticut, Rhode Island, Massachusetts, and New Hampshire; Maine and Vermont were not distinct colonies at this point) consisted primarily of the descendants of English immigrants rather than new arrivals from Europe. After economic conditions improved in England during the Restoration and as persecution of dissenting Protestants eased after the Glorious Revolution, fewer Puritans were motivated to leave the country. In addition, New England was a less attractive destination to those who did want to immigrate, because land in that region was scarcer, more expensive, more tightly controlled, and more vulnerable to Native American attack than elsewhere. Some New England colonies even discouraged immigration, passing laws that required ship captains to take responsibility for passengers who were "poor, vicious and infirm" and therefore potential burdens to their new communities.

New England colonies continued to grow after the Restoration in 1660, however, due to natural increase—a surplus of births over deaths. Because so many of the original migrants had come over in families, sex ratios were relatively balanced and most New Englanders married. With limited access to contraception, couples produced many offspring, on average about seven or eight infants per woman (see Singular Lives: Sarah Grosvenor, Pregnant Puritan). • At the same time, New England's cold climate and well-drained land limited the impact of disease and thus contributed to high average life expectancies relative to other American societies. In New England's farming villages in the seventeenth century, colonists who reached the age of twenty typically lived to around sixty-five. • High fertility and low mortality enabled a society founded by twenty thousand Puritans in the first half of the seventeenth century to grow into a populous colonial region even after the tide of migration stopped.

As New England families grew, the lands allotted to townships could no longer be subdivided to support all of their founders' descendants. Young men moved to newer towns, migrated westward and northward to unsettled areas, or left New England altogether. From 1670 on, more people moved out of New England than moved in.

CLIMATES AND ECOLOGIES

SINGULAR LIVES

Sarah Grosvenor, Pregnant Puritan

In 1742, a nineteen-year-old woman in the village of Pomfret, Connecticut, discovered that she was pregnant. Sarah Grosvenor and Amasa Sessions, the twenty-seven-year-old presumed father, were not married at the time. But that in itself was no longer remarkable in colonial New England, where premarital intercourse had become much more common. By midcentury, about 25 percent to 30 percent of brides in the typical New England town were already pregnant on their wedding night. Grosvenor and Sessions did not get married, however, although the two were members of prominent Pomfret families and would have made a socially suitable match. Nor did they seek another common solution to an unwanted pregnancy and arrange for the offspring to be supported by the community as an illegitimate child. Instead, Sessions hired a man named John Hallowell to prescribe an abortifacient drug. When the drug made Grosvenor ill, Hallowell attempted an abortion procedure, which caused a miscarriage. A month later, Grosvenor died.

It is hard to know how frequently women or couples in eighteenth-century America sought to terminate pregnancies. Ingesting abortifacients was sufficiently common that Grosvenor could simply refer to it as "taking the trade" when she confided the incident to a friend. Abortion by instrument was probably rarer, though such a procedure, if it took place in the early months of pregnancy, was not in itself a criminal offense in colonial Connecticut. Still, abortions were scandalous, in large part because they represented brazen attempts to conceal the sin of fornication, or sexual intercourse outside of marriage. Before 1700, New England towns had treated such sex as a crime, but by the time of Grosvenor's preg-

nancy, a new sexual double standard had emerged: Only women were prosecuted for fornication. Sarah Grosvenor might have agreed to "take the trade" to avoid being punished as a fornicator, to avoid the stigma of bearing a bastard, or for other reasons. But she ultimately seems to have agreed to the abortion procedure under heavy pressure from Sessions and Hallowell, convinced that an expedited miscarriage was necessary to protect her from mortal danger. In the end, however, it was the abortion itself that took Sarah Grosvenor's life.

The lethal abortion also brought Grosvenor's private relationships to public light. County magistrates began investigating Grosvenor's death in 1745, questioning her former lover, her relatives, and her friends and considering their culpability in her death. Though none of the Pomfret elders appear to have known anything, an inner circle of young people knew of Grosvenor's predicament, and her sister and cousin had secretly buried the fetus to conceal the abortion. A grand jury indicted only the doctor, Hallowell, however, for the "highhanded Misdemeanor" of attempting to harm Grosvenor and her fetus. Hallowell was convicted and sentenced to twenty-nine lashes and two hours of public humiliation, but he broke out of jail and fled the colony. He was never pursued or punished further. Amasa Sessions, who had hired him, remained a prominent and respected citizen in Pomfret.

Where in the Archives?

To reconstruct the tragic story of Sarah Grosvenor, historian Cornelia Dayton relied mostly on depositions and trial testimony recorded in the Windham County (Connecticut) Superior Court.

Last Remains. Apart from this simple tombstone, evidence of Sarah Grosvenor's short and tragic life survives in the court testimony of her friends, relatives, and neighbors. ©*Jessica Linker*

The sworn statements of many of the close relatives of Grosvenor and Sessions, along with the criminal charges against Hallowell, are preserved in Box 172, Record Group 3, Archives, History, and Genealogy Unit, Connecticut State Library, Hartford, Connecticut. They can be found on the University of Connecticut's History Department website (https://history.uconn.edu/).

Assignment

Read the indictments against Hallowell and the depositions of at least three witnesses, including Sarah's sister Zerviah Grosvenor and her cousins John Grosvenor and Ebenezer Grosvenor. Answer one of the following in 200–250 words:

1. How do the official indictments differ from the witness accounts in the way they speak about the act of abortion?

2. How do any two of the witnesses disagree in blaming Hallowell or Sessions for Grosvenor's death?

New England Family Values.   Large families, of the kind celebrated in this 1804 water-color family record, helped sustain population growth in the New England colonies long after foreign immigration slackened. *Gift of Edgar William and Bernice Chrysler Garbisch/National Gallery of Art*

Although New England life continued to revolve around small, close-knit, religiously homogeneous towns, increasing numbers of New Englanders after 1700 lived either on farms far removed from original settlements or in crowded commercial seaports.

DIVERSE IMMIGRANTS IN THE MIDDLE COLONIES

South of New England, relatively peaceful relations with Native Americans and prosperity linked to rising international prices for wheat made newer colonies more appealing to newcomers. New York, New Jersey, Delaware, and especially Pennsylvania attracted large numbers of immigrants in the eighteenth century, many from Scotland and northern Ireland. ● **Scots-Irish immigrants** included Scottish Presbyterians whose ancestors had settled in Ireland in the seventeenth century, but the term refers more generally to migrants from all sides of the Irish Sea. Driven mainly by poverty and land scarcity, they came from 1717 onward, forming the largest group of European immigrants to British America in the first half of the eighteenth century. Arriving as both free settlers and indentured servants, they made their way to the Shenandoah Valley of Virginia and the Carolina backcountry as well as to the Middle Colonies, drawn by the promise of cheap farmland. By the end of the eighteenth century, more than a third of the families listed in the census records of Pennsylvania and North Carolina had Scottish or Irish last names. ●

CROSSING BORDERS

Pennsylvania proved even more attractive to migrants from German-speaking lands. Close to thirty-seven thousand German immigrants entered British America between 1700 and 1750, more than twice as many as came from England in that period. German immigration to Pennsylvania had begun with Penn's recruitment campaigns of the previous century, and once Germans established communities there, relatives, neighbors, and coreligionists from Europe were more likely to join them. German colonists did not all emigrate from a single country (Germany was not a unified nation at this time) but came from Westphalia, Alsace, Bavaria, and the Rhine Valley. What they shared was the German language. English speakers in the colonies came to refer to these people as **Pennsylvania Dutch,** after the German name for the language, *Deutsche.* Many of the migrants had already moved several times back in northern Europe, but the departure for North America marked a more decisive life change. It also involved significant health risks, both at sea and in the port cities where most migrants disembarked. German-speaking immigrants to the Middle Colonies were even more likely than those from northern Britain to arrive in family units, and mortality among children was especially high during the voyage. Still, those who survived the passage were likely to live as well as or better than the relatives and neighbors they left behind.

By the mid-eighteenth century, European settlement in the Middle Colonies was even more ethnically diverse than it had been at the time of the English conquest of New Netherland (see Interpreting the Sources: Benjamin Franklin on the Population of British America). ● One thing the overwhelming majority of colonists shared, however, was a Protestant religious affiliation. Many were Presbyterians; others were Quakers, Lutherans, Anabaptists, Moravians, Mennonites, or Huguenots (French Protestants). But they all worshiped inside the broader Protestant fold. Some significant minority of Irish immigrants may have been Catholic, but if so, most kept that identity concealed. Britain's American empire was not hospitable to Catholic migrants in the first half of the eighteenth century, a point driven home by Parliament in

CONFLICTING FAITHS

1740, when it codified the process for becoming colonial citizens. By law, any free white man who resided in a British colony for seven years, swore allegiance to the empire, and had taken Communion in a Protestant church within the previous three months was eligible to own land and participate in elections. Soon after, Parliament revised the rules to clarify that Quakers counted as Protestants and to allow for the possibility of Jewish citizenship, but imperial immigration policy did not welcome Catholics. The Middle Colonies formed a kind of melting pot for Protestants. ●

CREOLES IN THE CHESAPEAKE

Colonial populations grew steadily in tobacco country as well. High mortality rates and imbalanced sex ratios had checked the natural increase of Virginia and Maryland for much of the seventeenth century, and those colonies had grown entirely through immigration. During the last three decades of the century, when overseas migration to New England slowed, migration to the Chesapeake remained strong; indeed, Virginia and Maryland were the two leading mainland destinations for English immigrants. Beginning around the same time, birthrates rose, sex ratios evened out, and colonists in the region began living longer on average. With a non–Native American population approaching sixty thousand, Virginia had become the most populous colony north of Mexico by 1700. Maryland lagged behind only Virginia and Massachusetts among England's mainland settlements.

After 1680, much of the population growth in the Chesapeake came from the forced migration of Africans. Africans and their descendants made up only 7 percent of the Chesapeake colonies' population in 1680. By 1750, that figure had risen to 40 percent. By 1710, the enslaved population in Virginia and Maryland already was reproducing itself (see Chapter 3), but planters there continued to purchase laborers at staggering rates. Close to thirty-five thousand Africans of diverse ethnic and geographical backgrounds were brought to the Chesapeake between 1700 and 1740, a number roughly equal to the entire combined populations of New York and Pennsylvania in 1700. Nonetheless, by 1750, 80 percent of enslaved Virginians and Marylanders had never seen Africa. This pattern fit the region's overall demographic change. Between 1680 and 1750, colonial society was being transformed into a society of creoles—people born in the colonies to parents of European or African ancestry.

The Chesapeake also became the chief destination for a new kind of bound labor. In 1717 and 1718, Parliament revised British criminal codes to encourage new forms of punishment as alternatives to execution. Specifically, the Transportation Act of 1718 authorized judges to exile felons to the American colonies. Over the next half century, close to fifty thousand **transported convicts,** mostly young British men convicted of minor crimes, crossed the Atlantic. Overwhelmingly, they were sold as indentured servants in Maryland and Virginia, where planters were anxious to prevent the formation of a Black majority.

Moravians in the American Interior. German-speaking Moravian missionaries baptize Lenape people in Bethlehem, Pennsylvania. *Niday Picture Library/Alamy Stock Photo*

AFRICANS AND EUROPEANS IN THE LOWER SOUTH

In the Lower South, planters' demand for slave labor created a Black majority from the early decades of settlement. South Carolina attracted relatively few European immigrants before the 1720s, despite colonial officials' attempts to increase the white population by paying bounties to ship captains who brought white male servants. South Carolina restricted these recruitment efforts to white Protestants and barred the purchase of convicted felons. Authorities worried that convicts would incite slave rebellions and that Catholics would betray the colony to nearby Spanish Florida. More generally, South Carolinians were not optimistic about the ability of Europeans to work in the

INTERPRETING THE SOURCES

Benjamin Franklin on the Population of British America

Born in New England in 1706, Benjamin Franklin ran away to Philadelphia at the age of seventeen and spent much of his adult life there. From his vantage point in the major port of Pennsylvania at midcentury, Franklin offered thoughts about the significance of immigration and population growth in America. In "Observations Concerning the Increase of Mankind, Peopling of Countries, etc." (1755), Franklin noted the relationship between cheap land and expensive labor in America and touted the growing colonial population as a boundless market for British goods. He predicted that within a century "the greatest number of Englishmen will be on this Side of the Water."

He worried, however, about the large numbers of non-English settlers that had come to the Middle Colonies: "Why should Pennsylvania, founded by the English, become a Colony of Aliens, who will shortly be so numerous as to Germanize us instead of our Anglifying them, and will never adopt our Language, or Customs, any more than they can acquire our Complexion." Having broached the subject of skin color, Franklin then shared some ideas that might surprise modern American readers.

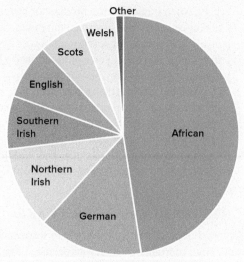

Immigration to British Mainland North America, 1700–1775. Question for Analysis: How might the fact that such a small percentage of immigrants in this period were from England have changed the character of colonial society? Source: Based on Aaron Fogleman, "Migration to the Thirteen British North American Colonies," *Journal of Interdisciplinary History* (Spring 1992): 691–709.

[T]he Number of purely white People in the World is proportionably very small. All *Africa* is Black or tawny. *Asia* chiefly tawny. *America* (exclusive of the new Comers) wholly so. And in *Europe*, the *Spaniards, Italians, French, Russians* and *Swedes*, are generally of what we call a swarthy Complexion; as are the Germans also, the *Saxons* only excepted, who with the English make the principal Body of white People on the Face of the Earth. I could wish their Numbers were increased. And while we are, as I may call it, *Scouring* our Planet, by clearing *America* of Woods, and so making this Side of our Globe reflect a brighter Light to the Eyes of Inhabitants in Mars or Venus, why should we in the Sight of Superior Beings, darken its People? why increase the Sons of *Africa*, by Planting them in *America*, where we have so fair an Opportunity, by excluding all Blacks and Tawneys, of increasing the lovely white and Red? But perhaps I am partial to the Complexion of my Country, for such Kind of Partiality is natural to Mankind.

Explore the Source

1. How does Franklin divide humanity by skin color? How many color groupings does he cite? Is skin color a racial classification for Franklin?

2. Why might Franklin have regarded Swedes and Germans as nonwhite?

3. What is Franklin's attitude toward Native Americans, whom he refers to as "Red"?

4. In the last sentence, is Franklin distancing himself from the intolerance of his remarks? Explain.

rice fields. The slave population, by contrast, continued to grow. South Carolina imported as many enslaved Africans between 1700 and 1740 as the two larger Chesapeake colonies combined.

The situation in the two British colonies that bordered South Carolina was quite different. North Carolina, which had broken away to form a separate colony in 1712, did not prove as conducive to rice cultivation. Parts of the colony's northeastern section belonged to the Chesapeake region, and farmers there grew tobacco.

Coastal areas were given over to pine forests and shipping. Slavery flourished in these regions but in much smaller units than in South Carolina. To the west, however, North Carolina was a land of small farms where slaveholding was uncommon. This region attracted some of the same types of European immigrants who flocked to Pennsylvania. Many of them, in fact, had arrived first in Philadelphia and then migrated south after 1740. Scots-Irish newcomers led this migration, followed by Germans.

Farther south, Georgia was created in 1732 as a haven for poor Britons and persecuted European Protestants. Founding leader James Oglethorpe prohibited slavery and limited land ownership and property inheritance in order to preserve the colony as a society of hardworking people who would defend the British Empire against invasion from the south. In its first two decades, Georgia welcomed just over two thousand overseas migrants, including debtors and convicts from England and small farmers from Austria and the Scottish Highlands. But wealthier settlers and migrating slaveholders from South Carolina rebelled against the founders' plans, lobbied Parliament, and forced the colony's trustees to legalize slavery and to cede control of Georgia to the British Crown in 1752. Georgia's population at the time was barely over two thousand. Subsequent migration would come mainly from other American colonies and from Africa.

A FARMING SOCIETY IN A COMMERCIAL EMPIRE

Although they hailed from multiple places in Europe and spoke in different languages, dialects, and accents, most immigrants who came voluntarily to North America in the century after the English Restoration had a common goal. They expected to acquire farmland. By and large, those expectations were fulfilled. Rates of landownership in the colonies were high compared to Europe, though they varied by region and declined over time. Free male colonists, many of whom had been landless peasants on the other side of the Atlantic, spread out with their households from the seaboard and became farmers. Farming families were ruled by paternal authority and sought to sustain themselves by growing all the crops and making all the goods necessary for their subsistence. Over the course of the colonial period, however, American farmers produced more goods for local trade. They also became increasingly attuned to patterns of long-distance commerce, centered in a handful of small coastal cities that connected the farms to a closely regulated network of transatlantic exchange.

LAND OWNERSHIP

European colonists saw land on the American continent as available to be owned. More than any other consideration, this is what induced them to uproot their lives and bear the costs and risks of a transatlantic journey. Land seemed available from a European perspective primarily because the eastern part of North America was more sparsely inhabited than the northwestern part of Europe, particularly after diseases ravaged America's indigenous population. But land availability was not simply a function of population density. Colonial laws, customs, and practices also made land easier to own than was the case either in areas controlled by native groups or in Europe.

Traditionally, Native Americans did not regard land as something that could be possessed outright—much as Europeans did not believe that individuals could buy or sell oceans and rivers. In most native peoples' view, individuals or groups could exchange specific use rights to a piece of land—say, for farming, grazing, or hunting—but these ownership claims did not last indefinitely and did not necessarily exclude other users or cover all land uses. From a very different cultural perspective, European societies also traditionally restricted the ability of individuals to own land. In much of Western Europe in the seventeenth century, landowners could not simply sell, give, or bequeath land at will, the way they could with food, animals, and other movable goods. Laws of entail (under which land could be passed on only to children) and primogeniture (under which an entire plot of land had to be passed, undivided, to an eldest son) were designed to keep land within a family's estate. In addition, land in Europe often came with long-standing obligations to feudal lords.

To encourage immigration, Britain's colonial charters stripped away many of these restrictions. Outside New England, colonists had to pay quitrents—small, perpetual taxes—either to the proprietor or directly to the British Crown, though these rents proved difficult to collect and often went unpaid. Most American colonists owned land as a **freehold,** which meant that it was viewed as the permanent and exclusive property of an individual (a freeholder), who was free to sell, trade, or give it to others. Departing from older European views of land, and dismissive of the different views of indigenous peoples, colonists turned land into private property.

By the end of the seventeenth century, land ownership was the norm in British America, except among those who were legally bound to work as enslaved laborers or servants on others' farms. The overwhelming majority of free men owned the land they farmed, either by having purchased a freehold or by simply squatting on it. Renting farmland was uncommon between 1660 and 1700, though it existed in pockets of Massachusetts, Maryland, and New York. These conditions had powerful and paradoxical consequences. Cheap land drew immigrants from Europe and emboldened native-born colonists to marry earlier and thereby produce more children. Both of those trends stimulated population growth, which pushed land prices higher. The higher prices concentrated land in the hands of large landlords and investors rather than freeholders. The ease with which colonists became freeholders in the seventeenth century threatened to undermine that way of life in the eighteenth century.

Older settlements in New England and New York were the first to experience these pressures, but a similar process took place in other colonies as well. During the first half of the eighteenth century, average farm size decreased and land tenancy became more common. At the same time, though, colonists pushed deeper into Native American lands for cheap farmland. Colonial governments encouraged them, offering land grants or tax relief to Protestants who would settle the backcountry and provide a buffer zone between the British colonies and their French, Spanish, and native neighbors. The westward drift of settlement offset some of the effects of overcrowding and land inflation, and as late as 1750, about two-thirds of the free men in all of Britain's mainland colonies owned land. No European society at the time came close to that rate of land ownership. This was the key fact that shaped social and economic life for white settlers in this period.

FARM HOUSEHOLDS: GENDER ROLES AND DAILY LIFE

The crucial building block of colonial society was the farm household, which formed around a male **patriarch.** The typical patriarch inherited or acquired arable land (suitable for growing crops), built a house, and commanded the labor of a wife, his unmarried offspring, and other dependents, who might include indentured servants, enslaved people, and wage laborers. In the Chesapeake, where people married later and died younger, households often incorporated a complex extended family of children, siblings, and widowed adults from multiple marriages. The core of the household, however, was a relationship between the patriarch and the woman, children, and other laborers who were legally subordinate to him.

Patriarchal relations had long roots in European society, but conditions in North America gave added force to the

Women in the Farm Economy. Colonial women used a spinning wheel, a device introduced many centuries earlier in India, to make yarn for fabric. *The Metropolitan Museum of Art, New York, Gift of Mrs. Russell Sage, 1909*

patriarchy. Farms in America were larger, more dispersed, and more autonomous than those in Europe. Unconstrained by rules of entail, the patriarch had greater power to dispose of his property as he saw fit. Though primogeniture remained common in America in this period, laws in New England and several other colonies allowed fathers to divide up property among several sons if they chose. Colonial patriarchs rarely bestowed real property (land) on daughters or other female kin, however. Even widows were unlikely to gain control of family resources and could be relegated to back rooms in houses owned by their sons. Land remained under the control of men.

Wives were subordinate to their husbands in the colonies and were expected to obey them, much as servants obeyed masters and children obeyed parents. Whereas men secured their independence through marriage and landowning, women became legally dependent as soon as they wed. A married woman could not make a contract, take someone to court, or possess property in her own right. Being unable to own land put farm wives in a precarious position, even as husbands were expected to love their wives and treat them kindly.

Still, women played important roles in the farm economy. Both women and men engaged in productive manual labor, though their tasks were generally separated. Men's work typically took place outdoors and focused on such activities as clearing, planting, weeding, harvesting, and herding. While their husbands, sons, servants, and enslaved laborers worked in the fields, farm women ran the dairy and egg operations, raised poultry, and tended food gardens. Soap and candle manufacturing were also women's work, as were spinning yarn and sewing garments. Weaving was a male domain in the seventeenth century, but in New England a decisive shift took place. By 1750, the typical New England farm had a loom operated by a woman.

Women also took charge of food preparation, which by the eighteenth century had become a more complex task on all but the poorest farms. After 1700, farm wives typically used more varied ingredients and cooked a range of different dishes to be eaten with specialized utensils (see Hot Commodities: Forks). Farm women also spent large portions of their lives bearing and raising children. Since

HOT COMMODITIES

Forks

John Winthrop, the first governor of the Massachusetts Bay Colony, owned a fork. This special utensil, which survives today, distinguished Winthrop from the mass of American colonists in the seventeenth century. A 1630 guide to what prospective colonists needed to bring to New England included a long list of household utensils: "1 iron pot; 1 kettle; 1 frying pan; 1 gridiron; 2 skillets, 1 spit; wooden platters; dishes; spoons trenchers." But no forks.

The fork was introduced by the Venetians around the sixteenth century (though it might have originated earlier, in Byzantium) and spread through the Italian peninsula among people who ate pasta. Forks did not become common in northern Europe until at least the seventeenth century, however, and they were adopted even later in the colonies. Forks do not appear in colonists' estate inventories before 1700, nor do they surface in archaeological digs. Well into the eighteenth century, forks were rare luxury goods in North America.

The absence of this simple kitchen implement suggests a very different world of food consumption. Colonists did not typically own any utensil to spear solid food and bring it to their mouths. Some owned knives, but unlike the older English knives that had pointed ends, colonists used newer-style English knives with round blades. Instead, food was eaten with fingers or with spoons. Seventeenth-century cuisine generally suited this arrangement, featuring stews, porridges, and mush that could be consumed out of bowls without cutting or spearing.

During the eighteenth century, colonial eating habits changed. For middling and wealthier farm families, separate dishes of meat, potatoes, and vegetables became more common. They were eaten on plates and tables with forks and knives rather than bowls and laps with spoons and fingers. The proliferation of plates, knives, and forks, mostly imported from Europe, made new food styles possible. But the rising demand for new utensils also reflected new tastes and desires—both for imported food commodities from Asia and the Americas and for the refined habits of bodily control associated with European elites. The fork, the rarest of those utensils in the beginning of the eighteenth century, soon became a required item in the kitchens of respectable farm households.

Think About It

1. Why might the fork have been adopted later than the spoon and the knife in both Europe and the American colonies?

2. Why was the fork a badge of respectability and refinement in the eighteenth century?

American Silver Fork, ca. 1740s.
This simple utensil, which entered colonial America as a luxury item, became the centerpiece of a new relationship to food among most British colonists. *Jay's photo/Getty Images*

---

women in the colonies married young (much younger than in Europe) and did not practice effective contraception, the typical farm wife spent two decades of her life giving birth every 2 to 2.5 years. Nonetheless, colonial culture did not treat mothering as a realm separate from the rest of farm labor. Childrearing was part of a woman's contributions to household production.

THE AGRICULTURAL ECONOMY: YEOMAN FARMERS AND THE SPREAD OF COMMERCE

Typical farm households in colonial America in 1700 grew most of the food they ate, sewed most of the clothes they wore, and manufactured the light household goods they used. Colonists aspired to the kind of self-sufficiency that has long been associated with the ideal—and the mythology—of the independent **yeoman farmer** or freeholder. Notwithstanding this ideal, rural Americans also engaged in various forms of trade. Most farmers bartered surplus produce with neighbors for particular goods, such as guns and iron farming tools, or for specialized services, such as midwifery and religious instruction. But some farmers also sold their crops for cash, which they accumulated in order to purchase farmland and livestock for their offspring (see How Much Is That? Cattle). In addition, colonists increasingly used cash to buy manufactured items imported from England under the protection of the Navigation Acts. After 1700, rural Americans began consuming a large volume of foreign-made goods, especially window glass, earthenware, and clothing—most of which they paid for by selling produce at local markets. Yet even as they participated in commercial transactions, most American farmers in the

How Much Is That?

Cattle

Pigs were the leading meat source in colonial America, but cows were even more prized—and more common. In addition to their value for beef and dairy products, cattle provided essential labor that fueled the farm economy. Even the most modest colonial farms kept at least one cow at any given time. Between 1730 and 1750, a yoke of oxen in Connecticut cost between 7 and 8 British pounds, which is roughly equivalent to between 1,600 and 1,700 dollars in today's currency.

colonial period devoted the bulk of their labor and attention to their own families' subsistence before worrying about the demands of distant customers.

Throughout the British colonies, however, market considerations shaped farmers' lives. In the southeastern part of the continent, farmers cultivated tobacco and rice for world markets and were acutely aware of fluctuations in the prices of those commodities. Farming on slave plantations in the South was essentially a commercial enterprise supported by long-distance trade in staple crops and human labor. Farther north and farther inland, farm households grew a more diverse range of crops and sold most of their surplus within their respective colonies. By 1750, many farmers in the Middle Colonies and the northern Chesapeake had begun to grow wheat for markets in Europe and New England. As they did so, their livelihoods became more dependent on political and economic developments in far-flung lands, even as they continued to see themselves as independent freeholders.

The other way in which farm households were drawn into the world of market relations was through the land itself. Paradoxically, the fact that land was broadly available for purchase—the very thing that enabled so many immigrant families and their descendants to become economically self-supporting—also turned land into a commodity with fluctuating values. **Land speculation** (buying land to rent it out, resell it, or control its resale value) had become common by the eighteenth century. In some colonies, land speculators amassed great estates. New York was an extreme case: Ten or eleven people owned about 75 percent of the land in New York in 1700. But throughout Britain's American colonies, the rising value of land encouraged private individuals to acquire more acreage than a single farm family could till.

URBAN CENTERS AND CITY PEOPLE

Economic stratification was far more pronounced in colonial cities, where merchants, artisans, wage workers, servants, and enslaved people lived in proximity to one another. Cities held less than a tenth of the colonial population during this period, but rural Americans felt their impact. Enslaved people and free immigrants typically landed in bustling ports before moving onto farms in the hinterland. Each colony's legislature and governing council met in an urban location. And cities organized the Atlantic trade that shaped life in this farming society. Urban merchants shipped the staple crops grown on rural plantations to foreign markets, and they imported manufactured goods, newspapers, and other scarce commodities. These imports eventually made their way to stores and market stalls in the farm towns and villages where most colonists lived.

Five substantial commercial cities emerged in Britain's mainland colonies before 1750: Boston, Newport (Rhode Island), New York, Philadelphia, and Charleston (South Carolina). They were stretched out along the Atlantic Coast, linking their respective hinterlands to a trade centered in and dominated by London. The five principal colonial cities were all small—in 1700 they ranged from about two thousand to about seven thousand in population—and performed many of the same economic functions, but they differed in some

Woman's Linen Chemise, ca. 1700. Imported linen clothing became common in America during the first half of the eighteenth century, in part because of rising standards of personal hygiene, which demanded garments that could be washed frequently. *Manchester Art Gallery, UK Manchester Art Gallery/Bridgeman Images*

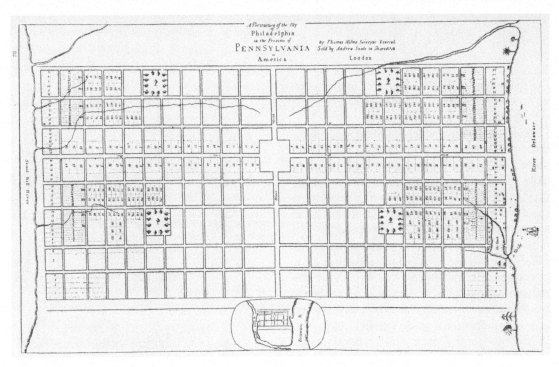

Philadelphia's Grid Plan. Philadelphia was distinguished by its network of straight streets intersecting at right angles. By 1700, geometrical order had become a dominant strategy of colonial town planning south of New England. *Archive Photos/Getty Images*

important respects. Boston, the oldest of the group (founded in 1630) and the largest town in British North America during this era, most resembled older European port towns. Boston's privately designed streets intersected at irregular angles and in haphazard patterns that gave it the congested appearance and feel of a medieval city. Philadelphia, by contrast, was created in 1682 on a formal grid plan. Newport and New York were closer to Boston, both in the time of their founding and in the layout of their streets, whereas Charleston, with its straight streets, resembled Philadelphia. In other respects, Charleston fit the model of colonial capitals in the British West Indies, busy port cities where enslaved Africans arrived and the staple crops they harvested departed. Philadelphia and New York were also entry points for new arrivals, but mostly for voluntary immigrants rather than enslaved people.

Thousands of colonists made their homes in a number of second-tier cities that grew in the first half of the eighteenth century. Some, such as Williamsburg (Virginia), New Bern (North Carolina), and Hartford (Connecticut), were seats of colonial government. Others, such as Salem (Massachusetts), Alexandria (Virginia), and Wilmington (North Carolina), were market towns. What all of those places had in common was a location on or near the eastern seaboard. Imagined from the inland farming settlements that made up the bulk of the colonies, urban society was a distant and barely visible bridge to the British Isles.

ENLIGHTENMENT AND AWAKENING

The colonies' growing and proliferating coastal cities were the conduits not only for trade and immigration but also for the arrival of new ideas and cultural influences from Europe. During the first half of the eighteenth century, urban printers and urban social gatherings helped spread the latest philosophical and theological developments from across the Atlantic. Two quite different but related intellectual movements would exert a powerful influence over colonial culture. One promoted a rational critique of received traditions; the other preached personal re-engagement with religion.

TAVERNS, NEWSPAPERS, AND INTELLECTUAL LIFE

Despite their modest size, colonial cities and towns were places of intellectual exchange and ferment. People, goods, and rumors from three continents circulated in the streets of these compact port towns. **Taverns** were especially important sites of information sharing in eighteenth-century urban life. Distinguished from alehouses, which catered to poorer customers and sold beer to go as well as on the premises, the eighteenth-century tavern was a more genteel institution, where middling and elite urbanites could drink wine and

87

engage in polite discussions of commerce and politics. In New York, committees of the legislature even held their meetings in a tavern.

POLITICS AND ENTERTAINMENT

● Licensed taverns multiplied and expanded in the middle of the century in the major cities. The fanciest of them were housed in elegant converted mansions located near the busy town docks. Called "public houses" (the origin of the term *pub*), taverns were licensed to provide food, drink, and entertainment to strangers, which typically included lectures or musical performances. In that sense, taverns were urban amenities that made colonial cities feel more like their European counterparts. And because they served as venues for strangers and locals alike, they were also places to express views about public affairs. In some colonies, taverns became centers of political dissent. ●

Printers also set up shop in cities and began producing the first **colonial newspapers.** Before 1700, governors and royal officials had prohibited the publication of news in the colonies, out of fear that the circulation of timely political information in print would lead to dissent and disorder. But in the years after the Glorious Revolution, Britain grew more confident in the political stability of its colonial system, and the need to promote commerce seemed to justify the small risks that newspapers might foment rebellion. The *Boston News-Letter*, generally considered the first real newspaper in England's colonies, began publication in 1704. Over the next few decades, similar weekly papers were introduced in New York, Philadelphia, Newport, Charleston, Williamsburg, and the Caribbean port cities of Bridgetown (Barbados) and Kingston (Jamaica).

● Colonial newspapers did not provide much local news, which was less urgent in small communities where information traveled quickly by word of mouth. Instead, the papers focused on reports from abroad, especially stories that would be of interest to their merchant readers. Commodity prices, ship arrivals, and developments in European politics and diplomacy dominated the news of the week. Urban newspaper subscribers were eager for reliable information about the British cities with which they traded, especially London, which remained the center of the world for many colonial merchants. Newspapers also included useful advertisements for local commerce, notices of runaway enslaved people and servants, and entertaining stories reprinted from the English press. ●

MEDIA AND INFORMATION

Newspapers also provided printers and their patrons a forum for influencing public opinion on local politics. For this reason, public officials strictly monitored newspapers

Boston News-Letter, the First Newspaper in British North America.   Its editor, James Campbell, was Boston's postmaster, and his paper originated as a series of handwritten reports to the governors of the New England colonies. In 1704, Campbell began printing it for wider circulation, using both sides of a single sheet. Note the absence of headlines or separate articles. Questions for Analysis: Why do you imagine the newspaper is reporting on the content of letters from overseas? *North Wind Picture Archives/Alamy Stock Photo*

in the early eighteenth century. In Massachusetts, newspapers were required to secure licenses, and the earliest Boston papers cleared each issue with the governor prior to publication. Benjamin Franklin's older brother James, publisher of the *New England Courant*, tried to operate without a license in the 1720s, but once his paper criticized the colonial authorities, he landed in jail. Banned from the business, Franklin evaded authorities temporarily by listing his younger brother on the masthead as the *Courant*'s publisher. In 1733, a Palatine German immigrant named John Peter Zenger began printing the *New York Weekly Journal*, the first political party newspaper in North America. Zenger printed political essays, mostly written or selected by the leader of a powerful faction hostile to New York's governor. Even some of the advertisements seemed to be satirizing the governor, who had Zenger arrested for the crime of publishing seditious libel.

When the **Zenger case** came to trial in 1735, his lawyer argued both that true statements should not be punished as libelous and that juries were entitled to judge the proper application of a law (rather than simply determining the facts in a particular case). Neither position had much support in English law, and the judge explicitly rejected both arguments. Nonetheless, the jury acquitted Zenger. Although this famous case was probably not very influential in the history of American libel law, it was celebrated at the time (and has been ever since) as a sign of growing popular support for the value of free expression and for the idea that a newspaper can be used to criticize the government.

ENLIGHTENMENT CULTURE

The rising confidence of urban publishers in their right to attack the regime in print was part of a larger set of developments in European thought known as the **Enlightenment.** Over the course of the eighteenth century, French, British, and German philosophers touted scientific experimentation, rational order, and individual reason as the proper way to understand both the natural world and civil society. Enlightenment ideas, which spread to North America during this period, challenged the authority of received tradition and emboldened intellectuals in the colonies to seek new truths through systematic inquiry and public debate. The illustrious career of Benjamin Franklin captured many of the themes and patterns in the American Enlightenment. Franklin was a self-educated urbanite who made scientific discoveries, engaged in philosophical

Imagined Interior of the Black Horse Tavern.   John Peter Zenger's political patrons gathered in this public space to toast the significance of their victory. Drawing from W. Harrison Baykes, "Old Taverns of New York," ca. 1915. *Collection of The New-York Historical Society*

speculation, published newspapers, founded libraries and intellectual clubs, ran the post office, and believed fervently in the power of writing and printing to spread the truth.

The Enlightenment directly undermined a number of reigning religious values in colonial life. Philosophical texts by early Enlightenment authors such as John Locke, Voltaire, and Jean-Jacques Rousseau encouraged readers to be skeptical of the authority of the clergy, to demand that religion appeal to reason rather than faith, and to look to scientific laws and observations of nature rather than to Scripture for evidence of divine will. Locke, who helped draft the original charter of the Carolina colonies, was an especially influential voice in America. His *Two Treatises on Government* (1689), written in the wake of England's Glorious Revolution, argued that political legitimacy comes from the consent of the governed, not from the biblically ordained powers of patriarchs. But the impact of the Enlightenment's critique of religious traditions affected more than just politics. Many urban colonists, like Franklin, as well as many elite Virginia planters embraced a deist outlook toward religious matters. **Deists** do not believe in a god who intervenes in the world. Instead, they see God's powers as built into the natural and moral order of the universe.

RELIGIOUS REVIVALS

Although some colonists embraced scientific rationality and what they called "reasonable religion," many more were influenced by European pietist movements that pushed in a different direction. **Pietism,** which promoted rigorous religious observance and stressed intense emotional prayer experiences, spread from German-speaking Europe to the Middle Colonies in the early 1700s. It was part of a broader trend toward popularizing and reinvigorating religious traditions through enthusiastic worship, which was emerging on both sides of the Atlantic and in various religious communities both within and beyond Christianity.

The American experience of pietism and revivalism, which historians call the **Great Awakening,** took place in multiple colonies from the early 1720s through the mid-1740s. In New Jersey and New York, Presbyterian minister Gilbert Tennent led revivals among Scots-Irish immigrants. Farther north, Congregationalist preacher Jonathan Edwards sought to stem the tide of religious skepticism and indifference in New England. Edwards moved audiences with vivid descriptions of hell and with his admonitions that individuals were utterly and precariously dependent on the creator. In his famous 1741 sermon "Sinners in the Hands of an Angry God," Edwards warned his

BEHIND THE IMAGE

John Wollaston was an English portrait painter who traveled to New York in 1749 and spent most of the next two decades in Britain's mainland colonies. Trained in London by artists in the rococo style, Wollaston generally stressed the elegance of his subjects, especially in their clothing. Whitefield, for his part, agreed to sit for several artists, but only after some deliberation about the propriety of doing so. He decided to use the lengthy sitting times required for a portrait "in beseeching the great God, by his holy Spirit, to paint his blessed Image upon his and my Heart."

WITHIN THE IMAGE

The painting's careful rendering of ① the clothing of Whitefield's listeners epitomizes rococo portraiture and emphasizes the refinement of the community to which he is preaching. Whitefield is shown enthralling ② a woman listening to one of his sermons in England. Although the evangelist reached massive crowds with his powerful voice and even larger audiences through published tracts, Wollaston's painting zooms in on the personal relationship between the charismatic minister and a woman in the church. ③ His outstretched hands suggest that the captivating power of his sermons lay in a bodily performance, not simply an inspiring religious message. The gesture also invokes the laying on of hands as a ritual whereby a holy person imparts spiritual gifts. Art historians have identified the enthralled woman with Elizabeth James, a thirty-six-year-old widow whom Whitefield married in 1741, though no other images of Elizabeth Whitefield survive to corroborate that hypothesis.

Portrait of George Whitefield by John Wollaston, ca. 1742.
Francis G. Mayer/Corbis Historical/Getty Images

BEYOND THE IMAGE

Whitefield crossed the ocean thirteen times in his life to maintain and extend his transatlantic ministry. Numerous portraits, like Wollaston's, circulated in the colonies as well. Paintings hung in the homes of wealthy colonists, whereas more modest followers of his preaching owned prints based on those paintings. All of these pictures of Whitefield contributed to his celebrity, long after he returned to England, by attaching a recognizable image of both his cross-eyed face and his expressive oratorical style.

Massachusetts listeners that "the God who holds you over the pit of hell, much as one holds a spider . . . over the fire, abhors you, and is dreadfully provoked."

The most popular and effective of the revivalist preachers was George Whitefield (pronounced *Whitfield*), an Englishman affiliated with the new Methodist movement. Beginning in 1739, Whitefield toured North America and became something of a celebrity, spellbinding colonists up and down the seaboard with his impassioned, extemporaneous oratorical style and a booming voice that could be heard at a great distance. In Philadelphia and Boston, Whitefield attracted crowds that were as large as the permanent populations of those cities.

● Tennent, Edwards, Whitefield, and other figures associated with the colonial revivals were not formally connected to a single movement. However, they shared a commitment to individual conversion experiences. Contemporaries dubbed them and their followers **New Lights,** as opposed to the Old Lights who worried about the excessive enthusiasm of the revivals and their tendency to embolden men and women to step out of their prescribed social positions. ● In some

CONFLICTING FAITHS

striking respects, the individualism of the Great Awakening resembled that of the Enlightenment. Although one movement preached rational study and the other valued total faith and emotional expression, both enjoined individuals to defy traditional authority and seek the truth for themselves. In that sense, the cause of John Peter Zenger, who also published the sermons of Tennent and Whitefield, was aligned with the evangelical culture of the pietists as well as with the more secular values of Benjamin Franklin. Both forces continued to shape the beliefs of American colonists over the course of the eighteenth century.

CONCLUSION

By 1750, well over a million people lived in Britain's mainland North American colonies, a number roughly equivalent to the population of Scotland at the time. American colonists had spread out across a long coast and well into an expanding backcountry. Though the colonies continued to differ markedly in population density, ethnic makeup, and religious orientation, and though they grew different crops on different kinds of farms and plantations, they were connected in many ways.

After the Restoration of the monarchy in 1660, England had acquired new territories and asserted control over a continuous ring of settlement. Since the Glorious Revolution of 1688, that control had focused on commercial exchange. And especially since the establishment of Great Britain in 1707, a diverse migration from Scotland, Ireland, and the German lands had fueled the colonies' growth and expanded the reach of an Atlantic commercial empire. From the perspective of someone like Benjamin Franklin, who had arrived in Philadelphia just a few years before the indentured servant William Moraley, Britain's American colonies seemed both fundamentally different from and intimately bound to England.

STUDY TERMS

Restoration
Anglo-Dutch War
Navigation Acts
mercantilism
Staple Act
Middle Colonies
Quaker migration
Dominion of New England
Glorious Revolution
Leisler's Rebellion
Scots-Irish immigrants
Pennsylvania Dutch
transported convicts
freehold
patriarch
yeoman farmer
land speculation
five substantial commercial cities
tavern
colonial newspapers
Zenger case
Enlightenment
Deists
pietism
Great Awakening
New Lights

FURTHER READING

A database of additional full-text readings is available through Power of Process for Primary Sources in Connect.

Bernard Bailyn, *The Peopling of British North America* (1986), sketches broad patterns in eighteenth-century immigration to the American colonies.

Kathleen Brown, *Foul Bodies* (2009), explores changing standards and practices of personal hygiene in early America.

Jon Butler, *Becoming America* (2000), surveys the changes in material, spiritual, and political life that helped form a new American identity.

James Deetz, *In Small Things Forgotten* (revised ed. 1996), demonstrates how archaeological discoveries illuminate the study of the material life of early America.

Karen Halttunen, *Murder Most Foul* (1998), studies the changing world views reflected in crime narratives of the colonial era.

David Hancock, *Oceans of Wine* (2009), traces the networks of consumption and culture that formed around the commerce in Madeira wine.

Allan Kulikoff, *From British Peasants to Colonial American Farmers* (2000), emphasizes the importance of land to British immigrants to North America.

Michelle Morris, *Under Household Government* (2013), examines family and sexuality in the Puritan colonies.

Mary P. Ryan, *Mysteries of Sex* (2006), includes a survey of changes in gender roles in colonial farm families.

Douglas Winiarski, *Darkness Falls on the Land of Light* (2017), captures and illuminates the ferment and enthusiasm of the Great Awakening in New England.

5 | Empires, War & the Transformation of Indian Country

Chapter Questions

1. In what specific ways were British colonists more thoroughly integrated into the British Empire during the eighteenth century?

2. How did the French and Indian War fit into the larger, global conflict among European powers?

3. Why did 1763 mark a tragic turning point from the perspective of Native Americans east of the Mississippi?

Emperor of the Six Nations. This 1710 painting by Dutch artist Johannes Verelst depicts Mohawk leader Hendrick Tejonihakarawa (his second name meant "Open the Door"), a major player in diplomatic relations with Britain. *Private Collection/The Bridgeman Art Library*

Eliza Pinckney kept in touch with her world by exchanging letters across an ocean. Pinckney, an elite Charleston resident partially responsible for the emergence of indigo as a major export crop, corresponded with friends thousands of miles away in London, which she saw as the center of her universe. Her own location in South Carolina, as she described it in 1762, was "the Wilds of America" in a "remote Corner of the Globe." Like many English-speaking colonists, she faced east, awaiting news and commodities from the capital of Britain's great empire. To her and her neighbors, the vast interior of the continent was "backcountry."

Time Line

1689-1697

King William's War (War of the League of Augsburg)

1702-1713

Queen Anne's War (War of the Spanish Succession)

1707

Act of Union unites England and Scotland as Great Britain

1711

Tuscarora War begins

1715

Yamasee War

1744-1748

King George's War (War of the Austrian Succession)

1754

French and Indian War begins

1754

Albany Congress proposes plan for intercolonial cooperation

1756

Seven Years' War begins in Europe

1762

Spain enters the war; Britain invades Cuba

1763

Treaty of Paris ends the war
Pontiac's Rebellion begins
King George III issues Proclamation of 1763
Paxton Boys massacre Conestoga in Pennsylvania

From the vantage point of Marie Madeleine Réaume L'archevëque Chevalier, the map of North America in the mid-18th century looked quite different. A prosperous and powerful Catholic Illini living among Potawatomi in what is now southwestern Michigan, she positioned herself at the center of a fur-trading geography that stretched north to forts along the Great Lakes and south to villages in the Mississippi River valley. Edicts from a distant French king might affect the fur trade, but the court at Versailles was not the hub of her world. Kin networks mattered more than colonial administration, and Chevalier shaped and managed those networks through marriage, baptism, and godparenting.

The continent looked different from the Carolina coast than it did from shores of Lake Michigan, and it looked even more different from London, Paris, or Madrid. In contrast to later periods of American history, colonists and Native Americans did not see themselves as inhabiting two completely separate worlds. The eastern portion of the North American continent was a heterogeneous mosaic of settlements, representing a wide array of ethnic groups, both native and transplanted. Political allegiances in these settlements could be complex. But four major powers—Iroquois, French, Spanish, and British—dominated the eastern half of the continent for much of the eighteenth century.

Of all the societies associated with these powers, Britain's colonial population was growing the fastest, doubling every twenty-five years during the eighteenth century as it spilled into new settlements. Still, other powers kept the expansion of the British in check, and frequent wars involving alliances of European and native forces preserved a balance among the antagonists. Europe's imperial conflicts provided indigenous peoples like Chevalier's Potawatomi kin with a survival map, while imperial growth helped sustain the identities that colonists like Eliza Pinckney used to make sense of their place in the world. Between 1754 and 1763, however, a more decisive war would alter that map forever.

RIVAL POWERS IN THE EAST

Farmers in Connecticut, artisans in Pennsylvania, and slaveholders in Virginia may have focused primarily on local relationships or on trade with England, but they were also living in a world shaped by imperial politics. From the perspective of England, Spain, and France, the eastern half of North America was an extension of their empires and another theater in their contest for power. The Iroquois League was the other dominant player in the political geography of the eastern portion of North America during the first half of the eighteenth century.

THE IROQUOIS LEAGUE AND BRITAIN'S NORTHERN COLONIES

The Haudenosaunee, the five-nation Iroquois League that had used its trading relationships with Dutch and English colonists to achieve military dominance during the mid-1600s (see Chapter 2), grew even more powerful as the century wore on. Following the bloody events of 1676–1677, when both New England and the Chesapeake were engulfed with violence, New York governor Edmund Andros initiated diplomatic negotiations with the Iroquoian Mohawk. Andros sought to broker peace between English colonists and Native Americans and expand his own political authority in the region. These negotiations established a pattern of councils and treaties between New York and the Iroquois League known as the **Covenant Chain.** Four other colonies eventually joined the diplomatic councils, which governed British–Native American relations during the first half of the eighteenth century.

In Covenant Chain negotiations, the Iroquois claimed to speak for all the native groups who traded or interacted with British colonists. The treaties gave the Iroquois security on their eastern front and access to the weapons they needed to attack fur-trading rivals to the west. On the other side, British colonies benefited from more stable partners in the fur trade and allies in their wars against the French. The Iroquois League grew by adopting captives from enemies in the Great Lakes region. The Iroquois also added a sixth nation to the League in the 1720s, following the **Tuscarora War** of 1711–1713, when an alliance composed of Swiss and German settlers, the colonial militias of North and South Carolina, the Yamasee people, and other native groups defeated the southern Tuscarora and burned their villages. The surviving Tuscarora migrated northward from the Carolinas to join the Haudenosaunee.

The Iroquois League proved a powerful ally for Britain's northern colonies over the course of a century of conflict

with other empires, but the Iroquois did not always do Britain's bidding. Indeed, when it served their purposes, Iroquois groups made their own peace with the French or with France's indigenous allies. Iroquois leaders understood the importance of not relying on a single European power and effectively gave both the French and the British Empires a reason to maintain good relations with the Six Nations. By around 1720, this strategy had succeeded not only in enhancing Iroquois power but also in securing greater peace between Native Americans and colonists (see Singular Lives: Sir Willian Johnson, Irish Mohawk).

SPAIN AND FRANCE IN NORTH AMERICA

At the dawn of the eighteenth century, England's Atlantic seaboard settlements were the continent's most populous colonies north of Mexico. Yet poised ominously at the edges of British colonial society were well-armed Spanish and French colonists and their native allies.

Spain's North American colonies in 1700 remained minor outposts at the northern edge of a vast empire centered in Mesoamerica, the Caribbean, and the South American mainland. The Pueblo Revolt of 1680 had checked the expansion of Spanish Jesuits into New Mexico, very few Spanish traders had settled in Texas, and the Florida missions had declined. Well into the eighteenth century, fewer than five thousand Spaniards inhabited these three colonies combined. But Spain was committed to preserving its Florida military bases, primarily to protect its Caribbean empire against the British. Consequently, Spanish Florida sought to extend its political influence over a number of southeastern native groups and bestowed gifts and noble titles on native leaders who had embraced Catholicism. Meanwhile, Native American groups seeking relief from Spain's authority and its labor demands found trading partners and military allies in the British colonies of South Carolina and later Georgia—both of which had been designed to challenge Spanish America.

France's North American empire was far more extensive than Spain's. French traders and missionaries prospered in New France, their scattered settlements stretching westward from Cape Breton Island on Canada's Atlantic coast through the St. Lawrence Valley and the Great Lakes. From there, French colonists extended southward along both banks of the Mississippi River through numerous trading villages in the Illinois territory and down to New Orleans, founded as a French city in 1718. Altogether, about 65,000 people (not counting the native

BEHIND THE IMAGE

Claude Chauchetière, a priest born in France, met Kateri Tekakwitha, a Mohawk-Algonquin convert to Catholicism, after they both arrived at the Kahnawake Jesuit mission south of Montréal in 1677. After Tekakwitha (baptized as Catherine) died in 1680, members of the mission reported visions of her apparition, and Chauchetière indicated he also experienced multiple such encounters, including one in which a voice urged him to produce an image of what he saw. Heeding the call, Chauchetière produced several portraits of her holding a wooden cross, though this oil painting is the only one that survived. The surrounding tapestry against which the painting is set dates from a later period.

Portrait of Catherine Tekakwitha, early 1680s, by Father Chauchetière.
Riccardo De Luca/Getty Images

WITHIN THE IMAGE

Chauchetière's painting sets the serene Catherine against a pastoral landscape, which probably differed markedly from the appearance of the Kahnawake mission and certainly deviated from images of Mohawk or Algonquin people as creatures of the forest. Although many later portraits of Tekakwitha assign her a dark complexion

and dress her in buckskin and feathers, this painting shows her as light-skinned and wraps her in a cloth tunic. Chauchetière (who knew what his subject looked like) may have been capturing Tekakwitha's actual appearance and customary dress, but these pictorial decisions also reflect the European-born painter's perception of Catherine as a traditional Catholic holy woman—rather than his European-born contemporaries' more typical perception of her as an uncivilized Native American.

BEYOND THE IMAGE

Noted during her short life for her piety and her vow of perpetual virginity, Tekakwitha was remembered after her death, in large part thanks to the efforts of Father Chauchetière, as a saintly figure whose intercession could perform miracles. Chauchetière's view of Tekakwitha received the ultimate validation in 2012, when she was canonized by Pope Benedict XVI as the first Native American saint. The painting, which had helped launch her on the journey to sainthood, remained in the Kahnawake, now the St. Francis Xavier, Mission, in Québec but it was featured (set against the tapestry shown here) in her 2012 canonization mass.

inhabitants) lived in French colonies in North America by 1750, at a time when Britain's mainland colonial population approached 1.2 million.

Compared to British America, the French presence, though sparse, was also less divided. French colonies did not have political conflicts with one another. French colonists also enjoyed much closer relations with Native Americans. Because New France's economic basis was animal furs and skins rather than staple agriculture, French settlers needed trading partners more than they needed native peoples' land. Moreover, their smaller numbers made the French more obviously dependent on cultivating alliances with Native Americans. The French, like the Spanish but unlike the English, lived among indigenous peoples, intermarried with native women, supplied native men with European goods (including weapons), and used these relationships to build an empire.

IMPERIAL WARS

Conflicts on the other side of the Atlantic shaped relations among the European colonies in North America (see Table 5.1). After King William III's ascent to the throne in 1689 (see Chapter 4), England renewed its rivalry with Catholic Europe and embarked on the first of a long series of costly wars with France, which would re-erupt periodically for more than a century. These were not contained, local conflicts between the two neighboring countries. In the early wars, England fought as part of large, multinational European alliances. Generally, France

SINGULAR LIVES

Sir William Johnson, Irish Mohawk

In the North American interior, far from the coastal towns founded in the seventeenth century, British colonists and Native Americans interacted often. William Johnson, an Irish immigrant who had settled in New York's Mohawk Valley, at the eastern edge of Iroquois territory, thrived in this environment. Born a Catholic in County Meath in Ireland, Johnson converted to Protestantism and set sail for New York in 1738 to help manage the estate of a wealthy uncle. Johnson became a successful fur trader and merchant and quickly forged connections in New York politics. But he cemented an even more useful political alliance with the Canajoharie Mohawk people. During King George's War, Johnson was able to draw on his influence and friendship with the Mohawk chief Hendrick Theyanoguin to organize bands of native men to fight on the British side, notwithstanding the Iroquois League's policy of neutrality.

Johnson's Native American ties were not simply diplomatic. He had learned Mohawk war songs, painted himself as a Mohawk warrior, and received a Mohawk name—Warraghiyagey, meaning "Doer of Great Things" or "Doer of Much Business." Johnson also fathered children with at least two Mohawk women, one of whom, Molly Brant, became his common-law wife.

These cultural bonds enhanced Johnson's standing in the British Empire rather than compromising it. He was appointed New York's agent for negotiations with the Iroquois. Later, during the French and Indian War, he became British Superintendent of Indian Affairs for the Northern Colonies and received the noble title of baronet. Yet despite his elevated social rank, Johnson remained a frontiersman, and he never set foot in the British capital. Instead, he amassed political power and wealth along the Great Lakes, becoming a major power broker along the frontier that separated—and connected—Iroquois country and British America. Johnson's career also epitomized the era in white–Native American relations when powerful polities engaged in frequent negotiations to avoid the widespread violence of the late seventeenth century.

Where in the Archives?

As a distinguished colonial official and the bearer of a noble title, Johnson left a heavy imprint on the historial record. Multiple volumes of his letters and papers were published almost a century ago, including *The Papers of Sir William Johnson* (Albany: The University of the State of New York, 1921–1965), found at HathiTrust (https://catalog.hathitrust.org/).

But another way to explore his complex identity and prodigious political influence is to examine three visual representations of him during the eighteenth century.

The painting titled *General Johnson Saving a Wounded French Officer from the Tomahawk of a North American Indian* by Benjamin West is housed at the Derby Museum and Art Gallery but available through Wikimedia Commons (https://commons.wikimedia.org/). The mezzotint engraving of William Johnson with the caption "Sir William Johnson: Major General of the British Forces in America" is also available through Wikimedia Commons (https://commons.wikimedia.org/). The painting titled *Sir William Johnson (1715–1774)* by Edward L. Mooney is housed at The New-York Historical Society (https://www.nyhistory.org/).

William Johnson. In this 1763 portrait, Johnson poses as a British nobleman. *Sir William Johnson (1715–1774). John Wollaston (1736–1767) 1750–752. Oil on canvas, ht. 30 1/16" × w. 25". Albany Institute of History & Art, gift of Laura Munsell Tremaine in memory of her father, Joel Munsell, 1922.*

Certifying Diplomacy. In this pictorial detail from a William Johnson certificate, British and Native American officials engage in a peaceful meeting. Johnson would bestow such certificates on his Native American friends and allies. *Science History Images/Alamy Stock Photo*

Assignment

Analyze the differences among the images in 200 words, considering the following questions:

Which aspects of his life do they choose to emphasize? Do they stress his nobility? His military valor? His Native American, English, or Irish identity?

TABLE 5.1 IMPERIAL WARS, 1689-1748		
Name of War in Europe	Name in British Empire	Dates
War of the League of Augsburg (also known as War of the Grand Alliance, Nine Years' War)	King William's War	1689-1697
War of Spanish Succession	Queen Anne's War	1702-1713
War of Austrian Succession	King George's War	1744-1748

was joined by Spain and by other Catholic allies, whereas the British had the support of Protestant forces in northern Europe. In each conflict, hostilities spread beyond Europe to wherever the rivals vied for control.

Beginning with **Queen Anne's War** in 1702, colonists and Native Americans were drawn into battle in significant numbers. The fight began over the proposed unification of the French and Spanish monarchies and lasted for more than a decade. European armies and navies clashed in far-flung parts of the globe as the two sides raided each other's possessions on the high seas and in the West Indies, Brazil, and North America. English forces from Carolina seized the opportunity to attack Florida, while the Spanish mounted a counteroffensive against Charleston. France ordered raids into New England, while the English launched an abortive naval expedition to seize Québec. Relations among various native groups proved crucial throughout this war. The Creek people joined the English attack on Florida for their own reasons, hoping to defeat the Appalachees, who were allied with Spain. The Mohawk and Abenaki tied to France carried out attacks against Puritan settlers in Maine and western Massachusetts. Notably, the French did not attack New York, not wanting to antagonize that colony's Iroquois allies, with whom they had recently signed a peace treaty.

In the end, Queen Anne's War produced no decisive shift in the balance of power among European empires in North America. In the treaty that officially ended the war in 1713, France ceded to Britain some territory in northern and eastern Canada, but Britain, Spain, and France all maintained their major prewar colonies. For Native Americans, on the other hand, the war enhanced the standing of particular confederacies, including the Creek peoples (who had defeated their enemies) and the Iroquois League (who had maintained their neutrality).

Following a period of relative quiet, Britain exported another long war to North America in 1739. In 1738, a British captain named Robert Jenkins appeared before Parliament holding his pickled left ear, which he claimed had been sliced off several years earlier by a Spanish coast guard official who was enforcing Spain's ban against British trading in the West Indies. The display fanned the flames of British nationalism, anti-Catholic hostility, and commercial ambition, and a year later Parliament declared war against Spain. Once again, fighting broke out on both sides of the ocean. English colonists in America signed up for a massive naval expedition to capture Spain's gold trade, but the assault on Spanish Cartagena (in present-day Colombia) failed disastrously. Farther north, British ships blockaded Florida, while soldiers from Georgia besieged St. Augustine. The Spanish broke the siege and counterinvaded Georgia.

The **War of Jenkins's Ear,** as this inconclusive Anglo-Spanish conflict was dubbed a century later, became part of a wider struggle with France and Spain over control of the Hapsburg monarchy in Austria. The North American theater of this War of the Austrian

Siege of Louisbourg.   Supported by the British navy, an attack force of New England colonists captured this pillar of Catholic power in Canada. *Print Collector/Hulton Archive/Getty images*

Succession, known as **King George's War,** further cemented the bonds between colonists and Britain's transatlantic empire. ● The only decisive military campaign in America took place in 1745, when forty-three hundred men, mostly from the New England colonies, captured the strategically significant French fort at Louisbourg on Cape Breton Island, Nova Scotia, giving Britain control over access to the St. Lawrence River. Many New Englanders saw the campaign as part of a Protestant crusade. As one Boston minister exulted, "a great Support of Anti-christian Power is taken away, and the visible Kingdom of CHRIST enlarged." ●

In the complex negotiations ending the war, Britain returned Louisbourg to the French in return for significant concessions in Europe and India. To soften the blow to New Englanders, Parliament covered the cost of the Louisbourg campaign, thus underscoring that Americans' local struggles were part of a single imperial operation. The Louisbourg campaign had embroiled the Iroquois League, as New York's governor pressed the Iroquois to abandon their neutrality pledge. Although the Iroquois resisted this pressure, the Covenant Chain was strained.

FRONTIERS AND BORDERLANDS IN INDIAN COUNTRY

In the eighteenth century, European empires controlled only a small portion of the territory that would eventually become the United States. Most of the continent, on both sides of the Mississippi River, remained Indian country—lands inhabited and dominated by the many indigenous peoples in North America. In Eastern North America, Indian country was a large area surrounded by a thinner ring of European settlements that were constantly advancing past their borders (see Map 5.1). There, different native groups, some of them new to this period, tried to preserve their independence through skillful diplomacy.

Farther west, where a small number of French traders and Spanish missionaries operated, Native American nations maintained firmer control.

ALLIANCE AND DIPLOMACY IN THE EAST

Amid the conflicts roiling the rival European empires, most of the eastern half of the continent remained inhabited by Native American groups. South and west of Iroquois territory, much of the American interior had been settled by smaller native groups who had migrated to lands depopulated by war and disease. In the northern reaches of Indian country, refugees from various Algonquian peoples who had been destroyed by the Iroquois in the mid-1600s fled west to the lands bordering Lake

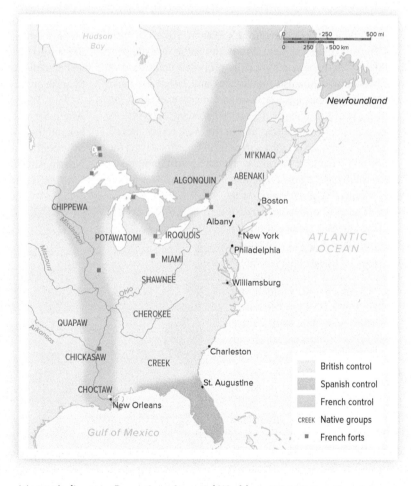

Map 5.1 Indigenous Power in an Imperial World, ca. 1720–1750.   East of the Mississippi River, native villages and groups still enjoyed effective sovereignty over most of the land. Rival colonial societies lay on the region's periphery.

Michigan. French traders and missionaries helped mediate conflicts among the refugees, who in turn used French communications networks (trade routes, linked forts, and missionary correspondence) to forge new alliances and create new clusters of villages. Major Native American groups of the upper Midwest, including the Ottawa, Miami, Potawatomi, and Fox, formed in this way around the beginning of the eighteenth century. They traded with the French, protected New France from the Iroquois League, and even identified with the French Empire, but they also established diplomatic relations with Iroquois groups and sold furs to the English in New York.

Similar patterns appeared throughout lands inhabited by indigenous peoples. In the Upper Ohio River valley, the Shawnee and Delaware peoples, driven west by land-hungry Pennsylvania settlers and their Iroquois allies, established new villages in the land between the French-allied native groups of the Great Lakes region and England's Middle Colonies. Farther southwest, the Choctaw group formed in present-day Mississippi, within the

Cherokee Chief Austenaco Donning Western Attire During a Visit to London, 1762. Austenaco, a famed orator, and two other Native American leaders met with King George III and sat for portraitist Sir Joshua Reynolds. Over one hundred fifty Native Americans made diplomatic journeys to Britain during the seventeenth and eighteenth centuries. *Hulton-Deutsch/Hulton-Deutsch Collection/Corbis/Getty Images*

orbit of French Louisiana. Most Choctaw villages allied and traded with the French, but others fought alongside the British. In the southeastern quadrant of the territory, the Creeks and Cherokee emerged in the eighteenth century as new and powerful multiethnic groups. The Creeks, who had been recruited and armed by South Carolina to attack Florida, became the region's leading military power. Different Creek villages allied themselves with French Louisiana and Spanish Florida, conducted trade with both empires, and reduced Creek dependence on Carolina. The Cherokee, who helped Carolina defeat the Creeks in the Yamasee War in 1715 (see Chapter 3), maintained closer ties to British America, but they played one British colony off against another and even pursued alliances with the French. These complex economic and diplomatic relationships were part of a common strategy

among eighteenth-century Native Americans. But they also reflected decentralized leadership in a Native American world where communities were on the move and ethnic identities were in flux.

NATIVE POWERS IN THE WEST

Between the Mississippi River and Pacific Ocean, indigenous people did not need to exploit any rivalries among European powers. In the West, native people rather than colonists held sway. Europeans lurked at the edges of this vast territory (see Map 5.2), with French migrants pushing in from Louisiana and Spanish migrants moving up from New Mexico. But French and Spanish colonists had to proceed carefully, eager not to run afoul of the groups and polities that dominated the region. Yet despite their small numbers and limited settlement, Europeans made a difference.

The rules governing encounters between whites and Native Americans on the other side of the Mississippi were perhaps clearest in southeastern Texas, where small numbers of French and Spanish colonists labored to gain permanent footholds in the early 1700s. France and Spain were not expecting to extract precious metals from the earth or to command plantation labor here. Instead, they were competing to establish relations with the powerful **Caddo** people, who controlled significant territory in what are now eastern Texas and Oklahoma, Louisiana, and Arkansas. French traders held the advantage over Spanish missionaries, since the French did not expect wholesale changes in the religious beliefs, family values, and sexual practices of the Caddo as a condition of doing business. In addition, French traders lived in families and intermarried with the Caddo—practices that made them easier to incorporate as allies within a native political system that stressed kin ties. Spaniards, by contrast, arrived in parties that were suspiciously all-male, though the Caddo were reassured by the ubiquitous images of the Virgin Mary

Map 5.2 Native American Powers in the West, ca. 1720–1750. Native American dominance was far more complete west of the Mississippi. Native people thus felt less need to play rival colonial empires off against one another.

villages and fairs, where they acquired the guns, ammunition, and horses that secured their military dominance. Western Sioux gradually incorporated European horses (see Hot Commodities: Horses) into their hunting and fighting in the first half of the eighteenth century, but guns and ammunition quickly shifted political relations between western Sioux and their neighbors.

In the southern plains, the Comanche migrated southward from the Rocky Mountains to track buffalo and traded hides for horses with Spanish settlers in New Mexico. Spain came to regret its role in the rise, in the eighteenth century, of the **Comanchería,** an expansive domain of Comanche influence that covered, in present-day terms, western Kansas, eastern Oklahoma, central Texas, and parts of New Mexico. Comanche raids would wreak havoc in Spanish (and later Mexican) settlements for another century. West of the Comanchería, the Apache also benefited from trade with neighboring New Mexico, where Spanish colonial authorities looked for allies against the French-connected Pawnee. New Mexico also shared a tense border with the Navajo, and as the Spanish colony grew slowly over the course of the 1700s, war and diplomacy with the Navajo became a major preoccupation.

At midcentury, European settlement in the western half of the continent remained light. French traders controlled the Mississippi River and were active along the Missouri, and French goods circulated through the Plains, Rockies, and Southwest. But no French colonies took hold farther west than east Texas. Spanish colonization was still confined to the South. Not until the last third of the century would Spain establish missions and military presidios along the Pacific Coast, which remained the most densely settled and least European-influenced portion of Western America. Only later, after the imperial map of the continent had shifted dramatically, would Father Junípero Serra found missions in San Diego (1769), Monterey (1770), San Francisco (1776), and elsewhere along the coast, laying the groundwork for the eventual urbanization of California.

they carried on their banners. From a native perspective, the presence of a woman in a diplomatic ceremony represented a promise of peace, and invoking the Virgin was a way of communicating that promise. Still, the Spanish came to understand that pictures of female saints might not suffice to put the native people at ease. When organizing an expedition to settle the San Antonio River in 1718, the viceroy of New Spain therefore requested only men with families, since "the Indians find it strange that the soldiers do not bring women." Outnumbered and vulnerable, Europeans in Caddo lands relied on diplomacy rather than force or intimidation.

Throughout the West, powerful native groups dominated. Beginning in the 1680s, bands of western Sioux swept through the northern plains, gradually controlling land from present-day Minnesota all the way west to the head of the Yellowstone River. Sioux hunting parties followed the buffalo migration during the summer and then moved to woodland areas to trap beaver. In the spring, they traveled east to French trading

HOT COMMODITIES
Horses

Romantic images of the Plains Indians feature noble warriors or hunters mounted proudly on their steeds. But where did Native Americans get horses? Like other indigenous North Americans, the people of the Great Plains had been nomadic pedestrians who domesticated dogs rather than horses for hunting assistance. In fact, horses had become extinct in the Western Hemisphere during the Pleistocene era. But horses came back to the Native Americans—from Europe.

Specifically, horses entered the American West through New Mexico, where Spanish colonists introduced them shortly after 1600. Spaniards found the hot, dry Plains grasslands unpromising for colonization. But this terrain proved hospitable to Spanish horses, whose North African breeding helped them survive arid summers.

Apache and Jumano peoples acquired New Mexican horses early in the seventeenth century through trade and theft, and the animals circulated in sprawling commercial networks, which reached as far away as Caddo villages in eastern Texas. More horses entered native hands in 1680 when New Mexicans left hundreds behind while fleeing the Pueblo Revolt. Soon after, the Comanche shifted to equestrian hunting, and their increased mobility both encouraged and enabled them to conquer their enemies' territory. Comanche power, in turn, helped spread equestrian culture through the Plains.

The equestrian revolution in the Plains had dramatic consequences. Horses were economically efficient, as they converted the region's abundant grasses directly into energy. They were politically powerful, as they allowed warriors to cover and govern larger stretches of territory. They lightened the burdens of nomadism, especially for native women, who had carried the materials of camp from place to place during the hunting season. And they created new trade patterns, serving both as a widely valued commodity themselves and as a means for transporting goods across great distances. Paradoxically, the horse was a European import that wound up helping some native people achieve prosperity and political autonomy in the face of European incursions. By the second half of the eighteenth century, horses had tipped the balance of political power from Spanish New Mexico to the Comanchería.

The spread of the horse came with serious costs, however. More efficient war making destroyed lives and subjugated many horse-poor native groups to a few horse-wealthy ones. In addition, equestrianism widened the

George Catlin, *Comanche Feats of Horsemanship*, Oil Painting, 1834-1835. The horse, originally a European import, became central to nineteenth-century Americans' romantic images of native life in the West. *SBS Eclectic Images/ Alamy Stock Photo*

gap—both in physical distance and in social status—between men's work and women's work, and higher battle fatalities skewed sex ratios in many villages. In the longer term, horses wreaked ecological damage by destroying grasslands, destabilizing bison populations, and disrupting long-standing patterns of economic subsistence.

Think About It

1. How might the introduction of horses have hurt Spain's colonization efforts in North America?

2. Why did Southwestern and Plains Indians value horses rather than other domesticated animals imported by the Europeans?

IMPERIAL CONNECTIONS IN BRITISH AMERICA

In some ways, the expansive empires that colonized North America were imaginary abstractions. All kinds of cues reminded Americans that they belonged to villages, towns, native groups, churches, colonies, extended families, or historical communities. But what made them feel part of an empire? This was an especially difficult question in the case of what was by far the largest group of European and African colonists on the mainland—those living in something called the British Empire. Great Britain was a new entity created by the 1707 Act of Union, and most people in Britain's mainland American colonies in the first half of the eighteenth century had never lived in the British Isles. The ties binding British colonists

Women in Baja California Dressed in European Clothing.
Spanish missionaries to the Pacific Coast extended the reach of
European consumer culture, as well as Catholicism. *Ignacio Tirsch.
The Drawings of Ignacio Tirsch, a Jesuit Missionary in Baja California.
Los Angeles: Dawson's Book Shop, 1972.*

to the empire in 1707 were loose, at best. By midcentury,
however, new connections among different British colonies linked them both to one another and to the imperial
center in London.

CONSUMER CULTURES

As much as any other connection, what
made the various colonies seem increasingly
British over the course of the 1700s was commerce. Both colonists and Native Americans
on the eastern part of the continent purchased consumer goods that had been produced overseas and brought to the colonies
through British ports on British ships, in
compliance with the Navigation Acts. Native
Americans living in territories that had been
claimed by Great Britain consumed European commodities, including weapons,
ammunition, iron tools, and woolen textiles. Purchasing such commodities did not
necessarily make Native Americans more
like Europeans. European manufacturers
designed lighter kettles, axes, and muskets for
native customers than for local markets,
whereas textile makers in Belgium and
England produced woolen "duffel," or
"stroud," cloth specifically for a Native American market. But all of these purchases had

an impact on native people's lives and made them dependent on trade relationships that tied them to colonists, traversed colonial boundaries, and crossed the ocean.

One of the most devastating commercial relationships
between eastern Native Americans and British colonists
involved liquor. Among all the popular European consumer goods in native communities, alcoholic beverages
were the ones that were literally consumed. Native villages might hold on to a brass kettle or a woolen blanket,
but a barrel of rum was depleted quickly—and tended to
stimulate more demand.

The **Indian liquor trade** developed slowly but steadily
in the English colonies during the seventeenth century
and had become a major force by the mid-eighteenth century. In the 1760s, rum produced in North America from
sugar harvested in the French and British West Indies
saturated native villages deep in the interior of British
America. Alcohol presumably brought pleasure, relief,
and inspiration to its Native American consumers, much
as it did to European colonists, and native people incorporated liquor into their festivals and rituals. But both
native and colonial observers testified to the horrific damage that came with the liquor trade as domestic violence,
illness, addiction, and political instability all followed distilled spirits into indigenous territory. But despite attempts
to regulate or ban the liquor trade, colonial merchants and

MANNER OF INSTRUCTING THE INDIANS.

"Manner of Instructing the Indians."   This early-nineteenth-century woodcut
shows how white Massachusetts settlers used alcohol to exploit the Mashpee people.
Scholars debate why liquor had such a disastrous impact on native communities.
Medical researchers find no evidence that Native Americans have a greater physiological susceptibility to alcohol abuse or addiction. *Collections of Old Sturbridge Village*

officials understood that without the liquor trade Native Americans would procure fewer skins and furs for European markets.

Indigenous people were hardly the only Americans to participate in what historians have called Britain's **empire of goods,** a system of commercial exchange that linked a widely dispersed population through the things they bought, consumed, displayed, and coveted. English colonists had long depended on imports to supply manufactured commodities that were not produced in North America. By the 1740s, many more of those commodities were available, and colonists demanded (and could afford) them. Colonial stores filled their shelves with unprecedented volumes and varieties of imported fabric, furniture, and utensils that appealed to colonists' rising aspirations to genteel living. Colonial merchants also imported spices, wines, dyes, metals, and other exotic items from places around the globe where British ships traded. Trade to the American colonies skyrocketed; from 1720 to 1770, the average colonist's consumption of British exports rose almost 50 percent. In the process, colonists were becoming more culturally English and more dependent on global exchanges managed by the British Empire.

Consumption connected colonists who hailed from distinct regions in Europe, worshiped in antagonistic religious traditions, and lived in radically different settings. Similar imported ceramic plates, glass mirrors, printed books, and silk gowns appeared in colonial homes from New England to South Carolina, in rural villages as well as port cities. Newspaper advertisements wrapped these consumer goods in an elaborate vocabulary of color, texture, and pattern that kept colonists abreast of the latest trends in British fashion and gave consumers new experiences of choice and control. By the 1760s, the expanding catalogue of British imports had shaped the material conditions of most colonists and reminded them how connected they were to a commercial empire.

Had Britain's American colonies manufactured more of their own goods, they might have been more isolated from the empire. British economic policies, however, gave British export merchants special access to American consumers and encouraged colonists to focus on exporting rawer commodities, such as timber, furs, and agricultural surplus.

Brocaded Silk Waistcoat, Spitalfields, England, ca. 1734.   The intricate, three-dimensional floral ornamentation is representative of new designs that emerged in the 1730s. Throughout British America, material life acquired a flashier appearance. Clothing, furniture, and wallpaper were available in brighter colors by midcentury. *Digital Image ©Museum Associates/LACMA, Licensed by Art Resource, NY*

Parliament also explicitly forbade the manufacture of specific goods, such as hats, in the colonies. Yet the bigger obstacle to colonial manufacturing was that because most free colonists wanted to become independent farmers, labor costs were high, and therefore domestic industries could not compete effectively with British products. Even as populations and per capita income grew, the colonies continued to import everything from paper and ink to nails and firearms. This shared dependence helped cultivate new connections among colonists.

● As part of its efforts to bind its American colonies to the commercial empire, the British government also took modest steps to build a communications infrastructure. In the seventeenth century, letters had been carried by individuals or collected and distributed informally by ship captains. In 1711, Parliament brought together the mail systems of England, Ireland, Scotland, and North America (both the mainland and the island colonies) into a single bureaucracy that could raise revenue for the empire. In principle, the postal system now connected residents of the different societies in British America, but only insofar as those residents were also part of a bigger network centered in London. Most colonists did not use this service regularly to correspond with England or with other residents of the empire, but the existence of a single channel of communication linking port cities on both sides of the Atlantic reinforced the claim that the colonies were part of a unified imperial realm. ●

MEDIA AND INFORMATION

MILITARY ALLIANCE

Britain's empire was a massive commercial operation, but it was also a military power ready to wage war on land and sea at any opportunity to gain an advantage over its rivals in Catholic Europe. These imperial conflicts thrust together residents of different British North American colonies, because all British settlements became potential targets for the empire's enemies. In periods of imperial war, then, American colonists were likely to feel especially British.

During these wars, militias from the different colonies fought on the same side—often under the command of British officers sent from London—against Native American and French forces. Further, imperial authorities established forts along frontier areas, which created lines of communication between colonies. In the 1750s, when conflicts in the Ohio River valley threatened to spread into a larger war with France, Britain's Board of Trade instructed its colonies to coordinate plans for defending the empire's holdings and to strengthen their alliance with the Iroquois League. Accordingly, in the summer of 1754, seven colonies sent delegates to a convention at Albany, which was selected because of its traditional role as a site of Covenant Chain negotiations between New York and the Mohawk. The **Albany Convention** marked an unprecedented affirmation of the common interests of different societies within Britain's growing empire.

Delegates in Albany endorsed a **Plan of Union,** proposed by Benjamin Franklin, to create a single governing authority for defense purposes. According to the plan, a Grand Council of delegates from thirteen mainland colonies would meet annually to consider security measures and to negotiate treaties with Native Americans that would be binding on all colonies. Franklin's proposal was not to create the beginnings of a new autonomous state but to tie the various settlements closer together as parts of a single empire. In any case, the Albany Plan was rejected unanimously by the colonies' assemblies, whose representatives feared that they would lose power. Critics of the proposed union also worried that the plan might entail taxation for common defense and doubted that the colonies could execute a unified policy toward Native Americans. On the native side as well, the Albany gathering bore no obvious fruit. Few non-Mohawk delegates attended, and none of the other Iroquois nations committed themselves to fighting

"Join, or Die."   Benjamin Franklin's political cartoon, published in the *Pennsylvania Gazette,* May 9, 1754, is most familiar as an icon of unity during the Revolutionary War, but it originally appeared at the time of the Albany Convention. *Library of Congress Prints and Photographs Division [LC-USZC4-5315]*

the French. Both the British colonies and their native allies were reluctant to commit to Franklin's vision of imperial unity.

THE FRENCH AND INDIAN WAR

Britain and its North American colonies experienced a brief period of relatively peaceful relations with other European powers after the War of the Austrian Succession. Then in 1754, the empire entered a new imperial war, the first to originate in the colonies themselves (see Map 5.3).

Violence between French and British soldiers in Ohio had escalated quickly in a North American conflict that British colonists would call the **French and Indian War.** It then spread into a global conflagration (known as the Seven Years' War of the Great War for Empire) that struck contemporaries as unprecedented in its scope and magnitude. As a Moravian missionary representing the Pennsylvania colony told an audience of Delaware people, "So long as the world has stood there has not been such a War." But not even the missionary could have anticipated the decisive impact that this event would have on North American politics.

WAR ERUPTS IN THE OHIO COUNTRY

Tensions along the borderlands between New France and the British colonies provided the spark that ignited the much wider war. Land-seeking British settlers and speculators were pushing west from Pennsylvania and Virginia into the Ohio country, while British merchants were beginning to trade with native groups whose allegiances the French could no longer afford to secure with gifts. In response, France began building forts to protect its claims to the region. The largest of these bastions, Fort Duquesne at the meeting of the Ohio, Allegheny, and Monongahela Rivers, was especially threatening to British colonists. French traders used the fort to supply weapons to the Delaware and Shawnee, and the colonists worried that the well-placed French stronghold would become a base for attacks on British lands.

In May 1754, a small force of Virginia militiamen led by twenty-two-year-old Major George Washington, along with

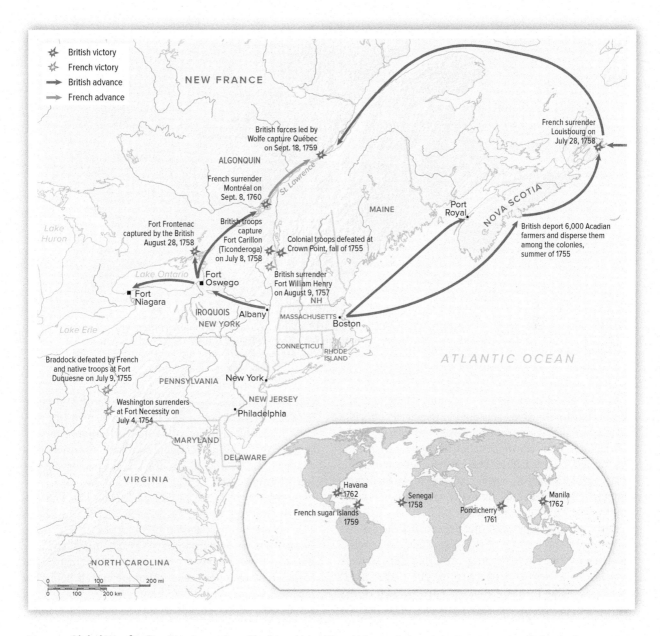

Map 5.3 Global War for Empire, 1754–1763. The Seven Years' War, which actually lasted nine years, counting all of its far-flung theaters, entangled European powers in conflicts as far away as North America, the West Indies, South America, West Africa, South Asia, and the Pacific Ocean.

Mingo warriors under the command of the Seneca half-king Tanaghrisson, initiated a surprise attack against French troops in western Pennsylvania and built Fort Necessity just southeast of Fort Duquesne. As British colonial and Iroquois delegates gathered in Albany to plan for the defense of their lands against the French and French-allied Native Americans, word arrived that Washington had been compelled by enemy forces to surrender the fort.

Clearly, Virginia was now at war, and royal authorities in London sent two regiments of Irish troops under the command of General Edward Braddock to support an invasion of the Ohio River valley. Braddock led a large, combined force of British army regulars and colonial militiamen (but no native allies) against Fort Duquesne in 1755, only to be routed badly at the Battle of the Monongahela. A smaller army of French, Ottawas, Ojibwa, and Potawatomi

Nineteenth-Century Engraving of the Fort William Henry Massacre. French officials offered to compensate native warriors with 2 gallons of rum if they would let the British prisoners go, but as one Native American explained to a Frenchman, "I make war for plunder, scalps, and prisoners. You are satisfied with a fort, and you let your enemy and mine live." **Question for Analysis:** What are the sympathies and perspective of this nineteenth-century artist? *Historicus, Inc.*

attacked the British, fatally wounding Braddock and thwarting the invasion. Washington managed to form a rear guard, disengage from the battle, and save a portion of the force from destruction, but Braddock's expedition had ended in utter failure. The French also captured the slain general's papers, which revealed the larger British military plan at the time—to capture strategic points along the Great Lakes and in Canada.

For the next three years, the French and their native allies racked up a string of victories. They took control of Lake Ontario in 1756 after capturing Fort Oswego on the lake's New York shore. From there, they drove south into New York and attacked **Fort William Henry** at the southern end of Lake George with a massive army in 1757. When the fort fell after a six-day siege, the French commander, Marquis de Montcalm, granted the surrendering army the right to leave with their arms and possessions as long as they pledged not to take up arms against France for eighteen months. Such generous terms had ample precedent in European chivalric practices, but the two thousand Native Americans who had joined the assault (many of whom had traveled hundreds of miles from their homes) felt entitled to their share of captives and war spoils. Acting on those grounds, the native soldiers attacked the British who were peaceably evacuating the fort. Although the ensuing massacre both frightened and mobilized British colonists, it also opened a breach in the alliance between French and Native Americans. Sensing that they played by different rules and had different priorities, the two sides grew reluctant to band together. This change of heart would have great consequences for the war's future course.

Across the Atlantic in Europe, meanwhile, France, Austria, Russia, Saxony, and Sweden banded together in 1756 to block the expansion of Frederick II of Prussia. Great Britain promptly joined the Prussian side, and now the British were fighting a war on two continents. The French took the upper hand in Europe as well, capturing the Mediterranean island of Minorca in the opening naval battle of the Seven Years' War and precipitating a political crisis in London that almost turned out Britain's governing administration. Soon the conflict spread through western and central Europe and as far away as India. From the British standpoint by 1757, however, the most troubling developments were taking place in North America, where France seemed poised to invade New England and conquer the continent.

THE TIDE TURNS

Britain's imperial fortunes improved dramatically in 1758 after two major shifts in policy transformed the war effort. First, colonists turned their attention to improving relations with the native groups in the Ohio country. At the **Easton Treaty conference** that year, the colony of Pennsylvania committed itself to protecting the Delaware people's land claims by prohibiting further white settlement north and west of the Alleghenies. Pennsylvania also returned some territory to the Iroquois League that had been ceded four years earlier. With the Ohio people no longer at war with Britain, and France's native alliances frayed, the balance of power in the region tilted. Slowly, the war in North America became primarily between French and British armies, and France's early advantage disappeared. Feeling vulnerable, the French even blew up Fort Duquesne rather than have it fall into enemy hands.

Britain's other crucial move was to turn to massive deficit spending, by borrowing heavily to subsidize the North American campaign, a policy advocated by Secretary of State William Pitt. Britain thereby offered colonists an inducement to assume a greater share of the fighting. Parliament would cover the rising costs of the war (for weaponry, provisions, and salaries) if the colonies would provide the manpower. As a result, after 1758, residents of the American colonies accounted for a majority of the enlisted military forces on the British side, putting the French, whose ranks were diminished by the flagging enthusiasm of their native allies, at a severe numerical disadvantage. New France's population of men of military age had barely reached sixteen thousand at the time of the war, but on the other side, fifty thousand residents of the British North American colonies joined the military effort in 1758 alone.

The new policies had a decisive impact. In July 1759, an army of about thirty-five hundred British soldiers and colonial militiamen, supported by nearly one thousand Iroquois soldiers, captured Fort Niagara, while British general Jeffrey Amherst led a successful attack on Lake George and forced a French retreat into Canada. Another British force besieged the fortress city of Quebec. French commander Marquis de Montcalm held off the invaders for two months, but in September 1759 the city fell to the British. The following year, when Montréal fell as well, the surrender of New France was complete. France's close native allies, the Seven Nations of Canada, also made peace with the British. By the close of 1760, Canada was in British hands.

THE END OF WAR

The surrender of New France did not conclude the war in Europe but there, too, Britain's new fiscal policies had borne fruit. By increasing its financial support to the Prussians and Hanoverians, who exchanged heavy blows with Russia and Austria and tied up French troops on the European continent, Britain was able to defeat thinning French forces in West Africa and the Caribbean in 1759 and off the coast of India in 1760. In an effort to check Britain's imperial expansion and prevent a radical shift in Europe's political balance, Spain entered the war on the side of France in 1762. Havana, the central port of Spain's lucrative Caribbean empire, then became a British target. Because the British navy had seized Spain's mail ships, the Spanish in Cuba had no idea that they were at war with Britain and were unprepared for the amphibious attack that came in June 1762. Fifteen thousand British troops, including approximately four thousand volunteers from New York and New England, laid siege to Havana for two months and ultimately captured the strategically valuable city. In October, Spain was forced to surrender the Philippine port of Manila to Britain as well.

Over the course of 1762, Britain's enemies began negotiating an end to the conflict. Whereas treaties concluding earlier imperial wars typically sought to restore some balance of power, the scale of the British victory, especially in the Americas, made such an arrangement unlikely in this case. Pitt hoped to impose a settlement that would permanently hobble France as an imperial rival. Other voices in British politics disagreed, fearing that a one-sided peace would isolate Great Britain from the rest of Europe and lead to future imperial clashes.

The two treaties ending the global conflict, both signed in February 1763, contrasted sharply. The Treaty of Hubertusburg, which focused on Europe, simply restored Austria's and Prussia's prewar borders. The **Treaty of Paris,** on the other hand, radically altered the geography of France, Spain, and Great Britain's overseas empires (see Figure 5.1). From a territorial standpoint, Britain emerged the big winner from the treaty negotiations. Indeed, in return for some important concessions in Africa, the Caribbean, and India, France transferred Canada and all French territory east of the Mississippi River to Great Britain. British North America now spanned the entire eastern half of the continent, from Hudson Bay down to the Gulf of Mexico (see Map 5.4).

Britain's territorial acquisitions would yield significant profits from the Great Lakes fur trade and the St. Lawrence fisheries. Had British negotiators been concerned primarily with international commerce, however, they never would have considered trading Havana and Guadeloupe, which exported more sugar than all British possessions combined, for cold stretches of Canada. But

Guadeloupe (captured from France in 1759); Grand Banks fisheries off Newfoundland, Canada

GREAT BRITAIN

Havana (captured from Spain in 1762)

Canada and territory east of the Mississippi River

Florida

SPAIN

FRANCE

Louisiana Colony

Figure 5.1 Key Territorial Exchange in the Treaty of Paris. In sheer land mass, French concessions to Britain were enormous. But France was able to regain control of most of the territories that had been captured in the war, including the Caribbean islands of Guadeloupe, Saint Lucia, and Martinique; the African slave-trading colony of Gorée; and trading posts in India. Spain retained Havana and Manila, which Britain had also taken during the conflict.

in 1763, the security of Britain's populous mainland colonies seemed paramount. Removing the French, with their Catholic missions and their diplomatic ties to the continent's indigenous powers, from North America could achieve that goal without destabilizing power relations in Europe.

Still, the treaty proved unpopular with many observers in Britain, and even with Secretary Pitt. By letting France keep its maritime possessions in the Caribbean and Newfoundland, Pitt observed, "We have given her the means of recovering her prodigious losses and of becoming once more formidable to us at sea." France would indeed recover from the war soon enough and become a formidable foe for the next half century, but the challenges of the Treaty of Paris to the British Empire would come as much from what the French gave up as what it retained. London now faced the political and financial costs of governing a much vaster colonial society.

A NEW IMPERIAL MAP

The year 1763 would mark the high point in American colonists' sense of belonging to the British Empire. It was also a turning point. As colonial leaders and British authorities faced the challenges of governing an enlarged domain, North Americans of different ethnicities,

religions, and national allegiances struggled to adjust to the decisions made by diplomats on the other side of the Atlantic. The most difficult adjustments came in Indian country, where many native groups rejected the Treaty of Paris and fought to preserve their independence. The Native American conflict that followed the British victory would drive a wedge between the interests of colonial settlers and those of the empire.

ASSESSING THE COSTS OF WAR

Britain's stunning and decisive victory in the French and Indian War came at a high price. Immense human sacrifices had been made, both by colonists and by British soldiers and sailors brought from across the ocean. In New England, no military conflict since King Philip's War had killed such a large share of the population. ● Britain's regular army had suffered at even ghastlier rates. Diseases had ravaged the redcoats, especially in the Caribbean. During the siege of Havana, for example, close to six thousand soldiers and sailors died, mostly from yellow fever, gastric illness, and other diseases. ●

DISEASE AND EPIDEMIC

American colonists and British residents weighed the relative significance of these sacrifices differently. Colonists claimed credit for having won the war. Some also wondered why they had put their lives on the line to capture Caribbean islands that would be used as bargaining chips among European powers. British soldiers, on the other hand, saw themselves as protecting the colonists, whom they regarded as ungrateful and often obstructionist. And British officers found colonial soldiers undisciplined—as General James Wolfe put it, "contemptible cowardly dogs." For their part, some colonial soldiers chafed under British martial law and bitterly resented the arrogance of their commanders from overseas.

The practical question of how to apportion the war's astronomical costs proved even more divisive. Britain's victories across the globe and its conquests in New France had been financed by loans from wealthy private investors. When the Seven Years' War started, Britain's national debt stood at 74.6 million pounds. By the time of the treaty, it exceeded 122.6 million pounds despite significant tax hikes during the war years (see How Much Is That? Britain's Postwar Debt). The annual interest alone on that sum amounted to more than half the national budget. The British government, now led by Prime Minister George Grenville, sought to pass some of this debt along to the colonies.

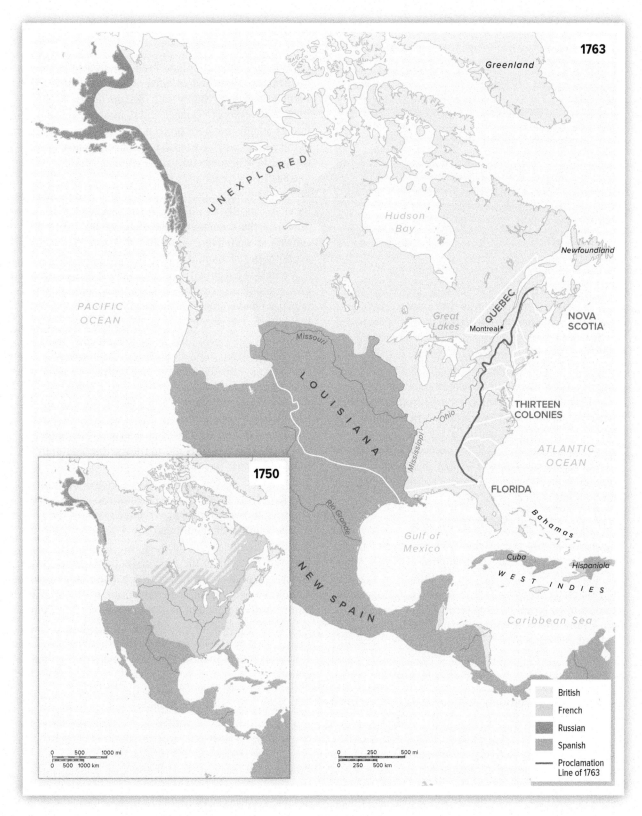

Map 5.4 North America as Envisioned Under the Treaty of Paris, with Comparison to European Land Claims in 1750. By removing the French from mainland North America, the treaty altered the European map of North America. Note that these maps, like the treaty itself, marked only European land claims, ignoring issues of Native American sovereignty and political power.

How Much Is That?

Britain's Postwar Debt

In 1763, Britain's national debt was 122.6 million pounds. That is equivalent to about 20.5 billion U.S. dollars in 2020. That figure may not sound staggering in the context of modern policies of deficit spending (the U.S. federal deficit in 2020 stood at 3.1 trillion dollars), but in relation to the size of Britain's national budget, the 1763 debt was much larger.

What made Grenville's policy especially tricky politically was the fact that colonists were used to paying significantly lower taxes than Britons in the home countries. To British eyes, this consideration only confirmed the equity of asking the colonists to contribute to the costs of administering and defending the empire. But to American colonists, who had come to expect minimal taxation, even a modest assessment felt burdensome. So when Parliament, in the 1764 **Sugar Act,** sought to shore up an import tax on West Indian molasses that the colonists had ignored or circumvented for decades, a firestorm of protest erupted (see Chapter 6). British attempts to raise revenues from American colonists plotted a course of deep political conflict.

POPULATIONS ON THE MOVE

The new map created by the 1763 treaty rewrote the boundaries dividing European empires in North America. But lands officially labeled as British on the new imperial map did not suddenly become English speaking, Protestant, and loyal to King George III of England. As news of the Treaty of Paris circulated through the continent, colonists and native people had to decide what difference the new boundaries made. Their decisions about whether and where to move shaped postwar North America as well.

Most native inhabitants of the lands contested during the war rejected and resisted the peace treaty, to which they had not been signatories (see the section Revolution in Indian Country), but several native groups in eastern Canada chose to migrate after the war. As British officials and settlers began moving into southern Quebec, the Abenaki, who had fought on the French side, headed to the margins of their earlier settlements. The Mi'kmaqs left their homes in Nova Scotia, either for the St. Pierre and Miquelon Islands retained by France or for distant parts of Newfoundland where British authority existed only on paper.

Britain's conquest of New France prompted an exodus of French soldiers and colonial officials, but most other French Canadians stayed put. Britain hoped to attract Protestant settlers to Quebec and to integrate that colony into its empire, but both projects faltered, in part because of the perception that French Canada remained culturally foreign. Few Britons and British colonists immigrated to Quebec in the years after the war, and although Britain set up a Protestant-controlled government that conducted its affairs mostly in English, French-speaking Catholics remained the dominant population. After 1763, French Canadians were living under British sovereignty without adopting British culture.

French colonists in the Great Lakes and Illinois posed a greater problem to the British, since trade, social relations, marriage, and cultural identity had integrated them with the indigenous people. Some British officials favored expelling French colonists from this region. Along the Mississippi River, many of them left voluntarily, crossing west (along with their native neighbors) into what was then **Spanish Louisiana.** Although Spain's flag now flew over the forts and cities in this colony, French colonial society largely persisted. The city of St. Louis was established in 1763 on territory that had just been ceded to Spain (though residents did not learn that fact until the following year). But its name, population, architecture, and overall character were distinctly French. Downriver, the older French city of New Orleans also fell to Spanish control, but French influences remained.

The transfer of Louisiana from France to Spain had further, significant consequences: It brought more enslaved Africans to the territory and reshuffled Native American politics in Texas, where the Caddo people could no longer exploit the competition between French and Spanish powers. But here, too, the removal of French power did not lead to the removal of French people or French culture. In fact, more French people moved to Louisiana under Spanish rule than when it was a French colony.

● One remarkable legacy of the postwar French migration is Louisiana's Cajun community. At the war's onset, British authorities in Nova Scotia, suspicious of the loyalties of a large group of French speakers in the settlement of Acadia there, exiled six thousand Acadians to English-speaking colonies farther south. Dispersed through North America in small groups, Acadians faced hostility wherever they landed. Virginia simply refused to admit them. Some sought refuge in France. Meanwhile, New England settlers had moved north to claim the exiled Acadians' farmland. By 1763, a far-flung **Acadian diaspora** of thirteen

CROSSING BORDERS

Colonial Legacies.   This 1909 painting of the famous Jackson Square in New Orleans shows the enduring imprint of both French and Spanish rule on the cityscape. The Cabildo (left) was the seat of Spanish colonial government after 1762, whereas the St. Louis Cathedral (center) reflects the earlier French presence, extending a tradition of Catholic churches on this site dating back to 1718. French architectural influence also appears on the Cabildo's mansard roof, added later. *The Picture Art Collection/Alamy Stock Photo*

CROSSING BORDERS

thousand refugees from Nova Scotia had settled in numerous communities on both sides of the Atlantic Ocean. Only three hundred of them had made their way to French Louisiana, but with the encouragement of Spanish authorities, Acadians began migrating to French-speaking Louisiana and formed a new Cajun culture there. Today, we identify that culture with a complex cuisine that incorporates Louisiana vegetables and various culinary influences from the surrounding Native American and African populations. •

In contrast to New France and Louisiana, Spanish Florida evacuated quickly once territory changed hands. Britain divided the territory into two colonies, West Florida and East Florida, and granted religious toleration to the three thousand Spanish subjects there. But Florida's colonists had shallow attachments to the region and were not eager to stay and test the limits of that toleration. With the financial support of the Spanish Empire, which offered them property in Cuba, Florida's colonial population moved south en masse to the center of the Spanish Caribbean.

As Native Americans, French, and Spanish sought their places within and beyond the expanded borders of British sovereignty, British colonists rushed north to Canada, south to Florida, and especially west into areas still controlled by Native Americans. Migrating settlers sought lands that now seemed accessible to them—in many cases, lands deep in the interior of the continent that lay well beyond the control of provincial governments. Adding to this flood of colonial settlers was a tidal wave of foreign immigration, which had begun in the prewar years and resumed following the Treaty of Paris. Emigrants came in especially large numbers from Scotland after the war and settled along the periphery of British America—in Georgia, the Carolinas, western Pennsylvania, upper New York, and Canada. Some of these areas were called the backcountry, but from another perspective they represented the advancing frontier of an aggressive settler society.

REVOLUTION IN INDIAN COUNTRY

The Treaty of Paris outraged the indigenous population of the region where British colonists were finding new homes. Native Americans had not participated in the treaty negotiations, nor did they consider themselves vanquished. Even those native groups who had fought alongside the French had done so for their own reasons and on their own terms. Moreover, they wondered, by what right could nations from across the ocean dispose of indigenous lands to settle their disputes? As a Delaware representative explained to an ambassador from Pennsylvania in 1758, "You white people are the cause of this war; why do not you and the *French* fight in the old country, and on the sea?"

But if Native Americans objected to the premise of the war, they also clearly saw the ominous implications of its resolution. Throughout the imperial wars of the eighteenth century, native groups had fought to preserve their independence by aligning themselves strategically with one of the European powers. The ascent of the British and the departure of the French spelled an abrupt end to that political strategy. Now, British forts arose on Native American lands in the trans-Appalachian West, and the indigenous people could no longer rely on European allies to dislodge the intruders. Native Americans' resentment of the new local power intensified once they realized that the British were not interested in gift exchanges or diplomacy. General Jeffrey Amherst, the British commander in chief, expected the native people to trade furs as dutiful subjects, not as allies—and given the urgent need for fiscal restraint, there was no room in the imperial budget for gifts.

In April 1763, an Ottawa chief named Pontiac convened a war council of Native Americans from the Great Lakes and the Ohio Valley, announcing a campaign to purge the land of the British. **Pontiac's Rebellion** drew on the teachings of Neolin, a Delaware prophet who exhorted native peoples of various ethnicities to band together under a common banner, return to their cultural roots, and "live without any Trade or Connection with the White people." Neolin's pan-Indian message lumped whites together, but to Pontiac some white people were more dangerous than others, and it was the transition from French to British power that alarmed him: "You see as well as I do that we can no longer supply our needs, as we have done, from our brothers the French." For Pontiac, the problem was less that trade with whites had become corrupting than that it had become exploitative: "The English sell us goods twice as dear as the French do, and their goods do not last."

Over the next few months, Pontiac and his men seized nine British forts spread over a vast region, and they besieged the city of Detroit for half a year. Native Americans killed five hundred British soldiers and hundreds of white settlers, reclaiming much of the land where the war had begun in 1754. Through much of the summer of 1763, the British Empire struggled to keep its hold on its western territories.

Committed to using all necessary measures to destroy his Native American enemies, General Amherst ordered his officers to take no prisoners. • He even contemplated the use of germ warfare, proposing to Colonel Henry Bouquet that the British "Send the Small Pox among those Disaffected Tribes of Indians." Two months earlier, the commander at Fort Pitt appears to have given blankets infected with smallpox to the Delaware people who had come on a diplomatic mission, but there is no evidence tying that event to Amherst. Historians debate whether British stratagems were, in fact, responsible for smallpox outbreaks during the spring and summer of Pontiac's Rebellion. •

By the fall of 1763, the war for independence was losing steam. William Johnson used his alliance with the Seven Nations of Canada to put diplomatic pressure on the indigenous groups allied with Pontiac to end the siege of Detroit. The following year, two British armies invaded Ohio, and the eastern groups of Pontiac's coalition made peace. Pontiac himself finally came to terms a year later. Amherst had been recalled to England, and his successors dealt more cautiously with the Native Americans, resuming gift exchanges and relying on diplomatic negotiations.

(vertical margin text) DISEASE AND EPIDEMIC

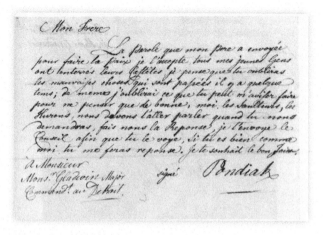

Letter Composed by Pontiac, 1763. The Native American rebel leader's letter, written in French, lifts the siege of Detroit. **Question for Analysis:** What is the significance of Pontiac's use of French? *Pontiac*

BRITAIN'S NEW NATIVE AMERICAN POLICIES

Although Pontiac's struggle for independence had failed to remove the British from Indian country, he succeeded in establishing the key point that Native Americans regarded Ohio and the Great Lakes region as their land. By capturing forts, besieging settlements, and killing colonists, the rebellion persuaded imperial officials that they could not rule all of the inhabitants as subjects of the British Crown. In October 1763, with Detroit still under siege, King George III promulgated a royal proclamation (see Interpreting the Sources: The Proclamation of 1763 and the Wampum Belt of 1764) establishing the Appalachian Mountains as the western border of Euro-American settlement. Thereafter, colonists could not settle or purchase land west of the **Proclamation Line of 1763** without special royal authorization. Designers of the new policy did not expect the line between white and Native American land to remain fixed, but they did intend to keep firm control over changes to the boundary.

British officials had several motivations for creating a partition between Native American land and the colonies. The Easton Treaty of 1758, which had helped turn the tide of the war, committed the empire to protecting the lands of its native allies, while the terms of New France's surrender obligated Britain to allow those Native Americans who had sided with the French to "be maintained on the Lands they inhabit." Britain also recognized that slowing the westward flow of white settlement would make the colonies easier and cheaper to administer and might redirect Anglo-Protestant migrants toward territories in Canada and Florida where European Catholics had dominated. But the violence ignited by Pontiac made the proclamation's goals

INTERPRETING THE SOURCES

The Proclamation of 1763 and the Wampum Belt of 1764

Britain's royal proclamation of 1763 aimed to solve an immediate crisis in Indian country, but it would have far-reaching consequences for relations between whites and Native American and colonial politics. For decades, this document regulated native peoples' claims in British North America and established both the legal basis and the legal limitations of those claims. Although the proclamation was a unilateral gesture on the part of the British Crown, and not a negotiated treaty, one year later, two thousand Native Americans representing twenty-four nations in British North America gathered in Niagara, New York, to ratify the new political order.

At the Niagara convention, William Johnson read the text of the proclamation, and the native delegates acknowledged it as the terms of a new peace. To express and codify their agreement, the Native Americans presented a Gus Wen Tah—a belt of purple wampum beads representing the respectful separation of British and Native American nations. Following are excerpts from the proclamation and a picture of a replica of the wampum belt.

And whereas it is just and reasonable, and essential to our Interest, and the Security of our Colonies, that the several Nations or Tribes of Indians with whom We are connected, and who live under our Protection, should not be molested or disturbed in the Possession of such Parts of Our Dominions and Territories as, not having been ceded to or purchased by Us, are reserved to them or any of them, as their Hunting Grounds.—We do therefore . . . declare . . . that no Governor or Commander in Chief in any of our Colonies of Quebec, East Florida. or West Florida, do presume, upon any Pretence whatever, to grant Warrants of Survey, or pass any Patents for Lands beyond the Bounds of their respective Governments . . . : as also that no Governor or Commander in Chief in any of our other Colonies or Plantations in America do presume for the present, and until our further Pleasure be known, to grant Warrants of Survey, or pass Patents for any Lands beyond the Heads or Sources of any of the Rivers which fall into the Atlantic Ocean from the West and North West, or upon any Lands whatever, which, not having been ceded to or purchased by Us as aforesaid, are reserved to the said Indians, or any of them.

And We do further . . . reserve . . . for the use of the said Indians, all the Lands and Territories not included within the Limits of Our said Three new Governments, or within the Limits of the Territory granted to the Hudson's Bay Company, as also all the Lands and Territories lying to the Westward of the Sources of the Rivers which fall into the Sea from the West and North West as aforesaid.

And We do hereby strictly forbid, on Pain of our Displeasure, all our loving Subjects from making any Purchases or Settlements whatever, or taking Possession of any of the Lands above reserved without our especial leave and Licence for that Purpose first obtained.

And We do further strictly enjoin and require all Persons whatever who have either wilfully or inadvertently seated themselves upon any Lands within the Countries above described or upon any other Lands which . . . are still reserved to the said Indians as aforesaid, forthwith to remove themselves from such Settlements.

And whereas great Frauds and Abuses have been committed in purchasing Lands of the Indians, . . . : In order, therefore, to prevent such Irregularities for the future, and to the end that the Indians may be convinced of our Justice and determined Resolution to remove all reasonable Cause of Discontent, We . . . strictly enjoin and require, that no private Person do presume to make any purchase from the said Indians of any Lands reserved to the said Indians. . . . [If] any of the Said Indians should be inclined to dispose of the said Lands, the same shall be Purchased only for Us, in our Name, at some public Meeting or Assembly of the said Indians.

. . .

Given at our Court at St. James's the 7th Day of October 1763, in the Third Year of our Reign.

Explore the Source

1. In what ways do these two kinds of primary sources, the text and the belt, differ?

2. How does the language of the proclamation reveal British attitudes toward Native Americans? Toward colonists?

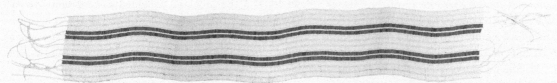

Replica Belt. The original 1764 diplomatic belt would have featured purple wampum arranged in this pattern. ©*City of Brantford*

Political Cartoon Criticizing the Quakers' Friendly Relations with Native Americans and Supporting the Paxton Boys, 1764. Quaker merchant Abel James distributes tomahawks to Native Americans from a barrel belonging to Quaker Party leader Israel Pemberton, who is shown embracing a native woman. James says, "Exercise those on the Scotch Irish & Dutch & Ill support you while I am Abel." Benjamin Franklin brandishes a purse of "Pennsylvania Money." *The Granger Collection, New York*

appear more urgent, because Britain could not afford perpetual war in unregulated territories. From the standpoint of the empire, restricting settlement was the price of peace in the western part of British America.

The Proclamation of 1763 did not automatically remove white settlers from western lands, or seal off the border to new arrivals from the colonies. The new British policy did discourage settlement, however, especially among land speculators who needed to have their land titles legally recognized in order to secure their investments. George Washington, viewing the proclamation as "a temporary expedient to quiet the Minds of the Indians," advised fellow speculators to scout out good land and stake their claims until the line moved westward or disappeared. Other colonists simply took their chances—and their guns—and moved west. In all of those cases, settlers' demands for access to western lands pitted them against the rule of the empire—and fueled a growing antipathy between Britain and the colonies.

Questions of policy towards indigenous peoples also divided the colonists themselves. On both sides of the new line, backcountry settlers advocated and implemented a harder, more violent approach to clearing Native American land, which sometimes put them at odds with coastal residents. In Pennsylvania, frontier settlers challenged the political authority of Quaker pacifists centered in Philadelphia. At the end of 1763, on the heels of the royal proclamation and in the midst of war with Pontiac, fifty Scots-Irish farmers from the town of Paxton in Lancaster County went on a killing spree, murdering Conestogas, a native group friendly to the colony, and mutilating their corpses. In January, these farmers, known as the **Paxton Boys,** led an army of five hundred through the streets of Philadelphia, demanding that the colony allocate money and soldiers to defend the frontier. No participant in the Paxton massacre was prosecuted, and the incident remained a vivid reminder of how difficult it would be to control violence between whites and Native Americans. Thus, despite the assurances of the Proclamation of 1763, British colonists and Native Americans continued to live in tense proximity on both sides of the Appalachians.

CONCLUSION

The French and Indian War was a watershed event in North American history. Most dramatically, the outcome signaled the end of the imperial conflict on the eastern half of the continent that many native groups had strategically exploited to maintain their political independence and hold on to their lands. After 1763, for the first time, native peoples faced a political map marked by a single eastern frontier, with British colonists advancing westward. The departure of the French also altered the position of the colonists in relation to Great Britain. More than half a century of imperial war and transatlantic commerce had brought the original English colonies closer to one another and more thoroughly identified with the empire and its military power. But now colonists no longer needed imperial protection against France. Instead, they saw a British state preparing to tax them and impeding their access to western lands.

Global conflict had impoverished France, leaving its regime vulnerable to a major revolution before the eighteenth century's end. But the settlement of the French and Indian War would hurt the victor as well. As he surrendered his country's North American colonies, the French foreign minister consoled himself with the prescient prediction that Britain would not be able to maintain control of its growing empire.

STUDY TERMS

Covenant Chain	French and Indian War
Tuscarora War	Fort William Henry
Queen Anne's War	Easton Treaty conference
War of Jenkins's Ear	Treaty of Paris
King George's War	Sugar Act
Caddo	Spanish Louisiana
Comanchería	Acadian diaspora
Indian liquor trade	Pontiac's Rebellion
empire of goods	Proclamation Line of 1763
Albany Convention	Paxton Boys
Plan of Union	

FURTHER READING

A database of additional full-text readings is available through Power of Process for Primary Sources in Connect.

Fred Anderson, *The War That Made America* (2005), provides a comprehensive account of the war as the major event in the lives of North Americans during the era.

Juliana Barr, *Peace Came in the Form of a Woman* (2007), demonstrates the importance of women to white–Native American diplomacy in the Texas borderlands.

T. H. Breen, *Marketplace of Revolution* (2004), illuminates the growth of Britain's empire of goods in North America.

Colin Calloway, *The Scratch of the Pen* (2006), casts 1763 as a pivotal year in the history of North America.

Pekka Hämäläinen, *The Comanche Empire* (2008), charts the growth of an overlooked political power in the American Plains and Southwest.

Daniel Richter, *Facing East from Indian Country* (2001), narrates the European colonization of North America from a native perspective and presents the French and Indian War as a turning point in that story.

Peter Silver, *Our Savage Neighbors* (2009), shows how fear of Native American attack united a diverse society of immigrants to the British colonies in the 1750s.

Susan Sleeper-Smith, *Indigenous Prosperity and American Conquest* (2018), emphasizes the economic achievements of native women in the Ohio River valley.

Richard White, *The Middle Ground* (1991), highlights the role of culture in the diplomatic politics of the Great Lakes region in order to rethink the history of white–Native American relations in North America before 1815.

Sophie White, *Wild Frenchmen and Frenchified Indians* (2014), explores how clothing, language, and religion blurred lines of racial identity in colonial Louisiana during this period.

1765–1781

6 | CRISIS & WAR

Chapter Questions

1. What were the colonists' central grievances, concerns, and beliefs in their growing rebellion against Parliament?

2. How does the Revolutionary War fit within a larger history of urban unrest and popular violence in the colonies?

3. What distinctive perspective did African Americans, both free and enslaved, have on the war?

4. How did the war unfold and progress, and what were its crucial turning points?

Toppling a Regime. Supporters of the colonial rebellion in New York City pull down the statue of King George III in 1776, as depicted by a nineteenth-century artist. *Private Collection/Picture Research Consultants & Archives*

Hauled into court in Salisbury, Connecticut, in 1765 for beating up two men over a business quarrel, Ethan Allen removed his clothing, raised his fist, and branded his accuser a liar. According to court records, Allen, his 6-foot, 4-inch naked frame towering above everyone else in the room, then announced "with a loud voice . . . that he would spill the blood of any that opposed him." The judge dismissed the charges in return for a promise that Allen would leave town.

Allen continued to run afoul of the local authorities in his next New England community, and in 1769 he bought cheap farmland from New Hampshire and resettled in the Green Mountain region (now in Vermont). Allen and his neighbors soon discovered, however, that their land was claimed by New York.

1765

Quartering Act passed
Stamp Act passed and protested

1766

Stamp Act repealed
Jenny Slew files one of the colonies' first freedom suits

1767

Townshend Duties passed

1770

All Townshend Duties repealed (except tax on tea)
Boston Massacre

1773

Tea Act passed
Boston Tea Party

1774

Intolerable Acts passed
Committees of Correspondence displace
British authority in Massachusetts
First Continental Congress

1775

Battle of Lexington and Concord
Lord Dunmore's Proclamation
Second Continental Congress
King George III declares thirteen mainland colonies to be in rebellion

1776

Thomas Paine's *Common Sense* published
Continental Congress declares independence from
Great Britain

1777

Iroquois end their neutrality in the Revolutionary War
British general John Burgoyne surrenders at Saratoga

1778

France declares war on Great Britain

1779

Spain declares war on Great Britain

1780

Netherlands declares war on Great Britain

1781

British forces surrender at Yorktown

When authorities from New York tried to evict them, Allen led a militia of men holding New Hampshire deeds, called the Green Mountain Boys, which waged a successful vigilante campaign against those who sought to enforce the authority of the colony of New York.

Ethan Allen and his militia are better remembered today for their role in the massive war that broke out in 1775 and that ultimately severed the links between Great Britain and thirteen of its American colonies. But the Green Mountain Boys did not begin with talk of political independence. Outlaw warriors in northern New England, Allen's men had their own agenda and might easily have stayed out of the war between the rebellious colonies and the British. At least one prominent Green Mountain vigilante even advocated fighting on the British side to help defeat their New York enemies.

The political struggles of the 1770s divided British America in complicated ways, engulfing and absorbing local conflicts as they unleashed violence up and down the eastern seaboard and beyond. The American Revolution, as these struggles came to be known, drew participants with varied goals and ideas, but over the course of the decade a powerful theme emerged. After the Green Mountain Boys captured the largest fortress in British North America in 1775 and ransacked its liquor supply, they toasted "the liberty and freedom of America." Rebellious colonists often used such language to explain their decision to take up arms against Great Britain. Words such as *liberty, freedom,* and *independence* meant different things to different people and reflected a range of ideological influences. But amid the carnage and chaos of the revolutionary era, such rhetoric helped cultivate a unified purpose among those colonists who sought to disentangle themselves from the political bonds that had defined their world up to that point.

THE IMPERIAL CRISIS

During the French and Indian War, the British government and its mainland American colonies had clung tenaciously to one another. But the war left a trail of mutual resentment and staggering debt, and the victory left colonists less dependent on British protection. In an attempt to govern its growing empire, Britain pursued two strategies that alienated colonial leaders and alarmed many segments of the colonial population. First, it stationed more troops in North America. Second, it transferred to American colonists some of the costs of governing the empire. Those two policies became the targets of a new and powerful political opposition in the colonies.

MILITARIZATION OF THE BRITISH COLONIES

British soldiers serving in the French and Indian War had frequently antagonized the colonists they were sent to protect, but Americans nonetheless understood why they were there. Even after the departure of the French in 1763, many colonists appreciated that British troops were suppressing Pontiac's Rebellion and conquering land on the western frontier. In 1765, however, a standing peacetime army of ten thousand British soldiers remained in North America.

In some parts of British America, the presence of redcoated soldiers was reassuring. In Britain's vast Caribbean empire, British warships protected island colonies from their French, Spanish, or Dutch neighbors while army garrisons supported white minorities against the persistent threat of slave rebellions. On most of the mainland, however, British colonies faced neither rival European settlements nor Black majorities. In those colonies, redcoats appeared to be a massive police force.

As he moved troops from Native American land to assume their permanent positions in the eastern settlements, Thomas Gage, commander in chief of Britain's American forces, faced the challenge of housing his men. He requested parliamentary authorization to seize both public and private buildings for this purpose. The British ministry passed the **Quartering Act of 1765,** which authorized the army to house soldiers in inns, livery stables, and houses that sold liquor. If the demand exceeded the capacity of those accommodations, soldiers could also be quartered in "uninhabited houses, outhouses, barns, or other buildings." To some colonists, the new law raised the specter of a military state imposing itself on the rights of private citizens.

TAXATION AND THE QUESTION OF REPRESENTATION

The Quartering Act was not only a military measure; it was a tax, since it required the colonies to pay for housing and feeding soldiers. In mandating that the colonies pay for the empire's military presence, Parliament was bypassing the elected assemblies that had always claimed the right to tax the colonists. Following on the heels of the Sugar Act (see Chapter 5), the Quartering Act was part of Britain's prime minister George Grenville's new program of raising revenue and asserting parliamentary supremacy over the colonial legislatures. Grenville's next move, the **Stamp Act** (1765), would prove even more controversial. Obligations to accommodate British troops and to pay customs on French molasses had precedents. But with the Stamp Act, Britain broke new ground in the colonies by imposing a direct tax that had nothing to do with the regulation of international commerce. Colonists had to pay a tax on all printed matter and every legal document—newspapers, books, pamphlets, almanacs, liquor licenses, land conveyances, college diplomas, wills,

Stamp Act Stamps, 1765. These one-penny stamps were used for newspapers and pamphlets. A similar tax had been in place in Great Britain for a long time, but imposing it in the colonies was a significant innovation in imperial policy. The tax hit especially hard in coastal cities, where printing presses were located. But legal documents and papers circulated deep into the interior, touching a broad segment of the population. *VCG Wilson/Fine Art/Corbis/Getty Images*

and decks of playing cards. These items were required to bear a special stamp verifying that the tax had been paid.

Almost immediately, the stamp tax, as it was known, ignited a major political crisis. Although the tax rate was higher in the West Indies than in North America, it was the mainland colonists who responded with outrage. Their grievance focused less on the financial burden of the tax than on what they perceived to be an assault on their traditional political rights as British subjects. Colonial politicians accused the Stamp Act of suppressing their free press by taxing newspapers and violating their rights to jury trials by granting military courts the power to try accused tax evaders. But most of all, they charged, the law infringed on the prerogatives of their elected assemblies and taxed colonists without their consent. Because colonists did not elect members of Parliament, the Stamp Act amounted to taxation without representation.

Opposition to the tax took different forms. Shortly before the new law was to go into effect, representatives from nine mainland colonies gathered in New York City, where they composed a petition. Addressing themselves to both Parliament and King George III, members of the 1765 **Stamp Act Congress** rejected the idea that a distant government could rightfully impose taxes on its American subjects. Although the petition was deferential in its tone and philosophical in its approach, by this point angry colonists had already engaged in less polite forms of resistance. In the thirteen oldest British colonies on the mainland (everything south of Canada and north of Florida), resisters formed groups called **Sons of Liberty** and mobilized large groups of supporters to take to the streets. In August, a massive crowd in Boston forced the resignation of Andrew Oliver, the colony's designated stamp agent, by hanging him in effigy, destroying his warehouse, and vandalizing his home. In New York, protesters went after the governor, burning his favorite chariot and intimidating him into surrendering the colony's supply of stamps. By the year's end, tax agents in twelve colonies had resigned. Royal officials quickly concluded that the Stamp Act would be unenforceable.

As reports of petitioning, defiant speeches, and violent protests reached Britain, the government faced added pressure from London merchants who worried about the effects of colonial boycotts on their business. Under the leadership of a new prime minister, Lord Rockingham, Parliament repealed the Stamp Act in 1766 and lowered the duty on molasses. At the same time, however, Parliament reaffirmed in the **Declaratory Act** that it had the authority to tax the colonies and that its laws were binding on "the colonies and people of America . . . in all cases whatsoever." Though the controversial tax was now dead, the crisis it had sparked was very much alive. The Stamp Act had unified diverse societies with varied economic interests and different histories of settlement—in opposition to the empire and in support of a principle that Parliament had now officially rejected.

IDEALS AND IMAGES OF LIBERTY

A new generation of colonial orators and pamphleteers, including Patrick Henry and Samuel Adams, rose to prominence during the Stamp Act crisis. They preached about *liberty*, which became the watchword of the resistance. Liberties, not shillings, the rebellious colonists insisted, were at stake in the dispute over taxation.

Opponents of the stamp tax meant various things when they spoke of liberty, including property rights, personal autonomy, and communal prerogatives. And they drew on different philosophical and historical traditions in arguing that British taxes and Britain's standing army threatened to enslave the colonists. The Patriots, as rebellious colonists began identifying themselves, invoked ancient ideals of the

Deacon Jacob Elliot's Liberty Tree, Boston.   Elliott's elm tree, on the corner of Essex and Orange Streets, became a patriotic symbol because of its role in the Stamp Act protest. The tree appeared on New England banners and flags during the 1770s. *Project Gutenberg Literary Archive Foundation*

Greek and (especially) Roman republics—a government with no monarch or emperor, a separation of powers, checks and balances among those powers, and great faith in virtuous, landowning, male citizens. They also cited English legal precedents, such as the Magna Carta (1215), which constrained the powers of the king, as well as the long history of settlements and charters that made up the English constitutional system of government. Many colonists spoke about "natural rights" in the language of English philosopher John Locke or the moral philosophers of the Scottish Enlightenment. Some borrowed concepts of liberty from Protestant theology, whereas others looked to the humanistic authors of the Italian Renaissance. In short, the ideals of liberty that the Stamp Act threatened had diverse origins and foundations.

Colonists paid special attention to opinions circulating in eighteenth-century England and saw themselves as participants in the ruling country's political debates. Critics of imperial policy began calling themselves **Whigs,** the name of Britain's pro-Parliament political party. They classified their colonial opponents as **Tories** after Britain's royalists, supporters of the king. One powerful strain of political rhetoric among the colonial Whigs echoed English essayists from earlier in the eighteenth century, who nourished a deep suspicion of the corrupting influence of political power and consumer goods. Liberty was always vulnerable, they believed, to the partisan schemes of professional politicians. Liberty was safe when political power lay in the hands of independent landowners whose votes could not be purchased or compromised because they shunned luxury and debt.

Well-educated critics of imperial policy discussed and disseminated these ideals of liberty in sermons, newspaper articles, and lengthy treatises on politics. But popular participation in the resistance movement depended on a broader cultural celebration of liberty, often involving rituals, ceremonies, symbols, songs, and images rather than learned texts. In New England, for example, colonists imagined liberty in the form of a tree—specifically, an elm tree on the property of Deacon Jacob Elliott in Boston. During the Stamp Act crisis, colonists renamed the large elm, originally planted in 1646, the **Liberty Tree,** because it was from its branches that tax agent Andrew Oliver dangled in effigy. The tree quickly became the symbol of the patriotic cause. A month after the big Boston riot, the Sons of Liberty convened under the elm, and all members received silver medals bearing an image of Elliott's tree.

Imagining Liberty. When New Yorkers celebrated the repeal of the Stamp Act in 1766, they erected a ship's mast, dubbed the Liberty Pole, at the center of their festivity. Liberty Poles and Liberty Trees suggested different things. Elm trees represented liberty as something old, firmly planted, and organically connected to the community, as well as a source of collective protection for those who gathered under its shade. Human-built poles suggested that liberty was something movable and flexible around which a diverse community could rally. But both trees and poles helped rebellious colonists imagine liberty as more than just an abstraction. *Science History Images/Alamy Stock Photo*

THE ESCALATING POLITICAL CONFLICT

Across the Atlantic, a change in the British prime ministry brought William Pitt, the man who had rescued the war effort a decade earlier, back to power. Beset by joint disease, Pitt put Charles Townshend, his chancellor of the exchequer (the national treasury), in charge of colonial policy. Townshend was eager to reduce the home country's military budget and at least as eager to back up the principle expressed in the Declaratory Act—that Parliament had complete legislative authority over the colonies.

The new tax bill Townshend pushed through Parliament in 1767, which became known as the **Townshend Duties,** introduced new import taxes on glass, lead, paint, paper, and tea. Because these were import duties rather than direct taxes, they did not provoke as immediate or violent a colonial response as the

Stamp Act. But merchants and other Whigs, especially in New England, still objected to the duties, because they recognized the bill for what it was: an attempt to raise revenue, not to regulate trade. Critics were especially galled by the new law's stipulation that some of the revenue would be used to fund the salaries of the colonies' governors and judges, so that those officials would be more independent of the elected assemblies and less susceptible to the popular protests that had destroyed the stamp tax. Colonial Whigs saw a conspiracy afoot to deprive them of their liberties.

Taking the lead, Samuel Adams drafted a petition in 1768 on behalf of the Massachusetts House of Representatives, calling on other British colonies to join in condemning the Townshend Act. Adams's **Circular Letter** acknowledged parliamentary supremacy, did not threaten independence, and attracted only mild support from a few other colonies. But the British government responded swiftly and forcefully. Lord Hillsborough, now directing colonial policy after Townshend's death, demanded that Massachusetts rescind the letter and ordered the dissolution of any colonial assembly that as much as received the Massachusetts petition. This policy backfired badly. Massachusetts legislators stood by the Circular Letter, and their counterparts in other colonies rallied to its defense. When the defiant colonial assemblies were dissolved, Whig rhetoric about an imperial design to suppress liberties in America seemed vindicated.

Reorganizing themselves, the Sons of Liberty in Boston began advocating boycotts of British imports as the best way to resist the empire's tax policies. **Nonimportation agreements** caught on only selectively among leading colonial merchants, but by 1770 they had cost Great Britain hundreds of thousands of pounds, whereas the Townshend Duties had yielded little in the way of revenue. In April of that year, Parliament repealed all of the taxes except for the one on tea. Despite the repeal, however, Britain was now locked in a political showdown with rebellious colonists. The empire's best hope was that divisions among and within the mainland colonies would make widespread political opposition impossible to sustain.

A DECADE OF POPULAR PROTEST

While Parliament and the colonial assemblies exchanged political maneuvers, a rising tide of angry protest swept through the colonies. Ordinary colonists engaged in daily acts of political expression and resistance. Some of it was directed at the imperial policies that enraged Whig politicians. But popular protest also focused on local grievances and targets, often dividing colonists rather than bringing them together. Both in cities and the countryside, political passions turned increasingly violent in the years following the Stamp Act controversy.

CONSUMPTION AND NONCONSUMPTION

The political fight between Parliament and the colonial legislatures over taxes and imperial revenue highlighted colonists' consumer habits. The population of the American colonies had grown so large, and their buying power so great, that Britain was counting on surcharges on the colonists' purchases of imported goods to defray the costs of administering the empire. On the other side, Whig opponents of the new tax policy relied on the threat of a boycott of British imports to provide leverage in their negotiations with the home country.

Urban merchants turned to nonimportation agreements after the Townshend Act of 1767, but at first these agreements were difficult to sustain or enforce. Merchants were reluctant to damage their partnerships overseas and afraid of losing business to local rivals or to other colonial cities. Over the next several years, however, the boycott movement strengthened as rebellious colonists expanded their strategy from nonimportation to nonconsumption. Whereas nonimportation was a deliberate action by large, urban buyers, **nonconsumption**—the decision not to buy or use items imported from other countries—entailed a change in the purchasing habits of ordinary men and women throughout the colonies.

The nonconsumption movement called on colonists to avoid all goods produced in Great Britain. Every purchase became a politically charged act, and every article of clothing advertised its wearer's allegiances in the crisis (see Hot Commodities: Homespun Clothing). In towns and cities in every colony, committees monitored the actions of importers and retailers and punished offenders. Patriots in Lancaster, Pennsylvania, for example, foreswore "any fellowship or correspondence" with merchants who sold imported goods—or with the consumers who bought them. In New York, nonconsumption activists covered an offending jewelry store with scaffolding. Elsewhere, store owners found their doors and windows smeared with excrement.

The campaign against British goods helped build local communities of activists who joined in shaming their neighbors, but an effective boycott also required long-distance communication and coordination among the colonies. In the same way that their shared consumer habits had helped American colonists identify with the

HOT COMMODITIES
Homespun Clothing

Among the many imported items that tied the American colonies to the British Empire, fabric was in far the most common. Imported clothing dominated American fashion in midcentury, and except for those who were enslaved, most colonists in the 1760s wore British textiles on their bodies every day. The nonimportation movement could not completely change this fact of colonial life, but it exerted powerful pressures to shop—and dress—differently. Opponents of British tax policies boycotted all kinds of popular consumer goods, but clothing was in a category of its own, both because of the importance of textile production to the British economy and because clothing was such a visible and loaded expression of one's identity and solidarity.

Homespun clothing was generally made of coarse linen or wool (or both), but there was no reason a garment manufactured in the colonies could not appear elegant. Several of the homespun clothes that survive from the late eighteenth century show fashionable cuts and fine tailoring. When George Washington appeared at his inauguration in an American-made suit of fine material and silk stockings, observers mistook his outfit for a foreign import.

For the most part, however, patriotic colonists reveled in homespun's conspicuous simplicity. But only if a homespun garment looked the part could it serve as a badge of support for revolutionary activism. In particular, older and simpler clothing—whether or not it was made from fabric spun in the colonies—best lent support to the cause, because it discouraged the impression that the wearer had violated the boycott. More generally, simple dress embodied a broader political ideal celebrated by the rebellious colonists, who associated luxury with aristocracy and effeminacy. In Benjamin Franklin's imagination, the model citizen of a republic appeared "in the plainest Country Garb; his Great Coat was coarse and looked old and threadbare; his Linnen was homespun; his Beard perhaps of Seven Days Growth, his Shoes thick and heavy, and every Part of his Dress corresponding." As has often been the case in American history,

Boy's Suit from Virginia, ca. 1780.
Though made of coarse, homespun cloth, this apparel was cut in the contemporary style.
The Colonial Williamsburg Foundation. Museum Purchase

the line between fashion and politics was thin in the era of the Revolution.

Think About It

1. How did the homespun movement empower ordinary colonists? How might it have oppressed them?

2. Why were clothes made in America likely to be of inferior quality in the 1760s and 1770s?

British Empire (see Chapter 5), their collective refusal to consume helped them identify with a broad resistance movement. Patriotic boycotts also led to contentious discussions about consumer culture. Nonconsumption advocates, including many Puritan preachers, cited the frivolity of luxuries and preached the virtues of self-sacrifice. Sometimes they cast aspersions on the particular commodities they wished to boycott. Whigs decried the unhealthful effects of tea, for example, and spread the unappetizing and xenophobic rumor that barefoot Cantonese workers stomped the tea leaves into their containers. Poorer colonists also used the nonconsumption campaign to criticize the spending habits of the affluent.

Women played prominent public roles in the colonial boycotts as debates about consumption politicized realms of daily life where women were active as both consumers and producers. Especially in wealthier households, women made significant purchases of imported goods, including clothing, tea, furniture, and utensils. Whig critiques of colonial dependence on British luxury goods often blamed upper-class women for their overconsumption and stigmatized the taste for luxuries as dangerous to manly liberty. Such stereotypes made it seem more urgent that female consumers join in the political protests. Women's labor, moreover, assumed even greater significance during the post-1765 crisis than before, because the success of the nonconsumption campaign hinged on the colonists' ability to replace British fabrics and clothing with American-made alternatives. Textile production had become women's work in the eighteenth-century colonial farm household, and women were now called on to increase their output of homespun cloth.

To publicize women's patriotic contributions to the cause, New England's Whigs organized spinning bees, traditional gatherings where women spun yarn or thread for clothing. Newspaper editors held up the spinners as symbols of the "industry and frugality of American ladies" and hailed their local contributions to "the political salvation of a whole Continent."

VIOLENCE IN THE COUNTRYSIDE

While consumer boycotts summoned the energies of Patriots in eastern towns and cities and connected their daily activities to public debates about taxation, Patriots in the colonies' rural interior were swept into very different political protests. Though these conflicts in the countryside had little to do with import duties or the rights of colonial assemblies, they contributed to a climate of instability and readied a cohort of rural American men for armed violence.

Rural violence was often the work of vigilante groups angry at seaboard elites, much like Pennsylvania's Paxton Boys, who had massacred Native Americans and besieged the colonial government in Philadelphia in the aftermath of the French and Indian War (see Chapter 5). Backcountry settlers in South Carolina organized in 1767 to demand government protection against cattle thieves and outlaw gangs. Calling themselves **Regulators,** they policed the frontier and administered extralegal punishments to individuals accused of crimes. Although South Carolina Regulators expressed local grievances, they spoke the same political language as Whig merchants protesting the Stamp Act. "We are *Free-men*–British subjects–Not Born Slaves," they insisted, demanding increased representation in colonial government. In neighboring North Carolina, a much larger Regulator movement expressed particular hostility to wealthy slaveholding elites and protested the legislature's decision to build a lavish governor's mansion in the capital of New Bern. By 1771, most white male residents of the North Carolina backcountry had joined in the violent protest, which withheld tax payment, disrupted court proceedings, and defied the authority of the colonial government.

The two Carolina Regulator movements met different fates. In part because colonial leaders in slave-majority South Carolina worried that violence in the countryside would create the conditions for another slave uprising like the Stono Rebellion of 1739, they sought to mollify the protesters by granting some of their demands. In North Carolina, where the threat of slave revolt seemed more remote and where the social conflict had already widened, colonial authorities violently suppressed the protests, executing leading Regulators and imposing a loyalty oath on Piedmont settlers.

Farther north, tenant farmers and rural squatters in New York's Hudson River valley organized both a rent strike and an armed rebellion in 1766, drawing inspiration from urban protests against the Stamp Act. Angry about high rents and evictions, farmers working plots owned by the Van Cortlandt and Livingston families threatened to murder their manorial landlords. Like the Regulators, rural New Yorkers organized militias and broke open local jails. British troops had to be called in to end their rebellion. The notorious **Green Mountain Boys** in northern New England (see chapter opening) also began as a band of farmers trying to protect their rights to stay on their land. And like other rural protesters in that period, they defiantly rejected traditional assumptions about deference to social elites or to established law and order. When New York's governor sought to enforce New York land deeds through a proclamation, Ethan Allen responded that the governor could "stick it in his ars." In the early 1770s, most Whig leaders in coastal towns and cities did not see such rural unrest as part of a larger defense of colonial liberties against British tyranny. Indeed, colonial legislatures were usually the targets rather than the leaders of backcountry rebellions. But armed violence in the continent's interior made the colonies much harder to govern and portended a wider unraveling of Britain's American empire.

URBAN CROWDS AND STREET THEATER

Protesters in large towns and cities were less likely to carry firearms than their rural counterparts, but their dense settlement made violent protest easier to organize and quicker to erupt. **Urban rioting** was an established tradition in eighteenth-century America, often associated with restoration of law and order rather than its subversion. Urban riots typically involved fifty to a hundred men and targeted property, destroying buildings or goods that were symbolically linked to a common grievance. Rioters claimed to be acting on behalf of the shared norms or values of the entire city and did not necessarily see themselves as lawbreakers. When rioters were poor, their critics would deride them as dangerous "mobs," a word that came from the Latin term *mobile vulgus*, meaning the fickle or unrooted common people. But one person's mob was another's legitimate crowd action.

The Stamp Act crisis initiated a major escalation in urban rioting. Riots became more frequent and more

Tarring and Feathering. This engraving, published in London in 1774, depicts two Bostonian Sons of Liberty torturing a British customs official: They poured hot tar over his bare skin and and then adhered feathers to it. Rioters sometimes amplified the torture by setting the feathers on fire. When victims eventually sought to remove the tar, their skin came off in chunks, introducing risks of serious infection.
Peter Newark Pictures/The Bridgeman Art Library

violent, and they involved many more participants, practically obliterating the blurry line between mob action and elite-sanctioned protest. Whig leaders sought to control the 1765 riots, but lower-class urbanites often set the tone, moving beyond attacks on stamps to express anger against the privileges of wealth. Twelve days after they forced the resignation of the stamp tax collector, rioters in Boston entered the stately home of Thomas Hutchinson, the chief justice of Massachusetts; tore down its brick walls; destroyed his furniture and many of his legal documents; emptied his wine cellar; and stole his cash. Samuel Adams condemned the "truly mobbish nature" of the attack, though many Bostonians on both sides of the conflict recognized it as a central part of the political protest against British authority.

Even after the Stamp Act was repealed, colonial cities became hotbeds of conflict and collective action. One historian has counted one hundred fifty different riots in the thirteen colonies in the second half of the 1760s. As with the rural unrest of the period, not every riot was directed against British rule, but they undermined authority, inflamed passions, and habituated colonists to both the threat and the reality of violence.

● Riots and demonstrations turned city streets into stages for political performances. Burning effigies, destruction of building facades, and loud shouting were common rioting strategies, because they dramatized the power of the crowd and brought shame upon political opponents. **Tarring and feathering** became a trademark shaming ritual during this period. Tories, haughty colonial officials, or merchants who violated nonimportation agreements might find themselves stripped naked, covered with tar and then feathers, and paraded in the streets. ●

Urban protests could turn brutal and destructive, but the relative absence of guns among the rioters made fatalities rare. The presence of more British troops on city streets in the late 1760s, however, introduced a more lethal element to the mix. On March 5, 1770, British soldiers guarding a customs house in Boston fired on a crowd of local laborers who were angrily heckling them and pelting them with snowballs and stones. Eleven civilians were struck by gunfire, five of them fatally. After a lengthy trial, the commanding officer and most of the soldiers involved were acquitted, but the **Boston Massacre** became a rallying cry for rebellious colonists.

THE TEA PARTY AND THE MOVE TO COERCION

Widespread social unrest helped set the stage for a dramatic and fateful urban demonstration in 1773 that fundamentally altered the course of imperial politics. After three years of relative peace between Britain and the colonies over tax policy, Prime Minister Frederick Lord North introduced a law to reinforce the last remaining Townshend duty, the tax on tea. North's principal goal

BEHIND THE IMAGE

Paul Revere, a silversmith and engraver, produced this iconic representation of a major escalation in the imperial crisis without having witnessed the violence on King Street. Neither had Henry Pelham, an engraver from whom Revere probably copied this image. Revere's print, titled *The Bloody Massacre Perpetrated in King Street,* went on sale in Boston a week before Pelham's quite similar *The Fruits of Arbitrary Power, or the Bloody Massacre.* Pelham accused Revere of having "plundered me on the highway."

WITHIN THE IMAGE

Revere's view of the violence blames ❶ the British soldiers for firing on ❷ unarmed men engaged in lawful assembly and offers his commentary on the scene by ❸ placing a sign reading "Butcher's Hall" over the coffeehouse above the redcoats. Pro-British accounts contest this version, and the best evidence indicates that British captain Thomas Preston stood in front of his men rather than behind them, in which case it would have been unlikely that he gave an order to fire on the crowd. ❹ Revere's placement of Preston makes the Patriot version of the massacre seem more plausible. Note that all of the civilians in the crowd appear to be white, despite the fact that Crispus Attucks, a man of African and native descent who had escaped slavery, was one of the casualties. Revere preferred an image of English-looking colonists having their rights trampled.

The Bloody Massacre Perpetrated in King Street (1770), engraved by Paul Revere. *Courtesy of National Gallery of Art, Washington*

BEYOND THE IMAGE

Revere's color engraving circulated quickly and had a profound impact on the revolutionary cause. Beyond its commercial success, his version of the Boston Massacre, as the event came to be known among Patriots, dramatized the threat to colonial rights and liberties and shaped popular views of the controversial clash. (For example, Loyalists at the time called it a riot, rather than a massacre.) During the revolutionary era, many Americans marked March 5, the date of the violence on King Street, rather than July 4, as the anniversary of independence.

was to bail out the British East India Company, a financially troubled and mismanaged private corporation that sold Chinese tea to British customers. North's **Tea Act** allowed the company to avoid export taxes, eliminate middlemen, and sell tea directly and inexpensively in America. Because the price would now be lower—even with the import tax—than Dutch tea smuggled into the colonies, North assumed that Americans would happily purchase East India tea and pay the tax. But the Sons of Liberty saw in North's move both an imperious insistence on Parliament's right to tax the unrepresented colonies and a sneaky plot to conceal the modest tax and induce colonists to pay for the British military presence.

Whig leaders called for tea boycotts, appealing to what was now a familiar strategy of consumer politics and urging colonists to abstain from tea drinking altogether. But

"Americans Throwing Cargoes of the Tea Ships into the River, at Boston," 1789 engraving. The men who boarded the *Dartmouth* and destroyed the tea represented a range of social backgrounds. They dressed as Native Americans to conceal their identities, intimidate their enemies, and achieve dramatic effects in the theater of urban protests. In addition, they might have wanted to claim a special connection with the American continent, as opposed to Britain (see Chapter 9). *North Wind Picture Archives/Alamy Stock Photo*

Americans were attached to their tea, and total abstinence was an unrealistic goal. And since a great deal of illegally imported Dutch tea was available in colonial stores, it would be impossible to enforce a social taboo against only those tea leaves that came from the British East India Company. Rebellious colonists therefore focused their wrath on the tea shipments, rather than the act of tea drinking, hoping to prevent the new product from landing in the first place. As tea shipments headed for the colonies in fall 1773, activists in the four major mainland port cities threatened the agents who had been specifically authorized to sell the tea. Agents in New York, Philadelphia, and Charleston, mindful of the rising tide of urban violence, decided to resign. Tea shipments to those cities went undelivered or never made it out of local storage.

In Boston, however, the colonial authorities stood firm. Massachusetts governor Thomas Hutchinson refused to allow the three tea-bearing ships to return to England without unloading their cargo. Like his opponents, Hutchinson saw the showdown over tea as a crucial test of imperial authority. On December 16, after an anxious stalemate that gripped the city for twenty days of public agitation, a well-organized band of one hundred to one hundred fifty men, disguised as Native Americans, climbed aboard the anchored ships, chopped open 342 tea chests with hatchets and axes, and unloaded their contents into Boston Harbor. The **Boston Tea Party,** as the incident would be named in the 1830s, destroyed about 10,000 pounds worth of property belonging to the East India Company (see How Much Is That? The Tea in Boston Harbor) and thwarted the hated tea tax.

The destruction of the tea broke new ground in urban protests to British tax policies, and both King George and Lord North called for a punitive response. Parliament passed four **Coercive Acts** in the spring of 1774, designed to reassert authority over its rebellious colony and compel Bostonians to compensate the East India Company for the tea. The new laws closed Boston's harbor and dismantled Massachusetts's self-government by abrogating its colonial charter and suspending all town meetings. Other controversial provisions of the laws protected royal officials from being tried for crimes in the colonies (where

How Much Is That?

The Tea in Boston Harbor

The 10,000 pounds worth of East India tea cast into Boston Harbor in 1773 is equivalent to about 1.8 million dollars in 2020.

popular anger might wield influence) and empowered the colony's royal governor to appoint and fire judges. Parliament also expanded the boundaries of Quebec and granted freedom of religion to Catholics.

The **Quebec Act** was not part of the Coercive Acts, except in the minds of rebellious colonists. Britain hoped to shore up the political allegiances of its loyal Quebec colony and further isolate Massachusetts and its supporters. But to some colonists, including Virginia land speculators such as George Washington, Thomas Jefferson, and Patrick Henry, the southward expansion of Quebec into the Ohio River valley was a painful reminder that British policy blocked western land settlement. The other outrage of the Quebec Act, especially in New England, lay in its accommodation to Catholics.

Whig leaders lumped together these five laws—the four Coercive Acts and the Quebec Act—as the "Intolerable Acts," but it was not immediately clear how rebellious colonists would express their intolerance. The British navy did not need the cooperation of Boston residents to close the port. But the new law amending the Massachusetts charter to make judges, sheriffs, and peace officers directly answerable to the royal governor proved more vulnerable to popular protest. When officials appointed by the British Crown tried to hold court sessions in Massachusetts, outraged farmers and artisans gathered en masse and physically prevented them from doing so. In Worcester County, more than forty-six hundred men from thirty-seven towns (about half the county's adult male population) marched to the county seat and blocked access to the courthouse. In other towns, royal officials were threatened and forced to resign. By October 1774, the British Empire no longer controlled the Massachusetts countryside.

MOBILIZING FOR REVOLUTION

Britain's leadership regarded the escalating rebellion in Massachusetts in 1773–1774 as a local crisis that could be contained. Massachusetts was only one of twenty-six British colonies in the Americas—one of eighteen on the mainland. For Americans enraged by the Intolerable Acts, the challenge lay in cultivating intercolonial ties and coordinating a response to British policies. As they corresponded, convened, and published about the infringements of their liberties, rebellious colonists in thirteen of the mainland colonies built a powerful resistance movement.

SPREADING THE WORD

Amid the intensifying crisis, opponents of British policy in North America established procedures and media for circulating news from one colony to another. Virginia took the lead in 1773, establishing a committee to maintain "Correspondence and Communication with our sister colonies," and within a few months almost every other colony followed suit. In Massachusetts, active correspondence committees at the township level had been organizing resistance within the colony since 1772. These **Committees of Correspondence** played an important practical role in the events leading up to the war and provided a model for connecting a dispersed population that had no history of regular contact.

British authorities and their supporters saw the correspondence committees as a revolutionary threat. Massachusetts Tory writer Daniel Leonard called them "the foulest, subtlest and most venomous serpent ever issued from the eggs of sedition." Earlier, colonists had used British communication networks to forge political ties. But by establishing independent channels of political contact, the new committees initiated a process of building a nation (see Chapter 7).

Perhaps the most salient achievement of the Committees of Correspondence was the call for a convention of colonial leaders in Philadelphia in September 1774 to respond to the British crackdown in Boston. Dubbing this gathering a "continental congress," organizers hoped to attract representatives from colonies throughout British North America. Twelve of the invited colonies answered the call (Georgia did not, nor did East and West Florida or any of the three Canadian colonies), sending fifty-six delegates to a meeting that would later become known as the **First Continental Congress.** Like correspondence committees, congresses were media of communication. Instead of circulating messages over distance, Congress convened select individuals from their scattered homes to a single location for a face-to-face encounter.

The fifty-six men who gathered in Philadelphia in 1774 were prominent figures in the various colonies; many of them had acquired renown as orators or pamphleteers in the Whig cause. But over seven weeks of discussion and deliberation, the delegates expressed different approaches to the crisis. More cautious representatives pushed the moderate measure of establishing a special American Parliament in which the colonists would be indirectly represented, but most delegates wanted a more forceful response to the Intolerable Acts. Still, they did not advocate independence from the British Empire. Congress called for peaceful redress of grievances, not armed rebellion, and delegates were careful not to burn all bridges back to where things stood before 1765. They addressed their petitions and resolutions to King George rather than to Parliament, as a way of both rejecting parliamentary authority and maintaining a posture of allegiance to the British Crown. Eager not to sever ties with the king, Congress blamed the current crisis and the repressive policies of the past decade on "the devices of wicked Ministers and evil Counsellors."

Though delegates spoke of liberties and rights, the overriding theme of the First Continental Congress was unity. Defying Parliament's attempt to isolate Boston for that city's seditious behavior, Congress officially resolved "that the town of Boston and province of Massachusetts Bay, are considered by all America as suffering in the common cause." As a concrete demonstration of this unity, Congress agreed to ban all British imports immediately and threatened to block all exports (except rice) to Britain, Ireland, and the British Caribbean the following year if Parliament did not repeal the Coercive Acts. These were momentous measures intended to weather a storm and restore an older colonial order. Only if the British government failed to address their grievances, delegates agreed, would the colonies regroup as a congress the following year.

THE BEGINNINGS OF WAR

Britain did not accede to the demands of the Continental Congress. Though several powerful voices in Parliament urged conciliation and compromise, they were

Exile of the American Company of Comedians to the West Indies. This painting, by Charles Willson Peale, depicts actress Nancy Hallam in 1771 playing cross-dressed as Fidéle in Shakespeare's *Cymbeline*. The Continental Congress expressed its collective disapproval of the theater, banning all plays throughout the colonies and for an indefinite period of time. Proscribing plays was intended both as a boycott of British theatrical culture and as a means of underscoring the solemnity and virtue of the patriotic cause. *The Picture Art Collection/Alamy Stock Photo*

outnumbered. Prime Minister North's government refused to repeal the Coercive Acts, as it had done with the Stamp Act and the Townshend Duties. Instead, North declared Congress an illegal assembly and ordered a naval blockade on the rebellious colonies to prevent them from trading with other nations. And in a move that was bound to lead to bloodshed, North also ordered General Gage to end the rebellion in Massachusetts by arresting its leaders and seizing its munitions supplies.

On April 18, 1775, Gage sent 700 soldiers on a night raid from Boston to the town of Concord, where rebel arms were stored. When they arrived the next morning, Gage's soldiers met Patriot militiamen who had been warned by riders from Boston that "the Regulars" were coming. The two forces exchanged fire, first in the nearby town of Lexington and then in Concord itself. The **Battle of Lexington and Concord** took the lives of 73 redcoats and 49 Massachusetts militiamen. Another 213 men were wounded in the clash. As British soldiers retreated toward Boston without having captured many weapons, more shots were exchanged and the toll rose. From one perspective, this event could have been seen simply as an especially bloody event in the waves of armed violence that had been rippling through the American countryside for a decade. But the involvement of the British Royal Army and the casualites they suffered ensured that the battle would have more dramatic implications. In the escalating dispute over Britain's imperial authority, Lexington and Concord struck many participants as an irreparable rupture.

● News of the fighting in Lexington and Concord spread quickly, by eighteenth-century standards, thanks to a network of express riders. Word had reached Connecticut and Maine by the next day, and New York City just three days later. As handwritten reports headed steadily south over the next two weeks by horse, passing from community to community as

MEDIA AND INFORMATION

far as South Carolina (1,000 miles from Boston), colonists gathered at taverns and meetinghouses to react to the event. It was important that these handwritten reports were signed by known members of correspondence committees, because the possibility of false information was all too real. Just six months earlier, mistaken intelligence from Boston had drawn thousands of New England minutemen to defend the Massachusetts capital against a rumored attack that never took place. But when the news of Lexington and Concord came to town, local Patriots respected the authority of the speedy relay network along which it traveled. •

News reports also hastened the spread of the fighting. Less than a month after Lexington and Concord, two distinct groups of New England militiamen (one commanded by Ethan Allen, the other by Benedict Arnold) converged on Fort Ticonderoga in New York and forced

a British surrender. Allen then took another fort, at nearby Crown Point (see Map 6.1). In capturing the forts, the rebellious colonists also acquired cannons, mortars, howitzers, and a significant volume of ammunition. By summer, Patriot forces were using some of those arms to besiege the British stronghold in occupied Boston.

Amid this violent unraveling of the empire, the political leaders of the rebellion reconvened as planned in Philadelphia, this time as thirteen colonies. But despite sharing a name with the first gathering, the **Second Continental Congress** differed significantly from its predecessor. By May 1775, hopes of peaceful redress had dimmed. The Second Congress was not an emergency session with a limited agenda but the beginning of an ongoing conversation among colonial representatives who together formed a makeshift government for the rebellion. Ultimately, this was the government that would cut ties with the empire, but for more than a year, Congress refused to do so.

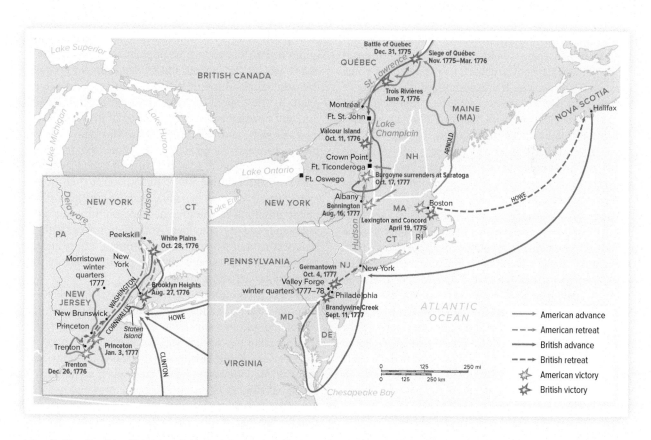

Map 6.1 Key Battles of the Revolutionary War, 1775–1777.   The war began in Massachusetts, but after a failed American attack on Canada, a major British invasion of New York shifted the center of the war farther south and west. Burgoyne's surrender at Saratoga in 1777 marked the end of this phase of the war. Question for Analysis: What geographical advantages did the British see in deploying troops to New York City?

Battle of Lexington, by Amos Doolittle, 1775.   The scene, painted by an artist sympathetic to the rebellion, shows the British firing on militiamen attempting to flee. *Art Images/Bridgeman Art Library/Getty Images*

It wasted no time, however, in taking command of the war against British rule. Congress created a **Continental Army** with eighty-eight battalions and appointed George Washington as general. It also authorized the printing of currency to pay for the war and sent representatives to negotiate alliances with Native American groups. Congress accounted for these actions in July with the Declaration of the Causes and Necessity for Taking up Arms, but it followed that declaration two days later with an Olive Branch Petition asking George III to intervene and restore peace to the empire.

Congress was walking a fine line in 1775, acknowledging that a state of war existed but officially still opening the door to a restoration of the colonies' political status within the empire. In the Olive Branch Petition, the representatives referred to themselves as "your Majesty's faithful subjects" and expressed hope for "a happy and permanent reconciliation." His Majesty was unmoved. On August 23, 1775, King George III declared the thirteen colonies to be in rebellion, marking a political point of no return in the imperial crisis. A year later, Congress would formally declare independence, instruct the colonies to refashion themselves as states, and embark on the project of building a nation (this story unfolds in Chapter 7).

MAKING THE CASE IN PRINT

As members of the Second Continental Congress began coordinating a massive military campaign to beat back British forces, other colonists waged a battle for public opinion. Patriots sought to popularize colonial grievances against Parliament and to drum up support for the war effort. Much of this discussion took place in print. By the time of the Second Congress, thirty-eight different newspapers were circulating in Britain's mainland colonies, and most of the men who printed those papers were early supporters of resistance to parliamentary taxation. The Stamp Act, after all, had been an attack on the printing trade. But whatever their financial interests or their personal politics, printers drew public attention to the dramas of revolution, war, and independence by flooding American towns with a steady stream of printed essays, sermons, letters, declarations, newspapers, and almanacs that broadcast the revolutionary changes afoot.

• The print medium was especially useful for this purpose, because it allowed authors to address their readership without appearing in public gatherings, without claiming any special social standing, and without identifying themselves personally. Anonymous or pseudonymous publication was a common rhetorical strategy in revolutionary America and had the added benefit of protecting authors from prosecution for treason. •

In January 1776, an obscure former corset maker who had recently emigrated from England authored a pamphlet entitled **Common Sense.** Under the cover of anonymity, Thomas Paine ignored the advice of friends

MEDIA AND INFORMATION

and boldly advocated independence, using colorful and provocative language to persuade American readers to abandon hopes of reconciliation and embrace their future as citizens of a democratic republic. While other pamphleteers claimed the rights of British subjects under the monarchy, Paine ridiculed the monarchy itself and bid farewell to the "so much boasted constitution of England." The first printing of *Common Sense* sold a thousand copies in a week, and it was reprinted quickly in other towns and cities, becoming the best-selling pamphlet in the history of colonial America. The remarkable circulation of *Common Sense* emboldened rebellious colonists to believe that they were advocating a popular cause. As one delegate to the Second Congress reported on his way back from North Carolina, the cry throughout the land was "Common sense and Independence."

MUSTERING ARMIES

In the war's opening months, colonists volunteered enthusiastically for military duty in the rebel forces. Some joined local militias, serving close to home for short terms while others enlisted in Washington's army. The difference between the two experiences was stark. Militiamen generally returned to their farms after the summer, were not forced to surrender entirely to the rigors of military discipline, and often elected their own officers. **Regulars,** as the full-time soldiers were called, typically enlisted for much longer stints, faced more brutal conditions, and suffered higher casualty rates. Regulars belonged to a professional, hierarchical army whose officers were appointed by Congress or by provincial governments. Rebel militias fought the opening battles of the Revolutionary War and would prove crucial to the American cause over the coming years, but Patriot leaders understood that without a full-time army under central command, it would be impossible to resist the British for long.

Deborah Sampson.   Sampson enlisted in the Continental Army under the name Robert Shurtliff. After the war, she went on a lecture tour and became a celebrity. This portrait appeared as the frontispiece of *The Female Review* in 1797. *Science History Images/ Alamy Stock Photo*

Most American colonists, whatever their political convictions, were reluctant to sign away their freedoms and join the Continental Army. By the end of 1775, once the initial war fervor had subsided, it had become more difficult to retain or replace those who had joined. Washington pushed for longer service terms, cash bounties to attract recruits, or more forceful measures to compel enlistment, but Congress resisted any measure that created a standing army of draftees or hirelings. A year into the war, however, as the British expanded their campaign beyond Massachusetts, Congress was forced to reconsider. By the end of June 1776, Congress was offering ten dollars to men who would enlist for three years. A couple of months later, the bounty was up to twenty dollars, plus a new suit of clothing and 100 acres of land to anyone who signed on for the entire war. In 1777, Congress also set minimum numbers of men that each state needed to contribute, prompting states to add their own material inducements to meet troop quotas. Maryland offered new recruits an additional forty dollars plus a pair of shoes and stockings. Later in the war, the incentive package for North Carolina recruits included "a prime slave." A Virginia law in 1780, signed by Governor Thomas Jefferson, promised "300 acres of land plus a healthy sound Negro between 20 and 30 years of age or 60 pounds in gold and silver." Such signing bonuses were attractive, especially to poorer colonists, but several states still needed to draft men to fill their quotas. The model of citizen soldiers volunteering to defend their freedom, an ideal cherished by Patriots, would not suffice in this war.

Still, many Continental soldiers enlisted—out of patriotism, financial need, thirst for adventure, or some combination of motivations. Young boys misrepresented their ages and defied the wishes of parents and masters when army recruiters came to town. Apprentices signed up, even though they could be forced to surrender to their masters any bounties they received for their service. And at least one woman, Deborah Sampson of Massachusetts, disguised herself as a man to take up arms against Britain. But for every enthusiastic recruit there were several disgruntled comrades. High rates of desertion and low rates of re-enlistment produced a serious problem of troop turnover. Although two hundred thirty thousand enlisted in the Continental Army over the course of the war, its active duty force rarely exceeded fourteen thousand at a single time.

For most of the war, the ranks of Washington's army were dominated by unmarried teenagers with few opportunities or responsibilities and other colonists without significant property. Some regiments included substantial numbers of recent immigrants, indentured servants, or transported convicts. George Washington officially prohibited the recruitment of enslaved or free Blacks, but as the conflict wore on, that policy was dropped. Approximately five thousand African Americans served in the Continental Army, mostly in northern regiments, and a much smaller number were admitted to state militias.

Commissioned officers, on the other hand, came from genteel social circles and considered themselves a breed apart. Severe differences in pay reflected and reinforced the social divide between officers and enlisted men in the Continental Army. Whereas a colonel received 75 dollars per month in 1778, the average private earned just 6.67 dollars. Class tensions within the American army contributed to the high number of mutinies, especially in the final years of the war.

On the other side, the British government could draw on long experience in mobilizing and training a large military force. By the summer of 1776, General William Howe had assembled more than thirty thousand soldiers under his command in New York City, the largest single military force in the eighteenth-century world. Britain relied even more heavily than the rebellious colonists on financial incentives and heavy-handed recruitment efforts to fill its ranks. Parliament lacked the authority to draft citizens for overseas campaigns, but the army and navy resorted to whatever measures were available, grabbing young men out of jails and poorhouses, pressing the crews of captured ships into British military service, and offering bounties to new recruits in Britain and Ireland. The British government also turned to its traditional German allies, especially the small German state of Hesse-Cassell, for supplies of professional soldiers. Close to thirty thousand Hessians, as these German-speaking soldiers were called, made up a major component of the British invasion force on the mainland, though their contracts exempted them from being shipped to the more dangerous Caribbean.

Much more effectively than the American colonists, the British also recruited enslaved African Americans. Before the war, British strategists had argued privately that a colonial rebellion would surely founder, because the empire could exploit tensions in a slaveholding society and provoke fears of slave insurrections. In the West Indies, such fears had helped contain anti-imperial protests, and Britain hoped a similar strategy might keep the southern mainland colonies out of any war. In April 1775, as Virginia slaveholders were moving toward armed resistance, Governor John Murray, Lord Dunmore, threatened them with an emancipation order. Dunmore had no real intentions of freeing people who were enslaved; a slaveholder himself, he did not wish to undermine the institution of slavery in British America. When his own enslaved persons took the bluff seriously and offered to fight against the rebels, a shocked Dunmore threatened to beat them if they raised the subject again. But once war erupted, British officials were less concerned with protecting slavery than with suppressing the rebellion. In November, Governor Dunmore, who had fled the capital and was now operating aboard a naval ship off the coast, declared martial law and proclaimed liberty for enslaved people who would bear arms for "His Majesty's Troops."

Lord Dunmore's Proclamation was no general emancipation order, since it officially applied only to young, able-bodied, enslaved males whose slaveholders were disloyal to the British Crown, but it had dramatic implications. Already a year earlier, a small number of enslaved people in Boston had offered their military services to the British in exchange for freedom, but Dunmore's new policy triggered a far more substantial movement toward self-emancipation in the South. On hearing the news, hundreds of enslaved African Americans (including many who were not fit for military service and thus not technically freed by the proclamation) fled plantations in the Norfolk (Virginia) area, eluded local slave patrols, and made their ways safely to British lines. Dunmore organized several hundred formerly enslaved people into a British Ethiopian Regiment. ● Tragically, many of the Black men, women, and children who took refuge with the British died as the result of a smallpox pandemic, which struck North America during the same years as the Revolutionary War. ●

DISEASE AND EPIDEMIC

As in earlier military conflicts on the American continent, both sides of the Revolutionary War sought to secure military support from Native Americans.

Lord Dunmore's Proclamation.   Dunmore's declaration appeared in a printed broadside poster distributed from a ship at the Norfolk harbor. The public display of the proclamation evoked the dreaded specter of a large-scale insurrection. *This image is available from the United States Library of Congress's Rare Book and Special Collections Division under the digital ID rbpe.1780180*

Individual native soliders could be found in one or the other army, but both the British commanders and the Continental Congress relied on diplomatic initiatives to whole native villages and communities, rather than trying to recruit individuals. Many Native Americans fought in the war, mostly on the British side, but they did so as part of their own armed units with their own political agendas (see the section Native Americans and the War).

MAKING WAR

At the outbreak of the war in 1775, both the British Empire and the rebellious colonists enjoyed distinct military advantages, and each side had some reasons for expecting a swift victory. Britain was the world's naval superpower, and its army was larger and better trained. The British could also exploit political and ethnic divisions within the diverse colonies. The Patriots, on the other hand, drew strength from their familiarity with the terrain and the ardor of local militias to defend their homelands. And although British politicians dismissed the fighting abilities of untrained colonists, the rebels doubted whether Hessian mercenaries would fight valiantly for a cause in which they had no obvious stake. American colonists also benefited from two important circumstances: As an indigenous independence movement, they could prevail simply by a stalemate, whereas the British needed to force a surrender and then reimpose their political will on a hostile population. Furthermore, Great Britain had powerful enemies in Europe who might be drawn into the conflict.

In the end, those last strategic considerations would prove crucial, but not before a long and drawn-out war ravaged the eastern part of the continent. British troops won significant battles and occupied major colonial cities for much of the war, but they could neither extinguish the rebellion nor contain the costs and risks of a war that threatened to engulf other parts of the empire.

EARLY CAMPAIGNS

In the months after Lexington and Concord, much of the fighting centered on Massachusetts. Howe's army attacked rebel troops stationed on Breed's Hill across the Charles River from Boston, and eventually drove them away (in a battle named for Bunker Hill, which lay nearby), but only after suffering heavy casualties. Howe remained in occupied Boston, awaiting reinforcements and planning another assault on New England. • Meanwhile, the Americans took the offensive with an **invasion of Quebec** in September 1775. The campaign, led by General Richard Montgomery and supported by Colonel Benedict Arnold, moved the conflict outside the rebellious colonies and stirred the passions of New Englanders by giving the struggle for independence the feeling of a religious crusade against Catholics. The day before embarking, soldiers assembled around Newburyport, Massachusetts, and visited the tomb of revivalist preacher George Whitefield

CONFLICTING FAITHS

(see Chapter 4), whose body had been laid to rest in a nearby church five years earlier. Pious American troops cut pieces of clothing from Whitefield's decomposed skeleton and took them along as holy relics. One army chaplain looked forward to the invasion of Catholic Quebec as an opportunity to "spread . . . the gospel through this vast extended country, which has been for ages the dwelling of Satan, and reign of Antichrist." ● Though animated by this religious purpose, many of the Newburyport soldiers fell to hunger and smallpox en route to Quebec. Nor did those who survived the journey fulfill their visions of Protestant glory. Arnold's men attacked the city of Quebec on New Year's Eve but were badly defeated.

The British offensive, meanwhile, focused on New York, where loyalism was stronger. Howe hoped to control the Hudson River, which divided New England from most of New York and from the rest of the colonies, in order to isolate the rebellious New Englanders and put a quick end to the war. Unprecedented numbers of British troops arrived at the southern tip of Manhattan in July 1776, just as the Continental Congress declared independence. Late in August, the British routed the Continentals at the Battle of Long Island, capturing over one thousand prisoners and forcing Washington's retreat to Manhattan. Understanding the strategic significance of the Hudson River, he ordered his troops to protect fortified positions on its two sides. But in November, Howe's pursuing army seized both Fort Washington (in what is now Manhattan's Washington Heights) and Fort Lee (in New Jersey) after a battle that resulted in the capture of more than twenty-eight hundred American soldiers. By December, Washington's armies were on the run again, moving westward across the Delaware River and south toward Philadelphia. The fate of the rebellion looked bleak.

As Howe momentarily halted his pursuit with the onset of winter, Washington crossed the Delaware again and attacked Hessian troops stationed in Trenton on December 26, capturing over nine hundred prisoners. Eight days later, after two more trips across the river, Washington's army defeated a British force at Princeton, prompting Howe to withdraw from most of New Jersey. These victories boosted morale and stemmed the tide of desertion from the Continental Army. ● Then in February 1777, Washington made a momentous decision to implement a mass inoculation program, designed to protect his troops from the smallpox outbreaks that had ravaged American troops up to that point. In violation of the laws of the Continental Congress, he used vaccines to immunize forty thousand soldiers within the year. ●

Washington had not offset the heavy imbalance of manpower and wealth that continued to favor the British, but by eluding disaster and surviving into a new year, the rebellious colonists were raising the costs and lowering the likelihood of Britain's bid to regain the allegiance of the colonies.

SARATOGA AND THE TURNING TIDE

After another year of heavy fighting, during which the British captured the colonists' new national capital of Philadelphia, Britain launched another major offensive to control the Hudson River, targeting the city of Albany, New York. In the summer of 1777, General John Burgoyne led seventy-eight hundred British soldiers and a smaller force of Native Americans on a long, southward expedition from Canada into the Hudson Valley. Burgoyne planned to converge with Howe, whose men would move north along the Hudson River from the British stronghold in New York. But Howe sailed south to Philadelphia, home of the Continental Congress. Washington was caught off guard; Congress was forced to flee inland to Lancaster, Pennsylvania; and Philadelphia fell into British hands. But Burgoyne would be as surprised as Washington by Howe's move.

Other reinforcements for the assault were arriving from the west, as an army of British soldiers, Hessians, Iroquois, and local Loyalists marched along the Mohawk River toward Albany. But they encountered heavy resistance at **Fort Stanwix**, a hundred miles west of Albany. A regiment of Continental soldiers held out inside the besieged fort until local militiamen, mostly German speakers whose ancestors had immigrated earlier in the century from the Rhine River region, joined the battle, as did Oneida soldiers who had broken from the Iroquois League to side with the Americans. The bloody fighting in and around Fort Stanwix illustrated the complex ethnic alignments of the Revolution, as Native Americans, Germans, and New York colonists fought on both sides. The strategic significance of the battle was simpler. By holding the fort, supporters of the rebellion stopped a key part of the Albany invasion in its tracks, foiling the British plan to capture the Hudson and divide the colonies into two, noncontiguous parts.

With no help forthcoming from Howe, Burgoyne was now on his own. He encamped at the town of Saratoga, his numbers and supplies depleted by a long journey that had been further slowed by the sabotage efforts of local militiamen. Soon after the Continental Army arrived, Burgoyne attacked on September 19 at Freeman's Farm, winning control of the field but suffering more casualties than the Americans. A second battle, on October 7, proved even costlier for the British, who retreated to Saratoga but soon found themselves surrounded. Burgoyne surrendered to the Americans on October 17, marking the formal conclusion of the **Battle of Saratoga** and bringing the invasion of Albany to an end.

POLITICS AND ENTERTAIN-MENT | ● As the news of Saratoga spread through the colonies, Patriots toasted the success of the rebellion and re-enacted "General Burgoyne's Surrender" in the form of a dance craze. ● Such premature celebrations soon subsided, but the reverberations of Saratoga would last longer. The defeat exposed Britain's war effort to criticism at home. And in France, reports of the American victory helped persuade King Louis XVI that the colonists' struggle for independence was viable.

FOREIGN INTERVENTIONS

Dreams of American independence, ironically, depended on international opinion and foreign diplomacy. Colonists sought the recognition and support of other nations, but none so badly as that of France, Britain's powerful, long-standing enemy. The French had been seeking an opportunity to avenge its defeat in the Seven Years' War, and French officials had, in fact, been counting on a political crisis in the American colonies to provide such an opportunity. But it was by no means clear in 1775 what role France might play in the Revolutionary War. Although the colonists' espousal of natural rights and representative government attracted certain French supporters of the Enlightenment, including the Marquis de Lafayette, most of the aristocrats in the court of King Louis viewed the democratic implications of the American Revolution with repugnance or trepidation. The Continental Congress published its Declaration of Independence in part to persuade the French of the legitimacy of the revolution. Still, in the first two years of the war, France provided covert military aid to the colonists but did not officially enter the conflict.

After Saratoga, France did not want to miss its chance to weaken Britain, especially in the Caribbean. Sensitive to the possibility that conciliatory moves from Britain might now lead to peace, France signed a defensive alliance with American representatives in February 1778. Under this agreement, both sides undertook not to make a separate peace with Britain until it formally recognized the colonies' independence. With French intervention seeming imminent, the British government dispatched a commission, led by the Earl of Carlisle, to negotiate an end to the war. Earlier in the year, Lord North had repealed the Tea Act and the Massachusetts Government Act (the abrogation of the colony's charter), but the **Carlisle Peace Initiative** went further, offering to roll back all post-1763 taxes if the colonists dropped their bid for independence. The alliance with France both emboldened and obligated the Continental Congress to reject those terms, however. Congress ratified the agreement with France, and in June the French declared war on Great Britain. Spain joined France in 1779, and a year later the Dutch followed suit.

Although it yielded no immediate results on North American battlefields, the support of Britain's European enemies instantly boosted the Patriots' prospects. French commitments made it less likely that Congress would go bankrupt, and French and Spanish threats to Britain's Caribbean colonies promised to tie up the British navy. A war on the American continent had turned global, again.

THE SOUTHERN CAMPAIGN AND THE BRITISH SURRENDER

While British and American diplomats adjusted to the shifting political landscape, each side pursued new war offensives. The Continental Army and the colonial militias turned their attention to the west, launching attacks in Indian country in 1778 and 1779. Edward Hand routed the Shawnee and Delaware near Fort Pitt, while George Rogers Clark drove into Illinois, capturing a British fort and seizing native villages. As Washington ordered an all-out attack on Britain's Iroquois allies in New York, North Carolina militias destroyed dozens of Cherokee villages in what is now Tennessee.

Britain, meanwhile, embarked on a new strategy for winning the war or at least salvaging a significant part of its mainland empire. Rather than isolate New England, the British now sought to capture the South. A **southern campaign,** the British hoped, would draw support from Loyalists, ignite fears of slave rebellions, and wrest control of the colonies' most valuable economic resources. Landing at the port of Savannah at the end of 1778, British soldiers propped up a new colonial government in Georgia. A year later, British generals Henry Clinton and Lord Charles Cornwallis sailed south from New York and invaded Charleston, where fifty-five hundred American soldiers surrendered to the British. Continental troops rushed south to thwart the invasion but were badly defeated in August, 120 miles north of Charleston in the Battle of Camden.

British successes in Georgia and South Carolina reflected the numerical strength of their forces, as well as valuable intelligence reports sold to them by Benedict Arnold, whose treason was uncovered in the fall of 1780. But Britain was not able to extend its control of the southern coast into the region's interior. The next phase of the campaign was a brutal civil war between Loyalists and Patriots in the Carolinas, where both sides committed vicious acts of torture and mutilation. Guerilla bands and militias on the American side gained the upper hand, winning significant battles at King's Mountain (North Carolina) and Cowpens (South Carolina). Unable to hold the Lower South, British general Cornwallis withdrew northward to Virginia.

Cornwallis captured Williamsburg, moved swiftly through Virginia's Tidewater region, and camped at the small tobacco port of **Yorktown** on the Chesapeake Bay in the summer of 1781, awaiting additional troops from New York. Learning that the powerful French fleet was sailing north from its main military ventures in the Caribbean, Washington devised a plan to surround Cornwallis. Instructing Marquis de Lafayette to detain the British troops in Yorktown, Washington headed south to Virginia with a French unit. Shortly before they arrived, Admiral Francois de Grasse's ships reached the Chesapeake Bay in time to cut off further British reinforcements and prevent Cornwallis from retreating. Surrounded by a larger French-American force, subjected to heavy bombardment, beset by food shortages and smallpox, and denied an escape route, the British surrendered on October 19, yielding approximately seventy-five hundred prisoners to the United States. The stunning American victory at Yorktown destroyed Britain's southern campaign. British forces still controlled New York and Charleston, but threats from France and Spain made Britain's position in North America difficult to sustain. The war, which was now deeply unpopular in England, shifted to the West Indies and to the negotiating table.

WHOSE REVOLUTION?

Fighting between France and Great Britain continued in the Caribbean and on the high seas for another two years, and George Washington feared another attack from British troops still staged in North America, but most Americans understood by the end of 1781 that the rebels had prevailed. Thirteen former British colonies would not be forcibly reintegrated into the empire. What this might ultimately mean for those living in North America remained unclear as diplomats negotiated peace terms and new state and federal governments developed (see Chapter 7). But the war itself shifted power relations among various groups of Americans.

WOMEN IN THE REVOLUTION

American women were formally excluded from military service in the American cause. Whig leaders of the independence movement did not advocate sexual equality or the rights of women to direct political representation. Nonetheless, women had both a role and a stake in the outcome of the revolutionary struggle. When war came, women found themselves swept into the chaos and violence of the period, even though few of them donned army uniforms. Thousands of women, mostly soldiers' wives, widows, or runaway servants, joined the military community as what were called **camp followers,** serving the Continental Army as nurses, cooks, and laundresses. Those women who remained at home faced difficult decisions about whether and how to support the war effort by concealing men and weapons or by providing food and lodging to soldiers and militiamen. Some women also served as spies for the Patriot cause (see Singular Lives: Patience Wright, Woman Under Cover). Finally, they participated by either supporting or discouraging the enlistment of their male relatives.

The war forced women of all classes to declare their political commitments and thereby muddied the neat lines that protected politics as the exclusive concern of elite men. What this portended for women's status in an independent United States remained unclear. Early in the war, Abigail Adams famously applied the Whig critique of power to the family. She admonished her husband, John, as a delegate to the Second Continental Congress, not to put "unlimited power in the hands of the Husbands." Observing that "all Men would be tyrants if they could," she warned that "Ladies . . . are determined to foment a Rebelion, and will not hold ourselves bound by any Laws in which we have no voice, or Representation." The Revolution did not, however, spark a widespread gender conflict.

SINGULAR LIVES

Patience Wright, Woman Under Cover

In 1772, during a lull in the imperial crisis, a young woman from New Jersey became a cultural sensation in London. Patience Wright was a young widow with five children to support and a talent for producing uncannily lifelike wax sculptures of people's heads. Hoping to make a living as a portraitist for the rich and famous, she secured a letter of introduction to Benjamin Franklin, then living in London, who showed her around town and promoted her work. Quickly, she amassed a substantial clientele, including lords, ministers, actors, and literary figures. By 1773, even the king and queen, whom Wright (raised as a Quaker not to respect social titles) referred to as "George" and "Charlotte," had sat to have their busts sculpted by this American woman.

Beyond her lucrative private commissions, Wright's fame and fortune grew with public exhibitions of her work. Some spectators came to see wax impressions of celebrities, much as they go to wax museums in London or Las Vegas today. But others were curious to see the product of Wright's unusual art. Word spread that Wright sculpted her subjects by studying their faces while holding the clay under her apron, keeping the material warm between her legs and concealing her work as she progressed, until finally lifting the apron to reveal, as if in a moment of birth, the fully formed head.

Over the course of the escalating conflict with the American colonies, Wright became notable in London for other reasons. Forthright about her sympathy for the rebellion, Wright fell from royal favor, and was even suspected of spying for the American cause. She maintained close relationships with a network of American supporters in London and welcomed American prisoners of war into her home. Biographers speculate that Wright may have passed information to her sister in Philadelphia by embedding pieces of paper into her wax sculptures. She never returned to her native land, dying in London in 1786 after a fall.

Where in the Archives?

Because of her unusual talent and performance style, Patience Wright achieved brief fame in newspapers on both sides of the Atlantic, and many articles describing her art survive. But she also shows up in the correspondence of famous Revolutionary leaders, including her promoter, Benjamin Franklin, and even George Washington. Letters to both men are housed in the

"The Heads of the Nation in a Right Situation," by John Williams, 1780. This political cartoon features Patience Wright admiring the decapitated heads of three British officials: "This is a sight I have long wish [sic] to see." The cartoon's title plays on the celebrity wax artist's last name. ©*The Trustees of the British Museum/Art Resource, NY*

Founders Online collection of the National Archives in "editions" called the Benjamin Franklin Papers and the George Washington Papers (https://founders.archives.gov/).

Assignment

Locate two letters to Patience Wright, one from Franklin and one from Washington, using the search feature on the Founders Online website:

1. Summarize each letter, 50–100 words per summary.

2. Compare each of the men's attitudes toward Wright and the significance of her work for the cause of independence, using details from the letters and your summaries, in 100 words. You may consider both the tone and the content of the letters.

LOYALISTS

Like many anti-colonial movements, the armed struggle for American independence was a civil war between two factions of colonists (see Map 6.2). Many **Loyalists,** as they called themselves, continued to see themselves as subjects of the British Crown and viewed the rebellion as illegitimate or undesirable. Loyalism was the dominant political stance among white colonists in Canada, Florida, Bermuda, and the British Caribbean, and some opponents of the rebellion in other colonies moved to those parts of the empire early in the crisis. But Loyalists also formed a substantial minority of the population in the thirteen rebellious colonies throughout the war. Some joined the British army or served in Loyalist militias or guerilla bands. Others lent material support to the British side. Yet others simply expressed their opposition to independence or refused to take loyalty oaths to the rebel governments.

American opponents of the rebellion were not restricted to a particular colony and did not all fit a common profile. Scholars estimate the number of Americans

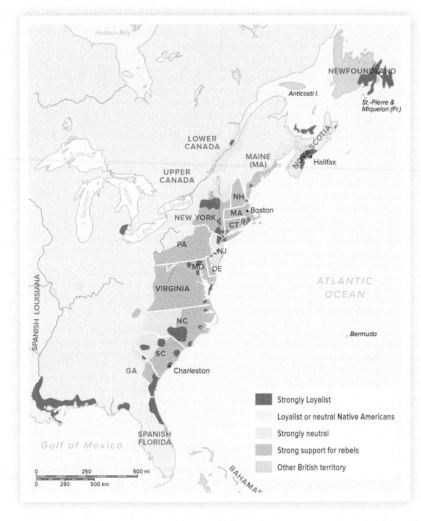

Map 6.2 A Civil War in Britain's American Colonies. Although the war divided families, towns, and colonies, loyalty to the empire was much stronger in particular regions.

fighting between Loyalists and Whigs in South Carolina was rooted in personal recriminations as much as competing views of parliamentary authority.

One common feature of many white Loyalist communities was their minority status. Men and women who felt vulnerable to the animosities of a hostile majority had a greater investment in royal protection and less optimism about a future under popularly elected governments. Immigrant groups who continued to speak Dutch or French tended to stay loyal, for example, as did some religious minorities. Specific religious minorities opposed the Revolution, or at least refused to participate, as a matter of faith. Quakers, Mennonites, Moravians, and others objected conscientiously to taking up arms, hiring substitutes, or paying taxes to support the fighting. Quaker meetings disciplined or expelled members for these practices, for taking loyalty oaths, or simply for celebrating Independence Day. Religious pacifists were seen as Loyalists and subjected to severe punishments, including property confiscation and imprisonment.

During the war, Loyalists of all persuasions suffered from punitive laws and hostile neighbors. After Yorktown, many began to emigrate. Overall, eighty thousand to one hundred thousand Americans fled or were banished for political reasons during the war era, many in mass emigrations in 1782 and 1783. Some wealthier Loyalists sailed to England, where the British government compensated them for their lost property. More sought new homes in other parts of British America, especially Nova Scotia. These Americans were refugees from a war they had lost, and from a colonial society that had vanished.

SLAVERY AND INDEPENDENCE

For the five hundred thousand human beings who were enslaved in the thirteen colonies at the start of the war,

who remained loyal to Great Britain during the war at less than one-fifth of the white population, and Loyalists were a persecuted minority in all thirteen colonies. But loyalism ran high in particular communities. During the war, Loyalists also concentrated in port cities, such as New York, Philadelphia, Charleston, and Savannah, occupied by the British army. Loyalism was sometimes associated with conservative political ideologies, but more often it reflected local conflicts and grievances. Many tenant farmers in New York's Hudson Valley opposed the Revolution in part because one wealthy landlord supported it. A formerly enslaved, now escaped, African American known as Colonel Tye led Loyalist guerrilla raids against Patriot slaveholders in New Jersey in part to settle old scores with men who had abused him. The brutal and protracted

the Revolution had special meaning. When Patriots claimed to be fighting to preserve their liberty against the threat of slavery, enslaved Americans paid close attention, wondering how their own freedom fit into this political agenda. Some British policy makers assumed that the rebels' ideas about freedom might undermine colonial slave systems, which is partly why they expected slaveholders to provide powerful conservative voices against the rebellion. Those expectations were partially confirmed in coastal Georgia and South Carolina, and more clearly vindicated in the British West Indies, where white colonists on the islands with the largest slave majorities showed the least enthusiasm for the independence movement. When a major slave revolt erupted in Jamaica in 1776, slaveholders there blamed it in part on all the talk circulating that year about the nobility of sacrificing one's life to avoid the fate of being enslaved. Few Whig essayists and orators in the mainland colonies ever made this link, however, and most of the revolutionary leaders accepted the institution of chattel slavery in their midst.

Many Black Americans, both free and enslaved, saw great promise in the independence movement. Especially in New England, Black preachers and writers embraced the cause of liberty and took white comrades to task for not extending their views on freedom to the plight of people living in slavery. Identifying with the Patriot cause, free Black men took up arms against Britain in disproportionate numbers in the North and played significant roles in the early violence in Massachusetts. Earlier in the imperial crisis, enslaved Blacks in Massachusetts took their enslavers to court, relying on liberty-minded juries to affirm their individual emancipation. Jenny Slew initiated one of the first of these **freedom suits** in 1766, persuading a court in Salem that having a white mother made her enslavement illegal. Others made different arguments, tailored to their circumstances. After 1773, Black New Englanders adopted the strategy of petitioning legislatures for general emancipation, arguing against the legitimacy of slavery altogether (see Interpreting the Sources: Antislavery Petitions in Massachusetts).

Whereas some enslaved African Americans in New England turned optimistically to the Revolution, far more enslaved people, especially in the South, saw prospects for freedom on the British side. For them, it was the war rather than the independence movement, that inspired dreams of liberation. As a political maneuver designed to frighten slaveholders into loyalty, Lord Dunmore's promise of freedom to African Americans in Virginia backfired. By harboring and arming fugitives from slavery, Dunmore united Virginia's slaveholders in opposition to the government and permanently severed their allegiances to the empire. But from the perspective of people living under the slavery regime in Virginia, Dunmore's Proclamation and similar orders by other British commanders were beacons of light. It was a life-changing opportunity for which many had been waiting. Throughout the war, whenever British forces occupied port cities in the North, enslaved men, women, and children sought refuge there.

When the heavy fighting shifted to the South after 1778, the scale of this migration exploded. By 1780, when British ships were traveling along rivers that fed into the Chesapeake Bay, word had circulated through Tidewater plantations and thousands of people in slavery began plotting their escape. A British naval raid along the Potomac River in 1781, for example, stopped in Mount Vernon, home of George Washington, where fourteen men and three women belonging to the American commander in chief climbed aboard. In all, some ten thousand enslaved people from Virginia fled to the British side between 1779 and 1781, constituting what some historians consider the greatest slave rebellion in U.S. history. For most of the participants in this **wartime slave rebellion,** the decision to run away proved fatal. A majority died of smallpox or various fevers that swept through the British camps. Others lost their lives to starvation or battle wounds during the siege of Yorktown. As the siege tightened, General Cornwallis decided to conserve supplies by sending thousands of Black men out of the fortified camp they had helped build. This gave them a chance to avoid recapture but exposed them to new perils. Probably no more than one out of six fugitives from slavery survived to the end of the war.

● Following the Yorktown surrender, it became clear that the enslaved people who had risked their lives for freedom by joining the British had chosen the losing side of the war. For many of the survivors, though, this decision had paid off. When Britain began evacuating, most of the formerly enslaved who had been promised freedom set sail on British ships, mostly for Nova Scotia. Free Blacks who had joined the British in New York also left the United States for Canada. Those African Americans who suffered most from the outcome of the Revolutionary War were those who belonged to Loyalist slaveholders. Thousands of such men, women, and children, mostly from Georgia and South Carolina, left the United States in bondage, destined for the sugar plantations of the West Indies. ●

CROSSING BORDERS

INTERPRETING THE SOURCES

Antislavery Petitions in Massachusetts

Slavery has been around for millennia, and enslaved people have resisted their bondage in countless ways. But petitions of enslaved men and women in Massachusetts during the 1770s broke new ground in attacking the fundamental injustice of slavery. The following passages are drawn from petitions to the Massachusetts colonial authorities in 1773 and the Massachusetts State House of Representatives in 1777.

I. Province of the Massachusetts Bay To His Excellency Thomas Hutchinson, Esq; Governor; To The Honorable His Majesty's Council, and To the Honorable House of Representatives in General Court assembled at Boston, the 6th Day of January, 1773. The humble PETITION of many Slaves, living in the Town of Boston, and other Towns in the Province is this, namely That your Excellency and Honors, and the Honorable the Representatives would be pleased to take their unhappy State and Condition under your wise and just Consideration.

We desire to bless God, who loves Mankind, who sent his Son to die for their Salvation, and who is no respecter of Persons; that he hath lately put it into the Hearts of Multitudes on both Sides of the Water, to bear our Burthens, some of whom are Men of great Note and Influence; who have pleaded our Cause with Arguments which we hope will have their weight with this Honorable Court. . . .

We have no Property. We have no Wives. No Children. We have no City. No Country. But we have a Father in Heaven, and we are determined, as far as his Grace shall enable us, and as far as our degraded contemptuous Life will admit, to keep all his Commandments: Especially will we be obedient to our Masters, so long as God in his sovereign Providence shall suffer us to be holden in Bondage.

It would be impudent, if not presumptuous in us, to suggest to your Excellency and Honors any Law or Laws proper to be made, in relation to our unhappy State, which, although our greatest Unhappiness, is not our Fault; and this gives us great Encouragement to pray and hope for such Relief as is consistent with your Wisdom, justice, and Goodness. . . .

We humbly beg Leave to add but this one Thing more: We pray for such Relief only, which by no Possibility can ever be productive of the least Wrong or Injury to our Masters; but to us will be as Life from the dead.

Signed,
FELIX

II. The petition of A Great Number of Blackes detained in a State of Slavery in the Bowels of a free & christian Country Humbly shuwith [showeth] that your Petitioners Apprehend that Thay have in Common with all other men a Natural and Unaliable [Unalienable] Right to that freedom which the Grat [Great] - Parent of the Unavese [Universe] hath Bestowed equalley on all menkind and which they have Never forfuted [forfeited] by Any Compact or Agreement whatever—but thay wher [were] Unjustly Dragged by the hand of cruel Power from their Derest frinds and sum of them Even torn from the Embraces of their tender Parents—from A popolous [populous] Plasant [Pleasant] And plentiful cuntry And in Violation of Laws of Nature and off Nations And in defiance of all the tender feelings of humanity Brough [Brought] hear Either to Be sold Like Beast of Burthen & Like them Condemnd to Slavery for Life—among A People Profesing the Religion of Jesus A people Not Insensible of the Secrets of Rationable Being

Manuscript Copy of a 1777 Petition of Enslaved Men and Women to the Massachusetts State House of Representatives. Prince Hall and eight other Black Bostonians presented this petition to the General Court, stressing that "your petitioners have Long and Patiently waited the Event of petition after petition." *Courtesy of Massachusetts Archives*

Nor without spirit to Resent the unjust endeavours of others to Reduce them to A state of Bondage and Subjection your honouer Need not to be informed that A Life of Slavery Like that of your Petioners Deprived of Every social Priviledge of Every thing Requiset [Requisite] to Render Life Tolable [Tolerable] is far [. . .] worse then Nonexistance.

Explore the Source

1. What are the shared arguments of the two petitions against the legitimacy of slavery?

2. How do the two arguments for freedom differ?

3. How does the later petition appeal to the ideals of the Revolution?

NATIVE PEOPLES AND THE WAR

Even more than the British Empire, which would continue to dominate trade with North America for decades, the biggest losers in the Revolutionary War were the two hundred thousand Native Americans living east of the Mississippi River. Native villages and nations took various positions during the course of the conflict. Many sought to remain neutral, but pressures from both armies and encroachments by American settlers often made this difficult. Representatives of the Continental Congress pushed the argument that Indian interests lay in ingratiating themselves with the region's emerging superpower and fighting against the British. In the fall of 1775, a diplomatic mission to Native Americans in the Ohio country explained that "the thirteen great Colonies of this Extensive Continent, Comprehending in the whole, at least One Million of Fighting Men, are now so firmly United and Inseparably bound together" that a fight with one colony would incur the wrath of the others. Some Shawnee and Delaware chiefs were persuaded by this threat, but many western warriors were not.

In the case of the powerful Iroquois League, the Americans hoped simply to keep them on the sidelines. "This is a family quarrel between us and Old England," one delegate told his Iroquois audience in 1775. Britain lobbied against this course, arguing that "the Americans . . . mean to . . . take all your Lands from you and destroy your people, for they are all mad, foolish, crazy and full of deceit." The Iroquois remained neutral until the spring of 1777, when the escalating conflict began drawing many warriors into the camp of their long-standing British allies. The war strained the League's political unity, however. While most fought for the British Empire, many Oneida and Tuscarora took up arms for the rebellious colonists. The Revolution ultimately ripped apart the Haudenosaunee, much as it did British America.

Like the majority of Iroquois, most powerful indigenous armies wound up siding with Great Britain, typically because their most pressing conflicts were with settlers who supported the rebellion. Cherokee, Creek, and Choctaw soldiers clashed extensively with American forces in the Southeast. After the war, Cherokee country even provided a haven for white Loyalists. Seminoles in

Agrippa Hull.   Hull was a free Black soldier in the Continental Army. This painting was based on a daguerreotype taken late in his life. *World History Archive/Alamy Stock Photo*

the loyal Florida colonies fought for the British Crown as well. All of these nations wound up in a worse position when their allies surrendered.

Regardless of whether they took up arms for Great Britain, the Revolution was a disaster in Indian country, destroying lives, ravaging land, and sowing dissension. It also armed American settlers, organized their militias, and gave them war experience, thus decisively tipping the balance of military power in the eastern half of the continent. Finally, the British had exerted a constraining force on the westward expansion of land-hungry Americans. As much as they had suffered from Britain's expulsion of the French in 1763, they would now mourn the departure of the British.

CONCLUSION

In less than two decades, Britain's North American empire had unraveled. In an attempt to pay back its war debts and finance the administration of its

territories, Britain had sent the colonists a tax bill. In response to that bill, colonial leaders articulated political ideas that undermined the authority of the home country and precipitated a standoff. Many British colonies backed away from the standoff, because they needed British protection more than they resented its costs. But in thirteen mainland colonies, majorities of the large and growing population of white settlers saw matters differently. Tapping into powerful sources of social conflict, advocates of independence found themselves in a bloody civil war and a protracted revolution.

The American Revolution took an enormous toll on those who lived in and around the thirteen colonies. Over twenty-five thousand soldiers died fighting for independence (approximately seven thousand from battle wounds, ten thousand from disease, and another eighty-five hundred in prison). Thousands more Native Americans and Loyalists were killed in battle and from disease, and as many as ten thousand enslaved African Americans died pursuing freedom in the chaos of the war. Even larger numbers of Loyalists fled the country. In 1781, even after the Yorktown surrender, civil war persisted in South Carolina, fighting continued in Indian country, and major American cities were under British occupation.

Alongside all of this violence and destruction, the rebellious former colonists were building something new. The new republic that would emerge from this crisis would be shaped by wartime traumas and experiences, but also by the nation-building project that took place in tandem with the Revolution.

STUDY TERMS

Quartering Act of 1765

Stamp Act

Stamp Act Congress

Sons of Liberty

Declaratory Act

Whigs

Tories

Liberty Tree

Townshend Duties

Circular Letter

nonimportation agreements

nonconsumption

Regulators

Green Mountain Boys

urban rioting

tarring and feathering

Boston Massacre

Tea Act

Boston Tea Party

Coercive Acts

Quebec Act

Committees of Correspondence

First Continental Congress

Battle of Lexington and Concord

Second Continental Congress

Continental Army

Common Sense

Regulars

Lord Dunmore's Proclamation

invasion of Quebec

Fort Stanwix

Battle of Saratoga

Carlisle Peace Initiative

southern campaign

Yorktown

camp followers

Loyalists

freedom suits

wartime slave rebellion

FURTHER READING

A database of additional full-text readings is available through Power of Process for Primary Sources in Connect.

Joseph Adelman, *Revolutionary Networks* (2019), charts the impact of printers on the independence movement.

Colin Calloway, *The American Revolution in Indian Country* (1995), examines the experiences of various Native American communities during the war.

Caroline Cox, *A Proper Sense of Honor* (2007), highlights social conflict within George Washington's army.

Kathleen DuVal, *Independence Lost* (2016), narrates the Revolution from the perspective of the Gulf Coast.

Douglas Egerton, *Death or Liberty* (2009), reconstructs the dilemmas of African Americans during the Revolution.

David Hackett Fischer, *Liberty and Freedom* (2005), shows how two key ideas of the revolutionary cause were represented visually.

Holly Mayer, *Belonging to the Army* (1999), reconstructs the world of female camp followers in the war.

Gary B. Nash, *The Forgotten Fifth* (2006), rethinks the significance of the war for African Americans, including those who joined the British side.

Andrew O'Shaughnessy, *An Empire Divided* (2000), explains why Britain's Caribbean colonies did not join in the revolt against the empire.

Ray Raphael, *A People's History of the American Revolution* (2001), offers a detailed survey of the crisis and the war, emphasizing the experiences of women, the poor, the enslaved, and Native Americans.

7 | MAKING A NEW NATION

Chapter Questions

1. What were the content, character, and composition history of the documents—the Declaration of Independence, state constitutions, Articles of Confederation, and U.S. Constitution—that established the new American republic?

2. How and in what ways was long-distance communication important to nation building?

3. Why and how did Americans become interested in plotting the geography of the North American continent?

I.

PROPOSED DIVISION OF THE WEST IN THE
PLAN OF MARCH 1, 1784.

Mapping the West, Imagining a Nation, 1784.
Historic Collection/Alamy Stock Photo

John Adams predicted in 1776 that the anniversary of independence would become a national birthday marked by "pomp and parade, shows, games, sports, guns, bells, bonfires, and illuminations, from one end of the continent to the other from this time forward, forever more." More than two centuries later, Adams's prophecy seems fulfilled in Fourth of July parades, battle re-enactments, backyard barbecues, afternoon baseball games, and shopping sprees of recent decades—except for the odd detail that he expected the celebrations to occur on July 2. Adams had not misread his calendar; he simply assumed

1776

Continental Congress declares independence

1776-1778

States create written constitutions

1777

Vermont constitution outlaws slavery

1781

Articles of Confederation ratified

1783

Treaty of Paris signed, officially recognizing the new nation's borders

1785

Land Ordinance divides western territories into gridded squares

1786

Violent political resistance erupts in western Massachusetts

1787

Northwest Ordinance prohibits slavery in the Northwest
Constitutional Convention gathers in Philadelphia
Constitution published

1788

The Federalist, arguing for ratification, appears in book form
Constitution ratified by nine states

1789

George Washington elected first president

1791

Bill of Rights added to the Constitution

1792

Post Office Act establishes federal control over a national communication network

that Americans would choose to commemorate the date when Congress passed a resolution declaring independence, instead of when it formally approved a written document to that effect two days later.

Adams's mistaken prediction reminds us how difficult it is to pinpoint in retrospect the moment when the new nation was born. Why do Americans not celebrate their independence on the April anniversary of the first shots fired at Lexington and Concord in 1775, or the act of Congress the following May that authorized the creation of new governments, or the framing of the first new state constitutions? Why not choose

the British surrender at Yorktown in 1781, the Treaty of Paris two years later, or the ratification of the Constitution in 1788?

Among the many turning points in the history of American independence and nation building, the events of July 4, 1776, do not immediately stand out. A signed, written text declaring independence did not suddenly introduce a breach between the colonies and the British Crown (which had already happened), nor did it instantly create a new national government (which would come years later). Yet this text and the moment it marked made a difference to the men of the Continental Congress who were charged with organizing the war effort. The tactic they chose was an act of communication that helped create a new nation. The military success of the rebellious colonists was only part of the process of making a new nation. July 4th commemorates the larger role of speaking, writing, and publishing in that process.

During the decade and a half following the Declaration, both leaders and ordinary participants in the revolutionary movement tried to make sense of the events of July 1776 and to back up the audacious claim that thirteen long-standing British colonies were now united as free and independent states. New governments had to be designed and implemented, new patterns of communication had to be established, new maps had to be drawn, and a new national identity had to be conceived, represented, and publicized. This period is often identified with two founding documents, the Declaration of Independence and the U.S. Constitution, which stand as powerful—and radically different—symbols of the birth of the nation. But these documents emerged in a larger context of discussion, conflict, and celebration. Nation building unfolded in committee meetings, public parades, newspapers, pamphlets, drinking rituals, popular novels, and the expanding media of communication.

DECLARING INDEPENDENCE

The **Declaration of Independence** has no formal status in American law. One cannot sue a neighbor or challenge a local ordinance on the basis of the pronouncements in the Declaration. Whatever power or authority it has enjoyed over the course of U.S. history is a function of its status as a sacred text that expresses the nation's founding ideals. But the Declaration did not become national scripture until the nineteenth century. By the twentieth century, the federal government would see fit to exhibit the original parchment text in a national shrine for visitors.

In its day, the Declaration's status was far less clear. Originally a statement by the Continental Congress, the Declaration was at the same time a personal pledge of commitment on the part of the delegates, a public indictment of King George III, and a strategic attempt to persuade the world (specifically, France, which Congress sought to recruit as a military ally) that the revolt against British authority was serious and legitimate. Members of Congress were not entirely certain what it meant to declare independence. Was Congress, as John Adams had suggested early in the process, simply declaring for the record a fact that already existed, or was it somehow bringing a new state of independence into being? This ambiguity persisted as the document circulated in multiple forms and formats across the rebellious colonies.

DECLARATION BY COMMITTEE

On June 7, 1776, Virginia delegate Richard Henry Lee presented a resolution on the floor of the Continental Congress "that these United Colonies are, and of right ought to be free and independent States." Because several delegations still had instructions from their colonies not to renounce allegiance to Britain, Congress decided to buy time by referring the matter to a smaller committee that would prepare a larger text. The committee consisted of five men: Thomas Jefferson (Virginia), John Adams (Massachusetts), Roger Sherman (Connecticut), Robert Livingston (New York), and Benjamin

Franklin (Pennsylvania), though Franklin was ill and probably did not participate in the initial deliberations. Jefferson, the junior member of the committee, was chosen as draftsman, charged with producing a case for independence in consultation with other committee members. The text he drafted was presented to Congress on June 28, and the independence resolution passed on July 2 by a vote of twelve to zero (with New York abstaining). But even after that vote, delegates spent the next two days tinkering with the document, making substantive changes and stylistic edits that Jefferson resisted and resented. A final version was then read aloud, accepted, and approved for publication.

It is hard to determine whether the Declaration was read aloud in Congress solely to secure final approval of its language, or whether the reading itself formed part of the ritual of becoming independent. If the Declaration was simply a legal enactment, like a declaration of war, then what mattered was simply that Congress had stated that the former colonies were now free states. But Jefferson himself took seriously the idea that he was drafting a text that would be performed before an audience.

National Shrine. The physical document that is identified with American independence had been treated somewhat carelessly by the State Department until 1921, when the Library of Congress took custody of the parchment. During World War II, the Declaration was transferred to Fort Knox under protection of the Secret Service and the U.S. Army. After its safe return to Washington, the Declaration entered airtight thermopane containers (with electronic helium detectors) in the National Archives. It remains a tourist attraction by day, but every night the document descends into a 55-ton vault of concrete and steel. *Photographs in the Carol M. Highsmith Archive, Library of Congress, Prints and Photographs Division*

Declarations were a special kind of speech act with a rich history in English politics. Unlike petitions, they did not appeal to the authority of a governing body. At the same time, they were more formal than ordinary announcements or pamphlets, which appeared with great frequency in colonial America. This particular declaration served multiple functions. It was supposed to rally popular support in the colonies for the war effort, justify the colonial cause to the "opinions of mankind," announce to other nations that the colonies were available for trade and military alliances, and formally nullify the authority of Great Britain over most of its North American possessions.

THE TEXT OF THE DECLARATION

Written in relatively plain language, Jefferson's draft sought to avoid the stately trappings of royal decrees and express the basic convictions of a broad populace. But for the founding document of a new nation, the Declaration of Independence is also notable for all the things it does not say. The text makes no mention of the history or purpose of English colonization (nothing about the travails of the Jamestown settlers or the lofty visions of the Puritans), omits any reference to the distinctive cultural identity of American colonists, refrains from commenting on the legitimacy of monarchy or aristocracy, and provides no blueprints for a new republican government—all subjects that could have been both contentious and

Early Draft of the Declaration of Independence. Thomas Jefferson was a timid and ineffectual speaker, but he valued the power of oratory and understood his task as draftsman of the Declaration as that of a playwright composing words that would be pronounced dramatically. This early draft included what might appear to be accent marks but were, in fact, Jefferson's way of instructing a speaker when to pause between words or phrases. *North Wind Picture Archives/Alamy Stock Photo*

distracting. Instead, the Declaration confines itself to a fairly specific political argument for revolution.

Though later generations would focus on select phrases from the opening, the bulk and the heart of the text consist of a list of charges against King George III. Like an indictment with dozens of criminal counts, the Declaration lists various "injuries and usurpations," including restricting trade, controlling immigration, imposing taxes, dissolving representative assemblies, maintaining a standing army during peacetime, hiring German mercenaries, and supporting slave revolts. Almost all of the charges refer to events of the previous two years. This timeless expression of the first principles of a new nation was, in fact, a timely political pronouncement.

The more memorable words of the Declaration appear in the opening paragraph. It speaks of the periodic necessity to change governments and appeals to the natural equality of "all men" with their inalienable rights to life, liberty, and the pursuit of happiness. Here, too, the Declaration was breaking little new ground. Jefferson's text drew on the writings of John Locke (the English philosopher who sought to justify the Glorious Revolution of 1688), on various Scottish Enlightenment thinkers, and most immediately on the model of fellow Virginian George Mason. Mason's draft for a state Declaration of Rights began with the claim that "all men are born equally free and independent, and have certain inherent natural rights, of which they cannot, by any compact, deprive or divest their posterity; among which are the enjoyment of life and liberty . . . and pursuing and obtaining happiness and safety." In elevating "the pursuit of happiness" to the same level as life and liberty, the Declaration of Independence (like the Virginia Declaration) was putting an important spin on the more common English trio of "life, liberty, and property." Both pursuing things and being happy would become central to American identity and ideology over subsequent generations, but even at the time the phrase struck a chord with the colonists. The pursuit of happiness—an idea drawn from Locke and other Enlightenment thinkers—was one of the few phrases in the Declaration's draft to which no delegate appears to have objected. Jefferson and his committee-mates were not coining novel terms or floating alien ideas. They were drafting language they hoped would express the prevailing sentiments of the revolutionary cause.

PUBLICIZING THE DECLARATION

The Declaration was composed for a larger world of public opinion. Although the simple act of writing, signing, or reading aloud this text might have fulfilled the Declaration's claim to "solemnly publish and declare, that these united colonies are and of right ought to be free and independent states," declaring independence would have meant little if it had been confined to the meeting in Philadelphia. John Hancock, president of the Continental Congress, took charge of the elaborate task of informing and persuading his fellow colonists from New England to Georgia that something momentous had taken place on July 4.

MEDIA AND INFORMATION

● Spreading the word that independence had been declared involved both writing and speech. According to congressional resolution, the Declaration was to be printed, so that copies could be distributed to assemblies, conventions, committees, and militias in every state. But once it arrived at those gatherings, the text would be proclaimed orally. George Washington ordered officers in New York to pick up copies of the text and read it to their soldiers "with an audible voice." Elsewhere, colonists gathered in courthouses, churches, and public squares to hear independence pronounced. ● In Philadelphia, not far from where the Declaration had been carefully composed and contentiously edited, a member of the local Committee of Safety performed the document from the balcony of an astronomical observatory to a chorus of cheers and bells. Colonists responded enthusiastically to these performances. Some communities defaced pictures of George III on tavern signs. New Yorkers destroyed a prominent equestrian statue of the king.

POLITICS AND ENTERTAINMENT

● Throughout the war, Americans re-enacted the dramatic script of July 4 in everyday acts of celebration. Especially common were festive rituals celebrating the thirteen free and independent states—thirteen gun blasts in a town square or thirteen toasts in a tavern (see Interpreting the Sources: Thirteen Toasts). All of this street theater was in turn reported in newspapers and pamphlets, which circulated along with copies of the Declaration itself, helping readers in one part of the continent imagine their celebrations as part of a unified national response. ● Men and women in the thirteen free and independent states experienced the act of declaration both as a piece of paper and as a shout in the street.

Jefferson's Portable Writing Desk. Originally just one member of a drafting committee, Jefferson came to be identified as the Declaration's author. *North Wind Picture Archives/Alamy Stock Photo*

STATE BUILDING

The first independent governments in U.S. history belonged to the individual states. Between 1776 and 1788, these new states united around a common fate and a collective war effort, but they did not form a single, coherent political entity. States made their own laws and devised their own political systems, drawing on their different colonial legacies as well as new ideas about legitimate and illegitimate uses of power. Nothing in the Declaration or in any of the other acts of the weak Continental Congress prescribed what exactly a proper republican government would look like. While the Congress, hamstrung by tight restrictions on its power, struggled to keep the states unified during and after the war, it fell to those states to bring a new political order into being.

THE FIRST CONSTITUTIONS

Even before the Continental Congress declared independence from Britain, it instructed the colonies to authorize and design new governments. Almost immediately, Patriots started amending their colonial charters or drawing up new **written constitutions**—some permanent, some designed simply to cover the war with Britain. Virginia and New Jersey adopted permanent constitutions within weeks of the congressional call. Over the next two years, eight other states would follow suit, and by the end of the war every rebellious ex-colony had some kind of new constitution in place. These documents are often overlooked in retrospect, but at the time they were recognized as the crucial instruments for change in American political life. The first state constitutions established the legal frameworks that would secure individual rights and determine who had access to wealth and power in the postcolonial era. They would also provide the bases for constitutional thinking at the national level.

Perhaps the most radical feature of the new state constitutions was the fact that they were written down in the first place. The noun *constitution* had not traditionally denoted a text, and the revered "English constitution" was not a document at all; it referred to the political system itself—to the distribution of power among different political institutions, as worked out in an assemblage of laws, charters, customs, and precedents. Colonists had grown accustomed to written documents (such as royal charters) that defined the terms and

INTERPRETING THE SOURCES

Thirteen Toasts

The era of confederation lasted until 1788, a full five years after the official end of the war. During that period, the question of whether the former colonies had become thirteen nations or one remained open. For the most part, the building of new governments and new societies took place at the state level, and former colonists likely saw themselves first and foremost as citizens of those states. But a larger national consciousness was spreading, reinforced by the circulation of printed material and by a postal network that crossed state borders. The practice of offering thirteen patriotic toasts at a tavern, which began as a ritual of wartime solidarity, continued into the 1780s as an expression of this new national consciousness. Although they were spoken to a room of people who knew one another, toasts were printed and reprinted in newspapers and circulated throughout the country.

Toasting rituals drew a wide range of participants into public life, including people who were excluded from voting, serving in the military, or holding office. In Northampton, Massachusetts, a group of women staged their own toasting ceremony to celebrate the conclusion of peace with Great Britain in 1783, after a men's celebration on the previous day paid insufficient attention to female contributions to the cause of independence. As reported in the newspaper, the assembled women drank to

1. Lady Washington.
2. The Congress.
3. A long continuance to our glorious peace.
4. The Thirteen United States.
5. Success to Independence.
6. May internal disturbances cease.
7. Trade and Commerce throughout the world.
8. Reformation to our husbands.
9. May the gentlemen and the ladies ever unite on joyful occasions.
10. Happiness and prosperity to our families.
11. Reformation to the men in general.
12. May the Protestant religion prevail and flourish through all nations.
13. May reformed husbands ever find obedient wives.

Source: Massachusetts Gazette, recorded in David Waldstreicher, In the Midst of Perpetual Fetes (Chapel Hill: University of North Carolina Press, 1997), 83.

Explore the Source

1. What tensions do you see among the various toasts, especially on issues of gender relations?

2. Whom do you imagine to be the intended audience for these toasts?

3. What do you think is meant by the phrase "reformation to the men in general"?

---

conditions of law and government, but those documents were subordinate to a larger system of royal and parliamentary authority that was not written down anywhere. Written constitutions promised to protect colonists against the abuses of power they had experienced under the English constitution, not only because printed texts could be easily circulated, consulted, and cited but also because they started from scratch.

Though they varied significantly from state to state, most of the original constitutions explicitly embraced the idea that legitimate governments drew their power from the consent of the people they governed and were obliged to respect certain **natural rights.** A majority of state constitutions explicitly listed these rights and their derivatives, which typically included civil liberties such as free speech, protection from unjustified searches and seizures, right to trial by jury, and the right to practice one's religious conscience (several states did, however,

maintain an established church). In the blueprints for most of the new governments, executive officers (governors) held much less power than their colonial predecessors, and in Georgia and Pennsylvania, the office was abolished altogether. Those two states also eliminated the more aristocratic upper chamber of the legislative branch, but most constitutions provided for **bicameral** (two-chambered) legislatures, which wielded unprecedented authority and were designed to be responsive to electoral pressures.

More significantly, most new state documents broadened participation in public life, by creating more elective offices, mandating more frequent elections, and reducing—but not eliminating—the property requirements for voting or holding office. In many states, close to half the adult white males became eligible to vote. Here, too, Pennsylvania's 1776 constitution was the most radical, granting suffrage to all taxpaying men (including free Blacks who qualified as taxpayers). In most states, the fact that only men could vote went without saying, though three states saw fit to make the condition explicit. New Jersey's state constitution, however, opened the door for unmarried women to vote, though that door would be slammed shut early in the next century. Despite such anomalies, the basic character of American politics in the early republic (the early *republics*, really) was established during this era.

In the process of building new states on the basis of abstract principles of rights and equality, the framers of these first constitutions faced the problem of slavery. Virginia, the state that held the largest number of enslaved African Americans, was careful not to pitch its influential Declaration of Rights too broadly. George Mason's draft had posited that all men were "born equally free and independent" and could not yield their natural rights, but the delegates at the convention added a phrase to make it clear that those rights were retained only by those who "enter into a state of society," which was understood to exclude those living in slavery. Framers of the **Vermont constitution,** on the other hand, took the occasion to outlaw slavery explicitly when they drafted their constitution in 1777. Vermont was a small territory (not officially recognized as a state until 1791), and its negligible enslaved population was a drop in the ocean of human bondage that spread over much of the nation. But the enactment was significant. Vermont was the first government to abolish slavery in the Americas, and its constitution was the first of the original state-building documents in the United States to extend the rhetoric of equality across racial lines. It was also the only one.

CONFEDERATION

Although the states crafted written constitutions, no comparable document existed at the national level. For five years after independence was declared, the Continental Congress operated without any formal authority. The purpose of having a single congress governing the thirteen unified states was explicit during wartime. Thirteen states needed a congress to manage the war effort (and to finance it by requisitioning and borrowing funds and by printing paper currency), to conduct international relations, and to run a postal network that crossed state borders. But as the prospect of military success came to appear more likely, it was not clear what kind of government a national congress should or could provide. Back in 1777, shortly after the American victory at Saratoga (see Chapter 6), Congress had passed what it called **Articles of Confederation,** outlining a structure for a weak central government of a collection of friendly states joined together for common defense. Though the Articles were not ratified by all the member states until 1781, Congress treated the document as a kind of constitution from the time of its initial passage. Since the Articles did not include any executive or judicial branches of government, Congress could act unilaterally to bring the new national government into being. In keeping with the idea that this was a confederation of sovereign states, each state delegation received one vote in Congress, irrespective of its size. When it came to raising funds for the war, states were assessed based on the size of their free populations, but Congress had no power to tax; it could only *ask* the states to contribute money.

A WEAK CENTRAL GOVERNMENT

The relative lack of power granted to the federal Congress under the Articles of Confederation was not an oversight. Recent experiences under British rule had left the leaders of the new states suspicious of strong governments and hostile to entrenched bureaucracies exercising authority across large geographical distances. The states certainly needed one another for protection and support, but that did not mean they wished to submit together to a federal authority located in a capital city. Significantly, the seat of national government migrated among four cities and towns (Philadelphia, Princeton, Annapolis, and New York) during the 1780s, never coming to rest long enough to create a genuinely national space. As the new federal government began its work, nation builders confronted some of the costs of this position.

The new multistate confederation and its weak central government faced the problems of how to repay war debts and how to control lands in the western part of the country. In dealing with the first of those challenges, Congress could only request contributions from the states, much as it had done during the war. States were not especially responsive to these requisitions. Only three of them came up with even half of their assigned quotas between 1781 and 1788. As an alternative to these inefficient requests, Congress proposed a tariff system, which it called an "impost," that would tax consumers indirectly by collecting 5 percent on the value of imported goods as they entered the country. But the measure needed the approval of all the state legislatures, and first Rhode Island and then New York withheld support.

The confederation's money woes were exacerbated by the general economic chaos of the period. During the war, the Continental Congress and the new state governments had issued close to half a billion dollars' worth of steadily depreciating paper money—notes that were not backed by any promise to redeem them in silver or gold.

The value of these **Continental dollars** had dropped precipitously by war's end, practically to a vanishing point. At the end of 1780, Continental money was trading at a discount of 100 to 1, which represented a 1,000 percent rate of inflation on bills printed between 1775 and 1779. As one farmer put it, wartime paper money was "no Better than oak leaves & fit for nothing But Bum Fodder."

Facing runaway inflation and a postwar depression, caused in part by a trade imbalance once foreign armies left North America and British merchants resumed exporting consumer goods, various groups of Americans in and out of government experimented with new strategies for advantage or survival. A few enterprising merchants from New York and New England began searching for new trading partners in China and along the Pacific Coast of North America. Other investors turned to speculating in the debts racked up by state governments during the war. Gambling that promissory notes from the states might eventually be worth something, speculators purchased these notes at heavy discounts from soldiers (and others who had been paid by the states for supplies) and placed considerable pressure on the new governments to repay them. Debtors, meanwhile, lobbied states to ease the money supply by printing more paper money. So did farmers, a group that included most white American families, who hoped that such a policy might boost crop prices. Seven states responded by issuing paper money in order to pay off public debts, which pleased both debtors and those who were owed money by the state but angered other creditors, who would be hurt by inflation. In Rhode Island, the legislature in 1786 authorized an especially large paper issue and declared it legal tender (at face value) for all debts—to the horror of merchants and lenders forced to accept previously worthless currency from customers and borrowers.

In Massachusetts, by contrast, where debtors wielded less influence in the legislature and where a strong tradition of tax administration had survived from the colonial era, the conflict played out differently. Massachusetts leaned on higher taxes rather than inflationary monetary policies to cover war debts, a preference that favored the interests of eastern merchants over western farmers. The state also imposed new direct taxes that further disadvantaged the rural interior. Several western counties erupted in armed revolt in 1786, often identified with Daniel Shays, a war veteran who was blamed by opponents for leading a rebellion. Shays was not, in fact, the leader of the angry farmers (who called their movement a "regulation," rather than a rebellion), though the name **Shays's Rebellion** survives. The rebels targeted the county courts, disrupting foreclosure proceedings where cashless farmers were losing their land.

They were poised to seize a federal arsenal in Springfield when a private army hired by Massachusetts governor James Bowdoin disarmed and imprisoned the rebels. This 1786 uprising put Boston Patriots in the awkward position of defending the rights of governments to forcibly suppress the resistance of taxpayers. The incident also dramatized the economic and political crisis facing the confederation.

Thomas Jefferson expressed his sympathy for the Massachusetts regulators in letters to several correspondents. "God forbid we should ever be 20 years without such a rebellion," he wrote. Jefferson's response was atypical among the leaders of the Revolution, but it reflected some more widely shared concerns about the dangers of a powerful and distant government. He considered the uprising in western Massachusetts a "rebellion honorably conducted," because it was rooted in the moral consensus of a local agrarian community and fit with that community's understanding of political events, however uninformed he thought they were. The lesson he drew was that state leaders needed to maintain better lines of communication with rural constituents, so that rural communities could remain both virtuous and engaged.

Other national leaders drew quite different lessons from this challenge to state government. To them, violence in western Massachusetts exposed the potential for anarchy latent in the recent rebellion and underscored the need for a strong central government that could collect revenues, set monetary policy, and support the kind of military force that could suppress an insurrection. Although Americans remained divided on these questions, the crisis in Massachusetts lent urgency to the complaints about the Articles of Confederation and called

Continental Bill Designed by Benjamin Franklin. Continental currency helped finance the war effort but was also intended to advertise and promote the cause of independence. This 6-dollar note, with its image of a busy beaver, encourages its readers and users to persevere ("Perseverando") in the struggle against Britain. As a symbol of industriousness, the beaver also suggests that hard work and productivity can turn a mere piece of paper into something of real value. *North Wind Picture Archives/Alamy Stock Photo*

attention to the difficulties of securing political assent in a geographically dispersed republic.

The westward drift of the American population posed other problems for the weak central government. Congress spent much of its energy during the 1780s trying to settle land disputes between states and impose treaties on the native inhabitants, who controlled much of that disputed land. In many ways, western lands dominated the politics of the era of confederation. The Articles of Confederation were only ratified in 1781 once Maryland was satisfied by Virginia's renunciation of its claims. Further cessions from various states offered the national government opportunities to remedy financial woes and design new states.

A NEW MAP

The new American nation was not simply a set of governments and political institutions. It also corresponded to a body of land. Separation from Britain did not automatically transform the appearance of this terrain, nor did it instantaneously change the way people lived on the land, but the Revolution had profound effects on the way land was imagined and described. In numerous ways, the first generation of independent American governments relied on maps to define the new nation.

IMAGINING A CONTINENT

The leading advocates of revolution did not speak much about the character of American land. But from the early days of the imperial crisis, leaders of the resistance to Britain had strategically invoked the idea that American colonies formed a continent as a way to get English-speaking colonists born in the Americas to see their interests and identities as united in opposition to those of Parliament. The word *continent* itself connoted a continuous landmass, cutting across various colonial borders, and emphasized the fundamental divide created by the Atlantic Ocean. This way of mapping the colonial world might seem natural today, but at the time it was something of a bold fiction to imagine all the different nations, societies, plantations, language groups, and faith communities living in North America as linked simply because they shared a continental setting. The very notion that British colonies were part of a single landmass stretching from the Atlantic to the Pacific was relatively novel at the time of the Revolution. For most of the previous two centuries, English mapmakers had typically represented North America either as a series of islands and peninsulas or as a separate region within a larger terrain whose contours were unknown.

The word *continent* gained currency in the 1770s and became crucial to the project of independence. Even though the thirteen colonial societies occupied only a small part of the vast expanse of North America, their leaders created *continental* congresses, mobilized a *continental* army, and attributed their political grievances to the continent itself. As one pamphleteer proclaimed in 1775, "Let English statesmen clamor for power . . . yet the continent

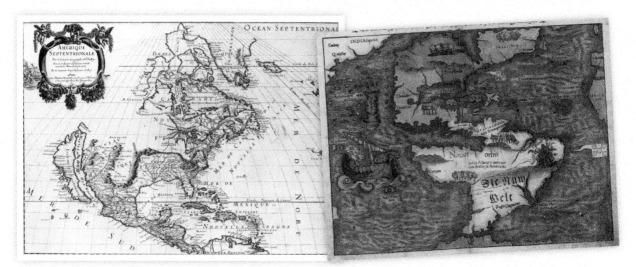

Earlier Views of North America. The image of the United States as a continent was something of a novelty in the eighteenth century. This 1669 map depicts a series of islands and peninsulas rather than a single landmass. *Bettmann/Getty Images*

This sixteenth-century Swiss map puts Mexico at the center of the American landmass and makes Cuba almost as large as the lands that formed the original United States. *Library of Congress Geography and Map Division [G3290 1550 .M8 Vault : HL 49-49]*

of America will contend with equal fervency." In Thomas Paine's *Common Sense*, the Continent (often capitalized) has needs, desires, and even bad habits. But perhaps the best evidence for this new attitude toward the continent lies in the special term that colonists adopted to describe themselves after the Stamp Act crisis. Over and over again, rebellious colonists identified as "Americans," a word that would soon become a national designation but was originally a geographical marker. By calling themselves Americans, as opposed to Virginians or Pennsylvanians, but also as opposed to Englishmen, Europeans, Christians, Baptists, colonists, or gentlemen, the founders of the new

republic were identifying with their continent (see Hot Commodities: Maps of the United States).

NATIONAL BOUNDARIES

Neither the Declaration of Independence nor the Articles of Confederation located the new republic geographically. But the third of America's important founding documents did define the new United States as a place on a map. In 1783, representatives of Great Britain and the new U.S. confederation signed the **Treaty of Paris,** officially ending the war (see Map 7.1). In recognizing the independence

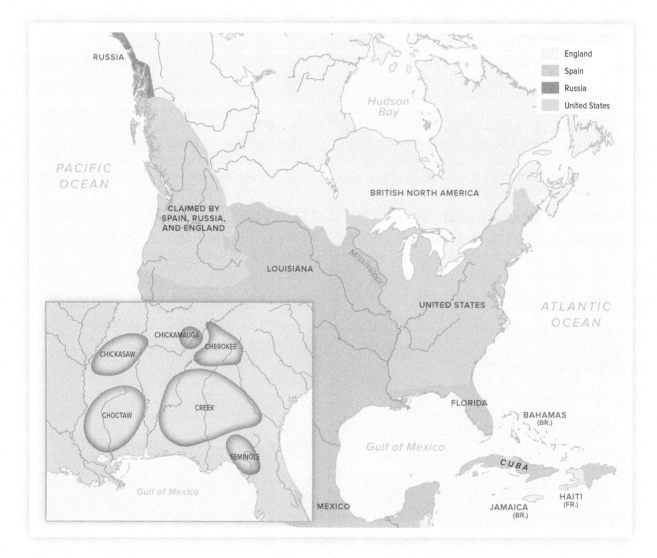

Map 7.1 Treaty of Paris, 1783. Diplomatic negotiations in Europe shifted the map of North America, but the new boundaries ignored the political reality that Native American groups still controlled large portions of the continent. In the southwestern portion of the new republic (see inset), nations not recognized in Paris remained dominant political players in the region.

HOT COMMODITIES
Maps of the United States

One of the remarkable innovations of the Revolution was a popular fascination with imagining what the new republic looked like. Often, new nations spread images of revolutionary leaders, buildings, or battleground sites, but after independence, and especially after the land ordinances, citizens of the United States took particular interest in maps. Jedidiah Morse's textbook *Geography Made Easy* (1784), written shortly after the Treaty of Paris, featured the first published map of the new nation. Cheap, single-sheet national maps became popular consumer items, and large wall maps hung in public offices, coffeehouses, and taverns. Images of the territory of the United States appeared on globes and in pocket atlases, popular almanacs, paintings, card games, and children's puzzles. The proliferation of maps was part of a broader trend toward greater geographical literacy in the late eighteenth century. Land surveying became an important occupation, almanacs began including more geographical data, and geography textbooks like Morse's sold quickly and extensively.

But maps were not simply informative; they were attempts to define the new republic. These nationalistic images stressed the identity between nation and continent, much like the new practice of naming towns, cities, and universities for Christopher Columbus or invoking the figure of Columbia for the United States. Maps also offered readers a graphic symbol of the United States not based in common language, religion, or history. The outline of the nation as a whole, typically without a ny stress on the borders separating individual states, became a recognizable icon, a logo for the new republic.

The nationalistic campaign faced an uphill battle, however. During the decades after the Revolution, British printers, mapmakers, and artists continued to dominate the production of the geographical images consumed in the new republic. Most maps used in American schools in the 1780s and 1790s continued to depict Europe as the center of the world, with the American continent at the periphery.

Picturing the New Nation. Whereas the Declaration of Independence and the Constitution presented the United States as a political entity, maps and icons, such as the one in this detail of a print honoring Benjamin Franklin, depicted the nation graphically as a landmass with a distinctive shape. *The Metropolitan Museum of Art, New York, Rogers Fund, 1926*

Think About It

1. Why might the map of the United States have become an iconic symbol for the new republic?

2. How might the spread of printed maps have contributed to the formation of a centralized federal government?

and sovereignty of the United States and "relinquish[ing] all claims to the government, propriety, and territorial rights of the same and every part thereof," the treaty identified the boundaries of the new nation with great precision (using prose rather than graphics). Article 2 of the treaty cites latitude degrees, distance measurements, and current flow patterns and refers by name to over a dozen different bodies of water. This was one crucial way to designate a new nation—by marking its international borders.

But mapped boundaries can be deceptive. A nation's borders might be recognized by one neighbor but not another. The United States may have relied on the Treaty of Paris to determine its northern border with British Canada, for example, but the treaty also granted the new nation a southern border with Spanish Florida, and Spain had not been consulted on that part of the treaty. The Spanish did not accept a map that divided Georgia from

Florida at the thirty-first parallel, nor did Spain recognize the treaty's authority to grant all U.S. citizens free navigation rights to the Mississippi River. In 1784, Spain barred American ships from the Mississippi and simultaneously cemented alliances with the Creek, Choctaw, and Chickasaw in the Southeast. Those native groups were also neighbors of the new United States, and they, too, had not been consulted on the terms of the Paris treaty.

- The confederation government could not simply take the paper boundaries of the new nation for granted. Shortly after the war's official end, Congress moved to establish a boundary with the six nations of the Iroquois League and occupied land in what is now western New York. Geographical and political ambiguity surrounded the negotiations. The confederation government and the state of New York each claimed rights to make a treaty with the Iroquoian nations. Meanwhile, the Iroquois maintained that their land lay between the United States and Canada whereas the Americans claimed it was surrounded entirely by U.S. territory and effectively conquered. • The resulting **Treaty of Fort Stanwix** (1784) ceded Native American land in the Ohio River valley held by native peoples to the United States. The treaty drew unsuccessful challenges from Shawnee, Delaware, and other groups who were not represented at the negotiations, and was ignored by the state government of New York, which proceeded to appropriate and sell the land. Such treaties made it clear that the new national government possessed the military force to impose international borders on individual native groups but still lacked the administrative capacity to dictate land use to the new states.

In the meantime, the national government needed to resolve boundary disputes between the states, many of which staked competing claims to western lands, far in excess of what their colonial population patterns might have suggested (see Map 7.2). Relying on geographical

vagueness in their original colonial charters, several states even had claims extending to the Pacific Ocean. Once the Treaty of Paris extinguished British claims to lands east of the Mississippi, states were in a better position to seize some of their western lands, but the national confederation also had its eyes on that prize. In 1781, Congress pressured Virginia, the largest state with the most extensive claims, to accept U.S. sovereignty over territory north of the Ohio River. Over the next five years, Massachusetts, Connecticut, New York, and Virginia ceded lands that gave the federal government control over the **Northwest Territory.** This was a major political victory for the new government and set the stage for an act of mapmaking that plotted the westward future of the nation.

LAND ORDINANCES

After the Treaty of Paris and the state cessions, Congress sought to extend the political and social institutions of the United States of America to new regions subject to its rule. The congressional delegate charged in 1784 with drafting a blueprint for the western lands under federal control was the same man who had been asked eight years earlier to draft a script for independence—Thomas Jefferson. In many ways, his second attempt at creating a nation on paper was even more ambitious than the first. Jefferson's grand plan for western development was adopted over the next three years in a series of congressional ordinances that organized land in the Northwest Territory and authorized the creation of new states that would join the confederation. Jefferson effectively drew a picture of the land west of the Appalachians as a blank slate of repeating patterns of identical square sections and subsections. Because Jefferson's plan structured land sales and influenced settlement patterns, this picture remains visible from the air, more than two centuries later, as one flies over the middle of the United States.

The first of these land ordinances, passed in 1784, established the basic plan, mapping out ten new,

Map 7.2 Western Land Claims and Cessions, 1784–1802. By persuading the states to drop claims on Native American–dominated territory relinquished by Great Britain in 1783, the confederation government assumed political control of an enormous and potentially valuable stretch of land.

self-governing territories beyond the jurisdiction of any existing states and that would eventually become states in their own right (see Map 7.3). Their boundaries followed straight lines rather than geographical landmarks (apart from the Ohio and Mississippi Rivers, which framed the entire territory). A year later, the **Land Ordinance of 1785** reduced the number of states that would emerge from this territory and introduced a more elaborate division of land: Each of the eventual states would contain townships 6 miles square, each township contained thirty-six equal sections of 1 square mile, and each section contained four square farm plots of 160 acres (or sixteen 40-acre farms). Congress stipulated further that at least one section in each township be reserved for education.

The final enactment, the **Northwest Ordinance** (1787), specified the procedures under which new states would form. Initially, a territory would be subject to the authority of an appointed governor, and once it reached a population threshold of five thousand free adult, property-owning males, its territorial government would qualify for a representative assembly. Once the free population reached sixty thousand, it could call a constitutional convention and apply for statehood. Congress also placed a significant restriction on these territories, which Jefferson had unsuccessfully proposed three years earlier. Slavery would be prohibited in the Northwest, though fugitives escaping across the Ohio River into the territory had to be returned to the South. This prohibition would have significant implications, not only for life and labor in the future states of Ohio, Illinois, Indiana, Michigan, and Wisconsin, but also for North-South relations in the United States and for future debates about the authority of the federal government to restrict slavery. For that reason, the Northwest Ordinance would be recognized by later generations as the singular achievement of the confederation. But Jefferson's larger vision of how the nation would expand is significant in its own

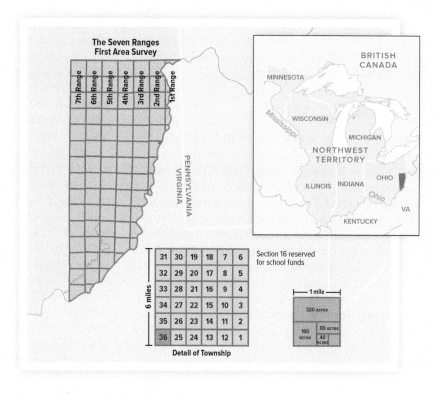

Map 7.3 Plotting the Northwest Territory. The land ordinances imposed a rectilinear grid on the nation's public lands, as shown in this detail from the projected map of southeastern Ohio.

right. The ordinances were not simply ground rules for political growth; they were plans for a new kind of American land that would extend indefinitely.

Jefferson did not invent the idea of a grid design—town and city plans in both Europe and the Americas had long expressed a preference for straight lines and right angles. But the Land Ordinance went further by mapping an entire territory (both urban and rural) as a single stretch of graph paper. Such a planning vision treated land as uniform and homogeneous, recognizing no distinctions of topography, demography, history, or proximity to centers of power. This was significant for at least three reasons. First, it was an appropriate vision for a democratic republic in which the use of land was not constrained by ancient laws, customs, or family claims. Second, it was a blueprint for a national real estate market, in which any plot of land could be easily bought and sold, even by someone who had never seen it. Third, it was a plan for migration, expansion, and conquest, since individuals, families, and communities could simply transplant themselves, relocating ever westward (often into Native American territory) to unknown places that were now likened to the places they left behind. In all these ways, the congressional plan for the Northwest captured and shaped larger patterns of American national development.

THE CONSTITUTION

Congress's success in mapping western territories and amassing a national domain of land did not solve the most pressing challenges of the 1780s. The Articles of Confederation had protected the sovereignty of the new states, in the process creating a central government with limited power to regulate the economy, maintain a strong army, or engage in effective international diplomacy. Congress might hope to sell western land, but without a stable currency or any existing revenue stream to cover the costs of a military, how was Congress going to enforce treaties with Native Americans or with Great Britain, negotiate with the Spanish for access to the Mississippi River, or maintain the allegiance and obedience of the hordes of settlers crossing the Appalachians? Meanwhile, even the state governments faced severe challenges to their authority from westward population drifts, which fed separatist movements in several states. Mounting dissatisfaction with decentralized government led, in 1786, to a meeting in Annapolis, Maryland, where delegates from five states discussed how to "remedy defects of the federal government" and specifically how to expand the power of Congress to regulate interstate commerce. The Annapolis gathering issued a call for a more elaborate national convention, and the disturbing news of the revolt in western Massachusetts produced a cascade of favorable responses from all thirteen states. By February 1787, Congress had thrown its own puny weight behind the proposal, calling it "expedient" for delegates to assemble in Philadelphia that May.

CONVENING THE DELEGATES

Calling a convention to amend the Articles of Confederation did not guarantee major changes in the structure of the nation. Most of the fifty-five delegates to the meeting shared a frustration with the impotence of the federal government; many also harbored a suspicion that the new state governments were excessively democratic. But this did not translate easily into a blueprint for reform. Much would depend on an unpredictable encounter among representatives from twelve states (Rhode Island declined the invitation to send delegates), who would deliberate in secrecy at the Pennsylvania statehouse.

Once a date had been set and delegates selected and charged, state representatives had to make the trek to Philadelphia. At the scheduled start of business, only the Virginia delegation had managed to muster, and they waited impatiently with their Pennsylvania hosts for several days before enough others arrived to form a quorum. Virginians such as George Washington and James Madison were irritated by the delay, but they seized the opportunity to set the convention's agenda and propose a model for a new federal government. The **Virginia Plan,** as it was called, envisioned a complete inversion of the relationship between state and federal government. Under the Articles, Congress represented sovereign states (a bit like the United Nations). Under this new plan, Congress would represent the people living in those states (more like Parliament). Congress would become a bicameral legislature within a three-branch federal government that included an executive officer and a judiciary, and each state's representation within both chambers of Congress would be proportional to its population. Congress would have the power to veto any state law and the authority to use military force against a state that defied a national law.

Though it was ultimately not adopted, the Virginia Plan framed the debate and forced the convention to wrestle immediately with big questions about representation, rather than considering more modest tweaks to the existing framework of national government. Delegates from smaller states (Connecticut, New Jersey, and Delaware), whose constituents would have lost representation under the plan, huddled quickly and devised a counterproposal—known as the **New Jersey Plan**—that reaffirmed the confederation's principle of giving each state an equal vote in the national government. Battle lines were drawn, and much of the summer would be devoted to working out a compromise, under which states would have equal votes in an aristocratic upper house (called the Senate), where members would sit for long terms and would not have to stand for direct election by the people, whereas representation in the lower house would be proportional to population.

TALKING ABOUT SLAVERY

The crucial shift toward proportional representation signaled a decisive break from the kind of nation envisioned in the Articles of Confederation. It also forced delegates to confront the explosive issue of how each state's population would be counted. As James Madison, one of the architects of the Virginia Plan, pointed out, the major political fault line in the United States was not between big states and small ones but between Northern and Southern states. The division arose "principally from the effects of their having or not having slaves." The North did, in fact, have people living in slavery in 1787, but the numbers were small enough to create a clear conflict between the two regions. When it came to apportioning representation in the lower house, Southerners wanted their population counts to include enslaved African Americans, whereas Northerners, not surprisingly, advocated counting only free persons.

Delegates ultimately settled on the infamous three-fifths clause, which credited states for 60 percent of their slave populations. This formula was not a novel suggestion; it had been introduced four years earlier when the Continental Congress was considering how to assess each state's financial burden. For tax purposes, of course, Northerners wanted the free and the enslaved to count equally, whereas Southerners took the opposite view. Delegates to the Philadelphia convention revived Madison's three-to-five ratio in 1787 as a way of calculating both political representation and tax assessment, but most of them understood that Congress was unlikely to engage in any direct taxation. The significance of the **three-fifths clause** is often misunderstood. It was neither an ingenious solution nor an expression of the mathematics of white racism but rather a familiar fraction for splitting a crucial political difference. From the perspective of the enslaved, the insult lay less in being counted as only three-fifths of a person than in being counted at all. Disenfranchised enslaved people had no interest in enhancing the political power of the states in which they were held as property. Crucially, the Constitution's three-fifths clause would provide a political bonus to slaveholders that would artificially amplify their voice in Congress and in presidential elections right up to the Civil War.

The immediate effect of the three-fifths proposal at the convention was to provoke one of the first national conversations about the legitimacy of human bondage. By 1787, the moral consensus that had supported African slavery in the Americas since the early years of European colonization had begun to fray in the North. And while Southerners, especially those from South Carolina, had repeatedly warned that any attempt to strip slaveholders of their chattel would instantly dissolve the national confederation, the dynamics of a face-to-face meeting with secret deliberations produced some frank discussion across a growing moral divide. Delegates from the South spoke openly and anxiously about the need for protection against the possibility that Congress would use its powers

of taxation to abolish slavery—and threatened on multiple occasions to leave the convention. Several delegates, mostly from the North, took the occasion to denounce slavery, which was, in the words of Pennsylvania delegate Gouverneur Morris, a "nefarious institution" that defied "the most sacred laws of humanity." Regional disagreements over slavery could not be cast simply as North versus South. Delegates from Virginia, where slave populations reproduced themselves naturally and slaveholders were no longer importing human beings from Africa or the West Indies, were willing to join New Englanders in criticizing the international slave trade, and Northerners from small states proved amenable to allying with small slaveholding states on that issue to thwart parts of the Virginia Plan. But these tense and testy discussions supported Madison's observation that slavery mattered more than size as an obstacle to redesigning the national government.

The ultimate resolutions of the slavery debate reflected the discomfort many delegates brought to the subject. Nowhere in the final version of the U.S. Constitution would the word *slave* or *slavery* appear, even though the document contains key provisions intended to protect the interests of slaveholders. The Constitution banned federal interference with the slave trade for twenty years and prohibited state and local governments from impeding the return of fugitives from slavery from other states. It also granted slave-rich states extra congressional representation based on their enslaved population—all without ever uttering the crucial word.

WRITING THE CONSTITUTION

By September 8, almost three and a half months after they began their work, delegates had arrived at a set of proposals for a completely new national government, one with enhanced powers and greater insulation from democratic influences. Many important features of the original Virginia Plan, including a bicameral legislature and a three-branch government, survived the long summer of caucusing and negotiation, but the power of the individual states was preserved in some important ways. Both the Senate and the presidency, an executive office chosen by a special gathering of prominent citizens (called an Electoral College), recognized the significance of states as fundamental units in the political order. State governments would have some control over their senators and presidential electors, and senators and electors would represent entire states rather than constituencies within those states. Still, the complex system of checks and balances proposed for the new national constitution entailed something much less like a league of states and more like a central government.

The last remaining item on the convention's agenda was to produce a written text that would describe and define the powers of the new government. Five delegates—Madison, Alexander Hamilton (New York), William Samuel Johnson (Connecticut), Rufus King (Massachusetts), and Gouverneur Morris (Pennsylvania)—formed the **Committee on Style,** which, like the five-man committee that drafted the text of the Declaration of Independence a decade earlier, was charged with choosing the right words to express the intentions of the larger convention. The committee, largely under the leadership of Morris, set about presenting, in crisp and economic language, the various agreements that had been reached over the summer, turning twenty-three provisions into seven main categories. This work was obviously more than just stylistic and editorial. How the Constitution was organized and the precise language it included would have far-reaching implications. And Morris's Preamble, which identified both the authority of the document (the people, not the states) and its goals (forming a more perfect union, securing the blessings of liberty), assigned a specific, overriding meaning to the text that a different introduction might not have claimed.

The precise wording of the text made a difference, and Gouverneur Morris could be said to have authored the Constitution in much same way that Jefferson is credited with authoring the Declaration (see Singular Lives: Gouverneur Morris, Ghost Writer). But few people (then or now) would identify Morris as the originator of the American Constitution, nor is it common to think of the Constitution as having an author at all. (James Madison is widely but misleadingly regarded as the architect of the Constitution, because he famously and vigorously defended its plan of government.) This is because the Constitution makes no claim to personal authority, speaking instead on behalf of an abstract "people." Whereas the Declaration was a pledge of personal honor and commitment on the part of specific individuals who were describing current events in urgent language, the Constitution speaks in a more impersonal voice. The words of the Constitution claimed to come directly from "the people"—not from the signers as individual speakers. All of this helps explain why the Constitution is essentially a printed rather than a written or performed text. Every printed copy of the Constitution has the same significance and authority.

RATIFICATION

The Preamble to the Constitution speaks confidently on behalf of "the people of the United States" and their desires, but, of course, the people had not yet spoken. The blueprint for a new government, which was first presented to the public on September 19, 1787, in a special issue of the *Pennsylvania Packet* newspaper, had been designed by a small and sequestered group of men, fewer than three-quarters of whom actually voted for final approval. The document did not even bear the official stamp of the existing Congress, which simply passed it along to the states without endorsement. Much work was needed to turn the text hammered out in Philadelphia into the supreme law of the land.

To take effect, the proposed Constitution (according to its own terms) would have to be approved by special **ratification conventions** in nine states, something supporters recognized would be a challenge. Almost immediately after the Philadelphia meeting adjourned, advocates of ratification, calling themselves **Federalists,** began organizing conventions in states where success seemed likely. Before the new year, Delaware, New Jersey, and Pennsylvania all ratified. The more interesting and important strategy of the Federalists was to refuse to allow any room in the ratification process for states to give input, propose amendments, express reservations, or vote on particular articles. All the states could do was accept or reject the published Constitution as it was written. This move was designed to prevent the chaos of having to renegotiate new compromises or resubmit amended versions of the text to additional conventions. It was also consistent with the fiction that the Constitution (which was going to set the rules of government, as opposed to being an act of government) spoke on behalf of the people, rather than on behalf of state assemblies or elected representatives. The ratification process presented states with a text written in the name of the people, and it was up to voters to claim the text retroactively or disavow having uttered it.

During the first few months of 1788, ratification battles blazed in several key states. Georgia, which favored a strong national government to protect its border with Spanish Florida, was an easy sell. Connecticut followed soon after, and Maryland and South Carolina also offered hospitable soil for Federalists. But larger states, especially Virginia, Massachusetts, and New York, posed more formidable challenges. **Anti-Federalists** were strong in those states and raised powerful objections to the proposed Constitution on grounds that it would create an oppressive central government that would trample on the rights for which the

SINGULAR LIVES

Gouverneur Morris, Ghost Writer

Politicians and scholars speak of the "framers" of the Constitution, appealing to their ideas and intentions in order to figure out the text's meaning. But who exactly framed the document is open to debate. One place to start is with the man who contributed most of the language that became the supreme law of the land.

Though his face appears on no currency and no state capitals bear his name, Gouverneur Morris left as powerful an imprint on the new nation as any of the more famous founders. Born into the ruling elites of New York in 1752, Morris joined the revolutionary cause and served briefly as a member of the Continental Congress during the war. But his shining moment came a decade later, after he was elected by the legislature in Pennsylvania to represent the state at the Constitutional Convention. Just thirty-five years old, Morris spoke more times at the convention than any other delegate, even though he missed an entire month of the deliberations while attending to private business back home.

Morris was an eloquent and provocative speaker, but he was even more effective as a writer and became an obvious choice to serve on the committee that drafted the Constitution. According to other participants, it was Morris who pared the resolutions and compromises produced on the convention floor into the finished product's compact and straightforward articles, which have become the focus of intense scrutiny and debate in American politics ever since. And it was Morris who penned the Preamble, which remains the most famous part of the original document.

Morris played no role in the ratification campaign and took no position in the new government. He spent most of the rest of the century in Europe, making money, following the French Revolution, and attending to his busy personal life. Morris would return to the United States to make two other great contributions to U.S. history. In 1807, he was appointed by New York State to a commission charged with mapping the future growth of New York City. Three years later, the same legislature named him chair of New York's Canal Commission, which recommended building a canal from the Hudson River to the Great Lakes. These two commissions would revolutionize market relations and urban life. One commission designed Manhattan's grid (see Chapter 8); the other created the Erie Canal (see Chapter 10).

Morris died in 1816, before the canal was built and before the gridded streets of New York were graded. But whereas he was optimistic about these projects, he was less sanguine about his other creation, the Constitution. Late in life, under different political circumstances, Morris came to rue the three-fifths clause and the power it gave to Southern states. Privately, he advocated a breakup of the union.

Morris's disenchantment with the Constitution he had written is a useful reminder of how hard it is to generalize about the framers. The fifty-five men who haggled in secret over the Constitution were very different from one another. And the man who came up with the words a nation would live by was hardly typical of the gathering. He was far more skeptical than most of his colleagues about the benefits of democracy. He championed a strong presidency in the face of delegates who were more comfortable with legislative authority. He was also far more committed to the rights of minorities. He loved cities and dreaded western expansion.

CONFLICTING FAITHS ● Like Thomas Jefferson (with whom he shared little else), he did not believe in an active god and was not a regular churchgoer. ● And he bitterly opposed slavery on moral grounds. What Gouverneur Morris meant by "a more perfect union" undoubtedly differed from what Madison would have meant by the same words. But Morris had simply come up with the phrase. Neither he nor any of the other delegates could determine its meaning.

Where in the Archives?

As a well-educated elite who held numerous public offices, Gouverneur

Founder of a Nation. While completing his famous sculpture of George Washington in full military dress, French sculptor Jean-Antoine Houdon used Gouverneur Morris, living in Paris at the time, as a body double. As in the Constitution he drafted, Morris's special role in the creation of this national icon is concealed from public view. *Witold Skrypczak/Alamy Stock Photo*

Morris produced countless written documents, which researchers have used to reconstruct his life. A two-volume collection of his correspondence and diary entries was published in the late nineteenth century: Anne Cary Morris (ed.), *The Diary and Letters of Gouverneur Morris* is available at the Online Library of Liberty (https://oll.libertyfund.org/).

But many of his most consequential contributions to U.S. history were spoken behind closed doors at the Constitutional Convention. For those contributions, we have to rely on James Madison's "Notes on Debates in the Federal Convention of 1787," housed in a collection of the Avalon Project of the Yale Law School (https://avalon.law.yale.edu/).

Assignment

Browse Madison's notes for August 1787 and notice how frequently and distinctively Morris spoke. Read closely his remarks on August 7, 8, and 9.

1. Write a 500-word response, producing evidence for Morris's views on the subjects of slavery and democracy.

Mercy Otis Warren (1728–1814), Anti-Federalist. Warren, a playwright and historian from Massachusetts, worried that the United States covered too vast a territory to be governed by a single legislature. Although women did not ordinarily vote and never held political office, elite women shaped public discourse about government affairs both in print and in polite conversation. *The Picture Art Collection/Alamy Stock Photo*

Revolution had been fought. A major theme in much Anti-Federalist rhetoric was long-distance communication. How could a government covering such a vast territory genuinely represent distant constituents and respect local customs and opinions? This concern was especially powerful among backcountry voters, who lived far from the centers of information exchange.

Federalists, on the other hand, were strong in cities and towns nearer the seaboard and capitalized on their strong support among printers, who were optimistic about a geographically expansive political culture in which citizens took an interest in distant developments and read newspapers. Arguments in favor of ratification dominated the press, most famously in New York City, where Madison, Hamilton, and John Jay collaborated on a series of eighty-five newspaper pieces published between October 1787 and August 1788. The first thirty-six pieces of *The Federalist* appeared together in book form that March, and the rest constituted a second volume published two months later. Though they formed but a small part of the larger print debate over ratification, the essays eloquently defended the proposed Constitution and, more significantly, offered what future generations would come to regard as the most reliable exposition of its political philosophy. The central theme of this philosophy was the idea that the Constitution represented a system of **checks and balances,** which would protect the new nation against oppression and corruption. *Checks and balances* referred not only to the division of the government into three branches with separate powers and different domains but also to the competition of heterogeneous forces, interests, and regions that *The Federalist* authors believed would prevent any one faction or social group from obtaining excessive power. In this way, its most influential supporters argued, the proposed Constitution would protect the new republic from too much democracy, too much aristocracy, and too much of anything else.

Arguments about ratification were not limited to the press. Both proponents and opponents staged rallies, celebrations, bonfires, and other symbolic expressions of support for their positions. In Carlisle, Pennsylvania, for example, Federalists assembled to fire a cannon to salute the Constitution, but they were met by a larger party of Anti-Federalists, who beat them up, burned an almanac in which the Constitution was printed, and set fire to the cannon itself. Whereas Anti-Federalists gathered to express the consensus of a local community, Federalists favored parades and processions that claimed to speak for more abstract collectivities, such as the new nation itself. Federalist street theater projected images of unity and wholeness and often used the ritual of the thirteen toasts. Once New Hampshire became the surprise ninth state to ratify, putting the Constitution into effect, Federalists tried to put pressure on Virginia and New York by offering only nine toasts.

Both Virginia (in June) and New York (in July) ratified the Constitution by extraordinarily close margins. In both cases, the promise of subsequent amendments to protect the rights of minorities and individuals helped sway opponents to support ratification. Federalists had refused to amend the text prior to the ratification process (since it would have unraveled the fiction that the Constitution preceded the political actions of the states), but once it was in place, the Constitution's leading advocates in Congress joined critics in supporting a **Bill of Rights,** which contains most of what Americans still regard as the essence of the original Constitution: freedom of speech, assembly, and arms-bearing, as well as freedom from state-established religion, unwarranted searches, self-incrimination, or cruel punishments. The Bill of Rights won congressional approval in September 1789 and, by the end of 1791, had met the requisite approval of three-fourths of the states. During that two-year period, North Carolina and Rhode Island also ratified the original Constitution, making good on the earlier boast of the delegates in Philadelphia. The Constitution had now been approved by the unanimous consent of the states.

The original U.S. Constitution, despite its limitations, would wield enormous influence on the development of law and politics both at home and abroad. It did not establish democracy (most Americans remained legally disenfranchised long after ratification), it did not espouse

The Preamble to the Constitution: We the People?
About one hundred sixty thousand voters participated in the selection of representatives to the state conventions that debated ratification. Perhaps one hundred thousand of those people voted, however indirectly, to accept this Constitution as the new supreme law of the land. By many measures, this was a remarkable democratic achievement, but the number of people who in any sense framed the Constitution falls far shy of the almost three million souls who composed U.S. society at the time.
Jon Helgason/Alamy Stock Photo

universal human rights (slavery was fully constitutional), and it did not guarantee basic freedoms of speech, press, assembly, and religion. But the Constitution did enshrine the fundamental principles of separation of powers and popular sovereignty that remain cornerstones of American government, and its model was adopted wholesale by other republican governments, from Venezuela to the Cherokee Nation, over the next several decades. In the longer term, the constitutionalist idea that national governments ought to be founded on and bound by a written text remains one of the most significant legacies of American nation building.

THE FIRST PRESIDENT

In keeping with its primary goal of creating a vigorous and energetic national government, the Constitution called for a chief executive who would wield more authority in American political life than any individual since independence was declared. Although no one campaigned for the job, George Washington seemed an obvious candidate by virtue of his broad personal popularity. Washington had participated in the Philadelphia convention but had frequently expressed his intention to retire from public life. Still, few doubted that he was the right man to unite the states and make the new office of president palatable to those who feared executive power.

After ratification, Washington maintained a reluctant posture, but the sixty-nine electors, representing eleven states (North Carolina and Rhode Island were not yet on board), did not hesitate to select him unanimously when they gathered in February 1789. The more complicated portion of the process was communicating this decision to the Confederation Congress in New York, so that the new president could be inaugurated. Due to frigid weather, it took two months to gather a congressional quorum, and the country was left in a state of limbo

without a functioning central government. Finally, on April 6, Congress opened the ballots and announced publicly that Washington had been elected. It would take another week before the president-elect was officially informed, but Washington had already begun to pack his bags for the move from Virginia to New York.

As he made his slow journey northward, Washington was celebrated in town after town with speeches, toasts, and parades. On the last day of April, the new president was sworn into office in New York's Federal Hall, taking his oath over a Bible brought from a local lodge of the Masonic Order, the secret society to which Washington belonged. After reading the oath prescribed in the Constitution, the officiating chancellor called out to the crowd below the gallery: "Long Live George Washington, President of the United States."

Having inaugurated a new chief executive with pomp and ceremony, the leaders of the republic faced the challenge of conferring dignity upon the office of the presidency without appearing to have replaced one king with another. Some of the founders, including the new vice president, John Adams, thought that the nation's honor called for Washington to be addressed with such majestic titles as "His Highness, the President of the United States, and Protector of their Liberties," but advocates of the simpler, republican-sounding "Mr. President" carried the day. The Constitution had clearly delimited the powers of the executive branch, but everyday decisions about protocol, dress, and conduct would also shape the character of the new government.

NATIONAL COMMUNICATION NETWORKS

Documents such as the Declaration of Independence and the Constitution did not simply lay political foundations for a new government; they were also part of a

BEHIND THE IMAGE

This pitcher made of white earthenware (a cheaper alternative to porcelain) was one of many mass-produced commemorative goods manufactured in England in the early 1800s for U.S. customers. Using a new technique called transfer printing, which pressed paper prints (made from inked copper plates) against glazed pottery, potters were able to transfer a wet image to the ceramic ware. Transferware prints from this period commonly responded to recent events in U.S. history, including the First Barbary War and the Embargo Act, and depicted topics such as population statistics, city plans, and election results.

Marketing Washington. Earthenware pitcher (ca. 1800–1810) honoring the first U.S. president. *The Metropolitan Museum of Art, New York, Gift of William H. Huntington, 1883*

WITHIN THE IMAGE

On one side of the pitcher, ⑤ George Washington accompanies ② Liberty, personified as a woman, who points to ③ a map of the American states, linking the ideals of the republic to the recognizable and towering figure of its first president. ④ Washington's name also appears on a wreath held aloft by winged, angelic creatures. and then again on the pitcher's other side, as part of a poem. ⑤ The poetic text, written by a blind Liverpool abolitionist who celebrated American independence, imagines an old farmer recalling the glorious history of the revolution—"how your Warren expired, how Montgomery fell, and how WASHINGTON humbled your foes." By referring to Joseph Warren and Richard Montgomery (two early American war casualties) as *your*, the pitcher proclaims its status as a salute from across the ocean, while its use of all-capital letters underscores the homage to Washington.

BEYOND THE IMAGE

Despite escalating tensions between Britain and the U.S. during the years leading to the War of 1812, Liverpool potters catered to the American market. The demand for commemorative kitchen goods supported a brisk trade in Liverpool transferware alongside other British goods, like textiles, designed for U.S. consumers. Such commerce connected American households into networks of international capitalism and habits of long-distance consumption, and they also shaped early U.S. identity. Buying a pitcher like this one was a patriotic gesture that advertised the figure of Washington (who had died shortly before the pitcher was produced) and cemented his place as a vehicle for imagining the new nation.

growing communication system. Their power depended on the proposition that citizens of the new republic, however dispersed over the map and however varied in personal circumstances, might imagine themselves as participating in a collective conversation. As the new nation emerged, American men and women contributed to this conversation by building a culture around printed texts. A wide range of printed novels, newspapers, and pamphlets offered definitions of what people living in the United States had in common, beyond their shared status as subjects of the new national government.

LITERATURE AND THE NEW NATION

The first writer to pose in print the question "What is an American?" was not a delegate to the Continental Congress, a signer of the Declaration, a pamphleteer for independence, or a framer of the Constitution. He was not a native English speaker, nor was he born in North America. Michel Guillaume St. Jean de Crèvecoeur had emigrated from France to Canada toward the end of the French and Indian War, subsequently adopted an English name, married a British colonist, and settled on a large plot of land in Orange County, New York. A Loyalist during the revolutionary crisis, Crèvecoeur left the United States in 1781. A year later, a London publisher printed his ***Letters from an American Farmer,*** a series of literary essays about American life and identity. Presented as the correspondence of a fictional Pennsylvania farmer named James to a genteel Londoner, James's letters celebrate an American society in which

Father for a Republic.   George Washington entered office amid lingering concerns that the new Constitution might bring back monarchy. The fact that Washington, who appears to have been sterile, sired no natural heirs may have helped allay some of those concerns. "Providence left Washington childless," as the nineteenth-century saying went, "that a nation might call him father." *Library of Congress Prints & Photographs Division [LC-DIG-pga-03236]*

people of humble origins can willfully remake themselves and achieve social and political equality through owning and cultivating land. To the question "What is an American?" James gives the now-familiar answer that American national identity grows out of economic and political opportunities rather than ethnicity, language, or religion.

Declarations, pamphlets, maps, and constitutions were ways of inscribing the new nation on paper and communicating it across distances. But much of what was written, printed, and circulated in the 1770s and 1780s, like Crèvecoeur's articulation of the American dream, took the form of literature. In published poems, plays, and works of prose fiction, American readers found entertainment, inspiration, and a shared literary culture.

As Crèvecoeur's example highlights, this culture was transatlantic. Texts, books, authors, and fictional characters routinely crossed the ocean in the early years of U.S. literature. In fact, most of the literature consumed by American readers before the nineteenth century was authored in Europe, and especially in England. British authors dominated the American literary marketplace in large part because the absence of copyright laws made it profitable for American publishers to produce cheap, pirated editions of foreign works, and English authors were the most accessible and best known. But part of

the reason there had never been any copyright legislation in colonial America was that the commercial value of American literature had never been very great. Despite high rates of literacy (among whites), American readers were dispersed widely in a country with poor roads and did not form a major book-buying market for most of the colonial era. In 1790, Congress passed the **Federal Copyright Law,** and though not many authors or publishers took advantage of it immediately, it signaled the beginnings of literary entertainment as a viable business in the United States.

WOMEN AND THE AMERICAN NOVEL

Novels were the most popular form of literary entertainment in the new nation. Although English novelists continued to dominate the trade, several popular and important American novels were published during the end of the eighteenth century. The distinction of being the first American novel is contested, but scholars usually bestow that honor on *The Power of Sympathy*, written by the American-born author William Hill Brown. Published in the United States by the influential Worcester publisher Isaiah Thomas in 1789, the year George Washington was inaugurated as the first president, Brown's novel did not achieve much notice during the author's lifetime. Several other novels from the 1790s made a bigger splash.

The most successful of these, Susanna Rowson's **Charlotte Temple** (1791), was written in England by an English author who had spent much of her childhood in America. Shortly after the novel appeared, Rowson moved (like her title character) to the United States, where her work sold an estimated forty to fifty thousand copies in two decades.

• The plots of many early American novels, including *The Power of Sympathy* and *Charlotte Temple*, feature the motif of seduction, a plot line that both entertained readers and evoked the fragility of the new republic. Would the new nation possess the necessary virtue to resist the corruption of its political institutions? In each story, a virtuous woman is enticed by a duplicitous lover into a morally compromising and socially damaging sexual relationship. • From the start, the national literature of the United States focused attention on questions of women's sexuality and education in the new nation. Brown dedicated his books to "the young ladies, of United Columbia" and claimed that his novel would "expose the fatal consequences, of seduction." Many critics, however, worried that the novels themselves were the seducers; they feared that as the title of one of many such attacks put it, novel reading was "a Cause of Female Depravity." Like other entertainment media in more recent periods, novels were suspected of thrusting young people into fantasy worlds that prevented them from becoming productive and respectable members of society. But within debates about novels at this moment in American history, critics were particularly concerned with the moral character of women. Whereas the Declaration, the Constitution, and other foundational texts of the nation-building period spoke only of men and rendered women invisible, female perspectives and experiences were central to the novel. Women figured in early U.S literature as authors, readers, and characters, as well as symbols of the new republic.

BROADCAST NETWORK

From the standpoint of the nation's founders, writing and print were crucial to sustaining America's republican

Susanna Rowson (1762–1824).
One of the leading novelists in the early United States, Rowson made a living as a professional actress and then as a school headmistress. She was unable to reap much of the profit generated by her best-selling novel, *Charlotte Temple*, which was not protected by international copyright agreements. *Susanna Rowson Papers, 1770–1879, in the Clifton Waller Barrett Library, Accession #7379-7379-c, Special Collections, University of Virginia Library, Charlottesville, VA*

experiment. To enable the exchange of ideas and information necessary for a national culture or a national politics, a dispersed population had to be connected through a regular system of communication. This was especially important in an overwhelmingly rural nation. Even though most of the founders lived in cities, they imagined the ideal America as a virtuous republic of independent landowners living at comfortable distances from one another and even farther from their seats of government. (Cities, they believed, were threats to the republic because of the potential for class conflict and mob violence.) How was a dispersed citizenry to become informed and involved in the affairs of government and society?

Five years after the text of the Constitution was printed and sent to the states, Congress enacted a monumental piece of legislation that would address this problem by creating a state-sponsored communication network. The **Post Office Act of 1792** put Congress in charge of selecting postal routes, protecting the privacy of the mail, and setting postage rates. More generally, the law laid the foundation for a broadcast network that would circulate political information on a national scale. By taking charge of the designation of routes, Congress could bring postal service to sparsely inhabited areas that might not have generated the mail business to pay for it. By proclaiming the invulnerability of mail to government surveillance, Congress encouraged a freer flow of ideas and information. But the most significant feature of the new, redefined U.S. Post Office was its subsidy for newspapers. Under the 1792 law, newspapers

How Much Is That?

News in the Mail

The price of sending a newspaper in 1792, adjusted for inflation, would have been 28 cents in 2020, roughly half the cost of mailing a first-class letter today.

could travel up to 100 miles for 1 cent and anywhere in the country for 1.5 cents (see How Much Is That? News in the Mail). Furthermore, newspaper publishers could send papers to one another free of charge. This provision determined the kind of mail system that would exist in the United States for the next half century.

● By making it cheap to circulate newspapers (and asking letter writers to pay high postage to subsidize that circulation), the federal government made it possible for citizens across the country to have access to political news. And by allowing newspapers to exchange free copies, the law made it likely that the content of that political news would be fairly national and uniform in character—since small-town papers would reprint the articles provided for them by their urban counterparts. The law thus created a relationship between the post and the press in the early republic that made information exchange quite different from that in later periods in two key respects. First, the mail would carry mostly newspapers rather than letters and would serve as a broadcast medium rather than an interactive one. Second, newspapers would be designed for distant readers as much as for local ones. ●

The tiny minority of Americans who lived in urban areas by 1790 occupied the front lines of the communication network. They received information faster, were more likely to produce the information consumed elsewhere, and were better integrated into the commercial practices that demanded and rewarded information exchange. But starting in 1792, the U.S. government mitigated some of those differences by turning thousands of towns and villages over an expansive terrain and a diverse society into distribution sites for national news.

MEDIA AND INFORMATION

Liberty in the Form of the Goddess of Youth, Giving Support to the Bald Eagle, by Edward Savage, 1796.
This illustration depicts a popular feminized allegory of the new republic. *Library of Congress Prints and Photographs Division* [LC-DIG-ppmsca-13641]

CONCLUSION

The revolutionary process of imagining a new nation out of thirteen very different colonies, which had begun two decades earlier with Committees of Correspondence, was in some important respects now complete. It would be misleading to describe that new nation as having been written into existence, because no piece of paper could by itself create the shifts in allegiance, identity, and authority that nation building entailed. Still, between 1776 and 1792, a series of written and printed documents—declarations, constitutions, pamphlets, maps, novels, and newspapers—circulated in the new republic and made the founding of the United States feasible, conceivable, and meaningful. Several of those documents framed the structure of new state and national governments. With their complex histories now often forgotten, they enjoy sacred status as instruments of historical change and keys to American national identity.

STUDY TERMS

Declaration of
   Independence

written constitutions

natural rights

bicameral

Vermont constitution

Articles of Confederation

Continental dollars

Shays's Rebellion

Treaty of Paris

Treaty of Fort Stanwix

Northwest Territory

Land Ordinance of 1785

Northwest Ordinance

Virginia Plan

New Jersey Plan

three-fifths clause

Committee on Style

ratification conventions

Federalists

Anti-Federalists

The Federalist

checks and balances

Bill of Rights

*Letters from an American
   Farmer*

Federal Copyright Law

Charlotte Temple

Post Office Act of 1792

FURTHER READING

A database of additional full-text readings is available through Power of Process for Primary Sources in Connect.

Martin Bruckner, *The Geographic Revolution in Early America* (2006), charts the new ways of writing about space during the colonial and early national periods.

Cathy Davidson, *Revolution and the Word* (1986), examines the importance of novels and novel reading to the founding of the new nation.

Jay Fliegelman, *Declaring Independence* (1993), places Jefferson and the Declaration of Independence within the context of eighteenth-century ideas about speech and performance.

Trish Loughran, *The Republic in Print* (2007), challenges the idea that the new nation formed a single reading public.

Pauline Maier, *American Scripture* (1997), demystifies the nation's founding document.

Eric Slauter, *The State as a Work of Art* (2009), explores the broader ideological setting for the ratification debates.

Will Slauter, *Who Owns the News?* (2019), puts the history of copyright in the new republic in a longer and broader story about property in information.

David Waldstreicher, *In the Midst of Perpetual Fetes* (1997), studies the practices and rituals that created national identity during and after the Revolution.

William Warner, *Protocols of Liberty* (2013), stresses the role of media and communications to the revolutionary era.

Kariann Akemi Yokota, *Unbecoming British* (2011), considers the everyday difficulties faced by the Americans in pursuing cultural independence from Britain.

8 | THE EARLY REPUBLIC

Chapter Questions

1. What were the impact and implications of the Haitian Revolution for the young U.S. republic?

2. When and how was slavery abolished in the North?

3. What two visions of America's national growth underlay the first party system, and how did the two parties differ on national policy?

4. How did the nation expand westward during the presidency of Thomas Jefferson?

Finding Their Way. The Lewis and Clark expedition, celebrated in this 1850 painting, reflected a particular vision of how the new nation might develop. *Private Collection/The Bridgeman Art Library*

In the decades immediately following the American Revolution, respondents to census surveys often lied about their age. This was not in itself remarkable; people had misrepresented how old they were in colonial times as well. What was new was that Americans were now more likely to pretend to be younger rather than older.

New attitudes toward age and aging do not suddenly appear with the publication of a declaration, the ratification of a constitution, or the signing of a treaty. Still, toward the end of the eighteenth century and the beginning of the nineteenth, a change took place throughout American culture—in law, art, and everyday language. Legislatures introduced mandatory retirement laws for public officials. New inheritance laws eroded the long-standing economic advantages of eldest sons. Fewer children were named for their grandparents. Family portraits began positioning parents and children on the same horizontal line. Clothing fashions shifted to emphasize youth and to show younger bodies to advantage. And finally, a new vocabulary

Time Line

1789
George Washington becomes first president
French Revolution begins

1790
Federal government moves to Philadelphia

1791
Slave rebellion erupts in St. Domingue

1792
Washington re-elected

1793
Yellow Fever epidemic hits Philadelphia
Louis XVI of France is guillotined

1794
Bethel church founded by Richard Allen in Philadelphia
Tax on whiskey incites Whiskey Rebellion

1795
Jay's Treaty helps prevent war with Britain but weakens Federalists

1796
John Adams elected president

1798
Alien and Sedition Acts

1799
Gradual abolition enacted in New York

1800
National capital moves to Washington, D.C.
Election of 1800 transfers presidential power to Republicans

1801
Jefferson takes office

1803
Marbury v. Madison establishes power of judicial review
Louisiana Purchase doubles size of U.S. territory

1804
Lewis and Clark expedition
Gradual abolition enacted in New Jersey
Independence declared in St. Domingue (Haiti)

1805
End of First Barbary War

1807
Embargo Act aims at halting European attacks on U.S. ships

1808
The Act Prohibiting Importation of Slaves takes effect

1811
Manhattan grid established

emerged for disparaging one's elders. Words like *geezer*, *fogy*, *codger*, and *fuddy-duddy* entered American speech around this time as contemptuous names for the elderly. Instead of venerating seniority, cultural biases began to favor those whose future lay before them.

Optimism toward youth suited the political climate of the early republic, where the founders harbored high hopes for a new nation with its own uncharted future. By the early 1790s, the Constitution was the law of the land, President Washington was beginning his second term in office, and the revolutionary movement to conceive a single nation out of thirteen colonies was largely complete. But the process of building that nation had only begun. Over the next two decades, the United States would establish new models for political competition and peaceful transitions of power. It would create an utterly new seat of national government and confront new dilemmas about slavery, race, and international relations. Most dramatically, the size of its territory would double, and Americans would move beyond the eastern seaboard in greater numbers than ever before. How all of this expansion and movement would change the republic was hard to predict. Building a nation required imagining new worlds.

Thomas Jefferson, who was the leading figure in national politics during most of this period, epitomized American optimism about new and imagined worlds. Even as he aged, he sympathized with this cultural trend toward celebrating youth. He once argued that constitutions ought to be reframed every two decades, so that no generation would ever be bound by the decisions of its predecessor. Although his political opponents detested Jefferson's fondness for innovation, most shared a sense that the new nation was an experiment for which the past offered only limited guidance.

THE PROBLEM OF SLAVERY

Africans had been enslaved throughout the Americas from the very beginnings of European colonization. In the mid-eighteenth century, however, critics (both free and enslaved) began to articulate publicly the view that slavery itself was inherently wrong. By the early national period, opponents of slavery were citing the libertarian ideals of the American Revolution and calling for slavery's destruction. At the same time, people in slavery and free people of color in St. Domingue (renamed Haiti in 1804) were fighting their own war of independence, invoking the same rhetoric of freedom and equality. In the 1790s, it suddenly seemed conceivable that the institution of slavery in the Americas was dying.

But any consideration of eliminating slavery in the United States threatened a major source of wealth in the new nation, and any discussion of emancipating enslaved African Americans challenged the unspoken premise that white men should control its politics and economy. Still, the early national era was marked by a serious reassessment of the long-standing system of racial slavery, a hardening of its geographical borders, and the emergence of large free Black communities in growing Northern cities.

SLAVERY SECTIONALIZED

Prompted by petitions from those living under the slavery regime (see Chapter 6) using the language of the new nation's founding documents, and emboldened by assertions of the dignity of labor among white workers, several states began putting slavery on the road to legal extinction during the decades following the Revolution. The institution was most vulnerable in the Northern half of the United States, where its scope had been limited. Enslaved people in the North were concentrated in towns and cities where labor was harder to control, free laborers resented the competition, and overall slave populations were relatively small. By the 1770s, only a couple thousand men and women were enslaved in New England (compared to over six hundred thousand in the other nine rebellious colonies and millions in the West Indies and Brazil), which lowered both the economic costs and the social implications of abolition. When the aspiring

state of Vermont became the first to outlaw slavery in 1777, fewer than two hundred people received their freedom. By 1787, slavery had also been made illegal in Massachusetts and New Hampshire, as well as in the Northwest Territory.

In other Northern states, larger enslaved populations made legislatures reluctant to free them outright, so plans were devised to end slavery more gradually. **Gradual abolition** became the dominant form of legal emancipation in all Northern states where significant numbers of men and women were enslaved. Pennsylvania provided the model in 1780, with a law that granted eventual freedom to the future offspring of enslaved persons. Any child born to an enslaved woman in Pennsylvania after the law took effect would become legally free at the age of twenty-eight. New York and New Jersey adopted similar laws, but significantly later and with much greater impact: More than thirty-two thousand people were still enslaved in those two states in 1800. Gradual abolition was passed in New York in 1799 and five years later in New Jersey, thus completing the legal dismantling of slavery in the North (see Map 8.1).

Although a new generation of African Americans achieved their freedom under gradual abolition laws during the early national era, some Northern slaveholders responded to the laws by selling their human property (illegally) to states where the institution was still alive and well. In addition, gradual abolition laws did not free any

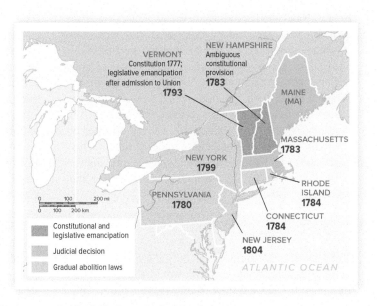

Map 8.1 Gradual Abolition in the North. In the decades following the Revolution, some states abolished slavery by legislative emancipation, others by judicial decision, and others by gradual abolition laws.

of the men, women, and children who were enslaved when the laws took effect. As a consequence, there were still people living in slavery in Connecticut as late as 1848 and in New Jersey as late as the Civil War. Nonetheless, the acts of Northern legislatures had the effect of stopping the growth of slavery in half of the nation.

For enslaved African Americans living in the South, the decades following the ratification of the Constitution did not lead to mass liberation, though many were granted freedom. Several leading Southern plantation owners openly favored gradual abolition, especially in the Upper South (Maryland, Delaware, Virginia, and North Carolina), where a downturn in the tobacco economy made slave labor—which could be costly to maintain and posed a perpetual threat of disorder or insurrection—less valuable. State legislatures in the Chesapeake region debated emancipation bills. None of these laws passed, but new rules made it easier for individual owners to emancipate their enslaved laborers. Rates of private **manumission** in Virginia, Maryland, and Delaware rose sharply between 1790 and 1810. (George Washington, upon his death in 1799, freed 124 people he had held as property.) By 1810, over three-quarters of Delaware's remaining Black population was free, and Baltimore's free Black population had increased seventeenfold.

Despite these gains, many more people were transported in slavery westward over the Appalachian Mountains than were liberated. In those twenty years, Maryland and Virginia sent fifty-six thousand enslaved people into Kentucky and another twenty-five thousand into Tennessee. Professional slave traders took some, but most were transported by their owners to work on new farms. In either case, the migration typically broke up a family, because slaveholders often divided up their human property when their children moved west and because enslaved families in the Chesapeake sometimes lived on multiple, neighboring plantations. During this period, coercive migration and interstate trade affected the lives of more people living under the slavery regime than all of the gradual abolition laws and individual acts of manumission combined.

HAITI'S REVOLUTION

The American Revolution was only the first in a series of revolutionary upheavals that would shake the great European powers and their colonies across the Atlantic. The second anti-colonial revolt in the Americas took place in St. Domingue, France's spectacularly lucrative sugar-producing colony on the western half of the island

Francois-Dominique Toussaint Louverture. Louverture, the son of an African prince, was a leader of the revolution in the French sugar plantation colony of St. Domingue, where slavery was abolished in 1794. Haitian rebels ultimately won independence from France in 1804. *Historic Images/Alamy Stock Photo*

of Hispaniola. The **Haitian Revolution** unfolded in stages and involved several competing groups. Mixed-race free people on the Caribbean island, who were classified in the French Empire as *gens de couleur*, demanded equal rights under a new constitution that had just been written in France. Poor whites wanted a voice in government, and the planter class hoped for greater colonial self-rule. In 1791, a fourth group entered the fray, as nearly two thousand of the colony's half-million enslaved people executed a well-planned attack on sugar plantations.

The combined effect of these eruptions was a protracted civil war. A well-educated, freed man named Toussaint Louverture emerged as the leader of a resistance force that would ultimately secure the abolition of slavery in 1794 and create the independent nation of Haiti in 1804. Haiti became the second democratic republic in the Americas (see Map 8.2).

News of the Haitian Revolution traveled quickly to the North American mainland, sparking fears of race war

Map 8.2 Slave Revolt in the Caribbean. The small island colony of St. Domingue lay well beyond the borders of the United States but had long occupied a central position in the Atlantic slave trade.

of violent revolution and eventually joining the city's free Black community. ● At the time, Philadelphia was the largest U.S. city, more populous than any other in the Western Hemisphere except for Mexico City. Philadelphia had been an obvious location for the major national gatherings of the revolutionary era and a frequent first stop for foreign visitors to the United States. Many of those foreigners were struck by the numbers of formerly enslaved African Americans on the streets of the American capital.

The number of formerly enslaved people living in Philadelphia skyrocketed in the 1790s, as free Blacks migrated northward from the Upper South, where legislatures fearing the ripple effects of the Haitian rebellion initiated repressive laws against them. Philadelphia's free Black community also included a number of runaways, who took shelter among abolitionists of both races against fugitive slave laws that mandated their return. Networks of free Blacks in Philadelphia also helped several visiting African Americans escape their bondage, including a woman named Ona Judge, who had been taken to the capital by her owner, President George Washington. Judge escaped to freedom in 1796, making her way to New Hampshire, where the president's agents sought unsuccessfully to recapture her. Nine months later, Washington's renowned cook, Hercules, absconded as well. Taking enslaved people to the nation's capital had become a risky proposition for their enslavers.

During this period, Philadelphia's free Black community developed a number of new institutions, most significantly a series of seven **Black churches.** These churches included the first Black congregations in the United States affiliated with the Episcopalian, Methodist, Presbyterian, and Baptist denominations of Protestant Christianity. Excluded from full citizenship, threatened by fugitive slave laws, and haunted by the specter of a prospering slave system in the South, free Blacks relied on their independent churches as a source of social support and an enduring political voice in the struggle against racial inequality.

The largest and most prominent Black congregation in Philadelphia, Richard Allen's Bethel church (founded in 1794), reflected in part the rising popularity of **Methodism,** an English Protestant movement founded in

and slave conspiracies. A white witness in Virginia claimed to have overheard two people enslaved in Richmond in 1793 plotting "to kill the white people soon in this place," just as Black people had done "in the French Island." In most Southern states, any Black person who spoke French was treated immediately as a security threat and denied entry at the ports. To enslaved African Americans and a growing number of sympathizers, the end of slavery in St. Domingue signaled that the institution might be destined to crumble elsewhere. To the men who enslaved others, the lesson of Haiti was that any end to slavery would be achieved or accompanied by bloodshed.

PHILADELPHIA'S EXPERIMENT

Events in Haiti sent shock waves throughout the United States. ● They also sent boatloads of white slaveholding refugees northward to American port cities, typically with their human property in tow. In Philadelphia, the nation's capital, about five hundred enslaved French-speaking people from St. Domingue arrived around 1793, bearing news

BEHIND THE IMAGE

Born in Germany in 1786, Johann Ludwig Krimmel immigrated to the United States in 1809, Anglicized his name to John Lewis, and taught drawing at a Philadelphia girls' school to earn a living. He joined an artists' club and began sketching and painting scenes of contemporary everyday life in Philadelphia, including several featuring African Americans. This scene portrays a Black woman selling pepper pot, a thick, spicy soup combining African, Caribbean, and local culinary traditions—and may have been inspired by a woodcut of a pepper pot vendor that appeared in a children's book in 1810.

WITHIN THE IMAGE

Krimmel's choice of subject matter reflects the ethnic diversity of Philadelphia, the economic opportunities that Black women pursued as an alternative to domestic labor, and the proliferation of urban food vendors. He reveals the diversity and cacophony of city life in several details: **1** The customers include two young women (apparently shocked by the spectacle and thus perhaps visitors from the country), **2** a lanky man in a top hat, and **3** an elderly man in a military uniform who may be a Revolutionary War veteran. Note also the contrast between **4** the joy of the vendor and the discomfort of her customers. **5** A dog, perhaps sensing the young women's apprehension, seems to be snarling at them.

BEYOND THE IMAGE

Pepper-Pot was part of Krimmel's first public exhibition and introduced the style and the themes that would

John Lewis Krimmel, *Pepper-Pot: A Scene in the Philadelphia Market* (1811).   *The Picture Art Collection/Alamy Stock Photo*

characterize his most famous work. By depicting groups engaged in the festivity of public gathering—markets, elections, taverns, weddings, and quilting frolics—Krimmel suggested to his audiences that the representative moments of American life exist in the hubbub of collective activity rather than in the stable portraits of exemplary individuals. His paintings, produced before the introduction of photography, continue to shape our images of the social history of the early national period.

---

the eighteenth century. The movement's presence was small in the United States at the time of the Revolution, but it grew quickly in the 1790s, spread by itinerant preachers, known as circuit riders, who embarked on evangelical missions through rural America. ● Methodist preachers sought converts across lines of race and class, and their style of worship, which emphasized lay participation and personal enthusiasm rather than the maintenance of social order, struck responsive chords among many disenfranchised Americans, male and female. Several notable leaders of minority communities in the first half

of the nineteenth century, including the Pequot William Apess (who would fight U.S. efforts to remove Native Americans from their lands) and the African American orator Sojourner Truth (who would become a leading voice in the abolitionist movement and an early advocate of women's rights) were Methodists. ● Richard Allen had converted to Methodism when he was still enslaved in Delaware. But in 1816, the Bethel church community broke with the Methodist establishment over issues of racial discrimination and formed the **African Methodist Episcopal (A.M.E.) Church,** with Allen as its first bishop.

CONFLICTING FAITHS

The A.M.E. Church would serve as the most powerful free Black institution in the decades before the Civil War.

DISEASE AND EPIDEMIC

● The networks of exchange connecting Philadelphia and Haiti carried more than just people and ideas. In July 1793, a deadly fever swept through Philadelphia, taking more than four thousand lives and exiling much of the surviving population to the countryside. The capital of the new nation was turned inside out, its municipal government disbanded and its population decimated. We now know that this catastrophic epidemic, spread by mosquitoes, had originated 1,500 miles away in the West Indies. ●

Philadelphia would not be the capital of the United States beyond the eighteenth century. But it remained the epicenter of American abolitionism for another two decades after the fever outbreak. Philadelphia would serve as the nation's principal urban laboratory for considering what the United States could look like if slavery were abolished and freed people joined whites in building a multiracial society. The violence and discrimination suffered by the Philadelphia Black community during the early years of gradual abolition in the North suggested that such a transition might not be smooth or peaceful.

THE BEGINNINGS OF PARTISAN POLITICS

As the home of the new federal government during the 1790s, Philadelphia also became a center of debate among national leaders with competing political visions. Already in President Washington's first term, divisions had emerged within the administration. By his second term, politicians and newspaper editors had begun organizing themselves into opposing camps with distinct approaches to national policy. Nothing in the Constitution called for the creation of political parties, and the Constitution's promoters had not expected parties to form in such a large and diverse nation as the United States. Parties had acquired a bad name among the founders, and in 1789, Thomas Jefferson took pride in the fact that he had "never submitted . . . to the creed of any party of men whatever." But a two-party system emerged quickly in the 1790s, and Jefferson stood at the helm of one of the parties. The division reflected serious disagreement over the character of the new nation, how powerful its central government ought to be, and how it should conduct foreign relations.

ALEXANDER HAMILTON'S ECONOMIC AGENDA

Disagreements over the future of the federal government under the Constitution began with money matters. As the nation's first treasury secretary, Alexander Hamilton sought to use federal power to encourage manufacturing, promote commercial growth, raise revenues for the national treasury, and fortify the political position of the central government. As a crucial first step, he wanted Congress to assume responsibility for debts incurred by the states during the war, a strategy designed to subordinate the states to the federal government and boost the country's credit rating. By presenting the new federal government as a responsible borrower, Hamilton hoped to persuade potential investors that U.S. bonds were safe places to put their money. This, in turn, would give the wealthy a vested interest in the republic's welfare and stability. Public debt, Hamilton argued, would form the "cement of our Union."

This call for debt assumption was bold, since the public debt was vast and could be paid off only by more borrowing. To pull this off, Hamilton proposed selling bonds and paying the interest on those bonds by collecting taxes. Critics objected to the plan on several grounds. Nationalizing state debts redistributed wealth from those states that had borrowed less (or had paid down their obligations) to those that had borrowed more. Small-debt states such as Virginia and Maryland resented having to bear the burden of big-debt states such as Massachusetts and Connecticut. Opponents of Hamilton's proposal argued further that covering the state debts would simply reward the wealthy speculators who had bought them at discounted rates from soldiers and farmers at the end of the Revolutionary War (see Chapter 7). Moreover, critics objected to Hamilton's plan for the same reasons he proposed it: They worried that debt assumption would make the central government powerful at the expense of the sovereignty of the individual states and that it would commit the new republic to a path of commercial growth. But Hamilton's supporters invoked the nation's moral obligation for debts incurred during the struggle for independence. With assumption advocates dominating the Senate and its opponents holding sway in the House, Congress faced a political impasse. Finally, at a 1790 dinner party hosted by Jefferson, a deal was struck whereby Southerners would support the assumption bill in return for key Northern votes in favor of placing the capital on the Potomac River, between the Southern states of Virginia and Maryland (see the section A Brand New Capital).

To pay down the interest on the bonds that Hamilton advocated, the federal government needed money. Under the Constitution, Congress could have raised funds through direct taxation (on land, property, or persons), but such taxes would have been difficult for a primitive federal bureaucracy to collect from a dispersed population that already paid property taxes to their state governments. Moreover, it would have entailed delicate negotiations over how to apportion the tax burdens of slave states.

Instead, Hamilton proposed **protective tariffs** on specific manufactured imports, such as textiles and shoes, which were designed to make American-made goods cheaper than their foreign competition. This would raise revenue while encouraging the growth of the nation's fledgling domestic industries, which were located primarily in New England. Hamilton argued that only by subsidizing the development of American manufacturing could the United States become a truly independent nation. Opponents, especially in the South, argued that such a tariff asked one region to subsidize the economy of another, and that American independence would come with widespread land ownership, not with industrial development. Hamilton's other revenue plan garnered more support, however. In 1791, and then again in 1794, Congress taxed a handful of goods that were deemed luxuries or vices, including snuff, sugar, and distilled spirits (see Hot Commodities: Whiskey).

The final component of Hamilton's economic plan was a **Bank of the United States** that would help circulate and stabilize paper currency in the new republic. Not a branch of government but a private, for-profit corporation chartered by the United States and modeled on the Bank of England, the bank would receive deposits from the federal treasury and then issue its own private bank notes, which could be used as legal tender for paying taxes. The government would own 20 percent of the bank's stock and appoint 20 percent of its directors, but the rest would be owned and controlled by private interests. Congress chartered the first Bank of the United States in 1791 (a second bank would be established in 1816; see Chapter 10), though opponents continued to question its legitimacy. Jefferson, Madison, and others argued that the Constitution did not authorize Congress to issue private charters or establish banks. Hamilton defended the bank on the grounds that Congress could adopt any means not prohibited by the Constitution to achieve its mandated objectives of regulating commerce and maintaining public credit. Debates over the bank exposed a wide gulf in Washington's cabinet between those who shared Hamilton's **broad construction** of the Constitution and those who favored a **strict construction** that limited the central government to actions enumerated explicitly in the original text.

THE FIRST U.S. PARTY SYSTEM

The polarization of views within the Washington administration over debt assumption, taxes, and banking split the original federalist supporters of the Constitution into rival factions, with Hamilton leading a group called the **Federalists** and Jefferson and Madison leading the Democratic-Republicans, also known as **Republicans.** (This is not the modern-day Republican Party, which originated in the 1850s.) The two parties embraced opposing visions of the nation's future. Federalists favored a strong national government and imagined a commercial economy operating out of thriving cities, earning the nation international respect and securing financial confidence in its new government. Their opponents, by contrast, valued an agrarian society of independent landowners and sought to protect those interests against the demands of urban merchants and financiers. Republicans, whose ranks included many who had opposed ratifying the Constitution in the first place, called for a restrained national government with modest expenditures and little need for revenue.

Although the rift between Federalists and Republicans began with debates over specific policies, the nation's first partisan divide reflected broad differences in outlook and ideology. Federalists worried about excessive democracy, whereas Republicans feared a reversion to monarchy. Federalists emphasized the lessons learned under the Articles of Confederation, when a weak central government left the republic divided and vulnerable. Republicans emphasized the lessons learned in the revolutionary struggle, when local liberties needed to be protected against a powerful and distant British government. Federalists aspired to build a nation that would rival and resemble Great Britain. Republicans were more likely to cite the British government and economy as models to be avoided. By later standards, these two rivals lacked the organizational structure of full-fledged political parties, but the division between Federalists and Republicans was significant and the parties appealed to different political constituencies. Republican positions were especially widespread among slaveholders in the South, small farmers in the mid-Atlantic states, and the more radically democratic urban artisans in the North. New England provided a stronghold for federalism. Washington himself tried to stay above the partisan fray, though most of his decisions as president aligned him with the Federalist cause.

FOREIGN REVOLUTIONS

The loudest clashes between the two parties erupted in the arena of foreign relations, where Federalists favored Britain and Republicans sympathized with France. This split reflected different understandings of the legacy of the American Revolution and played out in different responses to two other revolutionary movements. More than any other events that took place beyond America's new national

HOT COMMODITIES
Whiskey

Early National Grain Surplus. Tourists can visit George Washington's whiskey distillery, reconstructed at Mount Vernon. *Paul J. Richards/AFP/Getty Images*

In an effort to raise revenues in 1791, Congress acted on Hamilton's plan to tax whiskey and other spirits. Unlike tariffs, which could be collected by customs officials at the ports, the whiskey tax applied to a range of distilleries, large and small, across the country. When government officials tried to collect the tax in 1794 from farmers in western Pennsylvania, an area chronically short on currency and generally hostile to taxation, they met stiff resistance. Whiskey rebels intimidated tax collectors, mobilized their militias, and invoked the legacy of the tax protests against Britain. As many as seven thousand rebels gathered outside Pittsburgh but took no immediate action. Still, the **Whiskey Rebellion** was the first major act of resistance to federal authority under the Constitution. Eager to make a show of strength for the new national government, Hamilton and Washington personally rode out with thirteen thousand militiamen, and the rebellion crumbled without a fight.

Behind this political crisis lurked a larger development in American life:

an explosive growth in whiskey drinking. Congress might have targeted distilled spirits as luxurious vices, but whiskey drinking was becoming deeply ingrained in the daily habits of Americans across the socioeconomic spectrum. The late eighteenth and early nineteenth centuries marked a high point in alcohol consumption generally, and whiskey drinking in particular. During the first third of the nineteenth century, the typical American drank more alcohol than at any time before or after. In 1810, American distilleries were producing more than 3 gallons of distilled liquors— typically about 90 proof—for every man, woman, and child, and that figure does not include beer, wine, or cider. Overall, Americans consumed about twice as much alcohol per person in 1810 as they do now. Consumption levels would peak in the 1830s and then drop precipitously (see Chapter 12).

Whiskey flowed freely throughout American society during the early decades of the nineteenth century, though certain portions of the population drank more heavily. Women drank

less frequently than men and tended to prefer sweetened rum, hard cider, or alcohol-heavy patent medicines. In the South, Black people drank less than whites. Despite variations, alcohol was a basic feature of everyday life in this period. Even religious folk drank heartily by later standards. A Southern planter who wished to join the Methodist Church had to restrict his intake—within the acceptable daily quota of a *quart* of peach brandy. Drinking was an important social activity, an indispensable form of hospitality and camaraderie. To refuse a drink was to refuse to enter a world of equality and solidarity.

Historians have offered several explanations for the rise of drinking around the turn of the century, but the most important factor was the growth of whiskey production, which made liquor cheap and plentiful. American farmers were producing large surpluses of grain, especially corn, and whiskey was an especially efficient way to deliver corn to distant markets. A horse could carry six times the volume of corn in whiskey form, which was easier to store and far less likely to rot. Shipping grain in this form became even more profitable with technological improvements in the distilling process. Between 1802 and 1815, the federal government issued over one hundred patents for new devices to distill whiskey, which encouraged more farmers to become distillers. Once the Republicans repealed Hamilton's whiskey tax in 1802, the price dropped further. The result was a widespread drinking habit that would form a major part of American economy and culture.

Think About It

1. How did technological innovations affect whiskey consumption?

2. How have attitudes toward alcoholic beverages changed in the United States since the era of the early republic?

borders during this period, the Haitian Revolution and the French Revolution, two separate rebellions that overthrew ruling elites in the name of liberty and equality, tested the limits of the founders' beliefs in democracy and freedom.

The **French Revolution** was a political crisis that overturned centuries of absolute monarchy and established a period of representative government. The leaders of the new French government abolished feudalism and the traditional privileges of nobles and clergy and issued the Declaration of the Rights of Man and the Citizen, which echoed the American Declaration of Independence in announcing that government derives its power from the consent of the governed. When the uprising began in 1789, many Americans saw a reflection of their own venture in democratic nation building. But over time, the French cause claimed many more lives than were lost on all the battlefields of the struggle for American independence. Mobs of peasants and urban workers burned aristocratic country homes and rioted in the cities. Becoming more radicalized as a result of pressures from mobilized commoners, the French government ordered the execution of Louis XVI in 1793, and the bloodshed intensified as thousands of suspected political enemies were killed and others died in internal rebellions. Federalists were quick to draw from the French experience negative lessons about the dangers of democracy. Republicans, by contrast, remained faithful to France's revolutionary cause, despite the violence.

The French revolutionary government faced not only internal rebellions. By 1793, it was also at war with Britain, Spain, Austria, Prussia, and the Dutch Republic. Jefferson, who was secretary of state, argued that the United States should support France under the 1778 treaty of alliance that had been crucial to the success of the American Revolution, whereas Hamilton argued for suspending the alliance and maintaining relations with Britain, a key trading partner. President Washington, now in his second term, issued a proclamation of U.S. neutrality, but both the French and the British provoked the Americans and fueled the partisan debate. In 1793, the French minister Citizen Edmond-Charles Genêt went over the head of President Washington to enlist Americans to attack British ships and Spanish colonial positions. This meddling in American affairs undermined Washington's neutrality stance, infuriated the Federalists, and embarrassed Jefferson and the Republicans. Then in late 1793 and early 1794, British ships began blockading the West Indies and seizing American cargo vessels trading with the French. Britain's Federalist supporters were now on the defensive, and Alexander Hamilton persuaded Washington to send a special envoy to London to settle the dispute.

Supreme Court chief justice John Jay, a pro-British Federalist, returned in 1794 with a treaty that extracted a promise from the British to withdraw their troops from frontier posts in the Northwest Territory, as the Treaty of Paris had specified. **Jay's Treaty** also repaired the new nation's invaluable trading relationship with Britain, which had been broken by the Revolution, but it came at a political cost, because it appeared to betray the French. Moreover, Southern planters who had lost enslaved laborers to the British during the Revolutionary War complained that their compensation claims had not been sufficiently pressed. Republicans vilified Jay's Treaty, but Washington, although disappointed with the terms, supported it as important to avoiding war with Great Britain. The Senate ratified the treaty in June 1795.

Facing strong criticism for his support of the treaty, Washington dared the House of Representatives to impeach him. Many Republicans wanted nothing less. From their perspective, Washington had betrayed both France and the larger cause of revolution in his attempt to placate the British. In an effort to tarnish the president's previously glorious reputation, Republican printers republished a forgotten series of forged letters, allegedly written by Washington to a distant cousin in 1777, expressing doubts about the justice of the colonists' grievance against the British. Washington survived the threat of impeachment. Soon after, he affirmed his intention not to seek a third term, establishing a precedent that would remain until the presidency of Franklin Roosevelt in the twentieth century. The two parties promoted rival candidates, and in the first contested presidential election in U.S. history, Federalist John Adams became the nation's new chief executive. The candidate who ran a close second became his vice president—Republican Thomas Jefferson.

Washington's Farewell Address admonished his fellow Americans to avoid entangling alliances with other nations, but his successor inherited the difficulties that came with neutrality. Outraged by Jay's Treaty, France stepped up its attacks on American ships and suspended diplomatic relations with the United States. When an American delegation visited France in 1798 to restore the alliance, it was confronted with a series of demands, including a personal bribe to the French foreign minister. In reporting the incident to Congress, President Adams concealed the names of the three French diplomats involved with the letters x, y, and z. News of the incident, dubbed the **XYZ affair**, further strained Franco-American relations and plunged the two countries into an undeclared war at sea that lasted until 1800.

Partisan differences over foreign relations extended to St. Domingue. Federalists were sympathetic to Louverture's revolt against French rule, both because they were hostile to France (and sought to weaken the French position in the Americas) and because fewer Federalists owned enslaved people and hence were less concerned about the spread of emancipation or slave insurrection. Republicans, by contrast, sympathized with France and worried about the specter of an independent Black republic in the Caribbean that might undermine slavery in the American South. The rebellion in St. Domingue benefited significantly from the outcome of the election of John Adams in 1796. For four anomalous years, U.S. foreign policy was directed by a president who did not own people and did not come from Virginia. These four years coincided with a critical period in Haiti's independence struggle. Adams and his secretary of state, Thomas Pickering, supported Louverture, recognized his authority, and urged him to declare independence. American ships even bombarded counterrevolutionary forces. Moved largely by a desire to humiliate France and Jefferson's Republican Party, America's only Federalist administration helped establish an independent nation in Latin America that would become a symbol of Black freedom throughout the Americas. No president after Adams would even recognize Haiti—not until after the United States had endured its own civil war.

A PARTISAN PRESS

Like other policy clashes between the two parties, the debate over foreign affairs flowed through an elaborate network of **political newspapers.** Philadelphia was the central hub of news production during the 1790s and would remain so even after the government moved away in 1800, but newspapers sprouted up in every state of the union. Most newspaper publishers sympathized with the Federalist Party, but a handful of opposition papers began to flourish as well. Philadelphia's Benjamin Franklin Bache, the namesake grandson and protégé of America's most famous printer, published the *Aurora General Advertiser*, probably the most important partisan journal in the early republic. Bache did more than any contemporary political figure to tout the virtues of adhering to party principles—contrary to his grandfather's advice.

Another Republican printer, Matthew Lyon of Vermont, stirred even greater controversy. Lyon had emigrated from Ireland as an indentured servant, and he used his newspaper to launch an unlikely political career that got him elected to Congress. Federalists in Congress ridiculed the plebeian printer as a "beast" and a "fool," to which Lyon responded by spitting in the face of Representative Roger

Griswold of Connecticut. When Federalists failed to muster the two-thirds majority necessary to expel Lyon, Griswold resorted to beating his adversary with a hickory stick. Lyon's presence in Congress threatened the establishment, not only because of his background but also because he represented the potential of newspapers to stir up public opinion and tilt the balance of political power.

As tensions between the United States and France mounted in 1798 in the wake of the XYZ affair, Federalist leaders began to worry that critics of the administration would undermine the nation's security. Some blamed immigrant radicals, failed revolutionaries in their native lands who had allegedly come to sow disorder in America. But newspapers were especially worrisome to the Federalists. Abigail Adams singled out Bache's *Aurora* as a threat to national unity. "If that fellow . . . is not suppressed," she wrote to her sister, "we shall come to a civil war."

In spring 1798, Congress passed a series of laws designed to protect the nation against that prospect. Several of these laws, dubbed **Alien Acts,** targeted immigrants by extending the waiting period for obtaining citizenship from five to fourteen years and authorizing the president to detain or expel foreigners during times of war by executive order. Then, Congress addressed the problem of internal enemies by enacting a **Sedition Act,** which made it a crime to "conspire . . . to oppose any measure . . . of the government of the United States" or to "write, print, utter or publish . . . any false, scandalous and malicious" claims about the government. The Sedition Act criminalized dissent and seemed to

"Congressional Pugilists."   This cartoon depicts the fight between Federalist Roger Griswold and Republican Matthew Lyon in 1798. Lyon is shown brandishing iron tongs. *Library of Congress, Prints and Photographs Division [LC-DIG-ppmsca-31832]*

violate the First Amendment, but the Federalists who approved the bill in Congress and upheld its constitutionality in the courts argued that it was essential to protect the new nation. "Speech, writing, and printing are the great directors of public opinion, and public opinion is the great director of human action," one judicial supporter explained. There was no such thing as a harmless editorial in the press.

Under the new law, many of the major Republican newspaper editors were arrested, including Matthew Lyon, who was convicted and imprisoned for having charged the Adams administration with caring more about power, pomp, and flattery than the welfare of the people. Sitting in jail, Lyon won re-election to Congress.

• In the long run, the Sedition Act backfired, because it encouraged the spread of the opposition press it sought to control. Printers, especially Republican printers, were now more likely than before to present themselves as partisan political actors. Between 1798 and the election of 1800, Republican newspapers were cropping up throughout the country, and American news was increasingly divided into two contradictory and mutually unintelligible versions of current events. •

The Alien and Sedition Acts also aroused a libertarian counterattack from Republicans. In Kentucky and Virginia, the state legislatures sought to invalidate the laws, asserting defiantly the rights of states to resist or even nullify congressional laws they deemed unconstitutional. The **Kentucky and Virginia Resolutions** of 1798, which were secretly authored by James Madison and Vice President Thomas Jefferson, reflected a moment of uncertainty about the power of the central government and became foundational texts in the history of states' rights ideology. But no other states supported the resolutions, and a showdown over federal authority was averted. Ironically, Jefferson, Madison, and their partisans would soon hold the reins of federal power they had sought to limit.

"A BLOODLESS REVOLUTION"

The triumph of Thomas Jefferson over incumbent John Adams in the **election of 1800** was more than just a

Aaron Burr (1756–1836). Burr stubbornly refused to concede the presidency to Thomas Jefferson after the election of 1800, forcing the House of Representatives to decide the contest. Four years later, while serving as vice president, Burr killed Alexander Hamilton in a duel in New Jersey and managed to remain in office. Two years after that, he was arrested on charges of raising a private army in the West and conspiring to become emperor of a vast new nation extending from Ohio to Panama. *Pictures Now/Alamy Stock Photo*

changing of the guard. For the first time—and after thirteen months of intensive campaigning—control of the presidency shifted from one party to another, bringing to power men who had previously been branded as threats to national security. Jefferson saw his victory as a genuine revolution, on par with that of 1776, which had transformed the "form" but not the "principles of our government." To make the revolution complete, Republicans hoped to scale down the central government and set the new republic on a course that would break from European models of nationhood.

Two factors were critical to the outcome of this close election. One, which was noted repeatedly by both sides, was the power of the recently created Republican news network in influencing voters. The other was the Constitution's three-fifths clause, which significantly enhanced the voting power of Southern states by counting 60 percent of their completely disenfranchised slave population in determining their electoral votes. Without those bonuses, the states won by Adams would have yielded more electoral votes than those won by Jefferson, and the revolution would have been canceled. With the involuntary support of hundreds of thousands of people living in slavery, slaveholder Jefferson, disparaged by opponents as the "Negro President," took office.

The period between the November election and Jefferson's inauguration the following March was marked by grave uncertainty. Though the Republicans had outpolled the Federalists by 73 to 65 electoral votes, the Electoral College had failed to produce a clear verdict on the presidency, because Jefferson and his vice-presidential running mate, Aaron Burr, each received 73 votes. Electors were entitled to vote for both a first and a second choice (the latter would serve as vice president), and parties would instruct their electors to withhold one ballot from the vice-presidential candidate, so that he would come in second place. But a New York Republican neglected to play his part, producing a tie, and Burr refused to concede to Jefferson. The contest then moved to the House of Representatives, where a Federalist majority had to choose between two despised opponents. Only on the thirty-sixth ballot did Jefferson receive the required

MEDIA AND INFORMATION

support of nine state delegations. (By the time of the next presidential election, the Twelfth Amendment would prevent such a recurrence by separating the ballots of presidents and vice presidents.)

After Jefferson was officially elected, Adams devoted the final days of his term to appointing Federalists to positions as judges, diplomats, and military commanders before the Republicans took over. Adams and his newly installed Supreme Court chief justice, John Marshall, spent the month of February preparing and delivering commissions to 217 appointees, working right up to the waning hours of the day before the inauguration. Jefferson and the Republicans decried these tactics and the "midnight judges" that Adams had installed, but they honored all of the appointments that had been fully processed by the deadline.

William Marbury, one of the judges whose commission was not delivered in time, sued the Jefferson administration under the Judiciary Act of 1789 for refusing him the appointment. The Supreme Court (with the same Federalist John Marshall now presiding) ruled that the federal judiciary could not compel a president to process an appointment. More significantly, the Court ruled that the Judiciary Act voted into law by Congress violated the Constitution. *Marbury v. Madison*, decided in 1803, established the important principle of **judicial review,** under which federal courts claim the power to overturn acts of Congress they deem unconstitutional—a power the Constitution did not explicitly grant to the judicial branch. The case had a monumental impact on the future of American law and politics. In the shorter term, the entire ordeal of Marbury's contested commission captured something remarkable about the election of 1800 and the new system of political parties. Change at government's highest level, however bitter and contested, was conducted without violence and according to an understanding of the rule of law shared by both sides.

IMAGINED CITIES

Federalist and Republican visions of the new republic clashed starkly over the future role of American cities. From its founding, the United States was an overwhelmingly rural society, more so than any European nation at the time other than Poland. In 1800, only six places in the young nation had populations over ten thousand, and less than 4 percent of the country's population lived in them. Thomas Jefferson thought little of urban America and compared cities to "sores on the body politic." But to other founders, many of whom were urbanites themselves, American cities wielded power and importance beyond their number and size, because so much traffic

passed through them. Philadelphia was to the United States, Federalist financier Robert Morris wrote to John Hancock, "what the heart is to the human body in circulating the blood." But whether Americans saw their cities as bodily sores or vital organs, they recognized that urban areas were beginning to grow and proliferate.

Urban growth after the Revolution was not simply the result of migrations or natural increase. American cities were planned, plotted, and imagined. New towns on the frontier were built up in anticipation of future arrivals; older commercial cities on the seaboard were redesigned to accommodate sprawling populations that had not yet appeared; and brand new cities, such as the one that would become the U.S. capital, were projected onto the blank spaces of the national map.

A BRAND NEW CAPITAL

The founders of the new republic expected the federal government to be settled in a city, though which city remained an open question. Compared to European capitals during the same period, the nation's leading metropolis at the time was tiny. By modern standards, Philadelphia after the Revolution hardly seems urban at all. Its population in 1780 (about thirty thousand) would rank below that of Boynton Beach (Florida), Manitowoc (Wisconsin), and many small suburbs two centuries later, and its dense settlement could fit today within the boundaries of several major university campuses. Still, Philadelphia was a bustling, polyglot, cosmopolitan place. It was home to learned societies, a prestigious medical school, a thriving print industry, and the seats of both state and national government. Philadelphians controlled almost a quarter of the country's export trade, and eight Philadelphia newspapers produced much of the news that circulated nationally. If the selection of a national capital had been based on its eminence and influence—or on historical precedent—Philadelphia would have been an obvious choice.

Nonetheless, the national capital moved several times during and after the Revolution. And despite frustration with years of relocating their base of operations from place to place, few of the founders relished the idea of leaving the federal government indefinitely in the clutches of America's most populous and commercially powerful metropolis. In Philadelphia, many worried, the government might be susceptible to the pressures of democratic mobs on the one hand or commercial cliques on the other. Instead, the founders designed and built a new city, named after George Washington, to house their experiment in decentralized nation building.

The Constitution had called for the creation of a federal district that would not fall under any state's jurisdiction, but the question of where this district would be located was a point of conflict in Congress. Most of the participants in this debate agreed that the new capital ought to be located centrally, but the word *central* was open to disagreement. Did it refer to longitude, latitude, trade routes, settlement patterns, or national history? In an age when travel was slow and the national government's power over the states remained tenuous, Americans in different parts of the country worried about a capital that would be inaccessible to them or beholden to the interests of a rival region. Northerners—especially Pennsylvanians—lobbied for selecting a city at the country's demographic center (counting only white people). Southerners favored a mapmaker's definition of central, since that would recommend a site farther south than the eight places where national leadership had convened during and after the revolutionary crisis. In the deal that was struck to resolve the impasse over Hamilton's economic plan, Southerners won a site between Virginia and Maryland.

President Washington, who was designated to select the exact site, decided on a spot at the southernmost edge of the 105-mile zone he had been assigned by Congress. Rather than picking any of the existing towns in that district as the capital city, he chose a relatively uninhabited area, where he could create a majestic and thriving metropolis free of corruptions and conflicts of local community interests. The capital plan, designed by the French-born engineer Major Pierre Charles L'Enfant and selected (with several amendments) by the new national government, sought to rival the great urban centers of Europe in scope while embodying principles of rationality and order. (See Interpreting the Sources: Federalist and Republican Plans for a National Capital.)

Promoters of the new capital on the Potomac predicted that it would become the next Rome, attracting a population of one hundred sixty thousand within a few years. Washington and his commissioners were so enthusiastic about the city's prospects that they expected to build the city without any public financing. The plan was to buy an excess of land around the chosen site, announce the location, and then sell off the unneeded portion at a profit to pay for the construction of public buildings and urban infrastructure. From the beginning, then, Washington, D.C., was a speculative scheme of the sort that would become familiar in American urban history. For much of their history, cities in the United States have relied on the prospect of rising real estate values (rather than

more direct forms of taxation) to cover the costs of urban development. The Rome of the Americas would be built by the projected difference between what land was worth today and what it might be worth tomorrow.

Washington's bold scheme overestimated popular interest in living near the national government. At a special auction in 1791, with Washington, Jefferson, and Madison in attendance, only 35 out of 10,000 lots were sold. The results were no better a year later. Finally, the authorities staged a parade in 1793, and Washington himself stepped up to buy 4 lots, but few others were sold and the commissioners abandoned the auction strategy altogether. Maryland and Virginia had to provide loans to sustain the project.

D.C.'S HUMBLE BEGINNINGS

When the government moved to the new capital in 1800, only 109 buildings of brick or stone were standing. Few artisans were drawn to the area, and the commissioners had been forced to hire enslaved laborers from the neighboring plantations to help with construction. Physically, the town was rustic. Not long after her arrival, First Lady Abigail Adams got lost in the woods for two hours and had to hire a vagabond to guide her home. A group of congressmen returning from a dinner party lost their way in the bogs and had to wait until sunrise to return to the capital.

Apart from the postal system, the federal operation was quite small. When John Adams moved the executive branch of the federal government to the new capital in 1800, the entire records of the Departments of State, War, Navy, Treasury, and Justice occupied seven cases. The Washington, D.C., community was a small, tight-knit group as well. Congressmen and other public officials typically stayed in all-male boardinghouses, where they socialized together and often voted along similar lines. Supreme Court justices also shared temporary lodgings while the Court was in session.

Women were part of the capital scene, but mostly during the six-week social season. Several wives of prominent public officials who maintained year-round residences exerted influence on Washington, D.C., culture—and national politics—by cultivating and presiding over an elite parlor culture of parties and receptions where genteel social relations might be conducted and political alliances formed. More often, though, women were pushed to the sidelines of the public sphere of the new capital. Thomas Jefferson, who helped design the city, was especially hostile to the influence of women in politics. When he took over the presidency a year after the government moved there, he famously hosted all-male dinner parties where he enjoyed playing "mother" to his guests.

INTERPRETING THE SOURCES

Federalist and Republican Plans for a National Capital

Along with the Declaration of Independence, the Constitution, and the Bill of Rights, the design of the capital city ranks among the nation's founding documents. In creating a new capital from scratch, leaders of the early republic were able to imprint their visions of the United States onto paper and potentially onto public space. Republican Thomas Jefferson and Federalist Pierre L'Enfant offered contrasting plans for the city that would both house and represent the new national government.

Jefferson envisioned a simple grid of streets, with the main government buildings arrayed in a row across the capital's main street. In Jefferson's plan, the dots around the small city indicate the possibility of expanding the city, should the need arise. By contrast, L'Enfant's map called for a much larger city. Instead of setting aside space for future growth, L'Enfant boldly presumed that growth. And instead of adopting the repeating grid plan associated with Philadelphia (see Chapter 4), he drew on models of European imperial capitals, such as Versailles, France, which included diagonals, ovals, and circles. In L'Enfant's plan, different street grids are connected by diagonal avenues that traverse the city in multiple directions. L'Enfant's plan also divides the city into three separate centers of settlement, corresponding with the three branches of government.

George Washington opted for the more ambitious plan, though in revised form. And while the slow growth of the capital prevented many features of L'Enfant's imagined city from materializing, its landscape of broad, diagonal arteries; grand squares; and sweeping sight lines continues to distinguish it from other American cities built in the early nineteenth century.

Jefferson's Plan, 1791. Jefferson anticipated a simpler, more functional federal capital, though he left room in his plan for future growth. *Library of Congress, Manuscript Division [LC-us0074]*

L'Enfant's Plan, 1792. Federalist visions of the new capital emphasized grandeur and aesthetic appeal. *Library of Congress, Geography & Map Division [G3850 1792 .L4]*

Explore the Source

1. How does Jefferson's plan reflect the ideology of the Republicans?
2. Jefferson complained that L'Enfant's plan "glowed with an iconography of federal supremacy." What does that mean, and what features of L'Enfant's plan might have triggered that reaction?

For many years, Washington, D.C., remained a far cry from the New Rome envisioned by its designers. Not until the middle of the nineteenth century would the town begin to fulfill its original promise as a symbol of American grandeur with a full-year residential community.

THE URBAN FRONTIER

According to the mythology of westward expansion, white Americans trekked across the mountains as rugged individual frontiersmen or hardy family farmers and built primitive societies free of urban influences. In fact, the history of American settlement west of the Appalachians began with towns and cities. Before white farmers began tilling soil in the western reaches of the United States, and before settlers swelled the territorial populations in such places as Ohio, Indiana, Kentucky, Illinois, and Missouri,

entrepreneurs and government officials were mapping towns, incorporating cities, and projecting urban growth.

Cities were forceful impositions on the landscape. Some of these cities began as forts designed to support military conquest. But whether they were garrisons, fur-trading posts, supply centers, or commercial villages, cities like St. Louis, Cincinnati, Louisville, Pittsburgh, Lexington, and New Orleans formed an **urban frontier,** which was in place before farms were cultivated and before many of their states were admitted to the union. Cities created the possibility of a rural hinterland, and the rural hinterland in turn sustained the growth of cities.

Almost all of the earliest U.S. cities west of the Appalachians were located along major waterways. A typical example was Pittsburgh, whose location at the confluence of the Allegheny and Monongahela Rivers, where the

Washington, D.C., Around 1803. Hunters and farm animals appear on the streets of the new capital, within sight of the president's house. Question for Analysis: How does this image square with L'Enfant's city plan? *Library of Congress, Prints & Photographs Division [LC-USZ62-48766]*

Ohio River forms, had made it a contested strategic position in the battles among French, British, and Native American armies during the 1750s (see Chapter 5). Laid out as a city in 1764, Pittsburgh grew rapidly during the 1790s with the flow of migrants across the Appalachians. As new arrivals stopped in the city to sell horses and wagons and to buy food, furniture, and farm equipment, Pittsburgh became a significant marketplace and catered to a rising demand for manufactured goods. By 1811, iron making was a major local industry and several factories were busily producing nails, household utensils, farm implements, and machine parts. Pittsburgh soon surpassed Lexington in population, and a leading national business publication predicted it would become "the greatest manufacturing city in the world."

Pittsburgh eventually emerged as one of America's industrial centers, but the Ohio River city that would prove more immediately dominant was Cincinnati. Founded in 1788, fifteen years before Ohio entered the union, the "Queen City" became the central market for a vast hinterland, selling merchandise from Eastern cities and sugar, cotton, and molasses coming up from New Orleans. Cincinnati's population in 1810 was just over twenty-five hundred, but in the ensuing decades it would mushroom into the fifth largest city in the nation.

All of these cities contributed to and depended on the proliferation of riverboats, which carried people and goods along the region's major waterways. During the first decade of the nineteenth century, over twenty-five hundred boats were navigating the Ohio and Mississippi

Rivers at any given time, 90 percent of them traveling in the direction of the current. By 1811, the volume of river traffic had increased dramatically due to the introduction of **steamboat travel.** Robert Fulton initiated the American steamboat era in 1807 by sailing up the Hudson River from New York City to Albany in thirty-two hours. Four years later, Nicholas Roosevelt and his wife, Lydia Latrobe Roosevelt, brought steam travel to the rougher waters of the West. By making a successful voyage from Pittsburgh to New Orleans in 1811–1812, the Roosevelts demonstrated the viability of upriver boat travel in the West.

BOOSTERS, SPECULATORS, AND BANKERS

Inspired by the promising growth of Cincinnati, Pittsburgh, and other early river cities in the West, overland migrants plotted new sites. All along the Ohio River valley and the Great Lakes, ambitious promoters and businessmen laid out towns along grids and touted the glorious economic destinies of their imaginary communities to potential investors and residents. These **boosters,** as historians call them, were not simply investors trying to raise the value of Western real estate. They were active shapers of the frontier who analyzed climate and natural transportation advantages, developed theories about the gravitational pull that one city exerted on its neighbors, and made predictions about economic and demographic growth. Some of their assessments now seem quite prescient, others less so. For every Cleveland and Indianapolis, there was a

Robert Fulton's *Clermont* on the Hudson, 1813. Steam-powered riverboats became iconic symbols of the Western experience in the mid-nineteenth century. Their introduction in 1811 helped transform the economy and demography of the Mississippi and Ohio River regions. *The Granger Collection, New York*

Hygeia, a Lystra, and a Franklinville, towns that never made it despite what appeared to be compelling natural advantages and a burst of promotional energy.

What the boosters accurately perceived was the fact that new cities would vie with one another for economic and demographic superiority, even as they contributed to one another's growth. Close to two million Americans crossed the Appalachians during the first two decades of the nineteenth century, and most of them farmed. But the value of farmland in Ohio and Kentucky depended on markets for agricultural goods, and cities were crucial in reaching and shaping those markets. As cities got bigger, urban land values skyrocketed, and the boosters who successfully promoted the fortunes of their fledgling communities reaped considerable profits.

City growth along the urban frontier offered another reminder that life in the trans-Appalachian West was far from Jefferson's vision of a nation of simple farming folk. **Land speculators** rather than individual farmers bought up most of the plots sold by the federal government. In 1800, twenty-one speculators claimed one-fourth of Kentucky. Among them was the family of Supreme Court justice John Marshall. Many other founders and leaders of the new nation speculated in Western lands as well. Freed from the traditional laws and customs that prevented its transfer from one family or estate to another, land had become another marketable commodity.

Town boosting and land speculation were not the only new entrepreneurial opportunities in the growing urban frontier. At the beginning of the nineteenth century, bankers began to lobby states for charters to establish institutions that would provide white settlers with cash. Banks had to be chartered into existence by special acts of state legislatures, because banks actually created money. Before the Civil War, the United States had no uniform, government-issued paper currency. Instead, paper money consisted of the various notes of different state-chartered banks. When

manufacturers paid their employees or urban customers paid their grocery bills, they were likely using the bank notes of some individual bank, which were pieces of paper that the bearer could (in theory) take to that bank for redemption in silver or gold. Western states were attractive banking centers for investors who saw an advantage in having a remote location that would discourage people from ever presenting their bank notes for redemption (see Singular Lives: Andrew Dexter, Rogue Banker in the Wilderness).

As of 1790, the entire nation had a grand total of 4 banks. Thirty years later, the number had risen to 328, and many others had come and gone in the interim. Forty new banks were incorporated in Kentucky in 1818 and failed a year later. As long as buyers and sellers maintained faith in the bank's ability to redeem its promissory notes, bank currency would stay in circulation. Banks pumped money into local markets and financed much of the expansion of the American economy.

WALL STREET AND THE NEW YORK GRID

Maps of future cities on the Ohio River and charters for cash-poor banks in remote Michigan villages epitomized the exuberant ambitions of a new generation of merchants and planners. But commercial growth and speculation were not limited to the frontier. Many of the most daring and ambitious planners operated in the older cities on the eastern seaboard. There, too, the impulse to imagine urban growth was taking hold.

By the beginning of the new century, New York (which was then located entirely within the island of Manhattan) had surpassed Philadelphia as the nation's most populous city. The symbolic and practical center of New York's mercantile culture was the **Tontine Coffee House** on Wall and Water Streets. The Tontine was more than simply a place to drink coffee. It was a clearinghouse of information, both printed and oral, where merchants, lawyers, brokers, and civic leaders went to read newspapers, learn

SINGULAR LIVES

Andrew Dexter, Rogue Banker in the Wilderness

"Detroit in 1811," Engraving by Henry E. Downer.
In this engraving, based on a painting of Detroit by George Washington Whistler, Dexter's Detroit Bank is the third building from the right. *Courtesy of the Burton Historical Collection, Detroit Public Library*

Detroit was not one of the boomtowns of America's urban frontier. A French settlement founded a century earlier, Detroit was captured by the Ottawas and their British allies in 1763 and then given to the United States in 1796 as a provision of Jay's Treaty. In 1805, the federal government designated Detroit as capital of the new Michigan Territory, but white American settlement remained meager: The population totaled only 551, and English speakers were a minority. To live in Detroit, its governor wrote, was "to remove from the World, and barely exist."

For restless Boston schemer Andrew Dexter, Jr., Detroit's isolation and insignificance made it an ideal place to locate a bank. Born in 1779, Dexter descended from New Englanders and grew up in Providence, where he attended Rhode Island College (later Brown University). Graduating second in a class of promising young men, most of whom would become merchants and lawyers, Dexter moved to Boston, embarked on a successful legal practice, and married into a prosperous Boston family. But Dexter aspired to greater wealth and turned to the growing world of finance. Wresting control of a Boston bank in 1806, he acquired or established banks in other places farther west, including Michigan. Dexter's Detroit bank, the first such institution west of the Alleghenies, printed tens of thousands of dollars' worth of bank notes, sent them back to Boston, and began circulating them with the confidence that few New Englanders would ever trek to the Michigan wilderness to present the notes for redemption. As long as no one did so, Dexter and his friends figured, it would make no difference that the Detroit bank, like most of his financial institutions, held a much smaller supply of gold and silver than its notes promised.

Dexter used this scheme to buy land in Boston and finance the construction of Boston's Exchange Coffee House, which he hoped would become the major commercial center and stock exchange of the region. Upon its completion in 1808, Dexter's lavish Exchange was one of the tallest buildings in the United States. But the notes of the Detroit bank were soon discredited, its charter revoked, and Dexter's paper empire crumpled. Before the building opened for business, a disgraced Dexter fled to Canada ahead of his creditors, to whom he owed more than a half-million dollars. The Coffee House succumbed as well, destroyed by a massive blaze in 1818, which firefighting pumps could not reach due to the building's excessive height. Dexter ultimately returned to the United States, where he tried his hand at several unsuccessful ventures in the South, and died in 1837 after contracting yellow fever.

Where in the Archives?

Dexter and his financial shenanigans are the subject of Jane Kamensky's *The Exchange Artist* (2008). Like other secondary sources, Kamensky's book is based on evidence from primary sources produced during the period she describes, such as court records, private letters, genealogical tables, newspaper accounts, and images where Dexter's activities left their mark.

Because his most monumental achievement, the Exchange Coffee House, burned to the ground, Kamensky used contemporaneous travel writings to reconstruct its appearance and its place in the growing city of Boston. Her sources can be found at HathiTrust (https://www.hathitrust.org/):

- John Lambert, fl. 1811, *Travels Through Canada, and the United States of North America*, 3d ed., cor. and improved (London: Printed for Baldwin, Cradock and Joy, 1816).

- Charles Shaw, 1782–1828, *a Topographical and Historical Description of Boston: From the First Settlement of the Town to the Present Period; with Some Account of Its Environs* (Boston: Printed and published by Oliver Spear, 1817).

- [Samuel Lorenzo Knapp] 1783–1838, *Extracts from a Journal of Travels in North America, Consisting of an Account of Boston and Its Vicinity* (Boston: Printed by Thomas Badger, 1818).

Assignment

Read descriptions of the Exchange Coffee House in two of the following: Lambert (volume 2, pages 334–335), Shaw (pages 229–233), or Knapp (pages 8–9). View Thomas Wightman's 1809 drawing of the Exchange Coffee House at the New England Historical Society (https://www.newenglandhistoricalsociety.com/) in the article "Andrew Dexter Builds the 1st Skyscraper and Causes the 1st Bank Collapse." Answer the following questions in 300 words:

1. Which building features, as drawn by Wightman, do the written sources include or emphasize?

2. How do the two descriptions differ from one another, and how do they compare to the image?

Tontine Coffee House, ca. 1797. Full of printed publications and whispered rumors, coffeehouses like the Tontine (left) opened out onto a larger world of goods and ideas, but they were also local hangouts for people who already knew one another. It was at the Tontine, for example, that Alexander Hamilton met with friends in 1804 to discuss his upcoming duel with Aaron Burr, in which Hamilton was killed. *Francis G. Mayer/Corbis/Getty Images*

commodity prices, circulate mail, read incendiary pamphlets, arrange deals, and participate in public life. In 1792, a group of merchants who had been meeting in front of a sycamore tree on Wall Street to devise regulations for public trading of stocks set up shop inside the Tontine building, which had opened that year. This was the origin of the New York Stock Exchange.

Anticipating further growth in the city, New York State appointed a commission in 1807 to map streets and direct development on the rest of Manhattan. After debating many plans, in 1811 the commissioners published a map that would leave an enduring imprint on city life. Such a vision of a sprawling city covering the entire island was entirely speculative, much like the plan for Washington, D.C., or the maps of imaginary metropolises along the Ohio River.

PRESIDENT JEFFERSON AND WESTWARD EXPANSION

Despite its primitive setting in the sparsely settled national capital, the relocated federal government would embark on an ambitious course of national expansion. During the Jefferson administration (1801–1809), the United States took decisive steps in the transition from a set of seaboard settlements to a sprawling continental nation.

REPUBLICANS TAKE POWER

Thomas Jefferson had great expectations for what his revolution of 1800 might bring. In part, he saw his own election as a crushing blow to the monarchical tendencies and aristocratic sympathies of the Federalists, as well as to their program of military spending and high taxes. Once in office, he made a point of avoiding what he took to be the trappings of aristocracy. He abandoned such customs as riding in carriages, maintaining liveried servants, receiving foreign diplomats in special formal attire, and delivering State of the Union messages in person. More generally, he brought enthusiasm about the capacity of the leaders of the republic to remake the world on new foundations. "We can no longer say there is nothing new under the sun," Jefferson wrote shortly after the inauguration, "for this whole chapter in the history of man is new."

Many in the revolutionary generation shared Jefferson's suspicion of the dead weight of tradition. To the cohort that was coming of age as Jefferson took office, the allure of the new was even stronger. Jefferson sympathized strongly with this cultural trend. And many of his positions and policies favored the creation of blank slates that bore little imprint of the past. Perhaps nowhere was this clearer than in his long-standing interest in exploring and settling the American West. Jefferson was a cosmopolitan,

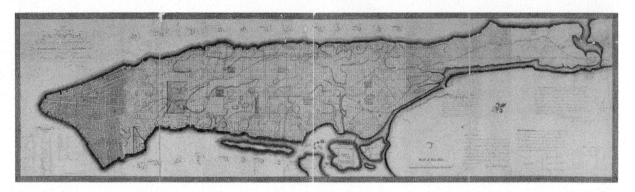

The Commissioners' Map of New York City, 1811.   For the first two centuries of its existence, New York was a dense and haphazardly planned collection of winding streets and irregular intersections. In 1811, when fewer than one hundred thousand people lived in Manhattan and settlement barely reached as far north as Houston Street, a commission proposed a grid plan for organizing all future development on the island. Unlike the plan for the nation's capital, the New York plan avoided ovals, circles, and broad, diagonal arteries. *Library of Congress, Geography & Map Division [G3804.N4:2M3 1811 .B7]*

Francophile intellectual, but he looked optimistically westward to an American future on a continent with which he was still largely unfamiliar.

THE LOUISIANA PURCHASE

Ever since the Treaty of Paris, American politicians had been troubled by the Spanish presence at the new republic's southern and western borders. Of particular concern during the 1790s was the fact that Spain controlled the mouth of the Mississippi River at New Orleans. As American settlers poured into Kentucky and Tennessee, establishing farms near rivers that flowed west, they pressured the federal government to secure free navigation rights on the Mississippi, so that they could ship crops down to the Gulf of Mexico and from there to Eastern markets. Some radical frontiersmen, including an obscure Tennessee politician named Andrew Jackson, who served briefly in Congress during George Washington's second term, threatened to move Kentucky and Tennessee into the Spanish Empire if the United States could not guarantee their access. For a while, Spain granted American farmers the right to ship their goods along the Mississippi through New Orleans and into the Gulf, as part of **Pinckney's Treaty** of 1795. But Spain revoked these privileges in 1802, and President Jefferson worried about the possibility of war.

As it turned out, Spain had secretly ceded Louisiana back to France two years earlier, though the Spanish were still maintaining a government in New Orleans in an effort to protect their other colonies. Meanwhile, France was having second thoughts about the value of the territory. By 1803, the French cause in St. Domingue was clearly lost (fifty to sixty-five thousand soldiers had been killed, mostly by disease), and the French emperor Napoleon lacked either the appetite or the resources for further military ventures in his American colonies. Furthermore, the loss of St. Domingue reduced the importance of Louisiana to the French, since Napoleon had valued his mainland colonies largely as a source of food, lumber, and animals for the lucrative sugar plantations in the Caribbean. Anticipating war with Britain, France was motivated to unload Louisiana to another power to avoid having to pay the costs of defending it against the British.

Jefferson had sought to purchase just the city of New Orleans, but Napoleon's representatives responded by offering Jefferson the entire Louisiana Territory, which stretched from the Mississippi to the Rocky Mountains, for the price of 15 million dollars (see How Much Is That? The Louisiana Purchase). Jefferson hoped to pay for his new Western lands not by tax revenue but by real estate speculation. The government could now trade land west of the Mississippi for Native American land to the east and sell that land to cotton farmers and speculators at a profit. The **Louisiana Purchase** treaty, signed in April 1803 and announced to the public on July 4 of that year, instantaneously doubled the size of the United States—at least on paper (see Map 8.3). Ironically, Jefferson's triumph was, in large part, the consequence of Toussaint Louverture's struggle against French colonial authority in Haiti, a revolt Jefferson feared, opposed, and sought to suppress.

How Much Is That?

The Louisiana Purchase

The 15 million dollars expended on the Louisiana Purchase in 1803 is roughly equivalent to 356 million dollars in 2020 currency, or about 67 cents per acre. The current commercial value of the land itself is difficult to assess, since some of it is zoned as parkland and thus not available for private sale, but typical rural land parcels in the state of Louisiana sell for thousands of dollars per acre.

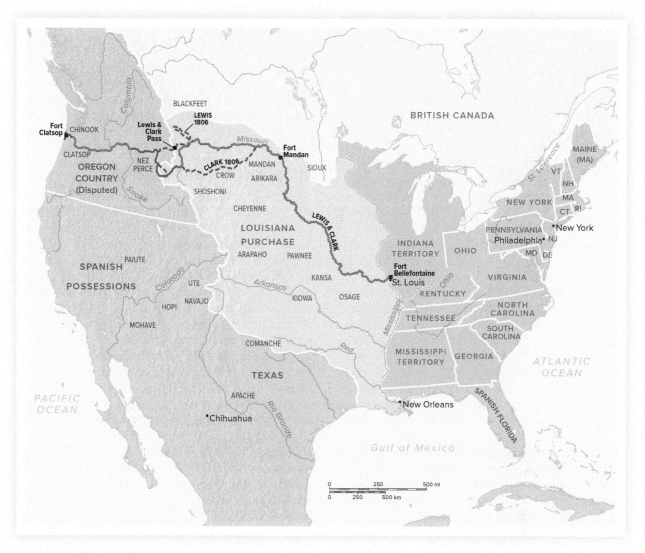

Map 8.3 Doubling the Size of the Nation. Jefferson's Louisiana Purchase was the most significant achievement of his presidency.

Jefferson seized this unexpected opportunity, despite his own doubts about whether the Constitution authorized the president to buy foreign land and expand the national domain, despite the prospect of opposition from Federalists, and despite the possibility that Spain might not recognize the sale. The last concern was particularly apt. Spain's secret deal with France to return the Louisiana Territory stipulated that the French would not cede the land to another party without offering it back to Spain first.

The allure of western expansion overcame these and other qualms. From Jefferson's perspective, the purchase (which he classified as a treaty, so as to keep within what he regarded as the strict limits of his constitutional authority) addressed a number of concerns in addition to the paramount goal of free access to the Mississippi. The prospect of this massive new terrain for agriculture assuaged

Jefferson's fears that the United States would urbanize and turn too quickly to manufacturing. Sudden territorial expansion offered the further benefit of dispersing the population and making it less likely for the new nation to be dominated by a strong central government.

LEWIS AND CLARK: REVEALING THE WEST

Jefferson also looked to the West to help solve what he and many other white Americans perceived to be the nation's Native American problem. He hoped to use territory on the other side of the Mississippi River to induce the Chickasaw, the Choctaw, and others to cede lands in the Lower Mississippi Valley. Finally, Louisiana promised to fulfill Jefferson's dream of locating a northwestern route across the continent to the Pacific Ocean.

In January 1803, before the French even broached the subject of Louisiana, Jefferson sent a confidential message to Congress asking for a modest expenditure to support an expedition of about a dozen men to travel up the Missouri River, exploring its full length, "even to the Western Ocean." Like the message, the expedition would have to be conducted discreetly, since the men would be traveling through foreign territory. Interestingly, Jefferson explained the need for exploring the Missouri in terms of white–Native American relations. Native groups, Jefferson observed, were increasingly refusing to cede lands. The only way to accommodate the "rapid increase of our numbers" was to transform the economic basis of native societies, so that they would abandon their policy of clinging tenaciously to territory coveted by whites. Jefferson's secret memorandum proposed persuading Native Americans to adopt agriculture and drawing them into networks of trade. An expedition along the Missouri would establish cultural contacts and develop commercial connections between the United States and the native people living along the river.

A few months after the secret message to Congress, the Missouri River mission acquired a much higher profile and far broader significance. Now the expedition would be surveying some of the newly acquired Louisiana Territory, about which white Americans knew very little. Jefferson entrusted the expedition to his private secretary, Meriwether Lewis, who asked his friend William Clark (a veteran of Indian wars in Ohio) to share the command of the party. Clark recruited a crew of Kentucky woodsmen from around the Ohio River to join a group already assembled by Lewis, and several others were added as the men made their way along the Ohio toward St. Louis, a French trading city that had just been transferred to U.S. control.

In the spring of 1804, Clark's crew traveled from St. Louis to the Missouri River city of St. Charles. From there, the Corps of Discovery, as the party would be called, traveled to Fort Mandan, North Dakota, and encamped for the winter before embarking on their epic westward expedition. The multicultural Lewis and Clark expedition included Southerners, Yankees, immigrants from Ireland and Germany, French Canadians, three men of Native American parentage, and an African American named York, who was enslaved to William Clark and never received any pay for his role in the project. At Fort Mandan, they were joined by a French Canadian named Toussaint Charbonneau and his pregnant Shoshoni wife, Sacagawea. Both served the expedition as interpreters, and Sacagawea's presence helped mark the mission as peaceful in the eyes of the communities they visited.

A year after leaving their camp at Fort Mandan, the Corps glimpsed the Pacific Ocean. Although they had not found a simple cross-continent waterway, they had identified a route between the Mississippi and the Pacific. Along the way, they had established relations between the United States and numerous native nations while amassing a treasury of geographical, botanical, and zoological knowledge that would fascinate Americans for decades.

CITIES ON THE MISSISSIPPI

When the United States acquired Louisiana from France, it took possession of a number of foreign cities that had been built along the boundaries of the French colonial empire. At the time, St. Louis was forty years old. Its location atop a limestone bluff just south of the junction of the Mississippi, Missouri, and Illinois Rivers had given the city strategic significance during decades of imperial conflict, but the population had grown slowly. St. Louis in 1803 consisted of about two hundred houses and a mostly French population of about a thousand people, two-thirds of whom were cousins. Still, it was the commercial center of the region and the gateway city to the vast land that Jefferson had added.

The real urban prize of the Louisiana Purchase, however, was New Orleans. The French had planned the city on the banks of the river in 1721, laying out a bounded grid of streets, about 1 mile wide and ½ mile deep. Later in the century, new suburbs (*faubourgs*) would be created beyond the original grid, which remained fortified. The city passed into Spanish hands in 1763, and Americans settled there in large numbers in the 1790s, but the culture remained predominantly French (see Chapter 5). When the United States took over New Orleans, it housed a population (including the *faubourgs*) of just over 8,000, of whom 2,773 were enslaved. Another 1,335 were free people of color, *gens de couleur libre* in the local terminology.
● Over the next six years, a large migration of refugees from Haiti (many of whom arrived in 1809 via Cuba) doubled the city's population, swelled its number of French speakers, and changed its racial composition. By 1810, over 63 percent of the residents of New Orleans were descended from Africans. ●

Whereas in the rest of the United States all descendants of Africans were typically classified as Black, the law and culture of New Orleans insisted on a more complex set of racial distinctions. Free people of color enjoyed a higher status than those with strictly African ancestry and were granted political rights and social freedoms denied free Blacks elsewhere in the South. White visitors were often struck by public romances between white men and women whose partially Black racial status would have rendered the relationship taboo or illegal in other states. At **quadroon balls,** elite white men paid

CROSSING BORDERS

A View of New Orleans Taken from the Plantation of Marigny,
by J. L. Bouquet de Woiseri, 1803. This painting depicts New
Orleans at the time it came under U.S. control. *Picture History/Newscom*

whose ships wished to participate in the lucrative Mediterranean trade. After independence, the United States made hefty annual payments to secure good relations with these Barbary states, as they were called. Despite the payments, in 1793 Algerian pirates boarded American ships and took 120 hostages in a bid to raise more money.

● Over the next three years, the fate of the captives became a cause célèbre, and accounts of their captivity dominated popular theater and literature. American newspapers reveled in lurid descriptions of Barbary cruelty and portrayed the Muslim world as uncivilized and despotic. ● After three years, the nation's first hostage crisis ended with a ransom payment of 1 million dollars.

POLITICS AND ENTERTAINMENT

After Jefferson's election, the pasha of Tripoli declared war on the United States in the hopes of extorting more money, and the new president responded by sending the navy to the shores of Tripoli. From a military standpoint, the U.S. expedition fared poorly. In 1803, an American battleship ran aground and required a daring rescue effort. Another attempt to blow up the Tripoli fleet literally backfired. Finally, an 1804 land attack succeeded in persuading the pasha that this war was costing more than it was worth. An 1805 peace treaty ended the first **Barbary War** (a second

admission (sometimes costly) to socialize with free women of color. These encounters could lead to arrangements whereby a woman of one-quarter African ancestry entered into an intimate relationship with a prosperous man of European descent in return for financial support. Despite the obvious constraints associated with such a relationship, the women involved would enter the ranks of fashionable New Orleans society.

Public life in New Orleans reflected this complex racial system, as well as the distinctive influences of Catholicism; West Indian dance, music, and clothing; Spanish architecture; and French laws. At the same time, New Orleans's geographical position in the urban frontier would place it at the center of the expanding U.S. economy over the coming decades, a hub city for the flow of goods, information, and enslaved populations.

CAPTIVITY AND THE EMBARGO YEARS

Jefferson's plans to reduce the federal debt, slash military spending, and scale back the activities of the central government were undermined by several developments during his presidency. The first decade of the century saw the new republic fight a war against North African pirates and struggle to avoid military showdowns with both France and Britain. Jefferson decided not to run for re-election in 1808, and his successor, James Madison, inherited a range of challenging predicaments. Complicated strategies of international diplomacy dominated national politics, framed a divisive debate about the slave trade, and hobbled a growing commercial economy.

WAR IN THE MEDITERRANEAN

Beginning in the late 1600s, the North African states of Morocco, Algiers, Tunis, and Tripoli controlled the Mediterranean Sea, exacting tribute from countries

Decatur's Conflict with the Algerine at Tripoli. In this retrospective portrait from the 1850s, the prominent historical painter Alonzo Chappel dramatizes the heroism of American naval forces and the barbarism of their enemies—represented, for example, by the pirates' clothing, facial hair, and unshod feet. *SOTK2011/Alamy Stock Photo*

war a decade later would finally release the United States from tribute obligations to Muslim states in the Mediterranean) and allowed Jefferson to save face. It also pushed many Republicans to abandon their opposition to maintaining a professional navy.

ENDING THE INTERNATIONAL SLAVE TRADE

American denunciations of hostage taking and white slavery on the Barbary Coast coexisted uneasily with American participation in the capture and enslavement of West Africans. Even many white Americans who were comfortable with owning people objected to kidnapping them in the first place. The U.S. Constitution explicitly protected the international slave trade from any congressional interference for two decades after ratification, but at the end of the Barbary Wars, that period was drawing to a close. Meanwhile, British opposition to slave trafficking was mounting and the Royal Navy was poised to use its power to abolish the international trade.

Jefferson's annual message to Congress at the end of 1806 called for legislation to ban the importation of enslaved people into the United States, and after considerable debate about the terms, Congress passed such a law, to take effect in the beginning of 1808 (the earliest allowable date under the Constitution). Many Southern slaveholders embraced the **ban on slave importation,** because it raised the value of the people they already owned—and because the enslaved population grew through reproduction in the American South (unlike every other slave society in the Americas, which depended on importation). But Southerners in Congress fought for lighter penalties for slave smuggling and did not want the government to grant freedom to Africans brought illegally to American shores. The final version of the bill allowed smuggled enslaved persons to be handled according to local custom and depended on Southern cooperation for its enforcement.

The ban on importing enslaved people did not threaten slavery in the American South. Over the next fifty years, many Africans would be brought illegally into the United States. And when over three thousand Black refugees from St. Domingue, claimed as property by white slaveholders, arrived in New Orleans in 1809, Congress voted to exempt them from the ban rather than emancipating or deporting them. Moreover, the ban had no impact on the bustling traffic in human beings that thrived *within* the nation's expanding borders. Still, the Black Philadelphia minister Absalom Jones preached a sermon when the new law took effect, proposing January 1 as an annual day of public thanksgiving to commemorate this historic achievement.

NEUTRALITY, IMPRESSMENT, AND EMBARGO

By far the most difficult diplomatic challenge of Jefferson's second term resulted from the Napoleonic Wars, which began in Europe in 1803. Initially, U.S. neutrality in this conflict between France and an alliance of Britain, Russia, and Austria was a source of economic boon. American ships were able to do business with both sides and took over shipping lines between France and its remaining Caribbean colonies. But as military conflict between France and Britain intensified, both antagonists began forbidding neutral ships from carrying goods to the other side. Moreover, both worried that America might provide military aid to the enemy.

In 1806, the British began boarding U.S. ships and searching them for suspected arms shipments or deserters from the Royal Navy. Overall, close to ten thousand sailors on American ships experienced forcible **impressment** into service for Britain between 1793 and 1814. More humiliating for the Americans, in 1807 a British warship sailing off the coast of Virginia opened fire on an American frigate that refused to submit to a search. Three Americans were killed and sixteen others wounded in this attack. Still Jefferson pursued a course of peace, hoping to avoid a war that would devastate the nation's economy, break the budget of the central government, and demonstrate the military impotence of the new republic.

As an alternative to war, Jefferson and the Republican Congress imposed economic sanctions on the belligerents. The Embargo Act, which passed Congress in December 1807, banned the importation of foreign goods and prohibited American ships from landing in foreign ports without special authorization. Subsequent laws were added to help the federal government enforce this draconian restriction. Jefferson believed that Americans could get by without European manufactured goods for the short time it would take Europeans to appreciate their dependency on American grain, tobacco, and cotton. He miscalculated. The embargo's most severe impact was clearly on the American economy. New England, where the shipping industry was headquartered, suffered most dramatically, but plummeting commodity prices in other parts of the nation spread the pain. Jefferson's embargo proved politically unpopular, and the Federalist Party began to show new signs of life, though the Republican secretary of state, James Madison, managed to win the election to succeed Jefferson in 1808, in part because the full brunt of the embargo had not yet arrived.

With Madison in office, Congress replaced the embargo with the **Non-Intercourse Act,** which opened up American commerce to all nations except France and Britain and promised to resume trade with whichever warring nation would respect U.S. neutrality. Napoleon seized the opportunity and suspended restrictions on American shipping, though French boats continued to intercept American cargo. In 1811, President Madison cut off trade with Britain.

At the same time, war between the United States and Britain-supported Native American alliances in the Northwest was putting further strain on Anglo-American relations. The stage was set for more direct conflict between the new republic and the empire to which it had once belonged.

CONCLUSION

The period between 1793 and 1811 witnessed a number of remarkable changes and innovations as the new federal government began to operate. Most dramatically, the United States doubled in size, extending across the contested Mississippi River (which it now controlled) all the way to the Rocky Mountains. Slavery was either banned or legally phased out in half of the country, and communities of free Blacks were growing in Northern cities. A new system of political parties emerged in response to marked differences over policy and ideology, and control of the central government passed peaceably from one party to the other. A new capital city was built on the banks of the Potomac. New networks of political newspapers began exploiting the postal broadcast system that had been set up in 1792, and ambitious speculators pushed the limits of a banking system that had barely existed at the start of the period. New cities sprouted up far from the eastern seaboard, and some two million men and women migrated to farmland within market reach of those cities. Some of those migrants went freely; others were brought in chains. On the international front, the French monarchy had crumbled and France had abandoned its main colonial projects in North America. One war had been declared against the United States by a foreign nation, whereas another, much larger storm was brewing. Though the nation was, by the most generous count, only thirty-five years old in 1811, American society, culture, and landscape had changed in some respects beyond recognition.

STUDY TERMS

gradual abolition	Alien Acts
manumission	Sedition Act
Haitian Revolution	Kentucky and Virginia
Black churches	Resolutions
Methodism	election of 1800
African Methodist Episcopal (A.M.E.) Church	judicial review
protective tariffs	urban frontier
Bank of the United States	steamboat travel
broad construction	boosters
strict construction	land speculators
Federalists	Tontine Coffee House
Republicans	Pinckney's Treaty
Whiskey Rebellion	Louisiana Purchase
French Revolution	quadroon balls
Jay's Treaty	Barbary War
XYZ affair	ban on slave importation
political newspapers	impressment
	Non-Intercourse Act

FURTHER READING

A database of additional full-text readings is available through Power of Process for Primary Sources in Connect.

Elizabeth Blackmar, *Manhattan for Rent* (1989), explores some crucial background for understanding the significance of the 1811 New York grid.

Simon Finger, *The Contagious City* (2012), provides a medical history of the Philadelphia yellow fever epidemic.

Jane Kamensky, *The Exchange Artist* (2008), presents the dramatic story of Andrew Dexter's Exchange Coffee House.

Catherine E. Kelly, *Republic of Taste* (2016), considers how judgments about art, theater, and architecture contributed to politics and national identity.

Roger G. Kennedy, *Mr. Jefferson's Lost Cause* (2003), reconsiders the Louisiana Purchase within the context of Jefferson's ideas about land, slavery, and freedom.

Susan E. Klepp, *Revolutionary Conceptions* (2009), shows how women began limiting family size in the early national period.

Sarah Luria, *Capital Speculations* (2005), interprets the ideas and ideologies behind the planning of Washington, D.C.

Jeffrey Pasley, *The Tyranny of Printers* (2003), offers a detailed guide to the political press in the early republic.

Jennifer Spear, *Race, Sex, and Social Order in Early New Orleans* (2009), reconstructs the complex racial hierarchies and sexual politics of the French, Spanish, and American city.

Ashli White, *Encountering Revolution* (2010), examines how the Haitian Revolution shaped attitudes toward slavery in the early republic.

9 | WAR, EXPANSION & INDIAN REMOVAL

Chapter Questions

1. In what ways were white–Native American conflicts crucial to the War of 1812?

2. What were the long-term consequences of the war for Native American life east of the Mississippi?

3. How did westward expansion relate to developments in the history of slavery, religion, and the American economy?

4. Why did American art and literature during this period emphasize Native American subject matter?

The Death of Tecumseh. An artist's interpretation of the death of the revolutionary Tecumseh at the Battle of the Thames in 1813. Tecumseh's death ended the pan-Indian alliance he had led against the United States. *Niday Picture Library/Alamy Stock Photo*

On a December night in 1829, a man in full native garb addressed a crowd in New York City. "MY CURSES ON YOU WHITE MEN," he shouted. "MAY YOUR GRAVES AND THE GRAVES OF YOUR CHILDREN BE IN THE PATH THE RED MEN SHALL TRACE!" At the close of his speech, the large audience responded with a thunderous standing ovation.

The speaker was not a Native American. He was a white Philadelphian named Edwin Forrest, who would become the first person born in the United States to earn an international reputation in the field of acting. And on this night in 1829, Forrest was appearing as the lead character in the premiere performance of a play called *Metamora; or, the Last of the Wampanoags*. The play, which retold the story of King Philip's War in 1675 (see Chapter 2), was a smashing success. Forrest made a hero out of the slain chief and emerged as a major celebrity. Why Forrest was portraying an American Indian on a New York stage in 1829, and why white audiences cheered Metamora's curse on their race, are important questions. Although set in the distant past,

1811

William Henry Harrison destroys Prophetstown at Tippecanoe
Construction begins on National Road
Devastating earthquakes occur along New Madrid fault

1812

Congress declares war on Great Britain

1813

Tecumseh killed at Battle of the Thames

1814

British capture Washington, D.C.
Andrew Jackson defeats the Redsticks at Horseshoe Bend
New England Federalists meet in Hartford
Treaty of Ghent formally ends the war

1815

Americans repel the British at the Battle of New Orleans

1816

American Bible Society formed
Second Bank of the United States chartered

1819

Jackson invades Florida
U.S. and Spain sign Transcontinental (Adams-Onis) Treaty
Financial panic and widespread bankruptcy strike the nation

1820

Congress enacts Missouri Compromise

1821

Sequoya devises Cherokee syllabary

1822

U.S. recognizes new independent republics in Latin America
Denmark Vesey and thirty-four others executed on charges of plotting a slave rebellion

1823

Monroe Doctrine propounded
James Fenimore Cooper publishes *The Pioneers*

1828

First issue of *Cherokee Phoenix* appears
Jackson elected president

1829

Metamora debuts at New York's Park Theater

1830

Congress passes Indian Removal Act

1835

Second Seminole War begins
Treaty of New Echota transfers Cherokee land

1838

Cherokee march westward in the Trail of Tears

Metamora opened just as the United States was preparing to exile tens of thousands of indigenous people from their homes in the South to lands west of the Mississippi River. Indian removal, as this government program was called, was the latest turn in a long and violent saga of white–Native American conflict, dating back to King Philip's War and beyond. But it also marked the culmination of a more recent war, one that had ushered in a new chapter in the growth of the young republic.

The War of 1812, as Americans call it, exerted a powerful impact on the nation's economic, cultural, and political development. But it is not often understood how much this event had to do with white–Native American relations. Although the official conflict was with Great Britain, its consequences were felt most clearly, both in the short and long term, by the native groups who lived between the Appalachian and Allegheny Mountains and the Mississippi River.

The real beginning of the War of 1812 came in 1811, when William Henry Harrison, the governor of the Indiana Territory, led a force of one thousand troops against an American Indian community located along the Tippecanoe River. The community, known as Prophetstown, had been a bastion of resistance among the cultures of the Northwest (and an important ally of Great Britain), and Harrison's victory was a major step in the struggle to clear the territories west of the Appalachians for white settlement. Over the next two decades, the new republic would experience a wide range of significant crises and changes, most of which related to the westward drift of the population, both free and enslaved, and the westward expansion of the market economy. Native Americans suffered grievously from these trends, and the fate of indigenous people in the eastern half of North America sparked debates among white Americans, shaping both national politics and popular entertainment. The theatergoers who flocked to see Forrest's *Metamora* on opening night witnessed the unfolding of that larger dramatic story.

TECUMSEH AND THE BEGINNINGS OF WAR

By 1811, it was clear that the outcome of the American Revolution had been disastrous for Native Americans living in the new republic. The colonists had revolted against, among other things, imperial attempts to create a buffer between American Indians and the colonies. Once the war was over, the victorious Americans regarded native lands as conquered territory. In response, several native groups had formed an alliance to halt American settlement of the Ohio River valley, but the U.S. troops defeated them at the Battle of Fallen Timbers in 1794 and extracted major land cessions the following year in the Treaty of Greenville. Thereafter, federal agents acquired legal title to vast swathes of native land through dubious negotiations with individuals who purported to represent tribal interests. Between 1802 and 1805, William Henry Harrison signed seven such treaties, acquiring title over considerable territory in the future states of Indiana, Missouri, Wisconsin, and Illinois at a rate of two cents per acre.

● In 1805, a new religious movement began to spread in the region. A Shawnee man named Tenskwatawa, who had struggled with alcohol addiction, received a revelation that inspired him to change his life and preach a message of spiritual renewal. Calling for a return to tribal traditions and a rejection of whiskey, imported goods, European foods, intermarriage with whites, and private property, the **Shawnee Prophet,** as he became known, attracted thousands of followers among the native groups of the Northwest Territory to his base of operations in a newly established village named Prophetstown (near present-day Lafayette, Indiana). ● The Prophet's older brother Tecumseh, meanwhile, built a parallel political movement to end the practice of ceding land to the United States. By 1811, Tecumseh's message had become a military rallying cry for Native Americans in different parts of the trans-Appalachian West. Meanwhile, swarms of white settlers were pouring into the region every year. A showdown was imminent.

PAN-INDIAN RESISTANCE

Tecumseh made the Prophet's idea of a cultural clash between American Indians and whites the basis for a new approach to geopolitics. He claimed that the continent's indigenous groups had a common identity and constituted a single political body. In this way, he hoped to avoid the question of which tribal leaders were authorized to negotiate deals with the United States. Tribal leaders did not have the authority to negotiate deals with the United States, Tecumseh argued, without the agreement of all native groups. Tecumseh, whose own ancestry was Shawnee, Creek, and white, identified not as a member of a particular tribal unit but as an "Indian." "All red men," he insisted, claimed an equal right to the land.

Tenskwatawa and Tecumseh's **pan-Indian** theme was not entirely original; arguments for unity among indigenous groups went back at least half a century (see Chapter 5). But Tecumseh was no ordinary leader. William Henry Harrison described him as "one of those uncommon geniuses, which spring up occasionally to produce revolutions." His message also came at a crucial point in the region's history, as the white population in Ohio was suddenly more than three times the number of indigenous people in all of the original Northwest Territory. With both the British and the French gone from the immediate area, native people faced the U.S. threat with more limited options for strategic alliances.

In 1809, after several native leaders from the Delaware, Miami, and Potawatomi groups ceded 3 million acres of Indiana land (including land inhabited by the Shawnee) to Harrison at the Treaty of Fort Wayne, Tecumseh pressed Harrison to rescind the deal. Harrison refused, arguing that a Shawnee man had no business commenting on the fairness or legitimacy of land cessions made by the Miami or Potawatomi. His diplomatic efforts rebuffed, Tecumseh devised an ambitious scheme for a confederacy that would unite northern and southern societies to forge a coordinated military response to American encroachment (see Map 9.1). In 1811, Tecumseh headed south toward Creek country to sell his plan.

Tecumseh, Composite Portrait by Artist and Historian Benson J. Lossing. This drawing was based on an 1808 sketch by French trader Pierre Le Dru. Lossing copied and modified the image, replacing Tecumseh's traditional dress with a British military uniform.
Question for Analysis: Why might the artist have changed Tecumseh's clothing?
North Wind Picture Archives/Alamy Stock Photo

CONFLICTING FAITHS

Map 9.1 Tecumseh's Diplomatic Mission. In the summer and fall of 1811, Tecumseh traveled both northwest to British Canada and south to Creek and Chickasaw country in present-day Alabama and Mississippi, traversing 3,000 miles in six months.

Tecumseh arrived among the Creek peoples at an especially portentous moment. That autumn, a brilliant comet (its tail measuring 100 million miles long) streaked across the Alabama sky, lending force to Tecumseh's claim that his cause had the blessing of the Great Spirit. By the time Tecumseh returned north, the comet's visibility had dimmed considerably, seeming to follow the charismatic leader home. ● In December, the first of several devastating earthquakes shook the continent. Though the epicenter was in New Madrid in southeastern Missouri, tremors could be felt in the nation's capital and as far

Reelfoot Lake and the Legacy of the Earthquakes. In February 1812, the third of the New Madrid earthquakes plunged enough marshland underwater to dam the Reelfoot Creek in northwestern Tennessee and create what is now Reelfoot Lake. Turning rivers into lakes transformed the New Madrid region from a bustling trade center to a sleepy swampland, but it also dramatized the apocalyptic nature of a seismic disaster that sparked spiritual crisis among both whites and Native Americans and contributed to the outbreak of the War of 1812. *Danita Delimont/Alamy Stock Photo*

away as Canada and Mexico. The quakes devastated the New Madrid region, causing homes to sink, islands to disappear, and the Mississippi River to reverse its course. But the larger environmental and spiritual impact was even more profound. The New Madrid earthquakes grabbed the attention of indigenous peoples throughout the vast region that Tecumseh was touring and lent support to the revivalist message that the Great Spirit was incensed by assimilation and land cessions. Tecumseh's war against the United States appeared to have divine sanction. ●

DIVISIONS OVER THE "CIVILIZATION PROGRAM"

Tecumseh's diplomatic journey to the South also coincided with rising internal conflicts among the Creek peoples. Ever since the Washington presidency, the federal government had been pushing a **civilization program,** designed to convert native inhabitants to European ways of living. The program was intended to absorb indigenous people into the new nation as equal citizens, but it also assumed that if Native Americans began using land differently, they might free territory for white settlement. In the words of Benjamin Hawkins, the government official who became the chief agent for Indian Affairs South of the Ohio in 1796, native groups needed to be introduced to "a new order of things." A big part of this new order was, literally, *things*—private property held and accumulated by individuals. But Hawkins also advocated a larger way of life involving agriculture, fences, reading and writing, European gender roles, and criminal punishments for individuals rather than groups.

As this new order made inroads among the Creek peoples, a mixed-blood elite prospered, accumulating considerable wealth (including enslaved people) and power. The disparity between the rich and poor became more apparent after a series of poor harvests in the first decade of the century. Hawkins secured the loyalty of several Creek leaders and warriors through government stipends and debt relief, which further alienated poorer Creek peoples from Hawkins and the United States. In addition, many were upset by U.S. plans to build a federal road through their land, increasing the westward traffic of white settlers and enslaved African Americans. By 1811, a civil war was brewing within the Creek Nation between supporters and opponents of the U.S. government.

U.S.-NATIVE AMERICAN TENSIONS EXPLODE

Tecumseh and his delegation went to Creek country bearing a pipe symbolizing warfare, but in the presence of Hawkins, Tecumseh appeared to counsel the Creeks not to accept it. A week into the visit, however, Hawkins left and Tecumseh showed his hand. At an assembly of Creek warriors, the gifted orator made a powerful case for American Indian unity and a return to traditional lifestyles. Many in the audience were swayed, including Hillis Hadjo, who would lead the Creek resistance movement. For the most part, however, Tecumseh did not persuade the leaders of the Southeastern groups to join his military alliance.

While Tecumseh was away on his diplomatic mission, Harrison attacked Prophetstown. Tecumseh had instructed his brother to keep the peace during his absence, but the Prophet could not resist the impulse to engage U.S. forces once they encamped outside the town. Harrison's army sustained many casualties, but equipped with superior guns they withstood the raid and proceeded to burn the abandoned native settlement to the ground. The **Battle of Tippecanoe** discredited the Prophet and destroyed his base of operations, but Tecumseh, who would not learn of the fighting for several months, was preparing for a much larger war.

THE WAR HAWKS PREVAIL

Tecumseh's military strategy depended on the revival of alliances with Great Britain, which had vacated the lands east of the Mississippi but still controlled Canada. In the summer of 1812, Tecumseh traveled north to Fort Malden, just across the river from Detroit, to meet with British officials who had promised him supplies in preparation for war. Relations between Britain and the United States had deteriorated rapidly during James Madison's first term, as the Americans sought to preserve their neutrality in the Napoleonic Wars while engaging in international commerce (see Chapter 8). The impressment of American sailors into the British navy, which seemed to imply that Americans were still subjects of the British Empire whenever they left U.S. soil, triggered national outrage. But only in 1811, with the looming threat of Britain's support for Tecumseh, did anti-British hostility reach a breaking point. A new generation of congressmen, many serving their first terms as representatives of southern and western constituencies, began clamoring for military action. These men, dubbed **War Hawks** by their opponents, included Kentuckian Henry Clay, South Carolinian John C. Calhoun, and other rising stars in the Republican Party. The War Hawks presented war as the only honorable response to Britain's humiliating attacks on American ships and sailors. But to its most ardent supporters, war also represented an opportunity to expand northward into British-controlled Canada and southward into Spanish-controlled Florida, where European powers supported Native American attacks against white settlers.

With rising political pressures from within his own party and the impressment of American sailors still fresh in popular memory, Madison sent Congress a declaration of war on June 1, 1812. A divided vote in Congress, the closest of any formal war declaration in U.S. history, reflected the crucial impetus for the **War of 1812.** In New England and the mid-Atlantic states, including areas that had suffered especially from Jefferson's embargo on international trade, support for the declaration was lukewarm. But among representatives from the South and the West, who were most concerned about the threat of Tecumseh's confederation, the war resolution passed with little dissent. Despite a recent lull in attacks on American ships, and despite the fact that Britain was about to suspend its blockade on ships doing business with France, the United States decided that the time was right to invade Canada.

THE WAR OF 1812: ESCAPING DISASTER

The War Hawks had predicted a quick and easy victory resulting in the annexation of Canada, but the United States was not prepared militarily for a fight with Britain and its native allies. The Americans suffered defeats near

Civilization Program. *The Picture Art Collection/Alamy Stock Photo*

BEHIND THE IMAGE

Scholars have questioned whether the unidentified artist who produced this 1805 oil painting ever visited the Georgia estate depicted, where Benjamin Hawkins lived with his common-law wife, Lavinia Downs. Hawkins served as the general superintendent of Indian Affairs South of the Ohio River for over twenty years and presided over a lucrative plantation. This portrait of the plantation slaveholder exhibits not his command of enslaved African American labor but rather his project of spreading the Civilization Program to the surrounding Creek society.

WITHIN THE IMAGE

Hawkins is shown instructing Creek individuals in the use of a plow, but by precept rather than example (❶ note his own genteel attire and bearing, far from that of a working farmer). Other details in the image confirm the painting's message that the Civilization Program was taking root in Creek country: ❷ Men rather than women are engaged in farm labor, and ❸ the only woman is engaged in child rearing; ❹ domesticated farm animals dot the pastoral landscape; and ❺ agricultural surplus is being collected.

BEYOND THE IMAGE

Idealized representations of the Civilization Program contributed to a growing sense during the years before the War of 1812 that the southwestern native groups (especially the Creek peoples and the Cherokee Nation) were on a path to assimilation that would ultimately clear land for the westward migration of American settlers. Such images would acquire more tragic overtones once the United States shifted to new policies of Indian removal more than a decade after Hawkins's death.

the border in Detroit and at Fort Dearborn (near the future location of Chicago) that summer, and the prospects for conquering Canada dimmed. Internal opposition to the invasion mounted as well, especially among the New Englanders, and Madison faced a strong re-election challenge in 1812. The battlefield moved south in 1813, and in 1814 the British attacked the eastern seaboard (see Map 9.2). Both sides scored significant victories and losses, but in the end the United States would survive this major test and succeed in fulfilling many of the War Hawks's central ambitions.

WASHINGTON, D.C., IS BURNING

After the initial British victories, American fortunes improved, especially on water. Commodore Oliver H. Perry defeated the British at Put-in-Bay on Lake Erie in September 1813. With control over the lake, U.S. forces were able to block supplies to British forts in Ontario. A month later, Harrison used Lake Erie to launch another invasion of Canada, defeating a Native American and British army along the Thames River. It was during this battle that Tecumseh, who had received a commission as brigadier general in the British army,

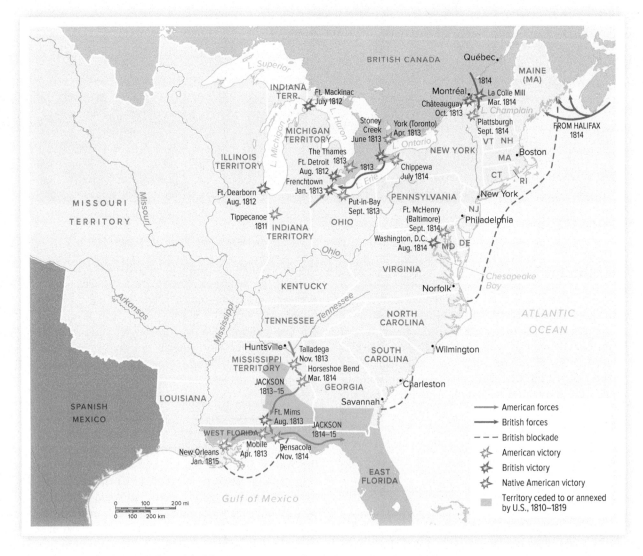

Map 9.2 Major Offensives of the War of 1812. Both the American invasion of Canada and the British counterinvasion of the United States ultimately failed. But U.S. victories against Native Americans in Alabama and Ohio proved crucial to the long-term consequences of the war.

was fatally shot in the chest. But soon thereafter, the U.S. army failed in an attempt to capture Montreal, whereas the British took Fort Niagara and burned the frontier city of Buffalo. The northern front of the war had reached a stalemate.

By the middle of 1814, the situation had changed again. British victories over Napoleon in Europe had freed up more troops for a North American surge. From the beginning, anti-war critics had warned that the invasion of Canada might provoke a counterattack against American towns and cities. Those fears now materialized. In August, ten thousand British soldiers moved on New York State but were thwarted in a crucial naval battle on Lake Champlain, which probably prevented a successful invasion of the Hudson River valley.

A second British invasion proved more damaging. On August 24, 1814, the British sailed into the Chesapeake Bay and attacked the nation's capital. First Lady Dolley Madison rescued her husband's papers from the invaders, but the presidential residence, the Capitol, a major newspaper office, and a federal arsenal were set ablaze. (The burning of public buildings was intended in part as retaliation for events in York, where U.S. troops had set fire to the Ontario parliament house.) After sacking Washington, D.C., the British proceeded toward Baltimore, the third-largest U.S. city. In a battle memorialized in what would later become the national anthem (see Interpreting the Sources: "The Defence of Fort McHenry"), the Americans succeeded in holding a key fort and the British withdrew, their mission unaccomplished. The British were joined by more than two thousand enslaved African Americans, who took advantage of the invasion to escape to freedom.

THE HARTFORD CONVENTION

As British forces drove into the heart of the country, anti-war sentiment intensified in the North. Connecticut and Massachusetts protested by withdrawing their militias from federal service while Federalist leaders throughout New England began organizing a political assault against Madison and the Republicans. At a secret Federalist meeting in December 1814, known as the **Hartford Convention,** delegates considered a call for New England to secede from the union, but that motion failed. Instead, they passed resolutions to scrap the three-fifths rule, limit presidents to a single term, bar the election of consecutive presidents from a single state, and require a two-thirds majority in Congress in order to declare war. Such constitutional amendments, Federalists figured, would

break the Virginia monopoly on the executive branch, reduce the power of the Republicans, and prevent the South and West from dragging the country into another disastrous expansionist war. While the delegation met in December, they elected not to publicize the platform until January—an unfortunate decision that would prove fatal for the party's prospects.

THE SOUTHERN FRONT

The one region where the Americans clearly prevailed was in the South. The social conflict that had been brewing within the Creek Nation intensified after Tecumseh's dramatic visit in 1811. Dissidents known as the **Redsticks** (after the red clubs they wielded), who had been inspired by Tecumseh's call for resisting U.S. authority, clashed with the forces of the Creek national council and attacked symbols of the new order—wealth, cattle, cotton, and mixed-race families. They also attacked whites, leading settlers to demand the "dismemberment" and "extermination" of the Creek Nation. After a devastating attack by the Redsticks against Fort Mims in 1813, the Creek peoples friendly to Hawkins called for U.S. military intervention. Tennessee general Andrew Jackson rose to national prominence by leading an army of white settlers, Cherokee, and Creeks against the Redsticks, in what is often called the **Creek War** but was part of the larger War of 1812. Jackson's invasion of Creek country (in present-day Alabama and Georgia) was a major theater of operation in the conflict between the United States and a British–Native American alliance committed to thwarting American expansion.

Jackson suffered numerous setbacks over ten months of fighting in Creek country. But in an exceptionally bloody battle, he defeated the Redsticks at **Horseshoe Bend** in March 1814. With the reluctant approval of the federal government, Jackson began dictating peace terms and redistributing Creek land, including that of the Creek peoples who had sided with him. Jackson forced his Creek allies to cede 23 million acres of land, which would become the heart of the Cotton Belt. The Creek peoples were driven into the northeastern corner of Alabama.

Jackson turned his attention next to Spanish Florida, where British forces had staged the third prong of their invasion (Spain was an ally of Britain). After landing in May 1814, the British joined forces with the Seminoles, who had been helping the Spanish repel American forays across the Florida-Georgia border since the beginning of the war. Once again, the conflict between the

INTERPRETING THE SOURCES

"The Defence of Fort McHenry" ("The Star-Spangled Banner")

Shortly after the attack on Washington, D.C., Francis Scott Key, a Federalist lawyer from Maryland, was sent to a British ship in the Chesapeake Bay to negotiate the release of a captured American physician. Detained on the ship while the British bombarded Fort McHenry, Key spent the night watching the battle. The following morning, when he saw the U.S. flag still flying over the fort, he drafted a poem on the back of a letter. Sold as a celebratory hand-bill under the title "The Defence of Fort McHenry," Key's poem circulated on the streets of Baltimore and was then set to the tune of a popular British drinking song with a daunting range of one-and-a-half octaves and performed by local actors in taverns. "The Star-Spangled Banner," as it came to be known, was among the most popular patriotic songs in nineteenth-century America, but it did not become the official national anthem of the United States until 1931, well after it had become a fixture at notable baseball games.

A Morning View of the Shelling of Fort McHenry. The thrilling spectacle of this British attack on U.S. soil has become enshrined by the national anthem as a symbol of American patriotism. *SuperStock/SuperStock*

The original poem contained four stanzas, only the first of which is widely performed. The poet begins by describing the experience of watching the bombardment from the ship and searching the next morning for a sign that the Americans have not surrendered. The second stanza answers the question—the flag is dimly seen and then comes into clear view—and offers an evocative description of the flying flag as a symbol of national resilience. The third stanza denigrates the British invaders for polluting American soil and disparages the mercenaries ("hirelings") and enslaved people in their forces. In the final stanza, Key cites the motto "In God is our trust," an early version of the phrase that would become the nation's official motto in 1956.

Oh, say can you see by the dawn's early light
What so proudly we hailed at the twilight's last gleaming?
Whose broad stripes and bright stars thru the perilous fight,
O'er the ramparts we watched were so gallantly streaming?
And the rocket's red glare, the bombs bursting in air,
Gave proof through the night that our flag was still there.
Oh, say does that star-spangled banner yet wave
O'er the land of the free and the home of the brave?
On the shore, dimly seen through the mists of the deep,
Where the foe's haughty host in dread silence reposes,
What is that which the breeze, o'er the towering steep,

As it fitfully blows, half conceals, half discloses?
Now it catches the gleam of the morning's first beam,
In full glory reflected now shines in the stream:
'Tis the star-spangled banner!
Oh long may it wave
O'er the land of the free and the home of the brave!
And where is that band who so vauntingly swore
That the havoc of war and the battle's confusion,
A home and a country should leave us no more!
Their blood has washed out their foul footsteps' pollution.
No refuge could save the hireling and slave
From the terror of flight, or the gloom of the grave:

And the star-spangled banner in triumph doth wave
O'er the land of the free and the home of the brave!
Oh! thus be it ever, when freemen shall stand
Between their loved home and the war's desolation!
Blest with victory and peace, may the heav'n rescued land
Praise the Power that hath made and preserved us a nation.
Then conquer we must, when our cause it is just,
And this be our motto: "In God is our trust."
And the star-spangled banner in triumph shall wave
O'er the land of the free and the home of the brave!

Explore the Source

1. Are there any words in the poem that provide clues to what Key might have believed to be the purpose of this second war with Britain?

2. If the Americans are defending Fort McHenry against British shelling, why does Key say, in the final stanza, "Then conquer we must, when our cause it is just"?

United States and a European colonial power merged with a conflict between white settlers and Native Americans.

CROSSING BORDERS

● In East Florida, the clash also pitted slaveholders in Georgia against fugitives from slavery living among the Seminoles. As increasing numbers of enslaved African Americans fled across the border, the Seminoles became a mixed-race group, and their settlements became centers of Black Native American alliance. ●

Although the British never got very far in their plan to arm and train Seminoles for an invasion of the United States, they built a fort along the Apalachicola River, 60 miles south of the U.S. border. After the war, the **Negro Fort,** as it came to be known, provided refuge for anxious Seminoles fearing another U.S. invasion, for defeated Redsticks fleeing Creek country, and for fugitives from slavery from Georgia and Alabama. But in the shorter term, Britain failed to capitalize on its Seminole alliance. In November 1814, Jackson attacked Pensacola, the capital of the separate colony of West Florida, and drove the British from the city.

WAR'S END: THE TREATY OF GHENT AND THE BATTLE OF NEW ORLEANS

In fall 1814, British authorities were looking to make peace. They had thwarted the U.S. invasion of Canada and humiliated the young republic by burning its new capital. But they had been less successful at defending their native allies in the Northwest, and that alliance had proved helpless in resisting the westward incursions of Americans in the South. Eager to bring to an end to a long war, Britain entered into talks with the Americans in Ghent, Belgium; no Native American representatives were invited to the negotiations. Britain agreed to return the forts it had seized during the war and to retain the original borders of the United States. In a treaty signed on December 24, both sides effectively abandoned the demands that had brought them into conflict in the first place. Most significant, Britain dropped its insistence on a buffer zone under Native American sovereignty between Canada and the United States, and the United States agreed to recognize all Native American rights and territorial claims from before the war. Had this latter provision been enforced, the Creek land cessions would have been invalidated. Instead, the Treaty of Ghent marked the end of British interference in U.S.–Native American relations.

Although the war ended officially in Belgium in December, news of the treaty did not reach the U.S. capital until February 13. It would take even longer to reach the Gulf of Mexico, which had become the main stage of the war. After withdrawing from Pensacola, British ships had moved toward New Orleans. There, on New Year's Day, 1815, they shelled the city but decided to delay a week before launching a ground invasion. Jackson was waiting for them with a force that included African Americans, Haitian immigrants, Irish immigrants, Choctaw warriors, French-speaking Louisiana militiamen, volunteers from Jackson's home state of Tennessee, and a band of pirates hostile to the British Royal Navy. The invading army outnumbered Jackson's by two to one, but due to the superiority of the American guns and some tactical errors by the British, the attack failed and the British soldiers were massacred. The remaining British forces sailed northeast and captured the American fort defending the city of Mobile, but soon thereafter news of the peace treaty arrived.

The **Battle of New Orleans** did not affect the war's outcome, at least not in the conventional sense of shaping the agreement that formally ended the conflict, which after all had been signed two weeks before the fighting took place. Nonetheless, the battle had important consequences. To begin with, the outcome of the war was not determined solely by what was signed at Ghent. Of equal importance was how the British, Native Americans, and Spanish would approach the United States in the coming years. From that perspective, the Americans' stunning victory in New Orleans made a statement that Native Americans in the Southwest were especially likely to notice. ● Furthermore, because news of Jackson's triumph reached Washington, D.C., and other Eastern cities before anyone in the United States knew about the treaty, the impact of the battle on American perceptions of the war was great. Rather than responding to an inconclusive treaty that cast doubt on why the country had declared war in the first place, Americans reacted first to accounts of Jackson's heroics, and that had important political ramifications. ●

MEDIA AND INFORMATION

By turning the war into an occasion for patriotic celebration, New Orleans made the Federalist convention at Hartford seem like a gathering of traitors. The Federalists would not survive the blow. At the same time, a new national hero was born in Andrew Jackson.

EXPANSION IN JAMES MONROE'S AMERICA

Having endured a long war and survived a foreign invasion, the Republican leadership exhibited a new spirit of optimism and urgency about the role of the central

The Hartford Convention in Political Caricature. This cartoon mocks the New England delegates gathering in Hartford as both eager to please the British and afraid to act. In the right corner sits King George III, encouraging the New England secession with promises of "plenty of goods to Smuggle; Honours, titles and Nobility into the bargain." *Library of Congress Prints and Photographs Division [LC-DIG-ppmsca-10755]*

government. Though the war had succeeded in clearing major obstacles to westward expansion, it had also exposed the weakness of the U.S. military, the risks of economic dependence on Europe, and the fragility of the nation's communication infrastructure. Republican War Hawks now took the lead in arguing for a nationalist program of expanded government activity, including defense spending, protective tariffs, transportation improvements, and a national bank—all measures Republicans had opposed before the war.

Madison was succeeded in 1817 by fellow Virginian James Monroe, who routed his Federalist opponent in the 1816 presidential election by an electoral margin of 183 to 34. The Federalists had been damaged by the successful resolution of a war they had opposed and were then preempted by the Republican embrace of economic policies they had favored. Monroe's landslide victory confirmed the demise of the Federalists as a national party. As the incoming president embarked on

a national victory tour, many observers looked toward a period of reconciliation. A Boston newspaper spoke of a new "era of good feelings," a phrase historians have used to denote the period of Monroe's presidency. But the decline of the two-party system of Federalists and Republicans did not put an end to factional divisions in American politics, nor did it ease tensions between different sections of the country. It simply meant that the most intense political battles at the national level took place within Jefferson's old party.

The period after the war was defined less by good political feelings than by efforts to consolidate U.S. control over all of the land east of the Mississippi. With Great Britain no longer supporting Native American resistance, a weakened Spanish Empire beginning to fall throughout the Americas, and an aggressive U.S. general riding a wave of national popularity, the Monroe years would mark a pivotal chapter in the history of American expansion.

INVASION OF FLORIDA AND THE EUROPEAN POWERS' WITHDRAWAL

Despite the Treaty of Ghent, the boundaries of the United States remained blurry and contested at the beginning of Monroe's first term. Monroe initiated talks with the British, who were still America's northern neighbors. In the **Rush-Bagot Treaty** of 1817, both sides committed to disarmament in the Great Lakes. The agreement, which was the first bilateral naval disarmament in the history of international relations, lasted until World War II, when Canada and the United States suspended the treaty to allow naval training. A separate convention the following year set the northern boundary of the Louisiana Purchase at the forty-ninth parallel (which currently divides the United States and Canada from the Minnesota/Manitoba border westward) and established joint British-American occupation of the Oregon Territory. Both of these diplomatic coups were the handiwork of Monroe's secretary of state, John Quincy Adams, who had also led the negotiating team at Ghent.

Facing south, the United States encountered a more difficult situation. The Spanish colonies of East and West Florida bordered the Gulf of Mexico all the way to the Mississippi River, blocking Southern American farmers' and merchants' access to Gulf seaports. Equally important, Florida was a refuge for escapees from slavery and dispossessed Native Americans from Georgia and Alabama.

From the beginning of the nineteenth century, U.S. presidents had sought to acquire Florida, both through diplomacy and by encouraging armed forays and rebellions. But none of these efforts succeeded in wresting Florida from Spain. An exchange of violent attacks between Seminoles and white settlers along the border in 1817 offered the Monroe administration a new opportunity. Andrew Jackson was summoned from Tennessee to lead a force into Florida to attack the Seminoles, but he was ordered not to attack any Spanish forts. Jackson had other ideas. Believing that the colony of East Florida should be ceded to the United States as reparations for the property losses of Americans, Jackson assembled a large army. Crossing into Florida, they killed Native Americans wherever they found them, including the Creek resistance leader Hillis Hadjo, who was tricked into boarding a U.S. riverboat flying the British flag. Then Jackson, either misconstruing or ignoring orders, moved toward the West Florida capital of Pensacola, alerting its residents that he would "put to death every man found in arms." The Spanish evacuated Pensacola and surrendered in a nearby fort. Jackson announced that he would occupy Florida until the Spanish proved that they could police the border.

Jackson's invasion of Spanish Florida, often called the **First Seminole War,** became a major international incident and a significant political crisis for Monroe, who needed to assert civilian authority over a military hero. Monroe called for the restoration of Spanish authority but refused to discipline Jackson. Meanwhile, Secretary of State Adams pressed the Spaniards on the point that they were unable to defend or police their colonies. After some negotiations, Spain and the United States signed the **Transcontinental Treaty of 1819 (Adams-Onis Treaty),** under which Spain ceded Florida, recognized the Louisiana Purchase, and agreed to a boundary between Mexico (a Spanish colony that had been waging rebellion since 1810) and Oregon that gave the United States access to the Pacific Ocean. In return, the United States agreed to pay 5 million dollars in private claims against the Spanish government and conceded that the Louisiana Purchase did not include disputed territory in what is now eastern Texas. Florida was now American territory, and another European power and Native American ally had left the eastern half of the continent.

LATIN AMERICAN INDEPENDENCE AND THE MONROE DOCTRINE

The Florida colonies were not the only ones slipping away from Spain. Independence movements had been gaining momentum in Central and South America since the Napoleonic Wars. Spanish rule had effectively ended in the southern cone of South America by 1818, and colonial authority was teetering both on the northern mainland and in Mexico. In 1822, the United States became the first outside power to establish diplomatic relations with the nation of Gran Colombia (comprising Panama, Ecuador, Venezuela, and Colombia). Immediately after, the United States recognized Mexico. The vast Spanish Empire in the Americas had been reduced to a couple of island colonies.

In 1823, however, Monroe heard rumors that a coalition of conservative European forces led by the Russian czar was poised to help Spain reconquer its lost American possessions. Facing this unsavory prospect, along with the threat of Russian expansion along the Pacific coast, Adams advised Monroe to introduce a new foreign policy in his annual message to Congress. The **Monroe Doctrine** held that the United States would not tolerate European interference with the sovereignty of nations in the Americas. The United States was now politically distinct from Europe, Monroe announced, and "the American continents are henceforth not to be considered as subjects for future colonization by any European powers." In return, America pledged not to intervene in Europe's internal political struggles or in the affairs of existing European colonies (such as Canada, Cuba, and Puerto Rico). The doctrine, which would have other important implications for U.S. foreign relations in later periods, was Adams's brainchild and marked the culmination of a ten-year diplomatic campaign to secure the larger objectives of the War of 1812. The doctrine was not only meant to warn the Spanish, French, and Russians against recolonizing Latin America; it was also designed to remove European nations forever as obstacles to America's westward expansion across the continent. Europeans were put on notice not to ally with the indigenous people who stood in the way.

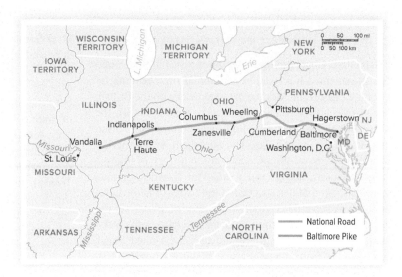

Map 9.3 The National Road.   Envisioned by Jefferson after the 1803 Louisiana Purchase as a continuous "line of communication" between the national capital and the city of St. Louis (newly added to the United States), the National Road was surveyed in 1811. By 1818, it had reached Wheeling, Virginia (now West Virginia), on the Ohio River. Because the bulk of the road west of the Ohio River was in the free states of the North, those states drew more migrants, visitors, and trade.

INTERNAL IMPROVEMENTS, ECONOMIC GROWTH, AND FINANCIAL PANIC

Following the war, Republicans committed themselves to a nationalist program of active government and embraced many of the policies previously associated with their political opponents. Even the aging Jefferson (no longer serving in government but following public life closely from the sidelines) seemed to shed some of his anxiety about commerce, industry, and big government. In 1816, the Republican-dominated Congress enacted a tariff to protect U.S. manufacturers against competition from foreign goods and authorized the creation of a second National Bank. Congress also appropriated one hundred thousand dollars to extend a national road that would link the eastern seaboard with the Mississippi River (see Map 9.3). The **National Road** (also called the Cumberland Road) connected the nation's eastern waterways to those west of the Appalachians and began a period of intense road building and canal construction in the United States (see Chapter 10).

All of these measures reflected Republican optimism about American westward expansion and the party's new vision of the nation as economically interdependent. Farmers and manufacturers, Easterners and Westerners, lenders and borrowers would all benefit, according to this new platform, from a sound money supply, a diversified economy, and what were called **internal improvements**—government investments in transportation infrustructure. Kentuckian Henry Clay dubbed this program "the American System"

and hitched his personal political fortunes to the promise of economic nationalism. John C. Calhoun, who would later be associated with the regional interests of the South, was also at this time a major proponent of a unified nation able to overcome the divisions of distance. "Let us, then, bind the republic together with a perfect system of roads and canals," he proclaimed. "Let us conquer space."

Most of the projects that Clay, Calhoun, and other nationalists envisioned were vetoed by Madison, who harbored doubts as to whether the Constitution authorized building canals and roads. His successor, Monroe, expressed similar concerns, and the era was marked by a conflict between supporters of federal subsidies for transportation and those who worried about their constitutionality or their costs. But both sides acknowledged the importance of long-distance transportation to economic growth.

The risks of growth and interdependence soon became apparent when a major depression struck the country, the first of several that would recur roughly every two decades over the course of the nineteenth century. Numerous factors contributed to the **Panic of 1819,** including a rise in foreign imports after the war, rampant land speculation, and a rapid increase in the money supply. Banks played an especially conspicuous role in the financial chaos of the postwar period. Congress had let the charter of Hamilton's Bank of the United States expire in 1811, ushering in a period of uncontrolled growth in the banking industry. The number of state-chartered banks in the

United States more than doubled during the war, and the new banks, mostly in the South and West, printed unprecedented volumes of bank notes without having to worry that a central bank would demand that they be redeemed in specie. In some cases, bank notes from west of the Appalachians had to be discounted by 50 percent for anyone to accept them.

After the war, the Republicans chartered the Second Bank of the United States to stabilize the money supply, but the new central bank was initially reluctant to press other banks to redeem their notes. Instead, the national bank issued large volumes of its own notes, funding loans for land purchases in areas, like Alabama, that had been conquered by the United States during the war. Steadily, the bank's capital was shifting westward and southward, as branches in the Northeast paid specie to redeem notes printed by the bank's other, more adventurous branches. Meanwhile, the value of American agricultural goods had begun to plummet on foreign markets, as Europe recovered from wars and bad harvests. Cotton prices, which had driven the land speculation in Alabama, fell in 1819 to less than half of their 1817 high. When the Bank of the United States started calling in loans and forcing state-chartered banks to do the same, farmers defaulted, land prices dropped, businesses failed, urban artisans lost their jobs, and an epidemic of foreclosure and bankruptcy swept the nation. The crisis likely accelerated westward migration, as white Americans from the East Coast, seeing poverty and diminished local opportunities, sought a new start on the other side of the Appalachians.

Some faulted the bank for the economic disaster, others complained of the inadequacy of the tariff protection, and others blamed American women and their fondness for luxury goods. Many farmers and artisans grew generally suspicious of the banks that appeared to create and nullify value arbitrarily. Interestingly, no one really blamed the Monroe administration, which was re-elected with all but one electoral vote in 1820.

MISSOURI AND THE NEW GEOGRAPHY OF SLAVERY

As the national economy suffered its first major depression, the political risks of westward expansion became clearer as well. The land ceded or surrendered by the Creek peoples, Choctaw, Seminoles, and Spanish during the second decade of the century included millions of acres that were especially suitable for cultivating cotton—and large-scale cotton producers relied on slave labor. In the northwestern corner of this cotton region, the removal of Native

American and European powers helped swell the Missouri Territory population (which included ten thousand people in slavery by 1820) to the point that it was eligible for statehood. As Congress deliberated in 1819 over whether to authorize Missourians to draft a constitution and begin the statehood process, slavery was the dominant subject.

Representative James Tallmadge from New York proposed a provision to make Missouri a free state. Specifically, the Tallmadge Amendment prohibited "the introduction of slavery or involuntary servitude . . . except for the punishment of crimes" and stipulated that anyone born into slavery in the new state would become free at age twenty-five. With every representative from the South voting against, the amendment still passed the House 78 to 76, but the Senate rejected it and Congress ended its year with the status of Missouri uncertain.

The stalemate over Missouri marked the rekindling of a fight over the balance of power between free and slave states that had flickered during the constitutional convention. Tallmadge offered his amendment to block what he called "the disproportionate power of the slave states." Southerners, in turn voted unanimously against the amendment, because they also saw this as a showdown over sectional power. If Congress could restrict slavery in Missouri, it could do the same in every new state that would be carved out of the Louisiana Purchase and thereby limit the value of slave property throughout the country. Perhaps more important, a free Missouri might put the entire institution of slavery in political jeopardy. Because each state received two Senate seats no matter the size of its population, maintaining the same number of free and slave states assured the South that Congress would never abolish slavery. The union in 1820 consisted of eleven states where slavery was legal and eleven where it had been either outlawed or gradually abolished. Missouri's status would tilt the balance.

A Republic of Roads. The mobility for which Americans were already famous in the early national era required the building of roads, which has been the leading form of public transportation investment throughout U.S. history. This watercolor depicts the hubbub outside a rural tavern in Maryland, near the eastern end of the National Road. *City of Baltimore*

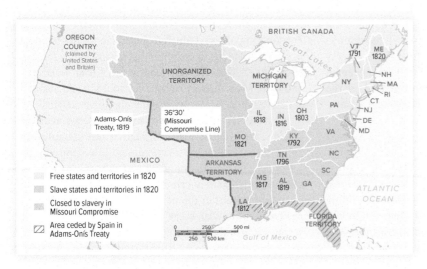

Map 9.4 The Missouri Compromise.   The compromise, intended to preserve political balance between slave and free states, presumed that slavery would continue to thrive only below a certain latitude.

When Congress reconvened in 1820, Senator Jesse Thomas, a Southern slaveholder now representing the free state of Illinois, suggested a compromise. Missouri would be allowed to enter as a slave state but would be counterbalanced by the admission of the northeastern (noncontiguous) portion of Massachusetts as the new free state of Maine. More important, Thomas proposed that Missouri be the only part of the Louisiana Purchase north of the 36°30′ latitude where slavery would be permitted (see Map 9.4). The two components of the **Missouri Compromise** were quite different. The first preserved the balance of power in the Senate through a policy of admitting new states in pairs. But the second provision made the future status of slavery contingent on geography rather than political balance in the Senate. By a three-vote margin in the House, this important compromise squeaked through.

In retrospect, the Missouri statehood crisis foretold the growing rift between North and South. To some observers, those implications seemed clear at the time. Thomas Jefferson likened the debates to "a fire bell in the night" that "awakened and filled me with terror." The geographical boundary recognized by Congress would only harden the moral divide of the slavery question, Jefferson noted, and the union would be doomed. Secretary of State John Quincy Adams, viewing the debate from the Northern side, also saw great portent and fantasized privately about a violent showdown over the question of slavery.

In the eyes of some Southerners, debates over slavery threatened their security by encouraging slave rebellions. Just two years after the Missouri Compromise, those fears

were stoked by news of a plot by enslaved and free Blacks to set fire to Charleston, South Carolina. The plot was pinned on a man named Denmark Vesey, who had been born into slavery in the Caribbean and brought to South Carolina as a boy. Vesey, a skilled carpenter and self-educated man, managed to purchase his freedom after winning a fifteen-hundred-dollar lottery prize in 1800 and rose to a position of influence within Charleston's Black community (see How Much Is That? Denmark Vesey's Lottery Prize). He had been inspired by events in Haiti and reportedly kept abreast of the congressional deliberations in 1819 and 1820. In 1822, Vesey was arrested, along with 130 other Black men, for planning what would have been the largest peacetime slave rebellion in American history. Using church meetings as a forum for gathering supporters, Vesey had allegedly designed the destruction of Charleston, the massacre of its white inhabitants, the pillaging of its arsenal, and a mass exodus of African Americans to Haiti. But the alleged plot was betrayed to the authorities, who convicted Vesey and thirty-four coconspirators in a secret trial and had them hanged. It stands as the largest number of executions carried out by order of a civilian court in U.S. history.

Because evidence of the plot came from coerced confessions, historians debate whether Vesey and his codefendants planned an armed rebellion. In any case, the irregular trials and interrogations suggest a moment of panic and hysteria among Southern whites, whose slave system was becoming more economically entrenched and more politically vulnerable (see Chapter 11).

How Much Is That?

Denmark Vesey's Lottery Prize

Adjusted for inflation, the prize would have the buying power of almost thirty-two thousand dollars in 2020—not exactly a jackpot but almost enough to buy a new car or a semester of tuition, room, and board at a private university.

NEW RELIGIOUS NEWORKS

Most Americans did not share Thomas Jefferson's sense of the momentousness of the slavery question in 1820. As American society expanded westward and settlers poured into territories wrested from Native Americans, the federal government consolidated control over the expanded nation. Meanwhile, forces outside the government worked to create a new religious culture across the country, building new religious networks that also connected the growing country. Northeastern Protestants used print to disseminate Christian ideas to a dispersed populace while evangelical preachers traversed the countryside, recruiting members to their growing denominations. Church membership doubled across the nation between 1800 and 1820, printed Bibles became standard fixtures in American homes, and a new spirit of religious enthusiasm took root in the South and the frontier, especially in areas cleared for white settlement by the war. These developments also presented opportunities for women to participate in public life at a time when men dominated electoral politics and long-distance commerce.

THE BENEVOLENT EMPIRE

By 1815, northeastern elites had lost their political foothold. Many former Federalists, facing the prospects of being shut out of national politics, turned to other strategies for influencing the republic and rescuing it from what they saw as the dangers of revolution. They pinned their hopes on religious institutions. • Unlike most European countries at the time, the United States had no official, government-sponsored religion. The Bill of Rights had prohibited Congress from establishing a national church, and once Republicans gained power in New England after the War of 1812, the official state churches in that region began to fall as well. The disestablishment and deregulation of churches created an open market in which a growing range of denominations, sects, and movements competed for souls and membership. •

CONFLICTING FAITHS

Without a central religious organization supported by public funds, a coterie of charitable societies and nongovernmental organizations emerged in the 1810s to boost religion on a national scale. Headquartered in Northern cities, these organizations tended to be multidenominational and controlled by laypeople rather than clergy. They focused on goals that were shared widely among Protestant churches, such as increasing biblical literacy, relieving poverty, supporting orphans, spreading the gospel across the globe, and suppressing prostitution. Some of the most important organizations founded during this decade included the American Bible Society (see Hot Commodities: Cheap Printed Bibles), the Sunday and Adult School Union (later the American Missionary Fellowship), and the **American Board of Commissioners for Foreign Missions** (ABCFM). As its name implied, the ABCFM sponsored missions to distant locations, including the Hawaiian Islands (laying foundations for the eventual American colonization of Hawaii), but much of its early emphasis was on the conversion of American Indians.

Together, the new organizations exerted significant influence in public life. Observers often referred to these institutions and their leadership as the **Benevolent Empire,** an unofficial religious establishment in a nation without an established church. The Benevolent Empire was an entirely Protestant affair and did not include the Catholics, Jews, Unitarians, or freethinkers living in the United States in the 1810s and 1820s. But for the most part, the establishment downplayed sectarian debates in favor of campaigns that spoke the language of universal salvation and humanitarian sympathy.

THE EVANGELICAL FRONTIER

Alongside the tract societies and missionary organizations that constituted the Benevolent Empire, America's evangelical churches embarked on campaigns to spread their message orally across the country. They were especially successful in the South and in southern parts of Ohio and Indiana—areas cleared for white settlement by native land cessions following the defeat of Tecumseh. The Methodist Church took the lead in this campaign, sending itinerant preachers, known as **circuit riders,** to small towns and farming communities, much as the American Bible Society disseminated printed books. • Typically, circuit riders were celibate men who traveled to otherwise isolated rural areas, preaching the gospel, recruiting converts, and organizing small religious communities known as "classes" to reinforce their message while on the road. By 1815, seven thousand classes had been established. By 1830, the number had more than doubled and almost half a million Americans belonged to them. Next to the postal system and the political press, the Methodist network of itinerant preachers and local classes ranks among the major early-nineteenth-century media of information exchange. •

MEDIA AND INFORMATION

Methodists also led the way in sponsoring another form of religious education—the **camp meeting.** These large gatherings attracted converts through powerful emotional appeals. The most famous of the revivals, at **Cane Ridge,** Kentucky, in 1801, lasted over a week and attracted a crowd estimated at between ten and twenty thousand.

HOT COMMODITIES
Cheap Printed Bibles

The ancient Hebrew and Greek texts that most Christians consider Holy Scripture have exerted great influence in America for centuries. When translated into English and bound together in a single volume, this corpus of texts is better known as "the Bible," and it has been the best-selling printed book in U.S. history. But Bibles have always come in different formats, and the business of making them has had its twists and turns.

Before the Revolution, English Bibles were not printed in America, because the British Crown held a copyright that forbade publishing them in the colonies. When the war for independence broke out, the colonists faced a Bible shortage, and the Continental Congress considered a desperate plan to import twenty thousand Bibles from Holland to address the crisis. After the war, American printers slowly entered the Bible business, but the big surge came in 1816, with the founding of the American Bible Society (ABS). Concerned about the spread of heretical religious ideas associated with the Enlightenment and the French Revolution, the ABS's founders sought to save the United States by increasing popular access to the printed translation of the Old and New Testaments. The ABS centralized production in New York City, adopted new typesetting technologies, and distributed the Bibles through a network of branches throughout the country. At a time when print runs of more than two thousand copies of a book were rare, the ABS produced twenty thousand English-language Bibles in its first year. Within two decades, the ABS was publishing over three hundred thousand Bibles a year.

Domesticating Scripture. In response to the success of the American Bible Society, rival publishers began offering more elaborate Bibles. Itinerant New England folk artist Joseph H. Davis painted small family portraits such as this one from 1836 depicting James and Sarah Tuttle. In many of the images, large family Bibles feature prominently among other symbols of domestic life. *Pictures Now/Alamy Stock Photo*

In 1829, the ABS committed to a goal of putting a Bible in every household in the nation over the next two years. The "General Supply," as this program was called, was an unprecedentedly ambitious venture in mass broadcasting. ABS Bibles were simple products, presenting the Scriptures in King James translation, without any additional commentary. The organization's evangelical Protestant supporters had great faith in the power of the book, as long as it made it into the homes of the nation's citizens. Unlike the Gideons International organization, which would begin distributing free Bibles in hotel rooms in the beginning of the twentieth century, the ABS rarely gave its goods away, on the theory that owners would value a Bible more highly if it had been paid for.

Although they were not free, ABS Bibles were very cheap, usually costing much less than a dollar. Other publishers, unable to match ABS prices, were forced to compete by producing Bibles with extensive commentaries, copious illustrations and maps, lavish bindings, and all kinds of supplemental historical information. The massive effort of northeastern evangelicals to make simple Bibles available to everyone thus had the secondary effect of prompting the spread of a new generation of fancier, illuminated Bibles, which became popular over the course of the nineteenth century.

Think About It

1. How did the proliferation of cheap printed Bibles change the attitudes of ordinary Americans toward sacred Scripture?

2. Did the American Bible Society's "General Supply" create the equivalent of a national religion?

Many of those in attendance experienced ecstatic conversion experiences; some fainted, shook violently, or barked like dogs. Camped out in tents on the hillside, the Cane Ridge community was by far the largest settlement in the state of Kentucky during the revival. Over the next forty years, numerous revival meetings appeared throughout the country. Camp meetings like Cane Ridge were early expressions of a later and larger trend toward mass revivals (known as the Second Great Awakening), which would take place in the Northeast during the 1830s (see Chapter 10). On the frontier, however, the revivals began earlier, reflecting the power of the Methodist religious network.

The spread of religious enthusiasm in rural America was not confined to a single denomination. Baptist communities, which were less centrally organized than their Methodist counterparts, flourished in many of the same rural areas. Presbyterians also established numerous new evangelical churches during this period. Other evangelicals sought to avoid denomination labels and simply called themselves "Christian." Several important American Protestant groups, including the Disciples of Christ, have their genesis in this anti-denominational Christian movement of the 1810s and 1820s. However they were organized or defined, American evangelical communities tended to emphasize broad themes of conversion and rebirth rather than finer points of theological doctrine. The spread of this kind of Christianity initiated a pattern in American religious life that remains visible today. The part of the country frequently referred to as the Bible Belt is the area that was influenced most by evangelical campaigns in the early nineteenth century. This development was not the result of the cultural isolation of rural communities but rather the opposite: Evangelicals in the South and the trans-Appalachian West were connected to growing networks of religious preaching and communication.

Jarena Lee. Born into the free Black community of Cape May, New Jersey, in 1783, Lee worked as a domestic servant in the outskirts of Philadelphia until she felt the call to preach. In the 1820s, she was traveling 2,000 miles each year as an itinerant preacher. *Fotosearch/Getty Images*

WOMEN, RELIGION, AND PUBLIC LIFE

In both the North and the South, in frontier churches and urban religious organizations, evangelical religious networks proved especially attractive to women during the decade after the war. Numerous female preachers, including Jarena Lee of the A.M.E. Church and the Methodist Phoebe Palmer, achieved renown as public speakers spreading the gospel. Ann Hasseltine Judson, who served with her husband as a missionary in Southeast Asia and translated parts of the Bible into Burmese and Thai, became one of the leading nineteenth-century American missionaries. Other women founded benevolent associations, organized charities, or served on the governance committees of local congregations.

During a period when women were excluded from politics, civic associations, and the professions, religion offered rare opportunities for public self-expression and communal distinction. Between 1810 and 1830, respectable women largely withdrew from many of the forms of public protest

and political speech (such as tavern toasts) that had been common in the revolutionary era. Only in the context of religious life were women able to address male audiences and present themselves publicly without fear of censure. When Fanny Newell, the wife of an itinerant Methodist preacher in Maine, decided to follow her husband's calling, she knew that her audiences would allow her to break a social taboo. "Whatever may be said against a female speaking, or praying in public, I care not," she would tell them, "for when I feel confident that the Lord calls me to speak, I dare not refuse."

Evangelical Protestants provided models for women's independent participation in public life. A few of them, including the writer and reformer Lydia Maria Child, became politically active on behalf of the rights of Native Americans, a major evangelical concern in the North. Significantly, the first organized petition campaign by women to influence national politics took place in 1830, and its goal was to resist a new initiative to confiscate native land.

CIVILIZATION AND REMOVAL

In the history of white–Native American relations in North America, the War of 1812 was a crucial turning point. During the negotiations following the initial Treaty of Ghent, Britain abandoned all serious resistance to U.S. westward expansion. Although the treaty had called for a return of native lands taken during the war, General Jackson ignored the treaty, Presidents Madison and Monroe were eager not to offend the hero of New Orleans, and Britain never pressed the point. Instead, the Creek theater of the war provided a model for a pattern of "treaties"—imposed mostly by Jackson—in which Native Americans ceded lands, white migrants moved in, and tribal territory was brought under the active jurisdiction of the federal government.

By 1820, the United States had consolidated control over all the land east of the Mississippi, but the question of what to do with the one hundred twenty-five thousand Native Americans occupying that land remained. Twelve years earlier, President Jefferson had promised native peoples that the "day will soon come when you will unite yourselves with us, join in our great councils, and form a people with us, and we shall all be Americans; you will mix with us by marriage; your blood will run in our veins and will spread with us over this great continent." But American leaders abandoned the assimilationist rhetoric after the war, and a new policy emerged. Instead of pressuring indigenous people to adapt to a new cultural order, the federal government sought to remove them altogether from the eastern half of the continent. Faced with forced exile from their homes, some native groups resisted, whereas others painfully complied with government orders. Responses to the policy were mixed in the white community as well, especially in the Northeast, where the new policy struck many observers as cruel or unnecessary. On both sides, the debates about white–Native American coexistence in the United States also reflected new ideas about national identity.

CIVILIZED NATIONS

The process of dispossessing and expelling Native Americans went most smoothly for the United States in Indiana, Illinois, and other parts of the old Northwest Territory. There, officials weakened resistance by bribing tribal leaders and settling debts, inducing many villages and tribal groups to relocate quietly. The Sac and Fox of the Great Lakes region, however, did take up arms and sought unsuccessfully to stop the American onslaught in the Black Hawk War of 1832. In the South,

resistance was more widespread. Five confederations in the South, the so-called **Five Civilized Tribes**—the Choctaw, Chickasaws, Creek peoples, Cherokee, and Seminoles—clung tenaciously to their land and forced the government to demonstrate how far it would go in order to clear land for white settlement.

Significantly, those southern tribal societies that resisted removal most nearly resembled their white neighbors. They were more settled and agricultural than northern Native Americans and had developed more sophisticated forms of centralized political authority. Many of their leaders were wealthy planters with mixed ancestry and English-sounding names, and Christianity had made significant inroads within their communities. The native groups that lived within the borders of Georgia, Florida, Tennessee, Mississippi, and Alabama, in other words, had by and large accepted the terms of the Civilization Program the United States had proposed as preconditions for equal citizenship and cultural integration.

The Cherokee Nation offers the most striking example of this pattern. The Cherokee were an Iroquoian group who had settled several centuries earlier in the southern portion of the Appalachians. At the beginning of the eighteenth century, they claimed control over an area of roughly 350 by 300 miles, from the Ohio to the Tennessee Rivers and from the Blue Ridge Mountains to the middle

Sequoya's Cherokee Syllabary, 1825, and *Cherokee Singing Book*, Printed for the American Board of Commissioners for Foreign Missions, Boston, 1846.   The new writing system was adopted almost immediately both by Christian missionaries and by traditional Cherokee medicine men. *North Wind Picture Archives/Alamy Stock Photo; Cherokee Singing Book. Printed for the American Board of Commissioners for Foreign Missions. Boston: Alonzo P. Kenrich, 1846. Division of Rare and Manuscript Collections, Cornell University Library*

of Tennessee. But between 1721 and 1806, the Cherokee, who fought on the losing side of the American Revolution, ceded over 97,000 square miles of land to American colonies or states and became a small and poor nation centered in northern Georgia. Over the next three decades, the Cherokee rebuilt their society in the shadow of the growing American republic.

Many Cherokee dressed like whites, spoke English, and embraced Christianity. A few were, in fact, white Loyalists who had fled to Cherokee country after the Revolution, but most were full-blooded Cherokee who had adopted European folkways and practices. The evangelical movement had reached them as well, and they worshiped as Methodists, Baptists, Moravians, Presbyterians, and Congregationalists. The Cherokee Nation also developed a written constitution in 1827 with a bicameral legislature and a tripartite government modeled explicitly on that of the United States. Finally, in imitation of their white neighbors, the Cherokee accommodated new ideas about racial hierarchy and instituted slavery. In 1830, about fifteen hundred African Americans were held as property by the Cherokee.

Most strikingly to outside observers, the Cherokee used a written alphabet—an 85-character syllabary devised in 1821 by a man named Sequoya. (*Syllabary* is the technical term for a writing system, like Korean, where individual characters represent entire syllables.) The **Cherokee syllabary** proved remarkably effective, and within about a decade most of the Cherokee Nation had learned to read, thus eroding one of the most culturally significant differences between whites and native people in Georgia. Sequoya's own life was a fascinating example of the complex paths that different Cherokee pursued in response to the shifting politics of U.S.–Native American relations. On the one hand, Sequoya was a traditionalist who shunned Christianity, did not speak English, and rejected acculturation in general. On the other hand, he fought on the side of Jackson in the Creek War, signed land treaties with the United States, and voluntarily removed to a reservation in Arkansas established by the federal government for the Cherokee after the War of 1812.

Sequoya's syllabary was a source of fascination to many Americans and made him a celebrity. With little success, white missionaries had sought to teach English-language literacy among the Cherokee. Sequoya's system, by contrast, seemed to answer the missionaries' prayers. Children who had struggled for years to learn to read English were able to master the syllabary in a matter of days. By 1828, the Cherokee had produced the first indigenous newspaper, the *Cherokee Phoenix and Indian's Advocate*, printed both in English and in Cherokee. In a very short time, the Cherokee had become a prominent advertisement for the willingness and capacity of traditional native societies to attain what white Americans regarded as civilization.

ANDREW JACKSON AND INDIAN REMOVAL

Southern Native Americans were unable to hold on to their land, despite their success in adopting and adapting to white culture. The fate of the Cherokee may have been sealed by the discovery of gold on their territory in 1828. But for all the native peoples in the region 1828 was an ominous year because of the election of Andrew Jackson as president. Jackson is often remembered more for his connections to the growth of mass democracy and party politics (see Chapter 10), but had made his name as an Indian fighter and began his presidency by transforming U.S. policy toward America's indigenous nations.

Jackson did not invent the idea of transporting Native Americans to territory beyond the Mississippi. Earlier presidents had contemplated schemes to separate indigenous people and whites or to induce the indigenous population to move west through land exchange. In 1825, President Monroe, just before leaving office, announced a new U.S. program to "remove" native groups "from the lands which they now occupy" to "the country lying westward and northward." But Monroe insisted that the removal must and would take place "on conditions which shall be satisfactory to themselves and honorable to the United States." During the term of John Quincy Adams, Monroe's successor, the federal government negotiated with different native communities in an effort to persuade them to trade their homeland. Both administrations followed U.S. law in treating indigenous groups as sovereign nations in their own right, and relations with them were established largely by treaty.

For Jackson, on the other hand, Indian removal was not simply a policy objective; it was a national security priority. He viewed the legalized presence of foreign nations within the borders of the United States as a potential danger and an affront to states' rights. Immediately after Jackson's election, Georgia, Alabama, and Mississippi seized the political opportunity and outlawed tribal governments. Supporters of the Cherokee sued the state of Georgia for interfering with the treaty obligations of the United States. In *Worcester v. Georgia* (1832), the Supreme Court under Chief Justice John Marshall ruled that the Georgia laws violated the territorial sovereignty of the Cherokee. But Andrew Jackson refused to enforce the court decision, and the Cherokee realized they could not count on the federal government to intercede in their conflicts with the states.

The **Indian Removal Act** became the major political initiative of Jackson's first term in office. In his first annual message to Congress in 1829, he pronounced the earlier federal policy of trying to convert indigenous peoples to "the arts of civilization" a failure. Jackson was clearly giving up on the Civilization Program. As for the southern Native Americans who had already acculturated, Jackson advised them to emigrate for their own good, since the federal government had no authority to stop Georgia, Mississippi, and Alabama from seizing their land or expelling them. Jackson repeated this theme in a message to two of the native groups. "Say to my red Choctaw children, and my Chickasaw children," he told an agent, "that their father cannot prevent them from being subject to the laws of the" states. He could only

help them if they moved to lands beyond the Mississippi, where their safety would be guaranteed "as long as the grass grows or the water runs." In 1830, Jackson asked Congress to pass the Indian Removal Act authorizing the president to negotiate and oversee the transfer of native groups remaining east of the Mississippi (see Map 9.5).

Not all white Americans shared Jackson's view that he was benevolently facilitating the next stage of an inevitable historical process. Jeremiah Evarts of the American Board of Commissioners for Foreign Missions led a nationwide campaign against the Indian Removal Act, calling upon Christians all over the country to lobby the federal government against committing what he regarded

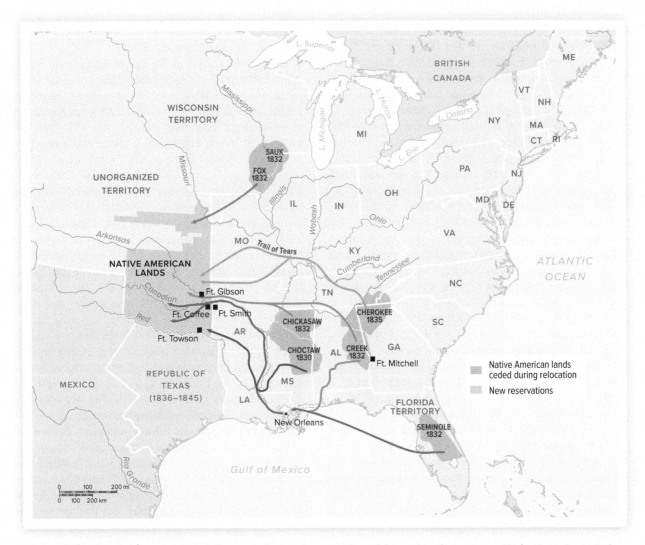

Map 9.5 Indian Removal. Advocates of the proposed removal program claimed that westward migration was in the Native Americans' own best interests. Andrew Jackson even compared removal to the larger pattern of voluntary mobility for which American society was becoming famous. "Doubtless it will be painful to leave the graves of their fathers," he conceded, "but what do they more than our ancestors did or than our children are now doing?"

as a grievous sin. Congressmen from New England, where evangelical sympathy for the Cherokee ran high and where native societies had already been dispossessed much earlier, voted overwhelmingly against the bill. Even a few Southerners, political opponents of Jackson, opposed the Removal Act. But Jackson's political capital was considerable and overwhelming support for removal in the Southeast proved decisive. In the House, the bill passed by a slim margin of 102 to 97.

Each of the five southern groups had its own exodus story, but the removal followed a pattern. First, the federal government pressured tribal leaders (or putative leaders) to trade their land by pointing out that if they refused, the states would take it, anyway. Once treaties had been signed, federal troops were called in to enforce the transfer. The Native Americans debated the best course of action, both in traditional tribal meetings and in the newer forums such as the *Cherokee Phoenix*. Some indigenous groups, like the Chickasaw and Choctaw, bargained for the best possible deal and then moved west (see Singular Lives: Pushmataha, Regretful Ally). Others stalled, practiced nonviolent resistance or, in the exceptional case of the Seminoles, waged a long war. That conflict, often called the Second Seminole War, lasted from 1835 to 1842 and cost the government tens of millions of dollars and fifteen hundred lives. In all, seventy thousand southern American Indians were uprooted from their ancestral homes.

The most elaborate and famous of these removals took place in Cherokee country, dragging on past Jackson's eight-year presidency. Jackson's removal policy divided the Cherokee. A Treaty Party, led by wealthy planters Major Ridge and his son John, favored rebuilding the Cherokee Nation in the West. The Cherokee National Council, led by John Ross, advocated resistance. Ross had helped initiate the legal battles for Cherokee rights at the U.S. Supreme Court, and afterward he led a delegation to Washington, D.C., to negotiate a deal that would allow the nation to remain in its homeland—or at least to delay removal until the political winds in Washington, D.C., could change. But the Jackson administration negotiated the **Treaty of New Echota** with the Ridge faction in 1835. Ross petitioned the Senate not to ratify the treaty, but to no avail, and U.S. troops began the process of rounding up the Cherokee for deportation.

CROSSING BORDERS

● From 1835 to 1840, an estimated sixteen thousand Cherokee citizens and the people they kept in slavery were forcibly exiled to the Oklahoma territory. Approximately four thousand died as a result of a set of marches in 1838, known as the **Trail of Tears,** which marked the brutal end of white–Native American coexistence in the eastern half of North America. ●

Lydia Maria Child (1802-1880). Like Washington Irving and James Fenimore Cooper, the novelist and reformer Child turned to the early period of white–Native American contact in the Northeast to tell a distinctively American story. But unlike the other two, Child took a more hopeful view of the possibility of integrating native peoples into American culture. *Archive Photos/Getty Images*

METAMORA, LEATHERSTOCKING, AND THE NEW AMERICAN CULTURE

While the U.S. government was gearing up to remove the five southern native groups, American theatergoers enthusiastically embraced the 1829 drama **Metamora,** which became one of the most widely performed theatrical productions in nineteenth-century America (see chapter's opening). The paradoxical popularity of *Metamora* on the eve of Indian removal was partly a matter of geography. New York spectators in 1829 who applauded Metamora's curse upon white people were far enough removed, both from the seventeenth century and from the frontier clashes that were erupting in their own time, to see Native Americans as something other than an immediate threat. In Georgia, by contrast, the play was less successful. The opening-night audience in Augusta, Georgia, hissed when Metamora chided whites for their treatment of his culture, and the play was boycotted.

When Tecumseh visited the Choctaw and Chickasaw in 1811 to rally support for his war against the United States, he encountered a powerful local chief named Pushmataha, who had distinguished himself as a Choctaw warrior and diplomat. Tecumseh's vision would set in motion a dramatic chain of events that transformed white–Native American relations in the United States, but it was Pushmataha's career that epitomized the dilemmas and experiences of Native Americans during the transformation.

In response to Tecumseh's 1811 appeal, Pushmataha pointed out that the Choctaw and Chickasaw had lived peacefully with the United States and had benefited from their contacts and exchanges with white Americans. Furthermore, he argued, it was foolish to declare war against "a people . . . who are far better provided with all the necessary implements of war . . . far beyond that of all our race combined." Yes, whites had committed "unjust encroachments," but the proper response was diplomacy, not warfare. Moved by Pushmataha's argument (or sharing his political outlook), the joint Choctaw-Chickasaw council rejected Tecumseh's appeal and supported the United States in the impending war. Pushmataha himself led a Choctaw force against the Creek Redsticks.

By 1820, however, Pushmataha had come to see things differently. His former ally, Jackson, was now pressuring him to trade 5 million acres of Choctaw territory in Mississippi for Western lands, which Pushmataha knew to be both barren and already occupied by white settlers. With Jackson making ominous threats and the Choctaw no longer able to seek alliances with Britain, Spain, or the Creek people, a reluctant Pushmataha was forced to accept the land exchange. Four years later, he led a delegation to Washington, D.C., in an unsuccessful effort to

lobby the federal government to evict white settlers from the new Choctaw holdings in Arkansas. While in the capital, he met with numerous statesmen and foreign dignitaries and sat for a portrait by the famous artist Charles Bird King. Later that year, he contracted a fatal virus and was buried with military honors in the congressional cemetery.

Pushmataha's final legacy to the history of white–Native American relations came through his friendship with the actor Edwin Forrest, whom he met in New Orleans in 1824. Forrest reported spending time with Pushmataha in the new western Choctaw territory and took an intense interest in the chief. One night, Forrest asked his friend to walk back and forth naked in the moonlight. Whatever else Forrest might have wanted to see, he was studying what he regarded as a perfect specimen of noble manhood. Forrest was preparing, in other words, for the role that would launch his career. When American audiences watched *Metamora*, they were seeing Forrest's impression of a character he probably based on Pushmataha.

Where in the Archives?

Pushmataha's attempts, late in life, to negotiate a better land settlement for the Choctaw Nation are preserved in the records of treaty negotiations of 1824 in Washington, D.C., and in a speech he made to Secretary of War John C. Calhoun.

The treaty negotiations appear in *Indian Affairs*, Vol. 2, pages 549–551, and are available through the Library of Congress's American, D.C., State Papers collection (https://memory.loc.gov/ammem/amlaw/lwsplink.html#anchor2).

***Pushmataha*, by Charles Bird King.** King's numerous portraits of Indian leaders, commissioned by the federal government, became popular attractions in an age when many white observers sought glimpses of what they saw as a vanishing race. *Lebrecht Music & Arts/Alamy Stock Photo*

Pushmataha's brief speech to Calhoun, in which he stresses history of friendly relations between the United States and the Choctaw Nation, is available in William Jennings Bryan's *The World's Famous Orations*, Vol. VIII. America: 1761–1837, through Bartleby Great Books (https://www.bartleby.com/268/).

Assignment

Read the transcripts of the negotiations and the speech and answer the following questions in 200 words each:

1. Does Pushmataha's position in these negotiations with the United States affirm Choctaw sovereignty, submission to the United States, or a combination?

2. Where do Pushmataha's delegation and Secretary Calhoun find common ground, and where are they in conflict?

Nonetheless, the theatrical splash of *Metamora* was not primarily a reaction to Indian removal; it was about the culture of white America. *Metamora* was written by John Augustus Stone in response to a prize competition created by the actor Edwin Forrest. The up-and-coming Forrest wanted to promote dramatic arts in the new republic to boost his career and to prove that legitimate theater could be produced in the United States. He invited American playwrights to submit a script that he would perform, stipulating only that "the hero or principal character shall be an aboriginal of this country." Forrest wanted to portray a Native American so that the play would seem authentically American. His sympathetic portrayal of an Algonquin warrior was intended to identify not with American Indians against Puritans but rather with *Americans* against Europeans. Northern audiences responded enthusiastically to this declaration of cultural independence.

● *Metamora* stands in a long tradition in American popular culture, including the Boston Tea Party, of using indigenous people to claim American-ness. Forrest's drama spawned a rash of American Indian plays of varying types on stages all over urban America in the nineteenth century. ● Biographies of native chiefs became popular at the same time, as did Native American characters and themes in American fiction. Lydia Maria Child entered the literary world in 1824 with *Hobomok*, a novel about a loyal and honorable Massachusett in colonial times who befriended the English and married a white woman. More famously, James Fenimore Cooper's *The Pioneers* appeared in 1823—the first of five historical novels known as **The Leatherstocking Tales.** Cooper was the first commercially successful American novelist, working at a time when Europeans regarded the United States as a cultural wasteland. As late as 1820, a prominent British journal asked provocatively, "In the four quarters of the globe, who reads an American book?" In the beginning of the decade, Washington Irving's short stories impressed critics in both Britain and the United States, but Cooper's novels, like Forrest's performances, marked a coming of age for American arts.

Cooper's *Leatherstocking* novels developed the character of Natty Bumppo, a white frontiersman raised among Native Americans. Bumppo (also called Hawkeye, Leatherstocking, Pathfinder, and Deerslayer) has no trace of native descent but has been made stronger and nobler by his relationships with native people. Cooper saw indigenous people as tragic figures doomed to extinction

Edwin Forrest as Metamora: Engraving After Mathew Brady Photograph. Brady's photograph, ca. 1860, was taken long after Forrest appeared in this role. Forrest was known for his muscular calves, featured here under his form-fitting pants. *Colaimages/Alamy Stock Photo*

through violence, but he also saw white American culture as reaping the benefits of contact with the native civilization. The double message was that American Indians and whites were fundamentally different but also that the history of white–Native American relations had made Americans different from the English.

Novels like *The Pioneers* and plays like *Metamora* were figuring out in the 1820s what gave the United States a distinctive character. In part, this was a way of persuading other Americans to attend homegrown theater and read their compatriots' literature. But it also reflected a new interest in both American and European thought regarding the idea—often associated with the term *romanticism*—that every nation has a special spirit, which its art ought to represent. Native Americans were crucial to this project of forging a uniquely American culture. Significantly, romantic ideas about American Indians were spreading at a time when whites were giving up on the older project of absorbing them into the new republic.

CONCLUSION

By 1830, it was clear that the second war between the United States and Britain had been more than just a failed American attack on Canada or a valiant attempt to restore American pride. In retrospect, both whites and indigenous people recognized that the War of 1812 had dealt a decisive blow to Native American life in North America. The United States had defeated a major uprising, expelling the American Indians' European allies and consolidating control over half the continent. The territory cleared for white settlement had in turn, become a major area of growth for both Southern slavery and evangelical Protestantism. The westward spread of slavery also provoked a political crisis over the admission of new states and intensified the pressure to confiscate Native American land. The rise of national organizations to promote evangelical values and practices produced some opposition to that confiscation, but ultimately a new program of Indian removal prevailed. Uprooted from their homes and exiled to the western territories, indigenous society east of the Mississippi had been destroyed. At the same time, Native Americans began to play an increasingly prominent symbolic role in white popular culture, helping Americans of European descent define what was distinctively American about the societies they were building.

In 1814, when U.S. diplomats were negotiating a treaty with Great Britain, the War of 1812 might have struck many American observers as misguided or inconclusive. Viewed with the hindsight of two decades, however, the conflict that began in 1811 with an attack on Tecumseh's followers appeared far more momentous. It had affirmed American independence from Great Britain, destroyed the first political party system, reshaped the U.S. map, laid new foundations for American art, ended the possibility of peaceful coexistence between whites and native people east of the Mississippi, and brought to a power a new political movement identified with the war's hero.

STUDY TERMS

Shawnee Prophet
pan-Indian
civilization program
Battle of Tippecanoe
War Hawks
War of 1812
Hartford Convention
Redsticks
Creek War
Horseshoe Bend
Negro Fort
Battle of New Orleans
Rush-Bagot Treaty
First Seminole War
Transcontinental Treaty of 1819 (Adams-Onis Treaty)
Monroe Doctrine
National Road
internal improvements
Panic of 1819
Missouri Compromise
American Board of Commissioners for Foreign Missions
Benevolent Empire
circuit riders
camp meeting
Cane Ridge
Five Civilized Tribes
Cherokee syllabary
Worcester v. Georgia
Indian Removal Act
Treaty of New Echota
Trail of Tears
Metamora
The Leatherstocking Tales

FURTHER READING

A database of additional full-text readings is available through Power of Process for Primary Sources in Connect.

Daniel Walker Howe, *What Hath God Wrought* (2008), surveys the political history of this period, with an emphasis on communications.

William G. McLoughlin, *Cherokee Renascence in the New Republic* (1992), details Cherokee attempts to protect their land by embracing U.S. models.

David Paul Nord, *Faith in Reading* (2004), considers the role of religious publishers as pioneers of American mass media.

Amanda Porterfield, *Conceived in Doubt* (2012), presents the growth of new religious institutions as an attempt to contain doubt and skepticism.

Alisse Portnoy, *Their Right to Speak* (2005), describes women's political activism in the debates over Indian removal.

Karl Raitz and George Thompson (eds.), *The National Road* (1996), sets the first major federal road-building project in the context of the American culture of mobility.

Claudio Saunt, *A New Order of Things* (1999), demonstrates the impact of the new economic order on the Creek before, during, and after the war.

Claudio Saunt, *Unworthy Republic* (2020), narrates the expulsion and dispossession of Native Americans in the 1830s.

Alan Taylor, *The Civil War of 1812* (2010), interprets war as a conflict among residents and immigrants in the eastern Great Lakes region over their relationship to the British Empire.

Conevery Bolton Valencius, *The Lost History of the New Madrid Earthquakes* (2013), reconstructs the seismic event that shook most of the nation at the beginning of the war era.

1825–1844

10 | MARKET SOCIETY & THE BIRTH OF MASS POLITICS

Chapter Questions

1. In what ways was the expansion of voting rights around the 1820s significant but limited?

2. What was the nature of the pageantry, violence, and partisanship of mass democracy?

3. How were canal building, urbanization, and the spread of market relations connected?

4. What major innovations shaped big-city life?

5. What new religious movements and trends emerged in the Erie Canal region?

First State Election in Detroit, 1837. Electoral politics had become a popular activity for men of different classes by the time of this election. *Artokoloro/Alamy Stock Photo*

A man walked into a bar in a small Maryland town just after election day in 1834 and made loud, disparaging remarks about the supporters of Senator Henry Clay, the leader of the party that opposed President Andrew Jackson. "Big Bill" Otter, as the man called himself, was a burly plasterer from nearby Emmitsburg who loved causing trouble, and he succeeded that day in provoking one of the Clay partisans in the bar. The offended man called Otter a liar and insisted that "there was as good Clay-men as Jackson-men." When Otter refused to retract his remarks, the Clay man challenged him to a fight. "I told him I could not fight," Otter recalled in his autobiography, "but I can beat any Clay-man belonging to the party in the United States at *butting*." The two men grabbed each other by the ears and butted heads violently. To the great amusement of the other bar patrons, Otter flattened his adversary. The Clay

Time Line

1821
New York State constitution enfranchises most adult men

1824
House of Representatives elects John Quincy Adams president

1825
New York State completes construction of the Erie Canal
Gas lamps appear on the streets of New York

1828
Andrew Jackson defeats Adams in election of 1828

1830
Congress passes Indian Removal Act
Joseph Smith founds the Church of Jesus Christ of Latter-day Saints
Charles Grandison Finney stages major revival campaign in Rochester, New York

1832
South Carolina nullifies the federal tariff
Jackson vetoes the rechartering of the Second Bank of the United States

1833
New York Sun introduced

1834
Whig Party formed

1836
Helen Jewett murdered in New York

1837
Economic panic triggers six-year depression

1844
Millerites prepare for the imminent return of Jesus Christ
Joseph Smith killed by anti-Mormon mob in Nauvoo, Illinois

man asked for a rematch, which produced the same result. By the end of the evening, Otter had head-butted another man and then the Clay supporter again. Finally, Otter bought drinks for everyone in the bar.

William Otter's postelection brawl was a sign of the new political times. A rural artisan born in England, Otter had minimal formal education and bore little resemblance to the men who had dominated politics

in earlier periods of American history. And for most of his early adulthood, Otter did not take much interest in affairs of state. But in 1828, Otter became a citizen in order to vote for Jackson. Six years later, he was defiantly expressing his political views at a tavern. And one year after that, the hard-headed William Otter was elected to public office. Ordinary men like Otter blustered their way into the political world during the second quarter of the nineteenth century, transforming politics from an activity reserved for the elite to an enterprise for the masses.

These years were a period of intense democratization, at least from the perspective of white males like Otter. Participation in elections skyrocketed. New political parties were born, attracting a passionate identification that led men to violence on election days, not only in rural taverns but also in the streets of the nation's cities. These developments are sometimes associated with the presidency of Andrew Jackson, who spoke of the common man and appealed to the expanded electorate. But Jackson's opponents also participated in the new, boisterous culture of participatory politics.

The expanding world of politics was connected with the spread of trade networks and the growth of cities. As new transportation links brought much of the country into commercial contact, rural Americans forged closer ties with the nation's cities, and older patterns of work and leisure in those cities began to change. During this period, New York emerged as a symbol of a new and distinctive metropolitan way of life. But through much of the Northeast and Midwest, both farmers and city dwellers were participating in activities and institutions, including political parties, labor unions, and religious revivals, that connected them to masses of anonymous strangers.

ANDREW JACKSON AND DEMOCRACY

By modern standards, the United States did not begin as a democracy. In the new American republic, there was no monarchy, nobility, or system of hereditary privilege. But this did not mean that the mass of people determined the actions of the government. The active engagement of large numbers of poor and middle-income Americans in the affairs of state (one of the hallmarks of democracy in the modern world) began in the second quarter of the nineteenth century. Historians sometimes call this development **Jacksonian Democracy,** but the term is potentially misleading. Jackson's rise to political power was more the consequence of the democratization of American politics than its cause. Still, throughout his presidency, Andrew Jackson symbolized and articulated the growing belief that politics should be driven by the opinions of masses of white men.

UNIVERSAL MANHOOD SUFFRAGE

At the beginning of the nineteenth century, the right to vote or hold public office was linked closely to wealth. In 1800, all but three states required its citizens to own a certain amount of property in order to vote. Outside of New England, few public offices were directly elected; most were either appointed or chosen by representatives. When an office was up for popular vote, the men who stood for election were likely to come from an elite social stratum. Although ordinary Americans could affect the course of political events as soldiers, consumers, rioters, or parents, most did not do so as voters.

During the first quarter of the century, all of this began to change. The six new states that entered the union between 1816 and 1821 (Indiana, Illinois, Alabama, Mississippi, Missouri, and Maine) adopted constitutions with laxer voting requirements than those of the original thirteen. And several older states amended their constitutions to expand the electorate. In some cases, these constitutional changes were fueled by conflicts between Federalists and Republicans or between rival Republican factions seeking to gain electoral advantage by adding new voters to the rolls. But whether it was the result of democratic ideals or political stratagems, the new trend in state constitutions turned voting into a more broadly shared right. The **New York State Constitution of 1821,** for example, extended the franchise to all adult white male citizens who paid state or local taxes, served in the militia, or worked on the highways. This covered 80 percent of the adult men in a state where, just a year earlier, only one-third of them had been eligible to vote for governor. By 1824, only four states still imposed significant property requirements for voting.

States were also expanding the number of elected government positions. Governorships, which generally had been determined by the legislature, were increasingly subject to popular vote. By the 1840s, it was even common for judges to be elected. States also changed the way presidents were chosen. In 1800, only a third of the states picked presidential electors based directly on a popular vote. By 1832, when Jackson stood for re-election, every state except for South Carolina conducted a popular vote for the presidency.

The expansion of voting rights and voting opportunities during this period marked the arrival of **universal manhood suffrage.** This nineteenth-century term did not mean that everyone could vote; it meant that one got to vote by virtue of being a man, as opposed to a child, a woman, or an enslaved person. The exclusion of children is often taken for granted, but the new suffrage laws of this era typically barred everyone under the age of twenty-one (and in some states, under twenty-five) at a time when life expectancy was much shorter than it is today. Because the median age in the United States in 1824 was seventeen, most people were kept out of the political process for reasons of age alone. The exclusion of women may have seemed natural to many Americans at the time (though some women had voted in New Jersey from 1776 to 1808), but it acquired new significance once men of all classes began voting. Politics became associated with masculinity in the nineteenth century, which shaped the way it was conducted and understood.

For African Americans, both free and enslaved, the limitations of universal manhood suffrage were far clearer. The same period that brought democratic opportunities to white males closed them down for free men of color. The New York constitution that removed property requirements for whites in 1821 made a point of imposing them on African Americans. New Yorkers of African ancestry had to possess two hundred fifty dollars' worth of property in order to vote, a restriction that barred all but 298 of the state's 30,000 Blacks. Pennsylvania's new constitution in 1838 affirmed that the right to vote, which earlier constitutions had granted to "freemen," explicitly meant white freemen. Black men also lost the legal right to vote in Connecticut, Rhode Island, and North Carolina. And no new state admitted after 1819 (except for Maine, which had been part of an older state) granted voting rights to African Americans. Free Black men resisted their exclusion from electoral politics and asserted themselves in the public life of Northern cities, but most were shut out of the newly expanded political process of the Jacksonian era.

New immigrants from Europe, by contrast, enjoyed significant voting rights under the new state constitutions of this period. In Illinois, adult white males who had been living in the state for six months could vote, whether or not they had become U.S. citizens. Between 1825 and 1850, massive numbers of Americans entered an unfamiliar world of electoral politics, taking part in what had previously been an elite activity. No longer a class privilege, voting was now linked to race and gender.

JACKSON'S RISE

In some respects, Andrew Jackson was an unlikely champion of these democratizing trends in American politics. Born in the Carolina backcountry in 1767, Jackson became a lawyer and moved west to the frontier city of Nashville in 1788, where he established himself as a successful land speculator, owned a plantation with over one hundred enslaved people, and married the daughter of the city's founder. He served briefly in Congress in the 1790s, belligerently advocating the interests of Western farmers and merchants who sought free access to the Mississippi River. After he returned to private life, the War of 1812 drew him back to public service, and this time he earned nationwide adulation for his role in the Battle of New Orleans. Although his name remained the subject of popular legend into the next decade, Jackson stayed out of politics, spending much of the period brooding over perceived mistreatment in connection with his unauthorized ventures into Florida (see Chapter 9). By all appearances, Jackson's glory days were behind him.

An unusual set of political circumstances returned Jackson to the national spotlight. As Monroe's final term in office drew to a close in 1824, no obvious heir was apparent and a number of candidates emerged. John Quincy Adams, who was Monroe's secretary of state (a traditional stepping-stone to the presidency), had distinguished himself in various diplomatic crises and challenges and might have been the presumptive choice. But after the Panic of 1819, voters and Republican Party leaders were more preoccupied with domestic affairs than with foreign relations, and Adams's perceived hostility to slavery cost him support in the South. A number of slaveholding candidates emerged, including William Crawford (a states' rights advocate who wanted to return to the fiscal conservatism that had dominated the Republican

platform before the war), Henry Clay, and John Calhoun (both of whom supported the party's turn toward internal improvements and the national bank). In previous elections, the Republicans had selected their presidential candidates at a congressional caucus—a gathering of all the party members in Congress. But with a growing spirit of democracy in the air and the party no longer worried about uniting against a Federalist opposition, the caucus had come to seem more aristocratic and less necessary. Less than a quarter of Congress attended the caucus, and its endorsement of Crawford was of doubtful value. For the first time since its formation in the 1790s, the Republican Party could not coalesce around a single candidate.

In 1822, the crowded presidential field was joined by a surprise contender. In an attempt to block a local rival, a group of Tennessee politicians nominated the hero of New Orleans, and to everyone's surprise Jackson's candidacy caught on in Pennsylvania and North Carolina. The **election of 1824** pitted four viable candidates. Jackson, who had been careful not to commit himself on any of the big issues of the day, fared best, but no one managed to win a majority of the electoral votes, which meant that according to the Constitution the race would be decided by the House of Representatives. Henry Clay was Speaker of the House and wielded considerable influence, but the representatives had to select from the top three electoral vote getters—Jackson, Adams, and Crawford. Clay directed his supporters to back Adams (to whom he was closest ideologically), and by the margin of a single vote in the New York delegation, Adams won. When Clay was subsequently named secretary of state, Jackson and his allies decried the so-called **corrupt bargain** that had determined the outcome and denied Jackson the presidency.

John Quincy Adams, son of the second president, was an accomplished statesman with a grand vision for an expanding national government. But the charge of having entered the White House through a backroom deal dogged his presidency, as did the perception that he was an elitist who felt that public officials should not be, in Adams's own infamous words, "palsied by the will of our constituents." An outraged Jackson, who had declared himself the champion of those constituents and their will, wasted no time preparing for a rematch in 1828. An army of newspapers friendly to Jackson organized a national public relations campaign, some of it quite vicious. In addition, Adams's slaveholding opponents had learned not to repeat the mistake of dividing their votes among several candidates. In an election that drew three times as many voters as in 1824, Jackson won handily. At the age of sixty-two, the military hero had refashioned himself as

Campaign Broadside, 1828. The contest between John Quincy Adams and Andrew Jackson featured smear campaigns in the press. Jackson's supporters labeled Adams an aristocrat for buying billiard tables for the White House and accused the president of having procured young virgins for the czar. Pro-Adams editors, in turn, called Jackson an adulterer. Both sides evoked the specter of a fragile republic in danger of dissolving. *Question for Analysis:* What does this cartoon suggest about the character and reputation of Jackson (standing)? *Library of Congress, Prints and Photographs Division*

a "man of the people" and become the first president from a state west of the Appalachians.

PATRONAGE, PEGGY EATON, AND JACKSON'S FIRST TERM

Jackson's long campaign against President Adams was more than just an attempt to undo the results of an irregular election. Jackson's supporters were building a new national coalition to replace the Jeffersonian party that had splintered by 1824. Once in office, Jackson's major contribution to the new political system was the practice of using government patronage to reward partisan loyalty. Previous presidents had appointed friends and supporters to vacant positions in the government, but Jackson was the first to dismiss large numbers of federal

officeholders on assuming the presidency. He defended the new policy as a reform rooted in the democratic principle that civil servants should rotate rather than forming an entrenched entitled class. Jackson's critics saw a power grab that threatened to debase civil service. The **spoils system,** as it was called, used the appointive power of the presidency to strengthen party unity and to make partisan affiliation crucial to those who aspired to participate in public life. This system would structure the distribution of federal jobs for the next half century.

At the top level of the cabinet, Jackson favored those who showed great personal loyalty. Early in Jackson's first term, their loyalty was tested when he named as his new secretary of war a Tennessean named John Henry Eaton, an old friend who had managed Jackson's campaign. Shortly before the inauguration, Eaton had married a much younger woman whose husband had committed suicide a few months earlier. Because Margaret (or Peggy) Eaton was rumored to have been Eaton's mistress while still married to her husband, prominent women in the capital, including the wives of cabinet members, ostracized Peggy Eaton and refused to admit her into polite society. Jackson insisted on Eaton's innocence and likely felt great sympathy for Eaton, since his own wife, who had died before he was inaugurated, had been wounded by accusations that she had not been legally divorced when she married Jackson. He also resented the fact that the women of Washington, D.C., were making the rules and defying his orders. Ultimately, he called for the resignation of his entire cabinet (excluding the postmaster general, whose wife had not participated in the boycott) in order to resolve the conflict. The **Peggy Eaton affair** underscored the importance of personal relations to the new administration and had significant political consequences in both the short and the long term. In addition to forcing a major turnover in the executive branch, the scandal boosted the political fortunes of Martin Van Buren, a widower who socialized freely and cheerfully with the Eatons, and introduced a breach between Jackson and Vice President John Calhoun, whose wife had spearheaded the boycott. Van Buren, not Calhoun, would inherit Jackson's political mantle and succeed him to the presidency.

While the Eaton scandal simmered, Jackson was devoting himself to Indian removal (see Chapter 9). After winning that battle, however, Jackson took on two other causes that would come to define his presidency: one related to federal-state relations and the other to finance. First came the **nullification crisis,** which reinforced the growing animosity between Jackson and Calhoun.

Calhoun led a revolt by South Carolina against an 1828 increase in the federal tariff on imports that protected Northern manufacturers from foreign competition but hurt cotton growers. Unable to persuade Congress to scrap the tariff, Calhoun anonymously authored a paper that put forward the doctrine that an individual state could nullify any federal law that it deemed unconstitutional, much like the Kentucky and Virginia Resolutions of 1798 (see Chapter 8). In 1832, when Congress replaced the 1828 tariff with a new one that provided little relief, the South Carolina legislature declared that the tariff law would no longer be operative in the state and no customs would be collected there.

Though Jackson was a vocal advocate of states' rights and had allowed Georgia to ignore the Supreme Court when it came to Indian removal, in this case he insisted on the supreme sovereignty of the federal union and labeled the actions of South Carolina treasonous. He secured congressional authorization for the Force Bill, which would allow him to use the military against South Carolina if necessary; he then ordered warships to Charleston harbor. Congressman Henry Clay worked out a compromise tariff bill that persuaded South Carolina to withdraw its nullification, but the point had been made on both sides. South Carolina, which would become the first state to secede from the union three decades later, was on record claiming the right to void an act of Congress. And Andrew Jackson was on record as being willing to wage war against those who defied his authority.

THE BANK WAR AND THE PANIC OF 1837

Jackson's battle against Calhoun and nullification was quickly eclipsed by his political showdown with the Second Bank of the United States. The bank had recovered from the mismanagement of its early years and from the political fallout over the Panic of 1819. The Supreme Court had ruled that its charter did not violate the Constitution, and by 1823 the bank was on solid financial footing under the astute management of Nicholas Biddle. When Jackson took office, the bank was regulating the nation's currency supply to the satisfaction of most of the financial community and the economy was enjoying relative stability. But Jackson came out in opposition to the bank, arguing that it concentrated power in a private corporation.

Fearing that Jackson might cause trouble for the bank when its charter expired in 1836, Biddle and his congressional supporters decided to have the bank apply for early renewal in 1832, so that Jackson would have to approve the new charter or jeopardize his re-election prospects later that year. Jackson took this as a mortal challenge. When Van Buren visited the president in the White House, he found Jackson lying on a couch. "The bank, Mr. Van Buren," he whispered, "is trying to kill me." He then pressed Van Buren's hand and added "but I will kill it."

The bank's charter bill passed easily, and Jackson responded by vetoing it. Over the previous forty years, presidents had used this power a total of nine times, and only three times involving important legislation. Jackson vetoed twelve acts of Congress, often citing constitutional grounds. This was perhaps the most significant growth in presidential power associated with Jackson's presidency. More strikingly, the veto message was a venomous and incendiary attack on the central bank, calling it an unfair monopoly that exacerbated the division between rich and poor. "The rich and powerful too often bend government to selfish purposes," Jackson proclaimed, and the bank was just another example of government-supported exploitation of the poor. The bank's supporters considered the veto message so outrageous that they reprinted and circulated thousands of copies, hoping it would help Jackson's opponent, Henry Clay, in the election of 1832. But Biddle and his allies had misread the popular mood. In a campaign that was in part a referendum on Jackson's passionate opposition to the Bank of the United States, the president was re-elected overwhelmingly.

Why Jackson hated the bank so passionately is the subject of debate. Even within Jackson's own cabinet, there were sharply divided views on what was wrong with Biddle's bank. Some Jacksonians opposed banks in general because banks printed bank notes and created money out of nothing (see Chapter 8). But others objected to the national bank precisely because it regulated other banks and made it *harder* for them to print money. Jackson's veto message probably appealed both to Western voters who wanted easier access to credit and to artisans who mistrusted the world of banks and paper.

After the election, three years still remained on the bank's charter, and Biddle was determined to muster sufficient congressional opposition to overturn the veto. Jackson, meanwhile, sought to destroy the bank even before its charter lapsed. Over the objections of two secretaries of the treasury, whom he fired, Jackson ordered that the federal government withdraw its money from Biddle's bank. Both the rhetoric of the charter veto and Jackson's long-standing discomfort with banks suggested that the president might propose a public alternative for storing government funds and regulating the currency

INTERPRETING THE SOURCES

Bank Notes

We are now so accustomed to paper money that we think of the green bills in our wallets simply as cash. But before the Civil War, the U.S. government did not print money and there was no such thing as uniform paper currency. The pieces of paper that circulated as money during this era were printed by hundreds of private banks chartered by the states in which they were headquartered (see Chapter 8).

Bank notes came in all sizes, colors, and denominations, and no one was required by law to accept them at face value in a transaction. The three-dollar bill pictured here promises that the bearer can exchange the note for three dollars' worth of specie (gold and silver). As long as everyone—storekeepers, landlords, neighbors, and friends—believed that the note *could* be redeemed for specie, it would continue to circulate as three dollars.

As cities grew, commercial exchanges proliferated, banks multiplied, and more men and women labored for cash wages, bank notes such as this became more common features of everyday life. Some of the hostility to the Bank of the United States reflected the frustrations and suspicions of Americans who were newly dependent on this chaotic system.

Explore the Source

1. What does the image on the bill represent, and why might it have been chosen?

2. If the owner of this bank note wanted to cash it in for gold or silver, what would he or she have had to do?

3. Why was it important for bank notes to bear personal signatures?

Three-Dollar Bill, 1850s, Mount Vernon Bank, Providence, Rhode Island. Bank notes from before the Civil War appeared in a bewildering array of denominations, including 1 cent, 9 cents, 12½ cents, and 3,000 dollars. *RI Currency*

supply. Instead, federal money was simply redeposited in twenty-three state-chartered private banks, many of them owned by associates of well-connected men in Jackson's circle of Democratic advisers. Biddle responded to the **deposit removal** by calling in loans and raising interest rates, thereby limiting the amount of paper money in circulation. This retaliatory act triggered a temporary recession and seemed to confirm Jackson's charge that the bank abused its excessive power for private gain and political influence. The larger problem for Biddle was that without the government deposits the national bank could exert little control over private banks and the money supply. Private banks printed more money and approved risky loans to investors eager to profit from Western lands offered by the federal government (see Interpreting the Sources: Bank Notes). Speculative lending, speculative borrowing, and speculative land purchasing created a major bubble in the economy.

Many of Jackson's supporters had seen his attack on the bank as an indictment of paper money and unearned wealth, but the **bank war** now appeared to have been an act of deregulation, allowing state-chartered private banks to do whatever they wanted. Jackson sought to tame the speculation by requiring payments at federal land offices to be made in gold and silver, but this drained gold and silver out of the banks, exposing them to the risk of not being able to redeem their notes. As Biddle's bank died, Britain's banks tightened the reins on American borrowers, gold and silver stopped flowing in to the United States from abroad, and in 1837 the American economy collapsed for the second time in less than twenty years.

The **Panic of 1837** was the result of a complex set of developments in the international economy, but it was seen by many at the time as the result of the Democrats' mismangement. Van Buren, who was elected to succeed

223

BEHIND THE IMAGE

This pro-Jackson cartoon was printed in New York as a lithograph in 1834, after Jackson had vetoed the bank's renewal of the Bank of the United States and had been re-elected to the presidency. Five years earlier, the artist, French immigrant Anthony Imbert, had produced the first political cartoon using lithography, which would become a major medium of political commentary over the course of the nineteenth century. Imbert's depiction of the bank war might have been his last copyrighted lithograph, as he died five months after its publication.

WITHIN THE IMAGE

Several details mark the cartoon's sympathies. ① Jackson appears as the champion of popular tastes and ordinary Americans, personified by ② frontiersman Joe Tammany, wearing a coonskin cap and shouting his support: "Hurrah my old yellow flower of the forrest, walk into him like a streak of Greased lightning through a gooseberry bush!" The large whiskey bottle by Tammany's feet also identifies Jackson with the common man and rugged masculinity. By contrast, supporters of ③ Nicholas Biddle include ④ an overweight woman, Mother Bank, holding a bottle of port wine and personifying the bank as a bloated institution. ⑤ A caption explains that "several long and severe rounds were fought" and "immense sums" wagered. Framing the showdown over banking policy as a bare-knuckle prize fight between scantily clad men before an audience of gamblers suggests how many Americans (including the antagonists) might have seen the debate.

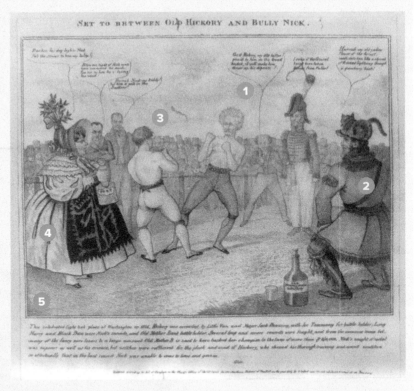

Bank War. *Library of Congress Prints and Photographs Division [LC-USZ62-9650]*

BEYOND THE IMAGE

Imbert was the most prolific producer of lithographic cartoons during the years of Jackson's presidency, and his images, which sold cheaply by the thousands, helped shape popular impressions of Jacksonian politics. Jackson's identification with the common man was already a well-worn cliché by the time this cartoon appeared, but specific elements of Imbert's rendition of democratic politics (coonskin hats, whiskey guzzling, boxing matches, muscled men) would be reinforced by other artists, contributing to the iconography of Jacksonian America. Jackson's enduring reputation as a frontier populist reflects images, and not just political rhetoric.

Jackson in 1836, suffered politically from the economic collapse, but the consequences for the nation as a whole were far more devastating. The ensuing depression lasted for more than six years, the longest and most severe downturn in American history until the Great Depression almost a century later. Business failures began in New Orleans and then spread both through the southwestern part of the country and to New York along the circuits of the cotton trade. Land values declined precipitously (real estate lots in New York worth 480 dollars late in 1836 sold for 50 dollars seven months later), wages plummeted for those workers lucky enough to hold on to their jobs, and despair spread across the country. As the philosopher Ralph Waldo Emerson saw it, "the land stinks with suicide." In many ways, the scenes were reminiscent of the smaller collapse in 1819. But by 1837, even fewer Americans were insulated from the instability of the market economy.

DEMOCRACY AND EQUALITY

As Jackson left office in 1837, he continued to rail against banks and paper money. But he took comfort in the fact that in America "the planter, the farmer, the mechanic, and the laborer . . . the bone and sinew of the country . . . [owned] the great mass of our national wealth." Jackson was fond of flattering the common people, but he was not alone in describing the United States in the 1830s as an egalitarian society. European visitors to Jackson's America routinely remarked on the absence of social hierarchy, the blurring of class divisions, and the broad distribution of economic opportunity. Some of these foreign observers liked what they saw, whereas others found it alarming, but traveler after traveler repeated the same observations: Americans dress in their Sunday best on a daily basis, people eat meat three times a day, and anyone's son might become the equal of any other's. Political democracy, it seemed, brought with it social and economic equality.

But how equal were conditions in the United States during this period of mass democracy? When making their observations, European visitors tended to bracket the enslavement of over two million African Americans or the subordinate roles of Blacks and women throughout the country. But even among white men, political democracy did not necessarily produce economic equality. Tax records from the period suggest that contrary to Jackson's claim, a small percentage of the population controlled most of the nation's wealth, whereas a majority of Americans owned no taxable property whatsoever. Moreover, most of the wealthy had been born wealthy, whereas most of those reared in poverty remained poor.

There are several possible explanations for Europeans' exaggerated perceptions of equality in Jackson's America. First, visitors may have seen what they expected to see in a country that represented novelty and social fluidity. Second, America was being compared to Europe, where fewer individuals owned land and the divide between rich and poor was more extreme. Finally, even though few Americans were wealthy, many ordinary citizens adopted the refinements that in Europe belonged only to the elite. These signs of privilege included not only clean clothing,

protein-heavy diets, and literacy but also architectural refinements that might have been especially impressive to foreign visitors, such as parlors, open staircases, carpets, and fenced yards with trees and shrubs.

PARTICIPATORY POLITICS AND THE SECOND PARTY SYSTEM

Jackson's presidency ushered in a new era of mass participation in electoral politics, and expanded voting rights among white men were only part of the explanation. Before the 1830s, even most people who were eligible to vote declined to participate, especially in national elections. But by 1840, close competition between national parties would lead to turnouts over 70 percent for presidential elections, a trend that would last through much of the century. Elections became popular festivities, and party politics drew the kind of boisterous participation and intense loyalty now more commonly associated with sporting events.

A SECOND PARTY SYSTEM

The Age of Jackson was an age of political parties. Having unseated Adams by building a new national coalition over a long campaign, Jackson's supporters sought to turn that coalition into a powerful party. Its lead architect was the New Yorker Van Buren, who had controlled a powerful statewide party organization centered in Albany. The national party created around Jackson's candidacy in 1828 differed from the Republicans and Federalists of the first party system. The **Democrats,** as Van Buren's party would come to be known, were organized from the grassroots up through a system of nominating conventions at the county and state levels, and regulated by rigid commitments to party unity.

Van Buren reasoned that the country would be better served by competition between two large, national parties than by a diffuse system of local factions and animosities. The clashes between national parties would help American voters identify and express political differences over what constitutes proper government. Van Buren also preferred party rivalries to regional ones. If Jefferson's alliance between artisans and small farmers in New York and slaveholders in Virginia could be revived and extended westward, the nation might avoid a split over slavery.

As the new Jackson alliance solidified, his opponents began reassembling and remodeling the New England–based coalition of nationalist Republicans who had supported Adams. The first rival party to tap into anti-Jackson sentiment was the **Antimasons,** who organized initially in response to a disappearance in upstate New York. William Morgan, a former member of a Masonic lodge, was rumored to have been abducted and murdered as he was preparing to publish the secrets of that international fraternal order, which had included many of the nation's founders. Antimasons accused Masons of conspiring to undermine the republic by keeping power in the hands of an elite secret society. As their message of transparent government spread west from New York, it attracted voters who suspected Jackson (a Mason) of being a despot. In 1831, the Antimasons introduced the now-standard practice of holding a national convention to set the party's platform and nominate candidates.

Three years later, Jackson's opponents would form a new national party, which they named the **Whigs,** after the British party that had voiced opposition in the eighteenth century to excesses of executive power. For the next twenty years, Democrats and Whigs would compete throughout the country in both national and state elections and their rivalry would shape political debate. For this reason, historians describe the period between the presidency of Jackson and the collapse of the Whigs during the 1850s as the era of the **Second Party System.**

By 1840, the Whigs had adopted many of Van Buren's tactics and created a successful national party on the Democratic model. That year, the Whigs held their first national convention and nominated for the presidency William Henry Harrison, who had led the attack on Tecumseh's followers at Tippecanoe in 1811. Though Harrison had been born into a wealthy slaveholding family in Virginia and owned a stately home in Ohio, the Whigs celebrated him as a simple frontiersman who drank hard cider and lived in a log cabin. The Whigs, like their rivals, won their first presidential election by nominating an Indian fighter from the War of 1812 and giving him populist credentials.

But Whigs and Democrats were not simply mirror images of each other. They differed on important issues and appealed to different constituencies. Though both parties were committed to national expansion, Whigs tended to support federal interventions in the economy, such as government-sponsored improvements in transportation or tariffs to encourage domestic manufactures. Democrats, by contrast, were more enthusiastic about using federal power for territorial acquistion. Whigs tended to embrace the evangelical values of the Benevolent Empire, whereas Democrats courted Catholic immigrants and advocated religious pluralism. Neither party criticized slavery, but Democrats were far more committed to its preservation and placed greater emphasis on white supremacy.

Part of what made the Second Party System so stable in this period was the fact that the Whigs and Democrats were nationally competitive. Between 1834 and 1853, the Democrats won 54 percent of the seats in Congress, although Whigs won slightly more popular votes for president. Unfortunately for the Whigs, both of the men they elected to the presidency, Harrison in 1840 and Zachary Taylor in 1848, died early in their first terms. The Democratic Party may have dominated national policy making in the 1830s and 1840s, but elections were close enough to maintain the enthusiasm of partisan loyalists on both sides and to discourage the formation of third parties.

CAMPAIGNING IN PRINT

Parties relied heavily on newspapers, pamphlets, and books to broadcast their message to voters. In every state capital in the union, both Whig and Democratic Party organs printed candidates' speeches and rebutted rivals' claims in great detail, drumming up voter interest well in advance of election day. In addition to these standing newspapers, parties produced special periodicals to support particular campaigns. In 1844, before the national conventions, sixty-three papers were published for Henry Clay (Whig) and forty-three for James Polk (Democrat). All of these papers enjoyed cheap postage rates courtesy of the federal government.

By the 1830s, biographies had also become a staple of the new political culture, as campaigns used candidates' life stories to appeal to voters. Because overtly campaigning for oneself was frowned upon during this period, candidates did not authorize these biographies and often claimed to have nothing to do with them. Democratic biographies tended to describe their nominees as ordinary men from humble beginnings who rose to prominence through hard work, whereas Whigs emphasized natural abilities and heroic service to the country. Whig biographies were also far more likely to stress a candidate's moral values, intense religious faith, and abstinence from alcohol. Significantly, campaign biographies paid little attention to the family relationships of their subjects and assigned women little, if any, role in the formation of their character. The men described in these books lived in a masculine world, much like the political arena in which they competed (see Hot Commodities: Davy Crockett and His Almanacs).

Democratic Election Tickets, 1828.   Though they appear to be campaign leaflets, these were actually ballots. Paper ballots in the nineteenth century were slates rather than menus. Instead of selecting from a range of candidates, voters selected a "ticket" and simply dropped it into a box. Parties printed these ballots, which discouraged ticket splitting (voting for candidates from different parties for different races). In these examples from Maryland, a voter would be selecting Jackson for president while casting votes for John V. L. McMahon and George H. Steuart, Jacksonians running to represent Baltimore in the state legislature. Question for Analysis: Compared to modern ballots, do you think these tickets presume more or less knowledge on the part of the average voter about candidates for office? *Library of Congress*

ROWDY ELECTIONS

In modern democracies, voting is the special ceremony through which the people are entitled and expected to express their will. But for most Americans in the nineteenth century, voting was not the sober, conscientious, private practice we now associate with that ceremony. Voting did not take place in curtained booths; it was performed publicly, often in crowded streets, town squares, county courthouses, or village taverns. In seven states, men exercised their franchise vocally. But even **paper ballots,** which were in use in most states by the middle of the nineteenth century, did not shield a voter's preferences from public view. On the contrary, ballots during this period were printed by the political parties themselves, often on distinctively marked or colored paper, and distributed by campaign workers to voters in front of the polling site. Ballots looked like and functioned as campaign paraphernalia.

   ● The festivities leading up to election day offered additional opportunities to foster and celebrate party loyalty. Both parties staged rallies and demonstrations in public spaces, featuring banners, floats, and torchlight parades. Except for the crucial fact that they were overwhelmingly male, these rallies resembled religious revival meetings lightly clothed in a common political goal. Speakers made high-pitched, emotional appeals

about the battle between good and evil, and partisans engaged in lots of singing. ● Attendance was often enormous. At one 1840 gathering in Ohio, William Henry Harrison addressed a crowd of Whig supporters estimated at one hundred thousand. These outdoor mass meetings relied on pithy slogans to define party positions and offered dramatic spectacles that allowed average citizens to feel included in massive contests, where each individual's vote was unlikely to determine the outcome.

Alcohol flowed freely on election days. Local candidates or party officials treated voters to rounds of drinks as a way of securing partisan loyalty and producing the revelry appropriate to the occasion. Urban elections were especially drunken and violent. During New York's 1834 municipal elections, thousands engaged in fistfights in the streets, bricks were thrown, gunfire was exchanged, and one side even raided the city arsenal for weapons. When the polls finally closed, city militias had to escort ballot boxes to City Hall.

Drinking, fighting, and gambling reinforced the popular notion that politics was a masculine affair. When Illinois Democratic congressional candidate William May was accused of adultery in 1834, he did not deny the charge. Instead, he responded that his accuser was "some spindle-shanked, toad-eating, man-granny, . . . some *puling* sentimental, *he*-old maid whose cold liver and pulseless heart, never felt a desire which could be tempted." In the age of universal manhood suffrage, rugged masculinity was deemed a political virtue by much of the electorate.

For other Americans, however, all the alcohol, revelry, and violence marked what was undignified and corrupt about politics. To many observers, especially native-born Protestants and women, the entire political process seemed tainted. Caroline Kirkland, in an 1839 novel set on the Michigan frontier, mocks the local politician as an ignorant, mercenary man who cares more about getting elected than about any issue. He gets his start in politics by selling hard-boiled eggs to voters on election day as an eight-year-old. "From eggs he advanced to pies, from pies to almanacs, whiskey, powder and shot, foot-balls, playing-cards, and at length," Kirkland informs her readers, "he brought into the field a large turkey, which was tied to a post and stoned to death at twenty-five cents a throw." Men like this epitomized the crude world of politics that many refined Americans found distasteful.

HOT COMMODITIES

Davy Crockett and His Almanacs

POLITICS AND ENTERTAINMENT

As the Whigs organized in opposition to President Jackson, they searched the political landscape for their own popular Western hero. They found David Crockett, a frontiersman from Tennessee who had fought under Jackson against the Creek peoples and had entered politics in the 1820s.

Long before Davy Crockett became a coonskin-wearing character on a Walt Disney television show in the 1950s, he was a real person from East Tennessee who parlayed his local popularity into a political career and served in Congress for three terms over the period 1827 to 1835. His opposition to Jackson's Indian removal policy led to his election defeat in 1831, but he triumphed again two years later and, with the help of Whig journalists and publishers, presented himself to a wide audience in a series of popular autobiographies designed to boost his prospects for national office. Crockett's autobiographies told of hunting bears and tricking his neighbors, but they also attacked Jackson's military record and economic policies. Like Jackson, Crockett portrayed himself as an ordinary man of extraordinary qualities, with virtues and wisdom acquired and demonstrated in frontier life rather than in books, academies, or cosmopolitan social settings. And like Jackson, he depended on a national publishing network to get this message out to voters.

Crockett never fulfilled his political ambitions or those of his Whig promoters. Though he toured the Eastern states in 1834 to build support for a possible bid for the presidency, Crockett's political star faded after he lost his seat in Congress in a close election a year later. Tired of Tennessee politics, Crockett left his home and moved farther south. "Since you have chosen to elect a man with a timber toe to succeed me" (his Jacksonian opponent had a prosthetic leg), Crockett reportedly announced, "you may all go to hell and I will go to Texas." Crockett did indeed move to Texas, where he was killed in 1836 at the Battle of the Alamo (see Chapter 11).

As a cultural icon, however, Davy Crockett enjoyed great success. The process of turning a Tennessee politician into a mythical figure began in his own lifetime. In 1830, a New York writer named James K. Paulding created a play entitled *The Lion of the West*, which featured a new comic character named Colonel Nimrod Wildfire, a powerful hero who was half man, half alligator and exposed the pretensions of the snobby and effete. Even before the script had been finished, rumors were identifying Nimrod Wildfire with Congressman Crockett. When the play came to Washington, D.C., Crockett rose appreciatively from the audience and exchanged bows with his stage counterpart. Already in 1830, Davy Crockett was a character in American theatrical entertainment.

Congressman David Crockett, 1833. Crockett's rise to political prominence in the early 1830s epitomized a new age in American politics. As the aristocratic French traveler Alexis de Tocqueville observed with horror, "The inhabitants of the district in which Memphis is the capital sent to the House of Representatives an individual . . . who has no education, can read with difficulty, has no property, no fixed residence, but passes his life hunting, selling his game to live, and dwelling continuously in the woods." *Barney Burstein/Corbis/VCG/Getty Images*

Davy Crockett, Cultural Icon. The cover of *Davy Crockett's Almanack,* 1837, features the Crockett character in a wildcat skin cap, a year after the real Crockett died in the Alamo. The man featured in the illustration is actually the actor James Hackett, who had played Colonel Wildfire on stage. *National Portrait Gallery*

By 1835, Crockett's autobiographies had been joined by an immensely popular series of *Davy Crockett's Almanacks,* which continued to be issued for twenty years after his death by urban publishers in the Northeast who had no interest in the politics of the deceased man for whom the almanacs were named. These comic almanacs presented Crockett as a human-animal superhero who kills wild beasts and takes on their qualities. Graphically violent and gory, many of the Crockett tales describe sadistic behavior toward Native Americans. Whereas the real David Crockett had stood up to Jackson on Indian removal, his comic alter ego would kill a Native American by chewing through his jugular vein and letting him bleed to death.

Think About It

1. Was David Crockett primarily a politician or a popular entertainer?

2. What does it teach us about American politics during the 1830s that a congressman became the basis for a comic superhero celebrated for sadistic violence?

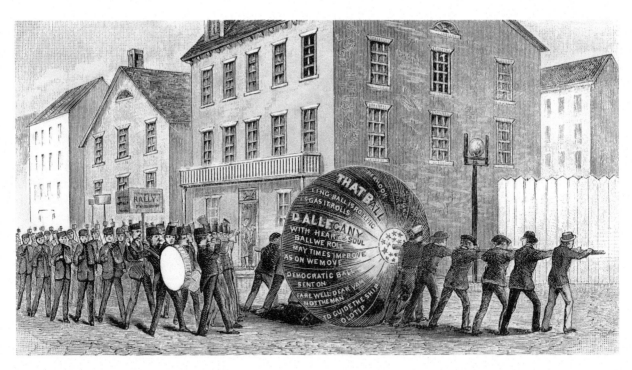

Rally for William Henry Harrison.   The phrase "keep the ball rolling" has its origins in the 1840 presidential campaign. The line "that swift the ball is rolling on" was used in a Harrison campaign song. Some Whig clubs then built what they called "victory balls," 8- and some-times 12-foot balls of canvas, leather, and tin, which they painted with campaign slogans and rolled in rallies and parades. The Tippecanoe Club of Cleveland, Ohio, rolled one such ball across the state. *North Wind Picture Archives/Alamy Stock Photo*

Still, most of those who were eligible to vote did so duti-fully, even if it meant holding their noses on the way to the polls.

MARKETS AND CITIES

The rise of mass politics coincided with three other revolutionary developments in American life: the growth of commerce, the quickening pace of transportation and communication, and the emergence of big cities. Commerce was hardly new in the 1820s. For centuries, Americans had been buying and selling land, people, sta-ple crops, and other commodities. But in the early nine-teenth century, new patterns of producing, transporting, distributing, and consuming goods changed the daily eco-nomic lives of most Americans, especially in the North, bringing them into a national network of regular commer-cial exchange. Similarly, although cities had existed in North America for many centuries, a handful of places emerged in this period as the nation's first large, imper-sonal metropolises. Some of these changes were part of the complex process known as **industrialization,** which in its early phases did not primarily involve machines and factories. Industrialization simply meant the reorganiza-tion of the production process by employers through the division of labor.

CANALS AND THE TRANSPORTATION REVOLUTION

Artificial waterways powered the growth of the American economy. Because transportation was much cheaper and faster on water than on land, **canals** sped the circulation of goods across the country and brought more people and places into commercial contact. Though canals were known in different parts of the world well before the nineteenth century, they had been used sparingly in the United States. After the end of the War of 1812, state governments, merchants, and entrepreneurs embarked on a major canal-building spree. As late as 1820, the total mileage of canals in the United States was lower than 100. But over the next three decades, Americans carved out more than 3,000 miles of new waterways, mostly with

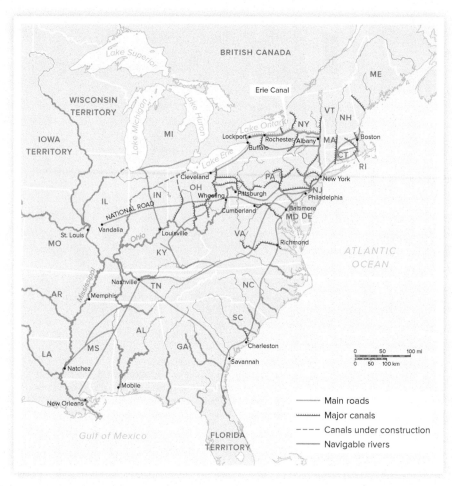

Map 10.1 Canal Network, 1840. Three states (New York, Pennsylvania, and Ohio) were responsible for most canal construction.

Buffalo on Lake Erie. The canal thus allowed for a continuous navigable water passage from the Atlantic Ocean to the Great Lakes. On October 26, 1825, Clinton celebrated this triumph of both civil engineering and public finance with a "Wedding of the Waters" ceremony in New York City. At the largest public celebration in any U.S. city to that point, Clinton poured a keg of water from Lake Erie into the ocean. In a palpable way, the world was becoming more connected.

The Erie Canal was crucial to the development, during the 1830s and 1840s, of a domestic market within the United States for agricultural produce. No longer would the growth of the American economy depend primarily on foreign trade. Other factors contributed to this development as well, including the proliferation of steamboats, which sped shipping schedules; the westward migration of farmers, which opened new land to cultivation; and the introduction of mechanical reapers, which allowed farmers to harvest larger crops. But canals enabled farmers in the interior of the country to raise crops and livestock for consumers along the eastern seaboard. In turn, canals also opened up new rural markets for manufactured goods from Eastern cities. Canals integrated farmland west of the Appalachians into a national water transportation network—and into the market economy.

Though canal construction was costly by the standards of government spending at the time, the investments paid off. New York State brought in five times as much in toll revenues as it owed in interest on debt incurred to finance the project. By 1837, Clinton's Ditch had paid for itself. Even more significant was the canal's impact on the state's economy. A year after the canal's completion, shipping costs from Lake Erie to Manhattan had dropped from one hundred dollars a ton to under nine dollars. Within five

public funding. Much of the construction took place in just a few states, but those canals, together with others dug in the Northeast and Midwest, linked most of the country's major rivers and lakes by the middle of the century (see Map 10.1).

In New York, Governor DeWitt Clinton persuaded the state legislature to fund what would become the nation's busiest and most profitable artificial waterway, the **Erie Canal.** Construction began on the Erie Canal in 1817 and ended in 1825, two years ahead of schedule. "Clinton's Ditch," as it was skeptically dubbed, began in the state capital of Albany on the Hudson River, which flows south to New York City and empties into the Atlantic Ocean. Wending its way north and west from Albany for more than 363 miles, the Canal passed over nineteen stone aqueducts and relied on eighty-three locks to raise water levels, ultimately reaching its terminus at

years, farmers in western New York could sell wheat for a profit in New York City. ● The new economic equation changed the face of the state. Places that had been wilderness were cleared of trees to make room for farmland and to supply firewood and lumber to the new market towns that were sprouting up along the canal route. Small frontier towns like Buffalo mushroomed into sizable cities, and the brand-new city of Rochester quickly emerged as a major processing and manufacturing center. Beyond the borders of the state, the Erie Canal changed the economy and ecology of the Great Lakes region. ●

Canals were but one component of a national transportation network that carried people and commercial goods. This network, which consisted of paved roads, steam-powered riverboats, and government-contracted mail carriages, also sped the flow of information (see Map 10.2). Apart from smoke signals, carrier pigeons, and a few experiments with optical telegraph relays, information traveled in this period only as fast as human beings.

● This meant that improvements in transportation were, by definition, improvements in communication. One measure of the impact of the new transportation network is how quickly people in various parts of the country received national news. When George Washington died in 1799 in Alexandria, Virginia, no one in New York City knew about it for a full week. The news took thirteen days to reach Boston and twenty-four days to reach Cincinnati. Just three decades later, President Jackson's State of the Union address would reach New York in 15.5 hours, Boston in 31 hours, and Cincinnati in just over two days. For those Americans living near these hubs of information exchange, shorter time lags meant new experiences of long-distance connection. It was now possible and meaningful to imagine that two related events could be happening simultaneously in different parts of the country. ● All of this was before the emergence of a national railroad system and before the introduction of the electromagnetic telegraph. Those advances

CLIMATES AND ECOLOGIES

MEDIA AND INFORMATION

Canal Country. "A new state of things is taking place in consequence of the opening of the New York and Ohio Canals," observed a young man from central Pennsylvania as he passed through Ohio in 1830. "Wheat etc. will now command the land and the country is beginning to assume a new appearance. . . ." Between 1820 and 1846, land values along the canal's route grew 91 percent. Like other canals of this era, the Erie Canal was a minimum of 4 feet deep and allowed boats to be dragged by animals traveling alongside the canal on a towpath. Canal boats traveled at slow speeds, but the reduced friction allowed a single animal to tow 50-ton barges. *Niday Picture Library/Alamy Stock Photo*

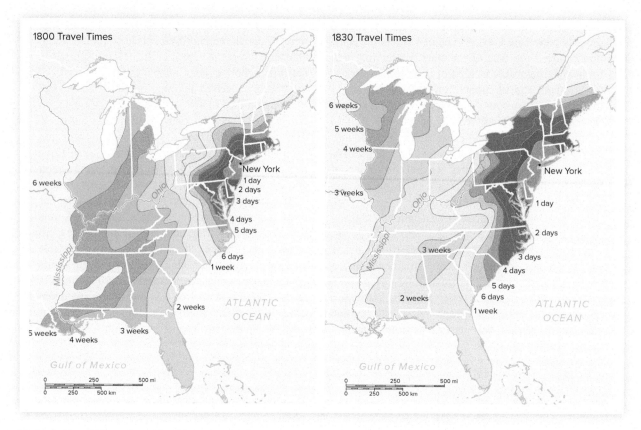

Map 10.2 Travel Times from New York, 1800 and 1830. Persons, goods, and information traveled along the same routes. For Americans living in the rural interior of the country, news arrived in the hands of a less steady stream of travelers, and current events unfolded along a much slower time line than for those in coastal cities. But the real distances between places were diminishing rapidly, well before the railroad or the telegraph.

would happen soon enough. But already in 1840, a revolutionary change had taken place.

URBANIZATION AND CITY GROWTH

Market expansion along the new transportation routes facilitated one of the most important developments in nineteenth-century American history: the transformation of the United States from a rural society to an urban one. When the Erie Canal was completed, the vast majority of Americans lived on farms and in villages. City life remained a minority experience in North America, as it had been for all of recorded history. The 1820 census found that only 7 percent of the population lived in settlements of twenty-five hundred people or more. Over the next hundred years, that proportion would increase steadily, finally reaching a majority by 1920. Many historical factors contributed to this century-long pattern of **urbanization,** but the spread of the market economy was pivotal. The

transportation revolution helped convert wilderness into farmland, but it also created new economic opportunities in the cities where agricultural goods were processed, exchanged, and distributed. Before 1830, Cleveland was a tiny village, and Chicago was not even incorporated, but state-funded canals had turned them (and countless lesser-known towns across the North and Midwest) into commercial centers by the middle of the century.

At the same time, the United States was becoming urban in another sense as well. What had made the early American republic a society of towns, villages, and farms was not simply the low percentage of people who lived in cities but also the low number of major cities overall and their relatively modest size. In 1800, only six places in the nation had more than 10,000 people, and the largest cities claimed barely 60,000. By comparison, London's population at the time was 865,000, and Paris had over 500,000. By midcentury, however, big-city life would become a central part of American culture.

TABLE 10. 1   LARGEST U.S. CITIES BY POPULATION: 1820, 1860, AND 2020

1820		1860		2020	
City	Population	City	Population	City	Population
New York	123,706	New York	813,669	New York	8,622,357
Philadelphia	63,802	Philadelphia	565,229	Los Angeles	4,085,014
Baltimore	62,738	Brooklyn	266,661	Chicago	2,670,406
Boston	43,298	Baltimore	212,418	Houston	2,378,146
New Orleans	27,176	Boston	177,840	Phoenix	1,743,469
Charleston	24,780	New Orleans	168,675	Philadelphia	1,590,402
Northern Liberties, PA	19,678	Cincinnati	161,044	San Antonio	1,579,504
Southwark, PA	14,713	St. Louis	160,773	San Diego	1,469,490
Washington, D.C.	13,247	Chicago	112,172	Dallas	1,400,337
Salem, MA	12,731	Buffalo	81,129	San Jose	1,036,242

The first modern metropolis in the United States was New York, which became the nation's most populous city at the end of the eighteenth century and has remained so ever since. New York grew quickly in the first quarter of the century, benefiting from transportation links to Britain that gave it competitive advantages over other eastern seaports. But in 1825, New York was still a compact settlement on the southern tip of Manhattan. The opening of the Erie Canal cemented the city's position as the nation's commercial capital by giving it superior transportation access to the West and making it the major inlet for foreign trade. • Over the next thirty-five years, New York's population quintupled to more than eight hundred thousand, swelled by the arrival of rural Northeasterners and foreign immigrants seeking better economic opportunities. By 1860, the population of Manhattan (Brooklyn remained a separate city until 1898) exceeded that of twenty of the thirty-three states in the union. •

New York was the largest of nine major American cities that had grown to over one hundred thousand by the 1860 census (see Table 10.1). Five of these cities were on the Atlantic Coast, three (Cincinnati, St. Louis, and New Orleans) were located on major rivers, and another

CROSSING BORDERS

(Chicago) fronted one of the Great Lakes. All were connected through the national network of water transport. Significantly, relatively little of the period's urban growth took place in the South, which benefited much less directly from the new canal projects and, because of the prevalence of slavery, did not attract large numbers of wage laborers. The largest Southern cities lay on major waterways at the periphery of the region (Baltimore, St. Louis, and New Orleans). As a whole, the South was a less urban society; its cities were fewer, smaller, and farther between.

CITIES, CROWDS, AND STRANGERS

America's growing cities were not simply bigger in the 1830s than they had been before; they were different social environments. Whereas even the nation's largest urban centers had been compact communities in which people recognized one another (see Chapter 8), cities were now places where newcomers experienced the pleasures, dangers, and alienation of modern anonymous living. It was during this period that residents and visitors in U.S. cities took notice of the **urban crowd.** Edgar Allan Poe, who was a product of this new urban setting, drew upon the mysteriousness of the crowded metropolis to create the modern detective story during the 1840s. In the first of his urban mysteries, "The Man of the Crowd" (1840), Poe's narrator follows an anonymous old man through city streets at night, trying unsuccessfully to figure out his story. Cities had become worlds of strangers.

Several new institutions contributed to the creation of this new urban environment in a handful of big U.S. cities between 1825 and 1835. The first was fixed-route public transit, which allowed strangers to navigate the city without having to know or communicate with other people. The horse-drawn **omnibus** (the word was later shortened to *bus*) provided regular service along New York's Broadway beginning in 1829. Within a few years, urban transit companies were operating omnibuses in Boston; Philadelphia; Baltimore; New Orleans; Washington, D.C.; and Brooklyn. Omnibuses were soon joined by street railway cars, also powered by horses. Transit systems contributed to the sprawling growth of American cities by expanding the distances people could conveniently travel between home and work.

The second major urban innovation was commercial nightlife, which was marked by the introduction of **gaslight.** Baltimore was the first city to light its streets with gas lamps in 1817, and New York had adopted the practice by 1825. By later standards, gas lamps provided only partial illumination and created none of the spectacle that would be associated with electrified cityscapes at the end of the century. Nonetheless, it signaled an important change. In earlier periods, city streets were largely empty after nightfall, but the new technologies of outdoor illumination served a growing market for late-night entertainment. Restaurants, bowling alleys, oyster bars, saloons, cheap theaters, dance halls, and various commercial sex venues catered to this market and changed the look and feel of nighttime. By midcentury, observers and reformers were describing what went on in cities after dark in sensational terms. One popular journalist decried "the fearful mysteries of darkness in the metropolis—the festivities of prostitution, . . . the haunts of theft and murder, the scenes of drunkenness and beastly debauch." Put less dramatically, the gas-lit city offered many city dwellers, especially young men, a new world of nocturnal activity that we now take for granted.

THE RISE OF THE PENNY PRESS

In addition to streetcars and gas lamps, city people relied on daily newspapers to guide them through unfamiliar urban environments. Newspapers were not new in the second quarter of the nineteenth century, but they were proliferating rapidly and attracting much greater readership. Between 1830 and 1840, the number of daily papers in the United States doubled, and their circulation rose proportionately. This trend was closely related to the rise of the Second Party System. With an expanded electorate and intense competition between the two parties, Democrats and Whigs were especially motivated to found newspapers. Many papers, especially outside of big cities, were essentially party organs that brought in little revenue.

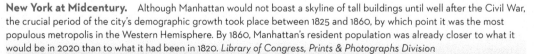

New York at Midcentury. Although Manhattan would not boast a skyline of tall buildings until well after the Civil War, the crucial period of the city's demographic growth took place between 1825 and 1860, by which point it was the most populous metropolis in the Western Hemisphere. By 1860, Manhattan's resident population was already closer to what it would be in 2020 than to what it had been in 1820. *Library of Congress, Prints & Photographs Division*

But if the party emerged victorious at the polls, newspapers' publishers were rewarded with government printing contracts. Other factors contributed to the growth of print journalism, including innovations in transportation, printing, papermaking, and corrective eyewear. But probably no cause was as important as the increased participation of ordinary men in partisan politics.

In big cities, daily news consumption was especially widespread. In New York, one copy of a daily newspaper appeared for every 16 residents in 1830. Twenty years later, the ratio had dropped to one for every 4.5 residents, and the ratio was one to 2.2 on Sunday. But the bigger change was in the kind of papers that circulated. In 1833, twenty-three-year-old journeyman printer Benjamin Day introduced the first daily to sell for a penny, the **New York Sun,** and within a few months it became the most popular paper in the city. At the time, the leading metropolitan papers of the time cost six cents and relied on subscriptions by merchants and lawyers. The *Sun* offered a smaller, cheaper product to a mass readership and employed an army of newsboys to hawk individual copies of the paper in the streets on a daily basis. This model of cheap news spread quickly to other big cities and changed the news business.

The **penny press** initiated new, less affluent readers into the daily habits of reading the news. Some of the early cheap dailies also had ties to working-class politics, but after the Panic of 1837 many of those publications folded. The penny papers that survived the depression attracted readers from different classes and usually disclaimed any formal identification with particular political parties. Newspapers like the *New York Sun*, the *Boston Daily Times,* and their many followers appealed to a wide local readership by offering popular stories, descriptions of city life, and classified advertising that helped ordinary city dwellers find work, entertainment, services, and consumer products.

The cheap dailies introduced a new brand of journalism to modern urban life. Though they continued older traditions of covering national politics and listing ship arrivals, penny papers pioneered the use of sensational stories to boost circulation. Two years into its existence, the *New York Sun* ran a series of articles, allegedly reprinted from a Scottish scientific journal, describing recent discoveries of life on the moon. • The articles' detailed reports of spherical amphibians that rolled instead of walking, blue goats with single horns, two-legged beavers, and short, hairy men with bat wings turned out to be fiction, but during the height of the 1835 Moon Hoax controversy, the *Sun*'s circulation soared to almost twenty thousand, making it in all likelihood the best-read daily newspaper in the world. •

MEDIA AND INFORMATION

More often, the leading news stories covered in the penny press were closer to home and rooted in real events. Typically, these stories revolved around sex and violence. Probably the most talked-about news event in urban America during the first decades of the cheap daily press was the 1836 murder of Helen Jewett, a New York sex worker (see Singular Lives: Dorcas Doyen, Tabloid Victim). Accounts of Jewett's life, descriptions of her corpse, and detailed coverage of the trial and acquittal of her accused killer dominated the penny papers, boosted their circulation, and established their new, modern role as an authoritative source of information for events of perceived public interest.

WORK, UNIONS, AND CLASS STRUGGLE

Big cities were also transformed during this period by changes in the workplace brought about by industrialization. At this early stage in industrial development (pre–Civil War), only about 10 percent of the labor force was engaged in manufacturing, and most of those workers spent their days in small workshops, making things with their hands, not with automated machinery. In these workshops, industrialization took the form of new strategies for reorganizing craftwork.

Urban employers (master craftsmen and entrepreneurial manufacturers) devised new ways to make the labor process more efficient and profitable, and these new methods changed the customary patterns and rhythms of work and leisure. They eliminated traditional practices such as drinking on the job and Monday absenteeism; they increasingly bought workers' time rather than their products; and they measured that time with new precision.

Employers also began rationalizing and **deskilling** the production process, dividing it up so as to minimize the amount of skilled labor required. Instead of training apprentices to master various parts of a trade, which they could perform with greater skill and reward over the course of their working lives, masters assigned certain parts of a trade to skilled craftsmen and other parts to workers who would continue to perform just that task. Clothing production, for example, was broken down into cutting, a relatively skilled occupation, and sewing, which could be contracted out to less skilled workers. Shoemaking, similarly, became two distinct tasks. Women were hired to stitch the upper half of shoes for lower rates of pay than men received to construct the outsole, shank, and heel.

The combined effect of deskilling and tighter managerial control was to reduce artisans' expectations for advancement within an occupation and to weaken the

SINGULAR LIVES

Dorcas Doyen, Tabloid Victim

In the weeks after she was found bludgeoned to death in her bed at a high-end brothel, a woman known as Helen Jewett was probably the most famous person in New York City. Jewett was murdered at the dawn of a new era in the history of American journalism, and the city's cheap newspapers filled their columns with information and misinformation about Jewett and speculation about the crime. Every day, new stories appeared in print, describing a prostitute of unparalleled beauty and charm, who read the poetry of Lord Byron and won the hearts of the rich and famous until her tragic demise.

Behind the sensational stories, the woman who adopted the work name "Helen Jewett" led a life that fit some more ordinary patterns in the history of the growing American city. Dorcas Doyen was born in Maine to a poor rural family and worked from a young age as a domestic servant for a judge in Augusta. Forced to leave when it was discovered that she was a sexually active teenager, Doyen moved to larger cities and began working in brothels. She arrived in New York in 1832 at the age of nineteen, part of a tide of young New Englanders migrating in search of social and economic opportunities.

Doyen was just one of many young women who tried to make a living in New York's expanding sex trade, which became more visible and popular during the first half of the nineteenth century. Pushed by low wages to consider alternative or additional work, increasing proportions of women sold sex for money. Though few catered to as elite a clientele as

Doyen, a number of women in the trade enjoyed considerable autonomy and accumulated significant assets.

Yet sex workers also faced serious risks in nineteenth-century cities. To reduce the dangers of infection and violence, prostitutes sought protection in brothels. But brothels were often attacked, and the women who worked there did not enjoy the full protection of the law. Her accused killer, Doyen's former lover, Richard Robinson, got away with murder in part because the judge presiding over his trial instructed the jury to disregard the testimony of women in the sex trade. Though Robinson faced a mountain of incriminating evidence, the only witnesses who could place him at the scene of the murder were, of course, sex workers.

Where in the Archives?

Doyen was one of many sex workers in New York in the 1830s. What we know about their circumstances and careers comes largely from police records and the writings of anti-prostitution reformers. But in Doyen's case, news reporting on her murder and the trial of her alleged killer thrust the details of her life into public view.

Because her extensive correspondence with Richard Robinson was introduced into evidence at the trial and then published a decade later in the popular crime press, we have access to printed copies of forty-three letters she wrote to him. Those letters can be found in five issues of the *National Police Gazette* from 1849, which is available through select libraries.

Helen Jewett. The original black-and-white version of this popular image of Jewett was printed shortly after her death. Readers of the story unfolding in the press would recognize the letter under her belt as a hint that she was delivering a message to Richard Robinson, the man charged with her murder. *Hum Historical/Alamy Stock Photo*

But in a fictionalized account of the murder, *The Lives of Helen Jewett and Richard P. Robinson,* published in 1849, George Wilkes and H. R Howard included several letters from the actual Jewett-Robinson correspondence. The account is available through HathiTrust (https://www.hathitrust.org/).

Assignment

Read Chapters 30–33 (pages 105–115) and pay special attention to the letters between Jewett and Robinson shortly before the murder. In 300 words, address the following question:

1. What is surprising to you in the way the sex worker and her client write to each other?

association between manual labor and a life calling. This was a dramatic shift in the world view of American craftsmen. Elite craftsmen with access to credit and capital withdrew from the workplace and became manufacturing entrepreneurs, and others in the same craft faced a future of wage labor. Many urban workers now identified less with the masters in their own trades and more with those at the same skill level and hierarchical status in other trades.

Beginning in the 1820s, workers in large cities responded to these changes by organizing labor unions. Philadelphia artisans took the lead in this movement, banding together to defend what a group of striking bookbinders called "their inalienable right . . . to affix a price on the only property we have to dispose of: our labor." Tradespeople had asserted their right to set prices on their work before, but only in the second quarter of the nineteenth century did American artisans from different trades coordinate their efforts on the grounds that they were all workers. Labor activists established a **General Trades Union** in New York in 1833, and over the next few years General Trades Unions sprouted up in more than a dozen U.S. cities. Most workers in New York belonged to such a union in the mid-1830s, as did significant proportions of urban working people elsewhere. During a three-year period between 1833 and 1836, American workers went on strike 172 times and were usually successful. Overall, the decade leading up to the 1837 financial collapse marked a high point of union struggles, before hard times, increased foreign immigration, and the use of state force to break strikes diminished the power of organized labor.

Strikes often expressed local grievances, but the central theme of union activity in the 1830s was control over the workplace, and especially the length of the workday. The **ten-hour movement** was a powerful organizing issue for American labor. Pay standards might vary from craft to craft and from city to city, but capping the workday at ten hours was something all workers could support. By the 1840s, unions and their political supporters had succeeded in establishing a ten-hour norm, beginning a century-long trend toward shorter working days in the United States.

Alarmed by changes in the workplace, urban artisans also turned to electoral politics. Workers' parties formed in Philadelphia and New York in the late 1820s. New York's labor party, led by a radical who advocated abolishing the private sale or rental of land and granting 160 acres to every man and unmarried woman, attracted considerable support in the 1829 elections. But soon thereafter, labor parties were absorbed or coopted by the Democrats. Urban workers often assumed leadership positions in those local Democratic factions that were more critical than the national party of the emerging industrial order.

Though the new industrial order took hold mostly in small workshop settings, a factory system did appear in a handful of much smaller cities in New England, where innovative technologies were used to convert raw cotton into finished fabrics. The most famous of these textile processing plants were in Waltham, Massachusetts, where the first fully integrated textile factory appeared in 1814, and nearby in Lowell. The **Waltham-Lowell system** employed female workers, mostly single women from New England farm families, and housed them in tightly regulated dormitories. Lowell was widely celebrated as a model of technological progress and worker contentment, and it attracted numerous young rural workers for whom a wage of approximately three dollars a week represented a significant economic opportunity (see How Much Is That? Textile Factory Pay in 1830). By the late 1830s, however, working conditions had deteriorated, and several disenchanted mill employees became labor activists. By the mid-1840s, mill companies had begun replacing New England farm girls with immigrants,

Time Table of the Holyoke Mills. Though they were unusually large, New England textile mills represented a growing trend toward precise timekeeping at the workplace. Mill operatives worked long hours, six days a week, regulated by an elaborate schedule of bells, beginning in this case at 4:40 A.M. *The Granger Collection, New York*

who were less likely to agitate for better wages and working conditions. These developments were well publicized at the time, but in the larger scheme of American labor and American urban development, Lowell was anomalous.

MILLENNIALISM AND AWAKENING

The era of canal building and early industrial development also saw the accelerating spread of evangelical Christianity. Church membership doubled between 1800 and 1835 relative to the population, and much of that growth took place in the last few years of the period. Americans were also turning to new religious ideas and movements beyond the borders of the major Protestant denominations. Large segments of American society were becoming more intensely religious while market relations, party politics, wage labor, and urbanization were eroding traditional patterns of living and laying the foundations of a modern culture.

REVIVALS ALONG THE CANAL ROUTE

Religious revivals and mass conversions, which had begun earlier with camp meetings, circuit riders, and tract societies (see Chapter 9), reached a climax after the opening of the Erie Canal. This was the height of what historians call the **Second Great Awakening,** when a charismatic Presbyterian minister named Charles Grandison Finney became the most successful evangelist in the nation. Finney was a lawyer in western New York who had attended church infrequently before he underwent a sudden conversion experience in 1821 and decided to preach. As he informed one of his clients, "I have a retainer from the lord Jesus Christ to plead his cause, and I cannot plead yours."

Finney looked around him at the world being remade by the canal and saw mushrooming towns and cities, Americans uprooting themselves continually in search of new prospects, and new work patterns removing young men from the scrutiny of their families. He decided the time was right for an evangelical campaign. In the part of western New York that came to be known as the **Burned-Over District** because of the religious enthusiasm that blazed through the canal region, Finney staged a series of revivals, culminating in a six-month stint in the booming city of Rochester in 1830 and 1831. He then moved to New York City, where he began preaching to massive audiences in a renovated theater. Over a long career, Finney was credited with bringing about the conversion of half a million souls with his emotional appeals and his message that contrary to orthodox Calvinist doctrine, human beings were moral free agents who could will their own salvation. He also transformed the conversion experience from a private moment in the individual conscience to a public event—one that competed with the new forms of commercial entertainment in the region's growing cities.

● At first, the religious old guard was hostile to Finneyite revivalism and worried about what they saw as a threat to the hierarchies of class and station that secured social order. In 1827, Reverend Lyman Beecher threatened Finney that if the evangelist tried to bring his revivals to Connecticut and Massachusetts, he would "call out the artillery-men." But as the market revolution spread, conservative clergymen overcame their scruples about revivalism. ● Four years after Beecher issued his threat, he was inviting Finney to speak in his own church. Following Finney's spectacular success in Rochester, Beecher declared his achievements "the greatest work of God, and the greatest revival of religion, that the world has ever seen."

The cultural impact of Finney's revivals was considerable, especially among middle-class, native-born Whigs in the North (see Chapter 12). Another group for whom the Second Great Awakening proved empowering was women. Religious worship provided the principal public occasions in which women rivaled or outnumbered men. In most Protestant churches, women formed a majority of those testifying to conversion experiences, signing church covenants, or becoming full members. Women began playing a larger role in determining the religious allegiances of their children. They also were able to assume more prominent positions in public religious life.

CONFLICTING FAITHS

Charles Grandison Finney Preaching to a New York Audience on Broadway. Using spectacle, advertising, and showmanship, Finney's revivals offered religious excitements that might counteract what he called "the great political and other worldly excitements" of the age. *Artokoloro/Alamy Stock Photo*

AMERICA AS SACRED SOIL: JOSEPH SMITH AND MORDECAI NOAH

While Finney's preaching revitalized American Protestantism, other religious visions were also taking root in the Burned-Over District. Joseph Smith, Jr., born in 1805, was a farm boy living near Palmyra, New York, when he began receiving revelations warning him to resist the local churches and await further instructions. At the age of seventeen, he announced to his family that an angel had directed him to golden plates buried at the top of a nearby hill. A few years later, after the Smith family lost their farm, young Joseph received permission from the angel to exhume the plates, along with special stones for translating the texts inscribed on them. Neighbors supported Smith during the two years he devoted to producing the text, which became the **Book of Mormon.** Published in 1830 and written in a style similar to the King James

translation of the Bible, the Book of Mormon describes the flight of a tribe of ancient Hebrews to the Americas, many centuries before Columbus. Jesus had appeared to them after his crucifixion, and their story held the key to restoring the true religion after eighteen centuries of collective error in worldwide Christendom.

Smith's vision and his sacred text helped reunify his disintegrating family during a time of economic upheaval along the canal route. It also formed the basis for a new patriarchal faith and a new **Church of Jesus Christ of Latter-day Saints,** which he established in 1830. The church appealed to many of his neighbors, and then to a community in Ohio, which Smith soon joined and absorbed. But Ohio was simply a temporary sojourn for Smith, who had announced in 1830 that the Saints (as Smith's followers called themselves) would gather in a new Zion in northwestern Missouri.

● Beset by dissension and financial troubles after the Panic of 1837, Smith took his flock westward to Missouri, and then in 1839 to Illinois, where they built a thriving city centered around a majestic limestone temple. In each of their homes, the Mormons, as Smith's followers were also called, faced persecution, sometimes for religious heterodoxy but mostly for being clannish or for seeming to form their own cooperative societies that existed apart from the laws of their neighbors. Ultimately, in 1844, Smith and his brother were killed by a mob. By then, Mormonism had become a sizable religion outside mainstream Christianity. ●

Some of the early appeal of the Mormon Church can be understood in the context of the social and economic struggles of local farmers hoping to restore a world of patriarchy and community that was threatened by the coming of the Erie Canal. But Mormonism, which is the oldest surviving non–Native American religion born in the United States, was also, at its core, a profoundly American faith. Whereas the New England Puritans had sanctified the land they colonized as a blank slate on which a model community might be transplanted, Mormonism placed the American continent at the center of its sacred geography. According to Smith's teachings, the Garden of Eden had been located in Jackson County, Missouri, and the resurrected Christ had appeared on American soil. Mormons saw what Europeans had called the New World as both a parallel Old World already graced by divine revelation and a new Zion where the Second Coming would be centered.

Around the same time that Smith was visited by his angel, a different utopian vision of America as the center of the world came to Mordecai Manuel Noah. A prominent Jewish playwright, newspaper editor, and politician from New York City, Noah sought to bring all of world Jewry to a colony on Grand Island in the Niagara River near Buffalo. On the day after the Jewish New Year in 1825, Noah appeared at a Buffalo Episcopal church as a "Judge of Israel," dressed in crimson silk robes he had borrowed from a New York production of Shakespeare's *Richard III*, and proclaimed to a gathering of mostly non-Jewish spectators that a city of refuge for Jews was hereby established. Named **Ararat,** after the place where the ark of the biblical Noah had come to rest following the flood, Mordecai Noah's colony was intended to attract persecuted Jews from foreign locales to a settlement along the Erie Canal. Nothing came of the ambitious plan, which was generally ignored or ridiculed in Europe, where most Jews lived. Ironically, however, Noah's dream that the United States would become a haven for European Jews and a center of Jewish life and culture would materialize over the next century.

THE END OF TIME

In different ways, both material progress and religious upheaval inspired many American Christians to suspect that they were living in apocalyptic times. **Millennialism,** which is the belief in the imminent arrival of the thousand-year reign of Christ and the angels on Earth prior to the Last Judgment, took different forms in American culture in the 1820s and 1830s. Some believed that the millennium was at hand because human beings had brought it about through moral, political, or scientific advances. Others believed that the millennium would begin miraculously and for no reason discernible to humanity. Either way, many Americans believed that the end was near. Joseph Smith had proclaimed in 1835 that "fifty-six years should wind up the scene." Others were even more optimistic or impatient. Various utopian communities, evangelical revivals, and new religions emerged during this period, and they all drew upon the rising millennial expectations of men and women living in the Northeast.

In 1831, a Baptist preacher named William Miller declared that 1843 would be the last "sure year of time" and that Christ would return to Earth by April 18, 1844. Miller based his prediction on an interpretation of the Book of Daniel, rather than on any local sign, but the widespread millennial expectations around him made this prediction seem more plausible. His followers, known as **Millerites,** circulated millions of pages of tracts and preached to half a million listeners in summertime tent meetings between 1842 and 1844. April 18, 1844, came and went without any discernible messianic arrivals, but the Millerites concluded that there had been a miscalculation and that the advent would occur the following Yom Kippur, the Jewish Day of Atonement. With a new target date, Millerites quit their jobs, settled accounts, and rushed to get baptized. But at the foretold moment, Miller's followers were disappointed. Many of them kept the movement alive under new leadership and became the Seventh-Day Adventists.

Other notable millennialist sects created during this period included the followers of Robert Matthews, a former carpenter in New York, who decided he was a Jewish messiah and called himself the Prophet Matthias. He convinced three wealthy merchants to bankroll his utopian community in the early 1830s, which attracted the formerly enslaved woman who would later take the name Sojourner Truth. Matthews was ultimately imprisoned for fraud, one of the first major scandals covered obsessively in New York's penny papers. Equally notorious were John Humphrey Noyes's Perfectionists, who believed that the Second

Coming had already taken place. Noyes had been converted by Finney in 1831 and ultimately concluded that conversion produced complete release from sin. In 1841, he struck out on his own to start a small community in Vermont, where members shared property and practiced what he called "complex marriage" (every man in the community was simultaneously married to every woman), until Noyes was prosecuted for adultery and fled to Oneida, New York.

CONCLUSION

The United States was not yet an industrial power in 1845, and by later standards it was not especially democratic. But market relations and a more participatory political system had begun to erode older patterns of social hierarchy. In the twenty years after the opening of the Erie Canal, enormous changes had taken place across much of the country—at the ballot box, on the farm, in the workshop, at church, and in city streets. A new party system associated with the rise of Andrew Jackson put politics at the center of new mass rituals among white men. Farmers in the continent's interior labored to the uncertain rhythms of distant markets. Artisans and entrepreneurs reorganized the way goods were manufactured. Increasing proportions of Americans crowded into cities and built new kinds of urban communities, including a crowded commercial metropolis in New York. For some men and women, these changes appeared so dramatic as to call for radical adjustments in religious outlook. But even for those who clung to older communities and world views, new political, economic, and social realities were making the country seem both more massive and more interconnected.

STUDY TERMS

Jacksonian Democracy	Erie Canal
New York State Constitution of 1821	urbanization
	urban crowd
universal manhood suffrage	omnibus
election of 1824	gaslight
corrupt bargain	*New York Sun*
spoils system	penny press
Peggy Eaton affair	deskilling
nullification crisis	General Trades Union
deposit removal	ten-hour movement
bank war	Waltham-Lowell system
Panic of 1837	Second Great Awakening
Democrats	Burned-Over District
Antimasons	Book of Mormon
Whigs	Church of Jesus Christ of Latter-day Saints
Second Party System	
paper ballots	Ararat
industrialization	millennialism
canals	Millerites

FURTHER READING

A database of additional full-text readings is available through Power of Process for Primary Sources in Connect.

Peter Baldwin, *In the Watches of the Night* (2012), tracks the growth of nightlife in American cities.

Edward J. Balleisen, *Navigating Failure* (2001), describes the impact of bankruptcy after the Panic of 1837 on perceptions of success and failure in American economic life.

Patricia Cline Cohen, *The Murder of Helen Jewett* (1998), provides a thorough account of the intriguing and tragic life of antebellum New York's most famous murder victim.

Vincent DiGirolamo, *Crying the News* (2019), presents a thorough account of the rise of the American newsboy.

Alexander Keyssar, *The Right to Vote* (2000), tells the tangled history of suffrage extension in the United States.

Bruce Laurie, *Artisans into Workers* (1997), synthesizes the history of and labor movements during the era of industrialization.

Andrew Robichaud, *Animal City* (2019), highlights the centrality of animal life to American cities in the early nineteenth century.

Mary Ryan, *Civic Wars* (1998), describes the vitality of outdoor political life in large U.S. cities in this period.

Charles Sellers, *The Market Revolution* (1991), explains the political and religious developments of the period as responses to the incursion of market relations values into everyday life.

Jeffrey Sklansky, *Sovereign of the Market* (2017), analyzes the ideas at stake in the debate about commercial banking in the Jacksonian era.

Laurel Thatcher Ulrich, *House Full of Females* (2017), explores the experiences of women in the early years of Mormonism.

1831–1844

11 | SLAVERY & THE SOUTH

Chapter Questions

1. How did the spread of cotton cultivation alter the lives of people living in slavery and their enslavers in the South?

2. How did the slave system affect Southerners who were neither slaveholders nor enslaved?

3. How did family, community, and religious outlook shape men's and women's lives in the South?

4. In what ways were the 1830s a pivotal decade in the political status of slavery in the United States?

"Old Sarah," Tintype Photograph. The experiences of millions of enslaved African Americans triggered new conflicts in antebellum America. *Universal History Archive/Universal Images Group/Getty Images*

In February 1831, a solar eclipse darkened the midday sky of Southampton County, Virginia, home to the enslaved Baptist preacher Nat Turner. Looking skyward, Turner later recalled, he saw "white spirits and black spirits engaged in battle" while "the thunder rolled in the Heavens, and blood flowed in streams." Turner had waited years for such an omen, ever since a revelation that the day was coming when all the world's hierarchies would crumble. In preparation for the earthly version of the battle he observed in the heavens, Turner recruited several associates. That August, a black spot appeared on the sun, and crimson flames lit the sky. Judgment Day had come.

Turner's enslaver and his enslaver's family were the first to die on the early morning of August 22. Over the next two days, Turner led about sixty enslaved people as they murdered at least fifty-five white men, women, and children on nearby farms. Virginia militias and white vigilante groups mustered quickly, killing Turner's followers on the spot or after capture. Turner himself, however, escaped. A manhunt ensued, and newspaper

Time Line

1829
David Walker publishes *Appeal . . . to the Coloured Citizens of the World*

1831
William Lloyd Garrison begins publishing *The Liberator*
Nat Turner leads a slave rebellion in Virginia

1833
American Anti-Slavery Society formed
British Parliament abolishes slavery in Britain's colonies

1835
Antislavery petitions spark controversy in Congress
Charleston lynch men raid the post office to destroy antislavery publications
Second Seminole War begins

1836
Houses passes the gag rule, preventing the discussion of slavery
Santa Anna defeats Texan rebels at the Alamo
Texas declares independence from Mexico

1839
Joseph Cinqué leads a mutiny of kidnapped Africans aboard the *Amistad*

1841
Supreme Court rules in favor of the *Amistad* captives

reports placed him across state lines or hidden in a swamp between Virginia and North Carolina—an area where those fleeing slavery survived on frogs, terrapins, and snakes. Finally, two months after the insurrection, Turner was discovered hiding in the ground close to home, camouflaged by branches and leaves. In short order, he was convicted and hanged.

The year 1831 marked the beginning of a new era in the history of Southern slavery. For some whites in the tobacco-growing Chesapeake, Turner's rebellion dramatized the dangers of holding large numbers of African Americans in bondage. For most whites in the larger cotton-producing region of the South, however, the lessons were different. As the international demand for cotton soared in the 1830s, so did the value of slave labor. And to most slaveholders, Turner's

revolt pointed not to the dangers of enslaving people but to those of criticizing slavery. For though he claimed to have seen omens in the skies, it was suspected that Turner, who could read and write, had been inspired by signs of a different kind—those of a growing antislavery movement in the North. Earlier that year, a white Bostonian began publishing a weekly newspaper calling for the immediate and uncompensated emancipation of every enslaved person in the United States. Two years before, a free African American had published a powerful critique of slavery and raised the specter of those living in slavery rising up against their enslavers. Although there is no evidence that Turner had seen either publication, slaveholders perceived new dangers in allowing those they owned to read, write, and even preach the gospel.

Once a small part of a hemispheric slave system, the American South became one of its main stages in the second quarter of the nineteenth century. From the Caribbean to South America, slave systems were falling. In the American North, slavery was nearing extinction as a result of full or gradual abolition laws. As slavery became the "peculiar institution" specific to the Southern states, slaveholders grew less tolerant of anything that might threaten their regime. By the 1840s, more than two million people were being held as property under that regime, many of them living far west of the world turned momentarily upside down by Nat Turner. Under the constraints of a rigid system of labor discipline and racial subordination, enslaved people helped build a new culture in the South. At the same time, the entrenchment of Southern slavery, in both the economy and national politics, would begin to unsettle the truce between slave and free states that had prevailed since the Missouri Compromise. In a remarkably short period, slavery would become a bitterly divisive issue in American life.

THE WORLD OF COTTON

The persistence and expansion of slavery in the United States were driven, above all else, by cotton. When the tobacco market collapsed at the end of the eighteenth century, many prominent Southerners began to rethink the region's commitment to human bondage. As relentless tobacco cultivation exhausted Southern soil, plantation owners questioned the economics of chattel slavery. Thomas Jefferson expected slavery to wither away as planters diversified their crops and relied less on gang labor. But cotton changed the script. Beginning in the final decades of the eighteenth century, demand for this raw material grew in the industrial centers of England, where textile production had become mechanized. English manufacturers sold cotton goods to expanding markets throughout the European continent, as well as in Africa, Latin America, and India. As Southern planters focused on supplying this growing global trade, slave labor acquired greater value. Enslaved people were on the move again, uprooted from their homes and treated as chattel within the U.S. slave trade.

COTTON BECOMES KING

Very little cotton had been cultivated on American soil during the colonial period. As late as 1790, annual cotton production in the United States amounted to only three thousand bales. Yet over the next fifty years, cotton would become the dominant staple crop of the South and the nation's leading export. Eli Whitney's invention of the **cotton gin** (short for *cotton engine*) in 1793 often gets credit for launching the South as cotton supplier to the world, since the gin separated cotton fibers from the seeds more quickly than could human hands alone. It was especially useful in the processing of the short-staple variety of cotton, which grew well in the interior of the country but was difficult to process by hand. The impact of Whitney's machine has been exaggerated, however. Other cotton gins had existed before Whitney's, and short-staple cotton cultivation had already begun to expand. The machines most responsible for the cotton kingdom were the steam engines that powered textile mills in England. The cotton gin was more the *consequence*, rather than the cause, of growing interest in cotton cultivation.

Neither cotton gins nor steam-powered textile factories instantaneously created a cotton kingdom. Annual cotton production in the United States rose steadily from 178,000 in 1810 to three hundred thousand in 1820 and to seven hundred thousand in 1830 as cotton plantations spread westward into land that had been acquired from France and Spain or wrested from the Cherokee and the Creek peoples. By 1860, Southerners were harvesting over 4 million bales of cotton each year, which amounted to 68 percent of the world market.

A number of factors put the South in a position to take advantage of the rising global demand for cotton. ● Though cotton is a sturdy, nonperishable plant that can be shipped across long distances, it grows only in certain climates. Land in the United States north of 37° latitude lacked the soil conditions, rain patterns, and number of frost-free days per year to sustain cotton cultivation. Southern landowners were also able to command enslaved laborers working in field gangs and thus could grow cotton more efficiently. ● The turn to cotton cultivation between 1790 and 1830 breathed new life into Southern slavery during the same period when Northern states were abolishing the institution.

As cotton production took off after 1830, it became the backbone of the regional economy of the U.S. South. Unlike tobacco, rice, and indigo, cotton thrived far from the seaboard, on all kinds of terrain south of 37° latitude. Whereas sugar and rice cultivation required large investments in expensive machinery, even small-scale slave operations could grow cotton at a profit. Although a small group of cotton plantation owners controlled significant proportions of the region's wealth, they represented a tiny fraction of the slave-holding class. The vast majority of slaveholders during the antebellum (pre–Civil War) period owned fewer than twenty people, and the cotton trade benefited them, too, even if they lived in parts of the South that did not produce cotton (see Map 11.1). Slaveholding tobacco farmers in Virginia, for example, had a stake in the cotton boom because it raised the value of their human property. By 1840, the economic relationship between cotton and slaveholding was so direct that one could determine the price of an enslaved person by multiplying the price of a pound of cotton by ten thousand.

Although cotton made slavery especially profitable in the South, it also tied the slaveholding states to the larger national economy. Because it accounted for more than half the nation's exports, cotton paid for the

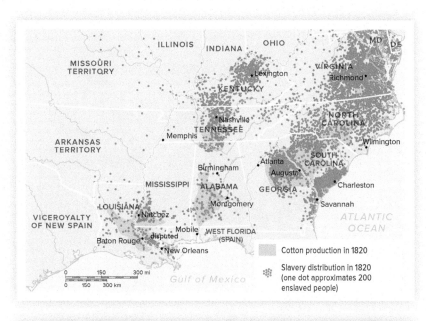

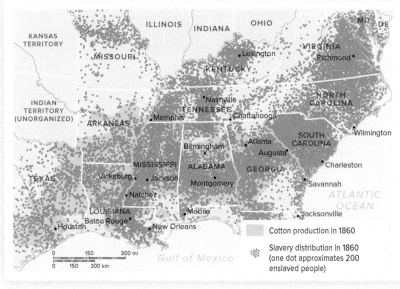

Map 11.1 Cotton and Slavery, 1820–1860. The spread of short-staple cotton cultivation refashioned the map of slavery in the United States in a few decades. South Carolina remained a center of large slaveholdings, but new concentrations of enslaved African Americans emerged in the rich-soil areas of central Alabama and Mississippi.

slave South its distinctive economic character, but it also cemented new bonds of national economic interdependence.

THE DOMESTIC SLAVE TRADE

On January 1, 1808, it became illegal to import enslaved people into the United States (see Chapter 8). However, as the international slave trade ended, the domestic slave trade intensified. ● Between 1790 and 1860, slaveholders relocated some 1 million human beings from Virginia, Maryland, and the Carolinas to states in the interior of the country. Some of these men, women, and children traveled with their owners, as entire plantations relocated to cotton country. But two-thirds of the migration took the form of interstate commerce—enslaved people were sold to new owners in other states. The number of African Americans sold across state lines in the seven decades between the ratification of the Constitution and the beginning of the Civil War exceeded the number of Africans who had been brought to the thirteen colonies or to the United States during the entire history of the international slave trade. ●

To slaveholders in the exporting states, the domestic slave trade was a major source of income. For a new class of professional slave traders, the transfer of half a billion dollars in human property was a big and well-organized business. But to the enslaved people involved in this trade, the march westward was a dreadful experience, which typically entailed being manacled to one another and confined in pens or ship holds for long

nation's imported goods and stimulated industry in the North. New York City was the leading distribution center and outlet for the cotton trade, and its fate as the nation's commercial capital was bound up with cotton—and with slavery. Cotton thus gave the

periods. Being sold also meant being uprooted from home and separated, often permanently, from parents, children, spouses, kin networks, lovers, and friends. About one in four interstate slave sales during this period severed a first marriage, and one in two destroyed a nuclear family. Furthermore, laboring conditions in Deep South locales such as Alabama's cotton fields and Louisiana's sugar plantations were often more brutal than those in the Upper South. For all these reasons, threats to sell people westward "down the river" could be especially traumatizing and effective.

The possibility of sale framed the experience of slavery during the antebellum period. For slaveholders, the slave market determined the value and liquidity of their property. For the enslaved, it undermined the stability of their most intimate relationships. Many white Southerners considered slave sales distasteful and the professionals who executed those sales disreputable. But the domestic slave trade lay at the foundation of slavery. As much as physical punishment, work without wages, inferior legal status for oneself and one's offspring, or lifetime obligation to an enslaver, the prospect and possibility of being sold as property defined what it meant to live in slavery in the antebellum South.

Slave Coffle. Enslaved people in the South were an intensely mobile population, and their dispersal made it both more difficult to maintain local communities and easier to forge loose bonds of common African American identity. This engraving depicts a coffle (a line of human beings shackled to one another) in Washington, D.C., around 1815 (note the uncompleted Capitol building in the background), though the image probably dates to the 1850s. *Hulton Archive/Getty Images*

POWER AND CONTROL UNDER SLAVERY

Over 2 million men, women, and children lived in slavery in the United States in 1830, almost all of them in the South. By the time of the Civil War, the slave population would approach 4 million. There was no single experience for all of them. Many enslaved people picked cotton in the fields; others grew hemp, wheat, corn, rice, sugar, or tobacco; and still others performed domestic service, mastered crafts, preached the gospel, managed others, or worked in factories. Some labored in large slave gangs and lived in areas with high Black populations, whereas others belonged to slaveholders who owned a small number of people and lived in towns with large white majorities.

Despite this range of experiences, however, enslaved people across the South shared the experience of living in a society dominated by free whites. Overall, about one-third of the South was enslaved, though the proportion was lower in the Upper South and higher in the Deep South. Most of the white majority did not own enslaved people (see Figure 11.1) but considered them to be their inferiors, in need of surveillance and subordination. Enslaved people in the South thus had to negotiate a brutal system of labor exploitation without the kind of communal support available to enslaved populations in other parts of the world.

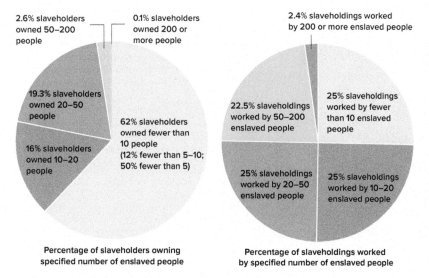

2.6% slaveholders owned 50–200 people

0.1% slaveholders owned 200 or more people

19.3% slaveholders owned 20–50 people

62% slaveholders owned fewer than 10 people (12% fewer than 5–10; 50% fewer than 5)

16% slaveholders owned 10–20 people

Percentage of slaveholders owning specified number of enslaved people

2.4% slaveholdings worked by 200 or more enslaved people

22.5% slaveholdings worked by 50–200 enslaved people

25% slaveholdings worked by fewer than 10 enslaved people

25% slaveholdings worked by 20–50 enslaved people

25% slaveholdings worked by 10–20 enslaved people

Percentage of slaveholdings worked by specified number of enslaved people

Figure 11.1   Slavery in the American South, 1840. Questions for Analysis: From the perspective of the enslaved, how uncommon was it to live in a household with twenty or more others, also enslaved? From the perspective of Southern slaveholders, how common was it to own twenty or more workers?

PLANTATION LIFE

For about half of those living in slavery in the South, life centered on the **plantation,** a large farm where crops were grown primarily for sale in distant markets rather than for local consumption. Some toiled on large sugar, cotton, or rice plantations where absentee slaveholders commanded the labor of more than one hundred enslaved workers. But in the antebellum era, most people in slavery lived and worked on smaller farms, with fewer than thirty others, whose owners lived on the property. This meant that slaveholders; their wives, overseers, and white children; and the enslaved lived side by side and sometimes knew one another intimately, though on grossly unequal terms.

On most plantations, the slaveholder's family occupied the big house, whereas enslaved people slept in crude, one-room log cabins. On larger plantations, the slave quarters formed rows that displayed the wealth of the slaveholder but also emphasized the disparity in living conditions of whites and Blacks. Slave clothing was also crude, consisting of two to four work suits made from a coarse fabric, known as "Negro cloth," that was manufactured in the North and sold to slaveholders.

In areas other than shelter and clothing, the enslaved tended to benefit more directly from the living standard of their enslavers. They ate more nutritiously than did people enslaved in the colonial period and received better

medical care than most Southern whites who were not slaveholders. For these reasons, enslaved African Americans grew taller and lived longer than people enslaved in the Caribbean, whose slaveholders did not typically reside nearby. More generally, those in slavery in the South experienced better basic material conditions than forced laborers in other societies but had to endure much greater surveillance and interference in their daily lives and were far more vulnerable to sale and forced migration.

About three-quarters of those enslaved on plantations, both male and female, worked as field laborers, toiling six long days (from dawn until dusk) every week, often driven by the lash to produce at an especially intense pace. On Sundays, most fieldworkers had the day off and some used it to cultivate crops for their own use. Many of those who did not work in the fields, especially children, old men, and women, were house servants, who worked less intensively but with less time off. Smaller numbers served as blacksmiths or carpenters, and they were among those most likely to derive satisfaction from their work. Men who labored as slave drivers or foremen experienced elevated status on the plantation, and though they risked earning the animosity of other enslaved people, more often assumed leadership roles in slave communities. Perhaps the most respected occupations, from the perspective of the enslaved, were preaching and healing, since those skilled services were directed primarily toward others living in slavery, but these were not full-time responsibilities.

Whatever their occupation or their worksite, the enslaved were subject to a system of discipline that relied on the threat of violence. Enslavers, mistresses, and overseers frequently whipped their human property, and both the lash and the lacerated back became powerful symbols of the evil core of slavery in the rhetoric of abolitionists and the recollections of those formerly enslaved. Whippings and other forms of **corporal punishment** were often conducted publicly as a shaming ritual, but the humiliation undoubtedly paled beside the sheer physical torture of some of these tactics.

The Lash. In an autobiography that told of his successful escape from slavery, Henry Bibb included engravings and illustrations from abolitionist sources that graphically depicted the violence of Southern slaveholding. Here, two scenes of punishment—the whipping by an enslaver and the beating of an enslaved woman by her mistress—suggest the pervasiveness of that cruelty. *Everett Collection/Newscom*

Slaveholders administered punishments such as holding people's heads under water, having them mauled by dogs, or castrating them. One North Carolina slaveholder was charged in court with beating a pregnant woman "with clubs, iron chains, and other deadly weapons" over a four-month period that ended only with her death.

Most slaveholders condemned such sadistic excesses, but even those who prided themselves on kindness admitted to regularly beating their human property. Slaveholders had an interest in limiting the abuse so as not to damage the productivity (or resale value) of enslaved workers, but the fact that states passed laws against "cruel punishment" suggests that economic interest alone was not sufficient to prevent torture and physical abuse. After escaping slavery, Henry Bibb described the ingenious use of a hickory paddle specially designed for beating without inflicting wounds that would be detectable by neighbors or prospective buyers. The paddle was "bored full of quarter-inch auger holes, and every time this is applied to the flesh of a victim, the blood gushes through the holes" or a blister forms. Bibb and others would be tied up and doubled over during the beating while the paddle struck "those parts of the body which would not be so likely to be seen by those who wanted to buy slaves."

Historians have applied the term **paternalism** to the system of plantation authority in the antebellum South. To describe slaveholders as paternalistic is not to call them benevolent or to label slavery mild. Rather, it means that slaveholders knew intimately the people they enslaved, took an active and meddlesome interest in their lives, regarded them as childlike inferiors who needed protection, and felt entitled to exert absolute authority over them. This produced a complex set of constraints and loopholes for those in bondage to negotiate, and helps explain some features of slaveholder behavior that at first seem bizarre or inconsistent. The same Louisiana slaveholder who would order mass whippings of all his field laborers simply to instill discipline, for example, also bought them valued Christmas presents from New Orleans. Many slaveholders claimed to love their enslaved workers and would later be shocked to discover, during the Civil War, that these people no longer wished to work for them.

FAMILY LIFE AND SEXUAL RELATIONS

Many enslaved men and women sought the comforts of family life, but Southern laws did not recognize their marriages, and the domestic slave trade did not respect their familial bonds. Men—husbands and fathers—were especially vulnerable to sale, which may have contributed to the frequency with which people living enslaved named their sons after fathers and grandfathers. As a rule, families on larger plantations stood a better chance of remaining intact.

When given the opportunity, the enslaved managed to form lasting family relationships. They cared about patterns of extended kinship and, unlike their white neighbors, avoided marriages with first cousins. The most cherished family ties were those between parents and children. And contrary to a well-entrenched misconception, enslaved children in the antebellum period were mostly raised in two-parent households. Slaveholders had their own reasons for facilitating family formation. Enslaved people with family ties on the plantation were less likely to flee or rebel. Furthermore, both marriage and the prospect of marriage tended to encourage reproduction. In part because they had such a clear interest in the marital life of their labor force, slaveholders intervened frequently by banning marriages off the plantation, for example, or by punishing infidelity. People living in slavery also disapproved of extramarital affairs but did not share the white society's stated discomfort with premarital sexuality.

Living within their enslavers' households, enslaved people also had to negotiate the sexual demands of whites. Most interracial liaisons in the antebellum South involved white men and enslaved Black women, and many were not consensual. Because Southern laws did not define the rape of an enslaved person as a crime and because slaveholders had considerable control over the living conditions of their human property, women on the plantation faced a constant threat of sexual assault. Harriet Jacobs fled her North Carolina home to avoid the unwanted sexual advances of her enslaver and the recriminations of his humiliated wife. Celia, an enslaved woman in Missouri, killed her slaveholder/rapist and went to the gallows. Far more commonly, sex between white men and Black women resulted in an increase in the slave population. In her famous diary, the patrician mistress Mary Boykin Chesnut of South Carolina complained that "like the patriarchs of old our men live in all one house with their wives and concubines, and the mullatoes one sees in every family exactly resemble the white children."

Some slaveholders and the people they held in bondage formed long-term romantic relationships, and in a few instances enslaved men had such relationships with white women. In general, Southerners of both races seem to have been slightly more tolerant of interracial sexuality during this period than they would be after emancipation. But it is important to remember that all those encounters took place within an unequal relationship in which enslaved people had no legal protection against sexual coercion and violence.

ENSLAVED BY THE STATE

Local communities and state governments shared the slaveholder's interest in maintaining discipline, preventing insurrection, and defending the Southern slave system against outside criticism. After the Turner rebellion, state legislatures in the South intensified their efforts to regulate the lives of the enslaved. On the one hand, new laws interfered with the slaveholder's control of his plantation, setting minimum standards for food and shelter and making it illegal for enslavers to murder or mutilate the people they owned. At the same time, the states passed other laws limiting the movements of enslaved people and prohibiting them from possessing firearms or assembling without white supervision, even for religious services. Most states also made it illegal for whites to teach those living in slavery how to read or write, because legislators feared that a literate enslaved person could forge a pass allowing him or her to travel away from an enslaver (see Hot Commodities: Slave Passes), communicate across distances to other enslaved people, and fall under the influence of antislavery literature.

Restrictions on slave behavior were better enforced than restrictions on slave treatment. All Southern states maintained **slave patrols,** whose responsibilities included catching runaways, breaking up large or otherwise suspicious gatherings, and monitoring the movements of Black people. African Americans traveling through the countryside, free or enslaved, could expect to be apprehended by patrollers ("paddyrollers") asking for their papers. Recalling his enslaved childhood almost seven decades after emancipation, a North Carolinian saw the patrollers as "jes' like policemen, only worser." Patrol service was compulsory in several states, and both poor and rich white men staffed these patrols.

Perhaps the most significant initiative in Southern slavery after 1830 was a new series of laws making it harder for people to achieve their freedom. State legislatures stemmed the tide of private manumissions that had taken place during the decades after the Revolution (see Chapter 8) by limiting the rights of slaveholders to grant or sell freedom to their enslaved workers. States in the Deep South explicitly forbade private acts of emancipation. Whereas the number of private manumissions soared in other societies where slavery remained legal through this period, such as Cuba and Brazil, they declined sharply in the American South. By 1840, free Blacks made up only 8 percent of the South's total Black population, and a mere 3 percent in the Deep South.

New laws also targeted free Blacks, restricting their work options, denying them the right to testify against whites, prohibiting their association with enslaved people, requiring them to carry proof that they were not enslaved, and in some cases even forcing them to leave

HOT COMMODITIES
Slave Passes

In an age before passports, driver's licenses, and Social Security numbers, one class of Americans was nonetheless required to carry identification papers. Already in the seventeenth century, slave societies were using passes to track enslaved people who were away from their owners. In the antebellum South, this practice was institutionalized to the point that anyone traveling without such a pass was liable to be arrested.

A slave pass was essentially a letter of introduction from a slaveholder to an unknown white reader, authorizing the person carrying the pass to be out of the enslaver's immediate physical control (which was necessary if slaveholders wished to send them on errands). A typical pass was a handwritten note like the following sheet found in the papers of a Missouri slaveholder:

> *Gentilmen let the Boy Barney pass and repass from the first of june till the 4 To Columbus OM for this date 1852*
>
> *Samuel Grove*

This surveillance system highlighted three important facts about slave life in the South. First, because patrols monitored the movements of enslaved people in order to protect communities from insurrection, Blacks could expect to be routinely inspected. Second, because slaveholders offered substantial rewards for the retrieval of runaways, even white people not serving on patrols might have an incentive to ask a traveling African American for proof of identity. Third, because most of the free population was literate (the best evidence suggests that approximately 70 percent of the white men in the antebellum South could read) and most of the enslaved population was illiterate (somewhere between 5 and 10 percent

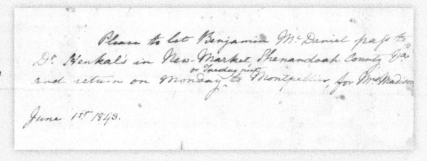

Slave Pass. This document grants permission for Benjamin McDaniel to travel to "Dr. Henkal's" in New Market, Virginia, on Thursday, June 1, 1843, and to return to Montpellier, Virginia, the following Monday or Tuesday. ©*Schomburg Center, NYPL/Art Resource, NY*

could read), the pass system could function in theory as a private communication medium among white people, borne on the bodies of Blacks.

But slave passes were imperfect tracking devices. Without other means of corroborating identity, a pass written for one could be used by another. Or those with legitimate but restricted passes could get a literate friend to alter the date, so that it could be used more flexibly. More generally, passes were highly susceptible to forgery. An enslaved person with rudimentary writing skills could attempt to copy a handwritten message to visit a relative on another plantation—or to escape to freedom. Buying passes was also an option. A New Orleans newspaper claimed that "any negro can obtain a pass for four bits or a dollar, from miserable wretches who obtain a living by such infamous practices." Henry Clay Bruce, who spent the first part of his life enslaved in Virginia and Missouri, recalled that passes could be counterfeited even more cheaply and simply. Since many of the patrolmen he met in Missouri were themselves illiterate, Bruce and his fellow captives were able to pawn off pages of

discarded correspondence as legitimate passes.

Slaveholders worried about forged passes and called attention to this risk in advertisements for runaways who knew how to read and write. In their autobiographies, formerly enslaved persons made the same connection between literacy and freedom and recounted stories of fabricating passes and manumission papers in order to escape. But the obstacles, risks, and deterrents to running away were considerable, even for those with access to fake passes, and the number of successful fugitives was far smaller than the number who could read and write. Literacy was probably less instrumental in slave escapes than either slaveholders or abolitionists claimed. More often, the ability to fake a pass brought moments of relief and freedom within a life of slavery.

Think About It

1. Why was the South's enslaved population primarily illiterate?

2. Why did slaveholders often mention in runaway advertisements whether the fugitive could read?

Pass Inspection. Slave patrols acquired a reputation for viciousness that only grew in the years after 1830 as Southern states restricted the movement of both enslaved people and freed people. This image shows an African American man surrounded by armed paddyrollers and their dog while his pass is scrutinized by lamplight. *CORBIS/Getty Images*

the state or face re-enslavement. The Southern legal system did not merely protect the property rights of slaveholders; it protected a system of racial subordination.

SLAVE RESISTANCE

Working in small slaveholding units, living under the close surveillance of their enslavers, and surrounded by a powerful white majority, those enslaved in America were unable to overthrow the regime on the model of Haiti, or even to stage armed revolts with the frequency or magnitude of their counterparts in Cuba, Brazil, or Suriname. Historians have documented at least two hundred fifty revolts on American soil and another two hundred fifty aboard slave ships, but most were limited in scope or impact, peripheral in their location, or relatively early in the history of Southern slavery. In fact, after Nat Turner there was no significant slave rebellion inside the South until the Civil War, when enslaved men took up arms and fought on the side of the Union.

But the absence of armed rebellion did not mean that African Americans accepted their fate. In countless ways, the enslaved sought to resist enslavers' claims to their labor and their lives. Everyday incidents of work sabotage, malingering, and theft, which whites interpreted as evidence of innate laziness and mendacity, gave enslaved people a small sense of control over their working conditions. On rare occasions, and when pushed to intolerable limits, a person in bondage would even violently confront a slaveholder or an overseer. Paradoxically, a key opportunity for strategic resistance appeared at precisely the moment when enslaved people seemed utterly powerless: at the point of sale. When slave traders attempted to obtain the highest price for their human merchandise, they depended on cooperation, as people for sale could be interrogated by a prospective buyer. In the course of the transaction, the enslaved had the power to represent their own ages, personal histories, medical conditions, habits, and attitudes. In the process, they could even sabotage or facilitate a proposed sale.

The most straightforward rejection of slavery, of course, was the decision to run away. Exactly how many enslaved African Americans fled the South each year is hard to determine, but Southern newspapers were filled with advertisements for runaways throughout the period (see Interpreting the Sources: Advertisements for Runaways).

INTERPRETING THE SOURCES
Advertisements for Runaways

Because most people living in slavery could not write about their lives, historians have relied heavily on the writings of white observers for detailed information about the daily experiences of the enslaved. Slaveholders recorded many observations, though, of course, their impressions and beliefs must be read critically. One especially interesting source of information about how enslaved people appeared to their slaveholders comes in the form of newspaper advertisements for the retrieval of fugitives.

The following advertisements appeared in the *Baltimore Sun*, the most popular daily newspaper in that city, in the 1840s:

Ranaway from the subscriber, living near Towsontown, on Tuesday, 25th inst., a **NEGRO BOY** by the name of Henry Hilton, about 19 years of age, very dark, and of a sullen look; a small scar on the cheek, occasioned by a burn; had on a dark cassinet pants, blue frock coat, and fine Jefferson boots. The above reward will be paid if returned to me.

DANIEL LEE

December 5, 1845

TWENTY DOLLARS REWARD. Ran away from the subscriber, living in Baltimore county, near the Copper Factory, on the 8th of July, A **NEGRO BOY,** who calls himself Dick Johnson; he is about 5 feet high, and stout built—17 or 18 years of age, with large, heavy eyes, wide mouth, and has lost the toes of his left foot by frost. His clothes were of coarse linen. He was purchased two years ago from Capers Burns who carried on the soap and candle business on Saratoga Street. There is no doubt he is lurking about the city, as he has been seen once or twice lately up town. I will give the above reward to any one who will bring him home to me, or secure him in jail so that I get him again.

LEVI HIPSLEY, near Cub Hill Post Office

August 6, 1844

ONE HUNDRED DOLLARS REWARD. Ran away from the subscriber on or about the 2nd inst., a negro woman named Sophia, though called Sophy. Said runaway negro woman is between thirty eight and forty years of age; bears her age well, is rather above the middle height; of a bright mulatto color; her front teeth are bad, some broken out; speaks very pleasantly; has no marks recollected; and is a very good looking servant.

The above reward will be paid is said runaway is taken without the state of Maryland; a reward of $50 if taken within the state and out of Baltimore City, and $30 is taken within Baltimore City; in each case, said negress to be either returned to her owner or lodged in Baltimore county jail.

TOBIAS E. STANSBURY

Baltimore County, April 26

TWO HUNDRED DOLLARS REWARD. Ran away from the subscriber, living on the north side of Severn, at the Ferry, about sunrise on the morning of the 25th November, a Negro Man, who calls himself HENRY HAMMOND. He was formerly the property of Dr. Rea, from whose estate I purchased him about four years ago. He is about 29 years of age; about 5 feet 6 inches high; very bright color, but not a mulatto; has a scar from the bite of a dog on one of his legs, which was seared with an iron to prevent hydrophobia. The clothing which he took with him, as far as can be ascertained, was a black cloth body coat, and black pantaloons, not very much worn; and plain black Russian hat. His working clothes, which he had on, are, drab pantaloons, which several patches on them, and drab coat, bull woolly; and a pair of new coarse pegged boots. It is probably that he has a pass bearing the name of Samuel Wilson, (a deceased negro) from whose wife he endeavored to obtain said pass during the last summer.

I will give 200 dollars for apprehension of the above described negro, if he is taken out of the state of Maryland; and if taken in the state I will give $100 if safely lodged in jail or delivered to me.

GEORGE B. HAYDEN, Annapolis, Nov. 25

November 26, 1840

Explore the Source

1. What sorts of signs do these advertisements rely on to help readers identify runaways?

2. What might you conclude about the material conditions of slavery from the information contained in these descriptions?

3. How might the advertisements reflect the distinctive conditions of urban slavery?

BEHIND THE IMAGE

In one of the more ingenious methods of escaping slavery, Henry "Box" Brown had himself shipped from Richmond to Philadelphia in 1849 in a small, wooden crate. Emerging after a journey of 350 miles and twenty-seven painful hours, Brown asked, "How do you do gentlemen?" and promptly passed out. This unsigned lithograph was published in Boston in 1850 under the title "The Resurrection of Henry Box Brown at Philadelphia" and sold as a fundraiser in support of Brown's larger campaign to publicize his escape through lectures, dramatic re-enactments, magic shows, and a vast panorama exhibition entitled *Henry Box Brown's Mirror of Slavery.*

"The Resurrection of Henry Box Brown at Philadelphia," Unsigned Lithograph, 1850.
Library of Congress, Prints & Photographs Division [LC-USZC4-4659]

WITHIN THE IMAGE

The lithograph features some of the abolitionists who were present when Brown emerged, including ❶ James Miller McKim and ❷ William Still, modeled on the likeness of Frederick Douglass both of whom hold tools that might have been used to free Brown from his confinement. ❸ The $3' \times 2' \times 2.5'$ crate itself symbolizes slavery, even though it is the vehicle of Brown's escape. ❹ The evident astonishment of the man holding the basket shows the appearance of Brown, alive, to be a miracle that parallels and compounds his miraculous escape from bondage. ❺ The lid, marked with the words "This Side Up," reminds readers that Brown was a package, a humorous yet deadly serious metphaor—as a critique of the treatment of human beings as chattel.

BEYOND THE IMAGE

Fellow fugitive Frederick Douglass criticized Brown for revealing and celebrating the details of his escape in visual displays such as this. "Had not Henry Box Brown and his friends attracted slaveholding attention to the manner of his escape," Douglass wrote, "we might have had a thousand Box Browns per annum." Instead, Brown's escape was a singular event. Samuel Alexander Smith, the white Virginian who helped arrange Brown's shipment, was apprehended and incarcerated for unsuccessfully attempting to repeat the maneuver with another enslaved person.

By 1850, slaveholders were sufficiently concerned with the issue of captives escaping to the North that they pushed for the enforcement of national fugitive slave laws. Some fugitives, like the famous orator and author Frederick Douglass, used the **Underground Railroad,** a loose network of secret escape routes, sympathetic hosts, and experienced guides, on his way North, though in his autobiography Douglass was careful to conceal the identities of his collaborators.

Successful escapes from the plantation (like prison breaks in later periods) were far less common than their prominence in the popular culture of the time might suggest. Especially after Indian removal, few people lived enslaved near the borders of states or nations to which they might flee. The thousands who made it safely to the North, to Canada, or to Mexico during this period were, statistically speaking, a drop in the bucket of Southern slavery. More frequently, they found short-term relief by absconding to a nearby location to avoid or protest mistreatment. The practice of temporary escape was sufficiently common that in 1839 a South Carolina judge explained to a jury charged with deciding whether a slave dealer had sold defective property that "occasional flights of a slave from his master's service for special causes would not constitute any material moral defect."

URBAN SLAVERY

The South as a whole was an overwhelmingly rural region in the antebellum period, and the enslaved were a predominantly rural people. Nonetheless, in 1820, people living in slavery accounted for at least one-fifth of the residents of all major Southern cities, and considerably more in some of the largest ones. New Orleans had an African American majority at the beginning of the nineteenth century, and Charleston's population was 58 percent Black as late as 1820. But both the slave and the free Black populations of Southern cities declined over the next several decades, so that by the mid-1840s Southern cities were much whiter and slavery was a less integral part of urban life.

Still, for a significant number of enslaved men and women, city living was a possibility, and by many accounts it was a relatively desirable situation. Slave discipline was much more difficult to maintain in urban settings, where enslaved laborers were not engaged in land cultivation and were often contracted out to employers other than their legal owners. The **hiring-out system,** as it was called, meant that bosses' power over enslaved workers was restricted. Those who were hired out often lived out as well and chose their own landlords. Some were able to live in small Black communities at the periphery of Southern cities.

Frederick Douglass, who was enslaved in Baltimore in the 1830s, found urban slavery "a paradise" compared to life on the plantation. From his perspective, the relative freedom enjoyed by the urban enslaved stemmed from the fact that population density

Dueling Poster. The protocols of honor culture required the issuance of a written public challenge after a long period of negotiation between the representatives of two antagonists. In this 1817 broadside, William Tharp states that William Smith rebuffed a personal visit to demand the satisfaction of a duel. Smith, a merchant, apparently believed that Tharp, a laborer, lacked the social status necessary to make him an honorable opponent. When he caught Tharp posting notices of challenge on September 28, a fight broke out and Smith was killed. A jury later acquitted Tharp. Question for Analysis: Who is the intended audience for Tharp's poster? *The Granger Collection, New York*

shamed white slaveholders into adhering to higher standards of treatment.

For others enslaved in cities, the relative freedom of urban life had to do with the economic conditions of the city. Sally Thomas, born into slavery in Virginia, moved with her enslaver to Nashville, Tennessee, in 1817; hired herself out as a laundress; and managed to earn enough to start a laundry business. Renting her own home, signing contracts, possessing property, and negotiating her own social relationships on both sides of the color line (she conceived a child with John Catron, who would later serve on the U.S. Supreme Court), Thomas enjoyed a kind of virtual freedom, even while the state of Tennessee defined her as enslaved for all legal purposes. Such cases were far from the norm, but they reflected the greater fluidity of an urban cash economy.

Enslaved city-dwellers were also able to live among communities of free people of color. Much like other ethnic minorities in nineteenth-century America, free people of color chose city life over the country and depended on their own churches, fraternal orders, and benevolent societies for social and economic support. But as the number of those living in slavery in cities and away from their enslavers grew after the 1840s, Southern cities became much more clearly segregated into Black and white communities. In the absence of strict control by slaveholders, white society assumed the role, and both free and enslaved African Americans were subjected to more general forms of social surveillance.

SOUTHERN CULTURES

The antebellum South was organized around the economics of cotton, the demographics of slavery, and the legal regime of white supremacy. But the distinctive texture of Southern life was also a matter of culture. Because this culture was destroyed during the Civil War, it is sometimes viewed with nostalgia, as a simpler time of courtly manners and gracious living, at least for those at the top of society. Historians have constructed a more complex and less harmonious view of antebellum life, recognizing that several cultures existed within the South, each with distinct beliefs and rituals that shaped daily life.

CODES OF HONOR AMONG WHITES

As in most other slaveholding societies, the powerful men who ruled in the South put great stock in the concept of **honor.** Their traditional honor culture stressed the importance of personal reputation and relied on public shame, as distinguished from private guilt, to regulate conduct. The honorable gentleman's reputation rested on his ability to demonstrate strength, self-possession, generosity, and honesty in his dealings with others.

On occasion, the code of honor also required displaying a willingness to die in a duel to avenge an insult and maintain one's reputation. Brought to the United States by French naval officers during the Revolution, elaborate codes of conduct for duels (known as affairs of honor) took hold among both Northern and Southern elites. After the 1804 killing of Alexander Hamilton by Vice President Aaron Burr, however, popular revulsion toward dueling in the North limited its appeal and use. Dueling was illegal in every state by the 1830s, but in the South what was prohibited by law was sanctioned by custom. As Andrew Jackson's mother had advised him as a young boy, "the law affords no remedy that can satisfy the feelings of a true man." A man of honor, in other words, cannot rely on the law to restore his personal reputation.

Even a physically harmless gesture could be deadly serious to a man of honor. Southern gentlemen stood guard against slights that might bring about dishonor. Once during Andrew Jackson's second term, a disgruntled former naval officer assaulted Jackson in a ship cabin and attempted to pull his nose. Jackson chased away his attacker with a cane (and refused to have him prosecuted) but was more intent on persuading the public that the nose-pull had failed. Whenever his friend Peggy Eaton teased him about the incident, Jackson would grow quite serious. He would shake his fist, she recalled, and insist that "by the eternal God, madam, no man ever pulled my nose."

White women had honor, too, in the sense that they were vulnerable to being dishonored, but their honor consisted almost entirely in sexual chastity and fidelity and did not entitle them to avenge insults or serve in public life. In that sense, the culture of honor in the slaveholding South was a white male prerogative. Black women and Black men could not participate within this culture of honor because of their status as subordinates.

Southern conceptions of honor were rooted in the domination of other human beings, and even non-gentlemen could claim to be men of honor by owning a couple of human beings or simply by virtue of belonging to a privileged race. At the same time, the treatment of people in slavery was shaped in part by the dictates of a culture of honor. Plantation punishments—which featured public flogging, enslaved adults beaten by white children, and enslaved women beaten in the presence of their husbands—were not intended solely to secure obedience or heighten productivity. They were also humiliation ceremonies designed to exclude enslaved people from the claims to honor that were treasured by slaveholding men.

Honor culture was not unique to the South, but its prominence in the region's public life found little parallel in the North as the century wore on. ● The prevalence of honor codes among white Southerners may even help explain certain interesting cultural differences between the two regions, such as the lack of enthusiasm in the antebellum South for forms of entertainment that were popular in the North. White Southerners showed less interest in news stories and museum displays that celebrated lies and hoaxes, things that were not laughing matters to men of honor. Perhaps for similar reasons, one historian has argued, the sport of baseball, with its emphasis on such dishonorable habits as stealing and trying to elude capture, did not really catch on in the South until well after the Civil War. ●

CHRISTIANITY IN BLACK AND WHITE

The Southern culture of honor coexisted (not always peacefully) with the spreading influence of evangelical Christianity. Especially in the beginning of the century, Baptist and Methodist preachers were the enemies of the culture of honor, in part because they called for the rejection of pastimes and practices (like gambling, horse racing, and extramarital sex) that were part of being a gentleman. Also, the evangelical message encouraged forms of public behavior (like ecstatic conversion and enthusiastic surrender before the Holy Spirit) that were out of place in honor culture.

Evangelical preachers also threatened the dominant culture by putting power in the hands of young, unmarried ministers and pious women, and they frequently blurred the racial divide by emphasizing the need for all human beings to be saved. After 1830, however, as Baptist and Methodist churches in the South began to

POLITICS AND ENTERTAINMENT

grow, they became more accommodating of the social order, especially on the subject of slavery. Still, evangelicalism exerted a cultural influence that competed with the code of honor in defining proper masculine conduct for slaveholders.

Christianity made significant inroads among those living in slavery as well. Though their religious practices differed in many respects from those of Southern whites, Americans of African descent, by and large, adopted the religion of their enslavers between 1760 and 1850. By 1860, one in four enslaved people belonged to a church (as compared to one in three among whites), and many more attended services, heard sermons, or espoused Protestant Christian beliefs.

Although they embraced the religion of the surrounding white society, African Americans in the South were able to infuse Christianity with their own perspectives and circumstances and find within it various resources for dealing with slavery. By choosing particular denominations (mostly Methodist and Baptist), emphasizing particular themes and messages, and adopting particular styles of worship, the enslaved carved out a distinctive form of religious expression within what was in some respects a biracial church. Black Christians gravitated toward certain biblical texts, favoring the exodus narrative, jubilee laws (which called for the emancipation of enslaved people every fifty years), and the psalms of the Hebrew Scriptures, for example, over the injunctions to obedience in the Pauline epistles of the New Testament, which slaveholders were fond of invoking.

Enslaved people also brought to the new religion African patterns of call and response (in which a preacher or singer alternates lines with a larger chorus or audience), rhythmic singing, and vocal improvisation. Enslaved Christians also developed their own tradition of sacred music, known as **spirituals,** with lyrics that emphasized sorrow, the longing for freedom, and even the possibility of revolution. "He said, and if I had my way," one enduring spiritual intones, "If I had my way, if I had my way,/I'd tear this building down."

Slaveholders were divided about the impact of Christian practice on enslaved people. Most slaveholders were driven, both by religious belief and by desire for paternalistic control, to bring those they owned into the church. Few saw any inherent conflicts between Christianity and slavery, and most believed that churchgoing would increase obedience. Thomas Affleck, a slaveholder and an agricultural innovator, advised overseers that "an hour devoted every Sabbath morning to [enslaved persons'] moral and religious instruction would prove a great aid to you in bringing about a better state of things amongst the Negroes." Yet at the same time, some slaveholders worried that enslaved people who engaged in ecstatic worship and listened to preachers might resist authority on the plantation. Most

CONFLICTING FAITHS

"Red Set Girls, and Jack-in-the-Green," 1837. African traditions were preserved more easily in slave communities in the Caribbean, where African-born enslaved people formed a much larger share of the population. But Caribbean celebrations of festivals such as Jonkonnu, depicted in this lithograph by the Jamaican Jewish artist Issac Mendes Belisario, had modest counterparts in parts of the U.S. South. *Yale Center for British Art, Paul Mellon Collection, USA/The Bridgeman Art Library*

troubling, of course, was the specter of the Baptist preacher Nat Turner, whose religious visions had led to a bloody slave rebellion. Many slaveholders discouraged literacy among enslaved people, even though Protestant faiths stressed the importance of daily Bible reading and study. ● It is hard to know, of course, how Christian ideas actually shaped slave consciousness, but the best evidence suggests that overall it induced neither feelings of subservience nor impulses to rebel. Enslaved African Americans probably found within Christianity both reasons to accept their fate in the short term and grounds for expecting freedom in the indefinite future.

SLAVE FOLKWAYS

Christianity provided only some of the resources that African Americans used to build community and find meaning under the brutal conditions of their enslavement. Some in southern Louisiana practiced voodoo, a religious tradition that drew upon both African and French Catholic beliefs, and throughout the South, Christianity coexisted with other rituals and world views. Like many Southern whites (including many white Christians), enslaved people cultivated the knowledge of folk medicine, spirit worlds, dream interpretation, and magic. Particular men and women earned special status within the slave community for their skills as conjurers, fortune tellers, or herb doctors, but ordinary people also passed on this knowledge to their children.

Parents living in slavery also entertained and instructed their children with a rich body of folktales. Many of these tales featured talking animal characters, such as Fox, Wolf, Rooster, Bear, and the clever Br'er (brother) Rabbit. **Animal trickster tales** originated in Africa, but as they evolved in the retellings of enslaved African Americans, the animal figures acquired more human characteristics and aspirations. Animal tricksters, unlike the mythic heroes of nineteenth-century white American culture, relied not on superhuman size or strength but on their wits— and a cunning grasp of their adversaries' habits and weaknesses. Wolf traps the acquisitive Br'er Rabbit with a sticky Tar Baby, but Rabbit dupes Wolf into throwing him into a briar patch, where he can easily escape, by pretending to fear that fate more than any other. Tales in which weaker animals elude or overcome stronger ones had special appeal to subjugated people seeking opportunities for resistance and comfort.

In those special moments of respite from the demands of fieldwork, a culture of display and festivity developed in and around the slave quarters, especially on larger plantations. Every Sunday, for example, enslaved people dressed up in their best and most flamboyant clothing. The British actress Fanny Kemble, while living on her husband's Georgia plantation in the 1830s, ridiculed the multicolored Sunday attire as "the most ludicrous combination of incongruities," but African Americans valued these fashion displays as communal events and courtship rituals. Many who were able to cultivate their own small plots of land used the proceeds to buy special Sunday outfits. During the week, enslaved women packed their Sunday best in fragrant flowers and herbs. Enslaved African Americans also dressed up for weddings and funerals or on the handful of holidays that enlivened the slave calendar. In the festival of Jonkonnu (or John Canoe), which was observed around Christmastime during the antebellum period, bands of Black men wearing elaborate costumes and playing musical instruments marched through the countryside, entering plantation homes and asking white landowners for money or drinks. And throughout the South, slave communities enjoyed log-rolling or corn-shucking festivals at critical junctures in the work cycle.

THE CULTURE OF COMMON WHITE FOLK

Most white Southerners did not belong to slaveholding households. As a group, they represented a lower class, since this majority owned less than 10 percent of the region's wealth by the end of the antebellum period. But not all of them were impoverished. Some were subsistence farmers tilling poor soil in the hilly backcountry, far from the large plantations. Others lived in cities, including a growing population of foreign immigrants by the 1850s. But large numbers were more substantial landowners, often called **yeoman farmers,** who grew crops for market as well as for subsistence. Yeomen lived on small family farms where men, women, and children worked together, much like modest landowners in the Midwest, where slavery was illegal (see Singular Lives: Frances Webb Bumpass, Evangelical Editor).

Unlike the wealthy planters, and more so than independent farmers in the North, the common folk of the southern hill country still inhabited a world that was relatively cut off from the communication networks that were beginning to reshape the country in the 1830s and 1840s (see Chapter 10). By national standards, they had low literacy rates and were unlikely to engage in regular contact with people beyond their communities and

SINGULAR LIVES

Frances Webb Bumpass, Evangelical Editor

White women in the antebellum South played a variety of social roles, not all of which fit easily into the familiar stereotypes of plantation mistresses and farmwives. Frances Webb was raised in Virginia and North Carolina, where she was given a substantial education that included private tutelage in Greek. In 1839, at the age of twenty, she met an itinerant Methodist minister named Sidney Bumpass, and she married him in 1842. After a number of posts in different rural congregations, the Bumpasses opened a school in Greensboro, North Carolina, and in 1851 Sidney, who had acquired a printing press, began publishing a weekly Methodist newspaper. In December of that year, however, Sidney died from typhoid fever and Frances, a thirty-two-year-old widow, assumed the reins. Despite early opposition from the Methodist Conference, which considered a woman's stewardship of a newspaper unseemly, Frances Bumpass ran the *Weekly Message* for twenty years, focusing much of the paper's attention on subjects related to female education. From the perspective of women's literary history in the South, Frances Bumpass was a pioneer.

On the contentious questions of slavery and race, Bumpass was more conventional. Though she and her husband sought to spread Methodism to African Americans and opposed a white lynch mob that attacked free Blacks, they did not express fundamental objections to the racial order of the American South. Like most white Southerners, the Bumpasses were not slaveholders, and like many white evangelical leaders in the region, Frances focused her daily life on spiritual matters that had little to do with politics or labor arrangements. In her private writings, however, she expressed ambivalence toward the slave system. She wrote in her diary about "the evils of slavery" and spoke of the possibility of moving to a free state. But Bumpass did not necessarily mean that slaveholding was sinful or wrong; she simply saw enslaved people as difficult to manage. They are "trouble" to their enslavers, she elaborated, "vexing them, and causing much sin."

Most of all, Frances worried about the possibility of a slave revolt. Rumors of such a revolt in North Carolina in 1844 prompted her to confess to her diary of a tendency to "dwell too much on... imaginary scenes of murder." These images kept her up at night and, once she did fall asleep, they awakened her with sudden dread. She turned to her faith on such occasions, which helped her manage the fear of latent violence built into Southern race relations. Still, her frightened perspective offers clues as to how white Southerners, with no obvious material investment in slavery might have regarded the prospect of emancipation.

Frances Webb Bumpass. Like most nonslaveholding whites, this evangelical newspaper publisher had no wish to subvert the South's racial hierarchy. *Courtesy of Troy-Bumpas Inn Bed and Breakfast, Greensboro, NC.*

Where in the Archives?

Frances Webb Bumpass's imprint on the historical record comes, in part, from her editorship of the *Weekly Message*. But she also left behind correspondence, a diary, and miscellaneous writings, as did her husband, Sidney. Although much of this material is unpublished, selections were compiled and published in 1899.

Mrs. Frances M. Bumpass: Autobiography and Journal (compiled by Eugenia H. Bumpass, edited by F. A. Butler, published in 1899 by Publishing House M.E. Church, South) is available at HathiTrust (https://www.hathitrust.org/). The compiled journal begins in 1852, shortly after Sidney's death, and ends in 1898, weeks before Frances's death.

Assignment

Locate and read pages 29–45 of Bumpass's published autobiography and diary. In a short essay of 300 words, present evidence to make the case that these writings show Bumpass as being a product of either the Second Great Awakening or a slaveholding society.

---

families. Like enslaved African Americans, poorer white farming families in the South maintained a rich folk culture that reflected traditions from across the Atlantic. In parts of the South, the music of nonslaveholding whites, for example, with its five-tone scales and distinctive singing style, resembled that of the Scottish lowlands or southeastern England, where many of their ancestors had lived. The common folk of the South also tended to preserve traditional beliefs in ghosts, witches, conjurers, and weather omens.

Despite the great cultural differences separating planters from yeoman farmers and common white folk, whites in the South shared some basic convictions. Although nonslaveholding white men formed a majority of the Southern electorate, they never posed a serious threat to the institution of slavery. Some aspired to acquire enslaved people in the future and supported slavery for many of the same reasons that people who do not own real estate today nonetheless support the rights and privileges of homeowners. Other yeoman farmers, who may not have aspired to enter the ranks of slaveholders, nonetheless defended slavery, because they shared with the planters a world view that valued hierarchy and obedience. These farmers commanded the labor of women and children in their own families, rather than enslaved African Americans, and saw themselves as having an interest in maintaining social order. But whatever their views on slavery, most white Southerners regarded the prospect of emancipating African Americans as frightening. Accounts of violence in Haiti and the bloody example of Nat Turner reinforced the widespread notion that the end of slavery would lead to racial conflict. As one poor white man told a Northern traveler, "I reckon the majority would be right glad if we could get rid of the niggers. But it wouldn't never do to free 'em and leave 'em here. I don't know anybody, hardly, in favor of that." Poorer whites in the South benefited, at least psychologically, from the privileges of racial superiority in a mixed-race society. But probably many would have been happy to live like family farmers in Northern states such as Illinois, where Black people were not tolerated at all, either free or enslaved. What they did not want was to live with those emancipated from slavery.

SLAVERY, POLITICS, AND SECTIONAL CONFLICT

At various points in the late eighteenth and early nineteenth centuries, the practice of slaveholding had fallen under political attack. In the 1830s, however, new factors heated up the slavery issue. When Great Britain banned slavery in its West Indian colonies and slavery was dismantled in the new independent republics of South America (see Table 11.1), the South became the largest slaveholding society in the hemisphere. Together with the Russian Empire, with its millions of serfs, the American South was now closely identified with a form of labor discipline and class division that was being rejected by

TABLE 11.1 THE ABOLITION OF SLAVERY IN THE AMERICAS, 1777–1833		
State or Region	Date Slavery Outlawed	Means
Vermont	1777	Constitutional mandate
Pennsylvania	1780	Gradual abolition
Massachusetts, New Hampshire	1783	Judicial ruling
Connecticut, Rhode Island	1784	Gradual abolition
Northwest Territory	1787	Continental Congress
Upper Canada	1793	Colonial law
New York	1799	Gradual abolition
Lower Canada (Quebec)	1803	Judicial ruling
New Jersey	1804	Gradual abolition
Haiti	1804	Armed revolution
Argentina	1813	Gradual abolition
Gran Colombia	1821	Gradual abolition
Chile	1823	Legal prohibition
Mexico	1829	Legal prohibition
Bolivia	1831	Legal prohibition
British West Indies	1833	Act of Parliament

much of the modern world. Southern slaveholders and their political allies came increasingly under attack, both from Northern abolitionists who decried the injustice to enslaved people and from Northern politicians enraged by the political power of slaveholders. In this polarized climate, all three branches of the federal government became embroiled in new outbreaks of the slavery debate.

ANTISLAVERY RUMBLINGS AND ATTEMPTS AT CENSORSHIP

The Missouri Compromise in 1820 (see Chapter 9) had succeeded in keeping the issue of slavery off the congressional agenda for fifteen years. But in 1835, a Maine representative introduced a petition signed by 172 women in his district calling for the abolition of slavery in Washington, D.C., the only part of the country over which Congress had uncontested jurisdiction. In prior years, such a petition would have been referred to a committee and quietly disposed of without serious consideration, but the new spotlight on Southern slavery prompted the House of Representatives to avoid the petition altogether. This resulted in a series of maneuvers between Northern Whigs and proslavery Democrats (from both regions) over the question of whether Congress would even acknowledge the criticism of slavery in its chambers.

First, a representative from Vermont made a motion to print the petition, noting that the signers were respectable citizens, not members of some radical organization. In response, a New York Democrat moved to table the motion to print. Two days later, another New Englander presented another antislavery petition, and James Henry Hammond of South Carolina moved that the petition "not be received." This was unprecedented. Petitions from citizens went routinely unheeded but had never been refused altogether. House Democrats, seeking to avoid a sectional split within their coalition on the eve of the 1836 election, then passed a **gag rule** on all slavery petitions, requiring that they be tabled immediately after being presented by title. The gag rule, which remained in effect in the House of Representatives from 1836 to 1844, prevented the antislavery views of Northern citizens from being aired in Congress.

This crisis over antislavery petitions reflected Southern panic over the sudden rise of a radical abolitionist movement in the North. Northern reformers had criticized slavery before, but most of their efforts had focused on ending the slave trade, and their proposals to emancipate people from slavery had involved gradual schemes that enlisted the support and cooperation of slaveholders. The leading antislavery organization in the United States before the 1830s was the **American Colonization Society** (founded in 1816), which briefly united opponents of slavery and anxious slaveholders around a plan to relocate enslaved people to Africa. Opponents of slavery turned to colonization as the best chance for achieving emancipation in the South, whereas slaveholders saw in it a way to deport free Blacks who might otherwise encourage slave rebellions. Advocates in both regions also defended colonization as a way of bringing Christianity to Africa. The American Colonization Society succeeded in 1822 in establishing the colony of **Liberia** on Africa's west coast, and colonization briefly enjoyed widespread support among a range of prominent political leaders in both the North and the South. But by 1825, this alliance had begun to splinter. Slaveholders now saw colonization as part of a larger plan of emancipation, which they objected to on economic as well as ideological grounds. And for a new generation of abolitionists, colonization came to seem both racist and unlikely to end slavery.

Between 1825 and 1835, gradual approaches to ending slavery gave way to a new radicalism among both Black and white abolitionists. In 1829, the *Ethiopian Manifesto* of Robert Alexander Young, a free Black from New York, prophesied the imminent arrival of a Black messiah who would lead enslaved people to freedom and execute divine judgment against slaveholders. Seven months later, a free Black from Boston named David Walker published his *Appeal . . . to the Coloured Citizens of the World*, which explicitly rejected the idea of colonization. In 1831, a white New Englander named William Lloyd Garrison began publishing his antislavery newspaper, *The Liberator*, advocating the immediate and uncompensated emancipation of all enslaved people. In 1833, the American Anti-Slavery Society was formed, providing an institutional base for a new abolitionist movement.

● The new antislavery movement was based in the North, but white Southerners had reason to worry about the circulation of these ideas within their communities. Taking advantage of the low postage rate charged to newspapers, Garrison and the American Anti-Slavery Society inundated the South with their publications. During the summer of 1835, abolitionists sent over one hundred seventy-five thousand pieces of mail into the South, an amount equal to the entire output of the Southern periodical press. In certain rural districts, these abolitionist papers comprised the overwhelming majority of the printed information arriving each day by mail. ●

MEDIA AND INFORMATION

Southerners tried various means to dam the southward flow of abolitionist tracts and to prevent them from reaching African Americans. In 1831, Georgetown (in the District of Columbia) passed a law prohibiting free Blacks from taking copies of *The Liberator* out of the post office. If caught, they faced a twenty-five-dollar fine

Charleston Post Office.   Southerners accused abolitionists of "pour[ing] their poisons into the national chalice" and being accessories to the murderous rampage of Nat Turner. In this abolitionist depiction of the 1835 Charleston post office raid, a poster offering a "$20000 reward for Tappan" refers to a bounty set by the city of New Orleans on American Anti-Slavery Society founder Arthur Tappan. *Everett Collection Historical/Alamy Stock Photo*

and thirty days in jail. If they could not pay the fine, they could be sold into slavery for four months. In 1835, a group of Charleston citizens calling themselves **lynch men** raided the post office at night, confiscated an unsolicited mass mailing from the American Anti-Slavery Society, and burned the offending publications in the streets of the city, along with effigies of leading abolitionists, before a crowd of two thousand. Significantly, the South found an ally in the White House. President Jackson considered abolitionists "monsters" who fomented slave uprisings and deserved "to atone for this wicked attempt with their lives," and he instructed his postmaster general not to deliver antislavery publications unless a subscriber demanded them. In the event that someone did, his or her name would be published. With the federal government's blessing, local postmasters thus quietly censored the mail.

The mass circulation of new antislavery ideas formed the backdrop for the fight in Congress about how to deal with abolitionist petitions. The postal system was making it difficult to maintain a clear geographical barrier between the North and South, thwarting the South's attempt to control how slavery was discussed within its borders. So Jackson and his party tried to impede the flow of antislavery mail and suppress the discussion of petitions to Congress, whose records circulated in the national press. But the petition gag proved in some ways counterproductive. Former president John Quincy Adams, now serving in the House of Representatives, waged a strenuous campaign to affirm the constitutional right of petitioning, drawing more public attention to the debate over discussing slavery than it would otherwise have attracted. Abolitionist petition drives, now protesting the gag rule in addition to the earlier cause, garnered even more signatures. The tabled petitions filled a 600-square-foot room in the Capitol, from the floor to its 14-foot ceiling.

PROSLAVERY DEFIANCE

The Southern defense of slavery had assumed a new form by the 1830s. Whereas earlier many white Southerners had conceded that slavery was problematic or even undesirable, such views quickly became taboo. Fearing insurrections like Nat Turner's, responding to attacks from the North, and feeling isolated in the face of a growing international rejection of slavery, Southerners began to assert that their labor system was a blessing, not a curse. No longer a "necessary evil" or an "irremediable evil," slavery was now, in the words of James Henry Hammond, "the greatest of all blessings which a kind Providence has bestowed upon our glorious region."

Slavery's defenders often began with the observation that abolition was impossible. For one thing, the economic value of enslaved laborers was too high. The British government had ended slavery in the West Indies by compensating slaveholders. But how would the federal government come up with 900 million dollars to pay slaveholders in the South, when all federal revenues amounted to only about 25 million dollars a year? Furthermore, they argued, it would be impracticable to send 2 million enslaved people back to Africa and dangerous to leave them on American soil. But the **proslavery ideology** that flourished in the South after 1830 also relied on a large arsenal of arguments for why slavery was, in fact, desirable.

Some of the proslavery arguments had been around for a while, introduced in the North during the eighteenth century when slaveholding fell under moral attack there. Southern Christians cited the biblical laws permitting slaveholding, invoked the "curse of Ham" from Genesis (see Chapter 3) to explain the enslavement of Africans, and presented Black slavery as part of a divine plan to Christianize the heathens of Africa. But proslavery advocates also advanced newer arguments during the antebellum period. Increasingly, slavery was justified with reference to an innate racial inferiority of Black people, which Southerners supported with the latest scientific theories developed at leading Northern universities. In addition, Southern politicians and writers contrasted slavery with the wage labor system that was spreading in the North and in Britain, claiming that enslaved plantation workers were better treated than factory workers. These arguments would grow more elaborate as sectional tensions escalated in the 1850s (see Chapter 14).

THE SLAVE POWER AND CONSPIRACY THEORIES

Proslavery arguments may have bolstered white Southerners' commitment to their labor system, but it was the U.S. Constitution and the two-party system that provided the ultimate defense of slavery during this period. By counting 60 percent of the growing enslaved population, the Constitution's three-fifths clause inflated the South's representation both in Congress and in the Electoral College that determined the presidency. Had enslaved people been excluded from the count, Southern voices in Congress would have been fewer and the nation would have elected a very different set of presidents. Slaveholders held the office of the presidency for fifty of the office's first sixty-two years.

In a subtler manner, the party system protected slavery by allowing a solid faction within the Democratic Party to control national elections. Because Southerners held sway among Democrats, and because other Democrats remained more committed to the primacy of the party than to any other cause, Southern Democrats could set policies and nominate candidates. Northerners who rose to prominence within the party had to be acceptable to the South. Southerners wielded less power among the Whigs, but they, too, needed to remain competitive in the South to have a chance at winning national elections.

These circumstances lent credibility to a new rhetorical device that entered the American political vocabulary in the 1830s. Northerners began to speak of a **Slave Power,** an insidious force in American history through which a small circle of wealthy slaveholders manipulated the political system for their own benefit. The charge was first developed by abolitionists, but it spread quickly to mainstream Northern politicians who claimed no particular sympathy for the enslaved. What was evil about the Slave Power, from this perspective, was more the conspiratorial scheming and the acquisitive appetites of the slaveholding class and less the injustice of treating another human being as property. In this view, the primary victim of slavery was thus not the enslaved person but the free institutions of the American republic. Such arguments would help spread hostility toward slaveholders among nonabolitionists and would eventually create problems for Democrats in the North.

The Slave Power thesis was part of a larger trend in antebellum political rhetoric toward **conspiracy theories.** Perhaps because the nation was still relatively young and itself the result of revolution, Americans were quick to suspect secret plots to subvert the republic. Charges of conspiracy had a long history in Anglo-American politics, dating back to English fears of Catholic designs on the throne, and such rhetoric had played an important role in the American Revolution. But in the 1830s and 1840s, subversion charges were leveled much more promiscuously—at Catholics, Mormons, Masons, and the national bank. The escalating slavery conflict was especially ripe for such accusations. On the Southern side, conspiracy theories focused on the abolitionists, whom proslavery politicians accused of stealing enslaved workers and plotting slave rebellions. Southerners evoked the specter of secret midnight meetings, "where the bubbling cauldron of abolition was fulfilled with its pestilential materials, and the fire beneath kindled by the breath of the fanatics." Most provocatively, both sides alleged that conspirators of the other region were motivated by a desire to have sex with enslaved women.

One key difference between the competing conspiracy theories in the slavery debates of the 1830s, however, was the fact that abolitionists were a fringe minority in the North whose views were considered dangerously extreme of congressional deliberation and unfit for the U.S. mail. By contrast, leading slaveholders held major political positions throughout the South.

SEMINOLES, TEXANS, AND THE SLAVERY CONFLICT

The federal government sought to avoid conflicts over slavery during this period but generally acted in support of slaveholders' interests. Jackson's Indian removal policies had cleared the way for the expansion of the cotton kingdom, and his successors continued those policies. When the Seminoles in Florida resisted removal, the U.S. Army pursued them over the course of a seven-year guerilla war. By some definitions, Seminole resistance was a slave rebellion, since hundreds of escaped African Americans and many descendants of formerly enslaved people were part of the Seminole Nation. The federal government's extraordinary commitment to removing this single native group reflected the threat that a Florida haven for runaways posed to nearby slaveholders. The **Second Seminole War,** as historians often label the conflict, lasted from 1835 to 1842, the nation's longest military conflict before Vietnam. It ultimately forced the removal of three thousand Seminoles to Oklahoma, but it cost the federal government 20 million dollars, and fifteen hundred American soldiers died in the battle.

On the western frontier of the cotton kingdom lay Texas, a province at the outer reaches of the new nation of Mexico. Mexico had achieved independence from Spain in 1821, but Texas lay far from the Mexican capital and much of its territory was populated and controlled by the Comanche, Apache, or Kiowa. ● The Mexican government welcomed Anglo settlers to Texas, with the proviso that they obey Mexican laws, learn Spanish, and attend Catholic mass. Ignoring those conditions, many Southern slaveholders answered the call. Mexico abolished slavery in 1829 but declined to enforce the ban in Texas. By 1830, the coastal region of eastern Texas had twenty thousand white American settlers and one thousand enslaved African Americans brought in to grow cotton. Mexico grew alarmed and banned further migration, but Americans continued to immigrate illegally into Texas, and by 1835 they outnumbered Mexicans there ten to one. ●

Sensing their numerical power and fearing Mexican attempts to reassert control over the province, American settlers in Texas organized a rebellion. English-speaking whites objected to being taxed and complained of lack of military protection against Native Americans. But most of all, they sought to preempt enforcement of national laws, including the ban on slavery. In 1836, joined by several leading Mexicans in the region, they declared independence.

Mexican president Antonio López de Santa Anna led an attack against the rebellion and captured the rebel garrison in San Antonio at the **Battle of the Alamo.** Mexican troops killed all 187 defenders of the fort, including former congressman David Crockett. The Texans, regrouped under the command of Sam Houston, ambushed Santa Anna's army near the San Jacinto River and took the president prisoner. Threatened with his life, Santa Anna signed treaties recognizing Texan independence and agreeing to keep his troops south of the Rio Grande. The Mexican Congress refused to ratify this coerced agreement, and Mexico continued to claim Texas as its own territory.

Houston and the Texans expected the United States to annex the new independent nation, but the politics of slavery dictated a different response. President Jackson recognized that adding a new slaveholding territory would jeopardize Northern support for his party's presidential candidate, Martin Van Buren, on the eve of election. Jackson waited for his last day in office to recognize the Texas Republic, with a southern border at the Rio Grande, based on the coerced treaty. But neither he nor Van Buren proposed annexation. Texas remained an independent slave state, called the **Lone Star Republic,** for the next decade, enjoying friendly relations with the United States and attracting

Santa Anna's Surrender. This 1836 cartoon imagines Santa Anna and his brother groveling as they turn themselves over to Sam Houston. "I consent to remain your prisoner, most excellent sir!! Me no Alamo!!" the Mexican leader tells Houston—a depiction that undoubtedly pleased Texans and Americans who had taken "Remember the Alamo" as a battle cry. *Library of Congress, Prints & Photographs Division*

one hundred thousand American immigrants with generous land grants. The ultimate status of this disputed territory awaited resolution.

THE *AMISTAD* CASE

The Van Buren administration was not able to control the debate over slavery as smoothly when fifty-three Africans, sold to Portuguese merchants and taken illegally to the Spanish colony of Cuba, made their way through the U.S. justice system. On July 1, 1839, a twenty-five-year-old man from Sierra Leone, known as Joseph Cinqué, led a mutiny aboard the Spanish ship *Amistad* as it was transporting them from Havana to another Cuban port. Using a nail to pick the locks on his collar, Cinqué similarly freed the

other captives, and the group armed themselves with sugar cane knives and killed the captain. They ordered a Spanish slave merchant to sail back to Africa, but he steered a northward course and the ship was ultimately intercepted by a U.S. ship off the coast of Long Island. The American captain towed the ship to New London, Connecticut, and a federal judge ordered that the African captives be jailed in New Haven pending a determination of their legal status. Were they Spanish property? Were they pirates who had illegally seized control of a Spanish vessel? Or were they free human beings who had themselves been illegally seized by pirates?

President Van Buren and his secretary of state, John Forsyth, supported the Spanish government's insistence that the Africans were Cuban born and ought to be forcibly returned to their Cuban slaveholders. Because the

"Joseph Cinquez [Cinqué] Addressing His Compatriots on Board the Spanish Schooner *Amistad.*"   This 1839 lithograph by John Childs depicts the leader of the *Amistad* rebellion as a prophetic orator enthralling his audience on board the slave ship. *ABC/Photofest*

Spanish had signed a treaty with Great Britain honoring the British ban on the international slave trade, they could not admit that the captives were taken from Africa. But Van Buren was unable to keep the case out of the U.S. judicial system, where a federal court tried to determine whether the Africans were legally enslaved. Crucial to the captives' case was the argument that they neither spoke nor understood Spanish. The judge ruled that the captives had, in fact, been taken from Africa and that their enslavement was therefore not recognized by any law—American, Spanish, or international.

The Van Buren administration appealed the decision to the Supreme Court, where John Quincy Adams argued the Africans' case, invoking the Declaration of Independence and the natural right to rebel against slavery. In 1841, the Supreme Court upheld the decision in favor of the West Africans, setting free all of the *Amistad* captives except for a man named Antonio, who had

been raised enslaved in Cuba. The Court made clear, however, that wherever slavery was legal—which, of course, included the American South—no right of rebellion existed. Had the men aboard the slave ship been legally enslaved in Cuba, or in Alabama, they would have been returned to their enslavers.

For Northern audiences, the **Amistad case** dramatized the plight of enslaved people. It also underscored how difficult it was to draw rigid lines between legal slavery and illegal kidnapping. And as an event in foreign relations, the *Amistad* crisis demonstrated that changes in *international* slavery politics might affect the federal government's ability to manage the conflict between North and South. The Supreme Court's ruling thwarted the will of the president and alarmed slaveholders, but it also averted a possible war with the British, who might have imposed a blockade of Cuba, in defiance of the Monroe Doctrine.

CONCLUSION

During the fifteen years after Nat Turner's insurrection, the slave system in the South became more firmly entrenched. While enslaved African Americans struggled to carve out places of autonomy and comfort, their prospects for emancipation dimmed considerably. Despite a dip in the late 1830s, the cotton economy boomed and the market for slave labor made every enslaved person vulnerable to sale and forced migration. Paradoxically, the growth of cotton intensified some of the social and cultural differences between the North and the South, even as it made the two regions more economically interdependent.

Meanwhile, a polarized and vitriolic debate over slavery left slaveholders feeling increasingly insecure, despite the extraordinary political power they wielded. A tense and fragile peace held between the slave states and the rest of the country, but events like Texan independence and the *Amistad* rebellion showed how hard this peace would be to maintain. If the United States were to expand southward or westward, peace would have to be renegotiated.

STUDY TERMS

cotton gin

plantation

corporal punishment

paternalism

slave patrols

Underground Railroad

hiring-out system

honor

spirituals

animal trickster tales

yeoman farmers

gag rule

American Colonization Society

Liberia

lynch men

proslavery ideology

Slave Power

conspiracy theories

Second Seminole War

Battle of the Alamo

Lone Star Republic

Amistad case

FURTHER READING

A database of additional full-text readings is available through Power of Process for Primary Sources in Connect.

Daina Ramey Berry, *The Price for Their Pound of Flesh* (2017), follows the conflict between personhood and property over the life cycles of the enslaved.

David Brion Davis, *Inhuman Bondage* (2006), places the history of slavery in the antebellum South in the larger context of the end of slavery in the Americas.

Kenneth Greenberg, *Honor and Slavery* (1996), reinterprets the Southern culture of honor.

Ariela Gross, *Double Character* (2000), shows how enslaved persons' dual status as property and moral agent complicated legal disputes in the courtrooms of the Deep South.

Martha Hodes, *White Women, Black Men* (1999), examines illicit sexual relations between white women and Black men in the antebellum South.

Walter Johnson, *Soul by Soul* (1999), uncovers how the process and prospect of sale shaped slavery in this period.

Stephanie E. Jones-Rogers, *They Were Her Property* (2019), stresses the economic power of female slaveholders.

Lawrence W. Levine, *Black Culture and Black Consciousness* (1977), recovers and analyzes the meaning of enslaved people's folktales, music, and expressive culture.

Stephanie McCurry, *Masters of Small Worlds* (1995), studies yeoman farm families in South Carolina and considers their ideological relationship to slavery.

Leonard Richards, *The Slave Power* (2000), shows how the Southern defense of slavery shaped national politics through the workings of the Second Party System.

Manisha Sinha, *The Slave's Cause* (2016), offers a history of radical abolitionism beyond the antebellum United States.

Andrew J. Torget, *Seeds of Empire* (2015), chronicles the political revolution wrought by cotton and slavery in the Texas borderlands.

12 | 1831–1848
ERA OF MIDDLE-CLASS REFORM

Chapter Questions

1. What prominent middle-class reform causes emerged in the North during the 1830s and 1840s?

2. What ideological themes connected the temperance movement to abolitionism and to other reform causes?

3. How did these reform causes relate to the social and economic circumstances of Northern middle-class life?

4. How did new ideals of domesticity help give birth to a feminist movement?

Making a New Man. A father fulfills his family duties by signing the temperance pledge. *Photo Researchers/Science History Image/Alamy Stock Photo*

One night in 1842, a widow in Utica, a growing New York town along the Erie Canal, waited up anxiously for her son. When he failed to come home, she made her way to a local brothel and called to him through the locked door of one of the bedrooms. The brothelkeeper tossed the mother down a flight of stairs, but when she arrived at her home, her son was waiting for her, ashamed and repentant.

The story of the bold widow appeared in the reports of Utica's Female Moral Reform Society and presented a parable for an important development in Northern culture during this period. The fatherless son, like many young men who moved to the region's growing cities, lives free of paternal authority and enjoys the pleasures of the marketplace. His mother hopes to influence him at home but is forced by his absence to seek him out, taking her maternal authority to the sinful world of the brothel. Risking exposure to the vices of the city, entering spaces ordinarily barred to respectable women, and suffering physical abuse in the process, the mother persuades her wayward son to mend his ways. In publicizing this victory against promiscuity and prostitution, Utica's female reformers were also narrating their own efforts to go out into the world, shout

Time Line

1826

American Temperance Society forms in Boston

1830

Godey's Lady's Book introduced

1831

William Lloyd Garrison begins publishing *The Liberator*

1832

Ralph Waldo Emerson embarks on new philosophical path

1833

American Anti-Slavery Society formed

1834

Anti-abolitionist riots break out in the North

1836

Maria Monk's *Awful Disclosures* published

1837

Elijah Lovejoy killed in Alton, Illinois

1840

Abolitionists split over political action and the role of women

1844

Catholic-Protestant riots erupt around Philadelphia

1845

Frederick Douglass publishes his autobiography
Potato famine begins in Ireland

1848

Seneca Falls Convention enacts Declaration of Sentiments
Revolutionary movements in Europe reinforce anti-Catholicism
in the United States

rights, public education, and prison reform. Others might seem more utopian, such as pacifism and cooperative farming. Still others strike modern Americans as repressive or bigoted, such as Sabbatarianism and anti-Catholicism. The most popular reform movement was the temperance campaign, which sought to persuade people to abstain from drinking alcohol. The most socially and politically disruptive was abolitionism.

These different movements and projects shared some basic themes and appealed to particular populations. Antebellum reform causes attracted mostly native-born Northern Protestants in the 1830s and 1840s and reflected a larger outlook associated with the growing middle class. Middle-class Northerners distinguished themselves through their occupations, homes, family arrangements, gender roles, sober habits, and world view. Reform movements would help define their culture.

During this period, however, another powerful culture emerged in the Northern states. Catholic immigrants, many of them from Ireland, moved to the United States in unprecedented numbers, bringing different attitudes from those of the reformers and challenging their authority. The reformers' ideals became the subject of culture wars between natives and newcomers, which contributed both to the friction between Democrats and Whigs and to the brewing conflict between the North and South.

On the whole, Southerners steered clear of the reform movements and campaigns that spread quickly in other parts of the nation, both because those movements included antislavery voices in the North and because Southern slaveholders tended to be social conservatives. Reform remained controversial in the North as well, but a host of powerful campaigns to change individuals, communities, and government policy gained critical momentum and transformed American life.

outside of locked doors, and wield their motherly influence over a wayward generation.

By the 1830s, the North was full of men and women who called themselves *reformers*. Not all of them followed the intrepid example of the Utica widow, but most shared the optimism of the eminent philosopher Ralph Waldo Emerson, who achieved renown lecturing to packed houses. "What is man born for," Emerson asked, "but to be a Reformer, a Re-maker of what man has made?" Some of the causes that the reformers embraced appear, in retrospect, humane and progressive, such as women's

THE CULTURE OF REFORM IN THE NORTH

Reform movements took root among Northerners who formed what we would now recognize as a modern middle class. Members of this class worked in a variety of occupations and earned a range of incomes. Their swelling ranks included shopkeepers, small-scale merchants, factory managers, lawyers, doctors, teachers, clerks, and many others, along with their families. For the most part, they all regarded themselves as people who worked with their heads rather than their hands. As much as income level, this separation between manual and non-manual labor during the early phases of American industrialization (see Chapter 10) marked the divide between the working class and the middle class. Non-manual workers were more likely to receive salaries rather than hourly wages, they enjoyed greater prospects for advancement, and their work was more likely to require and reward entrepreneurialism.

Reform movements appealed especially to this class. Middle-class Americans did not own large farms and were not masters of inheritable trades. Instead, they aspired to transmit to their children those values, habits, and appearances that might secure their position in a new economy. They worried about how the spread of commerce and cities might undermine their children's character and foil this project. And they increasingly worried about threats to the social order posed by manual workers who did not attend their churches, live in their neighborhoods, or share their spheres of social influence. Reformist impulses reflected these concerns.

The middle-class men and women who called themselves reformers did not form a political party or build a single organization. They did not always agree on the merits of every reform cause nor did they unite around a strategy for pursuing reformist goals. What they shared was a confidence that righteous individuals should take responsibility for making themselves and their neighbors better people. Armed with this confidence and with an evangelical fervor, reinforced during the Second Great Awakening (see Chapters 9 and 10), about what was right and wrong, reformers set out to reform themselves, their communities, and the society at large.

SELF-IMPROVEMENT

One of the cornerstones of reform ideology was the ideal of individual self-improvement. Young adults, especially men, were encouraged to discipline their habits, develop their characters, and expand their horizons. Many influential thinkers espoused this ideal, but none so powerfully as Ralph Waldo Emerson, a Unitarian minister from Boston who resigned his pulpit in 1832, rejected organized religion and other traditional institutions, and celebrated individual intuition as the source of true knowledge. Emerson encouraged Americans to trust that intuition and rely on themselves. Along with Henry David Thoreau, Margaret Fuller, and other New England philosophers and critics known as **transcendentalists,** Emerson believed in human perfectibility and preached that God was present in humanity and nature.

Emerson spread his ideas about self-reliance as a touring lecturer, part of a network of adult education offerings known as the **lyceum movement.** Beginning in the 1820s, lyceum societies sponsored public lectures on science, literature, philosophy, archaeology, and other subjects through much of the North, and they were especially popular in New England and the Midwest. By the mid-1830s, attending lectures had become one of the most common and respected leisure activities among middle-class adults. Through these lectures, a corps of speakers on the lyceum circuit exerted a powerful influence over a dispersed population.

At a time when literacy was widespread but opportunities for formal education remained quite limited, most Northern cities and towns supported lyceums and debating societies. Larger cities also sponsored lending libraries and schools for workingmen. Young adults participated in these institutions not only for education and entertainment but also as a way of demonstrating their commitment to a project that many lyceum lectures stressed: making oneself better.

ASSOCIATIONS AND UTOPIAS

Even as lecturers preached individual self-reliance and self-improvement, members of the middle class assumed that young people stood a better chance of improving themselves in groups. Sponsors of lectures and debates were just a few examples of the voluntary associations that Americans formed in unprecedented numbers during the 1830s and 1840s. The small city of Utica, for example, with fewer than ten thousand inhabitants, listed forty-one of these associations in its city directory for 1832. Voluntary associations, which included an array of charities, benevolent societies, fraternal orders, self-improvement associations, and religious groups, encouraged sociability and strengthened peer cultures.

Associations in the antebellum North appealed to a mobile population seeking community, and the men and women who were drawn to the project of reform in this period wanted to build better communities and not just better individuals. In some cases, the impulse to improve communities led reformers to withdraw from the larger society. Millennial religious sects, such as the Mormons or the Perfectionists (see Chapter 10), were famous examples of movements to fashion new social communities from scratch, but a host of more secular communes and experiments in cooperative living arose during this period as well. Robert Owen, a Scottish industrialist worried about the social effects of the factory system, built a model industrial community in New Harmony, Indiana, in 1825. Rejecting private property, religion, and marriage, Owen attracted nine hundred colonists to his community. One of Owen's followers, his fellow Scottish socialist Frances Wright, bought land in western Tennessee and formed the community of Nashoba, on which she settled enslaved people she had purchased. They would earn their freedom in five years and would be encouraged to intermarry with whites. Wright's community fell apart after a few years, and she became a symbol of sexual license and heretical religious views.

The most famous of the **utopian communities** of this period appeared in 1841 in West Roxbury, Massachusetts, where Emerson, Fuller, and other transcendentalists established **Brook Farm,** a cooperative agricultural community committed to high thinking and plain living. Brook Farm lasted only a few years, as did the substantial number of American communities organized around the cooperative ideals of the influential French thinker Charles Fourier. Still, experiments in noncompetitive communal living continued to attract reformers who were disturbed by the spread of capitalism, at least in certain parts of the country. Only 2 of the 130 cooperative utopias founded in the United States between 1800 and 1860 were located in the South.

REFORMING THE STATE

Self-improvement programs and utopian communities were often associated with freethinkers (atheists and critics of religion), but the most popular and successful movements to change society at large grew out of religious forces and impulses. The first organized campaign to bring the nation's conduct in line with religious dictates was **Sabbatarianism,** the movement to enforce Sabbath observance. American Sabbatarians sought, first in 1810 and then more forcefully between 1826 and 1831, to bar the transmission of mail on Sunday. Travel

for any worldly purpose violated many American Protestants' convictions about proper Sabbath observance, and the postal service represented the secular realms of commerce and politics more generally. Moreover, since delivering and distributing mail was the federal government's main activity as far as most Americans could see, evangelical Christians selected the Post Office as the best place to launch a campaign to reform the government.

Sabbatarians mounted national petition drives, but they faced opposition from a number of groups. Merchants insisted that the disruption of mail service would make business difficult and retard economic growth. Freethinkers, non-Protestants, and Protestant evangelicals from newer denominations argued that legislating Sabbath observance amounted to state-sponsored religion and impinged on freedom of conscience. The Sabbath mails movement failed to achieve its goal (Sunday delivery would not be suspended until 1912), but it helped organize evangelical reformers and spread the powerful idea that because Americans were connected economically they belonged to the same moral universe and were responsible for one another's sins.

Several of the other campaigns to reform society through government action focused on the issue of punishment. Opponents of the death penalty organized an **antigallows movement** in the 1830s and 1840s, stirring up an evangelical fervor associated with other reform causes in the North. In the mid-1830s, Pennsylvania and New York abolished public executions, and Maine passed a law stipulating that criminals convicted of capital offenses be confined in a state prison for a year and that they be executed only on the issuance of a written warrant at the discretion of the governor. By midcentury, the antigallows movement had persuaded three state legislatures—Michigan, Rhode Island, and Wisconsin—to ban executions altogether, making them the first governments in modern times to abolish capital punishment on a permanent basis.

More generally, reformers questioned the use of violence as a means of correction. Traditional practices of corporal punishment came under attack in the North, where reformers believed that criminals would be corrected more effectively by moral influence, guilty conscience, and surveillance than by physical beating or public humiliation. Congress even considered abolishing the time-honored practice of flogging in the U.S. Navy, but the measure faced unanimous opposition among representatives from the South, where the lash remained a respected symbol of authority and social order. As alternatives to floggings and beheadings, Northern states built

Prison Reform. The Auburn Prison was built in 1816, and twelve prisons of this type were in operation in the United States by 1840. *Classic Collection/Alamy Stock Photo*

innovative **prisons,** which were intended not simply to keep offenders in custody while they awaited punishment (or until their debts were paid) but to remake them into law-abiding citizens. Philadelphia's Eastern State Penitentiary placed convicted criminals under solitary confinement and enforced silence, in the hopes that they would be moved to repent their misdeeds. The Philadelphia model drew much interest abroad, but most states built a different—and cheaper—kind of prison, modeled on the one in Auburn, New York. In Auburn-style prisons, inmates performed hard group labor, which was sold cheaply to private contractors to pay the costs of their incarceration.

TEMPERANCE AND SELF-CONTROL

The most popular of all the antebellum reform movements targeted entrenched traditions of drinking. By 1830, Americans were consuming more hard liquor per capita than at any time before or since—nearly triple today's rate. But over the next two decades, a temperance movement curbed national alcohol consumption and turned the refusal to drink into a badge of middle-class respectability. In dramatizing the evils of liquor,

temperance advocates also emphasized key ideological themes that would tie together many of the disparate reform movements in the antebellum North. The temperance campaign provided both common ground and formative training for activists in those other causes.

TAKING THE PLEDGE

As evidence mounted of the dire consequences of alcohol addiction for family life, workplace productivity, and individual health, reformers took aim at American drinking habits. In 1826, a group of New England ministers founded the American Society for the Promotion of Temperance and launched a national campaign to refashion the public image of alcoholic beverages. Drinks that had commonly been considered healthy were now stigmatized as "demon rum," a poison that led to poverty, crime, and violence. Though these reformers used the word *temperance,* they were not advocating moderation. Members of the new organization were asked to pledge commitment to the cause by marking a "T" for total abstinence next to their signature, hence the word **teetotaler.** Within seven years of its founding, the campaign claimed a million members.

Early temperance advocates pushed for legislation to limit the sale of alcohol, and over the next two decades they were able to boast of some modest successes, mostly in the Northeast. By 1855, thirteen states had enacted some form of alcohol restriction, though most of those laws were overturned in court. For the growing temperance movement, however, these legislative efforts were not the main battleground. The thrust of the movement lay not in the passage of restrictive laws but in the promotion and celebration of a sober lifestyle. Temperance groups such as the **Washingtonians** (founded in 1840) and the **Sons of Temperance** (1842) were not lobbying organizations seeking the attention of politicians; they were fraternal associations designed to recruit members to sign abstinence pledges. In the first six years of its existence, the Sons of Temperance grew to two hundred thousand paying members, all of whom had taken such a pledge.

The temperance organizations of the 1840s stressed moral suasion rather than coercion and believed that even confirmed drunkards could be rescued from a life of ruin. To support their members' attempts to resist liquor, they created alcohol-free entertainment and sociability, featuring picnics, parades, concerts, and dances (see Hot Commodities: Cold Water). This alternative popular culture competed with the three main venues of male-dominated social life during the period—the theater, the tavern, and the political party—in which drinking played a central role. The Washingtonians and Sons of Temperance mostly targeted men and promoted new ideals of masculinity, but they were joined in these efforts by auxiliary female groups: the Martha Washington Societies and the Daughters of Temperance.

Already by 1840, the national consumption of alcohol had declined by more than two-thirds. A profound transformation in everyday life was under way, yet the impact of temperance reform across the country was uneven. Most of the pledges came from New England, western New York, New Jersey, and Pennsylvania. In the South and West, and in urban

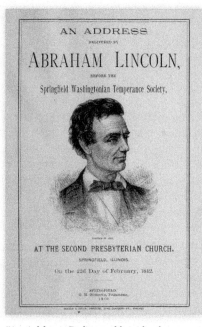

"An Address Delivered by Abraham Lincoln, Before the Springfield Washington Temperance Society."
There was some unintended irony in naming a temperance organization after George Washington, who had been a whiskey distiller, but the name reflected a desire to link alcohol reform to patriotism. Addressing a Washingtonian Society in Illinois in 1842, a young politician named Abraham Lincoln compared the "temperance revolution" to the revolution against Britain in 1776. In temperance, Lincoln proclaimed, "we find a stronger bondage broken, a viler slavery manumitted, and a greater tyrant deposed." *The Granger Collection, New York*

neighborhoods dominated by artisans, laborers, and immigrants, older patterns of drinking persisted. Alcohol continued to wreak havoc in Native American communities as well, though some native groups began to resist the liquor trade around this time. The Pawnee of the Great Plains regulated the supply of liquor, for example, and by the 1850s alcohol was totally banned from Pawnee villages. This was the result of powerful local leadership, however, rather than the influence of a national reform movement.

SENSATIONALISM AND THE PERILS OF DRINK

Temperance reformers hoped that a culture of sober camaraderie would support young men in their resolve to abstain from drinking, but they also turned to more sensational methods for sounding the alarm against alcohol. Reams of fictional temperance tales filled the pages of popular magazines during the 1840s, warning readers of the horrifying effects of alcohol on personal prospects and family tranquility. **Temperance novels** and plays enjoyed a heyday as well. Walt Whitman, before becoming a famous poet, began his literary career at the age of twenty-three with a novel entitled *Franklin Evans, or, The Inebriate* (1842). It sold more copies during the author's lifetime than any of his other publications. The novel concerned the travails of a young alcoholic from the North who visits a friend on a Virginia plantation, falls for an enslaved woman, and in a drunken state decides to marry and manumit her. Upon gaining sobriety, he regrets these actions, and he subsequently falls for a white woman from the North. His wife becomes jealous, murders her rival, and then kills herself. Such contrived, sensational plots were staples of temperance fiction in the 1840s. The most successful temperance author of the era was Timothy Shay Arthur, whose *Ten Nights in a*

HOT COMMODITIES
Cold Water

Water covers most of the Earth's surface, but its availability for human use can never be taken for granted. Even in our society, where access to drinkable water is considered a basic necessity, private water-bottling is big business. Only in the past century and a half have local governments in the United States assumed the burden of supplying water to their citizens. Before the middle of the nineteenth century, residents of big cities relied on communal wells, maintained their own cisterns, collected roof runoff, or purchased water from private companies. As populations grew, however, these methods proved inadequate to the changing demands of firefighting, public health, and personal hygiene. Between 1837 and 1848, Philadelphia, New York, and Boston all invested public funds in reservoirs and aqueducts. In a short time, water supply became a public utility.

Like other debates about municipal finance during this period, the question of whether government ought to intervene in the water business pitted poorer residents, who believed that the necessities of life should be shared by everyone, against wealthier residents, who advocated private competition. In this case, however, the supporters of public ownership found a powerful ally in middle-class reformers, who saw moral benefits in water. Starting in the 1830s, Northern reformers advanced new theories about the links between dirt and disease and touted the special

Cold Water Soldiers on Parade, 1848. Temperance reformers join in the celebration of the completion of Boston's first municipal water system. *Library of Congress, Prints & Photographs Division [LC-DIG-pga-02824]*

advantages of soft water (as opposed to the hard water that collected in wells) for washing food, clothing, and bodies. But the greatest advantage of clean water, reformers argued, was as an alternative beverage to alcohol. In the eighteenth century, distilled spirits had been considered a healthful complement to water—a mixer (or even a chaser!) that made water palatable and innocuous. By the 1830s, the conventional wisdom was shifting. By providing a clean water supply, governments would be removing one of the motivations for drinking liquor.

Temperance reformers supported public water projects as part of a larger campaign to turn clean, cold water into America's drink of choice. *Cold water* became a standard euphemism for events and organizations that shunned alcohol. Temperance societies called themselves cold water armies, staged cold water celebrations on July 4th, and sang cold water melodies that praised the virtues and pleasures of this alternative beverage. In an 1842 Washingtonian song, set to the tune of "Yankee Doodle," the final verse proclaims

> *I'll not touch the poisonous stuff,*
> *Since all the brooks are free, sir;*
> *Give me cold water, 'tis enough,*
> *That cannot injure me, sir.*

Think About It

1. Why did middle-class reformers not rely on private competition to provide water to urban residents?

2. What might have been some of the arguments against this reform?

Bar-Room (1854) became one of the best-selling American novels of the nineteenth century.

Temperance fiction frightened (and entertained) readers with stories of fortunes squandered, marriages sundered, and lives lost. Reformers also circulated images of crazed drunkards and the cowering victims of their violent outbursts. Finally, temperance lecturers sought to convert the masses by offering personal testimonies of the horrors of drinking. John B. Gough was a former actor who moved audiences all across the country with accounts of his drunken past and dramatic performances of the *delirium tremens,* a physiological

"The Drunkard's Home." This illustration, accompanying a temperance tale, dramatizes the threat that intoxicated men posed to their families. Temperance fiction often featured villainous husbands who beat their wives while under the influence and initiated their sons into the dangerous world of the tavern. *Chronicle/Alamy Stock Photo*

condition caused by alcohol abuse. Gough gained special notoriety in 1845, when he disappeared for a week in New York and was discovered seven days later, intoxicated, in a house of ill repute. Gough claimed that enemies had slipped a drug into his glass of cherry soda and dragged him to the brothel to discredit him. Much of the public appears to have accepted this explanation for his fall off the wagon, and Gough's career as a spokesman for the temperance cause continued to flourish. Gough's spectacular lapse reinforced the temperance message that alcohol was a dangerous foe that could never be vanquished permanently.

SEX AND THE SECRET VICE

Though the term *temperance* referred specifically to drinking, the campaign against liquor also stressed a broader ethic of **bodily self-control.** The impulse to consume alcohol was one of several appetites and instincts that needed to be suppressed. Reformers during this period worried especially about the sexual appetites of men. The middle-class male was expected to control his sexual instincts as well as his drinking habits.

Women reformers took the lead in an evangelical campaign against sexual vice. The American Female Moral Reform Society, which grew to more than one hundred chapters within ten years of its founding in 1834, targeted male depravity and challenged the traditional double standard that condemned prostitution and female promiscuity while condoning the sexual activity of men. In New York, the moral reformers organized a petition drive to persuade the state legislature to outlaw seduction. More generally, the moral reform movement sought to instill in men a new, chaste attitude toward their own sexuality.

Whereas the moral reform movement targeted men who patronized sex workers or seduced young women, others worried more about what men (and women) did when they were alone. Beginning in the 1830s, an antimasturbation movement took hold in the United States, as doctors, lecturers, and childrearing manuals initiated a public discussion of the dangers of what they called the solitary vice or **the secret vice.** Reformist tracts described the horrors of this widespread practice and linked it with numerous physical ailments and insanity. Temperance lecturer Sylvester Graham led the crusade, and other evangelical physiologists echoed his message, describing masturbation as the definitive problem of the age (see Singular Lives: Sylvester Graham, Diet Crusader). Reformers worried especially about very young boys initiating one another into the dark world of self-abuse, though Graham's disciple Mary Gove insisted that it was a common problem among girls as well. Much of the anxiety focused on boys living away from their parents and young men in cities who worked in the new economy. Masturbation, like drinking, was considered to be a dangerous habit that launched a young man down a steady path to ruin.

The masturbation scare of the 1830s should not be misunderstood as traditional superstition. Reformers who argued that masturbation caused debility, insanity, and death were not recycling old folk beliefs. They were espousing newfangled medical theories and citing the latest scientific studies in an optimistic attempt to change the world. Their emphasis on self-control linked their campaign to many of the other reform movements of their day. Reformers were not prudish men and women who were uncomfortable discussing sex. On the contrary, crusaders against the secret vice argued that masturbation needed to be discussed openly, not only between parents and children but in public life as well.

ABOLITIONISTS

A subset of the men and women who joined the temperance crusade also believed that slaveholding was sinful. **Abolitionists,** as they were called, remained a small group in the North throughout the 1830s and 1840s, but they hailed from the same evangelical circles as other, more popular reformers and stressed many of the same reform themes. Almost all abolitionists, both white and Black, advocated temperance, for example. But their radical views on slavery threatened the political compromises on which the federal union rested and challenged racial hierarchy in the North as well as the South.

IMMEDIATISM

What distinguished the new generation of abolitionist reformers that rose to prominence around 1830 (see Chapter 11) was their commitment to immediate rather than gradual solutions to the problem of slavery. From the 1790s to the 1820s, antislavery campaigns in both Britain and the United States had focused on stopping the slave trade or developing complex projects, such as African colonization (see Chapter 9) that enlisted the cooperation of slaveholders. By 1830, gradualist compromises had been discredited, attacked by Black abolitionists as racist and by slaveholders as too dangerous. In their place arose a powerful approach known by historians as **immediatism.** It was not the dominant view in the North, not even among those who found slavery repugnant. Though many Northerners objected to slave *trading* and viewed the political power of slaveholders with suspicion, the men and women who wanted to *abolish* slavery wherever it existed in the United States formed a tiny minority. Still, this new and radical ideology would frame the national slavery debate.

By the 1830s, abolitionists were calling for the immediate emancipation of all enslaved people, without compensation to slaveholders. This was a radical position by the standards of antislavery thought at the time. Britain's Emancipation Act of 1833, which ended slavery in the West Indies, offered 20 million pounds in compensation, to be supplemented for six years by the unpaid labor of Black "apprentices." Northern abolitionists, many of whom were evangelical Christians, wanted none of that. They were not interested in economic ramifications or political timetables. Slavery was inherently sinful and emancipation had to be instantaneous and unmediated.

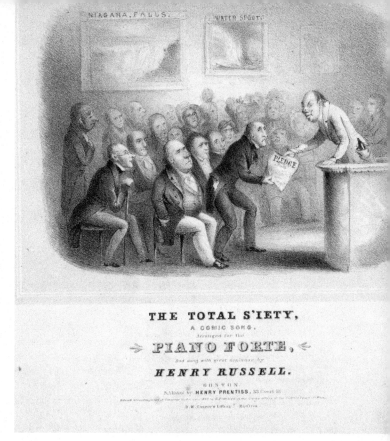

"The Total S'iety, a Comic Song," 1840. Temperance lectures persuaded countless audience members to sign pledges. Note how the drawing on this sheet music cover mocks the speaker as a drunken hypocrite, with a red nose and a bottle in his pocket, and lampoons the obsession with water. *John Hopkins University, Levy Sheet Music Collection, Box 099, Item 055*

Like a religious convert at a mass revival or a drunkard freeing himself from whiskey, enslaved people and slaveholders needed to break the chains of human bondage.

Abolitionism was not only a radical stance toward the slavery question; it was also a fundamental critique of the social order. Although most white Northerners, whatever they thought about slavery, held conservative attitudes toward American race relations, the abolitionists did not. Both Blacks like James Forten and Sojourner Truth and whites like William Lloyd Garrison and Angelina Grimké advocated racial equality. Garrison drew special notoriety for his views. When critics charged, as they often did, that abolitionists were driven by a desire for interracial sex, Garrison made it clear that he did, in fact, foresee and favor marriage between whites and Blacks.

Garrison and his most radical allies were countercultural critics. Although many of them had social and economic affiliations with an elite merchant class, and the evangelical religion they espoused had cultural prestige, their opposition to slavery put them at the margins of mainstream politics. For the Garrisonians, the sin of slavery

SINGULAR LIVES

Sylvester Graham, Diet Crusader

Among the many men and women who took the temperance podium in the 1830s, only one remains a household name. Sylvester Graham was a Connecticut-born physician and Presbyterian minister who began preaching against alcohol but broadened his message to attack masturbation and all habits that he believed led to drink, lust, and a general sapping of the body's vitality. According to Graham, the real problem was stimulation, and he urged his growing band of followers to abstain from coffee, tobacco, and frequent sexual intercourse—which meant more than a few times in one's life. (Graham himself was the seventeenth child of parents who clearly did not practice such restraint.) He also shunned meat, spices, snacking between meals, restrictive clothing, and soft bedding.

Graham's greatest notoriety came in the field of dietary reform. Reaching wide audiences through his popular lectures and books, he preached that the key to human happiness lay in the stomach. If people would adhere to a strict regimen of small portions of unstimulating food consumed at regular hours, they would be able to live long, chaste lives. Among the obstacles to such a life, Graham believed, was the refined white bread that was popular in urban settings. Graham invented his own bread recipe in 1829, using coarse whole-wheat flour and avoiding all chemical additives. The original Graham cracker, which was a good deal blander than its modern descendants, consisted of this special flour.

Though he was an idiosyncratic and controversial thinker, drawing the wrath of butchers and bakers and the ridicule of many of his contemporaries, Graham was in many ways the quintessential antebellum reformer. He preached temperance, bodily control, and chastity. He instructed young men on how to conduct more respectable lives and resist the temptations of the marketplace. And he believed that new medical notions could create happier human beings. In retrospect, many of his ideas seem more mainstream. Vegetarianism is no longer a novelty, and grocery stores in many parts of the country cater to those who prefer whole grains or unprocessed food. Even more Americans share Graham's faith that proper diet holds the key to health and happiness. Perhaps Graham's most enduring legacy appears on the American breakfast table. He had been a major proponent of early morning meals consisting of whole grains. One of his most influential followers, Dr. John Harvey Kellogg, experimented with flakes of different grains in an effort to find the perfect meal to lower the sex drives of the patients at his sanitarium. In 1906, Kellogg's brother Will began marketing the result under the brand name Corn Flakes.

Where in the Archives?

Graham was a prolific lecturer and author during the 1830s, addressing topics ranging from sexuality to food to cholera. Historians of reform draw upon these sources to understand his ideology and his influential message.

Sylvester Graham. Ralph Waldo Emerson dubbed Graham "the poet of bran and pumpkins." *Library of Congress, Prints & Photographs Division [LC-USZ62-123830]*

Sylvester Graham's *A Treatise on Bread, and Bread-Making* was published by Light & Stearns in 1837; his *A Lecture to Young Men, on Chastity* was first published in 1834 and is available in a second edition published by Light & Stearns: Crocker and Brewster in 1837; and both are available through Google Books (https://books.google.com/).

Assignment

Locate and read Chapters 1, 2, and 7 of *A Treatise on Bread* ("History of Bread," "Laws of Diet," "Who Should Make Bread") and pages 27–43 of *A Lecture to Young Men.* Answer the following questions in 200 words each:

1. How are Graham's perspectives on sexuality and bread related?

2. How does Graham connect health, morality, and social progress?

turned the nation's sacred symbols into objects of scorn. On July 4th, Garrison publicly burned a copy of the Constitution. Governments, churches, and even the Bible, whatever texts or institutions condoned slavery, became targets of the Garrisonians' wrath.

SLAVE TESTIMONY

Some of the most ardent and influential abolitionists were men and women who had been born into bondage. Formerly enslaved people were able to help the abolitionist cause by offering first-hand testimony about the brutal

"Am I Not a Man and a Brother?" This image was an icon of the American Anti-Slavery Society, the leading organization of immediatist abolition. Based on a design by British abolitionists in the 1780s, it originally appeared as a mass-produced miniature sculpture suitable for setting in jewelry. Questions for Analysis: Why is the man on his knees? Why might abolitionists have chosen to display this image rather than one of an enslaved man picking cotton, suffering corporal punishment, or rising up in rebellion? *Library of Congress, Prints & Photographs Division [LC-USZ62-44265]*

treatment they had received and by demonstrating their own humanity and their own capacity for citizenship. The most famous of these was Frederick Douglass, who escaped from his Maryland owner in 1838, settled in Massachusetts, and joined the American Anti-Slavery Society. Douglass was a sensation on the abolitionist lecture circuit, helping raise funds with his vivid accounts of plantation life. Audience members were sometimes drawn to his talks by skepticism that an African American raised in bondage could be so eloquent.

In part to dispel the suspicions they encountered on the lecture tour, formerly enslaved people like Douglass also published autobiographies. **Slave narratives,** as historians and literary critics call them, are invaluable sources of information about the experience of slavery, but they were also commercial publications designed to attract readers and yield revenue, often for the author. Moreover, they were abolitionist tracts designed to persuade readers of the evil of slavery in the American South. One of the most important strategies of the slave narrative was to prove its authenticity by naming actual slaveholders or by including letters from respected members of the white community asserting that the formerly enslaved person in question actually wrote the book. Proslavery apologists were quick to challenge the truthfulness—and the authorship—of published slave narratives. On one occasion, the American Anti-Slavery Society even recalled the autobiography of fugitive James Williams, because they could not corroborate the details of his story. Questions surrounding the authenticity of slave narratives continue to haunt scholars today. The now-canonical slave narrative of Harriet Jacobs, who wrote under the name Linda Brent, was widely believed to be have been composed by white abolitionist Lydia Maria Child until it was proved in the early 1980s to be Jacobs's own work.

MOB VIOLENCE

Unlike the advocates of other reforms, abolitionists were targets of major violence and repression throughout much of the North, especially in the years 1834–1838, when abolitionism was a new and disruptive force in national politics (see Chapter 11). **Anti-abolitionist riots,** often led by prominent members of the community, disrupted antislavery meetings and destroyed the homes and offices of the movement's leaders. Mobs also turned their wrath on churches where abolitionists preached and Blacks and whites prayed together. In 1837, rioters in Alton, Illinois, murdered abolitionist minister and editor Elijah Lovejoy as he sought to prevent the destruction of his printing press.

Mob leaders were often Democratic politicians eager to maintain their coalition with Southerners, and their posters criticized abolitionists for sowing sectional discord. But anti-abolitionists were also trying to control race relations in Northern cities. They targeted places where whites and Blacks socialized, and they decried abolitionists as amalgamationists—people who supported or desired interracial sexual unions. Participants in these riots also identified abolitionism with elitism, with England, and with the larger agenda of middle-class reform. A mob in Wilkes-Barre, Pennsylvania, for example, dragged an abolitionist named William Gildersleeve to the local tavern in 1839 and forced him to have a drink.

Farther south, slavery advocates were able to use the law, rather than mob violence, to suppress abolitionist activity. Local ordinances targeted antislavery publications and their authors. The Georgia legislature placed a bounty on Garrison, offering five thousand dollars to anyone who would bring him to Georgia to face criminal charges (see How Much Is That? Garrison's Bounty). Abolitionists steered clear of the South during the 1830s.

How Much Is That?

Garrison's Bounty

The five thousand dollars offered by Georgia for the apprehension of the abolitionist William Lloyd Garrison is equivalent to about one hundred fifty-six thousand dollars in 2020 dollars. By comparison, the FBI currently offers minimum rewards of one hundred thousand dollars for help apprehending the criminals on its Ten Most Wanted Fugitives list.

BEHIND THE IMAGE

Popular artist/cartoonist Edward W. Clay published this image a year after anti-abolitionist rioters in his hometown of Philadelphia set fire to a building where mixed-race gatherings took place. This was one of a series of cartoons produced by Clay during that year that ridiculed abolitionists and warned of the dangers of social encounters between whites and Blacks. The series title, *Practical Amalgamation*, warns readers that abolitionists don't simply reject white supremacy in theory but also intend to act on their beliefs. Most of the cartoons also include a depiction of or reference to William Lloyd Garrison.

Practical Amalgamation: Musical Soirée (1839), Edward W. Clay. *American Antiquarian Society, Worcester, Massachusetts, USA/The Bridgeman Art Library*

WITHIN THE IMAGE

The musical gathering shown here subverts what Clay's audience sees as the natural order of race relations. It takes place in a lavishly appointed home that 1 based on the landscape paintings on the wall, appears to be owned by African Americans. 2 Black figures dominate: They occupy the foreground and are participating in the festivities. 3 White guests are relegated to the background and are not participating in singing, and 4 the hunched white pianist seems like a servant rather than a performer. At the same time, 5 by presenting African Americans as having grotesque facial features, Clay ridicules their aspirations to social grace and gentility. 6 And by showing white men captivated by a Black female singer, Clay also reinforces the charge that abolitionism was motivated and characterized by desire for interracial sex. The tall white man in the rear of the scene appears to be modeled after Garrison.

BEYOND THE IMAGE

The *Practical Amalgamation* series, which circulated widely both in the Northeast and in England, was unusual at the time of its publication for its depiction of interracial intimacy, as well as for its focus on white, male abolitionists as leading figures in this drama. But it reinforced a new theme in anti-abolitionist rhetoric and conspiracy theory (see Chapter 11), which held that the white radicals who advocated immediate, uncompensated emancipation were motivated by pathological sexual desires.

INTERNAL DIVISIONS

As the abolitionist movement grew in the 1830s, members began to question two controversial parts of the new ideology. Garrison had advocated a policy of nonresistance, which meant that abolitionists, like other reformers, would rely on moral suasion rather than physical force to bring about social change. But for Garrison, it also meant not relying on state power or political elections. Abolitionists wrote petitions to Congress in the 1830s, but many of their leaders refused to support candidates for office and even opposed voting, since it implied cooperation with a slaveholding political system. This posture put the Garrisonians at loggerheads with **political abolitionists** like James Birney and Gerrit Smith, who saw in the political process an opportunity to exert significant influence over national policy.

Abolitionists also divided over the role of women in the movement. As in other antebellum reform campaigns, women participated actively in abolitionist efforts. Angelina Grimké, author of *Appeal to the Christian Women of the South* (1836), grew up in a slaveholding family in South Carolina and moved north, where she and her sister Sarah became antislavery lecturers. According to witnesses, Angelina Grimké could command the undivided attention of immense audiences for two hours at a time. Other women, including Lucretia Mott, Lydia Maria Child, and Abby Kelley, also assumed leadership positions in the American Anti-Slavery Society. But by the end of the decade, many supporters of the growing movement were objecting to the role that women were playing, criticizing both the practice of female abolitionists addressing mixed-sex audiences and their embrace of women's rights. When Kelley was appointed to a key committee of the American Anti-Slavery Society at its 1840 convention, a substantial minority of delegates bolted the room and formed their own organization. The **1840 schism** within the abolitionist ranks divided the Garrisonians, who were committed to sexual equality and opposed to political action, from those abolitionists who wanted to focus exclusively on slavery. One dissenter explained his resignation from the Board of Managers of the Massachusetts chapter of the American Anti-Slavery Society as follows: "The Society is no longer an *Anti-Slavery* Society *simply*, but . . . has become a *women's rights, no-government-Anti-Slavery Society*." The same year, political abolitionists launched the Liberty Party, a national political party defined entirely by its opposition to slavery. James Birney was the party's presidential nominee.

The two major issues over which abolitionists divided—the role of women and the legitimacy of political action—were closely related, because politics was a masculine arena in the antebellum period. Abolitionists who favored political action were urging reformers to focus on a world in which women had no legal voice and

POLITICS AND ENTERTAINMENT

● **Hutchinson Family Singers.** Like the temperance movement, abolitionism spawned its own theatrical culture. The Hutchinson family of New Hampshire (including the ten brothers pictured here) formed a popular singing group in 1840 and sang about slavery. They often performed at antislavery rallies and more generally identified with the reform causes of the era. "Yes we're friends of emancipation," the lyrics of their most famous song announced. "We are all teetotalers/And have sign'd the Temp'rance pledge." ● *Heritage Images/Hulton Archive/Getty Images*

men were the crucial audience. From this perspective, women who played an active role in the movement were entering a male preserve and behaving like men. For the Garrisonians, on the other hand, abolitionism was about moral suasion and not politics, so it was perfectly appropriate for women to be active in the movement. At the same time, the Garrisonians' rejection of political action was also a rejection of the violent, drunken masculinity that dominated mass politics. Like many others in the larger world of reform to which abolitionism belonged, key figures in the antislavery movement saw themselves as trying to create a different kind of man, more sober and self-controlled. Some of them also began to wonder whether the nation might be better served by a political process in which both men and women participated.

DOMESTICITY AND GENDER

The reform impulses that drove movements like temperance and abolition reinforced a growing interest among middle-class Protestants in the question of how to exert moral influence over other people. This was a particularly pressing issue when it came to their own children. Especially in towns and cities, middle-class fathers had little of the power enjoyed by traditional household patriarchs (see Chapter 4) who commanded family labor and controlled the inheritance of farmland. In a more mobile, market-oriented society, parents and community leaders sought new ways to shape character and cultivate marketable skills in the next generation. Around the 1830s, reformers began addressing those concerns by touting the home as a space of intimacy and tranquility presided over by a nurturing mother. Those who celebrated this ideal of domestic life promoted new roles for men and women and new beliefs about the significance of sexual difference that would have a powerful impact on modern American culture. The **cult of domesticity,** as historians call this ideology, spread through fashion magazines, holiday observances, and an expanding consumer culture. It also contributed, paradoxically, to the birth of the country's first feminist movement.

MEN'S AND WOMEN'S SEPARATE SPHERES

In earlier periods of American history, men and women had, of course, enjoyed different rights, assumed different responsibilities, and faced different challenges. But only in the nineteenth century did Americans come to believe that the sexes ought to occupy **separate spheres** of activity and influence. "Domestic life is a woman's sphere," an advice book from 1832 explained, "and it is there that she is most usefully as well as most appropriately employed." Men, on the other hand, belonged in the workplace, absorbed in the pursuit of financial gain. This was not a time-honored cliché but rather an outlook that was catching on, a reform idea.

Traditionally, the home had been a site of production where both men and women worked under the control of a male head-of-household. But by the 1830s, changes in the nature of work were making it possible to think of workplaces and domestic spaces as distinct. Especially in the more urban parts of the North, fewer workers lived with their employers or labored under the roof of a master. Those who worked for cash wages and produced for distant markets were less likely to perform that work where they slept and less likely to share that work with their blood relatives. At the same time, middle-class Americans were marrying later, having fewer children, and living in more tightly defined kin groups, often consisting of just a nuclear family. All of these conditions encouraged middle-class men and women to imagine the home as something opposed to work.

The home, according to the new apostles of domesticity, should be a female-dominated private zone insulated from the rough-and-tumble public worlds of the marketplace, the street, and the ballot box. Increasingly in the nineteenth century, middle-class homes were subdivided architecturally into a semipublic downstairs consisting of common areas and parlors and an upstairs consisting of private bedrooms and nurseries. Redefined in this way, the home now appeared as a feminine domain. In countless magazine articles, domestic manuals, advice books, and medical journals, authors of both sexes introduced the idea that women were naturally suited to private life. Catharine Beecher, perhaps the best-known author of housekeeping guides during this period, called domestic life "a woman's sphere" and discouraged her readers from venturing beyond its bounds. Earlier images of women as manipulative and domineering receded from mainstream culture—or were directed largely toward lower-class women and the sexually deviant women who filled the pages of sensationalist literature. In their place came images of women as vulnerable and infantilized. These were new beliefs, bolstered by the prestige of modern science. A medical professor explained to his exclusively male gynecology class in 1847 that the female head is "almost too small for intellect but just big enough for love."

What suited women to the task of running the home, according to the domestic reformers, was precisely this capacity for love. Loving mothers could build character in their children (and their husbands), because the objects of that love would be receptive to maternal influence and would wind up internalizing the proper values of sobriety, thrift, honesty, and self-control. Throughout the reform culture, men and women paid tribute to the shrine of what they called true motherhood.

Those who celebrated domesticity spoke of it as an oasis of personal relations unsullied by the conflicts of a materialistic world. But working-class Americans could not afford to live up to this middle-class ideal. Only a small minority of male urban artisans could support their families on a single income, and most poorer women left the home to work in factories, sweatshops, or, more often, as **domestic servants** in middle-class homes. Although the work of housewives was defined outside the wage labor model, household work was often wage labor when performed by an outsider. For home and work to become distinct in middle-class America, there had to be a pool of women available for low-paid work outside of their own homes. And for middle-class children to stay home longer, there had to be a pool of young girls entering the market at an early age to help service the domestic hearth. Domesticity thus reinforced class divisions—divisions that often overlapped with those of race and ethnicity. In the 1840s in Philadelphia, for example, one in five adult Blacks lived as a servant in a white household.

WHITE-COLLAR MEN

As the home became a feminine domain identified with middle-class women, middle-class men spent more time in places where they dominated. To the horror of reformers, some sought pleasure and camaraderie among men of different classes in the urban world of saloons, brothels, and theaters. Others enjoyed more respectable associations with members of their own class, such as debating societies and baseball clubs. Men could also carve out within the middle-class home some rooms of their own, such as a study or a library. But the most respectable masculine space within the new world of separate spheres was the office.

The office became the distinctive work environment for nonmanual workers during this era, especially for legions of young men employed as **clerks** in such businesses as dry-goods stores or banks. Though an entry-level clerkship might not pay much more than the wages of a young cabinetmaker or a tailor, clerks were apprentices in an expanding world of commercial opportunity, part of a new breed of middle-class employees whose identity came not from the craft they performed but from the prestige associated with commerce and capitalism. A clerk's tasks might be monotonous, but it was high-status work. In the clerical office, the young man demonstrated the kind of character and self-control that middle-class homes were supposed to instill.

Reformers enforced the link between respectable habits and the market economy through a new institution that produced and disseminated credit ratings. In 1841, an evangelical New York merchant named Lewis Tappan, who was prominent in the antislavery movement, opened the **Mercantile Agency,** the nation's first credit bureau. Starting out with his abolitionist friends, Tappan developed a vast network of informants scattered throughout the country, who supplied his office with financial reports and character references for tens of thousands of men engaged in commerce. Merchants eager to determine whether a firm or an individual buyer in a distant locale

Early Baseball Players. Baseball, modeled on an English children's game called rounders, was played by adults in American cities earlier in the century, but its history as an organized sport began in the 1840s. The first teams were middle-class fraternal clubs, such as the New York Knickerbocker Club, shown here. (Alexander Cartwright, in the middle of the back row, is often credited with having devised the original rules of the sport.) Clubs like the Knickerbockers enabled young men to enjoy respectable pleasures that did not involve gambling or violence. *The Granger Collection, New York*

was a good credit risk could purchase this information from the agency. Tappan's files, inscribed in large, red books held in New York, contained information about how much a man was worth and how reliably he paid his bills, but it also assessed his drinking habits, his personal life, and his moral reputation. The Mercantile Agency's success spawned numerous competitors, and Tappan's company eventually became Dun and Bradstreet, America's leading broker of credit information.

MAGAZINES, HOLIDAYS, AND CONSUMPTION

New ideals of femininity, masculinity, homemaking, and family life lay at the center of an expanding middle-class culture. This culture was spread not only in schoolrooms, lecture halls, and dining room tables but also in mass publications, such as advice books and periodicals. National magazines directed at female readers were especially important in disseminating ideas about domesticity and respectability. ● The first highly successful women's magazine, **Godey's Lady's Book** (founded in 1830), featured articles, stories, and poems by famous authors alongside fashion advice, architectural plans, and moral instruction. *Godey's*, with a circulation of one hundred fifty thousand by 1860, exerted an enormous influence on women's clothing styles, and the magazine became one of the principal arbiters of middle-class taste. ●

Magazines like *Godey's* instructed middle-class readers in the proper ways to dress, shop, socialize, mourn the dead, give gifts, and celebrate holidays. In fact, such magazines were at the center of new efforts to reform the calendar by promoting holidays that took place in the home and centered around the family. Sarah Josepha Hale, the editor of *Godey's*, waged a lifelong campaign to create a national holiday based on the religious thanksgiving fasts and feasts of New England Puritans. In 1863, Hale's campaign bore fruit, and Thanksgiving, which was already a popular middle-class custom in the Northeast, became an official observance identified with a domestic meal.

The **modern American Christmas** also emerged in this period as a family-centered holiday. Before the antebellum period, Christmas was a time of public drunkenness and outdoor revelry. Several of the American colonies had banned or discouraged the observance of December 25, in part because it was originally a pagan holiday but also because it was a time of social disorder. Between the 1820s and 1850s, Christmas was transformed into a family festivity celebrated largely indoors, focused on the exchange of gifts, and identified with the jolly figure of Santa Claus, who enters the home and rewards good children. By the 1830s, observers were already complaining that "All the children are expecting presents," and stores began bombarding potential customers with advertisements for Christmas gifts. Manufacturers, merchants, newspaper editors, and advertisers promoted the idea of Christmas as a time when material longings could be legitimately indulged and luxury items could be purchased and given as tokens of the kind of parental affection that was becoming the hallmark of the new middle-class family.

THE RISE OF FEMINISM

Though all the cultural emphasis on home and family imposed significant burdens and restrictions on American women, it also provided the basis for new arguments on behalf of women's rights. Celebrations of domesticity and motherhood assigned special significance to mothers in shaping the country's values and made women the guardians of social order. And all the talk about how men and women were fundamentally different creatures made it more plausible to argue that

Santa Claus Comes to Town.   Though nominally connected to a bishop canonized as St. Nicholas, the modern Santa Claus is an American figure, popularized in the 1822 poem "A Visit from St. Nicholas." By the 1840s, he had become a common commercial icon. In this 1850s illustration, which retains some of the revelry of earlier Christmas traditions, Santa visits "his young friends in the United States." © *North Wind Picture Archives*

MEDIA AND INFORMATION

Modeling Domesticity.   *Godey's* dress illustrations, which appeared in elaborate color plates at the time of the Civil War, heralded the arrival of the modern fashion magazine, but they were part of a larger reform campaign to spread the cult of domesticity to middle-class readers. *Reading Room 2020/Alamy Stock Photo*

critics of slavery had developed, invoking similar ideals of social inclusion, equality, and human rights. Early feminists also shared with the abolitionists a foundation in the evangelical churches, where women had been playing active roles since the beginning of the century. Abolitionism thrust women onto the stage of local and national politics and gave them valuable training in political organizing, fundraising, lecturing, and pamphleteering.

The campaign for women's rights gathered momentum in a series of conventions during the 1840s, the most famous of which took place in 1848 in Seneca Falls, New York. Organized by Lucretia Mott and Elizabeth Cady Stanton, the **Seneca Falls Convention** issued a Declaration of Sentiments, modeled explicitly on the Declaration of Independence, proclaiming the self-evident truth "that all men and women are created equal." Seneca Falls launched a feminist movement designed to secure equal status for women under the law. Feminist reformers focused on a few basic rights: Women ought to have legal control over their wages and property, the rights to form contracts and inherit, and equal rights to custody and guardianship over children. Finally, women ought to have the same right to vote in popular elections.

Woman suffrage became the most important goal of the antebellum feminist movement, the one demand that symbolized and could secure all the others. It was also the most controversial. A resolution demanding the vote for women barely passed the Seneca Falls Convention. Although other planks in the feminist platform met with some success in the state legislatures, suffrage did not. Even after the Civil War, when amendments to the Constitution enshrined and extended the principle of equal protection and expanded voting rights to include African Americans, women were still excluded from the electoral process.

The new feminist movement was most successful in securing women's economic rights. According to the prevailing legal doctrine of **coverture,** a wife was legally subsumed to the identity of her husband, bound to obey his orders and incapable of owning property, contracting her own debts, or appearing in court as her own legal person except under unusual circumstances. By the middle of the century, coverture was beginning to decline, especially in matters of property ownership. Mississippi passed a married women's property act in 1839, and by 1860, fourteen states had enacted similar laws allowing wives to control the property they had brought to the marriage or to acquire property while married that would not automatically belong to their husbands. Such reforms ran counter to the ideology of separate spheres, which stipulated that certain aspects

female purity suited women for moral leadership and not simply for subservience.

Northerners who were actively involved in the reform movements of the period were most likely to sympathize with such arguments. If maternal affection and moral suasion were the way to change the hearts and minds of drunkards, slaveholders, criminals, or wayward children, then women had a special moral authority to address social problems. But women active in causes such as temperance and abolition found the taboo against female participation in public life to be powerful. They also began to see more clearly the forms of second-class citizenship to which women were subjected. As Angelina Grimké wrote to Catharine Beecher, "the investigation of the rights of the slave has led me to a better understanding of my own."

By around 1840, a new feminist reform movement was emerging out of abolitionism. Early advocates of **women's rights** adopted many of the forms of social analysis that

Anti-Suffrage Cartoon, 1869. More than two decades after the Seneca Falls Convention, women were no closer to being able to vote. Popular lithographs continued to mock the prospect of female participation in political life as a threat to established gender norms and social order. **Questions for Analysis:** According to the artist, what is the problem with woman suffrage? *MPI/Getty Images*

of economic life belonged in the male domain. Other improvements in women's legal status fit with the new ideology. Most states began awarding custody of children to mothers rather than fathers during the antebellum era, but not on the grounds that men and women deserved equal rights. This new legal practice reflected beliefs that childrearing was crucial to social order and that mothers were naturally better suited to that task.

RELIGION AND IMMIGRATION

Even in the North, not everyone embraced the culture of reform. Radical movements, such as abolitionism and woman suffrage, certainly rankled the mainstream, but even the basic beliefs about self-control, character, and conscience that dominated middle-class culture at the

time were potentially controversial. Some of the biggest culture wars in the antebellum North pitted Protestants against Catholics. Reformers were overwhelmingly Protestant, and many of them saw Catholicism as an obstacle to reform. This view became more widespread during the 1830s and 1840s, just as Catholic immigrants were changing the demographic character of the country and challenging the assumption that America was a Protestant nation.

ANTI-CATHOLICISM

Though most Americans would now regard hostility to the Catholic Church as a form of bigotry, **anti-Catholicism** in the antebellum period was pursued by many native-born Protestants as a reform cause. Leaders of temperance, antislavery, and other reform crusades often portrayed Catholicism as a threat to the free institutions of the American republic, as a form of religious superstition that blocked the path to salvation, or as a conservative social force that prevented individuals from taking control of their own lives. These were common views in the United States at the time. New Englanders claimed a long tradition of anti-Catholicism going back to the Puritan founding of their colonies, but even in other parts of the country, a general fear of conspiracies (see Chapter 11) and foreign influences exposed Catholics to the suspicion that they were taking orders from the pope.

In the 1830s, anti-Catholicism began to intensify in the North. A number of factors contributed to this trend, including Catholic immigration to the United States, an international revival in Catholic piety and theology, and the general influence of evangelical Protestantism in American public life. In 1834, an anti-Catholic mob burned an Ursuline convent in Charlestown, Massachusetts, in response to a rumor that a nun was being held there against her wishes. Later that year, Samuel F. B. Morse, the man who would develop the electromagnetic telegraph and help introduce photography to the United States, published a series of letters claiming that European monarchs had enlisted the Catholic Church in a scheme to undermine democracy in the United States by encouraging Catholic immigration to the American West. The following year, the eminent minister Lyman Beecher (father of Catharine Beecher and the famous antislavery novelist Harriet Beecher Stowe), whose anti-Catholic sermons had helped inspire the convent attack, warned that Catholic schools in the United States were trying to indoctrinate American children for nefarious purposes. Then in 1836, Maria Monk's alleged exposé of her experiences at a Montreal nunnery (see Interpreting the Sources: The Awful Disclosures of Maria Monk), published with the support of powerful New England elites, became a phenomenal best-seller.

Anti-Catholic conspiracy theories found a receptive audience among reform-minded Protestants, and especially among abolitionists. Though the most radical antislavery voices criticized clergy and established religious authority more generally, abolitionists singled out the Catholic Church as an enemy of freedom comparable to the Slave Power. Abolitionists resented the fact that the Catholic Church accepted slavery, but like many reformers they also hated Catholicism on its own terms. "In this country, popery finds its appropriate ally in the institution of slavery," wrote an Ohio abolitionist. "They are both kindred systems. One enslaves the mind, the other both mind and body." Because Catholicism insisted on the infallibility of its own leaders, Protestant reformers charged, the Church is the natural enemy of democracy and human progress. On the other side of the divide, Catholic priests and intellectuals mistrusted the reform movements and their belief in the infallibility of individual conscience. Catholics, both in the United States and abroad, criticized Protestant reformers for having a naïve faith in human freedom, for elevating individuals over communities, and for favoring social changes that would lead to chaos, bloodshed, and true despotism.

Conflicts between Protestants and Catholics increased in the 1840s as the Catholic population of the United States grew. On the outskirts of Philadelphia, two bloody riots broke out during the summer of 1844 between Irish-born Catholics and native-born Protestants. Two Catholic churches and many homes were destroyed, and rioters on both sides were killed. Because the conflict pitted immigrant newcomers against **nativists** (advocates of the interests of native-born citizens and opponents of immigration), the riots are often categorized as nativist violence. But the core grievances on both sides of the Philadelphia riots had more to do with religion than with turf battles between recent arrivals and more established communities. Although nativism would become a powerful force in American politics in the 1850s (see Chapter 14), anti-Catholicism was even more widespread. And whereas virtually all nativists in the antebellum North were anti-Catholic, not all anti-Catholics were nativist. Especially after the Revolutions of 1848, when the Catholic Church played an important role in thwarting liberal nationalist uprisings in Europe, anti-Catholicism flourished among many Americans (including German immigrants, socialists, and land reformers) who had no sympathy whatsoever for nativism.

CONFLICTING FAITHS

IRISH IMMIGRATION AND THE POTATO FAMINE

Although anti-Catholic prejudice originated in global religious conflicts rather than ethnic hostilities in the United States, one American ethnic group bore the brunt of that prejudice. The experiences and perspectives of Irish Americans shaped the politics of evangelical reform in the antebellum era. The high point of Irish immigration to the United States would take place in the decade after 1845, but already by the 1830s the flow of immigrants from Ireland had struck most observers at the time as a

INTERPRETING THE SOURCES

The Awful Disclosures of Maria Monk

Of all the anti-Catholic writings produced in the United States, none was read more widely than a book entitled *Awful Disclosures, by Maria Monk, of the Hotel Dieu Nunnery of Montreal* (1836). Monk recounted her life in the Montreal convent, telling lurid stories of sex and murder while confirming her readers' suspicions that Catholicism was a religion that despised the Bible, kept its adherents ignorant, and thrived on secrecy. Like many other popular captivity stories of the time, including those of fugitives from slavery, Monk's book ends with a description of her escape from the convent.

Though *Awful Disclosures* was presented as nonfiction, Monk's tale would ultimately be exposed as a fabrication. Still, it sold three hundred thousand copies over twenty-five years, becoming one of the best-selling books by an American author before the Civil War.

Early editions of the book included a foldout map showing the interior and exterior layouts of the convent. Following are excerpts from the sixth chapter.

The [Mother] Superior now informed me . . . that one of my great duties was, to obey the priests in all things; and this I soon learnt, to my utter astonishment and horror, was to live in the practice of criminal intercourse with them. . . . Doubts, she declared, were among our greatest enemies. They would lead us to question every point of duty, and induce us to waver at every step. They arose only from remaining imperfection, and were always evidence of sin. . . . Priests, she insisted, could not sin. It was a thing impossible. Every thing they did, and wished, was of course right. . . . She gave me another piece of information which excited other feelings in me, scarcely less dreadful. Infants were sometimes born in the convent: but they were always baptized and immediately strangled! This secured their everlasting happiness; for the baptism purified them for all sinfulness. . . . How happy, she exclaimed, are those who secure immortal happiness to such little beings! Their little souls would thank those who kill their bodies, if they had in their power!

Explore the Source

1. What connections does the narrator make between Catholic religious ideas and the sex and infanticide that take place in the convent?

2. How might this text have been designed specifically to outrage readers who valued antebellum ideals of domesticity and motherhood?

3. Why do you think the author begins the book with detailed illustrations of the convent? How might the illustrations contribute to the book's message?

Sketch of Convent Exterior and Floor Plan of Interior. Monk's sensationalist publication claimed to take readers inside the hidden recesses of a criminal convent. *Courtesy of Canadiana.org*

dramatic change. Driven by land scarcity and overpopulation and drawn by cheaper overseas transportation, Irish men, women, and children moved to the northeastern part of the United States in large numbers in the 1830s, coming mostly from Catholic areas in southern and western Ireland. For the first time in U.S. history, a majority of Irish immigrants were now Catholic.

Irish Catholics in the United States identified strongly with their religion and not simply with their land of origin. The new immigrants built newspapers, such as the *Catholic Herald* in Philadelphia, the *Catholic Telegraph* in Cincinnati, and the *Pilot* in Boston, that addressed their readers as a specifically Catholic community. The leaders of the new immigrant communities were typically priests and bishops. By 1840, American Catholicism was already linked in the popular imagination with Irish immigrants living in the fast-growing cities of the North.

● In 1845, a natural disaster in Ireland prompted an exodus that would swell the Irish Catholic population in the United States to unimagined proportions. A fungus struck the Irish potato crop, which was the main food source of poor farmers who cultivated small plots of rented land controlled by English and Anglo-Irish landlords. The fungus charred the leaves of the potato plant and made them disintegrate. It wiped out 30 percent to 40 percent of the country's potato crop in 1845, and the following year it devastated the crop entirely. ● Ireland's potato harvests would not recover until the middle of the 1850s. By that point, the Irish **potato famine** had killed between 1 and 1.5 million people, out of a prefamine population of 8 million. ● Another 1.5 million came to America between 1845 and 1854, part of the greatest wave of immigration, as a proportion of the U.S. population, in the nation's history. In the process, Catholicism became the largest single religious denomination in America. ●

CLIMATES AND ECOLOGIES

CROSSING BORDERS

RELIGION AND THE COMMON SCHOOLS

Although many reform issues, including temperance and antislavery, contributed to the cultural clash between Protestants and Catholics, none proved quite so explosive as the emphasis that Protestants placed on the Bible. The Catholic Church had long been critical of the Protestant prescription of reading Scripture without commentary as a path to salvation, and Catholic leaders had long preached against Protestant Bible societies. This was an old conflict, but in the 1840s it moved to a new arena: the school systems of Northeastern cities.

Starting around 1840, a major reform movement to create **common schools** spread in the North, introducing the system of public education Americans now take for granted. Over the next twenty years, every Northern state would provide tax-supported, tuition-free education (free public schooling did not appear in the South until after the Civil War). But the earliest public schools were not secular. As with other reforms of the period, the impulse to make education free and universal had evangelical Protestant roots. Although Horace Mann, the leading champion of the common school movement, wanted the schools to be nonsectarian, he meant that the schools should not take sides among different Protestant denominations. Mann believed that children of different backgrounds and faiths would be exposed to what he took to be the common ground of Christian morality. He assured his supporters that the King James Bible would be part of the curriculum.

Catholics in the North did not share Mann's view that compulsory Bible reading was simply Christian morality, and they were reluctant to send their children to schools where they would be forced to read a Protestant version of the Bible. The leader of New York City's Irish immigrant community, Bishop (later Archbishop) John Hughes, organized a political party in the early 1840s to push for public funding of Catholic parochial schools, an idea that won the support of the state's governor. Philadelphia's Irish-born bishop tried the different tactic of filing a grievance with that city's school system, calling for the elimination of Protestant hymns and asking that Catholic children be allowed to read from a Catholic version of the Bible instead of the King James. His grievance triggered the bloody riots of 1844.

● Over the next fifteen years, bitter disputes over different translations of the Bible and different versions of the Ten Commandments spilled out of the classroom and into the political arena. Reformers did not want to give up on their commitment to expose all children, perhaps immigrants most of all, to what they saw as the core of Christian faith. But they did not want Catholic Bibles in their classrooms. And they especially did not want to use taxpayer money to support Catholic schools. To avoid giving such support, states ultimately decided to exclude religious instruction altogether from schools receiving public funding. ●

CONFLICTING FAITHS

CONCLUSION

By midcentury, movements promoting temperance, abolitionism, women's rights, universal education, and anti-Catholicism had become familiar features of public life in the North, as had a varied menu of self-improvement programs, cooperative communities, and social taboos. These were the product of a middle-class culture of reform that emerged during the same period when slavery was driving a wider wedge between the two sections of the country. The culture of reform did not go uncontested; it created new lines of social conflict and hardened old ones. But the broader assumptions about individual responsibility, social change, and family life that the reformers shared and reinforced were gaining power and influence. By midcentury, these ideas were reshaping everyday life in the North.

STUDY TERMS

transcendentalists
lyceum movement
utopian communities
Brook Farm
Sabbatarianism
antigallows movement
corporal punishment
prisons
teetotaler
Washingtonians
Sons of Temperance
temperance novels
bodily self-control
the secret vice
abolitionists
immediatism
slave narratives
anti-abolitionist riots

political abolitionists
1840 schism
cult of domesticity
separate spheres
domestic servants
clerks
Mercantile Agency
Godey's Lady's Book
modern American
    Christmas
women's rights
Seneca Falls Convention
woman suffrage
coverture
anti-Catholicism
nativists
potato famine
common schools

FURTHER READING

A database of additional full-text readings is available through Power of Process for Primary Sources in Connect.

Thomas Augst, *The Clerk's Tale* (2003), looks at the struggles of young middle-class men to establish their character and answer the moral demands of white-collar work.

Stuart Blumin, *The Emergence of the Middle Class* (1989), examines the development of a self-conscious American middle class in antebellum cities.

Justin T. Clark, *City of Second Sight* (2018), stresses the importance of images and visual culture to Boston's middle-class reform movements.

Nancy Cott, *Bonds of Womanhood* (1977), illuminates the relationship between the cult of domesticity and the emergence of feminism.

Bruce Dorsey, *Reforming Men and Women* (2002), emphasizes the importance of gender to reform movements in Philadelphia.

Karen Halttunen, *Confidence Men and Painted Women* (1982), studies the role of etiquette guides in spreading new standards of middle-class behavior.

April Haynes, *Riotous Flesh* (2015), analyzes the different reformers and theories that stigmatized female masturbation.

Amy E. Hughes, *Spectacles of Reform* (2012), highlights the role of drama and performance in abolitionist campaigns.

John T. McGreevy, *Catholicism and American Freedom* (2003), treats the conflicts between Catholics and Protestants in the antebellum era as a clash between ideas of freedom.

Mary P. Ryan, *Cradle of the Middle Class* (1981), documents how transformations in family life in the Erie Canal region laid the foundation for middle-class values.

Lisa Tetrault, *The Myth of Seneca Falls* (2014), traces the way the 1848 convention became a foundational moment in the struggle for woman suffrage.

13 | EXPANSION, NATIONALISM & AMERICAN POPULAR CULTURE

Chapter Questions

1. How did ideas about the United States's national destiny influence the decision to extend U.S. sovereignty over new territory?

2. What were the causes of the U.S.-Mexican War?

3. What major westward migrations occurred in the United States in this period, and how did they differ from one another?

4. How did communication, publishing, and popular entertainment shape American nationalism?

California News. War, conquest, and long-distance communications stoked the fires of westward expansion. *DeAgostini/Getty Images*

Writing in a New York literary magazine in 1845, James Kennard, Jr., posed a question of some importance to the magazine's elite readership. "Who are our National Poets?" he asked. Ever since 1776, Americans had been trying to declare their cultural independence. This required proving that American art expressed the particular genius of the American people. Beginning in the 1820s, white Americans often produced works of art and literature that featured Native American subject matter in order to distinguish American culture from that of Europe (see Chapter 9). But Kennard also wanted distinctively American artists, uncorrupted by the influences of other national traditions. Surveying the

Time Line

1844
Samuel Morse successfully demonstrates electromagnetic telegraph
James Knox Polk elected president on an expansionist platform

1845
Texas annexed
First postage reduction passed by Congress

1846
Congress declares war on Mexico
Britain and United States settle Oregon boundary
Associated Press created in New York
Brigham Young leads Mormon exodus to Utah

1848
Gold discovered in California
Treaty of Guadalupe Hidalgo signed
Nationalist revolutions break out across Europe

1849
Hyer-Sullivan boxing match becomes major sporting event

1853
Matthew Perry's expedition arrives in Japan

1855
William Walker assumes power in Nicaragua

the United States to stretch across the continent. By the time he left office four years later, his vision had been realized and the nation had doubled in size. Territorial growth was fueled in part by mass migrations of American settlers seeking cheaper land, but it was mostly the product of a major military invasion of Mexico. The U.S.-Mexican War would dominate Polk's presidency, unsettling the political rivalries between slave and free states and between Democrats and Whigs. The 1848 discovery of gold in the newly acquired territory of California accelerated both westward expansion and the political conflicts it triggered.

Kennard's essay also indicated the importance of popular culture to the new American nationalism. Actors, athletes, singers, and dancers enjoyed mass celebrity during the 1840s and 1850s, and their performances became occasions for building national identity. The particular performances that Kennard cited, which purported to represent plantation slavery, became especially significant. Minstrel shows ridiculed the bodies, voices, and experiences of African Americans, but they also spread new ideas about whiteness and helped define America's national identity. Even more genteel artists, such as novelists and poets, took an interest in the territorial growth of the United States.

Not all Americans supported the war against Mexico or clamored for westward expansion. For many Northern Whigs, for example, nationalism meant tightening the bonds of commerce and communication across the country rather than adding territories. They pushed for cheaper postage and celebrated the spread of telegraph wires and railroad tracks. But Americans in both parties and regions developed grander visions of the republic's historical destiny and global reach.

cultural landscape in 1845, Kennard argued that the real national artists were the enslaved. "The negro poets . . . in the swamps of Carolinas," he imagined, produced original poems, which were then reproduced by white actors in blackface and spread across the globe. This, according to Kennard, was American culture.

Kennard's essay was both playful and perverse, but his ideas reflected two important developments in American life by 1845. One was a rising confidence in the unique character of the United States and new expectations that the nation would continue to grow. The same year Kennard's essay appeared, a new president entered office committed to national expansion. James Knox Polk believed that it was the destiny of

MANIFEST DESTINY AND THE ROAD TO WAR

Nationalist movements in the United States looked to the west in the 1840s, imagining a country that spanned the continent. Access to the Pacific Ocean had been an explicit goal of the United States since before the days of the Lewis and Clark expedition (see Chapter 8). But now it was increasingly described as the fulfillment of the nation's destiny. Several powerful obstacles stood in the way of this destiny, however (see Map 13.1). The British still claimed the Oregon Territory, which had been ruled since 1818 under a "joint occupation" agreement with the United States. Farther south, various native groups, especially the Apache, Comanche, Navajo, and Kiowa, imposed their considerable military power over large regions. Even more of the Southwest lay within the political borders of Mexico, which held a population of around 7 million in the 1840s. In just a few years, the United States committed itself to the project of wresting enough land from these other powers to realize the dream of a transcontinental nation.

TEXAS AND THE POLITICS OF EXPANSION

By the 1840s, debates about territorial expansion had focused on the borderland with Mexico. Texas had declared independence from Mexico in 1836 (see Chapter 11), but the Mexican government refused to recognize either its independence or the Lone Star Republic's claim to extend all the way to the Rio Grande. Violence flared frequently between Texas and Mexico in the decade following

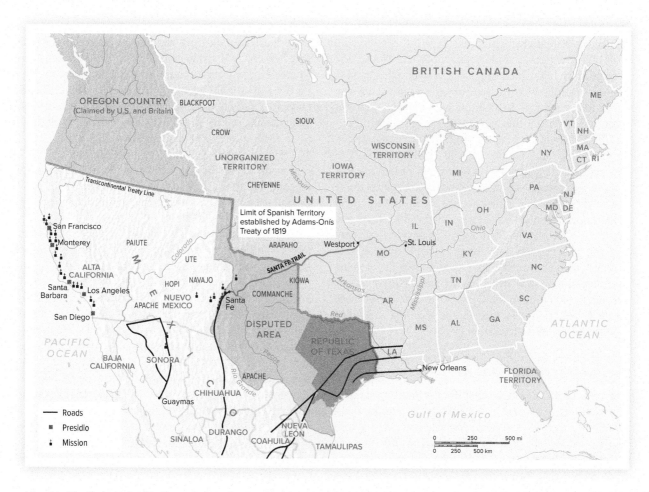

Map 13.1 North America in 1844. Between Mexico and the United States lay a disputed region that included the Lone Star Republic of Texas, whose borders and status Mexico did not recognize. In addition, powerful native polities held sway in much of northern Mexico and the U.S. West.

independence, which intensified tensions between Mexico and the United States. Ironically, Mexico had encouraged the emigration of white American settlers to Texas in the 1820s in an ill-fated attempt to impede U.S. expansion into northern Mexico and protect Mexicans from Comanche attacks. But now Texas was independent, dominated by English speakers with ties to the United States and desires to join the union. No longer a buffer, Texas was a prime target for foreign annexation and attack.

Though the prospect of annexing Texas appealed to many Americans, opponents argued that annexation was tantamount to declaring war against Mexico. Some also worried that taking Texas would embroil the United States in a struggle with the Comanche, who remained the major military power in that region. But the greatest opposition to annexation came from Northerners concerned about the spread of slavery and the balance of power between slave and free states. By 1840, the question of Texas had become the primary touchstone for sectional conflict over slavery.

During the Texas controversy, the White House was occupied by John Tyler, who succeeded to office in 1841 on the death of William Henry Harrison, just thirty-one days into his term. A slaveholding Virginia Democrat who had alienated the Jacksonian establishment in the 1830s by supporting states' rights, Tyler was tapped by the Whigs for vice president in 1840 in an effort to attract Southern support. He shared few of his new party's views, however, and they disowned him soon after he became president. Planning to run for re-election as an independent candidate, Tyler advocated adding Texas and instructed Secretary of State John C. Calhoun to prepare an annexation treaty with Texas in 1844. But Calhoun fanned the flames of the slavery controversy by arguing that annexation was necessary to foil British plans to encourage abolition in the Lone Star Republic. With the approach of the 1844 presidential election, a divided Senate rejected the annexation treaty.

THE ELECTION OF 1844

As both major parties headed toward their nominating conventions, it seemed possible that the burning question of Texas might not be a campaign issue. The Whigs rallied behind Henry Clay, who was known to oppose annexation but sought to avoid the controversy. On the Democratic side, former president Martin Van Buren was the presumed nominee, and he, too, intended to avoid the annexation question and run largely on the economic issues (such as bank regulation, tariffs, and internal

improvements) that had dominated the campaigns of the previous decade. But Van Buren faced opposition within his party, especially among annexation advocates. After successfully pushing a rule requiring the nominee to get a two-thirds majority of the delegates, the rebels threw their support to Lewis Cass of Michigan (an annexationist) and the convention was deadlocked. Finally, on the ninth ballot, a surprise candidate emerged. James Knox Polk, a Tennessee slaveholder who had been a protégé of Andrew Jackson, won the Democratic nomination and became the standard-bearer of a party suddenly committed to annexing Texas.

To shore up their support in the North, the Democrats called for the "re-occupation" of Oregon from Britain as well as the "re-annexation of Texas" (which Democrats claimed had been included in the 1803 Louisiana Purchase from France). Slavery was unlikely to flourish in the Oregon Territory, which was being settled by families planning to work the land themselves, and the eventual admission of a free state from the Northwest could appease Northerners by balancing out Texas. Polk's campaign trumpeted the Oregon cause as the centerpiece of the party's expansionist ideology. But everyone understood that a vote for Polk was a vote for taking Texas. This turn of events undercut President Tyler's hopes to win re-election as an independent. Rather than split the Southern vote, Tyler endorsed Polk and withdrew from the race.

Faced with an expansionist opponent, Clay could no longer dodge the Texas question. Trying to hedge his bets, he claimed to be willing to consider annexation if it could be achieved "without dishonor, without war, with the common consent of the Union, and upon just and fair terms." This position reassured none of the expansionists, but it alarmed slavery opponents in the North. In an extremely close election, voters opposed to slavery and annexation made a difference. Although abolitionist candidate James Birney, running on the Liberty Party ticket, polled only 2.3 percent of the total, he drew enough support away from Clay in Michigan and New York to secure victory for Polk (see Map 13.2). In one of the most consequential elections in American history, the Democrats recaptured the presidency and claimed a popular mandate for aggressive expansionist policies.

Before leaving office, President Tyler invoked this mandate and asked Congress to admit Texas to the union. Congressional Democrats were able to win approval for **Texas annexation** by treating it as an application for statehood, which required only a majority in both houses, rather than a treaty with a foreign nation, which required a two-thirds majority, which the Democrats did not have.

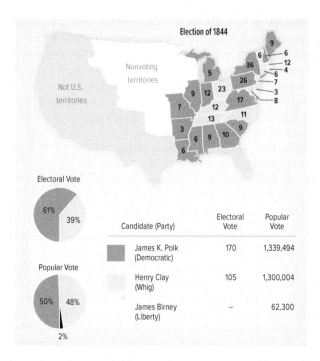

Map 13.2 Election of 1844.

John Quincy Adams, one of the bill's bitterest opponents, remarked that this maneuver had violated the Constitution, reducing it to "a menstruous rag." Over such objections, Texas entered the union, its status and borders still angrily contested by Mexico.

YOUNG AMERICA, RACE, AND MANIFEST DESTINY

As they contemplated and justified annexing and conquering western lands, Americans spoke explicitly about what they saw as the character of their nation. It was in this context that the famous words **Manifest Destiny** entered the political vocabulary. The phrase was introduced in the pages of John L. O'Sullivan's journal, *The United States Magazine and Democratic Review*, in 1839, probably by one of his writers, Jane McManus Storm, who published under the name C. Montgomery. In 1845, Storm used the term in widely circulated articles to argue for acquiring more territory. Annexing Texas, she wrote, would fulfill "our manifest destiny to overspread the continent allotted by Providence for our yearly multiplying millions." The American claim to greater Oregon was said to rest on exactly the same foundation—"our manifest destiny to overspread and to possess the whole of the continent which Providence has given for the development of the great experiment of liberty."

As both a political slogan and a political argument, Manifest Destiny meant a few things. First, expansionists were claiming that the westward spread of the United States was preordained by divine will. Second, the divine plan for the United States to expand was revealed not in sacred texts or prophecies but in the unfolding of history. Third, America was destined to expand in order to model and spread its free and democratic political institutions. Manifest Destiny expressed a utopian vision of the United States, propelled by the hand of God in history and introducing new political ideals to a changing planet.

Older countries might stake their claims to territory in the past—treaties, traditions, generations of occupancy— but the new ideologues of American expansion emphasized the future and touted the youth of the republic as a reason older nations ought to give way to U.S. interests. Expansionists in the late 1840s rallied under the banner of **Young America,** a name introduced earlier in the decade by the philosopher and lecturer Ralph Waldo Emerson. Significantly, the Young America moniker was adopted both by politicians advocating American expansion and by writers such as Herman Melville, Walt Whitman, and Nathaniel Hawthorne, who advocated a distinctive American literature (see the section National Literature).

But Manifest Destiny was a racial ideology as well. If America's youthfulness became an argument for why Great Britain ought to concede Oregon, what about Mexico, which was a new republic as well? Expansionists made many arguments against Mexican claims to greater Texas. Ultimately, however, what seemed to justify taking Mexican lands was the fact that Mexico was a racially mixed society that therefore did not share the national destiny of the United States. When John O'Sullivan and others celebrated the movement of settlers westward, they called it an "irresistible army of Anglo-Saxon emigration." In the words of a Maryland congressman, "We must march from Texas straight to the Pacific ocean, and be bounded only by its roaring wave. . . . It is the destiny of the white race, it is the destiny of the Anglo-Saxon race." Manifest Destiny meant white destiny.

WAR AND CONQUEST

Polk entered office with Texas already annexed and his eye on the Pacific Ocean. He hoped to acquire both the Oregon Territory and Mexican California in order to bring the harbors of San Diego, San Francisco, and the Puget Sound under U.S. control. Polk wished to avoid military conflict with Great Britain and acquire as much of Oregon as possible through negotiations while he prepared to invade Mexico. He expected war with Mexico to be relatively brief, since Mexico would not be able to defend its northern states while waging war against raiding Native American armies. Despite repeated battlefield victories, the Mexican War dragged on for seventeen months, taking many lives and provoking ominous political debates about the future of the union.

THE INVASION OF MEXICO

Mexico did not recognize the U.S. annexation of Texas. Moreover, Mexico disputed the boundaries that the United States had claimed for Texas, citing the traditional boundary of the Nueces River—not the Rio Grande, as Texans had asserted. For the United States to press its claim to the region between the two rivers, it would need to send troops into land that Mexico viewed as its own. Polk did so quickly, ordering General Zachary Taylor to take up a position along the Rio Grande. Predictably, Mexico's General Mariano Arista responded by attacking Taylor's men in late April 1846. When news of the attack reached Washington, D.C., Polk announced to Congress that Mexico had "invaded our territory, and shed American blood upon American soil." Facing a choice between accepting Polk's account of the conflict with Mexico and denying reinforcements to Taylor's army, Congress declared war.

Back along the Rio Grande, Taylor's and Arista's armies clashed for two days in the Battle of Palo Alto, where outnumbered U.S. troops took advantage of their lighter, more portable cannons to inflict heavy casualties. Mexican soldiers retreated across the river, Taylor maintained his position, and in September 1846 he besieged the city of Monterrey. Five months into the war, northeastern Mexico was under American control.

At the same time, Colonel Stephen Kearny led an expedition from Missouri into New Mexico, occupying Santa Fe two months before Taylor's siege of Monterrey. Three months later, Kearny marched into San Diego, California, entering a Mexican state where, farther north, the explorer John Frémont had initiated a revolt of American settlers against Mexican rule earlier in the year. Though the fighting was fierce, the two-pronged invasion of northern Mexico by Taylor and Kearny seemed to be working. In a final burst of resistance, General Santa Anna (whom the Americans had brought back to Mexico from Cuban exile in the hopes that he would negotiate a peace) mustered a massive army to expel the invaders from Monterrey. But in the Battle of Buena Vista (February 1847), Taylor's troops fought to a standstill, and Santa

Anna decided to withdraw southward. The Mexicans had missed their best chance to repel the invasion.

Despite the succession of victories, American war aims remained elusive. Had the United States simply wanted to annex and defend greater Texas, the conflict might have ended. But all along, Polk had wanted the invasion to force Mexico to negotiate a settlement that would cede New Mexico and California as well. In 1845, before the war began, he sent minister John Slidell to Mexico to offer cash for all of these territories (including 25 million dollars for California), but the Mexicans had rebuffed him, and a slew of U.S. military victories in the north had not changed their minds. The United States decided that the only way to force Mexico to negotiate would be to take the war south to the capital.

For the second phase of the war, Polk called on General Winfield Scott, rather than Taylor, to land a large force on the Gulf Coast city of Veracruz and march from there to Mexico City. Following lengthy preparations, Scott arrived in Veracruz in March 1847, occupied the city after an eighteen-day siege, and headed west. After defeating a force led by Santa Anna at Cerro Gordo in April, Scott's army moved slowly toward the capital. On September 14, Mexico City's authorities surrendered, and the U.S. flag was hoisted above the Mexican National Palace.

FOLLOWING THE WAR AT HOME

More than any prior war in American history, the conflict with Mexico unfolded in full view of the populace. Though it took place on foreign soil, the war engaged all Americans, because they had unprecedented access to its progress. This was the first war to be covered by the new mass medium of the cheap daily press (see Chapter 10). Newspapers all over the country actively relayed news from the front. In New Orleans, which was the principal staging point for troops, supplies, and information, nine daily newspapers competed for the most up-to-the-minute accounts of the war.

● The U.S.-Mexican War was also the first American military conflict to take place after the introduction of the electromagnetic telegraph in 1844 (see the section National Communication). Within weeks of the war's outbreak, messages could be exchanged instantaneously between New York and Washington, D.C. By the war's end, New York was connected via telegraph wire to Charleston, South Carolina. News could travel from New Orleans to the national capital within three days. Whereas just three decades earlier no one in Washington, D.C., knew of the Battle of New Orleans until weeks after it had taken place, residents of one

MEDIA AND INFORMATION

War News from Mexico, by Richard Caton Woodville, 1848. Americans gathered at post offices, telegraph offices, and newspaper offices to receive news of the war and discuss its progress. Most of these spaces were dominated by men, but note here the presence of a woman leaning out the window of the hotel to listen to the discussion. **Questions for Analysis:** What seems to be the perspective of the African American man and child in the foreground? Why might the artist have included them? *Library of Congress, Prints & Photographs Division [LC-DIG-pga-03889]*

MEDIA AND INFORMATION

city now formed something closer to a real-time audience for events in the other. Slow communication between President Polk and his officers on the Mexican battlefields continued to plague the chain of command and affect the conduct of the war, but many Americans, especially those living in cities, could experience the course of the conflict as a series of current events. •

Most Americans greeted the war news enthusiastically. The Declaration of War and the early successes at Palo Alto fanned the flames of patriotism throughout the country. Books, pamphlets, plays, and songs about the war proliferated, especially in the urban North. In New York theaters, actors and actresses interrupted their scenes to deliver passionate addresses in support of the war effort. Stores advertised special consumer goods, including Palo Alto hats and root beer.

War fever also helped swell the ranks of the army, which at the time war was declared consisted of barely seven thousand personnel. Young men quickly filled the fifty thousand spots called for by Congress, encouraged not only by the promise of generous land bounties in any territory that might be conquered but also by a variety of well-publicized patriotic gestures of local governments and businesses. Volunteers in Indiana were promised an extension on their taxes. As their home states met their quotas, men crossed state lines to volunteer for the war.

Soldiers came from all walks of life, including men who were not yet U.S. citizens and even a few Native Americans. • About half of the enlisted men were foreign immigrants, many of them Catholics from Ireland. The Mexican army sought to lure Catholic immigrant soldiers away from the U.S. military with pamphlets and posters, asking why they participated in the invasion of a Catholic country alongside "those who put fire to your temples in Boston and Philadelphia." •

CONFLICTING FAITHS

Some Irish immigrants switched sides, and close to three hundred of them were organized into the **San Patricio battalion,** which fought for Mexico in the battle of Buena Vista. The San Patricios were in the minority, however. Thousands of Irish immigrants fought for the United States (forming over a quarter of the soldiers under Zachary Taylor's command). The war gave them an opportunity to demonstrate their fitness for American citizenship—an opportunity denied to African Americans. By taking up arms against a Catholic country on behalf of their new country, Irish immigrants made a powerful claim to the destiny of white America.

WAR AND SLAVERY

From the start, the war had its critics in the United States. Many Northeastern Whigs vocally opposed Polk's claim that Mexico had started the war, and they denounced the invasion at every stage. As a young Whig congressman, Abraham Lincoln branded it a "war in conquest fought to catch votes" and repeatedly challenged the Democrats to identify the precise spot where U.S. soil had been attacked. The Massachusetts legislature branded the invasion "wanton, unjust and unconstitutional" and a "war against humanity." Nonetheless, Whigs continued to vote for war appropriations, claiming that they did not wish to deny the soldiers the support they needed.

The war's most outspoken opponents attacked it as a war for slavery. The abolitionist Frederick Douglass, formerly enslaved himself, railed against the "disgraceful, cruel, and iniquitous war with our sister republic." Henry David Thoreau refused to pay taxes to support the war, and the night he spent in jail for this defiance became the basis for his famous 1849 essay, *Resistance to Civil Government.* Radical abolitionist William Lloyd Garrison went so far as to root for the success of the Mexicans. "We only hope that, if blood has had to flow," he wrote, "that it has been that of the Americans."

Though most Northerners did not adopt such radical views, they were still attuned to the connection between the war and slavery. Some Northern expansionists who had supported Polk's aggressive stance on both Oregon and Texas began to wonder about Polk's priorities once they saw how differently the two frontiers were handled. Whereas the United States mounted a costly invasion of Mexico, Polk settled the Oregon question through diplomacy. After the British proposed a settlement at the forty-ninth parallel (far short of the Democrats'

campaign promise to push for all of Oregon), Polk submitted the **Oregon settlement** treaty to the Senate, where it was ratified in June 1846 with minor revisions. After the Oregon compromise, more Northern and Western Democrats began expressing doubts about the wisdom of war policy in Mexico. Manifest Destiny held broad national appeal, but the Mexican War was more popular in the South.

The sectional divide over the war came to a head in August 1846, when Pennsylvania representative David Wilmot proposed a rider to a war appropriations bill, prohibiting slavery in any of the Mexican territories that might be acquired in the war. Wilmot, a Democrat, was not an abolitionist and made it clear that his intention was to preserve the West as a place where white men could till the soil "without the disgrace which association with Negro slavery brings upon free labor." Polk expressed shock that anyone would see a connection between "slavery and making peace with Mexico," but Wilmot's Northern Democratic colleagues were eager to sever any possible connection between their support of the war and the westward extension of slavery. The **Wilmot Proviso** passed in the House, but the larger appropriations bill

The Hanging of the San Patricio Battalion Deserters at the Battle of Chapultepec, September 1847, **by Sam Chamberlain.** The immigrants who joined this battalion represented a small fraction of the 9,207 U.S. soldiers who deserted during the Mexican War as the war dragged on beyond most volunteers' expectations. This was the highest rate of desertion in any American war. *Herbert Orth/Time & Life Pictures/Getty Images*

stalled in the Senate. After the 1846 elections, when Whigs won control of the House, the Proviso passed there again, but Texas provided the necessary two-vote margin to defeat it in the Senate. Although the proviso never became law, ten state legislatures endorsed it, and it became a rallying cry for Northern Democrats uncomfortable with their party's slavery stance. The popularity of the Wilmot Proviso cast a political pall over the war effort, hinting that the addition of new territory might bring new troubles to Washington, D.C. It also augured deep fissures within the Democratic Party.

SURRENDER AND THE MEXICAN CESSION

Even after the fall of its national capital, the Mexican government (temporarily relocated to Querétaro, 125 miles away) refused to make land concessions that were satisfactory to the United States. Part of the problem was that by the end of 1847, the U.S. position was unclear, because American political opinion was deeply divided over what to ask for. Whigs now controlled the House of Representatives, and many Whigs opposed acquiring any new territory. Polk's long-standing war aim had been to wrest all of New Mexico and Alta California from the Mexicans and gain recognition of the Rio Grande as the border of Texas. But the success of the war had persuaded him that the United States should be able to get Baja California, too, along with much of what is now northeastern Mexico—as far south as Tampico (see Map 13.3).

Disagreement and uncertainty over how much territory to demand were not simply tactical; they reflected

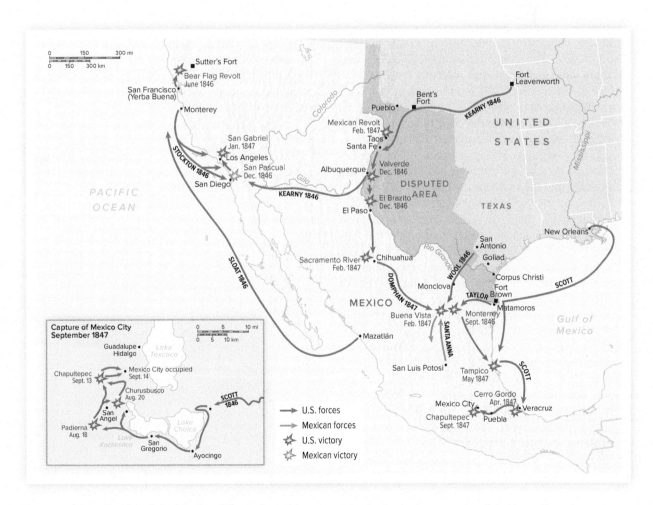

Map 13.3 Major Battles of the Mexican War. After sending troops into the disputed territory west of the Nueces River, the United States launched a multifront invasion of its neighboring republic.

ambivalence on the American side, even among the war's most enthusiastic supporters. Hard-liners framed their demands as compensation for the costs of the war. But their real justification for taking territory lay in the ideas of Manifest Destiny. All along, war supporters had spoken of the invasion of Mexico as expediting the removal of primitive peoples who were not making good use of the land—rather than vanquishing a foreign nation. "The Mexicans are *Aboriginal Indians*," one expansionist declared, "and they must share the destiny of their race." The fact that much of northern Mexico was still under the control of native nations seemed to support this notion, but Americans also emphasized the fact that Mexico itself was a mixed-race society, where the lines between European and native stock had been transgressed. From this perspective, many Democrats argued for taking possession of all of Mexico.

But the analogy between invading Mexico and removing indigenous peoples proved deeply misleading. U.S. soldiers encountered established cities, many of them older and larger than anything they had seen before. If the United States were to annex all of Mexico, what would they do with its 7 million inhabitants? Would they simply absorb the country and extend citizenship to people they considered racially inferior? Would they subjugate Mexico as a colony? Would they enslave the population or incorporate Mexico's system of peonage into the southern slave economy? Or would they, as one senator recommended, dispossess Mexicans and place them on reservations? All of these options were unpalatable to most Americans, and Polk pushed instead for taking only those portions of Mexico that would not force the federal government to choose between its commitment to white supremacy and its commitment to republican equality.

Polk had entrusted the task of securing a peace treaty with Mexico to Nicholas Trist, a former aide to Andrew Jackson. Unbeknownst to the president, Trist harbored deep objections to the U.S. invasion of Mexico and was far more eager than Polk to make peace. But Trist found negotiations with Mexico difficult, and in October 1847 Polk decided to recall him, partly as a tactical maneuver to make the United States seem less eager to make peace. The recall message (which was too sensitive to be conveyed via telegraph) took a month to reach Trist, who decided to ignore it. Two and a half months after being recalled, Trist reached an agreement with a new Mexican government. Under the **Treaty of Guadalupe Hidalgo,** signed in Mexico on February 2, 1848, the United States acquired 500,000 square miles of Mexican territory (not counting Texas), an area that covered the future states of California, New Mexico, Arizona, Utah, and Nevada and included the coveted Pacific harbors of San Francisco, San Diego, and Monterey. In return, the United States assumed 3.25 million dollars in private claims against Mexico and paid the Mexican government 15 million dollars (see How Much Is That? The Mexican Cession). The United States also agreed to grant citizenship to all Mexicans residing in the ceded territories, to assume responsibility for preventing all Native American raids into Mexican territory, and to prohibit the enslavement of Mexicans captured by Native Americans on either side of the new border.

Polk was furious with Trist for disobeying his orders and disappointed that the agreement did not wrest even more territory from Mexico. But with congressional opposition to the war mounting and guerrilla attacks against the U.S. invasion force taking a toll, the president submitted the treaty to the Senate, where it was ratified in March. After seventeen months, a long and costly war had come to an end. Not counting the treaty payments, the United States spent 98 million dollars on the war effort, far more than anyone had expected. More tragically, 12,518 U.S. soldiers were killed, most of them as a result of disease. This would be the last great burst of American territorial acquisition during the antebellum era (see Map 13.4).

How Much Is That?

The Mexican Cession

By the standards of the time, the 15 million dollars Mexico received for the lands ceded to the United States was trifling. It is dwarfed by the amount Mexico spent waging the war (nearly 100 million dollars, not counting pensions) and the amount the United States offered Spain (50 to 100 million dollars) later that year in an unsuccessful bid to purchase Cuba. In 2020 dollars, the sum represents approximately five hundred million dollars, or $1.49 per acre.

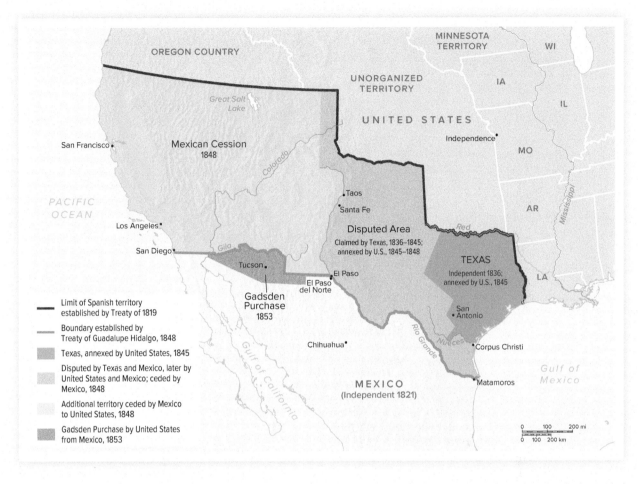

Map 13.4 The United States in 1854. After a decade of annexation, border settlement, war, and land purchase, the nation had extended its sovereignty over the continent and claimed its current continental borders.

EXPANDING WEST

America's westward expansion during the middle of the nineteenth century followed two paths. The United States used diplomacy and military force to extend its sovereignty over the western third of the continent, pursuing what politicians, journalists, and artists described as the nation's historical destiny. At the same time, westward expansion was the result of countless individual and group decisions by Americans and foreign immigrants to pick up stakes and pursue opportunities in those lands that the United States was in the process of conquering.

OVERLAND MIGRATION

● During the first third of the nineteenth century, the few Americans who traversed the South Pass of the Rocky Mountains had been fur traders. But in the early 1840s, two well-publicized expeditions established the feasibility of a 2,000-mile wagon voyage from the Missouri River to the Pacific Ocean in about six months. By 1850, the number of annual migrants on the **Overland Trail** had reached over fifty-five thousand. ●

Typical overland travel parties in the 1840s formed wagon trains each spring in what were called jumping-off cities along the Missouri River, namely Independence and St. Joseph, in Missouri, and Council Bluffs, Iowa (see Map 13.5). Most of the men and women who embarked on the Overland Trail were Midwestern white family farmers who lived in Missouri, Illinois, Iowa, and Indiana. They were transient people who had moved at least once before, often several times, in search of cheap, arable land farther west. Crossing the Rockies entailed a bigger commitment, however, since the supplies necessary for

CROSSING BORDERS

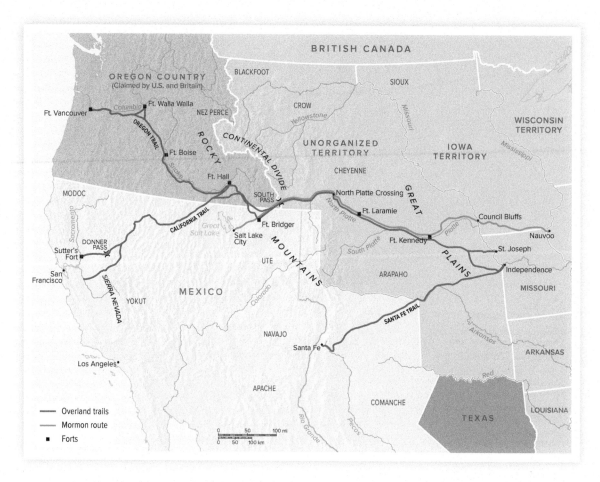

Map 13.5 The Overland Trail. Between 1846 and 1860, over two hundred thousand travelers trekked from the Missouri River across the Rockies to the West Coast, typically in canvas-covered wagons, each weighing between 2,000 and 2,500 pounds and pulled by teams of oxen and mules.

the journey cost about 600 dollars. But the lure of a homestead in Oregon was great, even before the United States took possession in 1846.

Overland migrants passed through Native American lands, including areas controlled by the relatively nomadic groups of the southern plains whose raids on northern Mexico had made it difficult for the Mexicans to resist the U.S. invasion. But Native American attacks on American travel parties were rare, especially before 1854. ● The route was not without risk, however. Diseases such as cholera took the lives of thousands of migrants. ● Overland travelers also needed to time their movements carefully. In 1846, for example, the **Donner party** started too late and took an ill-advised shortcut across the Utah desert, where many of their animals died, forcing them to cut loose wagons and supplies. They made their way to Truckee Lake (later renamed Donner Lake), the last serious mountain barrier, but

became trapped by heavy snowfalls for four months. The ghastly and well-publicized tale of their ordeal, including starvation and cannibalism, dramatized the perils of the Overland Trail.

GOLD DISCOVERED IN CALIFORNIA

Before 1848, Oregon was the primary Pacific destination of westward migrants. But in January of that year, while Nicholas Trist was in Mexico City negotiating an end to the war, James Marshall discovered gold in the middle of the Mexican state of Alta California, which Trist was at that very moment demanding from Mexico as the price of peace. The world did not immediately pay attention to Marshall's discovery at Sutter's Mill. But by June, word had spread to the San Francisco Bay region, where men left their homes, their military posts, and their ships in droves to pan for gold in the foothills of the Sierra Nevada. Later that summer, the news reached Hawaii and the west coast of Mexico. By the end of the year, newspapers all over the Atlantic seaboard were fanning the flames of gold fever. In less than twelve months, about eighty thousand people descended on California, now part of the United States. A year later, in 1850, California would draft a state constitution and enter the union as part of a national compromise over slavery (see Chapter 14). By 1854, Marshall's discovery had attracted more than three hundred thousand people to California.

The **California gold rush** differed from other migrations to the American West. Only a portion of the newcomers took the Overland Trail. Most arrived by ship, even those from the eastern half of North America. Some sailed around Cape Horn at the tip of South America; others traveled by steamship to Panama or Nicaragua; crossed the isthmus by foot, mule, and canoe (there was no canal in Panama); and boarded another ship on the Pacific side. Gold rush migrants were also far more heterogeneous in origin. In contrast to the white Midwestern farmers who packed the wagon trains of the more steady overland migration, those who followed the scent of gold hailed from many different places, especially Chile, Mexico, China, Australia, France, and the United States. The people who rushed to California between 1848 and 1854 thus had a very different relationship to the larger project of U.S. territorial expansion than homesteaders heading to Oregon. For some of the new arrivals, the journey to the Sierra was northward or eastward, rather than westward. For many of them, it was their first encounter with the United States.

Immigrants arrived in large numbers from the Cantonese-speaking parts of southern China, especially from the Pearl River delta, where the First Opium War had left a legacy of economic hardship. Most were young, single men bent on taking wealth back home. A minority were women, brought over to work as prostitutes in gold rush cities or in the mines. African Americans came as well, mostly in slavery and brought by their slaveholders to a territory in which the legal status of chattel slavery remained uncertain at first. The largest and most influential group of **forty-niners,** as the migrants became known, were white, English-speaking Americans, mainly from New England and the mid-Atlantic states. Mostly middle-class men, these gold seekers came as temporary migrants hoping to return to the communities from which they hailed with greater wealth and enhanced status. Few struck it rich, but gold brought people from all over the world and built new polyglot worlds on the California coast.

The other distinguishing characteristic of the gold rush migration was its gender imbalance. Men outnumbered women by as much as ten to one in the mining areas. Migrants complained of the absence of women and the domesticating influence they were supposed to provide. Prostitution flourished in the mines and especially in the growing cities on the San Francisco Bay and along the rivers, often involving women from France and China. But this only confirmed the sense of transplanted Northeasterners that they were living in a masculine world cut off from female society. Gold rush culture was rugged and male dominated; the major events of interest were, as one newcomer reported, "gambling, Duelling, Murdering, Lectioneering and Digging." There were also other, less violent expressions of this all-male culture. In the mining camps, men joined together for festive merriment and dancing, partnering up with one another. On one occasion in the town of Angel's Camp, half the assembled, marked by colorful patches on their pants, were ladies for the evening. But for most Anglo men, the absence of white, middle-class women was an excuse to construct a social world that featured the rough, same-sex pleasures of the bachelor culture that thrived in Eastern cities at the time.

Donner Lake in California's Sierra Nevada. One of the most famous tales of Western migration took place near here. Trapped by snow in this treacherous terrain, seventeen members of the Donner party tried to make it out of the mountains on foot but could not get beyond the snow on the western slope. Only seven of the seventeen survived, subsisting on the corpses of those who did not make it. Back in the main camps, thirteen migrants starved to death and became food for the others before the rescue parties arrived. *Dave Porter/Alamy Stock Photo*

NATIVE PEOPLE AND CALIFORNIOS

For the people who had been living in California long before the 1840s, the gold rush brought about even more momentous changes than the Mexican War. At the beginning of the decade, over one hundred fifty thousand Native Americans lived in California. This represented about half the size of the indigenous population just seventy years earlier, when Spanish settlement began introducing diseases to the region. But relatively few Hispanic colonists immigrated to California. Native Americans made up over 90 percent of the population in 1848, even after a malaria epidemic had almost wiped out native life in the Central Valley and after the U.S. invasion. The discovery of gold completely changed the demographic situation. Within a few years, whites outnumbered native people by about two to one.

Because Mexico had granted citizenship to the native population in 1824, California's indigenous inhabitants were eligible, in theory, to become U.S. citizens under the 1848 treaty. Instead, they were banished, relegated to second-class citizenship, or simply killed by private militias. California's government spent 1.5 million dollars on twenty-four distinct militia campaigns between 1850 and 1861, part of what the state's first governor called an inevitable "war of extermination . . . between the races." Attempts at genocide in California did not succeed, but the surviving indigenous population was greatly reduced. Their livelihoods disrupted by the tide of migrants, Native Americans developed new economic activities and resources, including stealing and selling horses but also performing their native identities in the immigrant towns. Within a few years of the gold rush, small groups of native people would dance in ceremonial regalia for spectators and then pass around the hat.

California's much smaller Mexican population, the **Californios,** already outnumbered by Americans even before California was ceded to the United States, also struggled to survive the onslaught of new arrivals (see Singular Lives: John Rollin Ridge, Cherokee Novelist). Although the new state constitution of 1850 granted rights only to "free white persons," this category included Mexicans of Spanish descent. Wealthy Californio rancheros, who had received substantial land grants from the Mexican government, were represented in the framing of a new state constitution and sought to define themselves as white in the eyes of the law. They held significant political power in southern California, where the gold rush had not diluted their strength. But after California joined the union, Anglos began challenging the rancheros' land titles in court and pressuring them to sell.

Farther north and inland, Anglo Americans used their superior numbers to muscle Mexicans (and other groups)

"California Gold Diggers: Mining Operations on the Western Shore of the Sacramento River," ca. 1849–1852.   This lithograph depicts the range of ethnicities and nationalities of the men who mined gold. *The History Collection/Alamy Stock Photo*

SINGULAR LIVES

John Rollin Ridge, Cherokee Novelist

When Andrew Jackson removed Native American communities from the Southeast, he promised them security in Western lands. But Southeastern Native Americans did not simply relocate and disappear. Facing internal divisions, conflicts with the native population of their new homelands, and the westward march of white American settlement and U.S. territorial sovereignty, groups such as the Cherokee enjoyed none of the peace promised by removal advocates.

The remarkable career of John Rollin Ridge, also called Yellow Bird, dramatized the dilemmas and fate of the Cherokee diaspora in the era of U.S. expansion. Ridge came from a distinguished and politically powerful Cherokee family. His grandfather had fought alongside Jackson in the Creek War, his father (who attended a missionary boarding school in Connecticut) became a prosperous land-owner and slaveholder, and his cousin Elias Boudinot founded the Cherokee *Phoenix*. All three signed the controversial Treaty of New Echota, which transferred Cherokee land to the United States, and moved voluntarily to Oklahoma in 1836, using their cash settlement with the United States to establish stores to serve the new arrivals. But when those Cherokee who had opposed the treaty arrived two years later along the Trail of Tears, the Ridge family became the targets of bitter animosity. In 1839, when John Rollin Ridge was twelve years old, treaty opponents executed his father in front of his eyes.

Young Ridge's white mother moved him to Arkansas and then sent him to be educated in Massachusetts. He returned to Arkansas at age twenty, took up the law, and like his father before him married a white woman. But the feud between the two Cherokee groups followed Ridge to Arkansas, and when he killed a man over a conflict about a horse, he decided to flee rather than face Cherokee justice. Ridge traveled first to Missouri in 1849, then a year later joined the exodus to California. After a brief and unhappy stint in the mines, Ridge turned to writing and in 1854 produced the first novel published by a Native American author.

Ridge's novel, *The Life and Adventures of Joaquin Murieta*, was based loosely on the life of a Mexican bandit who had become a legend in the American mining camps. In Ridge's version, Joaquin is a noble and honest Mexican miner who turns to crime to avenge the rape of his wife by white Americans. The novel condemns white racism and criticizes whites for failing to live up to the individualist values that Ridge admired in American culture. Ridge's attitude toward Mexicans seemed more ambivalent. Joaquin is a superhero, but the book's preface makes a point of distinguishing him from other, lesser Mexicans. On the surface, the novel raised questions about what it meant to be an American in this new land, but it also reflected its biracial author's own conflicted relationship to the United States. Despite Ridge's embrace of white civilization, he criticized the U.S. government's policies, clung to his Cherokee identity, aspired to launch a Cherokee newspaper, and longed to return to the Cherokee Nation, which he hoped would enter the union as its own state. Thwarted in that effort, Ridge remained a Californian. He died in 1867.

Where in the Archives?

In addition to *The Life and Adventures of Joaquin Murieta*, John Rollin Ridge published poetry and numerous pieces of writing in newspapers. He served as the editor for a number of California newspapers, including the *Daily National Democrat* in Marysville from 1858 to 1861.

John Rollin Ridge. In his most famous work, the Cherokee author, at the far left of this Cherokee delegation, celebrated a Mexican bandit in gold rush California. *Apic/Getty Images*

Three editorials by Ridge on U.S.-Native American relations and indigenous cultures were published in the paper and are available through Chronicling America, an archive of historic American newspapers maintained at the Library of Congress (https://chroniclingamerica. loc.gov/lccn/sn84038814/issues/): "Policy of the Government toward the Indians" (October 13, 1858, second page), "More about the Civilized Indian States" (February 24, 1859, second page), and "The Digger Indians" (April 13, 1860, second page).

Assignment

Locate and read the three editorials and write a short essay (400 words) describing Ridge's identity and ideology. Make sure to consider the following questions in forming your description:

1. Does Ridge see himself as assimilated?

2. Does he advocate Native American assimilation?

3. How does Ridge use the concept of civilization to evaluate white–Native American relations?

4. What is his perspective on Manifest Destiny?

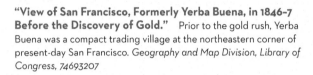

"View of San Francisco, Formerly Yerba Buena, in 1846–7 Before the Discovery of Gold." Prior to the gold rush, Yerba Buena was a compact trading village at the northeastern corner of present-day San Francisco. *Geography and Map Division, Library of Congress, 74693207*

San Francisco Harbor, Early 1850s. Almost overnight, San Francisco became a dense urban settlement. *Library of Congress Prints and Photographs Division [LC-USZC4-7421]*

out of the gold mines. In April 1850, the newly formed state legislature passed the first of two **Foreign Miners Taxes,** which imposed a prohibitive fee of twenty dollars a month on all non-American miners. It was ultimately reduced and then repealed, in part because of the organized opposition of European and South American gold seekers. A more modest imposition of the tax was reintroduced a year later, aimed largely at Chinese miners.

SAN FRANCISCO: INSTANT CITY

To get to the mines, most gold seekers passed through harbor towns on the San Francisco Bay, in the process creating a bustling urban society. The largest of these towns had been founded in 1835 by William Richardson, an independent entrepreneur of British birth who secured a private land grant from the Mexican government in the hopes of trading with small Mexican communities around the bay. Originally called Yerba Buena, the town was renamed San Francisco in January 1847, which may have contributed to the city's growth by identifying the new settlement with the more famous bay. At the time gold was discovered, about a thousand people lived in San Francisco; just eight years later, it was home to fifty thousand.

For many migrants, the booming economy of San Francisco was enough of a lure to detain or divert them from the mines. Wages in many sectors of the local

economy skyrocketed. Washing clothes became so expensive, for example, that some residents sent their laundry to Hawaii, while others simply bought new clothes when their favored garments got too soiled. One enterprising new arrival from New York brought with him fifteen hundred outdated copies of the daily *Tribune*, a two-cent paper, and sold them quickly and easily for a dollar each. Land values in the city soared, so that urban real estate became as much of a bonanza as mining claims. Some of these economic pressures and opportunities were the result of the sudden influx of gold. But many of them came from the compression of older patterns of urban growth into such a short time. "It's an odd place," a new arrival said of San Francisco in 1849. "[I]t is not created in the ordinary way but hatched like chickens by artificial heat."

Not all of the residents of San Francisco approved of the rough, masculine culture that characterized the instant city as well as the mines. Opponents of this culture, mostly middle-class, American-born Protestants, saw disorder both in the violent streets and in the corruption of the city's nascent political institutions. In 1851, they formed a **Committee of Vigilance** to execute "prompt and summary punishment" of public offenders. Over the next two years, they took ninety-one prisoners, exiling about a third of them from the city, whipping one, and hanging four others. Five years later, a more ambitious Committee of Vigilance arose. They captured a shipment of federal arms intended for the state militia and arrested the chief justice of the state's supreme court.

BEHIND THE IMAGE

Eliza Gilbert was born in Ireland, moved to Spain, adopted a Spanish name, and as Lola Montez enthralled European audiences with her "spider dance," in which she writhed provocatively and removed clothing while appearing to shake a spider off her body. Artist David Claypoole Johnston produced this cartoon around the time of her arrival on American stages, when Montez performed for three weeks at New York's forty-five-hundred-seat Broadway Theatre, the largest U.S. theater at the time. Montez achieved special success in gold rush San Francisco, where she personified the city's culture of male-oriented, sensational entertainment.

LOLA HAS COME!

ENTHUSIASTIC RECEPTION OF LOLA BY AN AMERICAN AUDIENCE.

"Lola Has Come." *Library of Congress, Prints & Photographs Division [LC-USZ62-108416]*

WITHIN THE IMAGE

Johnston portrays ① Montez as a graceful ballerina dancing in front of her stage manager while two other men ogle. Each of the three male spectators is identified with a text: ② The manager has pocketed his contract for "Half the House" (50 percent of the show's proceeds), while the oglers, poorly disguising their gazes, represent two kinds of readers. ③ One holds a copy of the New York *Herald*, a symbol of popular urban masculinity, and ④ the other struggles to attend to his *Sober Thoughts*, which proves no match for the sexualized display on the rehearsal stage. Such a reading would stress the dancer's power to overwhelm cultural opposition.

Alternatively, Johnston's cartoon could be interpreted as hostile to Montez, using ⑤ an empty house to undermine the aura of popular frenzy that surrounded her initial appearances and suggesting that she was unable to command the full attention of her audience.

BEYOND THE IMAGE

This image appeared in the January 1852 issue of *The Old Soldier*, a humor periodical published in New York City. Montez performed across the United States, including California, to sold-out venues. But critics often disparaged Montez's talent as a dancer or objected to the overt sexuality of her act. Some readers of *The Old Soldier* may have enjoyed a laugh at the dancer's expense, but images of this sort nonetheless fed popular fascination with a new generation of female sex symbols on stage.

For ninety-nine days, the committee ruled the city, jailing and executing men associated with gambling, commercial sex, political corruption, and the Democratic Party.

MORMON EXODUS

Oregon-bound families and gold seekers in California pursued new economic opportunities in the American West, but a large migration of Mormons from Illinois to the Utah desert had different motivations. After the murder of their prophet, Joseph Smith, in Nauvoo (see Chapter 10), Brigham Young took over the church, made provisional peace with the community's enemies, and led a **Mormon exodus** to a promised land in the West in 1846. In contrast to other overland travelers, Young chose a location where he figured the prospects for agriculture or mineral

CROSSING BORDERS

extraction were so poor that no one would bother them.

● Whereas other westward migrants were following or anticipating the progress of U.S. territorial expansion, the Mormons were seeking a distant refuge from the United States. From their perspective, the American continent was sacred, but the American nation was a place of persecution. The promised land near the Great Salt Lake was technically Mexican territory when Young arrived with the vanguard of his followers in 1847, but Young envisioned a society where the church held all political power and no other sovereign nation had real jurisdiction. ●

Young declared the existence of a state called **Deseret** and renounced any intention "to have any trade or commerce with the gentile world." The self-sufficient economy of Deseret depended on a complex system of irrigation works and a cooperative ethos that contrasted sharply with the competitive individualism of the California gold rush. By 1852, twenty thousand Mormon converts had settled in the Utah Territory, which was by that point part of the United States but largely ignored by the federal government. That year, Young first proclaimed publicly that the church sanctioned plural marriage (for men only), more widely known as polygamy. Outcry over this aspect of Mormon doctrine prompted the federal government to send troops to Utah in 1857 to assert U.S. sovereignty over the territory. More than a year later, after a prolonged standoff with federal forces and a massacre of non-Mormon overland migrants by a Mormon militia, the Mormon government negotiated a peace deal, agreeing to accept the sovereignty of the United States in return for a withdrawal of the troops and promises of freedom of religion in Utah.

NATIONALISM AND POPULAR THEATER

Most Americans living in the age of nationalist expansion did not enlist in Taylor's army, trek across the Rockies, or sail to California in search of gold. Many of them experienced nationalism and expansion primarily as ideas, sources of inspiration or humor, and subjects of conversation and debate. This period of war, annexation, and migration was also a time of major growth and consolidation in American popular culture. Americans of different classes flocked especially to the theater in the mid-nineteenth century, and stage performances became venues for spreading ideas about politics and nationality.

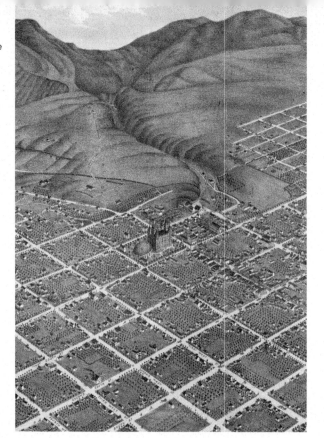

Bird's-Eye View of Salt Lake City, 1870. The temple city of the Church of Jesus Christ of Latter-day Saints grew almost instantaneously, holding forty-two hundred people within a year of its creation. But unlike San Francisco, Salt Lake City was a carefully planned urban space, where wide streets were laid out on a flat grid, land was divided by lottery, and real estate speculation was prohibited. *Library of Congress, Geography & Map Division, Washington [G4344.S3A3 1870 .K6]*

BOISTEROUS AUDIENCES

Theatergoing in U.S. cities during the first half of the nineteenth century was strikingly different from the quiet, decorous experience we now associate with dramatic entertainment. Instead of sitting in silent, rapt attention, audience members shouted, wandered around, got drunk, and engaged in all kinds of informal behavior—including spitting, throwing nutshells, and breastfeeding. When spectators disapproved of a performance, they might groan, hiss, shower the offending actor with fruits and vegetables, or wreak more serious havoc. When they approved, they might press an actor to repeat a line or an entire scene. On other occasions, audience members might caution a stage character to beware of some imminent danger, or they might suddenly disrupt a performance of Shakespeare with a rendition of "Yankee Doodle." Lights were left on, so that spectators could see and be seen. The audience was part of the show.

Significantly, these theater audiences tended to be male. Before the 1850s, respectable women saw plays only in the company of a male escort and tended to avoid the theater altogether. In most cities, prostitutes were admitted free of charge to a designated tier of the gallery, where they could negotiate and even consummate their business. ● But theaters, like saloons and polling places, were sites of public life where men dominated. This not only licensed drunkenness and rough behavior; it also marked theaters as appropriate places to air political views and allegiances. ●

POLITICS AND ENTERTAINMENT

P. T. BARNUM AND MUSEUM THEATER

Now remembered mostly for his later association with the American circus, Phineas Taylor Barnum was famous in his time as a curator of curious exhibitions, an impresario of popular entertainments, and a master of deceptions. Barnum was a founding father in the world of mass culture. He shaped and marketed commercial entertainment for multiple generations of Americans in the nineteenth century. Born in Connecticut in 1810, Barnum moved to New York City in his early twenties in search of opportunities to make money by catering, as he later put it, to "that insatiate want of human nature—the love of amusement." Barnum's opportunity came knocking in 1835 in the form of an enslaved woman named Joice Heth, who was reputed to be 161 years old and to have nursed George Washington. Barnum purchased her for one thousand dollars and peddled her and her bogus story throughout the Northeast. Thus began the career of America's greatest showman. Seven years later, Barnum had another major hit in the form of the Fejee Mermaid, which was actually made from the body of a fish and the head and hands of a monkey and exhibited to a skeptical but fascinated paying public as a major scientific discovery.

Such popular hoaxes, or humbugs as they were called, made Barnum a household name and drew customers to his **American Museum** on New York's Broadway. The museum would become the best attended entertainment venue in the United States by the late 1840s. For twenty-five cents, New Yorkers and the growing body of out-of-town visitors could tour a collection featuring exotic animals and fish, skeletons, ethnological artifacts, recent inventions, wax portraits, and various curiosities. Or they could observe a baby contest or enjoy the performance of the talented or freakish. Barnum's museum combined the zoo, the aquarium, the natural history museum, the circus, the lecture hall, and the art gallery.

In 1850, Barnum's museum also became an important theater. But instead of offering the typical stage entertainment of the era, Barnum dedicated the museum's lecture room to what he called "moral drama," a form of theater introduced in Boston a few years earlier by Moses Kimball. **Moral drama,** or "museum theater" as it was sometimes called, promised its patrons stage entertainment without the profanity or lewdness with which theater had long been associated. The plays were typically melodramas that reinforced the popular middle-class reform causes of the era (see Chapter 12). Titles such as W. H. Smith's *The Drunkard* and F. S. Hill's *Six Degrees of Crime; or Wine, Women, Gambling, Theft, and the Scaffold* reassured spectators that any depiction of vice would be framed by a morally instructive lesson. Museum theater managers also exerted tight control over their lecture halls, guaranteeing that the boisterous behavior of the traditional theater audience would not be tolerated.

These innovations were designed to make theatergoing a legitimate activity for women and families. Museum theater helped expand the American theater audience, repackaging the drama as a site of moral education, and redefining theater as a mixed-gender activity. By the end of the century, women would outnumber men in American theater audiences. More immediately, Barnum's lecture hall would provide the stage for numerous plays about slavery and race that would shape national debates in the antebellum era.

BLACKFACE MINSTRELSY

The new moral melodramas competed with Shakespearean tragedies and plays about the war in Mexico for the attention and disposable income of America's growing theater audiences, but no form of staged entertainment proved quite so popular in this period as **blackface minstrelsy.** Blackface entertainment took many forms in nineteenth-century America and proved adaptable to many different dramatic genres (including Shakespeare and moral melodrama), but its defining feature was the appearance on a public stage of a performer, typically a white man, with burnt cork or black paint on his face. Introduced in large Northern cities around 1830, it achieved the height of its popularity in the late 1840s and remained the dominant form of homegrown theater throughout the antebellum period and for some time thereafter. Blackface shows were immensely popular, but they also bore the stamp of elite approval. Minstrel troupes performed for several presidents, including Abraham Lincoln. It was the music of the blackface show that critics celebrated as America's national art.

Various blackface performers followed the same basic format, employed the same stock characters, and showcased many of the same songs and dances. American audiences through much of the North, Midwest, and far West were consuming essentially the same entertainment product (blackface was somewhat less popular in the South, in part because it was a primarily urban form of entertainment). The standard minstrel troupe featured four or five blackface performers wearing oversized, ragged costumes and armed with banjos, fiddles, bone castanets, and tambourines. The show typically consisted of a selection of songs; a medley of novelty acts, such as farcical dialogues, stump speeches riddled with malapropisms, and drag performances; and a narrative skit, usually set in the South, with dancing, music, and burlesque.

In these performances, the use of blackface was linked with representations of African Americans. The two stock characters who reappeared most frequently on the blackface stage popularized two stereotypes of Black America. **Jim Crow** (which was the name of both a character and a dance) was a happy-go-lucky, contented enslaved man living on a plantation. Zip Coon, his Northern counterpart, was an urban dandy, prone to mispronouncing or misusing big words, possessed of an inflated sense of social importance, and given to excesses of predatory sexual desire.

Much blackface performance rested on a foundation of racial contempt and animosity. White people dressed up as Black people and ridiculed their bodies, their speech patterns, their social aspirations, and their claims to human dignity—all before an appreciative white audience. Enjoying a blackface performance was a way of claiming one's whiteness, which is part of the reason the shows proved particularly popular among new immigrants from Ireland, who hoped to gain equality with their nativist detractors under the white banner.

But the appeal of blackface to urban audiences went beyond racism. Many of the skits and songs used blackface to mark the performance as popular rather than elitist. Jim Crow and Zip Coon were American types who exposed the pretensions of the well-born and often had the last laugh. As such, blackface performances helped white Americans declare cultural independence from Europe. In addition, under the protective cover of blackface comedy, bawdy burlesque humor could be indulged, and transgressive sexual pleasures, such as cross-dressing and homoeroticism, could be both expressed and disclaimed. Blackface also created a sense of common culture among a transient urban population. Many of the most popular songs from the blackface stage, such as "The Old Folks at Home," "My Old Kentucky Home,"

and "Oh, Susanna," drew on themes of displacement and longing for home (see Interpreting the Sources: "Oh, Susanna"). Finally, skits and songs about carefree characters leading undisciplined work lives may have appealed to an urban working class facing the early stages of industrialization.

Blackface promoters claimed that minstrel songs and dances were rooted in the slave experience. But blackface, like all popular American theater, was an urban phenomenon. Most minstrel composers grew up in frontier cities such as Pittsburgh and Cincinnati, and their initial audiences were in places like New York and Philadelphia. Blackface thrived in places of racial intermingling and was a product of the encounter between white performers and the free people of color who sang, danced, dressed expressively, paraded, and socialized in the public spaces of Northern and Midwestern cities. Famous African

Virginia Serenaders, Sheet Music, 1844. By the 1840s, blackface minstrel troupes were appearing in most big cities in the North, filling five huge theaters in New York, for example, where large auditoriums seated several thousand spectators. **Questions for Analysis:** Why does the title page show the Serenaders both in and out of their costumes? How do differences in posture reinforce the performers' ideas about racial difference? *Sheridan Libraries/Levy/ Gado/Getty Images*

INTERPRETING THE SOURCES

"Oh, Susanna"

It is difficult for modern readers to appreciate just how mainstream black-face entertainment was in the nineteenth century and how enduring its impact on American popular culture has been. Though its overt and crass racism might make it seem like a distant episode in the American past, much of what is now fondly remembered as classic American music had its origins on the blackface stage. The works of Stephen Foster are a good example. Foster's best-known songs, including "Camptown Races" (1850), "Old Folks at Home" (1851), "Jeannie with the Light Brown Hair" (1854), and "Old Black Joe" (1860), were written for the minstrel stage and designed to be sung with Black inflections and performed in blackface. The original lyrics of one of Foster's best-known compositions, "Oh, Susanna" (1848), show this connection explicitly:

OH, SUSANNA.

Written by S. C. Foster. Sung by Wood's Minstrels, 414 Broadway.

I've come from Alabama with the banjo on my knee,
I'm gwine to Louisiana my true lub for to see.
It rained all night the day I left, the wedder it was dry,
De sun so hot I froze to deff, Susanna don't you cry.

CHORUS AND REPEAT.
Oh, Susanna, don't you cry for me,
I've come from Alabama,
With the banjo on my knee.

I came from Alabama, Wid a banjo on my knee,
I'm gwyne to Louisiana, My true love for to see.
It rain'd all night the day I left, The weather it was dry,
The sun so hot I froze to death; Susanna, don't you cry.
Chorus:
Oh! Susanna, Oh don't you cry for me,
cos' I've come from Alabama, Wid my banjo on my knee
I jumped aboard the telegraph, And trabbled down the riber,
De lectric fluid magnified, And killed five hundred nigger.
De bullgine bust, de horse run off, I really thought I'd die;
I shut my eyes to hold my breath, Susanna don't you cry.

CHO: Oh Susanna...
I had a dream the odder night,
When ebery thing was still
I thought I saw Susanna A Coming down de hill;
The buck-wheat cake was in her mouth, The tear was in her eye;
Says I, "I'm coing from de south, Susanna, don't you cry."
CHO: Oh Susanna &c.
I soon will be in New Orleans, And den I'll look all round,
And When I find Susanna, I will fall upon de ground.
And If I do not find her, Dis Darkie'l surely die,
And when I'm dead and buried, Susanna, don't you cry.
CHO: Oh Susanna &c

Sheet Music for Stephen Foster's "Oh, Susanna" Born near Pittsburgh in 1826, Foster moved to New York and became the first American to earn a living by writing music. Although tens of thousands of urban Americans heard Foster's songs at blackface performances, many more encountered them in more intimate and informal settings, performed by amateurs who bought the sheet music. *Music-Images/Lebrecht Music & Arts/Alamy Stock Photo*

Explore the Source

1. Who is the speaker, and why might he and Susanna be living apart?

2. Does the song present the speaker in a sympathetic light?

American performers appeared on the blackface stage, and minstrel song lyrics referred to events and personages in the Black dance world. Less flatteringly, blackface publicized the forms of ridicule by which whites attacked the aspirations of emancipated urban Blacks to assert their freedom in public space.

● Although blackface was a mass entertainment form that drew fans from across the social and political spectrum, it enjoyed a special relationship with the ideology and culture of the Democratic Party. Most of the major minstrel performers and composers were identified with the Democrats.

Henry Wood, New York's leading minstrel promoter, was the brother of Benjamin and Fernando Wood, two of the leading Democratic politicians of the 1850s. Stephen Foster, blackface's preeminent composer, wrote Democratic campaign songs. ●
Blackface performances tended to embrace what the party stood for in the North—westward expansion, aggressive nationalism, anti-abolitionism, inclusive definitions of whiteness that accommodated recent immigrants, deep suspicion of reformers and evangelical pieties, and the championing of urban, working-class entertainment tastes in defiance of elitist prejudices.

NATIONAL COMMUNICATION

Much as the original creation of the United States had required new processes of communication (see Chapter 7), the territorial expansion of the American republic posed new communication challenges. The expanded nation required new infrastructure and new symbols of shared identity to bind together a diverse citizenry spreading to unfamiliar parts of the continent. Already in the 1840s, a network of railroad tracks was beginning to form in the Northeast. By the middle of the next decade, the railroad would thoroughly displace the canal system as the nation's most powerful force and most conspicuous symbol of economic consolidation and long-distance connection (see Chapter 14). But long-distance communication in this period was not simply about building roads, canals, or rail lines. Various important innovations in the way Americans communicated with one another facilitated the mobility of people and ideas in the era of national expansion.

THE TELEGRAPH

During the early decades of the nineteenth century, the time it took for information to pass between one part of the country and another had been radically reduced—by improved roads, artificial waterways, entrepreneurial news providers, and more frequent and dense patterns of travel and commerce. But generally speaking, information moved only as fast as the human beings or animals that conveyed it. The exceptions to this rule were various optical signal systems, which involved a series of visual displays relayed from one hill or tower to another. Optical telegraphy was expensive to set up and limited in its reach, but in 1837 Samuel Morse (a painter by training) and Joseph Henry (a physicist) had demonstrated the possibility of transmitting electromagnetic signals over wires. Morse, who secured a federal patent for the electromagnetic telegraph in 1840, synthesized and applied the discoveries and inventions of numerous scientists, promoted the new device with great vigor, and developed a code that would become the international language of telegraphy.

In 1843, Morse persuaded Congress to appropriate thirty thousand dollars for the construction of a telegraph line between Washington, D.C., and Baltimore. Though he squandered twenty-three thousand dollars of the grant trying to bury the wires below ground, Morse succeeded in building the line, and on May 22, 1844, he successfully transmitted the biblical phrase "What hath god wrought" across 40 miles. Morse expected the federal government to purchase his patent and regulate the use of the telegraph through the Post Office. He offered the patent for one hundred thousand dollars and tried to drum up support by staging chess games over the wires. But Congress refused, and Morse turned to private investors, who funded the rapid construction of telegraph lines. By 1850, 12,000 miles of telegraph wire stretched across the eastern half of the continent.

Because sending a message across these wires was extremely expensive—as much as one dollar per word in the early years—the telegraph did not transform the way Americans communicated with one another. Telegraphy was used mostly by merchants, bankers, and others who needed to check someone's credit, relay commodity prices, or lock in the terms of a commercial transaction. Nonetheless, the impact of Morse's device on popular culture was considerable, because the telegraph affected the way news was reported. In 1846, six major New York dailies agreed to share the costs of transmitting news from the Mexican War. This arrangement did not simply make it possible for New Yorkers to follow the war as it unfolded; it created the first wire service, called the Associated Press. Wire services created a new standard for speedy news flow and helped turn newspaper offices in large urban centers into major gathering spots for the reception of official information.

Although initially intended to harness the power of the telegraph for relaying war news, wire services could be used as well to turn other items of popular interest into mass media events. When boxers Tom Hyer and Yankee Sullivan squared off in a ten-thousand-dollar, winner-take-all prizefight 1849, the bout attracted considerable interest. Partisans of Hyer (a native-born Whig) and Sullivan (an Irish-born Democrat who would later die in a San Francisco jail, facing trial at the hand of the Committee of Vigilance) identified passionately with their respective champions and wagered an estimated three hundred thousand dollars on the outcome. ● Because prizefighting was illegal, the **Hyer versus Sullivan** match was held in a secret location in Kent County, Maryland, in front of only a few hundred spectators. But all over urban America, fans crowded around newspaper offices to hear the results relayed round-by-round. In this way, the telegraph helped create the modern sports event as a contest followed in real time by a national audience. ●

MEDIA AND INFORMATION

CHEAP POSTAGE

Although the federal government got out of the telegraph business, it continued to provide the infrastructure for

Hyer Versus Sullivan.   In this 1849 bare-knuckle fight, one of the first American sports events to be followed by a national audience, American-born Bowery butcher Tom Hyer (the taller boxer) knocked out Irish immigrant Yankee Sullivan in less than twenty minutes. *Free Library of Philadelphia/Bridgeman Images*

national communication through the U.S. Post Office. During this period, postal service underwent a major transformation, however. In its early decades, the Post Office had been used primarily by merchants to conduct business and by publishers to circulate newspapers. Up until the 1840s, the mail was important for ordinary Americans primarily as a source of news. Sending a letter to friends or relatives was a significant event reserved for special occasions, except for those wealthy enough to afford very high rates of postage. Sending a two-page letter traveling 400 miles—say, from Albany to Pittsburgh—would cost fifty cents—more than half the average daily wage of the time.

Beginning in 1845, a major change took place in the history of postal correspondence. Around the same time that private telegraph companies began assuming some of the role in news broadcasting and commercial exchange that had been the domain of the Post Office, Congress decided to enact **postage reform,** helping turn the nation's postal system into a popular interactive medium. According to a new law in 1845, letters would now be assessed primarily on the basis of weight rather than distance, and rates were lowered radically to five cents per half ounce for close distances and ten cents per half ounce for greater distances. The Postal Act of 1851 extended this reform by setting the basic letter rate at five cents for a half-ounce letter addressed to virtually anywhere in the country. If the sender prepaid the postage (for which purpose postage stamps had been introduced in 1847), it would cost only three cents. Proponents argued that the lower rates would be offset by the much higher volume of correspondence, because more Americans would develop new letter-writing habits. Lower postage was especially popular

among Whigs, who saw improvements in long-distance communication as essential to national expansion. But the reforms reflected a broader optimism that enough Americans would want to send letters across the expanding nation to justify the new strategy. The era of postal reform marked the emergence of the mail as a popular medium for maintaining personal relationships at a distance.

Postage reductions and westward expansion went hand in hand. Westward migrants were especially likely to want to correspond with those they had left behind. And events like the war with Mexico and the California gold rush dramatized the utility of a postal network for connecting temporarily separated family members. Forty-niners left for California with promises to send news (and wealth) back to their wives and children, and upon arrival they wrote frequently of their desire for news from home (see Hot Commodities: Photographic Portraits). On "steamer days," when mail from the Eastern states was unloaded, post offices in Sacramento and San Francisco became mob scenes.

NATIONAL LITERATURE

The decade after President Polk's election was also a time of explosive growth in American literature. An expanding publishing industry, headquartered in Northeastern cities, circulated unprecedented volumes of fiction. Americans read much of this fiction in serial installments in newspapers and magazines, or in cheap, soft-covered pamphlets sent in the mail. Because there were no international copyright laws (Congress was more interested in promoting the spread of reading than in protecting the property rights of authors), publishers could reprint

Mail Call. Post office lines in San Francisco and Sacramento were notoriously long, and reports told of men refusing offers of twenty dollars for their spot in line. Forty-niners were eager for news from home—and eager to show those they had left behind that their letters were more precious than money. Images of post office crowds were often designed as stationery in California and used for letters home. *North Wind Picture Archives/Alamy Stock Photo*

foreign works without having to pay royalties. But several American authors produced best-selling books as well. Female novelists such as Maria Cummins, Susan Warner, and Fanny Fern reached tens of thousands of readers in the middle of the nineteenth century with fiction that explored and celebrated the private feelings of their characters and focused on family relationships. This body of novels, often classified by critics as sentimental literature, included Harriet Beecher Stowe's antislavery novel *Uncle Tom's Cabin* (see Chapter 14), which would become the best-selling American novel of the century.

Stowe's novel also had elements of another popular fiction genre, often designated sensational literature and typically authored by men. Best-selling sensational fiction included the adventure stories and melodramas of the nativist author Ned Buntline, the soft-core pornographic novels of George Thompson, and George Lippard's *The Quaker City*. Lippard's 1845 novel promised to expose the "Secret Life of Philadelphia" and entertained readers

with stories of seduction, rape, murder, and the corruption of city life. Lippard was a prominent advocate of westward expansion and donated much of the money he earned from his literary career to a campaign for distributing Western land to the nation's urban working class. More generally, popular sensationalist fiction after 1845 celebrated the expanding American frontier as a place where adventurous men from different classes and regions could overcome their differences and unite under the banner of American manhood.

It was in this short period that the poets, novelists, and essayists now considered the giants of nineteenth-century literature produced their classic works. Herman Melville, Walt Whitman, Edgar Allan Poe, Emily Dickinson, Ralph Waldo Emerson, Henry David Thoreau, and Nathaniel Hawthorne were not nearly as well read in their day as Warner, Lippard, and Stowe, but by the middle of the twentieth century, they had become part of the American cultural canon and their work represented

HOT COMMODITIES
Photographic Portraits

When photography was introduced in France and Britain in 1839, its inventors and promoters imagined that it would be primarily suitable for still-life depictions and landscapes. There was little reason to expect the camera to be used for personal portraiture. The daguerreotyping procedure, named for the French inventor Louis-Jacques-Mandé Daguerre, could produce remarkably faithful images, but it required lengthy exposure times—five minutes to an hour in its early years. Even once exposure times were reduced to twenty seconds, the composure necessary to sit for a portrait could be excruciating. Daguerreotype artists would position their subjects against iron head rests, and many early portraits show men and women in apparent discomfort.

Nonetheless, portraiture quickly became the dominant use of the daguerreotype in the United States. By midcentury, 90 percent of the daguerreotypes taken nationwide were posed portraits of individuals or (less commonly) families. Portrait studios became big business, especially in cities. Within a decade of

Daguerre's invention, there were a hundred such studios in New York alone. And in the instant city of San Francisco, dozens of daguerreotype studios and salons appeared within a few years of the discovery of gold.

Daguerreotypes and wet-plate collodion photographs, which allowed for the mechanical reproduction of unlimited (and cheap) copies from a single negative, gave middle-class families the opportunity to emulate the traditionally genteel, even aristocratic practice of displaying the portraits of relatives and ancestors. They also allowed Americans on the move to maintain visual contact with friends and family living at a distance. After the postage reductions of 1845 and 1851, photographic portraits also became mobile.

Think About It

1. Why would photographic portraits have been especially popular in American cities and in California?
2. How might the circulation of photographic portraits have changed social relationships in the United States?

I Sell the Shadow to Support the Substance.
SOJOURNER TRUTH.

Sojourner Truth's Carte de Visite. After the introduction of photography, Americans could exchange calling cards that featured their own likenesses. By mid-century politicians, authors, and actors began using these cartes de visite as a form of publicity. The abolitionist orator Sojourner Truth used cartes de visite to support herself and raise funds for her cause. *Library of Congress Prints and Photographs Division [LC-DIG-ppmsca-08978]*

---

what critics call the **American Renaissance.** Their most enduring writing (including *Moby Dick*, *The Scarlet Letter*, *Walden*, and *Leaves of Grass*) first appeared in print in the years 1850–1855, when Americans were grappling with the implications of their expanded nation.

Several of the leading figures in the American Renaissance, including Melville, Whitman, and Hawthorne, were part of a New York–based literary circle that revolved around the nation's most famous expansionist journal, the *Democratic Review*. The journal's literary editor, Evert Duyckinck, became a spokesman for the Young America movement in American literature. Authors in this circle cared deeply about politics and attributed enormous political significance to literature. They were optimistic about the United States and eager to enhance its reputation, spread its influence, and expand its territorial sovereignty. They also championed nationalist republican movements in Europe (see the section The Revolutions of

1848), celebrated youth, supported the labor movement, and favored extending suffrage across class lines. But they were far cooler to middle-class reform causes, such as temperance, woman suffrage, and abolitionism; and like the blackface performers and promoters, they strongly identified with the Democratic Party.

THE AMERICAN NATION IN THE WORLD

Because the Mexican cession and the Oregon settlement added territories that extended the United States to the Pacific and established what are more or less the nation's current continental borders, it is tempting to think that the project of expansionism was complete and America's Manifest Destiny fulfilled. But nationalists in 1848 did not see it that way. Many American politicians, writers, and adventurers gazed with interest at other parts of the globe and saw new opportunities for American influence and new frontiers for U.S. expansion.

THE REVOLUTIONS OF 1848

On February 21, 1848, with news of the Treaty of Guadalupe Hidalgo freshly arrived at the U.S. capital, Americans learned of the Paris uprising that signaled the beginning of a new revolt against the French monarchy. This was the first of the **revolutions of 1848,** which erupted through much of Europe. Over the course of the year, liberal nationalist movements sought to establish republican governments within the multiethnic Hapsburg Empire centered in Austria. Uprisings in Hungary, Bohemia, German-speaking lands, the Balkan region, and the Italian peninsula declared independence from the Hapsburgs and envisioned a new era of liberal nation-states in central Europe. By 1849, however, some of the coalitions that had supported these uprisings had fallen apart, and conservative forces were able to restore Hapsburg rule.

American nationalists greeted the revolutions of 1848 enthusiastically. Many relished the prospect of the toppling of old European regimes. Some celebrated the idea that republican revolutions were extending an American empire of liberty eastward. When the exiled Hungarian nationalist leader Lajos Kossuth toured the United States in 1851, following the defeat of his revolution by Russian forces, he received a hero's welcome throughout the country. Supporters of the Young America movement were among Kossuth's loudest fans and portrayed him as the representative of American freedom in a world ruled by despots.

Kossuth hoped to parlay his American popularity into foreign aid that would enable him to launch a second revolution, but here he failed. Though private individuals donated to the Hungarian cause, the U.S. government was loath to antagonize the Hapsburgs and become enmeshed in European wars. And over the course of his visit, the Kossuth mania subsided. Irish Americans, many of whom saw Kossuth as an enemy of the Catholic Church, grew critical. Southerners worried that his speeches on behalf of freedom would embolden the critics of slavery. Kossuth was careful to avoid that topic, but this only alienated abolitionists, who accused him of pandering or hypocrisy. Unable to navigate the tensions of U.S. sectional politics, he headed back to Europe in 1852 without having achieved his real goal, but the American nationalism that had turned Kossuth into a star did not diminish.

FILIBUSTERS

The Treaty of Guadalupe Hidalgo did not satisfy many Americans' desires for territorial expansion. Democrats, in particular, clamored for further acquisitions and made expansionism a consistent plank in their party platform, even after the war. In 1848, they ran Lewis Cass for president against the Whigs's war hero, Zachary Taylor. Cass had advocated taking all of Mexico during the war and supported annexing Cuba as well. Cass was defeated by Taylor (who died in 1850 and was succeeded by Millard Fillmore), but Democrats continued to push for expansion into Mexico, Central America, the Caribbean, and the Pacific. When Democrats retook the presidency in 1852 with the election of Franklin Pierce, the United States pressed Mexico to cede more land, resulting in the Gadsden Purchase, and tried hard to wrest Cuba from the Spanish.

Where the U.S. government failed or refused to go, individual American citizens took matters into their own hands. The Mexican War triggered a rash of filibuster campaigns in which private armies used American territory and American expansionist ideals as a launching pad for invading foreign countries. Derived from a Spanish word meaning freebooter (pirate), American **filibusters** (the word denotes both invaders and invasions) entered British Canada, Mexico, Ecuador, Honduras, Cuba, and Nicaragua—and contemplated invasions of the Hawaiian Islands. These campaigns violated international law, which the United States had reaffirmed in the 1818 Neutrality Act, and the federal government officially disavowed them. But filibusters enjoyed significant popularity during the postwar years, in both the North and the South, especially among Democrats.

Filibusters were motivated by various desires for private gain, adventure, and masculine honor, but most of the men who led these expeditions also imagined that they would ultimately be extending U.S. sovereignty over new land. This was not an unrealistic expectation. After all, Texas provided a model for how a revolution by Americans acting without the sanction of their government could ultimately bring about annexation. The filibusters who invaded Cuba or Nicaragua anticipated a similar process as they sought to fulfill the nation's destiny.

Though thousands of Americans participated in the filibusters, they did not succeed. Joseph Morehead's foray into the Mexican state of Sonora was rebuffed in Baja California in 1851. California state senator Henry Crabb met his death while leading a similar expedition in 1857. Venezuela-born Narciso López founded the Junta Cubana in New York in 1848, attracting significant American support for his attempt at revolution in Cuba, but he was executed on the island in 1851. Tennessean William Walker seized power in Nicaragua from 1855 to 1857, but he was ousted and eventually shot to death in Honduras in 1860.

In retrospect, these ventures may seem foolhardy, but filibusters saw themselves as the vanguard of American imperial expansion, fighting on the side of history. They had no reason to believe that the pace of U.S. territorial acquisition would slacken. In 1853, the *Democratic Review* imagined the nation's borders creeping progressively southward into Mexico and spreading "a penumbra over the West Indies." Several years later, the magazine asserted that "no well-informed person entertains the shadow of a doubt" that Cuba and Mexico would become states in the growing union.

NEW COMMERCIAL FRONTIERS

Whigs were less eager to add new territory to a nation already beset by sectional controversy over the extension of slavery. Instead, they sought to expand the nation's power and influence by opening up new trade networks and building a commercial empire in the Pacific. Whig president Fillmore instructed naval commander Matthew Perry to sail to Japan with heavily armed ships, to pressure the Japanese to open up their ports to American traders. The first Perry expedition reached Edo (now called Tokyo) in 1853 and conveyed a letter from President Fillmore. A year later, a second expedition resulted in the signing of the Treaty of Kanagawa, under which Japan agreed to limited diplomatic and commercial relations with the United States. The United States would now be able to compete in the growing world of Pacific trade.

CONCLUSION

A decade after Congress voted to annex Texas, the United States was a sprawling, transcontinental nation with new links to the Pacific world. Many of its citizens expected further extension of the nation's borders and harbored ambitions for an expansive American empire. But even as things stood in 1854, the United States had become a very different place in a very short time. Territorial expansion attracted new streams of foreign migration and accelerated the dispersal of the native-born population. Various forces, including railroads, telegraph wires, cheap postage, print culture, and commercial entertainment, forged links among a mobile populace. But the era of nationalist expansion would pose new threats to the political unity of the country. By 1854, the compromises and coalitions that had contained sectional conflict over slavery were already straining.

STUDY TERMS

- Texas annexation
- Manifest Destiny
- Young America
- San Patricio battalion
- *Resistance to Civil Government*
- Oregon settlement
- Wilmot Proviso
- Treaty of Guadalupe Hidalgo
- Overland Trail
- Donner party
- California gold rush
- forty-niners
- Californios
- Foreign Miners Taxes
- Committee of Vigilance
- Mormon exodus
- Deseret
- American Museum
- moral drama
- blackface minstrelsy
- Jim Crow
- Hyer versus Sullivan
- postage reform
- American Renaissance
- revolutions of 1848
- filibusters

FURTHER READING

A database of additional full-text readings is available through Power of Process for Primary Sources in Connect.

Brian DeLay, *War of a Thousand Deserts* (2008), explains the importance of Native American raids to the course of Mexican history and the success of the U.S. invasion of Mexico.

Michel Gobat, *Empire by Invitation* (2018), reinterprets the appeal and ideology of the filibusters in Central America.

Amy Greenberg, *A Wicked War* (2012), chronicles the dramas and controversies surrounding the U.S. invasion of Mexico.

Darcy Grigsby, *Enduring Truths* (2015), explores the relationship between photography and abolitionism in the life of Sojourner Truth.

Albert Hurtado, *Indian Survival on the California Frontier* (1990), details the impact of Mexican and American settlements on native life in California.

Amy K. D. Lippert, *Consuming Identities* (2018), documents and analyzes the proliferation of images of people that took place in gold rush California.

Alexander Saxton, *The Rise and Fall of the White Republic* (1991), illuminates the connections between American popular culture and Democratic Party politics.

Benjamin Reiss, *The Showman and the Slave* (2001), sets P. T. Barnum's early success within the history of antebellum slavery and race relations.

Alberto Varon, *Before Chicano* (2018), reconstructs the ways Mexican American writers and thinkers imagined citizenship after 1848.

14 | A UNION UNRAVELING

Chapter Questions

1. Which events during the 1850s unsettled the conflict between proponents and opponents of the westward expansion of slavery?

2. How did changes in transportation infrastructure forge stronger connections between particular regions?

3. How did ideas about work, race, and religion shape the escalating sectional conflict?

4. What factors contributed to the breakdown of the two-party system?

Dismal Swamp. Fugitives from slavery often negotiated treacherous terrain, and their flight sparked political instability. *The Granger Collection, New York*

On June 2, 1854, life in the city of Boston ground to a halt as its inhabitants gathered to watch a single African American man walk down the middle of State Street on a Friday afternoon under armed guard. Anthony Burns, the man of the hour, was an enslaved Virginian who had run away to Boston and become an active member of that city's free Black community. But a month earlier, his putative owner, Charles Francis Suttle, had secured an arrest warrant for Burns under the controversial Fugitive Slave Act, which had been passed in 1850. Having been certified as the man named in the warrant, Burns was now in military custody, bound for the South.

From the moment Suttle's warrant was issued, Boston had been awash in agitation over the case. The city's abolitionists pursued a wide range of legal and extralegal strategies to secure Burns's release. Prestigious legal counsel, reams of inflammatory handbills, and impassioned exhortations from Protestant pulpits were mustered in his defense. There was even an unsuccessful attempt at armed rescue, in which

Time Line

genteel clergymen, Harvard law students, Black dock-workers, and prominent white attorneys wielded axes and pistols and mounted battering rams. Finally, several of Burns's supporters, both white and Black, tried unsuccessfully to purchase him from Suttle.

On the other side of this battle stood not only a Virginia slaveholder but also the federal government, which spent fourteen thousand dollars to secure Burns's return and demonstrate its commitment to the recapture of fugitives from slavery. Some of the Bostonians lining State Street on June 2 were on the government's side. A few were conservative elites and merchants in the cotton business who feared the turn to civil disobedience and sought to preserve good relations with the South. But more were Irish immigrants hostile to abolitionism and to the nativist Protestants who rallied to Burns's defense. Many of these immigrants staffed the marshal's guard and the militia. At the end of Burns's procession, gleeful militiamen taunted the fugitive with a chorus of the popular blackface minstrel song "Carry Me Back to Old Virginny." And with that, Anthony Burns boarded a ship and returned to slavery.

Anthony Burns was by no means the first fugitive from slavery to be recovered in the North after 1850, but his trial fired the imaginations of previously inert supporters of free labor. His forced return to Virginia (where he sat in a Richmond jail until his friends managed to purchase his freedom) also underscored a threat to national unity. The cases of those fleeing bondage unsettled the moral boundaries of slavery. The United States was half enslaved and half free, but those two halves were increasingly interconnected. Laws requiring the citizens of Massachusetts to enforce the claims of Virginia slaveholders punctured the illusion that free and slave states could peacefully coexist as separate worlds.

One of the central paradoxes of the 1850s was that Southerners and Northerners gravitated toward irreconcilably opposed positions on the slavery question, even as the nation became, in other ways, more unified. Economic ties, expanded communication, population movement, and most dramatically an emerging railroad system all reshuffled the national map, making distant places seem more connected. The emerging lines of long-distance connection tended to run along an east-west axis, however, forging relations and coalitions between Northerners and Midwesterners. Newly acquired Western territories, over a thousand miles away from the nation's capital, became the subjects of intense debate and strained the relationship between North and South.

The political system that had produced compromise in 1820 began to buckle under the weight of the Mexican cession of 1848, and sectional tensions escalated on a number of connected fronts: in the Western territories, in Boston, in Congress, and at the Supreme Court. National political parties that had attracted voters on both sides of this partition could no longer do so, and by the end of the 1850s a stark choice between two hostile positions would rip the nation apart.

COMPROMISES AND BOUNDARIES

The Mexican cession of 1848 extended U.S. sovereignty over foreign lands and fulfilled dreams of a transcontinental nation. But the new map of the United States raised novel questions about the character of that nation. As the federal government sought to organize its newly acquired territories and admit states into the union, the thirty-year political truce brokered by the Missouri Compromise broke down. Instead of extending the divide between slavery and free labor westward at the 36°30′ latitude, Congress relied on a complex set of new compromises to maintain the political balance.

THE ELECTION OF 1848

Although David Wilmot's 1846 proposal to ban slavery in any territory acquired as a result of the war against Mexico failed to become law (see Chapter 13), it provided the rallying cry for a new political movement in the North. Few supporters of the Wilmot Proviso advocated abolishing slavery where it existed or freeing any of the 3 million African Americans held in bondage. But they insisted that Congress had the right to regulate slavery in territories that had not yet become states, and most of

them wished to preserve the nation's Western lands as "free soil" for white settlers. As the 1848 election approached and the two major parties refused to embrace free soil principles, many Northerners embraced a **Free Soil Party,** nominating a ticket of Democratic ex-president Martin Van Buren and Boston's Whig leader, Charles Francis Adams (son of John Quincy Adams).

The Free Soil coalition drew many Wilmot Proviso supporters from both major parties, as well as more hard-core antislavery voters. But it failed to win any states and captured only 10 percent of the popular vote. Competing closely in both slave and free states were the two major-party contenders, war hero Zachary Taylor, a Louisiana slaveholder running on the Whig ticket, and Lewis Cass, a Michigan Democrat who favored aggressive westward expansion and did not seem to care whether slavery entered the new territories. Taylor narrowly won the contest, helped in part by the defections of Democrats in New York to Van Buren. The election seemed to demonstrate that the major parties could maintain their national coalitions even in the face of the slavery controversy. But the ominous appearance of Van Buren, the architect of the Second Party System (see Chapter 10), at the head of an army of rebellious Northern Democrats, foretold troubles for the political order.

THE COMPROMISE OF 1850

On taking office in 1849, President Taylor charted a course that seemed likely to help the North. Hoping to preempt controversy over slavery in the new territories, Taylor began pushing for immediate statehood for California and New Mexico, where American settlers had already adopted free-labor constitutions. Southerners in both parties protested this plan, however, and bitter debate over the expansion of slavery ensued.

Some Democrats proposed using the Missouri Compromise line and simply dividing the new territories between the North and the South (see Map 14.1). Missouri senator Thomas Benton, who had helped broker the original 1820 compromise, pinned his hopes on the geographical line and touted the special role of St. Louis as a central city that could lead the nation down a middle path on the slavery question. But congressional opinion was now more polarized than it had been thirty years earlier. The idea of cutting the national map in half and splitting the difference had become unacceptable to increasing numbers of Americans on both sides. Antislavery senators like William H. Seward spoke for a growing body of Northern politicians who would not countenance the

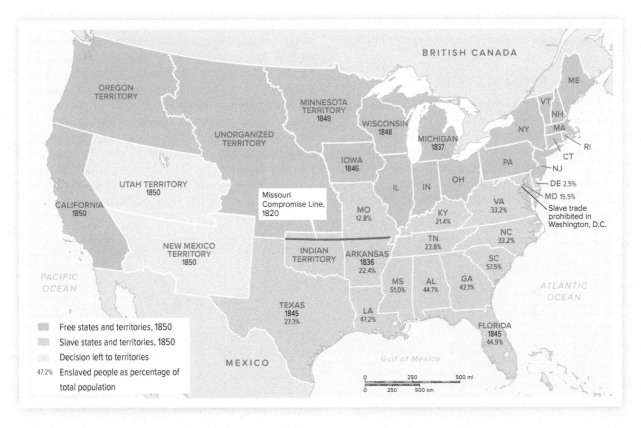

Map 14.1 The Compromise of 1850 (with the Missouri Compromise Line Shown). The compromise preserved the balance between slave and free states but introduced new principles for determining the status of slavery in the western half of the continent. Note that extending the Missouri Compromise line westward would have split California into two states with a border just north of Los Angeles.

introduction of slavery into any part of the country where it was not already legal. Proslavery spokesman John C. Calhoun, on the other hand, took the view that the federal government had no constitutional right to restrict slavery at all. During the 1850s, this view became the party line among Southerners known as **fire-eaters,** who felt that any concession on slavery would lead to abolition. A third position, which Cass had embraced during the presidential campaign, favored letting the status of slavery in the West be determined by **popular sovereignty**—a vote of a territory's local settlers.

After months of debate and the sudden death of President Taylor, Congress passed a series of laws, which together became known as the **Compromise of 1850.** Authored by an aging Henry Clay and refined by Stephen A. Douglas of Illinois, the compromise was a cluster of different measures that Congress enacted separately. The compromise appeared to give something to each side of the debate. It admitted California as a free state but determined that the status of slavery in the new territories of New Mexico and

Utah would be decided by popular sovereignty when they were ready for statehood. New Mexico also received a generous eastern boundary that had previously been contested by Texas. At the same time, Congress abolished the slave trade, but not slavery itself, in the nation's capital. As the linchpin of the deal, a stricter fugitive slave law went into effect, making it easier for slaveholders to recover their human property in other parts of the country.

Because the Compromise of 1850 contained so many different provisions, observers could (and did) disagree about which section's interests or which approach to the slavery question had prevailed. With the addition of California, free states now outnumbered slave states in the Senate. But slave states could hope to restore balance in the future, now that Congress had opened the door for popular sovereignty in the other Western territories. The South could also take comfort from the fact that Congress had still refused to abolish slavery anywhere, even in Washington, D.C., where it had sole jurisdiction. The clear losers in the debate were those who had favored updating and extending the Missouri Compromise. That model of managing the slavery conflict was now obsolete.

FUGITIVES FROM SLAVERY

By far the most controversial plank of the Compromise of 1850 was the **Fugitive Slave Act.** There was nothing new about the legal requirement that people legally enslaved in one state had to be returned to their owners, even if they escaped to another part of the country where slavery was illegal. Such a provision appeared explicitly in the U.S. Constitution. But the 1850 Fugitive Slave Act tilted the legal scales decisively against accused runaways and dramatically increased the obligation of citizens in free states to cooperate with slave catchers. According to the new law, someone charged with being a runaway was not entitled to a jury trial and could not use most customary forms of legal defense. Alleged fugitives could not contest the legality of slavery, nor could they even contest the claim that they were legally enslaved; the only permissible defense was that they were not the person listed on the warrant. The trial of an accused runaway would be a summary proceeding before a federal magistrate, enforced immediately and without

Debating the Fugitive Slave Act in Congress. In this 1855 engraving depicting debate over the Compromise of 1850, Senator Henry Clay speaks to his colleagues. The issue stirred passionate rhetoric like that of George Julian, a Free Soil representative from Indiana: "[If] I believed the people I represent were base enough to become the miserable flunkies of a God-forsaken southern slave hunter by joining him or his constable in the blood-hound chase of a panting slave, I would scorn to hold a seat on this floor by their suffrages, and I would denounce them as fit subjects themselves for the lash of the slave-driver." *GHI Vintage/Universal History Archive/Universal Images Group/Getty Images*

Broadside in support of Anthony Burns, 1854 Antislavery (and anti-Irish) posters rallied Bostonians to the defense of a fugitive from bondage. *Courtesy of the Trustees of the Boston Public Library/Rare Books*

possibility of appeal. The act also offered financial incentives for magistrates to certify a suspect as a fugitive and empowered federal marshals to require citizens' help in enforcing the law.

The Fugitive Slave Act took the slavery conflict from Congress to the towns and cities of the North and West. Slaveholders and their agents pursued runaways in border states, deep into New England, and as far away as California. In short order, New York, Philadelphia, Harrisburg, Syracuse, and Detroit became battlegrounds as fugitives, free people of color, and white abolitionists resisted the new law. In Christiana, Pennsylvania, armed African Americans killed two white men from Maryland who were trying to recover a fugitive. In Boston, which had been a magnet for people escaping slavery, as many as one-fifth of the city's Black residents were subject to being reclaimed as property under the Fugitive Slave Act, and many others worried about being mistakenly apprehended or falsely accused. A substantial portion of the community fled to Canada during the immediate aftermath of the Compromise of 1850. But most stayed, and Boston became the main stage for the fight over enforcing the new law. In 1851, Black Bostonians successfully rescued Frederick "Shadrach" Minkins from federal marshals and sent him to Canada. Two months later, the marshals prevailed in the recapture

of another Boston fugitive, Thomas Sims. And in 1854, the Anthony Burns case (see opening vignette) proved a galling defeat for Boston's antislavery community.

In the six years following passage of the Fugitive Slave Act, three runaways were forcibly rescued from their captors, whereas almost two hundred were returned to bondage. Both numbers are negligible in the context of more than 3 million enslaved people and over a thousand runaways a year. But the impact on white opinion in the North was far greater. By bringing the spectacle of enslavement to Northern soil, the Fugitive Slave Act gave credence to the abolitionist argument that slavery was not simply a Southern institution. Garrison and his followers had insisted since the 1830s that every citizen of the United States bore moral responsibility for slavery. After 1850, the logic of that position was especially compelling. Federal magistrates and marshals made it clear that slavery had legal legitimacy in Boston and Detroit, not just in Charleston and New Orleans. Individual states sought to nullify or thwart the Fugitive Slave Act, but it was a crucial part of the political compromise over slavery in the territories, and the federal government was committed to its enforcement.

UNCLE TOM'S CABIN

Against the backdrop of the new moral map created by the Fugitive Slave Act, Harriet Beecher Stowe was persuaded by her friends to write *Uncle Tom's Cabin.* Stowe grew up the daughter of Lyman Beecher, New England's leading Congregationalist minister. From age twenty-one to age thirty-nine, Stowe lived in Cincinnati, the largest city on the Ohio River, which was one of the major borders between free and slave states. Stowe's novel would reinforce the Ohio River's place in the popular imagination as the symbolic divide between Southern slavery and Northern freedom. In one of the book's most haunting scenes, the heroine (an enslaved woman named Eliza) flees across the frozen river, clutching her son Harry, with a slave trader in hot pursuit. But much of the novel describes the horrors of plantation life for those held in bondage on the other side of the water.

Stowe painted a picture of the South that emphasized the domestic slave trade and its tendency to break up enslaved families, but it also contained sensational descriptions of cruel and sadistic enslavers. The book also dealt with themes that were standard fare in the sentimental literature of the day (see Chapter 13), such as the nurturing home and courageous patience in the face of suffering. *Uncle Tom's Cabin* was serialized in the antislavery paper *The National Era* in 1851–1852 and then published as a book in May 1852. The novel was phenomenally successful. By 1857, half a million copies had been sold in the United States and over a million in England. No book other than the Bible was as widely purchased in nineteenth-century America.

Like the Fugitive Slave Act itself, *Uncle Tom's Cabin* brought vivid images of slavery to Northern audiences. Southern readers also paid attention to Stowe's novel and attacked it bitterly. Southern reviewers criticized her for describing slavery without ever having visited a plantation and charged that she must have been a depraved woman to make up such scenes of sensational cruelty from her own imagination. Others responded with novels of their own. Books like *Uncle Robin in His Cabin in Virginia and Tom Without One in Boston* (1855) and *New England's Chattels* (1858) made the proslavery argument that those enslaved in the South were better off than workers in the North. Some responses to Stowe's novel were less literary. In 1853, she received in the mail a package containing a dark-skinned human ear.

• *Uncle Tom's Cabin* was a media sensation, but its popularity did not necessarily mean that Stowe had persuaded her mass audience that slavery was immoral. Much of the American public knew Stowe's story and her characters through the theater, where Stowe had little or no control over the content. Within a year of the novel's publication, there were four versions on the New York stage, and another eleven in England. By end of the century, five hundred *Uncle Tom* companies would be touring the United States. About fifty people eventually saw the play for every one person who read the novel. *Uncle Tom* plays varied widely in their politics, and several of them changed the plot to downplay the novel's abolitionism. Several playwrights and theater promoters used *Uncle Tom's Cabin* as a vehicle for blackface minstrelsy (see Chapter 13), and many Northern theatergoers encountered Stowe's characters first as comic caricatures. An 1854 minstrel version of *Uncle Tom's Cabin* in St. Louis turned Stowe herself into such a caricature, dubbed Harriet Screecher Blow. •

Years later, Abraham Lincoln was reputed to have greeted Stowe with the observation that she was "the little woman who wrote the book that made this great war,"

because she mobilized humanitarian sympathy for the plight of the enslaved. But Stowe could no more control the meaning of her novel than she could direct the course of political events around her. *Uncle Tom's Cabin* became a major part of the culture of the 1850s, a touchstone in the polarizing debate over slavery. It did not, however, turn the North into a region of abolitionists.

RAILROAD NATION

The controversies over slavery in the territories and fugitives from bondage divided a nation that was in some respects more connected than ever before. America in the 1850s was linked by canals, telegraph wires, postal service, mass publishing, and ever-intensifying commercial contacts. But the most visible source and symbol of national connection was the railroad network. Abolitionists and fugitives from slavery used the metaphor of an Underground Railroad to designate a far-flung web of safe houses and accomplices through which tens of thousands of runaways from Southern bondage made their way to Northern states, Canada, Mexico, or the Bahamas.

• The above-ground system that inspired its name was also breaking down the walls that enclosed the Southern slave system. Railroad development affected perceptions of proximity; introduced new patterns of work, trade, and travel; mobilized the nation's labor force; stimulated heavy industry; and transformed the landscape of the country. Crucially, it forged special ties between free-labor states in the East and those in the West. In all these ways, the economic and social changes wrought by new transportation patterns during the 1850s further altered the map of slavery politics. •

THE RAIL NETWORK

Railroads had been part of American life since the 1820s, when horses pulled cars along the tracks of the Baltimore and Ohio railroad line. Those tracks soon accommodated steam locomotives, and governments began subsidizing the construction of new lines. By the end of the 1830s, the United States had more than twice as many miles of railroad track as all of Europe combined. Track construction slowed following the 1837 depression, but then rebounded on a much larger scale. Between 1848 and 1860, the United States became a nation of railroad lines. Track mileage soared during that period, from 5,000 to 30,000 miles, and a rail network centered in the Midwest surpassed the canal network as a conduit of long-distance travel and trade.

Railroad construction was not simply the result of new technologies. An extraordinary amount of private and public investment was necessary to finance the high initial costs of building the new train network. Railroad companies borrowed money from European banks, sold stock to farmers who lived along their routes, and benefited from extraordinary government munificence. State governments contributed 45 percent of the capital that financed the early construction of railroads. Starting in 1850, the federal government got in on the act as well, providing a land grant of several million acres to the Illinois Central railroad—the first of forty land grants to railroad corporations in the 1850s. By the end of the decade, the combined public and private investment in U.S. railroads had exceeded $1.1 billion (see How Much Is That? Railroad Investment).

The rapid growth of the rail network in the 1850s transformed American life in innumerable ways. By lowering the cost of transporting farm produce, the railroad brought new areas of the country into the orbit of long-distance trade. Canals had exerted a similar impact a generation earlier (see Chapter 10), but the railroad reached places that lay far from navigable waterways. Train transportation was also better protected than water travel against adverse weather conditions and afforded farmers more consistent access to urban markets.

How Much Is That?
Railroad Investment

The capital invested in railroad construction during the 1850s reached the equivalent of 27.3 billion dollars in 2020 dollars. This represented an unprecedented venture in transportation financing but would not stand out today, in an age of more complex infrastructural improvements. Boston's Big Dig project, which moved a major highway underground, was completed in 2007 at a cost of 24.3 billion dollars.

As rail lines spread, American farmers settled vast swaths of grassland west of the Great Lakes, planted wheat and corn, and created the prairie landscape that now characterizes much of the central and north-central region of the United States. Railroad companies actively encouraged this process, using posters, pamphlets, and handbills to attract settlers to the prairies adjacent to their lines.

By radically reducing the duration of journeys between parts of the country, especially in the North, railroads also changed popular travel habits, enabling new forms of vacationing and sightseeing and increasing the ease with which middle-class and elite Americans maintained

CLIMATES AND ECOLOGIES

The Bucolic American Locomotive, 1855. George Inness was commissioned by the Delaware, Lackawanna and Western Railroad to produce a work of art that could be used in the company's advertisements. Pictorial representations of the railroad typically showed rural scenes rather than urban settings and tended to integrate trains and tracks into a bucolic natural landscape. Because land was cheaper and labor more expensive in the United States than in Europe, American railroad lines often followed curved paths around natural obstacles, and this feature further linked the American railroad to rural rather than urban aesthetics. *PAINTING/Alamy Stock Photo*

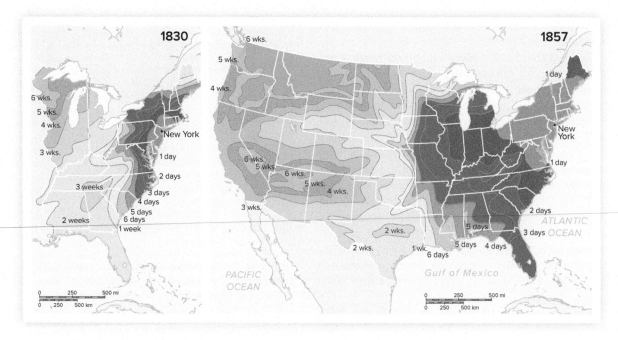

Map 14.2 Travel Times from New York City, 1830 and 1857. Before the railroad network was in place, a trip from Indiana or Illinois to New York City took two to three weeks, but by the early 1850s, it could be accomplished in less than two days.

relationships with distant friends and family. In the thirty years after the first railroad tracks were laid, trips that took weeks were reduced to a matter of a couple of days. By 1857, virtually the entire Northeast lay within a day's travel radius of New York City (see Map 14.2).

In contrast to Europe, where the railroad met significant opposition and resistance, Americans by and large celebrated the arrival of tracks and trains. In Europe, rail lines were superimposed on existing roads and highways and were often experienced as disruptions in the rhythm of prior ways of living, working, and moving. In the United States, by contrast, much of the rail network staked out new roads altogether and thus symbolized growth and expansion into new terrain. Urbanites and municipalities, worrying about steam explosions, restricted the use of railroad cars on city streets. At least in the period before the Civil War, however, most Americans tended to regard the new machines with considerable optimism. Whereas in Europe mechanical innovations were commonly associated with the breakdown of craft traditions and displacement of workers, mechanization in the United States appeared first and most conspicuously in the domains of transportation and agriculture rather than in industrial production. American journalists, critics, artists, and politicians commonly described new technologies as sublime works of art, and perhaps no

new technology impressed them more than the steam locomotive. An 1851 issue of the magazine *Scientific American* called the "sublime and terrific" spectacle of a large train, hurtling along at the profoundly unfamiliar speed of 30 miles an hour, "one of the grandest sights in the world."

By the 1850s, these large trains were speeding through every state in the union except for Arkansas (see Map 14.3), but the network was far denser in some regions than others. Eastern states such as Maryland, Pennsylvania, and New York had been centers of early railroad development, but by midcentury the focus of new construction had moved westward, with Ohio, Indiana, and Illinois leading the way. The other significant trend was that rail traffic tended to flow in an east-west direction rather than north-south. Rail cars transported commodities, tourists, and migrants along east-west routes and forged tighter credit relationships between communities along the Atlantic seaboard and those at similar latitudes in the Great Lakes, or along the Ohio, Mississippi, and Missouri Rivers. By the 1850s, one of the chief effects of the national rail network was to integrate the North with the West.

Nowhere was this integration clearer than in **Chicago,** which had been a tiny, fur-trading village in 1830 but by 1860 had become an industrial and commercial

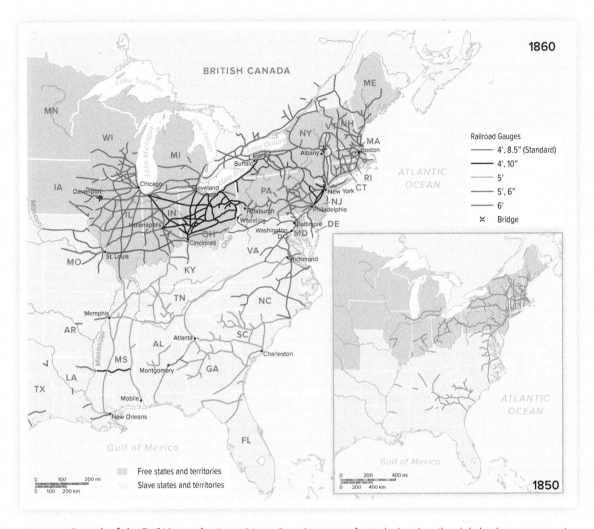

Map 14.3 Growth of the Rail Network, 1850–1860. Over the course of a single decade, railroads helped remap economic and social relations in the United States. The lack of track gauge alignment between rail lines on either side of Chicago assured that the city would remain a transfer point, not simply a stop, for freight moving across the country.

metropolis with a population of one hundred twelve thousand. The railroad was crucial to the spectacular emergence of Chicago. In 1848, construction began on the Galena and Chicago Union Railroad line, which quickly made Chicago the major destination for wheat grown north and west of the city (see Hot Commodities: Grain). Soon, eleven other rail lines would follow, linking Chicago to farms, towns, and cities in all four directions. Midwestern wheat farmers dispatched their goods and directed their energy toward Chicago, and through Chicago they were connected to regions and markets farther east.

Significantly, no railroad line ran *through* Chicago. Because it was either the eastern terminus or the western terminus of those eleven lines, Chicago provided the bridge between the two halves of the nation's rail network. And because it was also the major port on Lake Michigan, Chicago offered a transfer point between rail travel and water travel. These considerations put Chicago at the center of the nation's commercial map.

RAILROADS AND TIME

As railroad service proliferated, Americans acquired new reasons to care about exactly what time it was. The faster speed of train travel encouraged passengers to think in smaller increments of time, and the precise departure and

HOT COMMODITIES

Grain

The railroad empire centered in Chicago was built on grain. Farmers settling along the rail routes cultivated unprecedented volumes of corn and wheat with the hopes of sending it eastward via Chicago. By 1856, with skyrocketing European demand for wheat as a result of the Crimean War, 21 million bushels of grain passed through the city in a single year. Chicago was more than just a convenient stopover for agricultural products en route to distant markets. The city's grain business helped turn prairie crops into abstract commodities.

Along with the railroad itself, the invention that allowed Chicagoans to organize—and dominate—the grain trade was the steam-powered grain elevator, which was first used in Buffalo in 1842 and introduced in Chicago in 1848. The new elevators were enormous warehouses that used machines to load, weigh, and unload the vast quantities of grain stored there. Usually owned by railroad companies, grain elevators employed chutes to empty the contents of rail cars directly into their storage facilities. This radically reduced the costs of transferring the grain and gave Chicago a big competitive advantage over cities like St. Louis, which relied mostly on water transportation. Within a few years, Chicago's ten massive grain elevators were housing 4 million bushels of wheat at a time.

Grain elevators also mixed the grain from different farmers into one, undifferentiated mass that could be sold by weight. As long as buyers and sellers agreed that the grain in a particular elevator was of similar quality, one bushel was interchangeable for another and it was unnecessary to track the grain belonging to particular farmers. To facilitate this, a new, private organization called the Chicago Board of Trade (founded in 1848) established standards for distinguishing quality and established standards for each grade. Grain sellers received a receipt from an elevator for depositing a certain amount of grain of a particular grade, and they could then redeem their receipt for an equal quantity of similar-grade grain at any other elevator. Under this system, grain became a kind of money, and grain receipts a form of paper currency that could be exchanged by people who had no interest in actually owning grain, much as bank notes could circulate among people who had no intention of redeeming them for silver or gold. Elevator receipts also made it easier for speculators to bet on the price of grain. Buying a grain receipt was essentially an investment in grain, which the buyer could resell for profit or loss at a later date. And with the arrival in Chicago of the telegraph (in the same year as the elevator and the Board of Trade), Chicago grain receipts could be traded in places like New York. In the space of a decade, the same railroad network that caused wheat and corn to sprout all over the Midwestern prairie and turned Chicago into a city flowing with grain also created a second market in grain, far removed from farmers and crops.

Think About It

1. How did storing grain in elevators rather than in farmers' sacks change the way merchants thought about individual shipments of grain?

2. How might the efficiency of this grain elevator system have contributed to the perception on the East Coast that Chicago was the commercial center of the West?

---

arrival times that railroad companies advertised fostered new expectations of punctuality. Railroad whistles, like factory bells, were part of a growing cluster of cues that helped people in the mid-nineteenth century track time. "I watch the passage of the morning cars," noted Henry David Thoreau in his famous book *Walden* (1854), "with the same feeling that I do the rising of the sun, which is hardly more regular." More and more Americans could also consult clocks in their homes and watches in their pockets. The North dominated timepiece production, but clocks and watches had become common amenities throughout the country by the 1850s. Americans in all regions paid more attention to these devices and grew more likely to think of time as something that needed to be tracked mechanically rather than simply by astronomical observation or by attending to the natural rhythms of the day.

In the age of telegraphs and railroads, however, it quickly became a problem that clocks and watches in one place were out of sync with those in another town or state. If a passenger set his watch to noon in St. Louis, it would be ten minutes behind the clocks in Chicago by the time his train arrived. And if that passenger was also the train's engineer, the difference could make it hard to maintain schedules and avoid traffic jams or train collisions. Telegraphs exposed these time disparities as well. A merchant house in Philadelphia and a bank in New York might both close at 5 P.M., but if they tried to do business together over the wires, they might discover to their frustration that they actually closed at different times.

Telegraphs also offered a possible solution, however. Using telegraphy, railroad companies in New England began coordinating their schedules in 1849, agreeing to

James Palmatary's 1857 View of Chicago. Barely two decades after its incorporation, Chicago was a sprawling metropolis best depicted from an imaginary bird's-eye perspective. *Chicago History Museum/Getty Images*

use a time two minutes after the true astronomical time of Boston. British railroads had done something similar two years earlier, and it quickly set standard British time. Railroads had the effect of standardizing timekeeping in the United States as well, though it was not until 1883 that the railroads mapped out time zones for the nation and not until 1918 that the United States recognized that map and turned railroad time into official time. In the shorter term, however, railroad time coordinated the activities of those Americans along the Northern corridor who were integrated more intensively into the rail network.

INDUSTRY AND WAGES

The rail network also shaped the slavery conflict by accelerating the process of industrialization in the North. Track building spurred iron processing, fuel consumption led to coal mining, and the growth of commerce stimulated manufacturing. Faster travel opportunities and new travel routes encouraged laborers, including massive numbers of new immigrants, to move to U.S. cities for work opportunities. Outside the South, the railroads reinforced the steady rise in the proportion of Americans who worked for wages. In 1800, only about 10 percent of the U.S. workforce was employed on a wage basis; by

1860, the figure had become 40 percent. By 1850, for the first time, the number of wage earners in the United States exceeded the number of enslaved workers. Wage earners belonged to a new working class comprising men and women who were not bound to their employers but had no independent means of support. On average, they were paid less than most experts at the time thought was necessary to support oneself, and their wages declined, relative to inflation, over the course of the 1850s. Wage workers did not own their tools, could not set the value of their labor, had little in common with the people who employed them, and depended on their employers in unsettling ways.

Wage labor itself, rather than factory conditions, long hours, or mechanization, was the most controversial feature of the new world of industrial work. Wage laborers had long been stigmatized as dependent and vulnerable, and at midcentury they were becoming the norm in most states where slavery was illegal. Both proslavery ideologues in the South and labor leaders in the North spoke of **wage slavery** and compared the plight of immigrant workers in Northern cities to that of enslaved people on plantations (see Interpreting the Sources: George Fitzhugh on Industrial Labor). Arguments about wage slavery often created alliances between radicals who

327

INTERPRETING THE SOURCES

George Fitzhugh on Industrial Labor

When defenders of Southern slavery cited the impoverished conditions of laborers in the North or in England, their point was usually to liken "wage slaves" to "chattel slaves." Abolitionists were hypocrites, they charged, for condemning slaveholders while condoning the mistreatment of workers in their own backyards. Every society had a lower class that performed menial tasks, ran the proslavery refrain, so it was unfair and unwise to single out plantation slavery for censure. But as the political conflict over slavery intensified, Southerners began to insist that their own form of labor discipline was morally and politically *superior* to the industrial labor system emerging in the North.

For many critics of "wage slavery" or "white slavery," the Southern system was better because it confined slavery to a stigmatized race of people who did not deserve the benefits of freedom. But Virginian George Fitzhugh, perhaps the most radical proslavery ideologue of the 1850s, pursued the defense of slavery to its logical conclusion: Since slavery was really a benign system, then white workers would also be better off under its regime. In the process of defending the social and economic order of the South, Fitzhugh offered a critique of competitive capitalist society.

From *Sociology for the South, or the Failure of Free Society* (1854)

More than half of the white citizens of the North are common laborers, either in the field, or as body or house servants. They perform the same services that our slaves do. They serve their employers for hire; they have quite as little option whether they shall so serve, or not, as our slaves.... The socialists say wages is slavery. It is a gross libel on slavery. Wages are given in time of vigorous health and strength, and denied when most needed, when sickness or old age has overtaken us. The slave is never without a master to maintain him. The free laborer, though willing to work, cannot always find an employer. He is then without a home and without wages!

From *Cannibals All! or, Slaves Without Masters* (1857)

It is impossible to place labor and capital in harmonious or friendly relations, except by the means of slavery, which identifies their interests. Would [a northerner] lay his capital out in land and negroes, he might be sure, in whatever hands it came, that it would be employed to protect laborers, not to oppress them; for when slaves are worth near a thousand dollars a head, they will be carefully and well provided for. In any other investment he may make of it, it will be used as an engine to squeeze the largest amount of labor from the poor....

Free laborers pay one another, for labor creates all values, and capital, after taking the lion's share by its taxing power, but pays the so-called wages of one laborer from the proceeds of the labor of another.

Do not the past history and present condition of Free Society in Western Europe (where alone the experiment has been fully tried,) prove that it is attended with greater evils, moral and physical, than Slave Society? ...

But our Southern slavery has become a benign and protective institution, and our negroes are confessedly better off than any free laboring population in the world. How can we contend that white slavery is wrong, whilst all the great body of free laborers are starving; and slaves, white or black, throughout the world, are enjoying comfort?

Explore the Source

1. In what respects, according to Fitzhugh, do enslaved workers and wage workers share the same status?

2. By what standard does Fitzhugh consider enslaved workers to be better off than wage workers?

3. How might a critic of slavery respond to Fitzhugh's argument?

---

sought to improve the lot of white workers and wealthy slaveholders who sought to protect their property. Mike Walsh, an Irish-born labor radical in New York who was elected to Congress in 1852, was both a vociferous critic of capitalism and a staunch defender of slavery and the South.

In the South, the national rail network also had a significant impact on economic and social life but did not alter the labor system. International demand for cotton kept prices high during the 1850s, and the Southern economy boomed. Slavery was compatible with railroads, mechanization, and even mass production. Enslaved people worked in mills and mines as well as cotton fields. Thousands of enslaved workers in Virginia labored in factories in the 1850s, producing flavored plugs of chewing tobacco. But the economic success of slavery inhibited the spread of wage labor. As wage labor spread in the North, the difference between the North and South became increasingly framed in those terms. By the 1850s, Northern critics of slavery began using the model of wage labor to define what was wrong with slavery: Enslaved workers were not paid cash wages, did not sign contracts, and did not move freely from job to job in search of higher pay.

POLITICAL REALIGNMENT

From its inception, the Second Party System of competition between Democrats and Whigs had been designed to build national coalitions and forestall political conflicts between the North and South. The election of 1848 had exposed strains in that system, and the sectional truce that had been declared in the Compromise of 1850 was fragile from the start. By not extending the Missouri Compromise, Congress had signaled that the status of slavery in the Western territories would have to be settled by some new principle. Significantly, it was the spread of the rail network that brought conflicts to the fore. Territories on the western side of the Mississippi became major battlegrounds in an increasingly polarized and suddenly violent struggle over slavery. In the face of this challenge, Democrats and Whigs lost their grips on their coalitions and the nation inched closer to disunion.

KANSAS AND NEBRASKA

In the 1852 presidential election, the Democrats and their standard-bearer, Franklin Pierce, stood by the Compromise of 1850 and won a decisive victory with landslide margins in the Deep South. But the Compromise of 1850 had been vague on the crucial question of the day, which was whether and under what terms slavery would be introduced into the western half of the continent. Significantly, the admission of California, which straddled the 36°30′ line, implied that the geographical divide laid out in the Missouri Compromise would not extend to the lands taken from Mexico. California was a free state, because the gold rush had drawn settlers who supported a free-state constitution, not because of the Missouri line. Because the Missouri Compromise held little sway in the Mexican cession, Southerners may have imagined that it would ultimately become obsolete in the Louisiana Purchase as well, but this was far less clear.

The vast stretch of Louisiana Purchase land that had not yet been organized into territories was still sparsely settled in the early 1850s. Congress would have had no incentive to prepare these lands for statehood had it not been for the spread of the rail network. Prospects of a rail

line spanning the continent drew considerable interest after 1848. The Pierce administration pushed for the Gadsden Purchase (1853–1854), which added a small slice of the southern parts of present-day New Mexico and Arizona, to enable the construction of a line between New Orleans and San Diego and connect the South to the nation's Western territories. Politicians and investors in the Midwest envisioned a more northerly route. St. Louisans touted the advantages of their city as the gateway to the Pacific, and the state of Missouri invested massively in railroad construction throughout the decade in the hopes of boosting that prospect. But Chicago had already emerged as the leading western terminus of rail traffic from New York and the hub of an expanding regional rail network between the Ohio and Mississippi Rivers. Illinois politicians were in a strong position to nominate their leading city as a terminus for the western half of a transcontinental rail line. To facilitate this development, Stephen Douglas crafted a bill covering the entire unorganized portion of the Louisiana Purchase (from the western borders of Missouri, Iowa, and Minnesota to the Rocky Mountains), which he called the Nebraska Territory.

Seeking Southern support for his railroad vision and eager to promote popular sovereignty as a model for dealing with slavery in the West, Douglas included language in his Nebraska bill stipulating that "all questions pertaining to slavery in the Territories, and in the new states to be formed therefrom are to be left to the people residing therein." Worried that the bill would still add free states to the union, the South pressed Douglas for two key amendments. First, the law would repeal the provision of the Missouri Compromise that banned slavery north of 36°30′, so that slaveholders could move into the proposed Nebraska Territory. Second, the area under consideration would be split into two territories, Nebraska and Kansas, the latter adjacent to the slave state of Missouri and potentially attractive to slaveholders. With the strong backing of President Pierce, near-unanimous support from the South, and enough votes from Northern Democrats, the **Kansas-Nebraska Act** became law.

Outraged Northern politicians denounced the act as a violation of the sacred compact of the Missouri Compromise. Texan Sam Houston, one of the lone dissenters from the South, pointed out that Congress was also reneging on the promises made during Indian removal to reserve land west of the Mississippi for the permanent occupation of native groups exiled from their lands in the 1830s. As Houston observed ruefully, Kansas-Nebraska marked the official abandonment of the idea of a serious boundary between the United States and Indian country.

But few Americans focused on the implications of Kansas-Nebraska for the Shawnee, Delaware, or Chickasaw. The real outrage of Douglas's bill lay in its implications for the slavery controversy. On the same day that Anthony Burns was arraigned in Boston, Massachusetts senator Charles Sumner introduced a 200-foot-long petition signed by over three thousand ministers and written by celebrity author Harriet Beecher Stowe, calling the new law "a great moral wrong . . . a breach of faith . . . exposing [the nation] to the righteous judgments of the Almighty. . . ." As Sumner saw it, the one positive consequence of the bill was that by scrapping the Missouri Compromise (which abolitionists like Sumner saw as having been immoral in the first place), it made all future deals impossible: "Thus it puts Freedom and Slavery face to face, and bids them grapple. Who can doubt the result?"

The more immediate result, however, was a fatal blow to the Second Party System. The Whig Party had maintained ranks in 1850, but when Northern Whigs refused to support the Kansas-Nebraska Act, their Southern colleagues deserted the party. Enough Democrats had stood by Douglas's bill to make it law, but the 1854 congressional elections showed that Douglas and Pierce had miscalculated. Kansas-Nebraska alienated so many Northerners that the Democrats lost more than two-thirds of their House seats in the North.

THE KNOW-NOTHINGS

In the immediate wake of the collapse of the Whigs, the American Party, also known as the **Know-Nothing Party,** seized an opportunity. The Know-Nothings originated in a cluster of nativist secret societies, which coalesced in 1850 as the Order of the Star-Spangled Banner. Members of the order were committed to protecting the United States from what they saw as the menace of Catholic immigration (see Chapter 12). Tensions between native-born Protestants and Catholic immigrants, both Irish and German, ran high in the 1850s, often flaring into violence.

THE DEAD SERGEANT IN TWENTY-SECOND STREET.

Anti-Irish Caricatures in the Mainstream Press. This illustration from a book about the New York Draft Riots (see Chapter 15) draws on descriptions of Irishmen as having black skin and "brutish" or "simian" features. Here they are also depicted as inhumane, abusing the body of a militiaman killed in the rioting. *Bettmann Archive/Getty Images*

Hostility to Irish Catholic immigrants, in particular, reflected a number of forces and prejudices. Anglo Americans had inherited a long tradition of regarding Irish people as savage and inferior, and such views acquired more authority and prestige from new theories about racial difference. • For other nativists, the problem with Irish immigrants was more religious than racial. In the antebellum era, the Catholic Church became the focus of intense suspicion and hostility among temperance advocates, abolitionists, evangelical preachers, and other middle-class reformers (see Chapter 12), and nativists found common cause with those reformers who objected to Catholicism even if they welcomed immigration. • Finally, nativists could point to the growing political power of Irish and German Democratic voters in large U.S. cities, where immigrants and their children made up more than half the population.

In 1851, the Order of the Star-Spangled Banner created the American Party and shrouded its workings with secret rituals. "I know nothing" was a standard early response to queries about the party's membership and goals, which gave birth to the popular nickname. But by 1854, the Know-Nothing Party was operating in full view of the electorate and poised to capitalize on the Kansas-Nebraska crisis. In July 1854, American Party delegates from thirteen states promulgated a platform calling for restrictions on naturalization (the process of becoming a U.S. citizen) and the exclusion of Catholics from holding public office. Despite their focus on what seemed like a narrow political agenda, the Know-Nothings had significant appeal to party-less Whigs and disaffected Northern Democrats. Forty Know-Nothing candidates were elected to Congress, along with many more state legislators. The party swept through much of New England, replaced the Whigs as the major opposition party in most border states, and attracted significant chunks of the electorate in New York, Pennsylvania, and California. Know-Nothings even drew support in the South, where voters anxious to preserve the union looked to the American Party for a way out of sectional conflict.

In the Northeast, where anti-Catholicism and antislavery often converged, the Know-Nothings ran against the Kansas-Nebraska Act and became the party of middle-class reform. Know-Nothings captured the Massachusetts legislature and governorship in 1854, for example, and proceeded to implement antislavery and reformist goals. They enacted personal liberty laws designed to thwart the Fugitive Slave Act, abolished imprisonment for debt, passed child labor legislation, instituted a married women's property act, came close to abolishing the death penalty, and in April 1855 officially desegregated the Boston schools. In a mix of reform agendas that might seem stranger now than it did in 1854, the Massachusetts Know-Nothings also deported Irish paupers (establishing models for later immigration restrictions at the federal level) and sought to require immigrants to have twenty-one years of residency prior to voting. Outside of the Northeast, however, Know-Nothings did not run as an antislavery party. And in many parts of the country, the perceived threat of immigrants and Catholics was not powerful enough to organize an enduring political party. Within a couple of years, the Know-Nothings receded as a force in national politics.

BLEEDING KANSAS, BLEEDING SUMNER

By 1855, all eyes turned to Kansas, which had been designed by Congress as a territory where slavery might take legal root through popular sovereignty. Nothing in the congressional legislation specified exactly how the people of the territory would express their will. Who was eligible to vote in the elections establishing a new government in Kansas, and when would such elections take place? Partisans in the slavery conflict mobilized for a showdown with few clear rules.

● With railroad lines connecting the Atlantic seaboard to Illinois and Missouri, traveling to the Western territories from the Northeast was an easier proposition. A year earlier, twelve hundred settlers had been dispatched to Kansas by the Emigrant Aid Society, an antislavery organization based in Massachusetts. Thousands more settlers moved to Kansas under their own auspices from the Midwest, and most of them were committed to the goal of keeping slavery (and all African Americans) out of Kansas. These migrants were preceded, however, by western Missourians who crossed the border to vote for proslavery members of the new territorial legislature. David Atchison, a former Missouri senator, led the charge westward, urging his neighbors to "kill every God-damned abolitionist in the Territory" and protect the region against the Free Soil onslaught. ●

Although fewer than three thousand white settlers lived in Kansas at the time of the March election, more than sixty-three hundred votes were cast and the proslavery forces prevailed. Free-state voters immediately charged fraud on the part of Atchison's "border ruffians," declared the new legislature "bogus," and established a rival government. Kansas now had two territorial legislatures, enacting different laws and proposing competing state constitutions. The proslavery legislature, headquartered in the town of Lecompton, quickly passed laws making it a crime to speak against slavery and a capital offense to aid a runaway. Its rival, centered in the town of Lawrence, banned both slavery and free Blacks from the territory. Over the objections of the territorial governor, President Pierce recognized the Lecompton government, as did the U.S. Senate, whereas the House recognized the one in Lawrence.

Disputed elections often turned violent in antebellum America, but the scale and stakes of the Kansas conflict broke new ground. Armed proslavery Missourians, who had crossed the border before the election in order to vote, now did so to enforce the election's results. They were joined by other Southern settlers and supported by agents of the federal government. Free Soil settlers, for their part, requested help from supporters in Ohio, New York, and New England. Antislavery

Armed Free-State Supporters in Kansas, 1856. Antagonists in the slavery debate flocked to Kansas for what would appear in retrospect to have been a violent dress rehearsal for a far bloodier war. *Hulton Archive/Getty Images*

organizations sent Sharpe's rifles to Kansas, sometimes in crates marked "Bibles." The stage was set for a civil war.

After a series of smaller skirmishes, Lecompton men raided Lawrence in May 1856 and destroyed newspaper offices and the governor's house. In retaliation, an abolitionist named John Brown led an attack against proslavery settlers at Pottawatomie Creek, killing five people and mutilating their corpses. In the guerrilla war that ensued over the next few months, close to two hundred people were killed and 2 million dollars' worth of property was destroyed.

The fighting in what newspapers began calling **Bleeding Kansas** failed to resolve the legal status of slavery. Its principal effect on the larger debate was to replace abstract fears about geographical boundaries and popular sovereignty with concrete and frightening images of real enemies. Northern newspapers described boorish Missourians wielding bowie knives while the

South read about self-righteous zealots brandishing rifles.

During the height of the Kansas violence, Senator Charles Sumner of Massachusetts issued a venomous two-day attack from the Senate floor on "the crime against Kansas." In Sumner's words, the Missourians who had gone into Kansas to fight for slavery were "hirelings picked from the drunken spew and vomit of an uneasy civilization." Invoking familiar antislavery rhetoric about slaveholder lust, Sumner decried the South's "depraved longing for a new slave State." He singled out one Southern senator, Andrew P. Butler of South Carolina, as a liar whose fondness for slavery resembled a man chasing after a harlot.

From the perspective of Southern notions of honor, this was not simply political rhetoric; Sumner's words belonged to the class of insulting speech acts that could only be avenged by personal acts of violence. Sumner's goal had not been to antagonize anyone in the Senate chamber, much less to sway any of his colleagues' views on slavery. ● The real intended audience for this speech, which he had composed carefully, was the antislavery public who would read it in print. But three days after the speech, Butler's cousin, a young South Carolina congressman named Preston Brooks, approached Sumner as he sat at his Senate desk, preparing copies of the inflammatory text for mailing. After announcing that he had carefully read the contents of the speech, Brooks began beating Sumner over the head with a cane. The Massachusetts senator was trapped behind his bolted desk as Brooks continued to pummel him. By the time Sumner managed to pull the desk out from its moorings, his head had split open. Several senators tried to intercede, but two Southerners prevented anyone from getting to Brooks before Sumner had been beaten unconscious.

The shocking incident played out differently on the two sides of the sectional divide. Southerners saw Brooks as a hero, whereas Northerners turned Sumner into a martyr. A Northern majority in Congress censured Brooks, whereas a united South prevented his expulsion. Both men were enthusiastically re-elected by their constituents, though in Sumner's case this meant leaving his seat unoccupied for three years while he recovered from his head injury. Brooks's admirers sent him souvenir canes in the mail. ●

A new political party in the North, founded in 1854 during the Kansas-Nebraska controversy, seized upon the two events of May 1856 to launch their first presidential campaign. Calling themselves **Republicans,** the latest entrants to national politics invoked the specter of Bleeding Kansas and "Bleeding Sumner" to mount a sectional campaign that renounced all hopes of winning votes in the Deep South. To lead their ticket, the Republicans nominated John C. Frémont, who had helped wrest California from Mexican control. The Democrats replaced Pierce with James Buchanan, and the Know-Nothings nominated the former Whig president, Millard Fillmore. Buchanan won the election, but Frémont's showing was quite remarkable. As a first-time contender, the Republicans took a third of the popular vote without appealing to Southern voters. The results confirmed that Republicans had absorbed the remnants of the Liberty Party and supplanted the Know-Nothings among antislavery voters in the North. More ominously for the Democrats, Buchanan drew only 45 percent of the vote and lost most of the free states. Had the Democrats' northern opponents rallied behind one candidate,

MEDIA AND INFORMATION

Dred and Harriet Scott.   Shortly after the 1857 Supreme Court decision, the sons of Dred Scott's original owner purchased him and his family and manumitted them. Less than a year later, Dred died of tuberculosis. Harriet lived for another eighteen years. One of their daughters lived to be ninety-nine and died in the 1950s. *Library of Congress, Prints & Photographs Division (LC-USZ62-79305)*

a president could have been elected without a single electoral vote from the South.

DRED SCOTT AND THE END OF COMPROMISE

In his inaugural address, President Buchanan expressed the view that the status of slavery in the territories was really a judicial question that would be "speedily and finally settled" by the U.S. Supreme Court. What Buchanan had in mind was a legal battle over the fate of two Missourians, Dred and Harriet Scott. The case had been moving through the court system for eleven years and would finally be decided two days after Buchanan's 1857 inauguration.

Dred Scott was born into slavery around 1800 in Virginia and was taken westward by his owner, first to Alabama and then to St. Louis. After his owner's death, Scott was sold to an army surgeon named John Emerson, who took Scott with him to Illinois and then to the Wisconsin Territory, where Scott met and married an enslaved woman named Harriet Robinson. After brief trips elsewhere, Emerson decided to leave Dred and Harriet Scott in St. Louis, renting out their labor to others. Upon Emerson's death in 1843, his widow, Irene Emerson, inherited the estate and continued to rent out the Scotts. Dred Scott's many moves were not unusual among enslaved African Americans, and his circumstance as hired-out was common in a city like St. Louis (see Singular Lives: Elizabeth Keckley, Free Seamstress). But in 1846, Dred Scott took the uncommon step of suing for his freedom and that of Harriet and their two daughters, claiming that having lived in a free state and a free territory a decade earlier meant that he and Harriet were no longer enslaved.

Scott lost his first case on technical grounds in 1847, but three years later a St. Louis jury ruled in his favor. Irene Emerson's lawyers appealed, however, and the Missouri Supreme Court reversed the decision in 1852. Scott then initiated a new suit in federal court, this time targeting Irene Emerson's brother, John Sanford, who had been acting on his sister's behalf. (A Supreme Court official later misspelled Sanford's name on court documents, and the case would forever be known as **Dred Scott v. Sandford.**) The federal court upheld the state court decision, and Scott appealed the case to the Supreme Court in 1854. All the while, he and his family remained wards of the St. Louis County sheriff, who rented them out and held the proceeds in escrow pending a final resolution of the question of whether they were enslaved (in which case Irene Emerson was owed rent) or free (in which case they were owed wages). Ten years after the Scotts's original claim for freedom, their case was heard by the Supreme Court.

Arguments in the case of *Dred Scott v. Sandford* began in 1856. In May, the court decided to call a recess until after the presidential election and scheduled new arguments for December. At issue now was not only the freedom of the Scotts but also the more momentous questions of whether free Blacks had a right to sue in federal courts and whether Congress had been authorized to prohibit slavery in the territories. On March 6, 1857, Chief Justice Roger B. Taney, a former slaveholder who years earlier had served as Andrew Jackson's secretary of the treasury during the bank war, read the opinion of the court for a full two hours. Dred Scott was not entitled to sue, Taney ruled, because Dred Scott was Black. Black people were a degraded race, "so far inferior, that they had no rights which the white man was bound to respect." The founders had not intended the descendants of enslaved persons to become citizens, and free Blacks could not attain U.S. citizenship, even if they were citizens of individual states.

This sweeping claim could have ended the matter, but the chief justice (like President Buchanan) was eager to resolve the question that was on the minds of the electorate. Even though it should have made no difference to Scott's case, Taney proceeded to rule the Missouri Compromise unconstitutional and to deny that Congress could prohibit slavery in the territories. The clause in the Constitution authorizing Congress to regulate the territories applied only to those territories possessed or contemplated in 1787, according to Taney. Furthermore, he argued, enslaved people were property, protected against government seizure by the Fifth Amendment. This last claim meant that even leaving the slavery question to popular sovereignty was unconstitutional, since Congress could not grant a territorial government any authority that it did not possess. The Court as a whole supported Taney's decision by a seven-to-two vote, though the six concurring justices each wrote individual opinions, and they did not all affirm the entirety of Taney's rationale. But Taney was the chief justice, and his opinion appeared to be the law of the land.

FEAR AND CRISIS

Buchanan's confidence that the *Scott* decision had settled the slavery controversy once and for all was deeply misplaced. Instead, Taney's opinion became the centerpiece of sectional conflict. Republicans renewed charges of a Slave Power conspiracy that now also controlled the Supreme Court. Northern Democrats found themselves on the defensive and rifts within the party widened. As a presidential election loomed, an eruption of abolitionist violence in Virginia augured unimaginable bloodshed.

THE LINCOLN-DOUGLAS DEBATES

Senator Stephen Douglas's political career was instantly jeopardized by the *Dred Scott* decision. Having staked his fortunes on the ideal of popular sovereignty as a solution to the slavery problem, he now faced a Supreme Court decision that appeared to undermine it by completely deregulating slavery. A practical test of the status of

SINGULAR LIVES

Elizabeth Keckley, Free Seamstress

In October 1860, one month before the election that would bring Lincoln to office and spark Southern secession, the nation's capital turned its attention to a visit from the Prince of Wales, the nineteen-year-old who would later become King Edward VII of England. In preparation for a formal dinner honoring the prince, Elizabeth Keckley went shopping for elegant dress materials. A seamstress and fashion consultant for elite Washington clients, Keckley was selecting lace trimming for Mary Anne Randolph Custis Lee, the great-granddaughter of Martha Washington and the wife of Colonel Robert E. Lee, who had just led the force that quashed John Brown's rebellion.

Keckley had recently moved from St. Louis but would soon become a well-known figure in Washington, D.C., society. The following March, she met Mary Todd Lincoln at the new president's inauguration and was hired as the first lady's personal "modiste" (a fashionable dressmaker) and confidante. During the Lincoln presidency, Keckley designed Lincoln's event wardrobe and became one of her closest friends.

What makes the story of Elizabeth Keckley striking is the fact that just five years before Lincoln's election, she was enslaved. Born into bondage in 1818 near Peterson, Virginia, Keckley endured an especially brutal youth that featured savage beatings and repeated sexual assault. In 1847, her enslaver moved her to St. Louis, where he rented out her labor to local white families. Keckley developed her talents as a seamstress and cultivated a clientele and a network of supporters whom she would ultimately draw upon in her bid for freedom. Living in St. Louis also put Keckley in contact with the city's sizable free Black community, which by 1850 was more numerous than the enslaved population.

Keckley's life in St. Louis overlapped with that of the city's two most famous Black residents of the antebellum period, Dred and Harriet Scott. Keckley's main connection to the Scott case was through her owner, Hugh Garland, the lawyer who successfully represented Scott's owners in the Missouri courts. Garland was a steadfast supporter of the rights of slaveholders, and he was not eager to grant Keckley her freedom when she asked him to manumit her in 1850. But Garland needed cash, and after much resistance, he agreed to free Keckley in return for twelve hundred dollars. Over the next three years, Keckley worked in St. Louis to raise money for her own emancipation. In 1860, she moved to Baltimore and then to Washington, D.C., where she became active in Black philanthropic causes and a minor celebrity in the capital's social circles.

Where in the Archives?

Elizabeth Keckley's autobiography, *Behind the Scenes. Or, Thirty Years a Slave, and Four Years in the White House* (New York: G. W. Carleton & Co., 1868), is available at archives hosted by the University of North Carolina at Chapel Hill: Documenting the American South (https://docsouth.unc.edu/index.html).

A very different kind of evidence survives in the form of a quilt, probably produced by Keckley from Mary Todd Lincoln's

Elizabeth Keckley. Born into slavery in Virginia, Keckley found freedom in St. Louis and later became a successful businesswoman in the nation's capital. *Picture History/Newscom*

dresses. The White House Historical Association houses the textile (https://www.whitehousehistory.org/elizabeth-keckley), and a video from Kansas State University shows the image in detail and describes the quilt, materials, and pattern work (https://www.youtube.com/watch?v=yvaADt6HwxI).

Assignment

Read pages 43–55 and 76–90 of Keckley's narrative and examine Keckley's quilt. Identify three images in the quilt that you think might express or reflect some quality, experience, or attitude of Keckley's and explain the connection in three sentences each.

Lincoln-Douglas Debates, 1858. On the campaign trail, Lincoln tried to defend himself against charges of being an abolitionist and an amalgamationist: "Now I protest against that counterfeit logic which concludes that, because I do not want a black woman for a slave I must necessarily want her for a wife." *Bettmann/Getty Images*

Lincoln, who had emerged as the leader of the new Republican Party in the state. Raised in a yeoman farming family that had moved west from Kentucky to Indiana, and then to Illinois in search of cheaper land, Lincoln had become a store clerk and then a lawyer, embracing a middle-class culture marked by temperance, self-control, and self-education. On the subject of slavery, Lincoln had been a supporter of the Wilmot Proviso and marched in step with moderate antislavery opinion in Illinois. He bitterly opposed opening new territories to slavery, favored gradual emancipation where slavery existed, and spoke of a time when free Blacks might be colonized to West Africa, where they might enjoy their rights unfettered by racial prejudice.

Ordinarily, Douglas would have been a heavy favorite in this race. But widespread disenchantment with the Democrats in the wake of a major economic depression in 1857 made every Democratic senator vulnerable. Lincoln shrewdly challenged the incumbent to a series of debates, where he pushed Douglas to square his doctrine of popular sovereignty with Taney's decision in *Dred Scott.* Lincoln hoped to link Douglas to Taney and persuade Illinois voters that their free soil was not safe on his watch. Taking a text from the Gospels, "A house divided against itself cannot stand," Lincoln argued that the extension of slavery westward would ultimately bring slavery to free states as well: "I believe this government cannot endure, permanently, half slave and half free. I do not expect the Union to be dissolved—I do not expect the house to fall—but I do expect it will cease to be divided. It will become all one thing or all the other."

popular sovereignty came in 1858, when Buchanan sought statehood for Kansas under the proslavery **Lecompton Constitution,** which had not been submitted to popular ratification. The president, invoking *Dred Scott,* believed that slavery was now legal in the territories "by virtue of the Constitution." But Douglas continued to champion popular sovereignty and joined Republicans in blocking the statehood bill. Douglas stuck to his principle, but in the new political landscape created by Taney's decision, this now cost him Southern support.

Having stood up to the administration on the Kansas question, Douglas returned triumphantly to Illinois to campaign for re-election. His opponent was a former Whig legislator and congressman named Abraham

Douglas rejected Lincoln's dire predictions and insisted that new states could still decide the fate of slavery. In their Freeport, Illinois, debate, Douglas argued that although the Supreme Court barred settlers from outlawing slavery in the territories, settlers could still make slavery unworkable by refusing to enact laws

The Last Moments of John Brown, by Thomas Hovenden, 1884. Hailed and mourned by abolitionists in the Northeast and upper Midwest, Brown appeared to Southerners as a harbinger of mortal danger for whites living in a biracial slave society. *Peter Horree/Alamy Stock Photo*

election that year, Douglas still won narrowly. The victory was costly, however. Roger Taney and Abraham Lincoln had made Douglas choose between his short-term and long-term political futures. The Freeport Doctrine shored up his credentials in Illinois, but it thoroughly discredited him in the South.

JOHN BROWN'S RAID

On October 16, 1859, John Brown, the religious zealot who had massacred proslavery settlers in Kansas three years earlier, crossed the Potomac River from Maryland to Virginia with nineteen men, five of them African Americans. His immediate objective was to seize a federal arsenal in Harpers Ferry, Virginia (now West Virginia), and secure arms for a slave insurrection. Ultimately, Brown sought, in his words, "to purge this land with blood." In its first goal, **John Brown's raid** was a failure. Local militiamen surrounded the arsenal, a force of U.S. Marines led by Robert E. Lee arrived, half of Brown's party was killed, Brown himself was wounded, and all the survivors were captured. Enslaved people on nearby plantations did not take the raid as a cue to revolt, and the immediate threat was thwarted. Virginia convicted Brown of treason and conspiracy and hanged him on December 2.

necessary to protect it. The **Freeport Doctrine** was probably plausible and palatable enough to persuade his Democratic constituents that Douglas was not beholden to the Slave Power. Free of that grip, Douglas counter attacked with the devastating charge that Lincoln was an abolitionist who favored racial equality, two things Lincoln vigorously denied.

Since senators were not directly elected in this period, the 1858 Lincoln-Douglas race was determined by the elections for state legislators. Republicans drew more votes and gained more legislative seats, but because the Democrats held more of the seats that were not up for

Most Northerners, including most Republican officials, repudiated Brown's raid. But several abolitionists, both white and Black, had supported Brown's plan in advance and many others celebrated his effort after it failed. Abolitionist support for Brown alarmed white Southerners. Both Lydia Maria Child and Ralph Waldo Emerson compared Brown's martyrdom to that of Jesus and predicted that hanging him would turn the gallows and scaffold into sacred symbols. William Lloyd Garrison, who had always preached nonviolence, wished "success

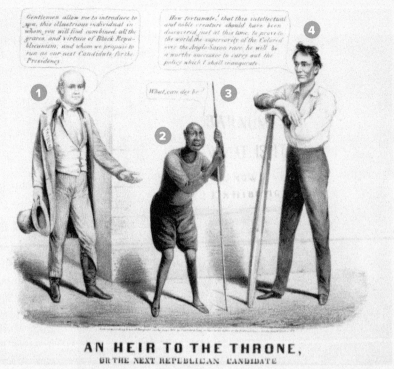

AN HEIR TO THE THRONE,
OR THE NEXT REPUBLICAN CANDIDATE

Currier and Ives Cartoon—Election of 1860. *Library of Congress, Prints & Photographs Division [LC-USZC2-2564]*

BEHIND THE IMAGE

Lithography, a technique of printing images and texts on paper from a stone or a smooth surface, was introduced in the late eighteenth century in Bavaria and quickly spread to the United States. The storied New York printmakers Currier and Ives produced thousands of mass-circulated lithographs between 1835 and 1907, including celebrity portraits, iconic scenes of middle-class holiday meals and baseball games, blackface humor, and political cartoons—all of which hung in homes, stores, firehouses, barrooms, and barns across the United States. Although this cartoon depicts Lincoln negatively, Currier and Ives produced many pro-Lincoln images; profit, not politics, was the focus of this printmaking firm.

WITHIN THE IMAGE

Published in 1860, the cartoon depicts ① Horace Greeley, antislavery editor of the New York *Tribune*, introducing an unnamed Black man of small stature as his running mate and eventual successor. ② Leaning on a walking stick, the unnamed man is meant to resemble the "What Is It?" exhibit from Barnum's Museum, advertised ③ on the wall behind, for which Barnum hired African American men, dressed them in fur suits, and asked viewers to decide "whether it is human or animal." ④ Lincoln also leans on a prop: a split fence rail. Raised on the frontier, Lincoln did split rails occasionally, and the Republican Party highlighted this aspect of his humble past in its presidential campaign. Here, however, Lincoln's fabled simplicity identifies him with an uncivilized brute. Split rails may also allude to the planks of the Republican platform, which, Democrats charged, concealed the party's abolitionism ("the policy" in Lincoln's comment in the cartoon). Praising the intellect of the What Is It?, Lincoln propounds the view that Blacks are superior to the "Anglo Saxon race."

BEYOND THE IMAGE

Readers of this cartoon could have been expected to recognize the popular "What Is It?" exhibit, which questioned the humanity of Black people. They would also have known that Lincoln's actual running mate, Hannibal Hamlin, was dark-skinned. The *Charleston Mercury*, a pro-slavery Democratic newspaper, claimed that Hamlin "had negro blood in his veins and . . . one of his children had kinky hair." Pro-Democratic cartoonists and speakers repeatedly focused on the racial politics of the election and referred to their opponents as Black Republicans.

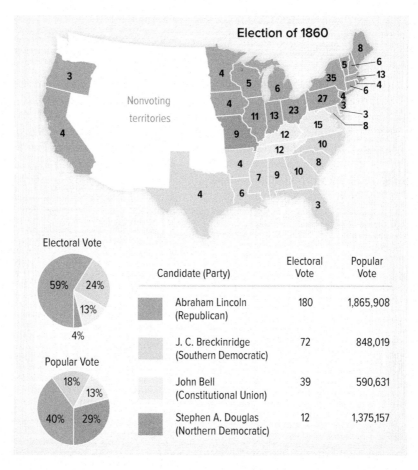

Map 14.4 Election of 1860. Douglas finished second in the popular vote but dead last in the vote that mattered.

Candidate (Party)	Electoral Vote	Popular Vote
Abraham Lincoln (Republican)	180	1,865,908
J. C. Breckinridge (Southern Democratic)	72	848,019
John Bell (Constitutional Union)	39	590,631
Stephen A. Douglas (Northern Democratic)	12	1,375,157

to every Slave insurrection at the South and in every country." On the day of the hanging, bells tolled in many New England towns.

If Nat Turner had initiated a period of proslavery defiance, John Brown brought it to a hysterical climax. One Atlanta newspaper announced that "we regard every man in our midst an enemy . . . who does not boldly declare that he believes African slavery to be a social, moral, and political blessing." Statements about slavery had become a matter of life and death.

THE ELECTION OF 1860

At the time of Brown's hanging, a presidential campaign was already under way. Predictably, the Democratic convention in Charleston, South Carolina, featured a showdown between Northern delegates who supported Douglas's program of popular sovereignty and Southerners who advocated federal laws protecting slavery in the territories. Douglas corralled the simple majority of votes to install a popular sovereignty plank in the party platform but lacked the two-thirds majority necessary to nominate him. Once the popular sovereignty plank passed, delegates from the Deep South bolted the convention. Douglas's supporters reconvened in Baltimore to nominate him, but Southern Democrats staged their own convention and nominated Buchanan's vice president, John C. Breckinridge of Kentucky, on a proslavery platform. More moderate Southerners, including former Whigs, turned to John Bell of Tennessee, who ran on the Constitutional Union ticket, which affirmed law and order over sectional concerns.

The decisive split in the old Democratic coalition left the South vulnerable to an antislavery takeover of the presidency. But to take advantage of this opportunity, the Republicans needed to sweep the North. Even more so than in 1856, the Republicans could expect no votes in the South. In most slave states, no Republican ballots would even be printed. Republicans understood that they would not be running against Breckinridge. Their real opponent was Douglas, whom they needed to defeat in nearly every free state. Rather than risk it all on a more prominent antislavery politician, like William Seward of New York or Salmon Chase of Ohio, they nominated Abraham Lincoln, whose moderate views on slavery and lack of association with nativism made him a safer choice. Lincoln was also from Illinois, a state that had become more prominent in the railroad era, whose eleven electoral votes might prove crucial to securing a Republican majority. Lincoln ran on a free-labor platform that offered Northern voters additional incentives to vote Republican that had little to do with slavery, including protective tariffs, homesteads, and internal improvements. The Republicans, not facing any nativist opposition and hoping to cut into the Democratic base, also affirmed the political rights of immigrants.

In a tense election that drew the largest turnout in U.S. history to that point, Lincoln captured the electoral majority (see Map 14.4). He won every state where slavery was illegal except for New Jersey (which he split with Douglas), and that was more than enough to win the election. Though his overall share of the popular vote was just 40 percent, Lincoln won majorities in the most populous states. Although Douglas ran competitively in much of the North, he won no free states outright. Divided between North and South, the Democratic Party was no longer a national force. Without its protection, slavery now seemed vulnerable to assault from the federal government.

CONCLUSION

Lincoln's election in 1860 was no ordinary shift in political power. For the first time in U.S. history, a president was elected on a platform that was explicitly critical of slavery. The Republicans had also seized the presidency without a single electoral vote from a Southern state, a sure sign that the South had lost its veto power over national policy. Equally ominous, from the perspective of the South, was the fact that the Democratic Party had splintered. During the three decades of sustained public debate about the legitimacy of slavery, both Northern and Southern Democrats had provided crucial political protection for Southern slaveholding. Without that protection, slavery now rested on shakier ground.

The collapse of the Democratic coalition was the result of many forces and circumstances. The Mexican cession, westward migration, and the California gold rush forced Congress to make new decisions about slavery in the territories. New political compromises stirred up conflicts that had been held in check by older political compromises. Meanwhile, foreign immigration had greatly increased the population (and the political power) of the free states, and new patterns of transportation and communication had made it harder to insulate one part of the country from another. The older model of compromise, which relied on geographical distance, was systematically dismantled over the course of the decade, first in the Compromise of 1850, then in the Kansas-Nebraska Act, and finally in *Dred Scott*.

By 1860, the map no longer provided a viable means of splitting political differences. Instead, American voters faced two radically different options. A Democratic Supreme Court proposed a bold solution that deregulated slavery in the name of the sanctity of private property. The new Republican opposition offered an alternative plan of regulating slavery and celebrating freely contracting laborers. In the new cultural and political landscape created during the 1850s, the Republicans won.

STUDY TERMS

Free Soil Party	Kansas-Nebraska Act
fire-eaters	Know-Nothing Party
popular sovereignty	Bleeding Kansas
Compromise of 1850	Republicans
Fugitive Slave Act	*Dred Scott v. Sandford*
Uncle Tom's Cabin	Lecompton Constitution
Chicago	Freeport Doctrine
wage slavery	John Brown's raid

FURTHER READING

A database of additional full-text readings is available through Power of Process for Primary Sources in Connect.

Tyler Anbinder, *Nativism and Slavery* (1992), connects the rise of the Know-Nothing Party to the shifting politics of slavery in the North.

Adam Arenson, *The Great Heart of the Republic* (2011), illuminates the special role of St. Louis in the sectional conflict of the 1850s.

William Cronon, *Nature's Metropolis* (1991), explains the rise of Chicago as an event in the larger environmental and economic history of its region.

Andrew Delbanco, *The War Before the War* (2018), highlights the conflicts over fugitives from slavery in the antebellum era.

Hidetaka Hirota, *Expelling the Poor* (2016), documents the exclusion and deportation of Irish immigrants by nativist state governments in the antebellum era.

Matthew Karp, *This Vast Southern Empire* (2016), documents the power of slaveholders in shaping an expansionist and nationalist foreign policy at the federal level.

John F. Kasson, *Civilizing the Machine* (1976), shows how Americans incorporated the railroad into their vision of the American landscape.

Michael O'Malley, *Keeping Watch* (1990), traces shifts in attitudes toward time in nineteenth-century America.

Amy G. Richter, *Home on the Rails* (2005), explores the relationship between domestic ideals and rail travel.

Ariel Ron, *Grassroots Leviathan* (2020), emphasizes the role of farmers and agricultural reform in shaping the ideology and ascent of the Republican Party.

15 | DISUNION & WAR

Chapter Questions

1. What course of events led from Abraham Lincoln's election to military conflict between North and South?

2. In what stages did Union war policy toward slavery and emancipation unfold?

3. What were the experiences and significance of Black soldiers in the Union army?

4. How did the war bring disorder and violence to Americans living far from major battlefields?

5. Through what media, new and old, did Americans on the home front experience the war?

Mourning Daguerreotype. A brutal war brought death and destruction to families across the country. *Library of Congress, Prints & Photographs Division [LC-DIG-ppmsca-36863]*

O n a Sunday in February 1862, much of the population of Nashville, Tennessee, was sitting in church when news arrived that the city was about to be attacked. Ministers released their congregations, but Nashville residents were unsure how to prepare for what lay ahead. Louisa Pearl described her neighbors "hurrying to & fro like crazy people." By the end of the day, the post office had closed, newspaper presses stood idle, and state government officials were escaping the city on trains. Soldiers charged with protecting the city prepared to leave as well, but first they seized horses, mules, and carriages; destroyed bridges; and looted private property. Banks shut, stores were emptied, and utter chaos reigned. Pearl began to hope that the invaders would finally arrive.

Time Line

1860
- Abraham Lincoln elected president
- South Carolina votes to secede from the United States

1861
- Confederate States of America established
- Confederate troops attack Fort Sumter
- First Battle of Bull Run (Battle of Manassas)
- Congress passes Confiscation Act

1862
- Battle of Shiloh
- U.S. Navy captures New Orleans
- Congress abolishes slavery in the District of Columbia
- Congress passes Second Confiscation Act
- Battle of Antietam
- Lincoln delivers the Emancipation Proclamation

1863
- U.S. begins forming Colored Troops
- Congress passes Conscription Act, instituting a federal draft
- Battle of Gettysburg
- New York Draft Riots
- Lincoln's Gettysburg Address

1864
- African American soldiers massacred at Fort Pillow
- Battle of the Wilderness
- Union general William T. Sherman's March to the Sea begins
- Lincoln re-elected

1865
- Confederate general Robert E. Lee surrenders to Union forces
- Lincoln assassinated

The army advancing on Nashville in 1862 marched under the banner of the United States. To most of the city's white population, however, the troops represented a foreign enemy. The political split between slave and free states in the 1850s had turned quickly into a brutal civil war between foes who saw each other as belonging to alien cultures. The reality, of course, was that the soldiers attacking Nashville and those fleeing the city had a great deal in common. Most men on both sides spoke English, shared a similar ancestry and religious identity, venerated the same founders, and claimed the legacy of the same American Revolution.

Those fighting for the Union in the Civil War saw themselves as continuing the revolutionary struggle to build a democratic republic based on majority rule, whereas their counterparts on the Confederate side saw themselves as reasserting the right to dissolve existing governments in order to protect local freedoms. Despite that stark ideological division, allegiances could shift and blur. In many parts of the country, people switched, suppressed, or misrepresented their loyalties over the course of the fighting, adding to the climate of chaos. The war divided neighborhoods and families, not just the nation.

But it was the division of the United States into two military apparatuses with massive armies that took the greatest and most unimaginable toll. Scholars now estimate that as many as seven hundred fifty thousand soldiers perished in the Civil War, more than the number who died in all other American wars combined between 1775 and 1945. Another fifty thousand civilians lost their lives as a result of diseases, food shortages, guerrilla warfare, and urban riots that accompanied the war. The death total was only the most tragic of the war's terrible consequences. Limbs were shattered, homes destroyed, fortunes squandered. The Civil War brought the United States unprecedented carnage, devastation, and chaos.

For many Americans, the war was also a time of possibilities. Southern whites in the eleven states that seceded from the United States built a new nation. At the same time, a federal Union now firmly controlled by Northern Republicans expanded the role of the central government in new directions. Most dramatically, enslaved African Americans found opportunities amid the carnage and chaos to renegotiate their relationships with their slaveholders, escape their bondage, take up arms against the slave regime, and turn the Union war effort, slowly, into a crusade against slavery.

SECESSION

With remarkable speed, the states in the Lower South responded to the 1860 presidential election by severing their ties to the United States. They left the union as individual states, claiming either the right to secede or the right of revolution, but they had no intention of remaining independent entities. By the time Lincoln took office, the rebellious states had coalesced to form their own rival government and were preparing for the possibility of war. Unionists devised plans to woo back the seceded states, or at least to prevent other slave states from joining them, but the incoming administration proved unable to reassure the South that slavery would be safe under a Republican regime. Within a month of his inauguration, President Lincoln had to decide whether to enforce federal authority in a rebellious South Carolina. When he did, shots were fired, more states seceded, and war began.

THE CONFEDERATION OF THE COTTON STATES

To most Southern whites, Lincoln's victory at the polls meant that the federal government was now in the clutches of a radical party that sought to destroy the South's way of life. Even though Democrats still controlled Congress and the Supreme Court, and even though Lincoln had insisted during the campaign that he had no desire to restrict slavery where it was already legal, leaders in the states most committed to slavery did not want to wait to see what the new government might do. Immediately after receiving news of the election, South Carolina's state legislature called a convention to consider the question of secession. By a vote of 169 to 0, the convention passed an ordinance on December 20, 1860, declaring that "the union now subsisting between South Carolina and other States, under the name of the 'United States of America,' is hereby dissolved." Though acting alone, South Carolinians saw themselves as the vanguard of a larger revolution to build a new nation. "The tea has been thrown overboard," a Charleston newspaper announced, "the revolution of 1860 has been initiated."

While South Carolina was voting to secede, other states in the cotton kingdom were working toward the same goals. Alabama and Mississippi dispatched representatives to the other slave states to drum up support for a Southern confederation. Secession commissioners, as these representatives were called, also came from South Carolina, Georgia, and Louisiana, lobbying more states to secede. Wherever they traveled in the South, the commissioners sounded the same basic themes. The "Black Republicans," as Southerners labeled Lincoln's party, intended to abolish slavery and elevate Blacks to positions of social and political equality. Commissioners also warned audiences that abolitionism would lead either to a race war or to the "amalgamation" of the two races. They were often preaching to the choir. Newspapers, ministers, and politicians in the Lower South were expressing and stoking the same fears. "Submission to Black Republicanism," one Alabama secessionist predicted, meant forcing "our wives and daughters [to] choose between death and gratifying the hellish lust of the negro." If the South wanted to avoid this dire scenario, delegates to these conventions argued, they needed to act preemptively. One by one, six more state conventions voted to secede. By February 1, Mississippi, Florida, Alabama, Georgia, Louisiana, and Texas had followed in South Carolina's footsteps. Three days later, delegates from the seceding states met in Montgomery, Alabama, and established the **Confederate States of America,** with a new constitution and Jefferson Davis of Mississippi as its president (see Map 15.1).

Though the seven rebellious states made it explicit that they were leaving the union over the issue of slavery, they defended their right to do so in terms of state sovereignty. Because states had ratified the U.S. Constitution, they argued, states could withdraw from it as well. But if the *justification* for secession lay in abstract principles of **states' rights,** the *causes* for which the Lower South was willing to risk the consequences of secession were slavery and racial supremacy. One month after the Confederacy was established, its vice president, Alexander Stephens, announced that the core principle of the new government was "the great truth that the negro is not equal to the white man; that slavery, subordination to the superior race, is his natural and moral condition."

THE UPPER SOUTH IN THE BALANCE

The seven states that formed the Confederacy in February 1861 represented only about half of the slave South. In eight other slave states (North Carolina, Virginia, Maryland, Delaware, Kentucky, Tennessee, Missouri, and Arkansas), arguments for secession fell short. Slaveholders made up smaller percentages of the white population in those states and consequently wielded less political power. In the larger cities in the Upper South, especially Baltimore, St. Louis, and Richmond, growing numbers of white artisans and European immigrants were unenthusiastic about slavery and indifferent to calls for a preemptive

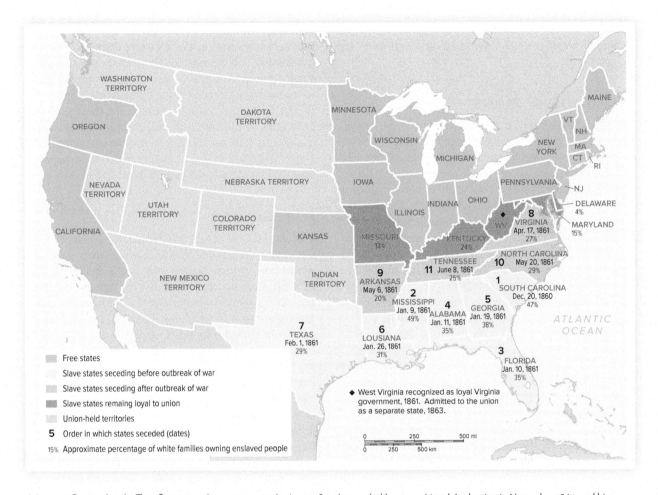

Map 15.1 Secession in Two Stages.   Seven states in the Lower South seceded between Lincoln's election in November 1860 and his inauguration four months later. Those in the Upper South did not secede until after the firing on Fort Sumter. Four other slave states remained in the union. Decisions to secede correlated to the extent of ownership of enslaved people.

strike against an antislavery agenda. Many slaveholders in the Upper South also supported staying in the union, because they worried that their property would be less safe if the nation split in two: If their states seceded, the North would have no political incentive to maintain or enforce federal fugitive slave laws. And throughout the Upper South, unionists touted the close economic ties that bound them to their Northern neighbors.

Secessionists tried to persuade nonslaveholding whites throughout the South that they also had a stake in the region's labor system. Slavery exempted poorer whites from belonging to the menial class, slaveholders argued. In the words of the governor of Georgia, "the poor white laborer . . . belongs to the only true aristocracy" in the South, "the race of *white men*." Upcountry farmers in the Lower South may have warmed to appeals

to racial supremacy, but those in the Upper South were less moved. Perhaps because several of those states had relatively small Black populations, the prospect of inter-racial unions, slave insurrections, and race war seemed less real.

Both the new Confederacy and Lincoln's government-in-waiting knew that the Upper South held the key to the fate of secession. By themselves, the seven seceded states faced grim prospects for resisting the United States. The eight northernmost slave states held more than half of the South's population and about two-thirds of the white men who would be asked to defend the region in the event of war. And though the Lower South was rich with cotton and human property, the Upper South accounted for most of the South's food supply and the vast majority of its industrial capacity. During the months between the establishment of the Confederacy and Lincoln's inauguration, both sides sought, above all, to avoid losing the Upper South.

COMPROMISE PLANS

As states began seceding, proponents of national reconciliation urged compromises that would reassure the South that slavery was safe. Outgoing President Buchanan, who denied that states had any right to secede but also denied the federal government the authority to compel them to stay, called on the North to help return fugitives from slavery, support plans to add Cuba as a slave state, and pass a constitutional amendment protecting slavery in all territories. Most Northerners refused to take this proposal seriously, deriding it as essentially the political platform of the Slave Power. Special committees in Congress, composed of men from both regions and both parties, gathered to consider other strategies. John J. Crittenden, a Whig from Kentucky, crafted a proposal in the Senate to assuage Southern fears with a series of irrevocable constitutional amendments. The first plank of the **Crittenden Compromise** would have prevented the federal government from ever interfering with slavery in the states where it was legal in 1861. The second plank would have barred Congress from outlawing slavery in the national capital—unless the voters there requested it and the neighboring states of Virginia and Maryland had already abolished slavery. The final piece of the plan permanently extended the geographical line of the Missouri Compromise.

Many prominent Republicans appeared willing to sign on to this compromise, but the president-elect instructed them not to. Lincoln told his supporters in Congress not to budge on the question of extending slavery into the territories. Other issues were negotiable, but not this one. The Senate rejected Crittenden's plan. Congress took other measures to stem secession, including the approval of a proposed constitutional amendment forever prohibiting the federal government from abolishing slavery in the states. Such gestures probably helped keep the Upper South in the union a little longer, but by the time Lincoln took office on March 4, 1861, neither the secessionists nor the Republicans were eager to compromise.

In his inaugural address, Lincoln insisted that secession was unacceptable and vowed to use "all powers at my disposal" to maintain federal property in the rebellious states. At the same time, he extended a hand to the Upper South, repeating his campaign pledge not "to interfere with the institution of slavery where it exists." Above all, he appealed to patriotism and to the "bonds of affection" uniting all Americans, to the "mystic chords of memory, stretching from every battle-field, and patriot grave, to every living heart and hearthstone, all over this broad land." Confederate leaders seized upon Lincoln's implied threat to use force against the South and labeled it a "Declaration of War." But the crucial audiences for the speech—the Democrats in the North whose support Lincoln would need in order to back up his threats and the unionists in the Upper South whose hand Lincoln needed to strengthen—seemed willing to give the new president a chance.

FORT SUMTER

Lincoln's quest to appear both firm and conciliatory faced a severe test the day after his inauguration, when he received word from the commanding officer at a federal garrison in South Carolina that supplies were running out. **Fort Sumter** lay 4 miles from the port city of Charleston, in the first state to have seceded from the union. Resupplying the fort would be read as an act of aggression and might nudge the Upper South into the Confederate fold. But evacuating the fort would appear to recognize the Confederacy and might embolden the Upper South to secede. Caught in this bind, but facing mounting pressure from Northerners to quash the rebellion, Lincoln announced his intention to dispatch unarmed ships carrying food supplies. The ball was now in the Confederacy's court.

Jefferson Davis anticipated that a federal invasion of the South would unite the region. Lincoln's gambit had dared Davis to fire the first shot, but as long as federal troops retaliated, the effect would be the same. As the secessionist Edmund Ruffin wrote in his diary in Charleston, "the shedding of blood will serve to change many voters in the hesitating states." Not wanting to fire on the unarmed supply boats, Davis ordered General P. G. T. Beauregard to take the fort before the boats arrived. On April 12, Beauregard's troops fired on Fort Sumter, and after thirty-three hours of bombardment, the undermanned garrison surrendered to the Confederacy.

In the North, the attack on Fort Sumter provoked an immediate outpouring of patriotic fervor. The outcry among Republicans was predictable, but even in Democratic strongholds, the image of the U.S. flag coming down under fire in South Carolina was too much to bear. Democrat Stephen Douglas captured the new mood: "Every man must be for the United States or against it. There can be no neutrals in this war, *only patriots—or traitors*." Lincoln's immediate call for seventy-five thousand militiamen to put down the rebellion was answered quickly and enthusiastically throughout the region.

Multilingual Union Recruitment Poster, New York. Lincoln's request for troops in April 1861 sought 75,000 militiamen, a tiny fraction of what would eventually be needed—but almost five times the size of the federal army at the time. Massive foreign immigration in the fifteen years before the war had given the free states a major population advantage, and the Union war effort depended on recruiting immigrants and their sons. Ultimately, more than 2.2 million men served on the Union side. *The Granger Collection, New York*

In the Upper South, by contrast, the militia summons had the opposite effect. Leaders in those states denounced Lincoln for authorizing an invasion of the South and made it clear that they would play no part in a crusade of "northern aggression." Two days after Lincoln called for troops, the crucial state of Virginia (the most populous in the South) voted to secede. Arkansas followed soon thereafter, as did Tennessee and North Carolina. Kentucky, Maryland, and Missouri ultimately remained in the union, but only after protracted political battles and—in the case of Missouri—armed clashes. Arguments for secession in those states described

the Lower South states as "sisters" and appealed to a widespread view of the South as a distinct culture threatened by strangers. Secessionists invoked this regional identity and spoke the language of loyalty and honor (see Chapter 11). But even after Fort Sumter, slavery remained the crucial factor in determining attitudes toward secession. Delegates who represented counties with higher enslaved populations voted overwhelmingly to secede. Delaware, with a tiny enslaved population, was the only slave state without a significant secession movement.

As the dust settled from the Fort Sumter bombardment, a new national map emerged. The Confederacy, with its capital now relocated to Richmond, Virginia, contained eleven Southern states, which held just under 30 percent of the nation's population; more than a third of the people living in the Confederacy were enslaved. In the three border states of Kentucky, Maryland, and Missouri, the U.S. flag still flew, but the population remained more divided. The vast majority of Americans lived farther north, in the other sixteen states. They clung to a vision of a single, unified nation.

THE CONFEDERACY UNDER SIEGE, 1861–1862

Badly overmatched in population, infrastructure, and resources (see Table 15.1), the Confederacy could count on one crucial advantage. Like the American colonists in their struggle for independence against Great Britain, the South did not have to conquer or occupy enemy territory; it simply needed to force a stalemate. The Civil War would be fought largely on Southern soil, and Confederate soldiers

TABLE 15.1 COMPARISON OF CONFEDERATE AND UNION RESOURCES		
Resource	Confederacy	Union
Population	39%	61%
Railroad mileage	34%	66%
Farms	33%	67%
Wealth produced	25%	75%
Factories	19%	81%

would be defending their homeland. But this tactical and psychological edge also meant that Southern towns, cities, and farms would bear the brunt of the conflict. Union forces invaded from multiple directions, leaving trails of death and destruction in Virginia and Tennessee and occupying territory along coasts and rivers in many parts of the South. In the first year and a half of the war, Confederate forces resisted the invasion effectively in the eastern theater, whereas the Union army advanced with greater ease on the western front. As casualties and costs mounted, both sides were disabused of their initial hopes that the war would be a quick affair.

PREPARING FOR WAR

Both the United States and the Confederacy were unprepared for the vast project of war making that lay ahead of them. The South needed to create a new national government and new national institutions (an army, a navy, a treasury, a post office) from scratch. But even in the North, where such institutions were already in place, the military was small, dispersed, and disorganized, and officer ranks had been thinned by Southern defections. Because federal bureaucracies were modest in size and not yet capable of coordinating a massive war effort, Northern states recruited and outfitted their own soldiers at the outset of the war. Different states negotiated separately with European arms dealers and domestic clothing suppliers, which proved costly and inefficient. Over the next few years, both the Confederacy and the United States would expand and centralize their government operations in order to deal with the unprecedented and unanticipated scale of the war.

Both Union and Confederate leaders expected the war to be brief, their confidence reflecting a mixture of

Civil War Uniforms. (Top) Uniform shell jacket of the 71st Pennsylvania Infantry; (bottom) Confederate uniform jacket made of homespun cloth. The different uniforms that various state regiments used during the early months of the war caused terrible consequences. In the 1861 Battle of Wilson Creek (Missouri), Union soldiers mistook a group of gray-clad Arkansas soldiers for Iowa volunteers, who also dressed in gray. After the Union men were massacred, Union commanders mandated the wearing of blue uniforms. *National Museum of American History, Smithsonian Institution, USAPhoto © Civil War Archive/Bridgeman Images*

political calculation and cultural prejudice. Southerners knew how difficult it would be for the Union to invade and occupy a territory of 750,000 square miles. They doubted that Yankees, whom they saw as cowardly and pragmatic, had the stomach for the fighting that would be required. Southern strategists and propagandists also argued that England's dependence on cotton would lead Britain to intervene in the war. Northerners, for their part, regarded the South as lazy and economically backward, incapable of sustaining a rebellion once the federal government committed to suppressing it. Republicans also saw secession as serving the agenda of the Slave Power, an elite cabal of fire-eating plantation owners. If federal troops made a show of force, many Union politicians figured, nonslaveholders in the South would refuse to fight, and more moderate voices in the rebellious states would prevail.

In keeping with their diplomatic objectives and their expectations of a short war, both sides downplayed the issue of slavery. Lincoln crafted the early war effort with an eye toward boosting Union strength in the border states. His goal was to quickly suppress a rebellion, not to precipitate a revolution in labor or race relations. If unionist leaders in Kentucky, Missouri, or Maryland interpreted the federal war effort as an attack on slavery, Lincoln warned, they might well switch sides. In addition, talking about slavery in the North ran the risk of turning the war into a Republican project, and Lincoln needed bipartisan mobilization. Jefferson Davis also had an interest in avoiding the subject of slavery. Great Britain was less likely to recognize the Confederacy if the Southern cause were identified with an institution that the British government had abolished in the West Indies and loudly opposed elsewhere. And once the Union army invaded, it was easy enough to recruit nonslaveholding white men by asking them to defend their homelands, without having to stress the benefits of white supremacy or the dangers of race war. As two governments prepared for a military showdown and two armies mustered near the Maryland-Virginia border, a silence surrounded the main political controversy that had provoked the crisis.

A THWARTED INVASION

Feeling pressure from newspapers and politicians in the North to invade Virginia, Lincoln directed General Irvin McDowell to devise an attack in July 1861. McDowell had thirty-five thousand men under his command, mostly untrained recruits nearing the end of their ninety-day commitments. His plan was to move against the twenty thousand Confederate soldiers defending the Manassas railroad junction in northern Virginia, about 30 miles from Washington, D.C. A victory there would disrupt the Confederate supply lines, demoralize the South, and pave the way for a march on the new capital at Richmond. But McDowell's troops moved too slowly; a spy ring in Washington, D.C., led by Rose O'Neal Greenhow alerted General Beauregard to the impending attack; and Union forces in the Shenandoah Valley failed to tie up a Confederate reinforcement army of eleven thousand men. By the time the invading troops reached Manassas on July 21, the two sides were roughly equal in size. At first, McDowell's forces seemed to prevail, but by midafternoon the tide had turned, and exhausted Union soldiers began retreating. The orderly retreat of companies turned quickly into the frenetic flight of individual men. A congressman, who had joined the crowds that had come down from Washington, D.C., to watch the battle, looked on with horror at the fleeing soldiers. "We called to them," he reported, "called them to stop, implored them to stand . . . ; no mortal ever saw such a mass of ghastly wretches."

The **First Battle of Bull Run,** named for the branch of the Potomac River where much of the fighting occurred, was a decisive victory for the Confederacy and a major event in the war. Compared to later Civil War battles, the number of casualties was modest, but the eight hundred soldiers from both sides killed on that day exceeded anything Americans had seen before. And the political and psychological impact of the chaotic retreat from Virginia ran even deeper. Southerners, finding confirmation of their view of a cowardly North incapable of manly combat, began celebrating their independence. One Richmond newspaper exulted, "The breakdown of the Yankee race, their unfitness for empire, forces dominion on the South. . . . We must adapt ourselves to our new destiny."

The North was deeply humiliated, and Lincoln and his generals dug in their heels for what they now accepted would be a much longer struggle.

Following Bull Run, Lincoln authorized the recruitment of a million soldiers to serve three-year terms and appointed George B. McClellan the commander of a newly formed **Army of the Potomac.** A skilled administrator, McClellan built a vast and well-disciplined force, though he was notoriously reluctant to take it into battle, perhaps mindful of McDowell's failed offensive. McClellan, a Democrat, also clashed with the Republican leadership—including Lincoln, whom he held in low regard and aspired to replace as president. To the great frustration of the Republicans, McClellan held back from attacking the South for months, apart from a single, disastrous foray in October 1861 at Ball's Bluff.

More than a year after Fort Sumter, and ten months after the Bull Run debacle, McClellan finally ordered a march on Richmond, moving one hundred thirty thousand soldiers to Norfolk (see Map 15.2). Confederate forces, led by Johnston and then by Robert E. Lee, blocked their onslaught in what was called the Seven Days Battle (June 25–July 1, 1862). The smaller Southern army suffered many more casualties, but McClellan withdrew his men back to Washington, D.C. Two months later, another Union assault on Manassas met with defeat. Lee then seized the offensive, hoping to take the war into Union territory and compel the North to surrender. On September 17, 1862, the bloodiest day in U.S. history to that point, the Union was able to claim victory in the **Battle of Antietam,** in Maryland, its first such success on the eastern front. But three months later, Lee's army defended its position near Fredericksburg, Virginia, killing or wounding thirteen thousand Union troops. As 1862 drew to a close, the Confederates had succeeded in keeping the invading army out of Virginia.

THE WESTERN FRONT AND THE NAVAL BLOCKADE

Although the U.S. Army of the Potomac faltered, Northerners found more cheering news from other theaters of the war. Under the command of General Ulysses S. Grant, Union forces moved into Tennessee in February 1862 and captured key river positions in battles at Fort Henry and Fort Donelson (see Map 15.2). Two months later, Grant prevailed again in the **Battle of Shiloh,** but at a cost that seemed astonishing at the time. Each side suffered about ten thousand dead and wounded. William Tecumseh Sherman, Grant's right-hand man, wrote home

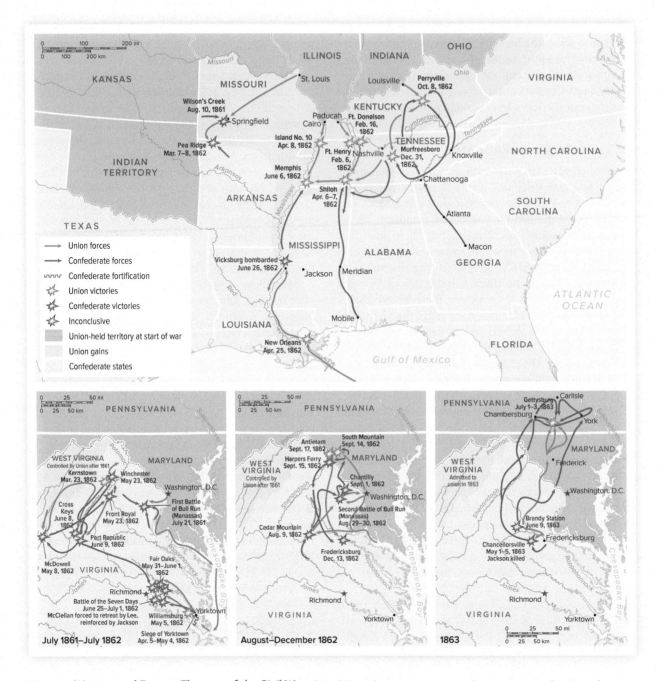

Map 15.2 Western and Eastern Theaters of the Civil War, 1861–1863. The Union army enjoyed great success in the West, where victories in Louisiana and Tennessee eventually gave the North control of the Mississippi River (see top map). By contrast, Confederate forces vigorously rebuffed the Union incursion into Virginia, the major eastern front of the first part of the war (see bottom maps).

about the spectacle of "piles of dead soldiers' mangled bodies . . . without hands and legs." The Union was winning in Tennessee, but the scale of the carnage persuaded many of the victorious Northern soldiers that the war would drag on. To Grant, the lesson of Shiloh

was that the Union could not be preserved "except by complete conquest."

The Union war effort also succeeded at sea. From the beginning, General-in-Chief Winfield Scott had advocated a strategy of isolating the South by blockading seaports and controlling the Mississippi River. Sealing off 3,550 miles of Confederate coastline was a tall order for the U.S. Navy, with few ships and no beachheads for supplying those ships. But Northern boats quickly captured key harbors in the south Atlantic and put the **naval blockade** into effect. In April 1862, the U.S. Navy took New Orleans, the South's largest port city. As a result of naval success and Grant's victories, large sections of the South were under Union control by the spring of 1862.

The Confederates sought to break the blockade by developing a new weapon: the ironclad warship. A redesigned wooden ship called the *Virginia*, outfitted with an armor plate, destroyed two wooden U.S. ships before being confronted by the Union's own ironclad, the *Monitor*. An inconclusive battle between the two ships on March 9, 1862, dampened Southern hopes of reopening their maritime trade. The South also counted on foreign intervention to end the blockade. Newspapers and politicians throughout the South urged planters to stop growing and shipping cotton, hoping this might induce textile manufacturers in Europe to pressure their governments to recognize the Confederacy. But this unofficial cotton embargo had the unintended effect of making the Northern blockade seem more effective, which in turn obligated Britain and France to respect it under international law. And as the war dragged on, the embargo impoverished the South and denied the Confederacy valuable resources. Meanwhile, European textile manufacturers survived without cotton from the South, both because they had stockpiled Southern exports before the war and because cotton from Egypt and India filled the void. France and Britain did not extend recognition and the blockade remained in place. Individual ships continued to make it through in both directions, but the Union's command of the seas devastated the Southern economy.

WEST OF THE MISSISSIPPI: NATIVE AMERICANS JOIN THE FRAY

Although most of the storied battles of the Civil War occurred in the eastern half of the country, fighting spilled into territories west of the Mississippi River as well. There, as in Tennessee, the Union army gained the upper hand. Confederate forces scored an early, bloody victory in the Battle of Wilson's Creek, near Springfield, Missouri, after which pro-Confederate Missouri militiamen were able to capture the southwestern part of that state. But federal forces soon drove them out, and Missouri remained in the union. Three Confederate states lay west of the Mississippi (Texas, Louisiana, and

Cherokee Leader Stand Watie.   After supporting John Ridge's Treaty Party and voluntarily moving west in the 1830s, Stand Watie organized a Native American regiment for the Confederacy and became principal chief of the Confederate Cherokee. ©*North Wind Picture Archives*

Arkansas), and by spring 1862, Union troops occupied parts of both Louisiana and Arkansas. Confederate general Earl Van Dorn tried to launch a northward attack from Arkansas into Missouri. He commanded a force of sixteen thousand, which included regiments of Cherokee and other Native Americans who had been exiled in the 1830s by Southern slaveholders (see Chapter 9) but now allied themselves with the Confederacy as their best hope for independence from the United States. In March 1862, Van Dorn's army was scattered by a much smaller Union force in the battle of Pea Ridge. The same month, Confederate forces that had marched from Texas into the territory of New Mexico were defeated by Union troops from Colorado. This failure, along with the resistance of Apache and Navajo peoples, blocked the South's attempt to expand westward during the war.

THE SLAVERY WAR

During the first two years of the war, Lincoln repeatedly insisted that the North was fighting to preserve the national union, not to abolish slavery. This position proved difficult to sustain. First, not everyone in the Union chain of command shared Lincoln's commitment to keeping the question of slavery out of the war. More importantly, the invasion of the South inevitably shook up relations among enslaved people and slaveholders, irrespective of official federal policy. Enslaved African Americans forced the issue by seizing their own opportunities to liberate themselves. By the end of 1862, Lincoln and the Republican leadership had come around to the view that winning the war might require emancipation.

SLAVERY AND WAR POLICY

At the start of the war, most Northerners supported Lincoln's policy of not undermining slavery in the South. In July 1861, as fighting erupted in Bull Run, the House and Senate passed resolutions affirming that the United States was fighting only to defend the Constitution and had no intention "of overthrowing or interfering with the rights or established institutions" of the South. Even abolitionists, who wanted nothing more than to overthrow the South's established institution, kept silent in 1861, understanding that only a unified North could wage this war and that war was most likely to accomplish their

goals. William Lloyd Garrison, invoking the words of Moses at the Red Sea, counseled the antislavery movement to "stand still, and see the salvation of God."

When Union forces entered the South, they were under strict orders to make good on Lincoln's reassurances. As the first waves of enslaved people sought refuge in Union army camps in Virginia and Missouri, Northern commanders confirmed the national policy of not harboring runaways. But from the start, many Union military personnel violated this policy. Some were motivated by their own antislavery convictions and by the growing clamor among Republicans in Washington, D.C., against the use of Northern soldiers as slave catchers. Others decided to employ or protect fugitives from slavery because they provided or promised valuable pieces of military intelligence.

Higher-ranking Union officers began questioning Lincoln's policy of noninterference, once it became clear that the Confederate war effort depended on enslaved labor. General Benjamin Butler decided to classify the enslaved men and women who escaped to Union camps in Virginia as "contraband of war." Butler's policy, which was endorsed quickly by the secretary of war, accepted the legitimacy of slaveholding while striking a blow

CROSSING BORDERS

● **Contrabands in Union Army Camp.** Enslaved African Americans seized the opportunity to flee to Union lines, hoping to secure freedom. In doing so, they helped transform the cause and nature of the conflict. ● *MPI/Getty Images*

against the South's slave system. Those enslaved in Virginia were indeed property, Butler seemed to concede, and like any other property used by disloyal citizens to support the rebellion, were subject to confiscation. With this rationale, Butler began sheltering and employing fugitives from slavery. The men, women, and children who went to Butler's camps were not legally free, but because they were **contrabands,** their slaveholders could no longer compel their labor or control their lives. In August 1861, Congress reinforced the policy with the first **Confiscation Act,** which authorized the capture of any property enlisted in the rebellion, including all enslaved people "employed in or upon any fort, navy yard, dock, armory, ship, entrenchment, or in any military or naval service." Then in March 1862, Congress prohibited army officers from returning enslaved escapees–a complete reversal of the original Union policy. For many enslaved men and women in the Confederate States, the invading armies represented an alternative to slavery.

Still, the Lincoln administration steered clear of larger plans to emancipate people from slavery during the first year of the war. When General John C. Frémont, the former Republican candidate for president, declared martial law in Missouri in August 1861, he announced that all enslaved people owned by rebellious slaveholders were hereby free. But Lincoln ordered Frémont to rescind the order. Secretary of War Simon Cameron raised the idea of arming those who were enslaved to help suppress the rebellion, but Lincoln rejected the recommendation and reassigned Cameron. As the fighting dragged on, however, Lincoln's approach shifted. Losing confidence that there was any point in cultivating unionist supporters in the states that had seceded, and slightly less worried about risking the support of the loyal border states, he moved gingerly (and always a step behind Congress) toward the position that preserving slavery might not be compatible with preservation of the union. He approached the subject cautiously, endorsing gradual, compensated emancipation in the slave states that had not seceded and sending freed Blacks out of the country.

EMANCIPATION

In April 1862, Congress abolished slavery in the District of Columbia. Slaveholders were to be compensated for their losses, and Congress backed Lincoln's goal of promoting the colonization of formerly enslaved people, yet the law was still a momentous development. A century after the rumblings of abolitionism had first appeared in American politics, and a year after the Civil War erupted, the federal government freed people from slavery through legislation for the first time. Over the next year, military realities would embolden the federal government to contemplate larger assaults on slavery. Two main developments propelled this process. First, as U.S. forces pushed deeper into the Confederacy, more enslaved people appeared in Union camps or fell into Union hands. Second, over the course of 1862, Northern politicians and military officials lost faith in the existence of unionist sentiment in the South. The Union army grew more dependent on Black labor and assistance and less committed to cooperating with slaveholders.

Back in Washington, D.C., Republicans reinforced the changes that were taking place on the ground in the South. In June 1862, Congress prohibited slavery in the territories and began preparing for the readmission of the northwestern portion of Virginia as the new free-labor state of West Virginia. A month later, Lincoln warned congressmen from the border states that slavery was likely to be destroyed in their states "by the mere incidents of the war." Congress then passed the **Second Confiscation Act,** which went much further than the first in authorizing the Union army to harbor runaways. Whereas the 1861 law had permitted the seizure of laborers being used in the Confederate war effort, the new act applied to the enslaved people of any slaveholders who supported the rebellion. Congress also passed the Militia Act, authorizing the army to employ "persons of African descent" in suppressing the rebellion and to emancipate those who accepted such employment. Lincoln then acted on this authorization, ordering his generals to seize enslaved persons in the Confederacy, employ them "for military and naval purposes," and pay them wages.

By the end of July, Lincoln had decided that the only way to defeat the Confederacy was to strip it entirely of its labor force and enlist Black support for the Union war cause. Rather than lure the seceding states back into the union by promising not to interfere with slavery, the North would threaten them with the slave rebellion they had feared most all along. Not wanting his new policy to appear as an act of desperation, Lincoln waited for a Union military triumph. When Lee's invasion of the North was blocked at Antietam that September, the president saw his chance. On September 22, 1862, Lincoln's **Emancipation Proclamation** declared that as of the new year, all people enslaved in rebellious states would be "then, thenceforward, and forever free." The South

Proclaiming Liberty. A Union officer addresses a crowd of formerly enslaved African Americans in Louisiana, many of them in military uniform, in the wake of the Emancipation Proclamation. *North Wind Picture Archives/Alamy Stock Photo*

was put on notice that the invading army was now formally allied with the enslaved.

On January 1, 1863, Lincoln signed the Emancipation Proclamation. Since it applied only to those states that had seceded and to the parts of those states that were not currently occupied by Union forces, the Proclamation did not abolish slavery in the United States. Still, its consequences were profound. In the North, Lincoln's order aroused the Democratic opposition, leaving Republicans politically vulnerable to the charge that they were waging a war for social revolution, not for the Constitution. In Europe, the same signals were greeted more enthusiastically and probably doomed any possibility that Britain or Russia (which had recently emancipated its serf population) would recognize the Confederacy. In the South, both

whites and Blacks took Lincoln's order quite seriously as a call to slave insurrection. General Beauregard threatened to retaliate by executing Union prisoners of war. Jefferson Davis called the Proclamation "the most execrable measure in the history of guilty man." ● Throughout the South, even in areas not covered by the Proclamation, those who had lived under the slavery regime rejoiced. News passed quickly through word of mouth along what contemporaries called a "grapevine telegraph" linking enslaved people across plantations, and several slaveholders reported first hearing about the Proclamation from them. In Northern cities and in occupied areas of the Confederacy, Black men and women ushered in January 1 as the dawn of a Jubilee, the biblical year of freedom for all enslaved people. ●

MEDIA AND INFORMATION

BLACKS IN THE UNION ARMY

Even before the Emancipation Proclamation, enslaved African Americans had been flocking to contraband camps, seeking both their own freedom and the opportunity to fight against the Confederacy. Abolitionists, Black and white, had argued for enlisting African Americans, hoping that by participating in the Union war effort, Black men might stake their claims to full and equal citizenship. Free Blacks had been excluded from militia service in the antebellum North, and Northern states refused to mobilize them during the first part of the war. But by 1863, the North's demand for men exceeded the supply of white volunteers. Brutal battles had depleted the Union ranks, and every successful incursion into Confederate terrain required a larger occupation force. Once the war became explicitly tied to emancipation, more whites in the North warmed to the idea of letting free Blacks in the North and contrabands in the occupied South put their own lives at risk for that war effort.

Black Americans—free and enslaved, Northern and Southern—had been contributing to the Union cause from the beginning of the war. They staged work slowdowns, conveyed military intelligence, aided Confederate deserters and fugitives from slavery, and left plantations. But the opportunity to serve in the Union army marked a turning point, both in the struggle for emancipation and in the course of the war. The recruitment of regiments of what the U.S. Army called **Colored Troops** began slowly, first in occupied Louisiana and South Carolina, and then in the New England states of Massachusetts, Rhode Island, and Connecticut. A few months later, the Lincoln War Department authorized other Northern states to follow suit. Free Blacks in the North quickly filled the new regiments that were established for them, but most of the Black military contribution would come from other parts of the country. Only forty-six thousand African American males of military age lived in the free states. More than twice that number were held in bondage in the loyal slave states, but these areas were specifically exempted from the Emancipation Proclamation. Mobilizing Black soldiers in the border states was a politically sensitive process, since it involved arming men who were legally enslaved, but Union recruiters fanned out to plantations in Maryland, Missouri, and Tennessee in 1863, and self-emancipating men enlisted in droves. Slaveholders tried unsuccessfully to slow the exodus, sometimes by threatening to punish the wives and children of men who enlisted, but the recruitment of enslaved people continued, and it severely undermined the slave regime.

Overall, one hundred eighty thousand African Americans, mostly escaped or confiscated from slavery and recruited from the border states and the Confederacy, fought in the U.S. Army, and another ten thousand in the U.S. Navy.

Black soldiers encountered significant discrimination in the Union military. The War Department refused to commission Black officers and insisted on paying lower wages to African American recruits. Whereas white soldiers earned a minimum of thirteen dollars per month, their Black counterparts received only ten dollars (regardless of rank). In late 1863, a South Carolina infantry regiment, led by Sergeant William Walker, protested the injustice of this arrangement by refusing to perform their duties. Walker was court-martialed and executed.

African American soldiers also faced special risks on the battlefields. The South refused to treat Blacks in the Union army according to the conventional rules of combat, and Confederate soldiers frequently shot at Black soldiers rather than taking them prisoner. As the *Arkansas Gazette* explained this policy, "we cannot treat negroes . . . as prisoners of war without a destruction of the social system for which we contend." In the infamous **Fort Pillow Massacre** (1864), Confederate troops in Tennessee slaughtered almost two hundred Black soldiers after they had surrendered. Officers (white or Black) who commanded the Colored Troops were also singled out for mistreatment. When Colonel Robert Gould Shaw, the white commander of the famous all-Black 54th Massachusetts Volunteer Infantry Regiment, was killed in South Carolina in 1863, the victorious Southern army refused to surrender his body for burial. When Captain Andre Cailloux, a free Black from New Orleans, fell while attacking a Confederate fort in Louisiana the same year, Southern snipers prevented Union personnel from retrieving his body during a truce. Cailloux's body lay unburied for forty-seven days.

How Much Is That?

Union Army Wages

The 10 dollars a month paid to Black soldiers represented a buying power equivalent to about 206 dollars in 2020 but the net pay, after deducting three dollars per month for clothing, would be about 150 dollars in 2020. The higher pay rate for white soldiers (from which clothing costs were not deducted) works out to a minimum wage of just over 268 dollars per month.

WHITE SOLDIERS' ATTITUDES TOWARD SLAVERY

The shift in Union war aims both reflected and affected the attitudes of white soldiers as well as Black ones. Most men who fought in the Civil War, on both sides, were neither enslaved people nor slaveholders. But they, too, cared about slavery and its relationship to the causes they were defending. From the time they joined the Confederate army, Southern men saw themselves as protecting their homeland against invasion, and the presence or prospect of free Black men with guns was a big part of what was threatening about the invasion. Already by 1862, a Confederate soldiers' newspaper insisted that "any man who pretends to believe that this is not a war for the emancipation of the blacks . . . is either a fool or a liar."

Union soldiers entered the war with a wider range of attitudes toward enslaved people. Most of the Northern men who signed up for battle hated slavery and blamed a slaveholding oligarchy for undermining the republic and starting the war, and many of them saw free labor as a big part of what was at stake in a war to preserve the United States (much as Americans would talk about fighting for free enterprise a century later). But only a minority saw the fate of 4 million people enslaved in the South as a cause worth dying for. Lincoln's new war policies tested the allegiance of most Union soldiers and, months after the Emancipation Proclamation, marked a low period in troop morale.

Over the course of 1863, however, many rank-and-file soldiers began to see things differently. Because anti-war Democrats, dubbed **Copperheads** by their opponents, attacked Lincoln for turning the Civil War into a crusade against slavery, those who criticized the Emancipation Proclamation risked being linked with the war's critics. Furthermore, the service of Black men in the Union military and their contributions to the war effort altered many Northern whites' perspectives on race relations. When Sam Evans of Ohio volunteered to serve with the U.S. Colored Troops in May 1863, for example, his father was aghast, writing that he "would rather clean out S__thouses at ten cents pr day" than assume such a "degraded" status. Sam explained that this was an easier way for him to become an officer, and he reminded his father that the new policy would save white lives. By the end of the war, however, both father and son supported Black enlistment as a matter of principle and advocated granting Black men the right to vote. Northerners who had despised abolitionism in 1862 came to endorse the goal of ending slavery in the South.

THE WAR'S MANY FRONTS

Though the Civil War is typically imagined as having taken place on bounded battle sites in rural America, the violence spilled over, blurring the lines between soldiers and civilians and touching the lives of men, women, and children across the country. Those who lived in the many paths traced by the clashing armies fell victim to stray bullets, errant cannon fire, or shells left behind. Especially in the South, civilians suffered at the hands of occupation forces. In the border states and in large cities, neighbors of different convictions and allegiances were swept up in guerrilla attacks, civil unrest, or violence between enslaved people and their enslavers. The mass movements of troops and refugees and the accumulation of carcasses and wounded bodies also accelerated the spread of disease. For Americans spared these ravages, the war's destructiveness was brought home by the loss of loved ones, the constant reports of death, and new, graphic depictions of the mounting carnage.

OCCUPIED TERRITORY

The Civil War was a brutal struggle for territory. For four years, Union and Confederate armies fought to control towns, cities, and large swaths of contested land, which meant that many parts of the country were subjected to **military occupation.** For most of the war, Union soldiers occupied much of Virginia, the Carolina coastline, southeastern Louisiana, middle and western Tennessee, and portions of Arkansas, northern Mississippi, and northern Alabama. These occupied areas included many of the South's major cities, such as New Orleans, Memphis, Nashville, Norfolk, and Alexandria. Later in the war, Charleston, Savannah, and Wilmington would also fall to federal forces. Overall, more than a hundred towns and cities in the South became Union army garrisons for at least part of the Civil War.

Federal military officials may have described their job as liberating the South from the clutches of secessionist oligarchs, but the South's white population regarded them as invading armies. No one knew for certain what life would be like under Yankee occupation, but popular stereotypes about the North may have predisposed white Southerners to believe rumors that the invaders were there to steal enslaved laborers, pillage property, and rape women. Hundreds of thousands of people lived under this army's occupation or fled their homes to escape such a fate. Slaveholders often sent valuable human property into the interior of the region to avoid financial loss. For those who remained, the reality of military occupation rarely lived up to their worst fears. During the early months of the occupation, Union soldiers actively enforced slave codes and even whipped those who disobeyed slaveholders. Overall, however, the effects of the invasion were devastating to Southern life. In cities and towns, trade was disrupted, employment opportunities disappeared, and food and fuel supplies were quickly depleted. In rural areas near the federal garrisons, farms and villages were vulnerable to raids for supplies, and in the zones that fell between the occupied territory and the Confederate-controlled interior, anarchy prevailed.

Even in parts of the South not under occupation, the war wrought widespread deprivation and periodic unrest. In the spring of 1863, food shortages and inflation led to rioting and looting in multiple Southern cities, mostly organized and led by women who were asserting their political power while their husbands were away at the front. In the Confederate capital of Richmond, hundreds of women took to the streets under the banner of "Bread or Blood" to protest high prices. The ensuing Richmond **bread riots** involved thousands of participants and rampant pillaging of stores and warehouses, prompting the governor to call out the state militia to restore order.

GUERRILLA WARFARE

In the slave states that remained in the union, Northern soldiers were still sometimes treated like occupying armies. When the 6th Massachusetts Volunteer Infantry passed through the streets of Baltimore after the attack on Fort Sumter, local whites rioted and killed four members of the regiment. In Missouri, which federal troops had kept in the Union fold in 1861, the Union imposed martial law throughout the war and tried more civilians under its authority than in all of the occupied states combined. Meanwhile, Missouri's Confederate sympathizers waged ongoing guerrilla campaigns against federal troops and their supporters.

Guerrilla warfare in Missouri was in some ways a continuation of the battles over slavery that had erupted across the border with Kansas in the 1850s (see Chapter 14). Pro-Confederate guerrillas, known as **Bushwhackers,** terrorized the Missouri countryside throughout the war period. Mostly very young men from farms, the Bushwhackers were loosely organized and had no formal connection to the Confederacy. But they targeted Union supporters and saw their own acts of looting, arson,

torture, and murder as part of a broader revolutionary struggle to defend their homelands against Lincoln's invasion. They were pursued both by Union troops enforcing martial law in Missouri and by Kansas regiments stationed along Missouri's western border.

Both in the border states and in the occupied South, soldiers and guerrillas added to the confusion by concealing their identities. In Mississippi, for example, Union scouts dressed in Confederate uniforms and pretended to be sick soldiers in order to acquire valuable information from white civilians. Many armed combatants did not wear uniforms at all and left it to their victims to figure out how thefts, beatings, rapes, or executions fit into the larger meaning of the war.

PRISONS, HOSPITALS, AND BURIAL GROUNDS

Most of the war's major battles lasted no more than a few days, but for many of the survivors, the end of a battle signaled the beginning of a new ordeal. Approximately six hundred seventy-four thousand soldiers were captured during the Civil War, and four hundred ten thousand were held in some form of military custody. Early in the war, the two armies sometimes released prisoners immediately, agreeing to parole equal numbers of men of corresponding rank. For a period in the middle of the war, large-scale prisoner exchanges were conducted at specified locations in Virginia and Mississippi. But by the middle of 1863, these arrangements had broken down, in part because of the Confederacy's refusal to accord Black soldiers the status of war prisoners but also because the Union authorities concluded that the South, with its much smaller population of eligible soldiers, needed the exchange more than the North did. By 1864, the number of war prisoners on both sides had soared. Over one hundred fifty compounds were established throughout the country to hold them, from Boston to Key West and as far west as New Mexico.

During the war, each side repeatedly accused the other of mistreating prisoners. Crowded into small barracks without adequate food or clothing, both Southern and Northern inmates suffered miserably. One Alabama artilleryman described the camp where he was incarcerated in Elmira, New York, as "nearer Hades than I thought any place could be." In Georgia's infamous **Andersonville prison,** thirteen thousand Union soldiers perished, from both disease and the violence of prison guards, between February 1864 and April 1865. (In 1865, the United States hanged Andersonville's commander, Henry Wirz, the only person executed for

INTERPRETING THE SOURCES

Walt Whitman's Condolence Letters

In December 1862, after the Brooklyn poet and journalist Walt Whitman learned that his brother George was among the wounded in Fredericksburg, he headed south to search for him. George Whitman was not badly wounded, it turned out, but Walt Whitman remained on the Virginia battlefield for eight days and then took a part-time job in Washington, D.C., so that he could devote himself to visiting military hospitals. By his own count, Whitman made six hundred hospital visits to somewhere between eighty thousand and one hundred thousand dying or wounded soldiers over the next three years. Among the services and comforts he offered these men, Whitman wrote condolence letters to the families of soldiers who did not survive. The following are excerpts from an 1863 letter to the family of a soldier from Breesport, New York, who had been a musician in the Union army:

Much of the time his breathing was hard, his throat worked—they tried to keep him up by giving him stimulants, milk-punch, wine &c—these perhaps affected him, for often his mind wandered somewhat—I would say, Erastus, don't you remember me, dear son?—can't you call me by name? . . .

I was very anxious he should be saved, & so were they all—he was well used by the attendants—poor boy, I can see him as I write—he was tanned & had a fine head of hair, & looked good in the face when he first came, & was in pretty good flesh too—(had his hair cut close about ten or twelve days before he died)—He never complained—but it looked pitiful to see him lying there, with such a look out of his eyes. He had large clear eyes, they seemed to talk better than words—I assure you I was attracted to him much—Many nights I sat in the hospital by his bedside till far in the night—The lights would be put out—Yet I would sit there silently, hours, late, perhaps fanning him—he always liked to have me sit there, but never cared to talk—I shall never forget those nights, it was a curious & solemn scene, the sick & wounded lying around in their cots, just visible in the darkness, & this dear young man close at hand lying on what proved to be his death bed—I do not know his past life, but what I do know, & what I saw of him, he was a noble boy—I felt he was one I should get very much attached to. I think you have reason to be proud of such a son, & all his relatives have cause to treasure his memory. . . .

I write to you this letter, because I would do something at least in his memory. . . . He is one of the thousands of our unknown American young men in the ranks about whom there is no record or fame, no fuss made about their dying so unknown, but I find in them the real precious & royal ones of this land, giving themselves up, aye even their young and precious lives, in their country's cause—Poor dear son, though you were not my son, I felt to love you as a son, what short time I saw you sick & dying here—it is as well as it is, perhaps better—for who knows whether he is not better off, that patient & sweet young soul, to go, than we are to stay? So farewell, dear boy—it was my opportunity to be with you in your last rapid days of death—no chance as I have said to do any thing particular, for nothing [could be done—only you did not lay] here & die among strangers without having one at hand who loved you dearly, & to whom you have your dying kiss. . . .

Walt Whitman to the parents of Erastus Haskell (Mr. & Mrs. SB Haskell), August 10, 1863

Explore the Source

1. What consolation does Whitman offer the dead soldier's parents about the conditions of his death?

2. Given the fact that hundreds of thousands of ordinary Americans died during the war and the sight of wounded patients became exceedingly common, what might be Whitman's point in calling men like Erastus Haskell "royal" and "precious"?

war crimes in the Civil War.) Overall, fifty-six thousand soldiers died in captivity during the Civil War, about 13 percent of the total number of inmates. Statistically, a soldier stood a better chance of survival on the battlefield than in a prisoner-of-war camp.

Soldiers who managed to avoid both battlefield death and imprisonment often wound up in military hospitals, which were established in towns and cities throughout the major war theaters. Richmond alone had thirty-four hospitals, the largest of which held eight thousand wounded and sick Confederate soldiers at a time. Union casualties filled an even larger number of hospital beds in the U.S. capital (see Interpreting the Sources: Walt Whitman's Condolence Letters).

The Civil War took place at a point in American history when techniques of killing had advanced more

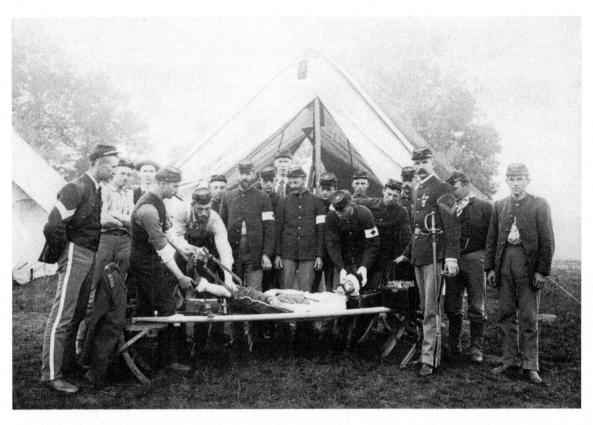

Amputation Procedure, Gettysburg, 1863. Surgeries were often performed outdoors for better lighting conditions. Doctors amputated fifty thousand limbs over the course of the war, and about 75 percent of the patients survived. Between 1861 and 1873, the United States awarded eighty-five new patents for prosthetic legs. *Thinkstock/Getty Images*

quickly than techniques of healing. Soldiers bore muzzle-loading rifles with three times the firing range of the arms that had been used in the war against Mexico just over a decade earlier. New, more powerful portable cannons, developed in France, mowed down soldiers in unprecedented numbers. Meanwhile, medical practices remained primitive by the standards of just a few decades later. Doctors understood very little about germs and antisepsis and spread numerous diseases through unclean instruments and hospital conditions. The availability of anesthetics encouraged doctors to amputate wounded and infected limbs, which probably saved many lives, but unsanitary surgical practices may have nullified some of the benefits. The scalpel used to stop an injured leg from infecting one body would spread the infection to another. • Soldiers, many of whom hailed from rural areas where they had been exposed to fewer diseases, succumbed to epidemics of measles, mumps, and smallpox, as well as recurrent outbreaks of malaria, typhoid, and dysentery. Twice as many soldiers died from disease as from battle injuries.

Disease swept quickly through the war-torn areas, paying no respect to the distinction between soldiers and civilians. Military camps, hospitals, and prisons became breeding grounds for contagion and produced staggering mortality rates. In crowded cities with transient populations, epidemics spread just as quickly. President Lincoln's eleven-year-old son, Willie, died of typhoid fever during the war, probably the result of water contamination in Washington, D.C. •

Dealing with the dead was as difficult as dealing with the injured and ill. Civil War battles yielded grotesque harvests of dead bodies, which needed to be disposed of, both out of respect for the deceased and out of concern for the living. Officials on both sides worried that leaving corpses to decompose on the battlefields would not only hurt troop morale but also imperil hygiene, because corpses might emit dangerous effluvia. Burying

DISEASE AND EPIDEMIC

DISEASE AND EPIDEMIC

Feeding the Wounded, Carlisle Barracks, Pennsylvania. Hospital service brought large numbers of women to the war front. Drawings and photographs of hospital scenes often highlighted the heroism of nurses and placed them in the foreground of military coverage. *Fotosearch/Archive Photos/Getty Images*

the dead was part of the burden of soldiering, usually borne by the victors, who controlled the field of battle after the shooting stopped. But the escalating casualty totals could easily overwhelm both the surviving army and the civilian population. At the Battle of Gettysburg in 1863 (see the section The War's End), three days of fighting killed seven thousand men and left twenty-two thousand others wounded. A local community of twenty-four hundred bore the impact of this carnage, which was compounded by the death of three thousand horses. About 6 million pounds of carcasses lay on the fields of this one Pennsylvania town. For several months, nearby residents walked around with peppermint oil or pennyroyal to combat the stench of death.

To address the enormous administrative and humanitarian challenges posed by all the death and suffering produced by war, an unusual private organization emerged on the Union side. Founded in New York at the start of the war, the Women's Central Association of Relief for the Sick and Wounded of the Army was an elite philanthropic organization in the larger tradition of antebellum reform (see Chapter 12), but in a time of expanding federal power and bureaucracy, the organization widened its goals beyond providing relief. Renamed the **United States Sanitary Commission** and authorized to act as a federal agency, it collected millions of dollars in private donations, but it turned its main attention to compiling vital statistics and hospital records, studying military hygiene, recruiting and training nurses, and supporting the Union war campaign by improving the health of Northern soldiers. Distinguished men from prosperous backgrounds dominated the organization's leadership structure, but the Sanitary Commission also provided opportunities for women to play significant roles in the war effort. Prominent commission nurses, such as Mary Livermore, Louisa May Alcott, and Katherine Prescott Wormeley, were among approximately twenty thousand Union and Confederate women who served as medical caregivers and helped turn the position of Civil War nurse into a platform for women's reform causes.

HOME FRONTS

Far from the cemeteries, military hospitals, garrison towns, and killing fields, Americans tracked the events of the war closely, like no prior event in the nation's history. As in the earlier war with Mexico, newspapers and wire transmissions relayed current military news, but the passage of fifteen years had increased the reach of the telegraph system and the circulation of the press.

Moreover, the massive mobilization of young men gave most readers, North and South, special reasons to attend

MEDIA AND INFORMATION

to the news. ● Newspapers regularly printed casualty lists, which friends and relatives of soldiers scoured nervously. In larger cities, newspaper offices posted the latest headlines as they came in via telegraph onto large bulletin boards that attracted large public gatherings during major battles. ●

Civilians also followed the war through three cultural practices that had spread before the war: letter writing, pictorial magazines, and photography. First, battlefields were connected to the home front through the mail. Civil War armies were the most literate mass fighting forces in history to that point (more than 85 percent of the soldiers could read and write), and the men who enlisted had grown up during the period when lower postage rates made the mail a popular tool for maintaining contact with distant friends and family. According to one estimate, soldiers in the Civil War sent or received an average of one hundred eighty thousand letters every day. Soldiers' correspondence provided readers back home with detailed information about army life and brought dreaded reports of injury or death. In the South, postal service was much less comprehensive and reliable. Nonetheless,

Confederate soldiers also spent much of their time writing letters, and Southern families anxiously awaited their arrival.

Second, Americans saw the war through a series of mass-circulation pictorial magazines that shaped the popular imagination of battles, armies, and the enemy, especially for Northern readers (see Hot Commodities: Civil War Board Games). These weekly publications, founded mostly in the 1850s, featured lithographed engravings and drawings of current events. Prominent papers included *Harper's Weekly*, the *New York Illustrated News*, and the spectacularly successful *Frank Leslie's Illustrated Newspaper*, which was selling as many as three hundred forty-seven thousand copies of a single issue by 1860. When the war broke out, *Frank Leslie's* (like most mass newspapers based in the North) decided to forsake its Southern readers and assume a pro-Union stance. The decision paid off handsomely, and *Leslie's* became the magazine of record in many Northern households. Even Union troops, with firsthand access to the events of the war, were avid consumers of the pictorial press. ● Southern readers, by contrast, had to make do with the much scantier offerings of the *Southern Illustrated News* (which had trouble hiring engravers and filled its columns mostly with text) and two other pictorial papers that operated only briefly. White

MEDIA AND INFORMATION

***A Burial Party on the Battle-Field of Cold Harbor*, by John Reekie and Alexander Gardner.**
Civil War photographs typically depicted still scenes before or after a battle. Question for Analysis: What might the photographer be trying to convey by arranging this posed scene of African American men gathering long-decomposed body parts? *Library of Congress, Prints & Photographs Division [LC-DIG-ppmsca-12615]*

HOT COMMODITIES
Civil War Board Games

The Civil War mobilized millions of soldiers, health care workers, merchants, couriers, refugees, and escapees from slavery, sending them great distances all over the continent. But a majority of the country remained at home. Americans on the home front imagined the conflict through a steady supply of media coverage and consumer goods—including pictures, songs, and mail envelopes with patriotic emblems—bringing the war into the parlors and living rooms of middle-class families, especially in the North.

Entrepreneurial publishers in Northern cities even produced and peddled Civil War games. Board games, many of them imported and adapted from India via Great Britain, had been growing in popularity in the United States during the nineteenth century, but the Civil War marked a major takeoff in the game industry. In 1860, Milton Bradley, a young New England inventor and entrepreneur, introduced a board game called the Checkered Game of Life, in which players advance strategically across a sixty-four-square checkerboard, following a journey from infancy to old age, navigating the ups and downs of fortune, and competing with other players in a search for individual prosperity. Bradley sold forty thousand copies of the game in its first year and parlayed that success into a company that became America's leading producer of board games. Much of that early success came from Union soldiers who took Bradley's portable box of backgammon, chess, checkers, and the Checkered Game of Life with them to distract and entertain themselves.

For those who stayed behind, games featured the war itself. Decks of playing cards depicted the rigors of camp life or featured pictures of fifty-two Union officers. The Game of Secession, a version of the ancient snakes-and-letters game genre and similiar to the modern Chutes and Ladders board game, followed the events of the political conflict. Another game, entitled The Game of the Rebellion, promoted itself by promising "Ladies, Gentlemen and Children a chance to 'fight the rebels by their own firesides.'"

Think About It

1. If the war brought death and destruction to so many American families, why were war games popular?

2. Why might Civil War games have been more popular in the North than in the South?

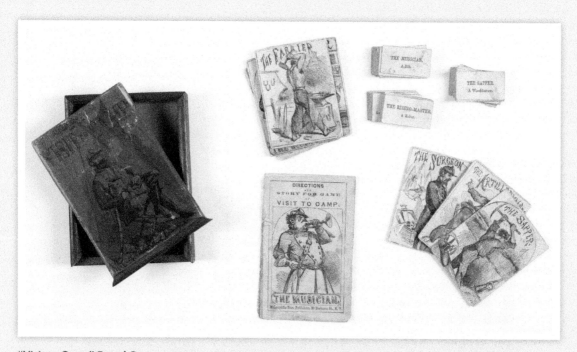

"Visit to Camp" Board Game. This game familiarized Northern consumers with important figures in Civil War military life, such as "The Surgeon," "The Sutler" (supplier of nonmilitary supplies to the troops), and "The Musician." *Courtesy, American Antiquarian Society*

Winslow Homer, "News from the War," from *Harper's Weekly*, June 14, 1862.   *The Picture Art Collection/ Alamy Stock Photo*

BEHIND THE IMAGE

Massachusetts-born artist Winslow Homer (1836–1910) was around twenty-five years old when the U.S. Provost Marshal's Office granted him approval to visit Union military camps at the front. Based on his observations there, Homer produced dozens of images for *Harper's Weekly*, a pictorial magazine founded in New York City in 1857. Homer spent about ten weeks in Virginia war zones in 1861 and 1862 and drew this illustration on his return to New York.

WITHIN THE IMAGE

Homer's illustration surveys the many media that provided war news. 1 In the central scene, a woman slumps over a parlor table, clutching a piece of paper. 2 The wires bordering the top of the image suggest that the paper in her hand is a telegraph; below the woman, the word *wounded* signals that she has received distressing news. Despite the insularity and serenity often associated with middle-class parlors (symbolized by the vined plant, caged songbird, and decorated folding screen), telegraphic communication exposes the home to the ravages of war. Other scenes focus on the mail. 3 At top

left, a sailor reads a letter while his comrade guards the precious cargo of correspondence "for the fleet." 4 At left center, an officer standing beside his horse holds official military communication. 5 A horse also appears beneath the mounted bugler, an older symbol of news. 6 By contrast, the lower right shows modern pictorial magazines (the *Harper's* masthead is discernible) flying from railroad cars to a crowd of soldiers desperate to read about the events in which they are engaged. 7 At bottom left appears an artist-reporter, like Homer, sketching two towering soldiers.

BEYOND THE IMAGE

"News from the War" appeared as a prominent, two-page spread in a mass-circulated magazine (*Harper's* had over two hundred thousand subscribers during the war era), and thousands more saw it second-hand. At a time when technological constraints made it unfeasible to publish photographs in newspapers, illustrations like this shaped the visual imagination of war throughout the North. 8 By including both his profession and the publication in which the drawing appeared, Homer highlighted his own place within the media landscape he was portraying, and he would go on to become one of the leading American painters of the nineteenth century.

MEDIA AND INFORMATION

Southerners could not stomach the Northern options, however. "The pictures in 'Harper's Weekly' and 'Frank Leslie's' tell more lies than Satan himself," wrote one Georgia woman in her diary. "I get in such a rage when I look at them that I sometimes take off my slipper and beat the senseless paper with it." •

Third, whereas pictorial magazines offered artists' perspectives on the war, the new medium of photography offered the promise of more direct access to the front. Because of the heavy equipment and lengthy exposure times entailed, **Civil War photographs** were not action shots of battle. Instead, they featured still scenes of camp life. Most of the photographs of the war front were exhibited and published by Mathew Brady, whose photo galleries in New York and Washington, D.C., introduced many Americans to the shocking spectacle of corpses piled on the fields of Antietam. • Brady was the most famous photographer of his era, and it was to Brady that President Lincoln turned, both in the presidential campaign and during his time in office, to help fashion his image. • But Brady did not take the classic war photographs that bore his name. Most were the work of Timothy O'Sullivan or Alexander Gardner, artists in Brady's employ. In all, Brady oversaw the production of some ten thousand photographic plates during the Civil War.

POLITICS & ENTERTAINMENT

THE WAR'S END, 1863–1865

For most Americans, at home or in uniform, the second half of this unimaginably long war brought only more destruction and grief. In hindsight, however, the Union war effort clearly turned a corner during the summer of 1863, as crucial battles depleted the Southern ranks and set up further Union incursions into Confederate territory. Lincoln regained the support of Northern voters, elevated a different general to supreme command of Union forces, and presided over the slow, bloody end of the conflict. All the while, his party was building a more powerful federal government, authorized not only to wage war but also to remake the nation.

KEY UNION VICTORIES

Though the North had occupied New Orleans and won decisive victories in Tennessee, General Grant still did not control the Mississippi River. After an unsuccessful attempt to capture the Confederate stronghold of Vicksburg, Grant decided in May 1863 to besiege the city. For six weeks, Confederate soldiers and Vicksburg residents suffered from hunger and disease, trying to survive on whatever food sources they could obtain, which reportedly included dogs, snakes, and boiled shoe leather. On July 4, Confederate general John Pemberton surrendered. As a consequence, the city of Vicksburg would not hold Fourth of July celebrations until after World War II.

Meanwhile to the east (see Map 15.3), General Lee's Confederate troops had won a major battle in Chancellorsville, Virginia, shortly before Grant began the **siege of Vicksburg.** Seeking to take quick advantage of the victory, Lee marched an army of seventy-five thousand men northward through Maryland and into Pennsylvania, hoping to inflict a heavy blow on the North, threaten Philadelphia and Baltimore, and force Lincoln to negotiate a settlement. On June 28, 1863, Union troops led by George Meade interrupted Lee's march near the town of Gettysburg, which was at the hub of several roads in the area. On July 1, the two armies began exchanging fire in what was to become the most famous battle of the Civil War. On the first day, the Confederate forces broke the Union lines, but the next morning brought Union reinforcements and the Northerners defended their elevated positions. Undaunted, Lee ordered an ill-advised frontal attack on Cemetery Ridge, the center of the enemy lines, led by General George Pickett, whose men stretched across an open field, forming a mile-wide target for Union cannons and guns. The killing on this last day of the **Battle of Gettysburg** brought Lee's casualties to twenty-eight thousand men, forcing him to withdraw to Virginia. Almost as many Northern soldiers were killed or wounded, but these were losses the larger Union army could more easily survive. Just one day before the fall of Vicksburg, Lee's invasion of the North ended in failure.

LINCOLN'S WAR

By many measures, the first half of Abraham Lincoln's term in office was a colossal failure. The union fell apart on his watch and the country was plunged into war. He seriously overestimated the extent of support for the union that could be rallied in the Upper South, and his attempts to placate slaveholders backfired. Then, two years into his term, his shift of course toward emancipation won him new enemies in the North. State legislatures in Indiana and Illinois passed resolutions calling for peace, and Copperhead leader Clement Vallandigham of Ohio

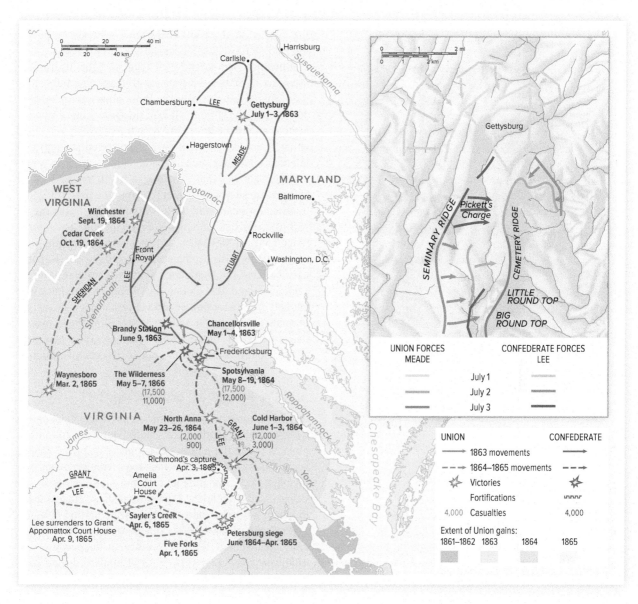

Map 15.3 The War in the East, 1863–1865.   The tide of the war shifted decisively after 1863, with key Union victories in both Virginia and the Southeast.

condemned the war on the floor of Congress. As support for the war ebbed, Lincoln suppressed civil liberties, using his military authority to order the arrest of anyone engaging in "disloyal" activities. He had Vallandigham arrested, for example, and expelled across enemy lines to Tennessee. (After the war, the Supreme Court would rule against one of Lincoln's tactics, the subjection of U.S. citizens to military tribunals in circumstances where civilian courts are in operation.) On the second anniversary of Lincoln's

inauguration, the South was still out of the union, more than a hundred thousand soldiers had perished, the nation's economy was in crisis, and Democrats were accusing him of having betrayed the Constitution.

A year before facing re-election, Lincoln seized the occasion of a ceremony dedicating a new national cemetery in Gettysburg to redefine the war effort. The main speaker at this event, held on November 19, 1863, was not the president but Edward Everett of Massachusetts, who

Mathew Brady's Lincoln. Brady's many photographs of Lincoln helped turn him into a broadly recognizable political celebrity unlike any previous president. *Library of Congress, Prints and Photographs Division [LC-USP6-2415-A].*

addressed a crowd of fifteen thousand for two hours. Lincoln followed with what was listed in the program as "Dedicatory Remarks" and consisted of ten short sentences. These remarks, which came to be known as the **Gettysburg Address,** paid homage to the men "who here gave their lives" at the nearby battlefield, so that the "nation might live." But in giving meaning to their sacrifice, Lincoln also made it clear what he thought the war was about. He did not mention the word *union.* Nor did he speak of the Constitution, which his political opponents invoked repeatedly in their attack on the war. Instead, Lincoln harked back to a moment before the Constitution. "Four score and seven years ago," he began, "our fathers brought forth on this continent a new nation, conceived in liberty, and dedicated to the proposition that all men are created equal." The nation was created in 1776, he reminded his listeners, with the Declaration of Independence. The founding ideals of that nation, which existed before individual states were formed, were freedom and equality. And the Civil War,

Lincoln insisted, would determine whether a nation founded on those ideals could survive.

Lincoln's Democratic critics ridiculed the "dishwatery utterances" of the Gettysburg Address and intensified their campaign to unseat him. Democrats ran on a slogan advocating "the Union as it was, the Constitution as it is," reminding voters that Lincoln's transformed war aims violated the Constitution (which protected slavery) and pursued a broader social agenda. The Democrats' problem, though, was that their slogan barely masked a split between those who favored a return to the pre-1861 union by suing for peace and those who advocated pressing on with the war but renouncing emancipation. They nominated General McClellan, who supported continuing the war, but they also produced a peace platform. Republicans battered the Democrats with the charge of favoring surrender, and the Union war fortunes had improved enough by the **election of 1864** to produce a wide margin of victory for Lincoln and increased Republican majorities in Congress. Lincoln's party was granted a new mandate to continue the war and pursue its national vision.

A NEW FEDERAL GOVERNMENT

Over the course of the long war, Republicans in Congress transformed a small, weak central government into a major force in the nation's economy. Part of the change lay in the war effort itself, which required mobilizing, supplying, and coordinating an enormous fighting force. But Congress also broadened the federal government's reach in other ways that had lasting impact beyond the war. With Southern Democrats out of the picture, Republicans created new revenue sources to finance the war, established welfare programs for veterans and their families, and stimulated economic growth through policies that favored business and encouraged western expansion (see Table 15.2).

Although many wartime laws would have far-reaching consequences, the most dramatic and controversial at the time was the **Conscription Act** (1863), which instituted a federal draft. Bypassing state governments, the law declared all unmarried white men between the ages of twenty and forty-five (and all married ones between twenty and thirty-five) eligible for forced military service. Congress passed the law in March 1863, at a low moment in the war, when the Union faced both a shortage of manpower and a crisis of morale. The Confederacy (despite its earlier espousal of states' rights) had instituted a national draft a year earlier, but in the North the Conscription Act was an unprecedented

TABLE 15.2 MAJOR FEDERAL LEGISLATION, 1862–1864

Legislation	What It Did	Significance or Postwar Consequences
Homestead Act (1862)	Entitled settlers (including immigrants who intended to become citizens) to 160 free acres of Western land after they had worked the plot for five years	Made it easier for small farmers to get land; over the next seventy years, more than four hundred thousand families acquired farms under this law; also encouraged westward migration and precipitated conflicts with Native Americans
Revenue Act (1862)	Established a national income tax, created the office of Commissioner of Internal Revenue, and outlined excise and sales taxes on dozens of items	Established both the IRS and the first progressive income tax in U.S. history
General Pension Act (1862)	Awarded pensions to disabled soldiers and their widows, children, and dependent sisters	Created a model for a social security system
Pacific Railroad Act (1862)	Awarded charters to the Union Pacific and Central Pacific Railroads to construct a transcontinental railroad, providing 100 million acres of public land for the project	Facilitated the growth of national markets and Western settlement (after completion of the railroad in 1869)
Morrill Land-Grant College Act (1862)	Provided federal support and public land to the states for establishing agricultural and mechanical arts (engineering) colleges	Facilitated the founding of research universities in every state, making higher education more accessible to a broader proportion of Americans
Act to Establish a Department of Agriculture (1862)	Established the Department of Agriculture, which was responsible for distributing information and seeds to farmers and collecting statistics on American agriculture	Paved the way for federal regulation of the crops that Americans grow and consume
Legal Tender Act (1862) and National Banking Act (1863)	Established a national currency and supported the market for federal government bonds	Created the United States's first uniform paper currency
Conscription Act (1863)	Instituted a federal draft for the first time in U.S. history	Formed the basis for drafts in future U.S. wars
Act to Amend the Laws Relating to the Post-Office Department (1863)	Made several changes to the postal service, including the introduction of free home delivery for forty-nine cities	Initiated the process of turning mail service into a standard feature of American residential life

exercise of federal power. Prominent Northern newspapers denounced the United States as "one grand military dictatorship." The most galling part of the law was a provision that allowed men to avoid military service by paying a three-hundred-dollar bounty or securing a substitute. This exemption had been intended to prevent a black market for substitutes, which would not benefit the government and would put the cost out of reach for most Americans. Indeed, when the substitution policy was rescinded in 1864, such a black market materialized, the cost of evading the draft skyrocketed,

and private companies exploited the situation. But the exemption had the effect of suggesting that military service was for poor men, not rich ones. The draft met resistance throughout the North, but the most deadly explosion of antidraft protest erupted in New York City, which for four hot days in July 1863 became engulfed in violence.

The **New York Draft Riots** were a mini Civil War deep in Union territory, in which Irish immigrants and other white working-class Democrats attacked the war effort and all symbols and instruments of Republican

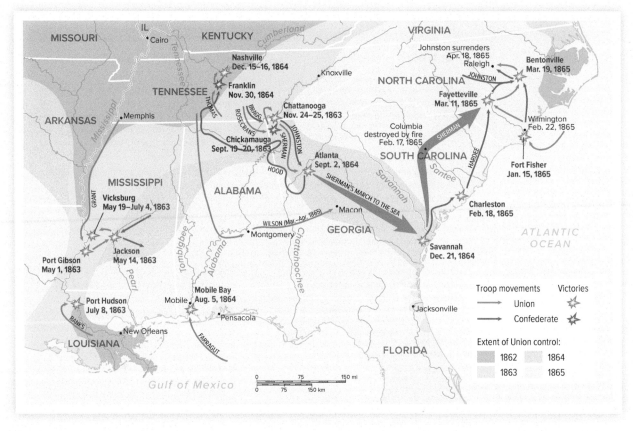

Map 15.4 The War in the West and Southeast, 1863–1865. While massive armies wore each other down in Virginia, Union forces prevailed decisively elsewhere, conquering major Southern cities.

Party rule. It also entailed a massive pogrom against the city's African American population. Rioters ransacked and torched the Colored Orphan Asylum, which housed over two hundred Black children. Black New Yorkers who could manage to leave town did so, and those who did not escape, including women, children, the elderly, and the infirm, risked being beaten, killed, or mutilated. For three days, chaos reigned in the city. Omnibuses and streetcars were idle, businesses were closed, stores were looted, and houses were burned. Companies protected their offices by stationing workers on rooftops with pots of boiling oil. Police were beaten to death. Rioters were bludgeoned with clubs, shot in the head, or tossed out of upper-story windows.

Finally, on the third day, Union troops arrived from Gettysburg, subdued the rioters, broke through the barricades, and occupied the city. The local government managed to quiet the draft resistance by paying substitution fees, and the federal draft proceeded. But over one

hundred people were killed in the riot—a small figure by the standards of the larger war but still the single bloodiest event in New York's history. Despite the urban insurrection, the federal government succeeded in administering a massive forced mobilization of men, providing a large enough army to win the war.

GRANT'S COMMAND

By the end of 1863, the Union had won another important victory in Tennessee, defeating Confederate forces at Chattanooga (see Map 15.4). Impressed with Grant's record, Lincoln brought him east to assume the position of general-in-chief. Grant's strategy was to capitalize on the North's manpower edge by pursuing all-out assaults, not releasing prisoners, and killing as many Confederate soldiers as possible. In May 1864, Grant engaged Lee's depleted forces in Virginia in two days of bloody fighting known as the **Battle of the Wilderness.** Grant then sought to move toward Richmond, but Lee cut him off at

Spotsylvania, where thousands more men fell. More carnage followed on June 1, at Cold Harbor. Grant was no closer to capturing the capital, but he also knew that a war of attrition benefited the side with a larger army.

While Grant and Lee battled in Virginia, Sherman moved from Chattanooga, Tennessee, into Georgia. On September 2, 1864, he captured Atlanta, one of the last industrial cities still under Confederate control. The taking of Atlanta was especially important, because it restored Northern confidence in Lincoln's conduct of the war and probably won him the election. Sherman's next move, however, was not against the remaining Confederate armies in the Southeast but against the Southeast itself (see Map 15.4). He moved his troops east toward Savannah, destroying bridges, factories, cotton gins, mills, railroad tracks, telegraph lines, and everything valuable that lay in his path.

The goal of Sherman's **March to the Sea,** as he put it, was to make the South "so sick of war that generations would pass away before they would again appeal to it." The march's devastating economic effects on the region's agricultural economy would persist for generations as well. More immediately, it crippled the Confederate war effort and crushed the morale of white Southerners. Thousands of enslaved Blacks, by contrast, greeted Sherman as a liberator and followed his army on their own march to freedom.

POLITICS AND ENTERTAINMENT

• **"Jeff in Petticoats: A Song for the Times."** One month after Lee's surrender, Union soldiers in rural Georgia finally captured Jefferson Davis, who had fled Richmond with his cabinet and remained a fugitive in the South. Because Davis reportedly disguised himself by wearing his wife's overcoat, Northerners ridiculed him as cowardly and emasculated. The six-verse song, published in 1865, became a hit in the North. • *Sheridan Libraries/ Levy/Gado/Getty Images*

SURRENDER AND ASSASSINATION

By the end of 1864, the Union troops had won another large battle in Nashville and Sherman's men had captured Savannah. Sherman then took the war back to South Carolina, where it had started almost four years earlier. As Columbia, the state capital, went up in a blaze, Confederate forces began evacuating the state, hoping to unite with other armies in North Carolina to stop Sherman. Meanwhile, Lee moved south from Petersburg, Virginia,

leaving the Confederate capital of Richmond exposed. Grant's armies took Richmond and attacked Lee's outnumbered forces as they retreated. On April 9, Lee surrendered to Grant at Appomattox Court House in Virginia, under generous terms that allowed Lee's men to keep their horses and effectively granted them immunity from treason charges. Over the next two weeks, other Confederate armies would abandon the cause as well. The Civil War was over (see Singular Lives: Jesse James, Confederate Guerrilla).

SINGULAR LIVES

Jesse James, Confederate Guerrilla

Few men rival Jesse James in the pantheon of American folk heroes. A Robin Hood figure who reputedly robbed banks to help the poor, the mythical Jesse James was a Wild West celebrity. The historical person behind the legend, however, came to his career of violence as a guerrilla fighting for slavery and the Confederacy in war-torn Missouri. Even by the standards of the Civil War, this was an especially dangerous place to be. Rent by bitter internal divisions and subject to martial law, Missouri lost a third of its population to death, exile, and displacement during the war. And for a teenaged guerrilla operating beyond the conflict's formal borders, the Civil War did not end in 1865.

Jesse James was born in 1847 in Clay County in northwestern Missouri to slaveholders with a small hemp farm. When war erupted, Jesse was barely a teenager, but his older brother Frank, aged eighteen, joined a local secessionist unit and fought against federal troops. After his unit was defeated in 1862, Frank James surrendered and returned home to Clay County, where he and his family lived resentfully under martial law and supported guerrilla attacks against their local adversaries. Frank spent much of the war in pro-Confederate Bushwacker gangs, and in 1864, his sixteen-year-old brother, Jesse, joined him. Their activities consisted mostly of killing farmers who supported the Union and fighting the Missouri State Militiamen who sought to enforce martial law. While serving under guerilla leader "Bloody Bill" Anderson, the James brothers looted the town of Centralia, Missouri, and shot unarmed Union soldiers and mutilated their corpses. After Anderson met his demise, Jesse James escaped to Texas with another Bushwacking gang.

In May 1865, a year after the war officially ended, James and his gang plundered their way back into Missouri, still fighting for the surrendered Confederate cause through an ongoing campaign of resistance and revenge against unionists. The campaign now included bank robbery. Archie Clement, the gang leader whom James had followed to Texas, became the prime suspect in an 1866 armed attack on a Republican-owned bank in Clay County, the first daytime bank robbery in U.S. history. James turned to robbing banks as well, targeting institutions owned by his political enemies and striking symbolic blows for the defeated causes of slavery and secession. For James, that war had begun a decade earlier in Kansas, when he was just a boy, and the accumulated grievances and vendettas assured that it would continue.

Where in the Archives?

Although James did not achieve fame or notoriety until his time as a bank robber, a number of sources record his activities during the Civil War. The following regional newspaper accounts of Bill Anderson's attack in Centralia, Missouri, indicate the gruesome horror of guerrilla warfare in Missouri. As was common at the time, newspapers from smaller cities frequently reprinted stories that appeared first in metropolitan centers better connected to telegraph networks. For this reason, news articles, unlike advertisements, did not vary much across a region. The Iowa and Indiana newspapers listed here, whose copies are digitized and available, represent typical Midwestern coverage of the violence.

The *Weekly Ottumwa Courier*, Ottumwa, Iowa (October 6, 1864), reprinted two articles from the *St. Louis Democrat*. The Iowa newspaper is available through Chronicling America, an archive of historic American newspapers maintained at the Library of Congress (https://chroniclingamerica.loc.gov/lccn/sn84027352/issues/).

The *Evansville Daily Journal*, Evansville, Indiana (October 12, 1864), drew upon a report from the *St. Joseph Morning*

Jesse James, Guerrilla Commander. James is remembered as a populist outlaw, but his depredations began as part of the Confederate war effort. *Library of Congress, Prints & Photographs Division [LC-USZ62-3855]*

Herald. The Indiana newspaper is also available through the Chronicling America collection at the Library of Congress (https://chroniclingamerica.loc.gov/lccn/sn86059181/issues/).

Assignment

Locate the accounts of the violence in Centralia in the two newspapers. This may take some effort: By modern standards, newspapers from this period lack prominent headlines or clearly defined sections. Typically, the biggest news stories would appear on the second page of a four-page issue, which is where both articles in the Iowa newspaper can be found. Less commonly, a story of this nature might make the front page, as in the Indiana case. As you read the accounts, consider whether Bill Anderson's raid should be considered part of the Civil War or marginal to it. Then complete one of the following lists:

1. List three pieces of evidence that Anderson and his gang saw the raid as a battle in the larger war between the Union and the Confederacy.

2. List three pieces of evidence that Anderson and his gang saw themselves as defending personal honor, expressing a personal vendetta, or engaging in acts of looting or plunder.

For African Americans in the South, the Confederacy's surrender confirmed what had been happening throughout the war. Slavery had been undermined steadily, first by the arrival of the Union forces, then by the actions of the enslaved, and eventually by the policies of the federal government. On every plantation in the South, this process played out differently. Many enslaved people left their homes, whereas others stayed, concealing their plans as they awaited the resolution of the conflict. Some took the opportunity to renegotiate the terms of their labor, and others sought to even old scores. In one dramatic scene in Virginia in 1864, three formerly enslaved people under the protection of Union general Edward Wild took turns whipping a slaveholder who had abused them. In different ways, most of the 4 million men, women, and children who had been held as property at the start of the war now enjoyed some measure of freedom or relief. Legally, enslaved people in the loyal border states had not been emancipated, but after the election of 1864, the enhanced Republican majority in Congress was able to pass a constitutional amendment to free them as well. On January 31, 1865, the **Thirteenth Amendment,** which banned slavery except as punishment for crime, was submitted to the states for ratification (see Chapter 16).

With the Confederate surrender and the abolition of slavery imminent, Lincoln now faced the challenges of reintegrating the rebellious states into what had become a very different nation. Without abandoning the position that secession was illegal and treasonous, he needed to devise a plan for granting amnesty to the millions who had supported the rebellion and the hundreds of thousands who had taken up arms against the United States. On April 14, Good Friday, Lincoln took time away from this project to attend a play at Ford's Theatre in Washington, D.C. During the play, an actor named John Wilkes Booth sneaked into Lincoln's box and shot him in the head. By the next morning, the president of the United States was dead.

Lincoln, long a controversial political figure, became an instant martyr throughout the North. His death seemed to stand in some way for all the suffering the nation had undergone, and perhaps to atone for all the violence it had perpetrated. In words that recalled Lincoln's own speech at Gettysburg but also compared his death to that of Christ, a Rhode Island minister captured a common theme in Northern eulogies: "One man has died for the people, in order that the whole nation might not perish."

CONCLUSION

By 1865, approximately 2.5 percent of the nation's population had been killed in the war (an equivalent loss today would exceed 7 million lives). In the South, where about one in five white men of military age perished, whole cities had been leveled. Communities in both the North and the South were awash in prosthetic limbs and covered in mourning crepe. The amount of money expended by the North alone in waging this war would have been enough to purchase every enslaved person in the South in 1861, set up each emancipated family with 40 acres and a mule, and compensate them for years of back wages. But, of course, slaveholders in 1861 were not interested in selling, and few white Americans, Northern or Southern, were willing to share the continent (let alone their own land) with 4 million free people of color. Few white Americans were interested in emancipation at all in 1861. But four years later, everything changed. What this change meant for national politics, the economy, and the lives of 4 million freed people remained profoundly uncertain.

STUDY TERMS

bread riots	Copperheads
Confederate States of America	military occupation
	guerrilla warfare
states' rights	Bushwhackers
Crittenden Compromise	Andersonville prison
Fort Sumter	United States Sanitary Commission
First Battle of Bull Run	
Army of the Potomac	Civil War photographs
Battle of Antietam	siege of Vicksburg
Battle of Shiloh	Battle of Gettysburg
naval blockade	Gettysburg Address
contrabands	election of 1864
Confiscation Act	Conscription Act
Second Confiscation Act	New York Draft Riots
Emancipation Proclamation	Battle of the Wilderness
Colored Troops	March to the Sea
Fort Pillow Massacre	Thirteenth Amendment

FURTHER READING

A database of additional full-text readings is available through Power of Process for Primary Sources in Connect.

Stephen Ash, *When the Yankees Came* (1995), covers life in the occupied South during the war.

Alice Fahs, *Imagined Civil War* (2003), focuses on the war as reflected in the popular literature of the period.

Brian P. Luskey, *Men Is Cheap* (2020), explores the labor market that shadowed Union soldier recruitment.

Stephanie McCurry, *Confederate Reckoning* (2010), shows the rising political agency of white women and enslaved African Americans during the war.

James McPherson, *Battle Cry of Freedom* (1988), remains the most influential and comprehensive narrative of the causes, course, and consequences of the war.

Chandra Manning, *What This Cruel War Was Over* (2007), examines soldiers' correspondence to explore their views toward slavery, secession, and the meaning of the conflict.

Heather Cox Richardson, *The Greatest Nation of the Earth* (1997), traces how the wartime Congress transformed the federal government and shaped the postwar nation.

Yael Sternhell, *Routes of War* (2012), places the dramatic movements of soldiers, deserters, refugees, and escapees from slavery at the center of the South's wartime experience.

T. J. Stiles, *Jesse James* (2002), presents the life of the famous Missouri bandit in the context of local guerrilla fighting and the Confederate cause.

David Williams, *I Freed Myself* (2014), argues that the enslaved initiated their own emancipation during the Civil War.

Garry Wills, *Lincoln at Gettysburg* (1992), interprets Lincoln's speech as a foundational moment in the remaking of the United States.

16 | SOUTHERN RECONSTRUCTION

Chapter Questions

1. What role did newly emancipated people play in setting the terms for political change in the South?

2. How did presidential and congressional Reconstruction plans differ?

3. In what ways did the new state governments in the South both fulfill and disappoint freed people's political aspirations?

4. Why did Reconstruction ultimately fail to enforce racial equality in the South?

A New South. Institutions like Richmond's First African Church helped build communities of freed people and encouraged optimism about the possibilities of a free and inclusive Southern society. *Interim Archives/Getty Images*

In May 1865, just a month after the Confederate surrender, rumors about the future of the South spread quickly along the Cotton Belt. Beginning on the Carolina coast, those recently freed whispered of a coming "Christmas Jubilee" in which the federal government would confiscate the slaveholders' plantations, divide them into small farms, and "give the land to the colored people." The rumor traveled quickly along the oral "grapevine telegraph" that had served as an informal communication network among enslaved people. Meanwhile, a different rumor spread among the South's white communities. Many white Southerners predicted that around Christmastime, armed Black mobs would seize the old plantations in a "Jubilee Insurrection."

As it turned out, neither jubilee came to pass. Although the federal government distributed some land to freed people, it did not embark on a large-scale confiscation of the plantations. Nor did the freed people rise up and take white people's property by force. But the rumors were opening shots in a struggle to determine how the South's devastated economy, culture, and political system would be reconstructed.

Time Line

1862

Wartime Reconstruction begins

1863

President Abraham Lincoln issues Emancipation Proclamation and Ten Percent Plan

1865

Congress sends Thirteenth Amendment to the states
Freed people celebrate emancipation in jubilee parades
Congress establishes Freedmen's Bureau
Lincoln is assassinated and Andrew Johnson becomes president
Presidential Reconstruction begins

1866

Congress passes Civil Rights Act
Congress sends Fourteenth Amendment to the states

1867

Congressional Reconstruction begins
U.S. Army undertakes largest voter registration drive in American history
Southerners elect racially inclusive governments

1868

House of Representatives impeaches Johnson
Ku Klux Klan begins night raids

1871

Jubilee Singers revive slave spirituals to great acclaim

1872

Official Memorial Day celebrations cease to mention slavery

1873

Supreme Court limits reach of the Fourteenth Amendment in *Slaughterhouse Cases*
African Americans massacred at Colfax County Courthouse
Ex-Confederate and Union soldiers commemorate the war together

1874

White militias mobilize against Black voters

1875

Congress passes Civil Rights Act

1876

Presidential election between Rutherford B. Hayes and Samuel Tilden leads to a deadlock

1877

Political bargain results in Hayes's presidency
U.S. Army stands down in the South
Last three Southern Republican governments fall

1878

Posse Comitatus Act prohibits the army from law enforcement

1883

Supreme Court rules Civil Rights Act of 1875 unconstitutional

For the freed people, the Civil War had been a war against slavery. If their hard-won freedom was to be meaningful, the federal government would have to give them access to the land of those who had kept them in bondage. With their own farms, freed people could reunite families, lead independent lives, and build strong communities. Ex-slaveholders sensed that their position was precarious. Rumors of a Christmas insurrection reinforced a racist solidarity against Black efforts to gain equality.

Freed people's efforts to define and claim their freedom, and former slaveholders' opposition to these efforts, lie at the heart of the era of Reconstruction (1862–1883). The term *Reconstruction* refers both to federal policies to reintegrate the states that had seceded and to the political, cultural, and economic revolution that took place in the South during these years. Reconstruction unfolded in three distinct phases. In the first, President Lincoln and Congress began debating how to bring the South back into the Union—well before the Northern victory had been declared. With the war won, Reconstruction entered its second phase, in which President Andrew Johnson suspended land distribution and former slaveholders tried to return African Americans to plantation labor. The final, dramatic phase began in 1866, when Republicans in Congress rejected Johnson's approach and set the South on the path to building a racially inclusive democracy. Vibrant Black communities emerged, built on the pillars of churches and schools, and Black men participated actively in all levels of government.

The South's new democracy soon came under attack. Every Reconstruction government had fallen by 1877, and by 1883 the Supreme Court had limited the scope of civil rights legislation. The nation's remarkable democratic experiment had all but collapsed. But African Americans' aspiration to landownership, autonomy, and full citizenship endured.

WARTIME RECONSTRUCTION

In 1862, just a year into the Civil War, President Lincoln and congressional leaders spoke of the need for a postwar plan of what they called "national reconstruction." Initially, **Reconstruction** simply referred to the legal terms and conditions under which the Confederate states would be readmitted to the union once they had surrendered. But as enslaved African Americans fled bondage and streamed across Union lines (see Chapter 15), they gradually turned slavery into a core issue of the war. Over the two and a half years following Lincoln's Emancipation Proclamation in January 1863, the president and Congress debated how to deal with the old Southern ruling class and ensure the freedom of formerly enslaved people.

LINCOLN'S TEN PERCENT PLAN

The Union's scorched-earth warfare pounded Southern cities and towns and tore up miles of railroads and highways. Farmland lay charred, and both sides stripped forests for fuel and materiel. After the war turned decisively in the Union's favor late in 1863, the need to formulate a thorough plan of reconstruction became urgent.

Lincoln and congressional lawmakers found no clear guidance in the federal Constitution for how to reclaim or readmit seceding states following a civil war or how to rebuild the economies, political institutions, and social fabric of the rebel states. The Constitution also gave no indication of whether the authority to reconstruct the union and the South lay primarily with Congress or with the president.

As Union lawmakers and leaders grappled with these thorny constitutional questions, they articulated two quite different conceptions of Reconstruction. In what came to be called the **Ten Percent Plan** (officially titled the "Proclamation of Amnesty and Reconstruction"), Lincoln argued that the authority to reintegrate the South into the union lay with the president and that harsh punishment was neither justified nor legal. The Confederate states might claim they had legally seceded from the union, Lincoln asserted, but in the eyes of the law they had not. Consequently, Southern state governments remained legitimate. Though he would later toughen his position, in 1863 Lincoln believed that taking a heavy hand against the South would prove counterproductive. The best way to help the South recover and to reunite the nation was to punish only the small minority of men who had led the Confederacy and welcome Southern lawmakers back into Congress.

Lincoln presented his plan in December 1863. Under this proposal, the rebel states would have to accept the end of slavery, and at least 10 percent of the number of voters in 1860 would have to swear loyalty to the union. Leaders of the Confederacy would not be allowed to hold office, but most other white Southern men would receive full amnesty and regain their political rights.

EARLY CONGRESSIONAL INITIATIVES

To implement his plan, Lincoln needed the consent of Congress, which had sole constitutional authority to seat (or reject) members of the House of Representatives and Senate. Northern Democrats and

Masters of Their Destiny. People fled slavery and poured across Union lines during the war. Accepting the end of the slave regime became the supreme condition for the Confederate states' readmission to the union. *Bettmann/Getty Images*

some conservative Republicans supported Lincoln's initiative. But it failed to impress moderate Republicans, and it bitterly disappointed a vocal minority known as the **Radical Republicans.** This congressional faction, made up largely of abolitionists, believed that the new rights of freed people might be imperiled if the process were hurried and that Southern elites might try to reintroduce slavery. Leading Radical Thaddeus Stevens also claimed that contrary to Lincoln's view that secession never occurred, the Confederates *had* left the union and had done so illegally. They could rejoin the union only by being readmitted as new states, Stevens concluded, something only Congress had the authority to do.

With the support of a number of moderates, Radical Republicans presented the **Wade-Davis Bill** of 1864 in an effort to slow readmission and assert congressional control over Reconstruction. Once the majority of a Southern state's voters pledged allegiance to the union, the bill provided for the president to appoint a governor and direct him to call a state election for a convention. The convention would craft a fresh state constitution banning slavery and permanently disenfranchising Confederate leaders. The only men who could participate in the convention were those who swore an oath they had not taken up arms against the federal government. Because so many white men had served in the Confederate military, this would have disqualified much of the prewar Southern electorate.

Lincoln considered the Wade-Davis bill a direct challenge to his authority and refused to sign it. Enraged, Radical Republicans and a growing cadre of moderates, in turn, enacted bold new laws aimed at ensuring emancipation. In January 1865, Congress passed the **Thirteenth Amendment** to the U.S. Constitution, which prohibited slavery and involuntary servitude in all forms except as punishment for crime. (This exemption allowed Northern states to continue their long-standing practice of putting prisoners to forced labor.) The Emancipation Proclamation had abolished slavery only in the rebellious states (not in loyal slave states) and as a wartime measure. The amendment, which Lincoln supported vigorously, would bring an end to legalized slavery in the United States.

Two months later, Congress established the Bureau of Refugees, Freedmen, and Abandoned Lands (or the **Freedmen's Bureau**) and charged it with overseeing Southern Reconstruction. Under the directorship of General Oliver O. Howard of the U.S. Army, the Bureau set about feeding millions of formerly enslaved people and poor white Southerners who faced starvation in the winter of 1865. These initiatives were reinforced on the ground when General Sherman issued Special Field Order No. 15, ordering the distribution of 40-acre sections of land to formerly enslaved people in the Union-occupied Sea Islands and Carolina Lowcountry. Under this plan, some forty thousand freed people settled on about 400,000 acres of land. Observing the mounting support in Congress for a more thorough Reconstruction of the South, Lincoln pragmatically endorsed certain demands of the Radicals—including giving propertied Black men the vote.

LINCOLN'S ASSASSINATION AND NORTHERN SENTIMENT

By April 9, 1865, the day that General Lee surrendered the Northern Department of the Confederate Army at Appomattox, Lincoln and Congress had agreed that the supreme precondition for the South's readmission into the union would be acceptance of emancipation. The South would be reconstructed and readmitted only as a free society. Beyond that certainty, however, a great deal of doubt remained about what course reunion might take.

John Wilkes Booth's shooting of Lincoln, less than a week after Lee's surrender (see Chapter 15), altered the political equation. When Lincoln died the following morning, waves of grief and fear swept across Northern cities and towns. Although Booth and his associates had acted alone, rumors spread that they had been part of a conspiracy to overthrow the federal government, halt the South's surrender, and reignite the war. Booth was indeed a Confederate sympathizer, but speculation about a Confederate plot had no basis in fact. Still, the rumors reinforced Northern antipathy toward the South's ruling class.

As public anxiety intensified, Lincoln's coffin was hoisted onto a funeral train. The locomotive embarked on a solemn, 1,700-mile procession from the capital through Philadelphia, New York, Buffalo, and Chicago before carrying Lincoln to his final resting place in Springfield, Illinois. Seven million mourners lined the route, and millions more saw photographs of the procession in the press. As the train wound its way west, public opinion swung decisively behind the Radical Republicans and their call for a thorough and exacting reconstruction of the South.

War and Disability. *Bowman, W. E. (William Emory/Library Of Congress)*

BEHIND THE IMAGE

John W. January, a Union army soldier from Illinois, ordered this cabinet card, a new, larger type of carte de visite (see Chapter 13) that was becoming popular in the years after the Civil War. Cabinet cards featured photographs of the individuals or companies who had commissioned them mounted onto thick card stock measuring 6.5 × 4.25 inches, and some included text on the reverse. January had lost his feet due to scurvy and gangrene while imprisoned in the South. Even before this card appeared, January had become a symbol of the suffering of Union soldiers in the mass media. In its June 17, 1865, issue, *Harper's Weekly* printed an article titled "Rebel Cruelties" that featured a drawing of January, lying emaciated and footless in a hospital bed.

WITHIN THE IMAGE

January displays ① both his amputated and prosthetic limbs, placing them side by side to expose the violence of his wartime wound. ② Though his dress and elegant furniture mark him as genteel, the prominent placement of the prosthetics and stumps announces his primary identity as a wounded warrior. ③ January wears what appears to be a medal of the Grand Army of the Republic, a fraternal organization of Northern veterans, though such cabinet cards were popular among Confederate amputees as well. ④ What made this card distinctive was the "Autobiography" on the other side, which provides a detail not implied by the photograph. In the text, January claims to have amputated his own feet, giving his common disability a special, heroic dimension.

BEYOND THE IMAGE

January's cabinet card was part of a larger campaign to publicize the conditions experienced by Union prisoners of war. Lecturing to Northern audiences (to whom these cards were sold), he re-enacted his self-amputation by detaching his prosthetics and exhibiting the pocketknife he had used to perform the surgery. January's account was disputed by a fellow soldier, who claimed to have performed the amputation and even published an alleged confession from January that he had made up the story to profit from lecturing. Quite apart from the controversy, the spectacle of lost limbs was a prominent part of public life in the postwar years. Injured and disabled men filled American towns and cities, prompting several municipalities to enact "unsightly beggar ordinances," prohibiting the exhibition of maimed or unsightly bodies in public space.

CLAIMING THE FUTURE

Northerners were hardly the only Americans to face uncertainty in the spring of 1865. In the South, the war had destroyed the legal right to buy, sell, and own human beings. But there was no consensus as to what freedom would mean in practice. In the first few years after the war, freed people, white farmers, planters, and the Freedmen's Bureau all explored the meaning of emancipation. They did so not only in political speeches and in the press but also in their everyday actions, parades, songs, and dress, as well as in the stories they told about slavery and the war that had led to its destruction.

FREED PEOPLE CLAIM THEIR FREEDOM

As it ended slavery, the Civil War wreaked havoc in the lives of 4 million people previously enslaved in the South.

> DISEASE AND EPIDEMIC
>
> • Approximately half a million of them escaped during the course of the conflict, and they were especially vulnerable to diseases that came with the mass mobilization of soldiers and refugees. Tens of thousands of formerly enslaved people died in a smallpox epidemic that erupted in Washington, D.C., in 1862 and spread to the Upper South over the next two years. • Those who remained on plantations during

the war suffered as well. Facing poverty, physical hardship, and a major medical crisis, freed people assumed the historic task of claiming their newfound freedom, performing hundreds of small acts that had been forbidden to them when enslaved. Freed people laid down tools, walked off plantations, and crisscrossed the countryside, looking for loved ones who had been sold and scattered under slavery. They gathered in abandoned halls, railroad cars, barns, cabins, and makeshift structures. It was during these early days of freedom that the rumors of land distribution circulated among Blacks in the rural South.

In cities, Black Southerners joyously celebrated their freedom with an important ritual from which they had been previously barred—the street procession (see Hot Commodities: Dressing for Freedom). In Charleston, Black clergy and the Colored Men's Twenty-First Regiment led a parade of ten thousand Black men, women, and children, lifting banners that proclaimed freedom and asserted the rights of Black men to vote. A flotilla carrying tableaux of the Old South, complete with auction block and actors playing the roles of enslaved people and an auctioneer, confronted white onlookers with the horror of their supposedly benign institution.

The prominence of uniformed Black soldiers in these parades asserted a claim to full citizenship—and signaled to white Southerners that Black communities were prepared to protect themselves by force if necessary.

Through the remainder of 1865, Blacks in the South exercised their new freedoms and began building their future as independent citizens. Formerly enslaved people overcame hunger, bombed-out roads, and a chronic shortage of money and credit to reconstitute their families, establish rudimentary schools, and found churches. Uncertain whether federal Reconstruction policy would protect them from white militias, freed men organized their own militias and drilled with the discipline many had learned in the Union army.

Above all, freed people made it clear that they no longer wanted to grow cotton for those who had kept them in bondage, not even for wages. Instead, they took steps to acquire small farms on which they could raise a few head of livestock and grow a variety of produce. Those who had escaped to the North during the war returned home with the hope of claiming the soil they and their forebears had tilled for generations. "Our wives, our children, our husbands has been sold over and over again to purchase the lands we now locates upon," declared one freed man. "[F]or that reason we have a divine right to the land."

Many pressed slaveholders for whom they had labored for the tools, stock, seed, and capital needed to fence and transform the war-ravaged land into working farms. Some even claimed back pay, although it is unlikely that they expected to receive it. As Jourdon Anderson, a man who had moved to Ohio, put the point to his former enslaver, "I served you faithfully for thirty-two years, and Mandy twenty years. At $25 a month for me, and $2 a week for Mandy, our earnings would amount to $11,680. . . . Please send the money by Adams Express."

For many people previously enslaved, freedom meant that families could now live together without fear of being separated by a sale, and Black men could assume their place at the head of the household. Like white fathers and husbands, the male head of house would assume the rights to discipline his children and wife and to claim responsibility for the household as breadwinner and decision maker.

In 1865, a small but growing number of freed people began to argue that Black heads of household should have the right to vote and hold public office. "Slavery is not abolished until the black man has the ballot," argued Frederick Douglass. For many Black Southerners, the ballot was both the supreme symbol of freedom and the

HOT COMMODITIES
Dressing for Freedom: Silks and Satins

On a spring day in 1865, a joyous crowd of Black people, clad in what one observer described as brilliant "silks and satins of all the colors of the rainbow," gathered on a main thoroughfare in Charleston, South Carolina. Just hours before, the revelers had been informed of their emancipation from slavery. They shed their work clothes, helped themselves to the fine suits and dresses of their former slaveholders, and headed into town to celebrate their freedom. Across the South, many formerly enslaved people marked emancipation in much the same way.

Going out publicly in colorful, fancy clothing was one particularly vivid means by which freed people staked a claim to full membership in American society. Under slavery, most had been compelled to wear relatively plain, white or undyed cotton garments suited to hard labor in the fields; their simple clothes also signaled to everybody that the wearer was enslaved (rather than a free Black person). Once free, they dressed up brightly and promenaded in town squares to exhibit their liberty—including the freedom to wear the clothing they pleased.

Dress remained an important form of self-expression and marker of identity during and after Reconstruction. Dressing stylishly also signaled a desire to participate as equals in consumer culture. Once stores reopened and trade with the North resumed, Southern Black women purchased fine textiles, buttons, and lace to sew into stylish dresses, bonnets, and blouses. Urban Black women sometimes modeled their clothing on the latest New York fashions, which they had seen in the new mass-circulation national magazines of the era. But many others incorporated fine materials into their own distinctive designs, blending expensive fabrics with

more affordable ones (including textiles and trim salvaged from upholstery and other household sources). Both poor and middling Black women dressed in "ladylike" ways that emphasized their femininity and respectability and asserted equality with whites. Parasols and crepe veils of the sort that adorned fashionable whites became popular accessories. Regardless of their trade or occupation, Black men wore topcoats and hats in public, particularly to church on Sundays. And men and women alike dressed to attend the theater and other public entertainments alongside whites.

Such stylish dressing frequently offended whites, who generally thought of African Americans as social inferiors whose attire should reflect their supposedly humble station in life. Some white men went so far as to violently cut new clothes off the backs of freed people, on the grounds that they were being "uppity"— aspiring to a social status above that of laborer. Other whites, who failed to see the historical significance of the colorful clothing, were appalled by the bright, new fashions. As Belle Kearney, the daughter of a former slaveholder put it, Black women had "bought brilliant-hued stuffs and had them made with the most bizarre effects." And some could not understand why even the poorest African Americans spent their precious wages on fashion. Why must Black people have "parasols when they ha'n't got no shoes?" chastised a Charleston proprietor. "Because,

Free Expression. Black Americans celebrated their freedom not only in formal speeches about slavery but also in music, dress, and their use of public space. This woman, in fashionable and tailored attire, exudes the self-assurance and pride that many African Americans expressed during Reconstruction—and many white people found threatening. *Smith Collection/Gado/Getty Images*

although we are poor, we are free," might have come the answer.

Think About It

1. Why might recently emancipated African Americans have valued clothing over other kinds of consumer goods, such as carpets, dishes, and pianos?

2. Why were many whites offended by the flashy outfits of freed people?

practical means by which African Americans would be able to protect their newfound rights.

RURAL WORLDS LOST: WHITE FARMERS

The war had been a calamity for the South's white yeomen farmers and their way of life. Many yeomen, especially in the Appalachian region, had opposed secession. But the Confederate government had conscripted vast numbers of them, and they had borne the brunt of the fatalities. As the war escalated and the Confederacy requisitioned their mules, crops, and supplies, many farming families were left all but destitute. "We are in this county as poor as people ever gets to be to live," lamented one Alabama farmer. For many of these families, a return to prewar farm life was all but impossible.

Many Southern farmers returned home in 1865 embittered with the planter class that had led them to war. Much like the freed people, they resisted having to go to work for planters as subordinated wage laborers producing food and raw materials for distant markets. Instead, their goal was to rebuild their own small farms, growing crops and raising livestock for themselves and the local marketplace. Many joined the local **Union Leagues,** the Southern chapters of the Northern Republican clubs that had been founded during the war in support of Lincoln's policies. These leagues worked hard to limit the immense political and social power of the planter elite. Some also joined the freed people in calling for a general distribution of the slaveholders' plantations. "We should tuk the land," wrote one white farmer, "[and] split it, and gin part to the [freed people] and part to me and t'other Union fellers."

PLANTERS AND POWER

Planters, the wealthy slaveholding class that had dominated Southern politics and society before the war, sought full restoration of their power, status, and way of life in the aftermath of the conflict. They had convinced themselves that slavery was a benevolent and Christian institution and that those they held in bondage had been quite content. Many were therefore shocked by the great joy of enslaved people in being freed. Even more perplexing was their refusal to continue working for them, even for wages. On one plantation in South Carolina, where freed people had divided the plantation into small farms for themselves, the former slaveholder was outraged by what he called their "recklessness and ingratitude." Many former slaveholding men and women misread the desire of freed people to work for themselves as indolence. "I don't think one does a really honest full day's work," wrote the

daughter of a wealthy Georgia planter. "They are affectionate and often trustworthy and honest, but so hopelessly lazy as to be almost worthless as laborers." Planters' most immediate desire was to force their formerly enslaved laborers back to work on their great cotton, sugar, rice, and tobacco plantations. They also wanted to ensure that Reconstruction did not destroy their political and economic power.

THE FREEDMEN'S BUREAU

As the freed people, yeomanry, and planters hashed out their visions of a new South in 1865, the Freedmen's Bureau extended the federal presence on the frontlines of Southern Reconstruction. The Bureau's tasks were complex and often contradictory. In a world turned upside down, it had to get food to millions of freed people and poor white Southerners, help refugees relocate their families, and secure civil peace. The Bureau also needed a way to identify and track the population it was assisting. This enormous project entailed persuading several million formerly enslaved people to adopt—and keep—a permanent family name and then register as many of the names as possible. In its first year, the Bureau was expected to do all this on an initial shoestring budget of just twenty-seven thousand dollars and with a staff of only a few hundred (see How Much Is That? Relief for Freed People).

Above all, the Bureau's mandate was to prepare those previously enslaved for a peaceful transition to freedom. Many Bureau agents drew on the abolitionist belief that a free society was one in which people voluntarily entered into contracts that imposed certain duties and obligations in return for certain benefits. Labor and marriage contracts were the focus of their efforts. Bureau officials shared the freed people's belief that freedom was connected with landownership, however. By November 1865, the Bureau had confiscated 850,000 acres of land and was ready to rent it out (and eventually sell it) to the freed people in 40-acre lots. The Bureau awaited orders from the federal government.

How Much Is That?

Relief for Freed People

In today's dollars, the value of the Freedmen's Bureau's budget of twenty-seven thousand dollars would be four hundred forty-five thousand dollars—a drop in the bucket compared with the magnitude of the South's devastation.

PATHS TOWARD RECONSTRUCTION

Divisions between congressional and presidential visions for bringing the South back into the union widened in the wake of Lincoln's assassination. Vice President Andrew Johnson, who succeeded to the presidency, was a yeoman farmer and unionist from the former slave state of Tennessee. A self-made man who loathed aristocracy, his political priority had been the permanent disempowerment of the Southern planter elite. "Damn the Negroes," he had declared during the war. "I am fighting those traitous aristocrats, their masters." But as it became clear that Black Southerners wanted full legal equality, Johnson reversed course and advocated restoration of the planters as the South's political leaders. This provoked outrage in Congress, and lawmakers eventually wrested control of Reconstruction from Johnson and set the South on the road to becoming the Western world's first truly racially inclusive democracy.

ANDREW JOHNSON AND PRESIDENTIAL RECONSTRUCTION

Early in his term, Johnson supported the abolition of slavery by requiring Southern states to ratify the Thirteenth Amendment as a condition for re-entry into the union. He did so not because he deemed slavery immoral but because it gave the planter class enormous power in Southern society and in the republic as a whole. On the question of whether Black people should have full political and civil rights, Johnson was blunt: "White men alone," he declared, "must manage the South."

Because Congress remained in recess for much of 1865, from April until December, Johnson moved forward with Reconstruction without congressional oversight. He appointed provisional governors in each of the Southern states and directed them to call constitutional conventions. In a series of executive orders, he mandated that white men could regain their property rights and vote for delegates to their states' conventions by taking an oath of loyalty to the United States. However, he disqualified Confederate leaders and those who owned property worth more than twenty thousand dollars. He also instructed state conventions to repudiate the debts of the Confederacy, a move that hurt planters who had invested their fortunes in war bonds. Although not as sweeping as the Radical Republicans' plan, Johnson's early initiatives seemed an important step toward dislodging the planter class from power.

Once it became evident by midsummer that the planters would not surrender their land and power without a fight, Johnson abandoned course. Rather than mobilizing a coalition of freed people, yeomen, and Republicans to take them on, he chose to incorporate the powerful ex-slaveholders into Reconstruction. He pardoned thousands of wealthy men disqualified under his original plan. He also authorized provisional governors to raise militias, thereby allowing planters to revive the old slave patrols and rearm ex-soldiers. Most critically, Johnson blocked the confiscation and division of plantations. He ordered that all confiscated land be returned to the planters.

● As Christmas approached and rumors of a massive transfer of land to the freed people circulated along the Cotton Belt, Johnson ordered the Freedmen's Bureau to inform the freed people that no large-scale redistribution would be forthcoming. ● The Bureau now urged freed people to sign labor contracts with the planters and return to plantation labor. "You must labor for what you get like other people," the officials warned. Those who helped themselves to planters' property could expect to be "punished with utmost severity." This reversal in federal policy resulted in massive displacements of African Americans. Some twenty thousand lost land in southeastern Virginia alone.

As a final concession, Johnson agreed to the planters' request that Union troops be gradually withdrawn from the South. Proof that Presidential Reconstruction had allowed the old slaveholding class to return to power came in the congressional elections of 1865. Every Southern state refused African Americans the right to vote. White Southerners elected twenty-four ex-Confederate lawmakers, state officers, and military commanders. Georgia voted the former vice president of the Confederacy, Alexander Stephens, into the U.S. Senate.

MEDIA AND INFORMATION

BLACK CODES

Under presidential Reconstruction policies, ex-slaveholders and Confederate leaders were also elected to state legislatures. With the exception of North Carolina, all the states of the former Confederacy enacted a set of laws known as the **Black Codes.** These laws gave Black Southerners the right to make contracts and use the courts, but they also attempted to turn the freed people into a compliant labor force for the planters. The codes denied freed people their own farms, prohibited them from hunting and fishing for food, and refused them access to money and credit (see Interpreting the Sources: Mississippi's Black Code, 1865). Some laws compelled all Black

INTERPRETING THE SOURCES

Mississippi's Black Code, 1865

Though they varied from state to state, planter-dominated governments throughout most of the South passed restrictive laws, called Black Codes, designed to re-establish their authority in the aftermath of the legal emancipation of people from slavery. Following is an example from Mississippi.

"Free to Work." Under the Black Codes, planter-dominated legislatures tried to force freed people, including children, to enter into year-long labor contracts for work they once performed when enslaved. *Papers, 1865, Accession #6060, University of Virginia Library, Charlottesville, VA.*

1. Civil Rights of Freedmen In Mississippi

Sec.1. *Be it enacted* . . . That all freedmen, free negroes, and mulattoes may sue and be sued, implead and be impleaded, in all the courts of law and equity of this State, and may acquire personal property, and choses in action, by descent or purchase, and may dispose of the same in the same manner and to the same extent that white persons may: *Provided,* That the provisions of this section shall not be so construed as to allow any freedman, free negro, or mulatto to rent or lease any lands or tenements except in incorporated cities or towns, in which places the corporate authorities shall control the same. . . .

2. Mississippi Vagrant Law

Sec. 1. *Be it enacted, etc.* . . . That all rogues and vagabonds, idle and dissipated persons, beggars, jugglers, or persons practicing unlawful games or plays, runaways, common drunkards, common night-walkers, pilferers, lewd, wanton, or lascivious persons, in speech or behavior, common railers and brawlers, persons who neglect their calling or employment, misspend what they earn, or do not provide for the support of themselves or their families, or dependents, and all other idle and disorderly persons, including all who neglect all lawful business, habitually misspend their time by frequenting houses of ill-fame, gaming-houses, or tippling shops, shall be deemed and considered vagrants . . . and upon conviction thereof shall be fined not exceeding one hundred dollars, with all accruing costs, and be imprisoned at the discretion of the court, not exceeding ten days.

Sec. 2. . . . All freedmen, free negroes and mulattoes in this State, over the age of eighteen years, found on the second Monday in January, 1866, or thereafter, with no lawful employment or business, or found unlawfully assembling themselves together, either in the day or night time, and all white persons so assembling themselves with freedmen, free negroes or mulattoes, or usually associating with freedmen, free negroes or mulattoes, on terms of equality, or living in adultery or fornication with a freed woman, free negro or mulatto, shall be deemed vagrants, and on conviction thereof shall be fined in a sum not exceeding, in the case of a freedman, free negro or mulatto, fifty dollars, and a white man two hundred dollars, and imprisoned at the discretion of the court, the free negro not exceeding ten days, and the white man not exceeding six months. . . .

3. Penal Laws of Mississippi

Sec. 1. *Be it enacted* . . . That no freedman, free negro or mulatto, not in the military service of the United States government, and not licensed so to do by the board of police of his or her county, shall keep or carry fire-arms of any kind, or any ammunition, dirk or bowie knife, and on conviction thereof in the county court shall be punished by fine, not exceeding ten dollars, and pay the costs of such proceedings, and all such arms or ammunition shall be forfeited to the informer; and it shall be the duty of every civil and military officer to arrest any freedman, free negro, or mulatto found with any such arms or ammunition, and cause him or her to be committed to trial in default of bail.

Source: Mississippi Slave Code, 1848, Hutchinson, Code of Mississippi, 512-17; 16.8; 16.9: §1, Vagrancy Act of Mississippi, 1865; Kermit L. Hall, Paul Finkelman, and James W. Ely, Jr., American Legal History: Cases and Materials (Oxford: Oxford University Press, 2010), 351–353.

Explore the Source

1. Why might white lawmakers have seized upon vagrancy as the focus of a Black Code?

2. What role do the authors of this code envision for people of color in the post-slavery South?

3. Why might lawmakers have banned marriage between Black people and white people?

Southerners to sign year-long labor contracts. One state's code banned freed people from performing any kind of labor besides plantation labor or domestic service. Black workers who quit their positions and looked for better wages and conditions faced forfeiture of all wages earned and could be forced to return to their original employer. Most codes required aspiring Black businesspeople to apply for costly licenses. Just as when they were enslaved, freed people were prohibited from hunting or bearing arms. African Americans could be arrested as vagrants if they begged, played games, or engaged in diversions from supervised labor. The codes also established a new category of racial crime: Discourtesy and other allegedly offensive behavior against whites by anyone classified as a negro were punishable by the old slavery method of whipping.

Black Southerners did their best to resist the codes and refuse exploitative labor contracts. "I ain't going to bind myself," one freed man in South Carolina informed a planter in late 1865, "not till I can see better." But when President Johnson made it clear that there would be no large-scale distribution of land, freed people reluctantly signed agreements. Prohibited from making an independent living, many had no choice but to return to work for those who had previously kept them enslaved. In Congress, however, the Black Codes backfired on their Southern authors. Both the codes and freed people's protests confirmed many Republicans' suspicions that the planters were reintroducing slavery through a back door.

CONGRESS TAKES CONTROL

Once Johnson's Reconstruction failed to purge the South of slavery and allowed ex-Confederates to retake power, moderate Republicans in Congress joined their radical colleagues in calling for a more aggressive plan of **congressional Reconstruction.** Radical Republicans believed that without universal male suffrage, Black Southerners' freedom was in perpetual jeopardy. People could only protect their rights, Radicals argued, when they were able to participate

The Face of Radical Reconstruction.
Congressman Thaddeus Stevens of Pennsylvania poses hand-on-heart above a law book placed on a floral tablecloth. Radical Republicans like Stevens claimed that law and morality required the redistribution of former slaveholders' plantations to the freed people. Questions for Analysis: What is the meaning of Stevens's pose? Why does he include a law book? *National Archives and Records Administration*

fully in elections and government. Unlike moderates, Radical Republicans were also passionately committed to land redistribution. In the view of Thaddeus Stevens, the government should seize all 394 million acres of the "70,000 proud, bloated and defiant rebels" and redistribute them to the freed people. By the end of 1865, a new coalition of moderates and Radicals in Congress stood opposed to presidential Reconstruction.

When Congress reconvened in December, the new coalition exercised Congress's constitutional right to refuse to seat the Southern congressmen elected under Johnson's watch. Lawmakers then established the powerful Joint House and Senate Committee on Reconstruction. In early 1866, the committee held public hearings on the mistreatment of freed people under the new Southern governments. On the basis of this evidence, the committee forwarded a series of groundbreaking laws. A new Freedmen's Bureau Bill granted that agency the authority to cancel the repressive labor contracts that many Black Southerners had been compelled to sign. In direct opposition to Johnson's policy, the bill also provided for the distribution of land to the freed people and established military courts to enforce their legal rights.

The Committee on Reconstruction also sponsored the nation's first civil rights bill, which granted **birthright citizenship** to all people born in the United States (except Native Americans) and conferred on them equal rights before the law. President Johnson vetoed both bills, on the grounds that they were an unwarranted extension of federal power over the states, but Republicans eventually had enough votes in Congress to override him and enact these landmark laws.

THE FOURTEENTH AMENDMENT, VIOLENT BACKLASH, AND IMPEACHMENT

In 1866, shortly after enactment of the Civil Rights Act, Congress passed the **Fourteenth Amendment** to the

Constitution and sent it to the states for ratification. This was the first comprehensive civil rights amendment since the 1780s and marked a significant departure from previous citizenship law. The amendment guaranteed birthright citizenship (again, Native Americans were excluded), making citizens of almost all people who had formerly been enslaved. The amendment guaranteed all citizens the full "privileges and immunities" of citizenship and equal protection of the laws at both state and federal levels. States were prohibited from depriving citizens of life, liberty, or property without first allowing them to defend those rights in a court of law.

The Fourteenth Amendment also made an important contribution to the electoral system. Any state that barred male adult citizens from voting in state or federal elections would be penalized by a reduction in its number of representatives and presidential electors. This sent a clear message to the South that the disenfranchisement of men on racial grounds would reduce the region's political power at the federal level. Despite the lobbying efforts of woman suffrage advocates, however, the amendment did not penalize states that withheld the franchise from women, which all states continued to do.

Congress sent the Fourteenth Amendment to the states, where a three-fourths majority was needed for adoption. To secure the necessary approval of Southern states, Congress stipulated that any state that ratified the amendment would be readmitted to the union. Johnson, meanwhile, opposed the amendment and urged his supporters to reject it. Ironically, Johnson's home state of Tennessee was the only one of the eleven former Confederate states to vote in its favor. It was readmitted in 1866.

The Fourteenth Amendment and the Civil Rights Act provoked a backlash of anti-Black violence across the South in the summer of 1866, with race riots breaking out in Memphis, New Orleans, and several other Southern cities. In New Orleans, a mob of white men, led by police, attacked Republican delegates on their way to a constitutional convention, triggering a spree of violence that left fifty people (mostly Black bystanders and constitutional delegates) dead and dozens more injured. Mob violence was often instigated by planters and merchants who sought to subordinate Black people to their employers and exclude them and white Republicans from political power.

Violent white opposition only strengthened the hand of Radical Republicans in Congress. The riots convinced remaining moderates that legal reform was not enough, and the federal government's slow response to the violence persuaded them that Johnson was abnegating his presidential duties. In December 1866, Congress took complete control of Reconstruction. Lawmakers began by establishing universal male suffrage in the Western federal territories and Washington, D.C. The following year, Radicals enacted the sweeping legislation they believed was crucial to the success of Reconstruction. The **Reconstruction Act of 1867** declared most of the governments established in the former Confederate states under President Johnson's Reconstruction policy to be illegal. The act divided the rest of the South into five districts, to be administered directly by federal military officers, who would do whatever was necessary to protect citizens' property and lives. Southern states were to call conventions, rewrite their constitutions to include universal male suffrage, and hold elections to elect new, racially inclusive governments. Finally, Congress mandated that Southern states could re-enter the union only once they had disenfranchised ex-Confederate leaders and granted the vote to freed men.

Radicals were reasonably confident that the U.S. Army would cooperate and enforce the act. Secretary of War Edwin Stanton was broadly sympathetic to their agenda, but Stanton answered directly to the president. Congress therefore enacted the **Tenure of Office Act** (1867), which prohibited the president from firing cabinet members whose appointment had required Senate approval. This precipitated a final confrontation between the beleaguered president and an ever-more confident Congress. Ignoring the law, Johnson attempted to hand Stanton his notice. Stanton refused and barricaded himself in his office for three days while House Republicans voted to impeach Johnson. In the Senate, the vote fell one short of the number needed to convict and remove the president. But impeachment effectively neutralized him. Free of Johnson's oversight, Stanton halted the withdrawal of federal troops from the South.

Johnson left office the following year as the country went to the polls to elect a new president. Former Union war hero and Radical sympathizer General Ulysses S. Grant defeated Democrat Horatio Seymour by a large majority in the electoral college but a slimmer majority of the popular vote (309,684 out of a total of 5,716,082 votes). Black voters played an important role in the election, rewarding the party that had been responsible for abolishing slavery and establishing civil rights. Consequently, Republicans became even more firmly committed to protecting Black suffrage, whereas the Democratic Party determined to limit it severely.

Black suffrage was not a popular cause in the North, and Democratic gains in the 1868 elections threatened doom for the Republicans. But with a new president

Memphis Riots, 1866. Whites who opposed Black rights torched a freed people's schoolhouse in this outbreak of anti-Black violence. *North Wind Picture Archives/Alamy Stock Photo*

firmly behind Radical Reconstruction and their party still controlling most state legislatures, Radical Republicans seized the opportunity to lock in their political gains through a constitutional amendment. The **Fifteenth Amendment,** which was passed in 1869 and ratified in 1870 after prolonged and extensive debate, provided that a citizen's right to vote could not be denied or altered by either state or federal government "on account of race, color, or previous condition of servitude." The third and final Reconstruction Amendment, the Fifteenth was aimed primarily at the South, but its provisions applied to the entire country. As with the Fourteenth Amendment, Congress declined to extend its legal protections to women. And by rejecting proposed language that would have prevented states from barring voters based on wealth or education, the amendment's sponsors opened the door to future schemes of Black disenfranchisement in the South. But in making racial discrimination at the polls unconstitutional and giving itself the authority to enforce Black voting rights across the nation, Radical Republicans secured an important victory.

TOWARD A RACIALLY INCLUSIVE DEMOCRACY

Freed people were overjoyed by the Reconstruction Act of 1867, which promised them true freedom and equality. In Southern cities, many defied the unfair contracts they had been forced to sign. They refused to sit in the back of streetcars and insisted on paying the same price as white people for the same goods and services. All over the South, African Americans convened spontaneous, mass meetings to mark the dawn of a new era. Itinerant lecturers and preachers, most of them Black but some white, carried the news to the countryside. Planters looked on as Black laborers walked off plantations, attended political rallies, and signed up en masse to join Republican Union Leagues, just as white farmers had done after the war.

Assembling in churches, schools, the woods, and the fields, Union Leagues initiated hundreds of thousands of Black Americans into political life. Organizers typically placed a Bible, a copy of the Declaration of Independence, and a farming implement on a table and then

Faces of a New Government.   Voters in the South elected delegates to rewrite their state constitutions. Forty-nine Black men served at the constitutional convention in Louisiana in 1868. *Library of Congress, Prints & Photographs Division*

solemnly administered oaths of allegiance to the league and the Republican Party. League orators then educated members about the electoral process and the system of government and held "colored men's conventions," which despite their name drew masses of women and children as well as men. Rural Blacks, meanwhile, turned the conventions and leagues into vehicles for putting education, labor, and especially land reform on the Republicans' political agenda. As one orator reminded the crowd at an Alabama convention, "Didn't you clear the white folks land?" "Yes," the crowd roared, "and we have a right to it!"

As Black Southerners mobilized politically, the U.S. Army set about registering Black men and other eligible voters in the former Confederacy. Sending a small crew of registrars all over the South, the Army worked closely with the Union Leagues to execute the biggest government-led voter registration drive in American history. Rural freed people once again laid down tools and flocked to towns, inspired by the hope that registration would finally lend them a political voice and lead to land redistribution.

Elections for delegates to the constitutional conventions in the South got under way in late 1867 and continued through 1869. Under military protection, between 70 percent and 90 percent of Southern Black men went to the polls, voting overwhelmingly for the party that had enfranchised them. About 75 percent of Southern white men participated, with the rest either boycotting the elections or being disqualified by their role in the Confederate rebellion. Republicans won a majority of delegates in every state.

When the first conventions finally met in the state capitals in the fall of 1867, the scene was nothing short of astonishing. Just three years earlier, slavery had ruled the South. Now, as one sympathetic British observer commented, "black men and white men sit side by side," to rewrite the political rules. These new constitutions were more democratic and egalitarian than anything Americans, North or South, had known before. Every new constitution guaranteed men their civil and political rights regardless of race. All also repealed the Black Codes. They reduced the number of capital crimes and abolished the punishment most symbolic of slavery—whipping—and the penalty of imprisonment for debt. Many constitutions contained provisions for public schools and poverty relief, and some established basic legal rights for women. At several conventions, freed men voiced support for giving women the vote, on the grounds that it was an "inherent right" of citizenship, but the measures failed to pass.

Although the conventions established legal equality, they did not mandate a systematic redistribution of land. With rural Black delegates a minority in many conventions, and many white Republicans anxious that land confiscation would provoke violence, redistribution proposals failed.

RECONSTRUCTION GOVERNMENTS

In the months following the constitutional conventions, Southerners mobilized to take part in racially inclusive elections for federal, state, and local governments. Whereas smaller Democratic and Whig Parties attracted planters and merchants, Republicans drew a large coalition of Blacks and whites. Black churches played a critical role as bases for Republican mobilization, as did the Union Leagues. Leaders soon emerged to express and press Black political demands.

Black candidates for office were drawn from diverse backgrounds. Some had been free and living in the South for generations. Others were Northerners, including fugitives from slavery who returned to the South after the war to participate in Reconstruction. Some worked for the Freedmen's Bureau, and others were educators, ministers, shopkeepers, or artisans. Notably, however, few candidates were drawn from the masses of impoverished freed people who had once slaved for the planters. Many rural freed people favored Black representatives who were literate or owned property, in the belief that they would more effectively advance the interests and aspirations of people formerly enslaved.

A broad group of white Republicans occupied many of the most powerful positions in state government. Southern Democrats derided this powerful white minority by calling them **scalawags,** slang for runty, useless farm animals. The white Republican coalition was comprised largely of upcountry yeomen who had been quietly building their own Union Leagues since 1865. A small number of planters and former Democratic leaders signed up as well, either out of the pragmatic conviction that the Democrats' future in the South was doomed by Black enfranchisement or out of support for the Republican ideology of legal equality and free labor. Aware that Northern Republicans were aggressively pursuing large-scale development in the American West, some ex-planters also considered the party more likely to attract Northern investment capital to the South.

"Electioneering at the South." Black candidates campaigned for office in the 1867 and 1868 elections, often at small gatherings such as the one illustrated here. Notice that women are in attendance but seated separately from enfranchised men. *Library of Congress Geography and Map Division*

Throughout the South, voters elected Republican-dominated legislatures in 1867 (see Map 16.1). These **Reconstruction governments,** which ruled from a few months to nine years, acted on the egalitarian principles in the new state constitutions. Many established universal male suffrage. Georgia, North Carolina, and South Carolina led the way on the nationwide movement to give married women the right to hold property and retain their earnings independent of their husbands.

Reconstruction governments established the South's first public schools, on the principle that a decent education is a right of freedom and the basis of democratic citizenship. Legislatures also directed the construction of hospitals, asylums, and penitentiaries and looked for ways to adapt these Northern institutions to the values of the new, democratic South. In North Carolina, for example, lawmakers rejected the practice of putting convicts to forced labor for private manufacturers and introduced a variety of programs designed to rehabilitate offenders.

• Whites from the North made up the rest of the South's Republican base. Southern Democrats referred to them as **carpetbaggers,** deriding them as impoverished and ill-educated scoundrels who had packed up all their worldly belongings in travel bags made of carpet and headed south to "fatten on our misfortunes." The great majority of former Northerners, however, were neither poor nor illiterate, and most had no interest in political office. A great number were Union veterans and some were aspiring farmers and artisans. Just like migrants to the West during this period, Northeastern families moved south in search of land, small business opportunities, or an agrarian way of life that industrialization and the rise of wage labor were threatening to destroy. •

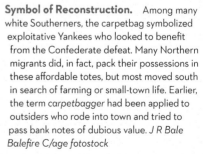

Symbol of Reconstruction. Among many white Southerners, the carpetbag symbolized exploitative Yankees who looked to benefit from the Confederate defeat. Many Northern migrants did, in fact, pack their possessions in these affordable totes, but most moved south in search of farming or small-town life. Earlier, the term *carpetbagger* had been applied to outsiders who rode into town and tried to pass bank notes of dubious value. *J R Bale Balefire C/age fotostock*

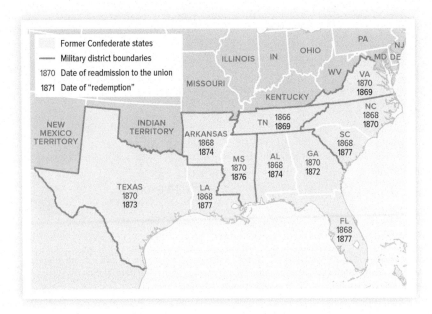

Map 16.1 Southern State Governments During Reconstruction. Every former Confederate state elected a Reconstruction government in 1867, and African Americans served in the legislature of every Reconstruction government in the South—in stark contrast to the situation in the North at the time. Reconstruction governments qualified Southern states for readmission to the union but were dismantled ("redeemed") in the 1870s.

Some states, including Texas, integrated their police forces. For the first time in American history, Black people wore law enforcement badges and exercised the protective and peacekeeping powers of the state. All these reforms were undertaken without federal funding.

Legislative changes also helped produce a new, racially inclusive legal culture in the South. For the first time, African Americans served on juries in large numbers and some served as judges. They made wide use of the court system to enforce their newfound rights, crowding courts that had once been off-limits. For Black women, who had legal but not political rights, the courts and the legal system became a vehicle to gain some measure of protection from intimidation and harm.

In the economic sphere, the new Republican state governments generally aimed to lessen the South's dependence on cotton, which had lost value when India, Egypt, West Africa, and Brazil entered the market during the Civil War. In 1868, lawmakers responded by looking for ways to encourage farmers and planters to plant different, more lucrative crops. They also invested in education in the hope that this would lead to diversification of the economy. And like Northern legislatures, they supported the construction of railroads, which would integrate their states into the national and global economy.

These economic policies side-stepped freed people's demands for land redistribution. In the end, the states made little effort to resettle freed men and poor whites on their own small farms. South Carolina made farms available at an affordable price to fourteen thousand African Americans, but this was the major exception. Some legislators worried that it would alienate white voters. Others argued that depriving planters of their property was illegal or immoral. Instead, most lawmakers preferred to assist rural freed people with legislation that protected them from undue exploitation by planters.

Although the states did not deliver on rural freed people's most pressing request, freed people nonetheless supported their new democratic government. The fact that Black men held office in these governments was itself highly significant. All told, over six hundred Black men served in Southern legislatures during Reconstruction, and sixteen in Congress. In 1870, Hiram Revels, a minister and educator who had helped raise Black regiments during the war, became the first African American elected to the U.S. Senate. Twenty Black men served as governors and high-ranking cabinet ministers. Black officeholding in the United States was groundbreaking, but white critics of Reconstruction overstated its magnitude. Although only 20 percent of all Republican officeholders during Reconstruction were Black, critics routinely disparaged Southern governments as "Negro rule."

RECONSTRUCTING SOUTHERN SOCIETY

By 1871, all the former Confederate states had met the requirements laid down by the Reconstruction Act and rejoined the union. The United States was whole, and the key political aims of Reconstruction had been fulfilled. But Southern Reconstruction was more than a political project. The workplaces, churches, schools, and other institutions that Black Southerners founded in the early years of peace set in motion lasting social and cultural change among freed people. African Americans carved out new identities, drew emotional and spiritual sustenance, and forged new forms of artistic and moral expression. Likewise, white communities underwent broad changes in these years, as many lost family farms and were drawn into the sharecropping system.

PATTERNS OF WORK

In the rural South, farm labor and daily life settled into new patterns, as landless Blacks and whites struggled to maintain some measure of independence. Such patterns varied by region. The rice-growing areas of South Carolina and Georgia typically adopted the task system, under which agricultural workers were paid a set amount for each task they performed rather than an hourly wage. On the sugar plantations of Louisiana, freed people worked under the contract system for hourly or weekly wages under close supervision. In the cotton and tobacco belts, where most Black Southerners lived, sharecropping emerged as the dominant mode of farming among both whites and Blacks. Sharecropper families rented part of a large plantation, where they lived and grew tobacco or cotton. At harvest, the family split the crop with the landowner as payment for rent. Sometimes, they also owed a portion to local merchants and planters in payment for seed and equipment.

Although sharecropping was not the system of freehold farming for which the freed people had hoped, it enabled them to live as families and to work without overseers. It also held out the promise of eventual ownership of land. In theory, a sharecropper could save enough money from the sale of his surplus crops to purchase his own farm. In practice, however, it was very difficult. Just 20 percent of Black Southerners owned land by 1877. Freed women's aspiration to withdraw from field and domestic service in order to work as wives and mothers in their own homes was partially realized in the late 1860s. But by the 1880s, over half of all Southern Black women were working for wages.

Sharecropping, along with the states' efforts to lay railroad track and reintegrate the South into the global economy, wrought significant changes in the Southern landscape. As great plantations were divided up and rented out as farms, some eight thousand stores sprang up across the Cotton Belt to meet sharecroppers' growing demand for food, farming supplies, and housewares. Country villages proliferated, typically following newly laid railroads along which cotton, farming supplies, consumer goods, and mail flowed.

As the global price of cotton recovered in the late 1860s, yeomen farmers and sharecroppers increasingly committed all their land to raising this "white gold." Despite states' encouragement of diversification, Southern farming became increasingly devoted to a single crop. Integration into the global marketplace meant that farmers and sharecroppers benefited from the rising prices of cotton. But they also became vulnerable to slumps. When the global price of cotton plummeted in the depression of 1873–1878, tens of thousands lost all their land and income. • Many growers abandoned the traditional practice of crop rotation (which allowed the soil to recover) in order to maximize production. This change depleted the soil of nutrients, and cotton crops grew less robustly and lost much of their resistance to pests, rot, and disease. • Monoculture had important social consequences, too. Sharecroppers' reliance on cotton made them more dependent on the merchants and planters who gave them credit and access to the global marketplace.

CLIMATES AND ECOLOGIES

THE HEART OF THE COMMUNITY: THE CHURCH

Other areas of Black Southern life thrived under Reconstruction. The churches that Blacks had created in the early days of freedom remained the only Black institutions not connected to planters and white authority. Indeed, churches continued to be the principal spaces within which freed people experienced and expressed their independence. Black ministers from the North spearheaded a missionary drive into the South, as did Northern branches of the Episcopal, Presbyterian, and Congregational churches. These missions resulted in the construction of hundreds of independent Black church buildings. Their commitment to teaching freed people to read and write also played a crucial role in lifting Black Southerners' reading literacy (but not writing literacy) rate from just 5 percent in 1870 to 70 percent by 1890.

In the countryside, visiting itinerant preachers tied sharecropping families together in networks that sometimes stretched over several counties. Traveling preachers

Freedmen's Bureau School, South Carolina.   Freed people's schools were both symbols of and training grounds for freedom, but attending them could be perilous. "When we sent our children to school in the morning," reflected Douglass Wilson, a formerly enslaved Union army colonel whose son was beaten by whites for attending school, "we had no idea that we should see them return home alive in the evening." *Corbis/Getty Images*

fostered the sharing of information and forged a larger sense of community among rural Black people. In both city and country, women came to occupy important positions of spiritual and institutional authority. Although barred from ordination as ministers, they organized missionary societies and literacy programs, and exercised considerable influence over church activities.

Black churches developed their own, distinctive theology. Free of the oversight of white ministers, rural congregants drew on the old folk religion they had secretly forged while living enslaved in the secluded "hush arbors" and "praying grounds" of the plantations. Black ministers built upon enslaved preachers' emphasis on faith as a source of resistance to oppression, and freed people carried forward the tradition of exuberant, expressive worship. Congregations clapped, danced, and sang old slave songs about freedom, as well as new gospel songs celebrating emancipation as the work of God (see Singular Lives: Ella Sheppard, Spiritual Singer). Firm in the belief that their faith had carried them through to freedom, congregants sang of the coming of a New Jerusalem: "See what wonder Jesus done / O no man can hinder me!"

SCHOOLS AND AID SOCIETIES

Much like churches, schools became a symbol of freedom and a central institution in the everyday lives of both rural and urban Black Southerners. Many freed people prized literacy, which had been forbidden under slavery, as the key both to economic and cultural progress and to spiritual salvation. Black people founded and staffed many schools, but Northern religious and reform organizations also played an important role, employing some fourteen hundred white teachers and missionaries for Black schools and donating thousands of schoolbooks. By 1870, there were four thousand freed people's schools, and over one in every ten freed youth attended them. Six years later, over half of all freed youth were in school. Some states tried to establish integrated schools, but white parents generally rejected them and the initiative failed.

Alongside churches and schools, freed people established a wide range of mutual aid societies, including organizations to help the sick and the elderly, savings banks, firefighting companies, tenants' clubs (to defend sharecroppers' rights), and labor associations. In the cities, where the Black population was doubling, freed people set up debating clubs, drama groups, and trade

SINGULAR LIVES

Ella Sheppard, Spiritual Singer

As well as participating fully in the world's first racially inclusive democracy, African Americans transformed American culture through a great surge of creativity in the performing arts. Although they remembered slavery as the brutal institution it had always been, Black musicians also recovered and celebrated the unique musical form created in slavery, the slave spiritual, which mixed African vocal styles with the language and imagery of English hymns. In the 1870s, Ella Sheppard and fellow musicians of the all-African American **Jubilee Singers** transcribed and performed dozens of these spirituals, introducing the nation and the world to America's first homegrown musical tradition.

Sheppard was born into bondage in Tennessee in 1851, and her experience of slavery inspired what became the most famous of the slave spirituals: "Swing Low, Sweet Chariot." One day, her mother discovered that their mistress had been bribing young Ella to spy on her. Reacting in "agony of soul and despair," Ella's mother tried to drown herself and her daughter. But an elder intervened, with the words that would later become the chorus of the well-known spiritual. Soon after, Ella's father, a formerly enslaved man who had saved enough to buy his freedom, paid three hundred fifty dollars to free Ella. When creditors threatened to re-enslave Ella's stepmother to satisfy debts, the family fled for Cincinnati. There, Ella took piano and singing lessons, becoming an accomplished enough musician to support her family after her father died in 1866.

Like many African Americans who escaped the slave states, seventeen-year-old Ella returned in 1868 to help build the South's new democracy. She taught piano in Nashville and used the proceeds to enroll at Fisk University (which had been founded by the American Missionary Association two years earlier for the purpose of educating freed people). As the pianist for the Fisk choir, Ella went on

Singing Freedom. The Jubilee Singers, with Ella Sheppard (seated at table, with long earrings), pose for the photograph that would be their carte de visite. *Library of Congress Prints and Photographs Division*

fundraising tours for the school in 1871, performing popular and classical standards and the occasional spiritual. The choir's mostly white evangelical audiences applauded respectfully for the standard tunes but cheered wildly for the spirituals. The director promptly changed the choir's name to the Jubilee Singers (in honor of emancipation) and Ella assumed responsibility for collecting and producing slave songs. The choir returned home with twenty thousand dollars—enough money to build a new campus.

Fisk became a distinguished liberal arts college and the Jubilee Singers toured the North and Europe to great acclaim. Commenting on the state of American music in the 1890s, the European composer Antonin Dvořák wrote of the choir's spirituals, "These beautiful and varied themes are the product of the soil. They are American . . . and [have] all that is needed for a great and noble school of music." In the 1910s, the choir recorded many of the spirituals that Sheppard had remembered and performed. Long after Reconstruction was defeated, these songs served as an important source for America's other distinctive contributions to music: jazz, the blues, rock 'n' roll, and rap.

Where in the Archives?

Because Ella Sheppard and the Jubilee Singers toured in an era preceding the spread of recorded sound, historians rely

on newspaper reviews and sheet music to reconstruct their performances.

The songbook *Jubilee Songs: As Sung by the Jubilee Singers, of Fisk University* (New York: Biglow & Maine, 1872) is housed in the Internet Archive (https://archive.org/).

The review "The Jubilee Singers. Immense gathering of Sunday-school Children," appeared in *The American Missionary*, volume 20, April 1876, pages 89–90, and can be found at HathiTrust (https://babel.hathitrust.org/cgi/pt?id=coo.31924066335856&view=1up&seq=421).

Another review, "The Jubilee Singers," appeared in *The New National Era*, a newspaper published by Frederick Douglass, on the third page of the March 28, 1872, issue. The newspaper is available through Chronicling America, an archive of historic American newspapers maintained at the Library of Congress (https://chroniclingamerica.loc.gov/lccn/sn84026753/issues/).

Assignment

Read all three sources and answer the following question in 400–500 words:

1. Would you classify the Jubilee Singers as popular entertainers, evangelical missionaries, or political activists? Support your response with evidence both from their lyrics and from the published accounts of their performances.

associations. These organizations formed a vital network among Black Southerners and laid a foundation on which they built strong, independent communities.

CHALLENGES TO RECONSTRUCTION

By 1870, Reconstruction had transformed culture, politics, and the economy in the South. Nine of the eleven ex-Confederate states had Republican legislatures. For the first time in the nation's history, a small but significant minority of Black men exercised authority as lawmakers, judges, sheriffs, and militia officers. Most freed people (like many white farmers) still believed that if they worked hard enough, landownership and full independence were possible. But in the early 1870s, the tide turned against the South's revolution. Harsh economic conditions bred resentment against the new governments, just as the federal government's resolve to ensure their success weakened. Across much of the South, the ideology of white supremacy tightened its hold.

THE AILING SOUTHERN ECONOMY

Republican-led state governments continued their efforts to rebuild the South and complete its transition from a slave society to a free labor democracy, but they could not do it alone. The Northern investment that was necessary to Southern Reconstruction never materialized, going instead to lucrative mining and railroad opportunities in the West (see Chapter 17). Northern businessmen distrusted the South's radically democratic governments and worried about the risks posed by white violence against Blacks. The South was "the last region on earth," despaired prominent Republican George Templeton Strong, in which "a Northern or European capitalist [would] invest a dollar."

The federal government did not help the Southern rebuilding effort. Like Northern investors, the government preferred to work with private corporations in the West. Southern states racked up massive debts as they opened schools and rebuilt towns, with some states' deficits quadrupling in just a few years. Legislators responded by raising taxes and attempting to broaden the tax base. But most Southerners were poor and possessed little in the way of taxable assets or income. State governments therefore turned to the elite planters who owned significant wealth. Higher taxes, in turn,

hardened the opposition to Reconstruction among planters, who also resented the tendency of Reconstruction governments to award building and other lucrative contracts to unionists.

Planters soon found allies among the growing number of poorer white farmers who had owned land before the Civil War but who had lost their farms due to debts acquired in the harsh economic climate. Although their predicament was the result of the cash-starved economy, crop failures, and the volatile global cotton market, white farmers tended to focus their frustration on closer and more concrete targets—Republican lawmakers and the freed people. Many blamed Reconstruction for depriving them of their land, freedom, and autonomy.

THE MAKING OF WHITE SUPREMACY

In these desperate economic times, the ideology of white supremacy gained momentum and exploded in spectacular acts of violence. Racial segregation of the sort that had been common in the private hotels, trains, and steamboats of the antebellum North quietly took root in many Southern states. Prominent Black Americans were often refused admission to first-class railroad cars and steamship berths. Oscar J. Dunn, the lieutenant governor of Louisiana, for example, was barred from traveling in a first-class railcar in his own state. Planters and white storekeepers often refused to do business with Black Republicans, and white state and county officials neglected to carry out the directives of Black superiors.

The ex-Confederate militias that President Johnson had allowed to rearm in 1865 morphed into secret societies and paramilitary organizations such as the White Leagues and Red Shirts. These groups frequently threatened, terrified, and beat African Americans who tried to vote or otherwise assert their independence. The **Ku Klux Klan,** led by ex-Confederate general Nathan Bedford Forrest, was the largest and most infamous of these secret leagues. Masking themselves in white sheets or colorful costumes, Klansmen galloped across the countryside at night, looking for Black men they considered a threat to white political and economic interests. On arriving at a victim's home, the Klan performed elaborate rituals of violence and humiliation that were designed to put Black men in their subordinate place. These performances drew on popular Southern theater, blackface minstrelsy, and folk music to stage terrifying dramatizations of white men's supposed superiority. Northern newspapers and leaflets reported these events in lavish detail, creating a national audience for the Klan's acts of terrorism.

POLITICS AND ENTERTAINMENT

● With its popular cultural references and skillful appeals to white racism and anxieties about Reconstruction, the Klan won instant support among white Southerners. Among those who joined were Democratic politicians, planters, members of smaller secret societies and paramilitary organizations, common criminals, and struggling white farmers, shopkeepers, and workers who feared competition from Black people. Musicians, circus performers, and actors also belonged, playing central roles in the Klan's highly theatrical performances. ●

While sending a chilling message to Black communities, the Klan's violent spectacles informed white Southerners that the defenders of white supremacy were on the march once more. Many quietly heralded the Klan as a patriotic liberation army and gave them aid and comfort. They heeded the Klan's call to join the Democratic Party and rebuild its political power.

Republican state governments were generally unable or unwilling to confront the Klan. But Congress passed the Enforcement Act of 1870, which prohibited the use of force or threat of force against anyone trying to vote or attempting to register to vote, and the Ku Klux

Klan Flag, ca. 1866. With a mythical beast and a Latin motto that invoked eternal truths recognized "always, everywhere, and by everyone," the Klan shrouded their bitterly contested agenda. Designing flags was part of a larger strategy of using ritual and performance to reassert white supremacy and drum up popular support without arousing Northern suspicions that they were reinstating Confederate rule. *Source: Chicago History Museum via Illinois Digital Heritage Hub*

Klan Act (1871), which gave the federal government broad powers to arrest and prosecute individuals who conspired to deprive citizens of their right to vote, hold office, or serve on juries. Under the act, federal officers prosecuted hundreds of Klansmen in North Carolina and Mississippi. And in South Carolina in 1872, the federal government sent troops into nine counties, arrested hundreds of Klansmen, and exiled two thousand more to bordering states.

The federal war on Klan terrorism weakened and dispersed the Klan insurgency. But in key respects, the Klansmen's job was done. By 1873, they had forged a new culture of white supremacy and crowned the Democrats the party of the white South. Five Southern states had been "redeemed" (won back by the Democrats). In addition, the Southern states' inability to stop Klan violence on their own signaled that Reconstruction could not survive without ongoing federal assistance.

REPUBLICANS DIVIDED

As the Klan battled the federal government in the South, some prominent Northern Republicans broke away to form the Liberal Republican Party. Although they supported the new constitutional amendments, Liberal Republicans criticized the Klan enforcement acts on the grounds that the laws vested excessive police power in the hands of the federal government at the expense of the states. Representing the growing middle class of the urban North, these Republicans also claimed that the South's racially inclusive democracy gave the "ignorant" laboring poor too much power. Liberals sought the re-enfranchisement of ex-Confederates, arguing that their exclusion from political life deprived the South of some of its "best men."

Republican governments in the South were weakened further by internal divisions. Most party members agreed on the necessity of equal civil rights, but they diverged on social and economic issues. Black Republicans tended to favor governmental funding of schools, infrastructure, and other public goods and supported higher taxes as a way of providing these things. White Republicans were more likely to object to tax increases. Many also objected to

African Americans assuming positions of leadership in the party. In some states, where Blacks formed a majority, they were able to force out white leaders who marginalized them. But many white Southern Republicans responded by abandoning the party.

THE DEATH OF RECONSTRUCTION

After 1873, the ailing Republican congressional coalition that had championed Southern Reconstruction finally fell apart. "Radicalism is dissolving—going to pieces," one Southern Democrat exulted quite accurately. Vigilante violence, legal setbacks, economic depression, and the hardening of Northern sentiment all combined to allow the Democratic opposition, known as **Redeemers,** to take control of the last remaining Reconstruction governments.

SOUTHERN MILITIAS MOBILIZE

The campaign of violence against Southern Blacks accelerated in 1873, despite the Klan's defeat. The single deadliest attack occurred on Easter Sunday, 1873, at the Colfax courthouse in Grant Parish, Louisiana, where armed White League paramilitaries attempted to unseat the newly elected Republican judge and registrar. Although a Black regiment of the state militia defended the building, it was overwhelmed when the league unleashed a cannon and set the courthouse on fire. By the end of the siege, more than 280 Black men lay dead, including 50 who had surrendered (just 3 white men lost their lives). The following year, the League armed about 14,000 men and marched on the Louisiana capitol, where they battled the state militia, overthrew the Republican government, and installed a white Democrat at its head. Federal troops put down the rebellion, but the spectacle of thousands of armed white men besieging a state government persuaded many white Northerners that the challenge of Reconstruction was too great.

The devastating effects of the Colfax massacre were reinforced in 1876, when the Supreme Court heard the appeals of three white men involved in the crime. The men had been prosecuted under the Enforcement Act of 1870 for depriving the victims of their civil rights. In *U.S. v. Cruikshank* (1876), the Court overturned their convictions on the technical grounds that the original charge had not identified race as the motivation for the massacre. The justices also ruled that the Fourteenth and Fifteenth Amendments did not authorize the federal government to prosecute and punish private organizations such as the White Leagues. Like the massacre itself, this decision emboldened white supremacists and confirmed suspicions that the federal government would no longer intervene on Black Southerners' behalf.

REMEMBERING THE WAR, FORGETTING SLAVERY

Northerners' support for Reconstruction depended, in part on their belief that the Civil War had been a struggle against slavery and that victory would not be complete until the freed men achieved full legal and political equality. Immediately after the war, Northern Memorial Day parades, speeches, war monuments, and graveyard services celebrated emancipation as the chief goal and sweetest fruit of victory. But after 1873, commemorations downplayed slavery. Instead, they underlined the necessity of forgiving the South. Unionists and Confederates had fought with equal valor, white Northerners emphasized, and now it was time to reunify as Americans. As one veteran Union officer put it, "over the grave of buried bygones, rejoice that . . . as soldiers and citizens, we know no North, no South, no East, no West—only one country and one flag." Memorial Day celebrations now enacted a collective forgetting of the Civil War as a war against slavery. Although some Northerners, including Frederick Douglass, objected, by 1876 few remembered that emancipation had been the war's central achievement.

A similar change also took place within the South. Under Reconstruction governments, Black and unionist militias had played prominent roles in the South's annual Decoration Day festivities, which celebrated the war for its destruction of slavery. But in the growing number of Democratic states, Decoration Day became a celebration of Confederate veterans and their heroism. Black citizens could march only at the back of the procession. In 1874, for the first time, white Northerners and Southerners participated in the same Memorial Day celebrations. Northerners now decorated the graves of Confederate and not just Union soldiers. Memorial Day became a tribute to a reconciled white nation.

This new approach to Memorial Day paralleled new political alliances between North and South. Liberal Republicans began to work with Southern Democratic

Honoring the Confederate Cause. Richmond, Virginia, held its first annual Confederate veterans' parade in 1875. The parades continued through the 1910s. *Library of Congress*

Redeemers to restore peace and commerce in the South. They agreed that mob violence would stop only when the federal government ceased to play an active role in the South and Black men no longer governed. As New York Liberal Republican E. L. Godkin put it, once the federal government departed, "the negro will disappear from . . . national politics. Henceforth the nation, as a nation, will have nothing more to do with him."

RECONSTRUCTION'S DAY IN COURT

In 1875, in one last bid in Congress to save Reconstruction, Radical Republican Charles Sumner sponsored legislation that outlawed racial discrimination in every state of the union. The **Civil Rights Act of 1875** declared that it was government's duty to treat people equally and justly, irrespective of their race, color, religion, nativity, or political belief, and that all people were entitled to the full and equal enjoyment of any public inn, theater, transportation system, or place of amusement. The law broke important new ground for protecting the rights of African Americans as consumers of goods and services.

But as Congress enacted Reconstruction laws, other parts of the government, especially the courts, blunted their impact. Federal circuit courts heard dozens of cases under the Civil Rights Act of 1875, but the federal government did little to enforce the law. It was left up to victims of racial discrimination to bring a lawsuit, and the expense of doing so discouraged legal action. In those cases that made it to court, judges did not interpret the act as a mandate to integrate public amenities. Instead, they took it to mean that public amusements and transportation systems were to ensure that separate, first-class accommodations were also available for people of color.

The Supreme Court further undermined Reconstruction, first by striking down state and federal loyalty laws, thereby opening the way for ex-Confederates to return to Southern politics. Subsequently, in the *Slaughterhouse Cases* of 1873, the Court ruled that the Fourteenth Amendment only protected the rights of federal citizenship and that the states were free to limit other rights (such as the right to education and welfare) on the basis of race. Three years later, in *U.S.* v. *Cruikshank*, the Court overturned the convictions of the perpetrators of the

Force Unmasked. Violence against Black voters and white Republicans intensified beginning in 1873. This cartoon satirizes the idea that elections in the South were free. *Bettmann/Getty Images*

Colfax massacre, ruling that the Fourteenth Amendment protected an individual's rights from violation by a state government, but not by private individuals and mobs. These cases made it clear that neither the federal government nor the federal courts were likely to protect the civil rights of African Americans. Southern Democrats would have a free hand.

THE ELECTION OF 1876

Sensing that Reconstruction's end was within reach, Southern Democrats in 1875 announced the **Mississippi Plan.** They openly called on their partisans to carry that state's upcoming election "peaceably, but by force if necessary." In a departure from earlier Klan tactics, heavily armed white militias deployed openly and without disguise, preventing some sixty thousand Black and white Republicans from voting and thereby securing a Democratic victory. In the wake of this success, Democrats in the remaining Republican states organized white electoral militias as well.

President Grant sensed the shifting political winds. Mindful of the 1876 election, he slowly withdrew federal support from Southern Republicans, withheld troops needed to defend Black voters from murderous mobs, and all but dropped enforcement of the Ku Klux Klan Act. Grant also quietly extended patronage to moderate Southern Democrats in an effort to build a new alliance.

Grant's effort failed. In 1876, a series of financial scandals in his cabinet tainted his administration and,

ironically, associated him with the Southern Republicans from whom he had tried to distance himself. Congressional Republicans took stock of Grant's plummeting popularity and settled on a mild-mannered conservative from Ohio, Rutherford B. Hayes, in the hope that his reputation for honesty would reunite the party and restore its tarnished name. The Democrats nominated Samuel B. Tilden, who had earned renown as the reformer who brought down New York City's corrupt Tweed administration (see Chapter 18).

Tilden carried all of the South's Democratic states and won the national popular vote by a margin of 250,000 (see Map 16.2). But in the electoral college, he fell 1 vote shy of the 185 needed to win the election. Both sides claimed victory in the three Southern states (South Carolina, Florida, and Louisiana) where Republicans still controlled the state governments but Democrats were gaining power, challenging

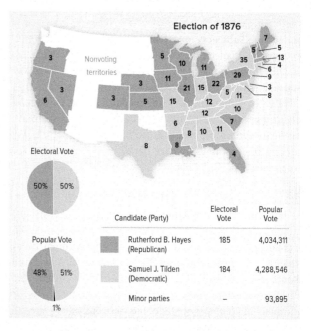

Map 16.2 Election of 1876. For the first time since 1824, the candidate with the most votes failed to win the presidency. But Hayes's victory was not simply the result of the peculiarities of the electoral college system; it was the fruit of a political deal that ended the nation's project of reconstructing the South.

Election Stalemate.   Congressmen and members of the public, including women, packed the U.S. Supreme Court chamber in 1877 to witness the proceedings of the electoral commission. Democrats refused to accept the commission's ruling that Rutherford B. Hayes had won the presidential election of 1876, and the outcome was instead decided in a secret meeting between Southern Democrats and Hayes's Republican allies. *U.S. Senate Collection*

the legitimacy of Black suffrage, and disputing the legislatures' certified election results. Only if all three states were counted for Hayes would the Republicans retain the White House. Neither party would concede defeat. Democrats warned gravely of raising militias and ominously declared, "Tilden or Fight!" Congress appointed an electoral commission to resolve the standoff. The commission voted eight to seven, along party lines, to declare Hayes the victor. Democrats resisted. But in March 1877, following a long, secret meeting between leading Southern Democrats and five Republicans close to Hayes, the Democrats capitulated and consented to a Hayes presidency.

The price the Republicans paid was something many Liberal Republicans had wanted for some time. In exchange for the presidency, the Republicans quietly consented to a "new Southern policy" that would leave white Southerners to run their own political affairs. Known as the **Compromise of 1877,** that agreement left freed people and the South's remarkable democratic experiment to the mercy of Southern Democrats and their militias. President Hayes ordered the last few U.S. troops in the South to stand down, and Democrats ousted the three

remaining Republican governments. The South had been "redeemed"; Reconstruction was dead.

BURYING RECONSTRUCTION

In 1878, Congress passed the **Posse Comitatus Act,** which prohibited the federal government from using the army to enforce the law—including laws that protected voters from violence and intimidation. Five years later, Reconstruction received a lethal blow when the Supreme Court heard the 1883 *Civil Rights Cases.* These cases arose from lawsuits brought by Black citizens in California, Kansas, Missouri, New York, and Tennessee who had been refused access to theaters, hotels, and railroad cars on account of their race. The Court ruled that the Fourteenth Amendment did not bar racial discrimination by a private business. It added that most of the Civil Rights Act of 1875 was unconstitutional, because the authority to protect citizens from discrimination lay not with the federal government but with the states. The Black press condemned the Court's decision as an ultimate betrayal of the Civil War and Reconstruction. Few white people commented.

CONCLUSION

Black Southerners played a central role in each of the three stages of Reconstruction, first while enslaved and then as freed people. During the war, it was people in bondage who forced the issue of emancipation onto the federal war agenda through their exodus across Union lines. President Lincoln subsequently resolved to expand wartime Reconstruction to include the abolition of slavery, the confiscation and redistribution of some former plantations, and stricter criteria for the readmission of rebellious states. Lincoln subsequently drafted a program for the construction of a more democratic South.

President Johnson put Lincoln's plan of Reconstruction on hold. Making clear that his opposition to Black enfranchisement was greater than his hatred of the planter class, he set about restoring former slaveholders to power. But freed people's refusal to comply with the laws enacted on Johnson's watch emboldened Republicans in Congress to reject restoration of the old ruling class and to help freed people build the world's first racially inclusive democracy. Congress passed key civil rights reforms and empowered the U.S. Army to enforce the law. As a result, men who had lived in slavery just a few years before served in the South's new government and on juries, the judiciary, and police forces.

Aware that Reconstruction would deprive them of their power, planters waged a bitter campaign against the South's Reconstruction governments. A growing cross section of white Southerners waged small-scale warfare against Black voters, white Republicans, and anyone who supported Black rights. Violence against Black Southerners wore down Northern voters' commitment to Reconstruction, and the Supreme Court further undermined Reconstruction by limiting the reach of key civil rights legislation. Facing economic hardships, many white Southerners who had not opposed Reconstruction blamed the region's misfortunes on Republican rule. And as memories of the war against slavery faded, more Northerners came to think of the Civil War as a tragic conflict among brothers rather than a heroic fight against slavery. They called for reconciliation with the white South.

As a result of all these factors—vigilante violence, legal defeat, economic depression, the hardening of Northern sentiment, and white people's amnesia about slavery—every Reconstruction government had fallen by 1877. The *Civil Rights Cases* of 1883 confirmed the end of an era. But Black Americans' aspirations to landownership, freedom, and full citizenship endured, as did the cultural institutions they established during Reconstruction. Although the scope of the Thirteenth, Fourteenth, and Fifteenth Amendments was severely limited, Congress did not repeal them. In the 1950s and 1960s, almost a century after their enactment, they would become indispensable tools of liberation for a new civil rights movement.

STUDY TERMS

Reconstruction	Fifteenth Amendment
Ten Percent Plan	scalawags
Radical Republicans	carpetbaggers
Wade-Davis Bill	Reconstruction governments
Thirteenth Amendment	Jubilee Singers
Freedmen's Bureau	Ku Klux Klan
Union Leagues	Redeemers
Black Codes	Civil Rights Act of 1875
congressional Reconstruction	*Slaughterhouse Cases*
birthright citizenship	Mississippi Plan
Fourteenth Amendment	Compromise of 1877
Reconstruction Act of 1867	Posse Comitatus Act
Tenure of Office Act	*Civil Rights Cases*

FURTHER READING

A database of additional full-text readings is available through Power of Process for Primary Sources in Connect.

David Blight, *Race and Reunion* (2001), illuminates the process by which white Americans came to accept white Southerners' view of the conflict.

Jim Downs, *Sick from Freedom* (2012), documents the devastating impact of war and emancipation on the health of freed people.

Laura F. Edwards, *Gendered Strife and Confusion* (1997), examines the impact of Reconstruction on private life and gender roles in a North Carolina county.

Eric Foner, *Reconstruction* (1988), remains the most systematic and detailed treatment of Southern Reconstruction.

Leon Litwack, *Been in the Storm So Long* (1979), considers the early phase of Reconstruction and the responses of freed people and ex-slaveholders to emancipation.

Erin Stewart Mauldin, *Unredeemed Land* (2018), explains how war and emancipation altered the Southern landscape and how ecological constraints shaped development of the South.

Elaine Franz Parsons, *Ku-Klux* (2015), highlights the Klan's use of popular entertainment forms.

Joseph P. Reidy, *Illusions of Emancipation* (2019), considers the transition from slavery to freedom through the lenses of time, space, and home.

Heather Cox Richardson, *West from Appomattox* (2007), argues that Southern Reconstruction was part of a larger nation-building project of that unfolded in the North and West as well.

Nicole Myers Turner, *Soul Liberty* (2020), recovers how religious organizing by Black Virginians laid a foundation for political action and community formation.

THE DECLARATION OF INDEPENDENCE

IN CONGRESS, JULY 4, 1776,

THE UNANIMOUS DECLARATION OF THE THIRTEEN UNITED STATES OF AMERICA

When, in the course of human events, it becomes necessary for one people to dissolve the political bands which have connected them with another, and to assume, among the powers of the earth, the separate and equal station to which the laws of nature and of nature's God entitle them, a decent respect to the opinions of mankind requires that they should declare the causes which impel them to the separation.

We hold these truths to be self-evident, that all men are created equal; that they are endowed by their Creator with certain unalienable rights; that among these, are life, liberty, and the pursuit of happiness. That, to secure these rights, governments are instituted among men, deriving their just powers from the consent of the governed; that, whenever any form of government becomes destructive of these ends, it is the right of the people to alter or to abolish it, and to institute a new government, laying its foundation on such principles, and organizing its powers in such form, as to them shall seem most likely to effect their safety and happiness. Prudence, indeed, will dictate that governments long established, should not be changed for light and transient causes; and, accordingly, all experience hath shown, that mankind are more disposed to suffer, while evils are sufferable, than to right themselves by abolishing the forms to which they are accustomed. But, when a long train of abuses and usurpations, pursuing invariably the same object, evinces a design to reduce them under absolute despotism, it is their right, it is their duty, to throw off such government and to provide new guards for their future security. Such has been the patient sufferance of these colonies, and such is now the necessity which constrains them to alter their former systems of government. The history of the present King of Great Britain is a history of repeated injuries and usurpations, all having, in direct object, the establishment of an absolute tyranny over these States. To prove this, let facts be submitted to a candid world:

He has refused his assent to laws the most wholesome and necessary for the public good.

He has forbidden his governors to pass laws of immediate and pressing importance, unless suspended in their operation till his assent should be obtained; and, when so suspended, he has utterly neglected to attend to them.

He has refused to pass other laws for the accommodation of large districts of people, unless those people would relinquish the right of representation in the legislature; a right inestimable to them, and formidable to tyrants only.

He has called together legislative bodies at places unusual, uncomfortable, and distant from the depository of their public records, for the sole purpose of fatiguing them into compliance with his measures.

He has dissolved representative houses repeatedly for opposing, with manly firmness, his invasions on the rights of the people.

He has refused, for a long time after such dissolutions, to cause others to be elected; whereby the legislative powers, incapable of annihilation, have returned to the people at large for their exercise; the state remaining, in the meantime, exposed to all the danger of invasion from without, and convulsions within.

He has endeavored to prevent the population of these States; for that purpose, obstructing the laws for naturalization of foreigners, refusing to pass others to encourage their migration hither, and raising the conditions of new appropriations of lands.

He has obstructed the administration of justice, by refusing his assent to laws for establishing judiciary powers.

He has made judges dependent on his will alone, for the tenure of their offices, and the amount and payment of their salaries.

He has erected a multitude of new offices, and sent hither swarms of officers to harass our people, and eat out their substance.

He has kept among us, in time of peace, standing armies, without the consent of our legislatures.

He has affected to render the military independent of, and superior to, the civil power.

He has combined, with others, to subject us to a jurisdiction foreign to our Constitution, and unacknowledged by our laws; giving his assent to their acts of pretended legislation:

For quartering large bodies of armed troops among us:

For protecting them by a mock trial, from punishment, for any murders which they should commit on the inhabitants of these States:

For cutting off our trade with all parts of the world:

For imposing taxes on us without our consent:

For depriving us, in many cases, of the benefit of trial by jury:

For transporting us beyond seas to be tried for pretended offences:

For abolishing the free system of English laws in a neighboring province, establishing therein an arbitrary government, and enlarging its boundaries, so as to render it at once an example and fit instrument for introducing the same absolute rule into these colonies:

For taking away our charters, abolishing our most valuable laws, and altering, fundamentally, the powers of our governments:

For suspending our own legislatures, and declaring themselves invested with power to legislate for us in all cases whatsoever.

He has abdicated government here, by declaring us out of his protection, and waging war against us.

He has plundered our seas, ravaged our coasts, burnt our towns, and destroyed the lives of our people.

He is, at this time, transporting large armies of foreign mercenaries to complete the works of death, desolation, and tyranny, already begun, with circumstances of cruelty and perfidy scarcely paralleled in the most barbarous ages, and totally unworthy the head of a civilized nation.

He has constrained our fellow citizens, taken captive on the high seas, to bear arms against their country, to become the executioners of their friends, and brethren, or to fall themselves by their hands.

He has excited domestic insurrections amongst us, and has endeavored to bring on the inhabitants of our frontiers, the merciless Indian savages, whose known rule of warfare is an undistinguished destruction of all ages, sexes, and conditions.

In every stage of these oppressions, we have petitioned for redress, in the most humble terms; our repeated petitions have been answered only by repeated injury. A prince, whose character is thus marked by every act which may define a tyrant, is unfit to be the ruler of a free people.

Nor have we been wanting in attention to our British brethren. We have warned them, from time to time, of attempts made by their legislature to extend an unwarrantable jurisdiction over us. We have reminded them of the circumstances of our emigration and settlement here. We have appealed to their native justice and magnanimity, and we have conjured them, by the ties of our common kindred, to disavow these usurpations, which would inevitably interrupt our connections and correspondence. They, too, have been deaf to the voice of justice and consanguinity. We must, therefore, acquiesce in the necessity which denounces our separation, and hold them as we hold the rest of mankind, enemies in war, in peace, friends.

We, therefore, the representatives of the United States of America, in general Congress assembled, appealing to the Supreme Judge of the world for the rectitude of our intentions, do, in the name, and by the authority of the good people of these colonies, solemnly publish and declare, that these united colonies are, and of right ought to be, free and independent states: that they are absolved from all allegiance to the British Crown, and that all political connection between them and the state of Great Britain is, and ought to be, totally dissolved; and that, as free and independent states, they have full power to levy war, conclude peace, contract alliances, establish commerce, and to do all other acts and things which independent states may of right do. And, for the support of this declaration, with a firm reliance on the protection of Divine Providence, we mutually pledge to each other our lives, our fortunes, and our sacred honor.

The foregoing Declaration was, by order of Congress, engrossed, and signed by the following members:

JOHN HANCOCK

NEW HAMPSHIRE	MASSACHUSETTS BAY	RHODE ISLAND	CONNECTICUT
Josiah Bartlett	Samuel Adams	Stephen Hopkins	Roger Sherman
William Whipple	John Adams	William Ellery	Samuel Huntington
Matthew Thornton	Robert Treat Paine		William Williams
	Elbridge Gerry		Oliver Wolcott

NEW YORK
William Floyd
Philip Livingston
Francis Lewis
Lewis Morris

NEW JERSEY
Richard Stockton
John Witherspoon
Francis Hopkinson
John Hart
Abraham Clark

PENNSYLVANIA
Robert Morris
Benjamin Rush
Benjamin Franklin

John Morton
George Clymer
James Smith
George Taylor
James Wilson
George Ross

DELAWARE
Caesar Rodney
George Read
Thomas M'Kean

MARYLAND
Samuel Chase
William Paca
Thomas Stone

Charles Carroll, of
Carrollton

VIRGINIA
George Wythe
Richard Henry Lee
Thomas Jefferson
Benjamin Harrison
Thomas Nelson, Jr.
Francis Lightfoot Lee
Carter Braxton

NORTH CAROLINA
William Hooper
Joseph Hewes
John Penn

SOUTH CAROLINA
Edward Rutledge
Thomas Heyward, Jr.
Thomas Lynch, Jr.
Arthur Middleton

GEORGIA
Button Gwinnett
Lyman Hall
George Walton

Resolved, That copies of the Declaration be sent to the several assemblies, conventions, and committees, or councils of safety, and to the several commanding officers of the continental troops; that it be proclaimed in each of the United States, at the head of the army.

THE CONSTITUTION OF THE UNITED STATES OF AMERICA[1]

We the People of the United States, in Order to form a more perfect Union, establish Justice, insure domestic Tranquility, provide for the common defence, promote the general Welfare, and secure the Blessings of Liberty to ourselves and our Posterity, do ordain and establish this CONSTITUTION for the United States of America.

ARTICLE I

Section 1

All legislative Powers herein granted shall be vested in a Congress of the United States, which shall consist of a Senate and House of Representatives.

Section 2

The House of Representatives shall be composed of Members chosen every second Year by the People of the several States, and the Electors in each State shall have the Qualifications requisite for Electors of the most numerous Branch of the State Legislature.

No Person shall be a Representative who shall not have attained to the Age of twenty-five Years, and been seven Years a Citizen of the United States, and who shall not, when elected, be an Inhabitant of that State in which he shall be chosen.

[Representatives and direct Taxes[2] shall be apportioned among the several States which may be included within this Union, according to their respective Numbers, which shall be determined by adding to the whole Number of free Persons, including those bound to Service for a Term of Years, and excluding Indians not taxed, three fifths of all other Persons.][3] The actual Enumeration shall be made within three Years after the first Meeting of the Congress of the United States, and within every subsequent Term of ten Years, in such Manner as they shall by Law direct. The Number of Representatives shall not exceed one for every thirty Thousand, but each State shall have at Least one Representative; and until such enumeration shall be made, the State of New Hampshire shall be entitled to chuse three, Massachusetts eight, Rhode-Island

[1]This version follows the original Constitution in capitalization and spelling. It is adapted from the text published by the United States Department of the Interior, Office of Education.

[2]Altered by the Sixteenth Amendment.
[3]Negated by the Fourteenth Amendment.

and Providence Plantations one, Connecticut five, New York six, New Jersey four, Pennsylvania eight, Delaware one, Maryland six, Virginia ten, North Carolina five, South Carolina five, and Georgia three.

When vacancies happen in the Representation from any State, the Executive Authority thereof shall issue Writs of Election to fill such Vacancies.

The House of Representatives shall chuse their Speaker and other Officers; and shall have the sole Power of Impeachment.

Section 3

The Senate of the United States shall be composed of two Senators from each State, chosen by the Legislature thereof, for six Years; and each Senator shall have one Vote.

Immediately after they shall be assembled in Consequence of the first Election, they shall be divided as equally as may be into three Classes. The Seats of the Senators of the first Class shall be vacated at the Expiration of the second Year, of the second Class at the Expiration of the fourth Year, and of the third Class at the Expiration of the sixth Year, so that one-third may be chosen every second Year; and if Vacancies happen by Resignation, or otherwise, during the Recess of the Legislature of any State, the Executive thereof may make temporary Appointments until the next Meeting of the Legislature, which shall then fill such Vacancies.

No Person shall be a Senator who shall not have attained to the Age of thirty Years, and been nine Years a Citizen of the United States, and who shall not, when elected, be an Inhabitant of that State for which he shall be chosen.

The Vice President of the United States shall be President of the Senate, but shall have no vote, unless they be equally divided.

The Senate shall chuse their other Officers, and also a President pro tempore, in the absence of the Vice President, or when he shall exercise the Office of President of the United States.

The Senate shall have the sole Power to try all Impeachments. When sitting for that purpose they shall be on Oath or Affirmation. When the President of the United States is tried, the Chief Justice shall preside: And no person shall be convicted without the Concurrence of two-thirds of the Members present.

Judgment in Cases of Impeachment shall not extend further than to removal from Office, and disqualification to hold and enjoy any Office of honor, Trust, or Profit

under the United States: but the Party convicted shall nevertheless be liable and subject to Indictment, Trial, Judgment, and Punishment, according to Law.

Section 4

The Times, Places and Manner of holding Elections for Senators and Representatives, shall be prescribed in each State by the Legislature thereof; but the Congress may at any time by Law make or alter such Regulations, except as to the Places of Chusing Senators.

The Congress shall assemble at least once in every Year, and such Meeting shall be on the first Monday in December, unless they shall by Law appoint a different Day.

Section 5

Each House shall be the Judge of the Elections, Returns and Qualifications of its own Members, and a Majority of each shall constitute a Quorum to do Business; but a smaller number may adjourn from day to day, and may be authorized to compel the Attendance of absent Members, in such Manner, and under such Penalties, as each House may provide.

Each House may determine the Rules of its Proceedings, punish its Members for disorderly Behaviour, and, with the Concurrence of two-thirds, expel a Member.

Each House shall keep a Journal of its Proceedings, and from time to time publish the same, excepting such Parts as may in their Judgment require Secrecy; and the Yeas and Nays of the Members of either House on any question shall, at the Desire of one fifth of those Present, be entered on the Journal.

Neither House, during the Session of Congress, shall, without the Consent of the other, adjourn for more than three days, nor to any other Place than that in which the two Houses shall be sitting.

Section 6

The Senators and Representatives shall receive a Compensation for their Services, to be ascertained by Law, and paid out of the Treasury of the United States. They shall in all Cases, except Treason, Felony, and Breach of the Peace, be privileged from Arrest during their Attendance at the Session of their respective Houses, and in going to and returning from the same; and for any Speech or Debate in either House, they shall not be questioned in any other Place.

No Senator or Representative shall, during the Time for which he was elected, be appointed to any civil Office under the Authority of the United States, which shall have been created, or the Emoluments whereof shall have been increased, during such time; and no Person holding any Office under the United States shall be a Member of either House during his continuance in Office.

Section 7

All Bills for raising Revenue shall originate in the House of Representatives; but the Senate may propose or concur with Amendments as on other bills.

Every Bill which shall have passed the House of Representatives and the Senate, shall, before it become a Law, be presented to the President of the United States; If he approve he shall sign it, but if not he shall return it, with his Objections, to that House in which it shall have originated, who shall enter the Objections at large on their Journal, and proceed to reconsider it. If after such Reconsideration two-thirds of that House shall agree to pass the bill, it shall be sent, together with the objections, to the other House, by which it shall likewise be reconsidered, and if approved by two-thirds of that House, it shall become a Law. But in all such Cases the Votes of both Houses shall be determined by Yeas and Nays, and the Names of the Persons voting for and against the Bill shall be entered on the Journal of each House respectively. If any Bill shall not be returned by the President within ten Days (Sundays excepted) after it shall have been presented to him, the Same shall be a Law, in like Manner as if he had signed it, unless the Congress by their Adjournment prevent its Return, in which Case it shall not be a Law.

Every Order, Resolution, or Vote to which the Concurrence of the Senate and House of Representatives may be necessary (except on a question of Adjournment) shall be presented to the President of the United States; and before the Same shall take Effect, shall be approved by him, or being disapproved by him, shall be repassed by two-thirds of the Senate and House of Representatives, according to the Rules and Limitations prescribed in the Case of a Bill.

Section 8

The Congress shall have Power To lay and collect Taxes, Duties, Imposts and Excises, to pay the Debts and provide for the common Defence and general Welfare of the United States; but all Duties, Imposts and Excises shall be uniform throughout the United States;

To borrow money on the credit of the United States;

To regulate Commerce with foreign Nations, and among the several States, and with the Indian Tribes;

To establish an uniform rule of Naturalization, and uniform Laws on the subject of Bankruptcies throughout the United States;

To coin Money, regulate the Value thereof, and of foreign Coin, and fix the Standard of Weights and Measures;

To provide for the Punishment of counterfeiting the Securities and current Coin of the United States;

To establish Post Offices and post Roads;

To promote the Progress of Science and useful Arts, by securing for limited Times to Authors and Inventors the exclusive Right to their respective Writings and Discoveries;

To constitute Tribunals inferior to the Supreme Court;

To define and punish Piracies and Felonies committed on the high Seas, and Offenses against the Law of Nations;

To declare War, grant Letters of Marque and Reprisal, and make Rules concerning Captures on Land and Water;

To raise and support Armies, but no Appropriation of Money to that Use shall be for a longer Term than two Years;

To provide and maintain a Navy;

To make Rules for the Government and Regulation of the land and naval forces;

To provide for calling forth the Militia to execute the Laws of the Union, suppress Insurrections and repel Invasions;

To provide for organizing, arming, and disciplining the Militia, and for government such Part of them as may be employed in the Service of the United States, reserving to the States respectively, the Appointment of the Officers, and the Authority of training the Militia according to the discipline prescribed by Congress;

To exercise exclusive Legislation in all Cases whatsoever, over such District (not exceeding ten Miles square) as may, by Cession of particular States, and the acceptance of Congress, become the Seat of the Government of the United States, and to exercise like Authority over all Places purchased by the Consent of the Legislature of the State in which the Same shall be, for the Erection of Forts, Magazines, Arsenals, Dock-yards, and other needful Buildings;—And

To make all Laws which shall be necessary and proper for carrying into Execution the foregoing Powers, and all other Powers vested by this Constitution in the Government of the United States, or in any Department or Officer thereof.

Section 9

The Migration or Importation of such Persons as any of the States now existing shall think proper to admit, shall not be prohibited by the Congress prior to the Year one thousand eight hundred and eight, but a tax or duty may be imposed on such Importation, not exceeding ten dollars for each Person.

The privilege of the Writ of Habeas Corpus shall not be suspended, unless when in Cases of Rebellion or Invasion the public Safety may require it.

No bill of Attainder or ex post facto Law shall be passed.

No capitation, or other direct, Tax shall be laid unless in Proportion to the Census or Enumeration herein before directed to be taken.

No Tax or Duty shall be laid on Articles exported from any State.

No Preference shall be given by any Regulation of Commerce or Revenue to the Ports of one State over those of another: nor shall Vessels bound to, or from, one State, be obliged to enter, clear, or pay Duties in another.

No Money shall be drawn from the Treasury, but in Consequence of Appropriations made by Law; and a regular Statement and Account of the Receipts and Expenditures of all public Money shall be published from time to time.

No Title of Nobility shall be granted by the United States: And no Person holding any Office of Profit or Trust under them, shall, without the Consent of the Congress, accept of any present, Emolument, Office, or Title, of any kind whatever, from any King, Prince, or foreign State.

Section 10

No State shall enter into any Treaty, Alliance, or Confederation; grant Letters of Marque and Reprisal; coin Money; emit Bills of Credit; make any Thing but gold and silver Coin a Tender in Payment of Debts; pass any Bill of Attainder, ex post facto Law, or Law impairing the Obligation of Contracts, or grant any Title of Nobility.

No State shall, without the Consent of the Congress, lay any Imposts or Duties on Imports or Exports, except what may be absolutely necessary for executing its inspection Laws; and the net Produce of all Duties and Imposts, laid by any State on Imports or Exports, shall be for the use of the Treasury of the United States; and all such Laws shall be subject to the Revision and Control of the Congress.

No state shall, without the Consent of Congress, lay any duty of Tonnage, keep Troops, or Ships of War in time of Peace, enter into any Agreement or Compact with another State, or with a foreign Power, or engage in War, unless actually invaded, or in such imminent Danger as will not admit of delay.

ARTICLE II

Section 1

The executive Power shall be vested in a President of the United States of America. He shall hold his Office during the Term of four years, and, together with the Vice President, chosen for the same Term, be elected, as follows:

Each State shall appoint, in such Manner as the Legislature thereof may direct, a Number of Electors, equal to the whole Number of Senators and Representatives to which the State may be entitled in the Congress: but no Senator or Representative, or Person holding an Office of Trust or Profit under the United States, shall be appointed an Elector.

[The Electors shall meet in their respective States, and vote by Ballot for two persons, of whom one at least shall not be an Inhabitant of the same State with themselves. And they shall make a List of all the Persons voted for, and of the Number of Votes for each; which List they shall sign and certify, and transmit sealed to the Seat of the Government of the United States, directed to the President of the Senate. The President of the Senate shall, in the Presence of the Senate and House of Representatives, open all the Certificates, and the Votes shall then be counted. The Person having the greatest Number of Votes shall be the President, if such Number be a Majority of the whole Number of Electors appointed; and if there be more than one who have such Majority, and have an equal Number of Votes, then the House of Representatives shall immediately chuse by Ballot one of them for President; and if no Person have a Majority, then from the five highest on the List the said House shall in like Manner chuse the President. But in chusing the President, the Votes shall be taken by States, the Representation from each State having one Vote; a quorum for this Purpose shall consist of a Member or Members from two-thirds of the States, and a Majority of all the States shall be necessary to a Choice. In every Case, after the Choice of the President, the Person having the greatest Number of Votes of the Electors shall be the Vice President. But if there should remain two or more who have equal votes, the Senate shall chuse from them by Ballot the Vice President.][4]

---

[4]Revised by the Twelfth Amendment.

The Congress may determine the Time of chusing the Electors, and the Day on which they shall give their Votes; which Day shall be the same throughout the United States.

No person except a natural-born Citizen, or a Citizen of the United States, at the time of the Adoption of this Constitution, shall be eligible to the Office of President; neither shall any Person be eligible to that Office who shall not have attained to the Age of thirty-five years, and been fourteen Years a Resident within the United States.

In Case of the Removal of the President from Office, or of his Death, Resignation, or Inability to discharge the Powers and Duties of the said Office, the same shall devolve on the Vice President, and the Congress may by Law provide for the Case of Removal, Death, Resignation, or Inability, both of the President and Vice President, declaring what Officer shall then act as President, and such Officer shall act accordingly, until the disability be removed, or a President shall be elected.

The President shall, at stated Times, receive for his Services a Compensation, which shall neither be increased nor diminished during the Period for which he shall have been elected, and he shall not receive within that Period any other Emolument from the United States, or any of them.

Before he enter on the execution of his Office, he shall take the following Oath or Affirmation:—"I do solemnly swear (or affirm) that I will faithfully execute the Office of President of the United States, and will, to the best of my Ability, preserve, protect, and defend the Constitution of the United States."

Section 2

The President shall be Commander in Chief of the Army and Navy of the United States, and of the Militia of the several States, when called into the actual Service of the United States; he may require the Opinion, in writing, of the principal Officer in each of the executive Departments, upon any subject relating to the Duties of their respective Offices, and he shall have Power to Grant Reprieves and Pardons for Offenses against the United States, except in Cases of Impeachment.

He shall have Power, by and with the Advice and Consent of the Senate, to make Treaties, provided two-thirds of the Senators present concur; and he shall nominate, and by and with the Advice and Consent of the Senate, shall appoint Ambassadors, other public Ministers and Consuls, Judges of the supreme Court, and all other Officers of the United States, whose Appointments are not

herein otherwise provided for, and which shall be established by Law: but the Congress may by Law vest the Appointment of such inferior Officers, as they think proper, in the President alone, in the Courts of Law, or in the Heads of Departments.

The President shall have Power to fill up all Vacancies that may happen during the Recess of the Senate, by granting Commissions which shall expire at the End of their next Session.

Section 3

He shall from time to time give to the Congress Information of the State of the Union, and recommend to their Consideration such Measures as he shall judge necessary and expedient; he may, on extraordinary occasions, convene both Houses, or either of them, and in Case of Disagreement between them, with respect to the Time of Adjournment, he may adjourn them to such Time as he shall think proper; he shall receive Ambassadors and other public Ministers; he shall take care that the Laws be faithfully executed, and shall Commission all the Officers of the United States.

Section 4

The President, Vice President and all civil Officers of the United States, shall be removed from Office on Impeachment for, and Conviction of, Treason, Bribery, or other high Crimes and Misdemeanors.

ARTICLE III

Section 1

The judicial Power of the United States, shall be vested in one supreme Court, and in such inferior Courts as the Congress may from time to time ordain and establish. The Judges, both of the supreme and inferior Courts, shall hold their Offices during good Behaviour, and shall, at stated Times, receive for their Services, a Compensation, which shall not be diminished during their Continuance in Office.

Section 2

The judicial Power shall extend to all Cases, in Law and Equity, arising under this Constitution, the Laws of the United States, and Treaties made, or which shall be made, under their Authority;—to all Cases affecting ambassadors, other public ministers and consuls;—to all cases of admiralty and maritime Jurisdiction;—to Controversies to which the United States shall be a Party;—to Controversies between two or more States;—between a State and Citizens of another State;[5]—between Citizens of different States—between Citizens of the same State claiming Lands under Grants of different States, and between a State, or the Citizens thereof, and foreign States, Citizens, or Subjects.

In all Cases affecting Ambassadors, other public Ministers and Consuls, and those in which a State shall be Party, the supreme Court shall have original Jurisdiction. In all the other Cases before mentioned, the supreme Court shall have appellate Jurisdiction, both as to Law and Fact, with such Exceptions, and under such Regulations as the Congress shall make.

The trial of all Crimes, except in Cases of Impeachment, shall be by Jury; and such Trial shall be held in the State where the said Crimes shall have been committed; but when not committed within any State, the Trial shall be at such Place or Places as the Congress may by Law have directed.

Section 3

Treason against the United States, shall consist only in levying War against them, or in adhering to their Enemies, giving them Aid and Comfort. No Person shall be convicted of Treason unless on the Testimony of two Witnesses to the same overt Act, or on Confession in open Court.

The Congress shall have power to declare the Punishment of Treason, but no Attainder of Treason shall work Corruption of Blood, or Forfeiture except during the Life of the Person attainted.

ARTICLE IV

Section 1

Full Faith and Credit shall be given in each State to the public Acts, Records, and judicial Proceedings of every other State. And the Congress may by general Laws prescribe the Manner in which such Acts, Records and Proceedings shall be proved, and the Effect thereof.

Section 2

The Citizens of each State shall be entitled to all Privileges and Immunities of Citizens in the several States.

A Person charged in any State with Treason, Felony, or other Crime, who shall flee from Justice, and be found in another State, shall on demand of the executive Authority of the State from which he fled, be delivered up, to be removed to the State having Jurisdiction of the crime.

No Person held to Service or Labour in one State, under the Laws thereof, escaping into another, shall, in

Consequence of any Law or Regulation therein, be discharged from such Service or Labour, but shall be delivered up on Claim of the Party to whom such Service or Labour may be due.

Section 3

New States may be admitted by the Congress into this Union; but no new State shall be formed or erected within the Jurisdiction of any other State; nor any State be formed by the Junction of two or more States, or parts of States, without the Consent of the Legislatures of the States concerned as well as of the Congress.

The Congress shall have Power to dispose of and make all needful Rules and Regulations respecting the Territory or other Property belonging to the United States; and nothing in this Constitution shall be so construed as to Prejudice any Claims of the United States, or of any particular State.

Section 4

The United States shall guarantee to every State in this Union a Republican Form of Government, and shall protect each of them against Invasion; and on Application of the Legislature, or of the Executive (when the Legislature cannot be convened) against domestic Violence.

ARTICLE V

The Congress, whenever two-thirds of both Houses shall deem it necessary, shall propose Amendments to this Constitution, or, on the Application of the Legislatures of two-thirds of the several States, shall call a Convention for proposing Amendments, which, in either Case, shall be valid to all Intents and Purposes, as part of this Constitution, when ratified by the Legislatures of three-fourths of the several States, or by Conventions in three-fourths thereof, as the one or the other Mode of Ratification may be proposed by the Congress; Provided that no Amendment which may be made prior to the Year One thousand eight hundred and eight shall in any Manner affect the first and fourth Clauses in the Ninth Section of the first Article; and that no State, without its Consent, shall be deprived of its equal Suffrage in the Senate.

ARTICLE VI

All Debts contracted and Engagements entered into, before the Adoption of this Constitution, shall be as valid against the United States under this Constitution, as under the Confederation.

[5]Qualified by the Eleventh Amendment.

This Constitution, and the Laws of the United States which shall be made in Pursuance thereof; and all Treaties made, or which shall be made, under the Authority of the United States, shall be the supreme Law of the Land; and the Judges in every State shall be bound thereby, any Thing in the Constitution or Laws of any State to the Contrary notwithstanding.

The Senators and Representatives before mentioned, and the Members of the several State Legislatures, and all executive and judicial Officers, both of the United States and of the several States, shall be bound by Oath or Affirmation to support this Constitution; but no religious Tests shall ever be required as a qualification to any Office or public Trust under the United States.

ARTICLE VII

The Ratification of the Conventions of nine States shall be sufficient for the Establishment of this Constitution between the States so ratifying the same.

Done in Convention by the Unanimous Consent of the States present the Seventeenth Day of September in the Year of our Lord one thousand seven hundred and Eighty seven, and of the Independence of the United States of America the Twelfth. In Witness whereof We have hereunto subscribed our Names.[6]

GEORGE WASHINGTON
PRESIDENT AND DEPUTY FROM VIRGINIA

NEW HAMPSHIRE
John Langdon
Nicholas Gilman

MASSACHUSETTS
Nathaniel Gorham
Rufus King

CONNECTICUT
William Samuel Johnson
Roger Sherman

NEW YORK
Alexander Hamilton

NEW JERSEY
William Livingston
David Brearley
William Paterson
Jonathan Dayton

PENNSYLVANIA
Benjamin Franklin
Thomas Mifflin
Robert Morris
George Clymer
Thomas FitzSimons
Jared Ingersoll
James Wilson
Gouverneur Morris

DELAWARE
George Read
Gunning Bedford, Jr.
John Dickinson
Richard Bassett
Jacob Broom

MARYLAND
James McHenry
Daniel of St. Thomas Jenifer
Daniel Carroll

VIRGINIA
John Blair
James Madison, Jr.

NORTH CAROLINA
William Blount
Richard Dobbs Spaight
Hugh Williamson

SOUTH CAROLINA
John Rutledge
Charles Cotesworth Pinckney
Charles Pinckney
Pierce Butler

GEORGIA
William Few
Abraham Baldwin

Articles in Addition to, and Amendment of, the Constitution of the United States of America, Proposed by Congress, and Ratified by the Legislatures of the Several States, Pursuant to the Fifth Article of the Original Constitution[7]

[AMENDMENT I]

Congress shall make no law respecting an establishment of religion, or prohibiting the free exercise thereof; or abridging the freedom of speech, or of the press; or the right of the people peaceably to assemble, and to petition the Government for a redress of grievances.

[AMENDMENT II]

A well regulated Militia, being necessary to the security of a free State, the right of the people to keep and bear Arms shall not be infringed.

[AMENDMENT III]

No Soldier shall, in time of peace, be quartered in any house, without the consent of the Owner, nor in time of war, but in a manner to be prescribed by law.

---

[6]These are the full names of the signers, which in some cases are not the signatures on the document.

[7]This heading appears only in the joint resolution submitting the first ten amendments, known as the Bill of Rights.

[AMENDMENT IV]

The right of the people to be secure in their persons, houses, papers, and effects, against unreasonable searches and seizures, shall not be violated, and no Warrants shall issue, but upon probable cause, supported by Oath or affirmation, and particularly describing the place to be searched, and the persons or things to be seized.

[AMENDMENT V]

No person shall be held to answer for a capital or otherwise infamous crime, unless on a presentment or indictment of a Grand Jury, except in cases arising in the land or naval forces, or in the Militia, when in actual service in time of War or public danger; nor shall any person be subject for the same offence to be twice put in jeopardy of life or limb; nor shall be compelled in any criminal case to be a witness against himself, nor be deprived of life, liberty, or property, without due process of law; nor shall private property be taken for public use, without just compensation.

[AMENDMENT VI]

In all criminal prosecutions, the accused shall enjoy the right to a speedy and public trial, by an impartial jury of the State and district wherein the crime shall have been committed, which district shall have been previously ascertained by law, and to be informed of the nature and cause of the accusation; to be confronted with the witnesses against him; to have compulsory process for obtaining witnesses in his favour, and to have the Assistance of Counsel for his defence.

[AMENDMENT VII]

In suits at common law, where the value in controversy shall exceed twenty dollars, the right of trial by jury shall be preserved, and no fact tried by a jury, shall be otherwise reexamined in any Court of the United States, than according to the rules of the common law.

[AMENDMENT VIII]

Excessive bail shall not be required, nor excessive fines imposed, nor cruel and unusual punishments inflicted.

[AMENDMENT IX]

The enumeration of the Constitution, of certain rights, shall not be construed to deny or disparage others retained by the people.

[AMENDMENT X]

The powers not delegated to the United States by the Constitution, nor prohibited by it to the States, are reserved to the States respectively, or to the people.
[Amendments I–X, in force 1791.]

[AMENDMENT XI][8]

The Judicial power of the United States shall not be construed to extend to any suit in law or equity, commenced or prosecuted against one of the United States by Citizens of another State, or by Citizens or Subjects of any Foreign State.

[AMENDMENT XII][9]

The Electors shall meet in their respective States and vote by ballot for President and Vice-President, one of whom, at least, shall not be an inhabitant of the same State with themselves; they shall name in their ballots the person voted for as President, and in distinct ballots the person voted for as Vice-President, and they shall make distinct lists of all persons voted for as President, and of all persons voted for as Vice-President, and of the number of votes for each, which lists they shall sign and certify, and transmit sealed to the seat of the government of the United States, directed to the President of the Senate;— The President of the Senate shall, in the presence of the Senate and House of Representatives, open all the certificates and the votes shall then be counted;—The person having the greatest number of votes for President, shall be the President, if such number be a majority of the whole number of Electors appointed; and if no person have such majority, then from the persons having the highest numbers not exceeding three on the list of those voted for as President, the House of Representatives shall choose immediately, by ballot, the President. But in choosing the President, the votes shall be taken by states, the representation from each state having one vote; a quorum for this purpose shall consist of a member or members from

[8]Adopted in 1798.
[9]Adopted in 1804.

two-thirds of the states, and a majority of all the states shall be necessary to a choice. And if the House of Representatives shall not choose a President whenever the right of choice shall devolve upon them, before the fourth day of March next following, then the Vice-President shall act as President, as in the case of the death or other constitutional disability of the President.—The person having the greatest number of votes as Vice-President, shall be the Vice-President, if such number be a majority of the whole number of Electors appointed, and if no person have a majority, then from the two highest numbers on the list, the Senate shall choose the Vice-President; a quorum for the purpose shall consist of two-thirds of the whole number of Senators, and a majority of the whole number shall be necessary to a choice. But no person constitutionally ineligible to the office of President shall be eligible to that of Vice-President of the United States.

[AMENDMENT XIII][10]

Section 1

Neither slavery nor involuntary servitude, except as a punishment for crime whereof the party shall have been duly convicted, shall exist within the United States, or any place subject to their jurisdiction.

Section 2

Congress shall have power to enforce this article by appropriate legislation.

[AMENDMENT XIV][11]

Section 1

All persons born or naturalized in the United States, and subject to the jurisdiction thereof, are citizens of the United States and of the State wherein they reside. No State shall abridge the privileges or immunities of citizens of the United States; nor shall any State deprive any person of life, liberty, or property, without due process of law; nor deny to any person within its jurisdiction the equal protection of the laws.

Section 2

Representatives shall be apportioned among the several States according to their respective numbers, counting the whole number of persons in each State, excluding Indians not taxed. But when the right to vote at any election for the choice of electors for President and Vice-President of the United States, Representatives in Congress, the Executive and Judicial officers of a State, or the members of the Legislature thereof, is denied to any of the male inhabitants of such State, being twenty-one years of age, and citizens of the United States, or in any way abridged, except for participation in rebellion, or other crime, the basis of representation therein shall be reduced in the proportion which the number of such male citizens shall bear to the whole number of male citizens twenty-one years of age in such State.

Section 3

No person shall be a Senator or Representative in Congress, or elector of President and Vice-President, or hold any office, civil or military, under the United States, or under any State, who, having previously taken an oath, as a member of Congress, or as an officer of the United States, or as a member of any State legislature, or as an executive or judicial officer of any State, to support the Constitution of the United States, shall have engaged in insurrection or rebellion against the same, or given aid or comfort to the enemies thereof. But Congress may by a vote of two-thirds of each House, remove such disability.

Section 4

The validity of the public debt of the United States, authorized by law, including debts incurred for payment of pensions and bounties for services in suppressing insurrection or rebellion, shall not be questioned. But neither the United States nor any State shall assume or pay any debts or obligation incurred in aid of insurrection or rebellion against the United States, or any claim for the loss or emancipation of any slave; but all such debts, obligations, and claims shall be held illegal and void.

Section 5

The Congress shall have the power to enforce, by appropriate legislation, the provisions of this article.

[AMENDMENT XV][12]

Section 1

The right of citizens of the United States to vote shall not be denied or abridged by the United States or by any State on account of race, color, or previous condition of servitude—

---

[10]Adopted in 1865.
[11]Adopted in 1868.

[12]Adopted in 1870.

Section 2

The Congress shall have power to enforce this article by appropriate legislation.

[AMENDMENT XVI][13]

The Congress shall have power to lay and collect taxes on incomes, from whatever source derived, without apportionment among the several States, and without regard to any census or enumeration.

[AMENDMENT XVII][14]

The Senate of the United States shall be composed of two Senators from each State, elected by the people thereof, for six years; and each Senator shall have one vote. The electors in each State shall have the qualifications requisite for electors of the most numerous branch of the State legislatures.

When vacancies happen in the representation of any State in the Senate, the executive authority of such State shall issue writs of election to fill such vacancies: Provided, That the legislature of any State may empower the executive thereof to make temporary appointments until the people fill the vacancies by election as the legislature may direct.

This amendment shall not be so construed as to affect the election or term of any Senator chosen before it becomes valid as part of the Constitution.

[AMENDMENT XVIII][15]

Section 1

After one year from the ratification of this article the manufacture, sale, or transportation of intoxicating liquors within, the importation thereof into, or the exportation thereof from the United States and all territory subject to the jurisdiction thereof for beverage purposes is hereby prohibited.

Section 2

The Congress and the several States shall have concurrent power to enforce this article by appropriate legislation.

Section 3

This article shall be inoperative unless it shall have been ratified as an amendment to the Constitution by the legislatures of the several States, as provided in the Constitution, within seven years from the date of the submission hereof to the States by the Congress.

[AMENDMENT XIX][16]

The right of citizens of the United States to vote shall not be denied or abridged by the United States or by any State on account of sex.

Congress shall have power to enforce this article by appropriate legislation.

[AMENDMENT XX][17]

Section 1

The terms of the President and Vice-President shall end at noon on the 20th day of January, and the terms of Senators and Representatives at noon on the 3d day of January, of the years in which such terms would have ended if this article had not been ratified; and the terms of their successors shall then begin.

Section 2

The Congress shall assemble at least once in every year, and such meeting shall begin at noon on the 3d day of January, unless they shall by law appoint a different day.

Section 3

If, at the time fixed for the beginning of the term of the President, the President elect shall have died, the Vice-President elect shall become President. If a President shall not have been chosen before the time fixed for the beginning of his term or if the President elect shall have failed to qualify, then the Vice-President elect shall act as President until a President shall have qualified; and the Congress may by law provide for the case wherein neither a President elect nor a Vice-President elect shall have qualified, declaring who shall then act as President, or the manner in which one who is to act shall be selected, and such person shall act accordingly until a President or Vice-President shall have qualified.

[13]Adopted in 1913.
[14]Adopted in 1913.
[15]Adopted in 1918.

[16]Adopted in 1920.
[17]Adopted in 1933.

Section 4

The Congress may by law provide for the case of the death of any of the persons from whom the House of Representatives may choose a President whenever the right of choice shall have devolved upon them, and for the case of the death of any of the persons from whom the Senate may choose a Vice-President whenever the right of choice shall have devolved upon them.

Section 5

Sections 1 and 2 shall take effect on the 15th day of October following the ratification of this article.

Section 6

This article shall be inoperative unless it shall have been ratified as an amendment to the Constitution by the legislatures of three-fourths of the several States within seven years from the date of its submission.

[AMENDMENT XXI][18]

Section 1

The eighteenth article of amendment to the Constitution of the United States is hereby repealed.

Section 2

The transportation or importation into any State, Territory, or possession of the United States for delivery or use therein of intoxicating liquors, in violation of the laws thereof, is hereby prohibited.

Section 3

This article shall be inoperative unless it shall have been ratified as an amendment to the Constitution by conventions in the several States, as provided in the Constitution, within seven years from the date of the submission hereof to the States by the Congress.

[AMENDMENT XXII][19]

No person shall be elected to the office of the President more than twice, and no person who has held the office of President, or acted as President, for more than two years of a term to which some other person was elected President shall be elected to the office of the President more than once.

But this Article shall not apply to any person holding the office of President when this Article was proposed by the Congress, and shall not prevent any person who may be holding the office of President, or acting as President, during the term within which this Article becomes operative from holding the office of President or acting as President during the remainder of such term.

This article shall be inoperative unless it shall have been ratified as an amendment to the Constitution by the legislatures of three-fourths of the several states within seven years from the date of its submission to the states by the Congress.

[AMENDMENT XXIII][20]

Section 1

The District constituting the seat of Government of the United States shall appoint in such manner as the Congress may direct:

A number of electors of President and Vice-President equal to the whole number of Senators and Representatives in Congress to which the District would be entitled if it were a State, but in no event more than the least populous State; they shall be in addition to those appointed by the States, but they shall be considered, for the purpose of the election of President and Vice-President, to be electors appointed by a State; and they shall meet in the District and perform such duties as provided by the twelfth article of amendment.

Section 2

The Congress shall have power to enforce this article by appropriate legislation.

[AMENDMENT XXIV][21]

Section 1

The right of citizens of the United States to vote in any primary or other election for President or Vice-President, for electors for President or Vice-President, or for Senator or Representative in Congress, shall not be denied or abridged by the United States or any state by reason of failure to pay any poll tax or other tax.

---

[18]Adopted in 1933.
[19]Adopted in 1951.

[20]Adopted in 1961.
[21]Adopted in 1964.

Section 2

The Congress shall have the power to enforce this article by appropriate legislation.

[AMENDMENT XXVI][22]

Section 1

In case of the removal of the President from office or of his death or resignation, the Vice-President shall become President.

Section 2

Whenever there is a vacancy in the office of the Vice President, the President shall nominate a Vice President who shall take office upon confirmation by a majority vote of both Houses of Congress.

Section 3

Whenever the President transmits to the President Pro Tempore of the Senate and the Speaker of the House of Representatives his written declaration that he is unable to discharge the powers and duties of his office, and until he transmits to them a written declaration to the contrary, such powers and duties shall be discharged by the Vice-President as Acting President.

Section 4

Whenever the Vice-President and a majority of either the principal officers of the executive departments or of such other body as Congress may by law provide, transmit to the President Pro Tempore of the Senate and the Speaker of the House of Representatives their written declaration that the President is unable to discharge the powers and duties of his office, the Vice President shall immediately assume the powers and duties of the office as Acting President.

Thereafter, when the President transmits to the President Pro Tempore of the Senate and the Speaker of the House of Representatives his written declaration that no inability exists, he shall resume the powers and duties of his office unless the Vice President and a majority of either the principal officers of the executive departments or of such other body as Congress may by law provide, transmit within four days to the President Pro Tempore of the Senate and the Speaker of the House of Representatives their written declaration that the President is unable to discharge the powers and duties of his office. Thereupon Congress shall decide the issue, assembling within forty-eight hours for that purpose if not in session. If the Congress, within twenty-one days after receipt of the latter written declaration, or, if Congress is not in session, within twenty-one days after Congress is required to assemble, determines by two-thirds vote of both Houses that the President is unable to discharge the powers and duties of his office, the Vice President shall continue to discharge the same as Acting President; otherwise, the President shall resume the powers and duties of his office.

[AMENDMENT XXVII][23]

Section 1

The right of citizens of the United States, who are eighteen years of age or older, to vote shall not be denied or abridged by the United States or by any State on account of age.

Section 2

The Congress shall have power to enforce this article by appropriate legislation.

[AMENDMENT XXVIII][24]

No law, varying the compensation for the services of the Senators and Representatives, shall take effect, until an election of Representatives shall have intervened.

---

[22]Adopted in 1967.

[23]Adopted in 1971.
[24]Adopted in 1992.

PRESIDENTIAL ELECTIONS

Year	Candidates	Parties	Popular Vote	% of Popular Vote	Electoral Vote	% Voter Participation
1789	**George Washington**				69	
	John Adams				34	
	Other candidates				35	
1792	**George Washington**				132	
	John Adams				77	
	George Clinton				50	
	Other candidates				5	
1796	**John Adams**	Federalist			71	
	Thomas Jefferson	Dem.-Rep.			68	
	Thomas Pinckney	Federalist			59	
	Aaron Burr	Dem.-Rep.			30	
	Other candidates				48	
1800	**Thomas Jefferson**	Dem.-Rep.			73	
	Aaron Burr	Dem.-Rep.			73	
	John Adams	Federalist			65	
	Charles C. Pinckney	Federalist			64	
	John Jay	Federalist			1	
1804	**Thomas Jefferson**	Dem.-Rep.			162	
	Charles C. Pinckney	Federalist			14	
1808	**James Madison**	Dem.-Rep.			122	
	Charles C. Pinckney	Federalist			47	
	George Clinton	Dem.-Rep.			6	
1812	**James Madison**	Dem.-Rep.			128	
	DeWitt Clinton	Federalist			89	
1816	**James Monroe**	Dem.-Rep.			183	
	Rufus King	Federalist			34	
1820	**James Monroe**	Dem.-Rep.			231	
	John Quincy Adams	Indep.-Rep.			1	
1824	**John Quincy Adams**	Dem.-Rep.	113,122	31.0	84	26.9
	Andrew Jackson	Dem.-Rep.	151,271	43.0	99	
	Henry Clay	Dem.-Rep.	47,136	13.0	37	
	William H. Crawford	Dem.-Rep.	46,618	13.0	41	
1828	**Andrew Jackson**	Democratic	642,553	56.0	178	57.3
	John Quincy Adams	National Republican	500,897	44.0	83	
1832	**Andrew Jackson**	Democratic	701,780	54.5	219	57.0
	Henry Clay	National Republican	484,205	37.5	49	
	William Wirt	Anti-Masonic	8.0		7	
	John Floyd	Democratic	101,051		11	
1836	**Martin Van Buren**	Democratic	764,176	50.9	170	56.5
	William H. Harrison	Whig	550,816	49.1	73	
	Hugh L. White	Whig			26	
	Daniel Webster	Whig			14	
	W. P. Mangum	Whig			11	
1840	**William H. Harrison**	Whig	1,275,390	53.0	234	80.3
	Martin Van Buren	Democratic	1,128,854	47.0	60	

Year	Candidates	Parties	Popular Vote	% of Popular Vote	Electoral Vote	% Voter Participation
1844	**James K. Polk**	Democratic	1,339,494	49.6	170	79.2
	Henry Clay	Whig	1,300,004	48.1	105	
	James G. Birney	Liberty	62,300	2.3		
1848	**Zachary Taylor**	Whig	1,361,393	47.4	163	72.8
	Lewis Cass	Democratic	1,223,460	42.5	127	
	Martin Van Buren	Free Soil	291,263	10.1		
1852	**Franklin Pierce**	Democratic	1,607,510	50.9	254	69.5
	Winfield Scott	Whig	1,386,942	44.1	42	
	John P. Hale	Free Soil	155,825	5.0		
1856	**James Buchanan**	Democratic	1,836,072	45.3	174	79.4
	John C. Fremont	Republican	1,342,345	33.1	114	
	Millard Fillmore	American	871,731	21.6	8	
1860	**Abraham Lincoln**	Republican	1,865,908	39.8	180	81.8
	Stephen A. Douglas	Democratic	1,375,157	29.5	12	
	John C. Breckinridge	Democratic	848,019	18.1	72	
	John Bell	Constitutional Union	590,631	12.6	39	
1864	**Abraham Lincoln**	Republican	2,218,388	55.0	212	76.3
	George B. McClellan	Democratic	1,812,807	45.0	21	
1868	**Ulysses S. Grant**	Republican	3,013,650	52.7	214	80.9
	Horatio Seymour	Democratic	2,708,744	47.3	80	
1872	**Ulysses S. Grant**	Republican	3,598,235	55.6	286	72.1
	Horace Greeley	Democratic	2,834,761	43.9	66	
1876	**Rutherford B. Hayes**	Republican	4,034,311	48.0	185	82.6
	Samuel J. Tilden	Democratic	4,288,546	51.0	184	
1880	**James A. Garfield**	Republican	4,446,158	48.5	214	80.5
	Winfield S. Hancock	Democratic	4,444,260	48.1	155	
	James B. Weaver	Greenback-Labor	308,578	3.4		
1884	**Grover Cleveland**	Democratic	4,874,621	48.5	219	78.2
	James G. Blaine	Republican	4,848,936	48.2	182	
	Benjamin F. Butler	Greenback-Labor	175,370	1.8		
	John P. St. John	Prohibition	150,369	1.5		
1888	**Benjamin Harrison**	Republican	5,443,892	47.9	233	80.5
	Grover Cleveland	Democratic	5,534,488	48.6	168	
	Clinton B. Fisk	Prohibition	249,506	2.2		
	Anson J. Streeter	Union Labor	146,935	1.3		
1892	**Grover Cleveland**	Democratic	5,551,883	46.1	277	75.8
	Benjamin Harrison	Republican	5,179,244	43.0	145	
	James B. Weaver	People's	1,029,846	8.5	22	
	John Bidwell	Prohibition	264,133	2.2		
1896	**William McKinley**	Republican	7,108,480	52.0	271	79.6
	William J. Bryan	Democratic	6,511,495	48.0	176	
1900	**William McKinley**	Republican	7,218,039	51.7	292	73.7
	William J. Bryan	Democratic; Populist	6,358,345	45.5	155	
	John C. Wooley	Prohibition	208,914	1.5		
1904	**Theodore Roosevelt**	Republican	7,626,593	57.4	336	65.5
	Alton B. Parker	Democratic	5,082,898	37.6	140	
	Eugene V. Debs	Socialist	402,283	3.0		
	Silas C. Swallow	Prohibition	258,536	1.9		

Year	Candidates	Parties	Popular Vote	% of Popular Vote	Electoral Vote	% Voter Participation
1908	**William H. Taft**	Republican	7,676,258	51.6	321	65.7
	William J. Bryan	Democratic	6,406,801	43.1	162	
	Eugene V. Debs	Socialist	420,793	2.8		
	Eugene W. Chafin	Prohibition	253,840	1.7		
1912	**Woodrow Wilson**	Democratic	6,293,152	42.0	435	59.0
	Theodore Roosevelt	Progressive	4,119,207	28.0	88	
	William H. Taft	Republican	3,484,980	24.0	8	
	Eugene V. Debs	Socialist	900,672	6.0		
	Eugene W. Chafin	Prohibition	206,275	1.4		
1916	**Woodrow Wilson**	Democratic	9,126,300	49.4	277	61.8
	Charles E. Hughes	Republican	8,546,789	46.2	254	
	A. L. Benson	Socialist	585,113	3.2		
	J. Frank Hanly	Prohibition	220,506	1.2		
1920	**Warren G. Harding**	Republican	16,153,115	60.4	404	49.2
	James M. Cox	Democratic	9,133,092	34.2	127	
	Eugene V. Debs	Socialist	919,799	3.4		
	P. P. Christensen	Farmer-Labor	265,411	1.0		
1924	**Calvin Coolidge**	Republican	15,719,921	54.0	382	48.9
	John W. Davis	Democratic	8,386,704	28.8	136	
	Robert M. La Follette	Progressive	4,831,289	16.6	13	
1928	**Herbert C. Hoover**	Republican	21,437,277	58.2	444	56.9
	Alfred E. Smith	Democratic	15,007,698	40.9	87	
1932	**Franklin D. Roosevelt**	Democratic	22,829,501	57.4	472	56.9
	Herbert C. Hoover	Republican	15,760,684	39.7	59	
	Norman Thomas	Socialist	881,951	2.2		
1936	**Franklin D. Roosevelt**	Democratic	27,757,333	60.8	523	61.0
	Alfred M. Landon	Republican	16,684,231	36.5	8	
	William Lemke	Union	882,479	1.9		
1940	**Franklin D. Roosevelt**	Democratic	27,313,041	54.8	449	62.4
	Wendell L. Wilkie	Republican	22,348,480	44.8	82	
1944	**Franklin D. Roosevelt**	Democratic	25,612,610	53.5	432	55.9
	Thomas E. Dewey	Republican	22,117,617	46.0	99	
1948	**Harry S. Truman**	Democratic	24,179,345	50.0	303	52.2
	Thomas E. Dewey	Republican	21,991,291	46.0	189	
	J. Strom Thurmond	States' Rights	1,169,021	2.0	39	
	Henry A. Wallace	Progressive	1,157,172	2.0		
1952	**Dwight D. Eisenhower**	Republican	33,936,234	55.1	442	62.3
	Adlai E. Stevenson	Democratic	27,314,992	44.4	89	
1956	**Dwight D. Eisenhower**	Republican	35,590,472	57.6	457	60.2
	Adlai E. Stevenson	Democratic	26,022,752	42.1	73	
1960	**John F. Kennedy**	Democratic	34,226,731	49.7	303	63.8
	Richard M. Nixon	Republican	34,108,157	49.6	219	
	Harry F. Byrd	Independent	501,643		15	
1964	**Lyndon B. Johnson**	Democratic	43,129,566	61.1	486	62.8
	Barry M. Goldwater	Republican	27,178,188	38.5	52	
1968	**Richard M. Nixon**	Republican	31,785,480	44.0	301	62.5
	Hubert H. Humphrey	Democratic	31,275,166	42.7	191	
	George C. Wallace	American Independent	9,906,473	13.5	46	

Year	Candidates	Parties	Popular Vote	% of Popular Vote	Electoral Vote	% Voter Participation
1972	**Richard M. Nixon**	Republican	47,169,911	60.7	520	56.2
	George S. McGovern	Democratic	29,170,383	37.5	17	
	John G. Schmitz	American	1,099,482	1.4		
1976	**Jimmy Carter**	Democratic	40,830,763	50.1	297	54.8
	Gerald R. Ford	Republican	39,147,793	48.0	240	
1980	**Ronald Reagan**	Republican	43,904,153	51.0	489	54.2
	Jimmy Carter	Democratic	35,483,883	41.0	49	
	John B. Anderson	Independent	5,719,437	7.0	0	
	Ed Clark	Libertarian	920,859	1.0	0	
1984	**Ronald Reagan**	Republican	54,455,075	58.8	525	55.2
	Walter Mondale	Democratic	37,577,185	40.5	13	
1988	**George H. W. Bush**	Republican	48,886,097	53.9	426	52.8
	Michael Dukakis	Democratic	41,809,074	46.1	111	
1992	**William J. Clinton**	Democratic	44,908,254	43.0	370	58.1
	George H. W. Bush	Republican	39,102,343	37.4	168	
	H. Ross Perot	Independent	19,741,065	18.9	0	
1996	**William J. Clinton**	Democratic	45,590,703	49.3	379	51.7
	Robert Dole	Republican	37,816,307	40.7	159	
	H. Ross Perot	Reform	8,085,294	8.4	0	
2000	**George W. Bush**	Republican	50,456,062	47.9	271	54.2
	Al Gore	Democratic	50,996,582	48.4	266	
	Ralph Nader	Green	2,858,843	2.7	0	
2004	**George W. Bush**	Republican	62,048,610	50.7	286	60.1
	John F. Kerry	Democratic	59,028,444	48.3	251	
	Ralph Nader	Independent	465,650	0.4	0	
2008	**Barack Obama**	Democratic	65,070,487	53	365	60.6
	John McCain	Republican	57,154,810	46	173	
2012	**Barack Obama**	Democratic	65,899,660	51.0	332	58.6
	Mitt Romney	Republican	60,929,152	47.2	206	
2016	**Donald J. Trump**	Republican	62,984,828	46.1	304	60.1
	Hillary R. Clinton	Democratic	65,853,514	48.2	227	
2020	**Joseph R. Biden**	Democratic	74,222,960	46.8	306	66.3
	Donald J. Trump	Republican	81,283,361	51.3	232	

Note: The final column reflects the percentage of eligible voters who participated in the election (VEP)—not Voting Age Population (VAP). Source: http://www.electproject.org/home/voter-turnout/voter-turnout-data

GLOSSARY

A

abolitionists Radical opponents of slavery, vilified throughout the country for their views on emancipation and racial equality.

Acadian diaspora Dispersion of French-speaking colonists from eastern Canada after the French and Indian War, which led to the formation of a Cajun community and culture in Louisiana.

adelantado Spanish term for "advance men" who organized conquest expeditions to foreign lands on behalf of the monarchy.

adjustable rate mortgages Home loans with rates of interest subject to change, the proliferation of which contributed to a real estate bubble and a massive default and foreclosure crisis in 2007–2008.

affirmative action Policy of advancing the educational and employment opportunities of members of groups that traditionally had been oppressed, exploited, and abandoned.

affluence gap Relative difference, which increased dramatically during the Gilded Age, the 1920s, and the late twentieth century, between society's wealthiest stratum and the average wealth of the majority.

African Methodist Episcopal (A.M.E.) Church Powerful Black church that broke with mainstream Methodism in 1816 over issues of race.

African slave trade Term commonly used by historians to designate long-distance commerce in human laborers from Africa, south of the Sahara, especially between 1500 and 1800.

Agricultural Adjustment Act New Deal law that reconstructed the farming sector by paying farmers to plant fewer acres and raise less livestock, which consequently displaced many tenant farmers.

agricultural depression Economic depression that struck farmers in the 1920s as depressed prices for meat and produce led to a wave of farm foreclosures.

agricultural revolution Major shift in subsistence among North Americans, beginning around the tenth century, as many native societies turned to planting corn and legumes for their principal food sources.

AIDS Coalition to Unleash Power Organization, formed in 1987 by gay men and their supporters, that lobbied for anti-discrimination laws, government investment in AIDS research, and public education about AIDS.

Air Pollution Control Act 1955 law authorizing states and local governments to regulate air pollution.

Albany Convention 1754 meeting between British mainland colonies to discuss a defensive military alliance among themselves and the Iroquois League.

Alien Acts Series of laws, enacted during the Adams administration, that targeted immigrants, in part by extending the waiting period for citizenship.

Allied Powers Military alliance in World War I, consisting of Britain, France, Russia, Japan, and Italy, which the United States joined as an "associated" power.

al-Qaeda Loose coalition of radical Islamists who have waged terrorist warfare against the United States since the 1990s.

America Name given to a presumed continent by German cartographer Martin Waldseemüller in 1507, after Florentine businessman and navigator Amerigo Vespucci.

America First Foreign policy approach, used by Donald Trump, that rejected multilateralism and was based on pragmatic self-interest.

America First Committee Isolationist organization that argued (before Pearl Harbor) that U.S. involvement in World War II would be detrimental to national interests.

American Board of Commissioners for Foreign Missions National society that facilitated Protestant missions among Native Americans and around the world.

American Civil Liberties Union Legal advocacy group founded during World War I to defend dissenters in the wake of increased government surveillance and suppression of free speech.

American Colonization Society Organization that resettled African Americans in Africa, and which created a temporary alliance between slaveholders and some antislavery Americans.

American dream Popular perception, dating from the Gilded Age, that any individual in the United States who works hard and shows initiative will prosper and be happy.

American Expeditionary Force U.S. military force that invaded Mexico in 1914 in response to diplomatic tensions between the United States and the administration of Victoriano Huerta.

American G.I. Forum Civil rights organization, formed by Latino veterans in the mid-twentieth century, that used the court system to combat racial discrimination and segregation.

American Indian Movement Indigenous peoples' civil rights group founded in 1968 that emphasized socio-economic improvement and a message of "Red Power."

American Museum P. T. Barnum's massive museum in New York City, which featured exotic specimens, curiosities, theater, and other forms of popular entertainment.

American Recovery and Reinvestment Act 2009 fiscal stimulus package designed to cope with widespread unemployment due to the Great Recession.

American Renaissance Term used by literary critics for the period in which many works of American literature now considered masterpieces (including a number in the early 1850s) were produced.

American way   Idea, first promoted by big business at the 1939 World's Fair, that the ideal society was one in which government played a limited role in the economy and where responsible corporations provided jobs, good wages, advanced technology, and consumer choice.

American Woman Suffrage Association   Woman suffrage organization that lobbied for women's enfranchisement at the state level.

Americans with Disabilities Act   1990 civil rights law that prohibited employers from discriminating against people with mental or physical disabilities and stipulated suitable accessibility in such spaces as businesses, schools, and restaurants.

Amistad **case**   Court case determining the legal status of African captives who had led a mutiny on the Spanish ship *Amistad* in 1839.

anarchism   Diverse set of political philosophies—originating in Early Modern Europe, adopted in Gilded Age America, and resurgent in the anti-globalization and Occupy movements—that advocates the dissolution of the state and the creation of stateless societies made up of voluntary egalitarian associations.

Andersonville prison   Confederate military prison in Georgia during the Civil War, in which over thirteen thousand Union soldiers perished from disease or violence.

Anglo-Dutch War   Seventeenth-century military conflict between England and the Netherlands that resulted in English control of New York.

animal trickster tales   Folklore developed by African Americans living in slavery, often defined by a motif of weaker animals overcoming or outwitting stronger animals.

anti-abolitionist riots   Episodes of mob violence against abolitionists, especially frequent from 1834 to 1838, resulting in the destruction of property and bodily injury.

anti-Catholicism   Religious, cultural, and political antipathy toward Catholics, which played a large role in mid-nineteenth-century nativism and middle-class reform.

Antifederalists   Opponents of ratifying the U.S. Constitution.

antigallows movement   Nineteenth-century prison reform movement against public execution, which succeeded in persuading three states to ban the death penalty entirely.

Antimasons   Minor political party that formed in opposition to Andrew Jackson and advocated transparency in government.

anti-miscegenation laws   Laws under which most states in the nineteenth century prohibited interracial marriage and in some cases interracial sex.

Apollo space program   NASA spaceflight program, initiated in the 1960s, that put American astronauts into Earth's orbit and achieved the first moonwalk in 1969.

Arab Spring   Series of pro-democracy protests in the Middle East and North Africa in 2011, resulting in regime change in some countries and contributing to civil war in Syria.

Ararat   Mordecai Noah's proposed colony near the western terminus of the Erie Canal, which he imagined as a refuge for persecuted Jews across the world.

Army of the Potomac   Union army formed under the command of George B. McClellan after the defeat at the First Battle of Bull Run.

Articles of Confederation   System of American governance prior to the Constitution, notable for creating a weak central government.

assembly line   Manufacturing process by which parts are sequentially added to the product, whether by humans, automated machines, or a combination of humans and machines.

Atlantic Charter   1941 agreement between the United States and the U.K. that established a blueprint for the post-WWII world order.

attack ads   Electoral advertisements that began appearing in the 1980s and emphasized the negative attributes of the opposing candidate rather than the positive attributes or policy positions of the preferred candidate.

automation   Replacement of manually operated systems with robotic and other automated systems, improving business efficiency but leading to the loss of unskilled and semi-skilled manufacturing jobs and the decline of labor unions.

avant-garde   French term, literally meaning "advance guard" and entering American English after World War II, referring to innovative and experimental art, people, ideas, and ways of life.

B

baby boomers   Americans born between 1946 and 1964, a period in which the national birthrate temporarily rebounded from the historic low of the 1930s.

Back to Africa movement   Black nationalist program, promoted by Marcus Garvey, that transported African Americans to Africa to build Liberia.

Bacon's Rebellion   1675–1676 uprising by colonists in Virginia, caused by white-indigenous relations and class conflict.

Bakke **v.** *Regents of the University of California*   1978 court case in which the Supreme Court approved of affirmative action in the university's admissions policy but ruled that numerical quotas based on race were constitutionally prohibited.

balance of power   General principle, dating back to Early Modern Europe and still influential today, that international peace prevails only when rival states or alliances are equally powerful.

ballot initiative   Progressive Era reform, still in force in twenty-four states and the District of Columbia, that enables citizens to force a public vote on a particular issue, provided that they gather a certain number of voters' signatures.

ban on slave importation   1808 law, after which slavers depended on natural increase and illegal importation to buoy America's enslaved population.

bank notes   Various notes of private banks before the Civil War, which could serve as currency promising to pay the bearer a certain quantity of specie (silver or gold).

Bank of the United States Private corporation, and a major component of Alexander Hamilton's economic platform, that would stabilize and circulate currency in the early United States.

bank war Political conflict, involving Andrew Jackson and Nicholas Biddle, over the rechartering of the Second Bank of the United States.

Barbary War 1801–1805 war between the U.S. and North African states, resulting from an attempt to extort money from the United States.

Bataan Death March Forced relocation of U.S. and Filipino prisoners of war by the Japanese army in the Philippines in 1942, during which ten thousand prisoners died.

Battle of Antietam Civil War battle in 1862 in Maryland that was the bloodiest day in U.S. history to that point and which yielded a Union victory.

Battle of Gettysburg Civil War battle in 1863 in Pennsylvania that thwarted Robert E. Lee's Northern invasion and cost roughly fifty thousand lives.

Battle of Lexington and Concord 1775 armed conflict between British troops and colonists, which many viewed as an irreparable rupture between the empire and the thirteen colonies.

Battle of Little Big Horn Significant Sioux victory against U.S. military forces led by George Armstrong Custer during the Great Sioux War of 1876–1877.

Battle of New Orleans Andrew Jackson's assault at the end of the War of 1812, which boosted American nationalism but had no effect on the formal resolution of the conflict.

Battle of Saratoga Defeat of the British campaign to take Albany, which helped turn the tide of the war in the Americans' favor.

Battle of Shiloh Civil War battle in 1862 in Tennessee, a victory for Union forces under Ulysses Grant, which produced a level of carnage that shocked military officers.

Battle of the Alamo 1836 Mexican military attack on Anglo Texans who had declared independence from Mexico.

Battle of the Wilderness Inconclusive Civil War battle in 1864 between the forces of Ulysses Grant and Robert E. Lee, illustrative of Grant's military tactic of a war of attrition.

Battle of Tippecanoe Armed conflict between the followers of Tenskwatawa and William Henry Harrison, resulting in the destruction of Prophetstown.

Bay of Pigs Site of a failed 1961 U.S.-backed invasion of Cuba to overthrow Fidel Castro.

Beats Mid-twentieth-century poets and writers who condemned the banality of American consumerism, politics, and mass culture.

Beirut barracks bombing 1982 bombing of American and French barracks in Beirut by the Islamic Jihad Organization.

Benevolent Empire Network of national Protestant organizations in the early republic that were committed to the spread of Christianity and to various philanthropic goals.

Beringia Region encompassing a land bridge from Asia, across which some of the first humans to inhabit the Americas migrated.

bicameral Having two legislative chambers, typically one higher than the other.

Bill of Rights Conventional name for the first ten amendments to the U.S. Constitution.

biotechnology Use of science and technology to improve biological systems, industry, and agriculture, coming into prominence in the 2000s.

birtherism Groundless right-wing nativist belief that Barack Obama was not born in the United States.

birthright citizenship Citizenship that is legally conferred on birth within the territorial limits of a state or nation.

Black churches Independent churches developed by free Black communities after the 1780s, through such denominations as Episcopalian, Methodist, Presbyterian, and Baptist.

Black Codes Laws passed immediately after the Civil War by Confederate legislatures seeking to return freed people to a condition akin to slavery.

Black Lives Matter Decentralized protest movement that emerged in the early 2010s, largely concerned with social justice and violence against Black Americans.

Black nationalism Ideology that advocates Black solidarity, racial superiority, and separatism.

Black nationalist Adherent to a form of Black pride, popularized by Marcus Garvey and the Universal Negro Improvement Association, that advocated development of the Black community and racial separatism.

Black Panther Party for Self-Defense Black political organization founded in Oakland, California, in 1965 that developed social programs for the Black community and clashed with the police and government.

Black Power Ideology and social movement, which emerged in the 1960s, that advocated Black solidarity.

blackface minstrelsy Extraordinarily popular brand of theatrical entertainment in nineteenth-century America, featuring performers wearing burnt cork or black paint on their faces.

blue-collar strategy Largely successful attempt by the Republican Party, beginning around 1968, to court historically Democratic union voters by stressing cultural issues and themes such as patriotism, traditional gender roles, and hostility to the counterculture.

bodily self-control Cultural ideal, central to many antebellum reform causes, that valued suppressing violent impulses and bodily appetites.

Bolshevik Revolution Overthrow of Russia's provisional government in 1917 by communist workers' associations, culminating in establishment of the Union of Soviet Socialist Republics (USSR) in 1922.

Bonus Army Large group of World War I veterans who demanded early payment of bonuses in 1932 and to whom Herbert Hoover responded with violence.

Book of Mormon Sacred text first published by Joseph Smith, Jr., in 1830 on the basis of a religious vision.

boosters Civic-minded businessmen who promoted the prospects and fortunes of rival frontier cities in the nineteenth century, typically where they lived and owned property.

Boston Massacre Significant 1770 urban riot, resulting in British troops firing on American colonists.

Boston Tea Party Urban protest against enforcement of the Tea Act, resulting in the destruction of tea and the escalation of the crisis in imperial politics.

Boulwarism Approach to corporate culture, implemented by General Electric in the 1950s, that championed pro-business policies and conservative, free-market ideology.

braceros Mexican workers, or "helping hands," invited into the United States during World War II to fill the labor shortage caused by military conscription.

bread riots Incidents of organized resistance and looting in Southern cities during the Civil War, typically led by white women, protesting high prices and inadequate food provisions.

Briggs Initiative Failed 1978 California ballot proposition that would have authorized the firing of public school employees for engaging in homosexual "conduct" or for defending gay rights.

broad construction Approach to constitutional interpretation that favors granting the federal government any powers consistent with its general charge as long as those powers are not explicitly restricted by the Constitution (*see also* strict construction).

Brook Farm Transcendentalist utopian community established in 1841 on the principles of cooperation, simple living, and high intellectualism.

Brown v. Board of Education of Topeka, Kansas Landmark 1954 court case in which the Supreme Court ruled that the racial segregation of schools violated the equal protection clause of the constitution.

Buffalo Bill's Wild West show Touring performances, popular in the 1880s that celebrated pop-culture archetypes of the Anglo-American West.

Burned-Over District Area in western New York, along the Erie Canal route, where religious revivals were particularly influential during the Second Great Awakening.

Bush Doctrine American military policy, under George W. Bush, that asserted the right of the United States to attack any nation harboring people classified as terrorists.

Bushwhackers Pro-Confederate guerrillas who operated in Missouri and eastern Kansas during the Civil War.

busing Court-ordered programs that transported schoolchildren from one part of a city to another to achieve racial desegregation.

C

Caddo Powerful indigenous people in the region of present-day Texas and Louisiana who exploited French-Spanish competition during the first half of the eighteenth century.

Cahokia Center of the Mississippian civilization, in present-day Illinois, with large earthwork mounds and a population of ten to twenty thousand.

California gold rush Stream of global migration to California between 1848 and 1854, spurred by the discovery of gold.

Californios Hispanic population of Mexican California, born before the United States acquired the region.

Camp David peace treaty 1979 accord between Israel and Egypt, brokered by the United States.

camp followers Women who attached themselves to military units, often serving as nurses, cooks, and laundresses.

camp meeting Outdoor, multiday mass revival held in a rural area.

canals Artificial waterways, which were a major feature of the nineteenth-century transportation revolution.

Canary Islands Islands claimed during the fifteenth-century Castilian Reconquista, resulting in the devastation of the indigenous population, the Guanches.

Cane Ridge Large 1801 Methodist camp meeting in Kentucky, among the first nineteenth-century religious revivals.

cap-and-trade Market-based strategy for curbing climate change that incentivized polluters to limit carbon emissions.

Captain America Heroic comic book character introduced during World War II in support of U.S. intervention.

CARES Act Biggest economic stimulus in history, enacted in 2020 in response to economic dislocation caused by the COVID-19 pandemic.

Carlisle Peace Initiative Britain's proposal to end the Revolution, rejected by the Continental Congress, which stipulated no colonial independence.

carpetbaggers Derisive name for white Northerners who moved south during Reconstruction to take up farming or start a small business and who often carried their belongings in a bag made of carpet.

Central Powers Military alliance in World War I, consisting of Germany, Austria-Hungary, Bulgaria, and the Ottoman Empire.

Chaco Canyon Largest city of Ancestral Puebloans, located in present-day New Mexico, which housed a population of several thousand.

chain stores Retail outlets that operated under the same brand and management and helped spread mass consumption from the 1920s onward.

Charlotte Temple 1791 bestselling novel by Susanna Rowson that emphasized romantic seduction and its consequences.

chattel slavery Labor system in which human beings are held captive, bought, and sold as movable property.

checks and balances Idea that various kinds of political equilibrium will prevent any one branch of government or political interest from seizing too much power under a new constitution.

Cherokee syllabary Writing system devised by Sequoyah, which enabled widespread literacy in the Cherokee nation.

Chicago Major American city whose growth was entwined with the spread of railroad networks in the mid-nineteenth century.

Chicano Movement Twentieth-century social movement that sought to secure civil rights, anti-discrimination, and socio-economic improvement for peoples of Mexican descent.

Chinese Restriction Act 1882 law limiting Chinese immigration and reaffirming the prohibition on Chinese naturalization.

Christian Coalition Conservative Christian organization, founded by Pat Robertson, that influenced the Republican Party in the 1980s and 1990s.

chunkey Popular Cahokian hoop-and-pole game that became a major part of Mississippian culture.

Church of Jesus Christ of Latter-day Saints Church founded by Joseph Smith in 1830, the followers of which are commonly called Mormons.

circuit riders Itinerant Methodist preachers sent around the country to evangelize, especially in sparsely settled regions.

Circular Letter 1768 petition by Samuel Adams requesting British colonies to join in condemnation of the Townshend Duties.

Citizens United v. *Federal Election Commission* 2010 Supreme Court ruling in which the Court allowed for corporations or other special-interest groups to spend large sums on political campaigns.

City Beautiful Movement Social movement, started in 1893, that asserted a link between urban aesthetics and moral behavior.

Civil Rights Act of 1875 Legislation, sponsored by Charles Sumner, that outlawed racial discrimination in public spaces.

Civil Rights Act of 1964 Civil rights legislation that prohibited discrimination in employment and public facilities.

Civil Rights Cases 1883 cases heard by the Supreme Court, which ruled that much of the Civil Rights Act of 1875 was unconstitutional and that the Fourteenth Amendment did not bar private businesses from practicing racial discrimination.

Civil Service Act 1883 legislation, designed to combat political patronage, that placed candidates for federal positions on the basis of competitive examinations.

Civil War photographs Wartime photographs, most of which were exhibited and published by Mathew Brady, that featured scenes of death and camp life.

Civil War veterans' pension system First U.S. federal welfare program, which provided pensions to Union veterans and their dependents through a tariff on imported goods.

Civilian Conservation Corps Popular New Deal initiative that provided young men (and smaller numbers of women) work in wilderness areas and parks.

civilization program U.S. initiative to convert Native Americans to European ways of living, including private property, agriculture, literacy, and European gender roles.

clerks Lower-level office workers, usually young men, whose labor was associated with respectable, middle-class social status in the mid-nineteenth century.

Coercive Acts Controversial laws implemented after the Boston Tea Party to reassert Britain's control over Massachusetts colony.

Cold War Military, economic, cultural, psychological, and political rivalry between the United States and the Soviet Union following World War II.

colonial newspapers British American newspapers that provided commercial information and influenced local political opinion.

Colored Troops Civil War regiments of African American troops, formed after the Emancipation Proclamation, which encountered significant discrimination in the Union military.

Columbian exchange Massive transfer of people, animals, plants, microbes, commodities, ideas, and information across the Atlantic Ocean in the decades following Columbus's voyages.

Comanchería Region dominated by the Comanche people during the eighteenth and early nineteenth centuries, extending from western Kansas through much of New Mexico.

Committee of Vigilance Group formed in San Francisco in 1851 and 1856 to police and punish men engaged in gambling, commercial sex, and political corruption.

Committee on Public Information Government agency that used advertisements, films, and other media to shore up popular support for American involvement in World War I.

Committee on Style Group of state delegates, led by Gouverneur Morris, tasked with drafting the U.S. Constitution.

Committee to Re-elect the President Organization that supported Richard Nixon's 1972 presidential re-election campaign, which engaged in deceptive practices and illegal activities.

Committees of Correspondence Independent intercolonial communication network developed in 1773, which alarmed British authorities and Tories.

common schools Publicly supported, tuition-free schools that proliferated in the North during the 1840s.

Common Sense 1776 pamphlet by Thomas Paine that advocated American independence and was printed widely throughout the colonies.

Comprehensive Anti-apartheid Act 1986 legislation, passed by Congress over Ronald Reagan's veto, that divested capital from apartheid South Africa.

Compromise of 1850 Bundle of legislation, including California's admission as a free state and the Fugitive Slave Act, born of political debates over slavery in the Mexican Cession.

Compromise of 1877 Political agreement that resolved the contested election of 1876, whereby Republicans gained the presidency and Democrats gained full control of Southern state governments.

Comstock Act 1873 censorship law spearheaded by Anthony Comstock, which policed items sent through the mail deemed to be obscene.

Comstock Lode Silver deposit, discovered in 1859 in present-day Nevada that attracted speculators to invest significantly in mining companies and operations.

Coney Island Resort and amusement park outside New York City that became a popular site of leisure for the urban working class in the late nineteenth century.

Confederate States of America Government formed in 1861 by secessionist states over the issue of slavery.

Confiscation Act 1861 U.S. law, reinforcing wartime contraband policies, that authorized the capture of any Confederate property used in the rebellion, including enslaved human beings.

Congress of Industrial Organizations Confederation of labor unions that, unlike the rival American Federation of Labor, organized by industry rather than on an occupational basis and admitted unskilled workers, women, communists, Mexican Americans, and Black Americans.

Congress of Racial Equality Civil rights organization founded in 1941, which notably protested the segregation of interstate and public transportation.

congressional caucus Nominating process in the early republic in which congressmen from the same party designated presidential candidates.

Congressional Reconstruction Phase of Reconstruction during which Congress rather than the president directed the reconstruction of the South.

Conscription Act 1863 U.S. law instituting the first federal draft but allowing for the hiring of substitutes.

conservative think tanks Research and political advocacy organizations that emerged in the mid-twentieth century and propagated conservative ideologies such as free enterprise.

conspiracy theories Beliefs in coordinated, secretive plots to subvert the republic, which figured prominently in antebellum slavery politics.

conspiracy theories Beliefs that a small cohort of people secretly plot to manipulate political institutions or upend an existing social order.

consumer rights Set of rights that consumer advocacy groups first defined and demanded in the 1890s, such as a customer's right to safety and to full, truthful product information.

containment Strategy, the foundation of U.S. foreign policy during the Cold War (1947–1989), of confining communism to the Soviet Union and blocking the expansion of Soviet influence and power

Continental Army Military body formed by the Continental Congress, largely composed of young unmarried men and more genteel commissioned officers.

Continental dollars Wartime money, printed by the Continental Congress, that was essentially worthless by the end of the war.

contrabands Fugitives who escaped from slavery to Union camps during the Civil War and were declared freed from their owners on the model of enemy property captured during war.

Contract with America Republican campaign platform, leading up to 1994 midterm elections, in which Newt Gingrich promised low taxes, welfare reform, balanced budgets, and term limits, defining the party's policy agenda for the rest of the decade.

convenience foods Prepackaged, processed food products that became popular in the mid-twentieth century and sold in high volume at supermarkets.

Copperheads Democrats in the North who sought to end the Civil War.

corporal punishment Punishment inflicting bodily pain, such as whipping, flogging, or castration, often employed by slaveholders as a mechanism of control.

corrupt bargain Jacksonians' charge of collusion between Henry Clay and John Quincy Adams to fix the outcome of the election of 1824.

cotton gin Machine that separates cotton fibers from seeds, which facilitated and accelerated the South's fixation on cotton produced using slave labor.

counterculture Sociological term for the unconventional attitudes, desires, values, and ways of life that many U.S. youth adopted in the second half of the 1960s.

court-packing President Franklin D. Roosevelt's controversial plan (never implemented) to appoint up to six additional Supreme Court justices so as to expand the number of pro–New Deal liberals on the bench.

Covenant Chain System of diplomatic negotiation between British colonies and Native American groups during the first half of the eighteenth century, led by New York and the Iroquois League.

coverture Long-standing legal doctrine that subsumed a married woman's identity to that of her husband.

COVID-19 Deadly disease caused by a coronavirus that emerged in 2019, triggering a global pandemic that killed over six hundred thousand Americans and disrupted public health, economies, and everyday lives on a global scale.

Coxey's Army Group of roughly five hundred unemployed people, led by populist Jacob Coxey, who participated in the first march on Washington, D.C., and demanded unemployment relief.

Creek War War against the Redsticks, led by Andrew Jackson and allied Cherokee and Creeks, during the War of 1812.

creole Term applied to people of foreign ancestry born in colonial territory, such as the children of Europeans or Africans in North American colonies.

Crittenden Compromise Senator John Crittenden's failed 1861 proposal that suggested, in part, permanently barring the federal government from interfering with slavery in states where it was then legal and extending the Missouri Compromise line.

cross of gold Phrase used by William Jennings Bryan in the election of 1896 to appeal to rural voters and defend silver.

cruising Form of socializing that emerged in the 1950s in which teens drove around town in small groups with no single destination in mind and for the purpose of having fun and was later adapted to refer to the practice of walking the streets in search of a casual sexual partner.

Crusades Series of religiously motivated military expeditions by European Christians in the medieval era to seize control of Jerusalem and other lands held by non-Christians.

Cuban missile crisis International crisis in 1962 ignited by Soviet installation of nuclear weapons in Cuba, which raised tensions between the United States and USSR and heightened the threat of nuclear war.

cult of domesticity Term used by historians for the popular celebration, mostly in antebellum Northern middle-class culture, of the ideal home as a morally nourishing, female-dominated sphere.

culture wars Term coined in the 1980s to describe the clash of value systems that characterized that decade but that has also accompanied most other periods of rapid economic and political change.

D

Dawes Severalty Act 1887 legislation that divided reservation lands, designed to transform indigenous people into private property owners and assimilate them into American society.

D-Day June 6, 1944, when Allied forces landed in German-occupied Normandy, France, to carry out Operation Overlord.

de facto **segregation** Separate and unequal treatment of minorities, especially African Americans, despite the absence of racial segregation laws.

Declaration of Independence Text, primarily authored by Thomas Jefferson, that signified the Continental Congress's commitment to independence from Britain.

Declaratory Act British Parliament's assertion in 1766 that it had the authority to tax the American colonies.

decolonization Process by which colonial peoples in Asia, Africa, the Middle East, and the Caribbean demanded and won their independence from European rule in the three decades following World War II.

Deepwater Horizon Oil rig that exploded in 2010 and emptied 5 million barrels of oil into the Gulf of Mexico, creating an environmental and economic disaster.

Deferred Action for Childhood Arrivals Government program, introduced in 2012, that delayed deportation proceedings for Dreamers and gave them a right to apply for work permits.

Deists Adherents of a religious outlook (but not an organized church or denomination) that sees evidence of God in the natural world rather than in special acts of divine revelation and intervention.

Democrats Major political party organized around the candidacy of Andrew Jackson and under the leadership of Martin Van Buren, which emerged in the Second Party System.

department store parades Boisterous public processions sponsored by businesses and department stores, such as Macy's, that were popularized in the 1920s and celebrated consumerism.

deposit removal Andrew Jackson's redepositing of federal money in state-chartered private banks, which escalated his administration's conflict with the national bank.

deregulation Abolition or suspension of regulations, after 1980, that were designed to stabilize the economy and protect consumers, workers, and the environment but that business considered cumbersome, costly, or ineffective.

Deseret Mormon state declared by Brigham Young in Utah, which depended on large-scale irrigation and cooperative living.

deskilling Subdivision of craft labor into smaller components, at least some of which require less skill.

détente From the French word for "relaxation," a policy of easing tense political relations, especially between the United States and the Soviet Union in the 1970s.

diaspora Geographically dispersed community linked by a shared identification with or attachment to a distant homeland.

digital divide Gap between people with access to the Internet and all it has to offer and those without access.

Digital Revolution Mass digitization of information and widespread adoption of the Internet and cell phones.

disco American music genre most popular in the urban nightlife of the 1970s, characterized by flashy dancing and musical elements of funk and soul.

Dodd-Frank Act 2010 reform, enacted during the Great Recession, limiting the investment activities of banks.

dollar diplomacy Term coined by Theodore Roosevelt to describe President William Howard Taft's policy of pursuing U.S. business interests overseas and gaining access to foreign markets by extending loans to foreign governments.

domestic servants Workers, usually poorer women, who worked in the homes of more economically independent families.

Dominion of New England James II's attempt in the 1680s to reorganize English colonies north of Maryland into a supercolony.

Donner party Ill-fated group of American emigrants whose deadly trials were publicized to illustrate the dangers of overland travel.

dot-com crash Sudden drop in the share prices for technology stocks in March 2000, which ruined many Internet businesses, eviscerated the NASDAQ index, and ended a period of exuberant optimism about the digital economy.

Double V campaign Black freedom movement campaign during World War II that linked victory over fascism abroad and victory over racism at home as two sides of the same democratic coin.

Dreamers Millennials and members of Gen Z who were brought to the United States as children by undocumented immigrant parents.

Dred Scott v. Sandford 1857 Supreme Court case that denied African Americans U.S. citizenship and asserted that slavery could not be legally regulated in the territories.

Dust Bowl A wheat-growing region of the Southern plains in which drought conditions and over-plowing led to destructive dust storms and mass out-migration.

E

Easton Treaty conference Meeting that improved Pennsylvania's relationship with the Delaware and Iroquois League during the French and Indian War.

Economic Opportunity Act of 1964 Welfare reform that battled poverty by equipping lower-income Americans with skills and education through such programs as the Jobs Corps.

Eighteenth Amendment Constitutional amendment banning the manufacture and sale of alcoholic beverages, promoted by women reformers and prohibitionists.

eight-hour work day Length of the workday, demanded by workers and unions in the Gilded Age and Progressive Era, that became standard for workers in many industries during the New Deal.

1840 schism Fracturing of the antislavery movement over the role of women and the legitimacy of political action.

election of 1800 Close election between Thomas Jefferson and John Adams, producing the first transition of power between political parties.

election of 1824 Tightly contested presidential election that was determined by the House of Representatives and resulted in John Quincy Adams's victory over Andrew Jackson.

election of 1864 United States presidential contest between Abraham Lincoln and Democratic challenger George B. McClellan, which Lincoln handily won.

election of 1896 Presidential contest between William Jennings Bryan and William McKinley, in which debates about the gold standard and free silver figured prominently.

election of 1980 Presidential election in which Republican Ronald Reagan defeated Democrat Jimmy Carter in a landslide victory.

election of 2012 Presidential election in which incumbent Democrat Barack Obama defeated moderate Republican Mitt Romney in the popular and electoral vote despite outsized Republican campaign spending.

election of 2020 Presidential election in which Democrat Joseph Biden, with running mate Kamala Harris, defeated incumbent Republican Donald Trump, who falsely claimed that widespread voter fraud had contributed to his loss.

Emancipation Proclamation 1863 proclamation, issued by Abraham Lincoln, that declared all enslaved people in rebellious states to be free, but did not abolish slavery in the United States.

empire of goods Term used by recent historians to describe the way consumption linked dispersed colonial populations to one another and to the British Empire during the eighteenth century.

enclosure movement Trend in England around 1700 toward fencing off pastures and converting land traditionally held in common into exclusive private property.

encomienda Exploitative labor regime that Spanish conquerors imposed on native populations in the Americas.

energy crisis Shortage of energy resources that precipitates a social or political problem by making it difficult or expensive to light and heat homes and businesses or to fuel transportation vehicles.

English Civil War Violent political conflict in the 1640s that divided English society and deposed the English monarchy.

English Reformation Rejection of the Roman Church and papal authority by Henry VIII and Elizabeth I.

Enlightenment Broad European intellectual movement in the seventeenth and eighteenth centuries promoting reason, the scientific method, religious skepticism, and the exchange of new ideas.

Environmental Protection Act 1970 law creating a federal agency devoted to environmental issues.

Equal Rights Amendment Constitutional amendment guaranteeing equal rights regardless of sex, which was never ratified and was subject to fierce cultural, religious, and political debate in the 1970s.

Equal Rights Amendment Proposed constitutional amendment, initially promoted by the National Woman's Party, for legal rights regardless of sex.

Erie Canal The first major United States canal project, which connected the Hudson River to Lake Erie and was central to the development of the American commercial market and the growth of New York City.

ethnic revival Rise of ethnic pride movements in the 1970s, especially among the descendants of eastern and southern European immigrants.

ethnonationalism Nationalist sentiment or ideology rooted in the idea that the nation is limited to or defined by a particular ethnic or racial group.

evil empire Ronald Reagan's term for the Soviet Union framing adversarial U.S.–Soviet relations in moral terms of good and evil.

Executive Order 9066 Executive order creating military zones in the United States in which Japanese nationals, Americans of Japanese descent, and the Unangan (Aleut people of Alaska) were forcibly relocated and interned.

Exodusters African Americans in 1879 who, in response to the defeat of Reconstruction, embarked on what they called a Great Exodus from the South to Kansas.

expansionist Name preferred by Gilded Age and early Progressive Era advocates of U.S. empire-building because of the popular association of imperialism with unpopular European monarchies.

F

Fair Deal Harry Truman's term to describe and promote his plans to extend the New Deal.

fall of Saigon Invasion and capture of Saigon by North Vietnam in 1975, which ended the civil war in Vietnam, though not the larger fighting in the region.

Farm Security Administration New Deal agency designed to assist displaced tenant farmers but which failed to stem their Dust Bowl migration and alleviate economic insecurity.

farming frontier American farmers' westward migration onto the Great Plains and elsewhere, sped by federal distribution of Western lands after the Civil War.

Federal Copyright Law 1790 law that helped make domestic American publishing a profitable business enterprise.

Federal Reserve Act 1913 law creating the Federal Reserve system, centralizing the nation's banking, and creating greater federal control of the money supply.

Federalists In the 1780s, proponents of the new national constitution and a stronger federal government; a decade later, a national political party that championed strong central government.

Fifteenth Amendment Constitutional amendment granting citizens the right to vote regardless of race or a previous condition of servitude.

Fifth Freedom Idea that, in addition to President Franklin D. Roosevelt's fundamental Four Freedoms, there was the freedom of economic choice—that is, the freedom to undertake economic actions, including buying and selling, without government regulation.

filibuster Any attempt to block or delay Senate action on a bill or other matter, often by debating it at length or offering multiple procedural motions.

filibusters Unauthorized expeditions by private armies into foreign lands, either for profit or for political ideals such as U.S. expansionism.

Filipino insurgency Armed uprisings and episodes of violent resistance in the Philippines after Spain transferred control of the islands to the United States in 1899.

final solution Nazi regime's name for the Holocaust's deadliest phase, from 1942 to 1945, during which it carried out the execution of 12 million Jews, communists, Poles, Slavs, Roma (gypsies), gays, Jehovah's Witnesses, and other minorities.

fire-eaters Southern defenders of slavery who adopted increasingly intransigent and belligerent postures in the 1850s.

fireside chats President Franklin D. Roosevelt's publicity technique of using the new medium of radio to bypass the conventional news media (the press) and communicate directly with voters.

First Battle of Bull Run Civil War battle in 1861 in Virginia that was a major early victory for the Confederacy.

First Continental Congress 1774 meeting of colonial representatives, which sought peaceful redress of colonial grievances and espoused themes of unity, but not independence.

first hundred days Period immediately following a president's first inauguration, which, beginning with Franklin D. Roosevelt, has been held by voters and the news media to be a crucial period for establishing the president's priorities, leadership style, and legislative agenda.

First New Deal Franklin Roosevelt's initial response to widespread economic crisis, some key programs of which met with criticism from big business and unfavorable Supreme Court rulings.

First Seminole War Andrew Jackson's highly controversial invasion of Spanish Florida in 1819.

Five Civilized Tribes Designation applied to those Native American groups in the Southeast (the Creek peoples, Cherokee, Chickasaw, Choctaw, and Seminoles) that appeared to have embraced key aspects of white American culture, including settled agriculture and literacy.

five substantial commercial cities Major seaports and conduits of British Atlantic commerce before 1750: Boston, Newport, New York, Philadelphia, and Charleston.

flapper Young woman who openly transgressed the gender and class conventions of the 1920s through her dress, comportment, use of makeup, and assertive sexuality.

Food Administration Government agency, established in 1917, that oversaw Allies' food supply and encouraged Americans to boost food production and reduce household consumption.

Fordism Economic system, named after auto manufacturer Henry Ford and dominant from 1945 to the 1970s, that paired mass production with mass consumption by ensuring that industrial workers were optimally efficient and well paid (to enable them to purchase consumer goods).

Foreign Miners Taxes California tax on non-U.S. citizens in 1850, an effort to exclude gold-seekers of other nationalities from the mines.

foreign-language newspapers Non-English newspapers published in the United States that helped sustain ethnonational communities.

Fort Pillow Massacre 1864 Confederate massacre of nearly two hundred Black soldiers after they had surrendered.

Fort Stanwix Fort defended against British troops during the Revolution by a multiethnic force of Germans, New York colonists, and Native Americans.

Fort Sumter U.S. fort in South Carolina that was attacked by the Confederacy in the first military action of the Civil War.

Fort William Henry Site of a massacre of British soldiers by French-allied native people during the French and Indian War.

forty-niners Gold seekers during the California gold rush.

Four Freedoms Universal freedoms defined by President Franklin D. Roosevelt in a 1941 speech: freedoms of worship and of speech and freedoms from fear and from economic want.

Fourteen Points Woodrow Wilson's principles for a postwar peace settlement, which included calls for free trade, self-determination, and an international association to ensure states' security.

Fourteenth Amendment Constitutional amendment decreeing birthright citizenship for all persons born on U.S. soil, except Native Americans, and protecting the basic rights of all citizens from infringement by the states.

Franciscans Spanish priests belonging to a particular order, empowered by the Ordinances of Discovery to pursue the religious conversion and submission of the Pueblos.

free enterprise Libertarian economist Friedrich Hayek's name for the business sector, which, he argued in the 1940s, was the origin and guarantor of freedom itself and should therefore be free of almost all legal constraints.

free silver Political slogan coined by farmers and mining companies of the late Gilded Age who called for the unlimited minting of silver coins, which would have reduced farmers' debts and increased mining profits.

Free Soil Party Political party, formed in 1848 by a coalition of Democrats and Whigs, that opposed extending slavery to Western territories.

free trade zone Designated area of a foreign country, increasingly common in the late twentieth century, in which American and other companies are permitted to land, reconfigure, manufacture, and re-export goods without paying taxes or export duties.

Freedmen's Bureau War Department agency established after the Civil War, that was tasked with facilitating the transition to freedom of formerly enslaved people.

freedom rides Civil rights demonstrations started by CORE in 1961, in which activists traveled throughout the South to test the enforcement of court-ordered desegregation on public busses.

freedom suits   Legal petitions for freedom presented by enslaved African Americans during the revolutionary era to colonial or state courts.

Freedom Summer   Civil rights campaign in the summer of 1964 in which volunteers registered Black voters throughout the South.

freehold   Form of land ownership (common in the modern West) in which an individual can buy, sell, bequeath, or exchange the land at will.

Freeport Doctrine   Political strategy suggested by Stephen Douglas in defense of popular sovereignty, which held that settlers could practically strip slavery of necessary legal protections even if they were legally prohibited from outlawing it.

French and Indian War   North American theater of the Seven Years' War, which diminished France's imperial presence and provoked new conflict between native people and settlers.

French Revolution   Political crisis that overthrew the French monarchy and informed partisanship and foreign policy in the early United States.

frontier thesis   Historians' name for the popular theory, advanced by Frederick Jackson Turner in 1893, that the experience of westward expansion freed Americans from outdated European customs and instilled in them a love of democracy.

Fugitive Slave Act   Controversial 1850 law strengthening the legal obligation to return escapees from slavery to their owners.

G

G.I. Bill   1944 act that offered veterans numerous benefits, including education, job training, and housing.

gag rule   Rule prohibiting discussion of a particular topic, most famously the House of Representatives' limitation on petitions relating to slavery during the 1830s.

Gaither Report   1957 government report detailing the USSR's military and technological advances, which impelled the United States to liberally invest in science and technology.

gang system   Method of labor management used on tobacco plantations— for example, enslaved laborers work together in teams under the scrutiny of a foreman or an overseer (*see also* task system).

gaslight   Artificial light, which notably revolutionized the experience of nightlife in cities.

gay pride parades   Public exhibitions celebrating gay relationships and identities, which first became popular in the early 1970s.

General Trades Union   Multi-city labor union founded in 1833 by a coalition of artisans from various trades.

Generation X   Generation of Americans that followed the baby boomers and defined themselves as distinct from hippies, the counterculture, and mass protest movements.

Generation Z (Gen Z)   Generation of people born after 1996, notable for left-leaning political activism and widespread use of social media networks.

genome   Genetic material, which became subject to new techniques of digitized sequencing and analysis that revolutionized medical and genetic research in the late 1990s.

Gentlemen's Agreement   1907 diplomatic agreement between the United States and Japan, in which Japan consented to restrict the emigration of Japanese laborers to the United States.

gerrymandering   Practice, common but increasingly controversial in the Gilded Age, of setting electoral districts to the advantage of one's own party.

Gettysburg Address   Abraham Lincoln's address at the dedication of a cemetery in Gettysburg, which emphasized the nation's founding ideals of freedom and equality.

Ghana   Dominant West African kingdom between the eighth and thirteenth centuries that controlled significant gold deposits and established extensive trade routes.

gig economy   System of employment that became prominent in the 2010s, in which workers relied on independent contracting facilitated by web-based applications and services.

Gilded Age   Term coined by Mark Twain and Charles Dudley Warner, and later adopted by historians, to describe the period 1865–1895.

globalization   Complex and controversial process, under way since the 1960s but intensifying since 1980, by which certain national barriers, particularly those constraining money, goods, and ideas, are lowered or disassembled.

Glorious Revolution   Bloodless regime change in England in 1688 that resulted in William III's and Mary II's taking the throne of James II.

Godey's Lady's Book   Influential nineteenth-century magazine, founded in 1830, that shaped the lives of middle-class women.

gold standard   Monetary system, in operation in the United States between 1879 and 1971, under which paper notes were convertible into a predetermined quantity of gold.

gradual abolition   Process by which slavery ended legally in many Northern states, typically by laws that declared children born to enslaved people after a certain date to be free and that liberated those already enslaved once they reached a particular age.

Great Awakening   Historians' name for a series of religious revivals and pietist movements in various British American colonies in the second quarter of the eighteenth century.

Great Chicago Fire   1871 fire that destroyed much of Chicago and, in its aftermath, inflamed class tensions and anxieties about industrial growth in cities.

Great Migration   Movement, between 1910 and 1970, of over 6 million African Americans out of the South into the cities of the West, Midwest, and Northeast.

Great Mississippi Flood   1927 natural disaster that was met with a massive relief effort led by Herbert Hoover (who failed to protect and aid displaced Black Americans).

Great Puritan Migration   Historians' name for the movement of tens of thousands of Puritans from England to the American colonies (mostly New England and the Caribbean) from the late 1620s to 1640.

Great Sioux War of 1866-1868 Plains war between the United States and the Sioux, Cheyenne, and Arapaho, which resulted in a Sioux victory against American encroachment.

Great Sioux War of 1876-1877 Plains war that broke out after the discovery of gold in the Black Hills, ending in a Sioux defeat.

Great Society Lyndon Johnson's domestic policies aimed at stemming poverty and racial injustice.

Green Mountain Boys New England farmers who engaged in protest and vigilante violence against colonial authority figures in New York.

greenback Paper currency first issued during the Civil War (by the Union) to stabilize the economy.

greenhouse gases Gases, such as carbon dioxide and methane, that alter the Earth's climate and became fixtures in discussions of climate change after the 1980s.

growth liberalism Theory behind Lyndon B. Johnson's War on Poverty (1964-1968) that government-funded education and vocational training programs would get the unemployed back to work and out of poverty and dependence.

guerrilla warfare Irregular style of military engagement, used especially by pro-Confederates in the Civil War, featuring loosely organized acts of arson, looting, or murder.

Gulf of Tonkin Resolution 1964 resolution passed by Congress that authorized the United States to engage directly and militarily in Vietnam.

Gullah Patois (blended language), developed by enslaved people in parts of the South Carolina Lowcountry, with many African words and linguistic features.

H

Haitian Revolution Complex colonial uprising against France in the sugar colony St. Domingue, resulting in Haiti becoming an independent Black republic in 1804.

Harlem Renaissance Diverse cultural movement of the 1920s—centered in Harlem, New York—in which African

American writers, musicians, and artists defied racism and embraced Black pride.

Hartford Convention Anti-war delegation of Northern Federalists, in which they floated secession and devised strategies to weaken Southern Republicans' political power.

Haymarket Affair 1886 bombing at a workers' rally in Chicago, which contributed to increased nativism and widespread suspicion of anarchism, radicalism, and the Knights of Labor.

Hays Code Guidelines established in 1934 to regulate the content of Hollywood films, including bans on depictions of sexual passion, homosexuality, and interracial relationships.

Helsinki Accords 1975 international agreement, considered a major easing of Cold War hostility, that recognized the sovereignty and boundaries of European states in the Eastern Bloc and expressed a commitment to universal human rights.

Hernandez v. *Texas* 1954 court case in which the Supreme Court ruled that all racial groups were entitled to equal protection according to the Fourteenth Amendment.

hiring-out system Practice, common in Southern cities, of renting out one's enslaved worker to another white employer in return for wages.

Home Affordable Modification Program Federal program introduced in 2009 to help homeowners facing foreclosure due to the Great Recession.

homeless Americans People without permanent residence, usually due to socio-economic dislocation, whose plight was particularly pressing during the Great Depression and again throughout most of the 1980s.

Homestead Act 1862 law that facilitated U.S. western expansion by making 160-acre lots of land available to American citizens.

honor Cultural ideal cited by historians and anthropologists as central to the values of elite whites in the antebellum South.

Hoovervilles Shantytowns, satirically named after President Herbert Hoover, that unemployed Americans set up during the Great Depression on

the periphery of cities, typically alongside rail lines and near city dumps.

Horseshoe Bend Battle in which Andrew Jackson's forces defeated the Redsticks, resulting in a massive territorial cession to the United States.

House Un-American Activities Committee Conservative congressional group that, starting in the late 1930s, investigated leftists and communists and sought to discredit some New Dealers.

Hull House Chicago community center founded in 1888 by Jane Addams and devised to culturally uplift the urban poor and immigrant populations by exposing them to middle-class volunteers and ideals.

humanitarian crisis Event in which mass death or suffering is thought to be under way or imminent yet avoidable, provided that governments, relief agencies, and/or citizens take action.

Hurricane Katrina Devastating storm that struck the Gulf Coast in 2005, flooding the city of New Orleans, killing more than eighteen hundred people, and bringing shame to a federal government that responded poorly to the crisis.

Hyer versus Sullivan 1849 bareknuckle boxing match, which urban Americans around the country followed in real time thanks to the telegraph.

I

"I can't breathe" Words spoken by African American man Eric Garner as he was fatally choked by a police officer, which became a rallying cry for Black Lives Matter.

illegal alien Category, originating with the Chinese Exclusion Act (1882) and reinforced by the National Origins Act (1924), denoting a person who has entered the United States illegally.

immediatism Radical ideology of American abolitionists who favored the immediate and uncompensated emancipation of all enslaved people.

Immigration Act of 1924 Restrictive immigration legislation that set quotas limiting the number of immigrants permitted into the United States and reinforced "illegal alien" as a legal category.

Immigration and Customs Enforcement (ICE) Federal agency that became controversial during the Trump presidency for conducting aggressive immigration raids and deportations.

Immigration and Nationality Act of 1965 Legislation that abolished the national origins quota, which had been particularly prejudicial to immigrants from southern and eastern Europe, Asia, and Africa.

impressment Forced conscription of men into naval service, a practice the British were frequently accused of carrying out on American ships in the early nineteenth century.

Indian liquor trade Settler commerce that developed in the British colonies and that observers decried for its destructive effects on native peoples.

Indian New Deal New Deal initiative that ended allotment for indigenous peoples and empowered tribal councils.

Indian Removal Act Cornerstone of Andrew Jackson's first term that rejected civilizationist policy in favor of voluntary or forced relocation of native peoples.

Industrial Workers of the World Labor union that appealed to immigrants, women, and African Americans and whose aim was to seize the means of production from capitalists.

industrialization Reorganization of an economy and a society as it turns toward large-scale manufacturing, typically involving the specialization, subdivision, and mechanization of traditional production processes.

installment plan System of consumer credit consisting of a series of regular payments, popularized in the 1920s after its adoption by General Motors.

Insular Cases 1901–1904 Supreme Court cases on territorial incorporation, concluding that persons born in American-occupied territories do not automatically receive constitutional rights.

internal improvements Government-subsidized projects, such as roads and canals, designed to facilitate economic development and bind a country together.

international human rights movement Informal network of dissident political groups in different countries and of nongovernmental organizations that seek to hold governments and other entities accountable to universal standards of human rights, a concept that drew increasing power and prestige in the 1970s.

International Monetary Fund International organization formed in 1944 at Bretton Woods to stabilize and facilitate the global financial system.

internationalists Commentators and policy makers, particularly during the 1930s, who criticized isolationism and argued that the United States should play an active role in international relations.

Internet Global system of computer networks, introduced in the 1960s by the U.S. military, that became a mass medium for global digital communication in the 1990s.

Internet piracy Originally, in the 2000s, the music industry's term for the unauthorized duplication and sale over the Internet of copyrighted music and subsequently used for the illegal Internet duplication of any and all copyrighted material.

Interstate Commerce Act of 1887 Legislation that helped establish federal regulations, such as fair prices and conditions, for railroads.

invasion of Quebec Unsuccessful American military campaign against Britain in 1775, which some Americans interpreted as a religious war against Catholics.

Iran-Contra scandal Political scandal caused by the Reagan administration's covert funding of Contra fighters in Nicaragua through arms sales to Iran.

iron curtain Popular term, coined by British prime minister Winston Churchill in 1946, to describe the ideological barrier and physical boundary between Soviet-dominated Europe and Western Europe.

Iron Palace A.T. Stewart's department store, which opened in New York in 1862, and pioneered a model of consumer aesthetics and retail practice followed in urban America during the Gilded Age.

Iroquois League A powerful political bloc of indigenous nations that formed in the region south of Lake Ontario before the arrival of Europeans in North America.

ISIS Militant Islamic organization that supplanted al-Qaeda as a dominant actor in Middle Eastern conflicts and the War on Terror during Barack Obama's presidency.

J

Jacksonian Democracy Common but potentially misleading scholarly term for the culture of mass political participation that President Andrew Jackson both championed and symbolized.

Jackson-Vanik Amendment 1974 U.S. law that withheld trade privileges from nations that denied citizens the right of emigration.

Jamestown English settlement in Virginia whose colonists successfully cultivated tobacco, secured an alliance with Powhatan, and warred with Opechancanough.

Jay's Treaty 1795 U.S. treaty with Britain that improved the countries' relations but fueled partisanship between Federalists and Republicans.

Jim Crow Both a standard dance and a stock character on the blackface stage.

Jim Crow laws Collective term for the legal system of racial segregation and discrimination that characterized the South between the late nineteenth century and the mid-1960s.

jingoism Pejorative term for a form of extreme patriotism, first identified in connection with British imperialism in the 1870s and later popularized in the United States by critics of U.S. expansionism.

John Brown's raid John Brown's attempt in 1859 to seize a federal arsenal and spark a slave insurrection, for which he was executed but subsequently lionized by antislavery Americans.

Johnson County War 1892 conflict between small ranchers and cattle barons in Wyoming, resulting in the murder of several ranchers.

Jubilee Singers African American choir formed in the 1870s that toured internationally and performed and transcribed many slave spirituals.

judicial review Judges' assessment of the constitutional validity of acts by the executive and legislative branches of government.

K

Kansas-Nebraska Act Controversial 1854 law permitting territorial residents to determine the future of slavery in parts of the Louisiana Purchase.

Kefauver Committee Congressional sub-committee, convened in 1954–1955, that condemned the portrayal of teenage sexuality and delinquency in popular culture.

Kentucky and Virginia Resolutions Resolutions, secretly authored by James Madison and Thomas Jefferson, that sought to invalidate the Alien and Sedition Acts by limiting the authority of the federal government.

Keynesianism Branch of economics, developed by John Maynard Keynes and applied in the United States in 1933–1980, in which government stabilized the economy by actively stimulating consumer demand and investing directly in the housing sector, agriculture, industry, interstate transportation, and science and technology.

Keystone XL pipeline Proposed oil pipeline between Canada and Texas that critics charged would threaten the environment and indigenous sovereignty and sacred sites.

King George's War North American theater of the War of Austrian Succession, which helped cement bonds between British colonists and their empire.

King James Bible Scripture produced during the reign of James I in an effort to standardize Bible-reading practices.

King Philip's War Major military conflict among New England colonists, the Wampanoags, and other native peoples, from 1675 to 1676.

Kitchen Debate Impromptu televised debate between Nikita Khrushchev and Richard Nixon on the socio-cultural significance of American household goods and technologies.

Knights of Labor National workers' union that became popular in the 1880s and sought to create solidarity among productive laborers.

Know-Nothing Party Political party, also known as the American Party, formed in 1851 and known for secretive rituals, virulent nativism, and anti-Catholicism.

Ku Klux Klan White supremacist group that first formed during Reconstruction, utilizing tactics of violence and intimidation against the Black community.

L

La Caroline Huguenot colony established in Florida in 1564 and attacked by Spain to consolidate Catholic rule in the region.

Land Ordinance of 1785 Ordinance that specified the elaborate division of land for states and townships in the Northwest Territory.

land speculation Buying or owning land with the intention of selling it at a profit.

Latin Christendom Dominant religious community of western Europe in the medieval period, spread across much of the continent and unified under the authority of a pope in Rome.

League of Nations First intergovernmental organization, operating from 1919 to 1946, to promote peace and a system of collective security based on negotiation and arbitration.

Lecompton Constitution 1858 proslavery state constitution for Kansas, based on disputed election results and supported by President James Buchanan but rejected by other Northern Democrats.

Leisler's Rebellion 1689 uprising in New York, led by Jacob Leisler, in support of the Glorious Revolution.

Lend-Lease Act 1941 law authorizing the United States to supply materiel to countries whose protection the president deemed vital to U.S. defense.

Letters from an American Farmer Crèvecoeur's 1782 collection of literary essays that pondered early American identity and the virtues of American society.

Levittown Standardized, prefabricated, and relatively affordable housing that was important to mid-twentieth-century suburbanization.

liberal (modernist) Christianity Diverse body of thought that gained popularity among urban Protestants in the late nineteenth and early twentieth centuries and that emphasized the importance of active interpretation in the reading of Scripture.

liberal internationalism Foreign policy philosophy, invoked by Barack Obama, that emphasized global U.S. leadership, international diplomacy, and multilateralism.

libertarianism Body of thought, initially influential among a small segment of the American business elite in the 1950s, holding that individuals own themselves and have a moral right to acquire property and that the state should simply keep the peace and protect private property.

liberty bonds War bonds sold to raise capital during World War I and the subject of a large-scale publicity campaign.

Liberty League Group of financiers and industrialists who condemned the First New Deal.

Liberty Tree Trees, usually elms and oaks, that the Sons of Liberty designated as symbols of liberty and organized public protests around.

Little Ice Age Cooling period, beginning in the early fourteenth century that likely contributed to the abandonment of Mississippian cities.

lobbyists Representatives of corporations, foreign governments, or private individuals who seek to influence legislators' political behavior.

Lone Star Republic Independent state of Texas, which permitted slavery and enticed U.S. immigrants with land grants.

Long Depression 1873–1879 economic recession that depressed large swathes of the economy and created new conditions for class and racial conflict.

long telegram 1946 message from diplomat George Kennan that warned of future Soviet expansion and conflict and formed a basis for American Cold War policy.

Lord Dunmore's Proclamation Royal governor of Virginia's pledge to offer liberty to enslaved men who took up arms against the colonial rebellion.

Louisiana Purchase France's territorial cession brokered by the Jefferson administration in 1803, doubling the size of the United States.

Loyalists Name adopted by colonists who favored rapprochement with Great Britain and the maintenance of colonial relations during the Revolutionary era.

Lusitania British passenger ship sunk by a German U-boat in 1915, killing 1,195 people, an event which American conservative nationalists cited as an argument for war.

lyceum movement Antebellum network of adult education programs in the North and Midwest featuring lectures on philosophical and academic topics.

lynch men Group of Charleston citizens who confiscated and burned mass mailings of the American Anti-Slavery Society in 1835.

lynching Illegal but unpunished execution of Black Americans commonplace between 1880 and the 1930s that enforced the subordinate status of Black people in Southern society.

M

maize Corn, first grown around 5000 BCE in present-day Mexico, that supported many North American agricultural societies.

make America great again Ronald Reagan's 1980 presidential campaign slogan, which represented a revival of conservative politics.

"Make America Great Again" Donald Trump's 2016 presidential campaign slogan, which implied nationalist and nativist politics.

Mali Powerful West African kingdom whose rulers adopted Islam and established limited intercourse with Portugal before collapsing in the fifteenth century.

Manhattan Project Top-secret U.S. government project that enlisted physicists to develop the atomic bomb during World War II.

Manifest Destiny Popular ideology from the 1840s maintaining that the United States was divinely ordained to expand to the Pacific Ocean.

Mann Act 1910 legislation criminalizing the transportation of women across state lines for prostitution, as well as other, vaguely defined immoral sexual behavior.

manumission Legal emancipation of an enslaved person by his or her slaveholder.

March on Washington for Jobs and Freedom Massive, televised civil rights demonstration in Washington, D.C., in 1963, notable for featuring Martin Luther King, Jr.'s "I Have a Dream" speech.

March to the Sea General William Tecumseh Sherman's 1864 military campaign in Georgia, in which Union forces systematically destroyed any property in their path.

Marshall Plan U.S. program to aid the European economic recovery after World War II and stem the spread of communism into Western Europe.

mass consumption Economic and cultural system, which took root in the nineteenth century and became dominant in the twentieth century, that produces an ever wider array of commercial goods and services and promotes the idea that personal happiness can be attained through the acquisition of material goods.

mass shootings Violent incidents that became politically and socially salient in the 2010s, in which an assailant armed with a gun attacked a group of people.

Massachusetts Bay Colony Largest New England colony, whose Puritan leaders touted commitment to piety and communal living.

Maverick Law 1884 law, passed in Wyoming Territory, that made unbranded, wild cattle the legal property of wealthy cattle barons.

Mayflower Compact Agreement signed aboard the *Mayflower* by forty-one Pilgrim men, binding them together as a political body.

McCarthyism Originally Senator Joseph McCarthy's policy of identifying and purging from government and the

culture industries any persons suspected of being communist; subsequently any form of persecutory investigation that stifles free speech or is motivated chiefly by partisan politics.

McClure's Affordable, nationwide magazine that published writing by muckrakers such as Ida Tarbell.

Me Decade Journalist Tom Wolfe's derogatory label for the 1970s as a time of excessive individualism.

Medicaid Government-funded health care, enacted in 1965, that covered the medical expenses of lower-income Americans.

Medicare Government-funded health care, enacted in 1965, that covered the medical expenses of senior citizens.

meetinghouse In New England colonial towns, the central building where religious services and public affairs were conducted.

Mercantile Agency First credit bureau in the United States, founded in 1841 by middle-class reformer Lewis Tappan.

mercantilism Term coined by economists in the eighteenth century for the belief that a nation's military and political well-being depended on an active regulation of international trade, generally toward such goals as increasing exports, decreasing imports, and securing a net influx of gold and silver.

Mesoamerica Geographical region, encompassing Central Mexico and Central America, where a variety of ancient complex civilizations flourished before European contact.

mestizo Offspring of colonial Spanish immigrant men and indigenous women who populated Mexico and Central America.

Metamora Popular 1829 play, starring Edwin Forrest, that drew on broad national interest in Native American identity during the Indian Removal era.

Methodism Protestant denomination, spread by itinerant preachers that appealed to many disenfranchised Americans.

#MeToo Social movement, built on social media, that emerged in 2017 encouraging women to publicly discuss experiences of sexual assault.

Meuse-Argonne offensive   Major military campaign in World War I and largest in U.S. military history, wherein AEF and Allied forces pushed Germans out of France, resulting in German calls for an armistice.

Mexican immigration   Migration from Mexico, often a target of regulation by American legislators and nativists.

Middle Colonies   English colonies on the Atlantic seaboard between New England and the Chesapeake (New York, New Jersey, Pennsylvania, and Delaware).

Middle Passage   Forced transatlantic journey of African captives bound for slavery in the Americas.

midterm elections of 2018   Elections during Republican Donald Trump's presidency that resulted in Democrats' gaining control of the most diverse and gender-balanced House of Representatives in U.S. history.

military occupation   Territories, cities, or towns subject to provisional rule by armed forces.

military-industrial complex   Dwight D. Eisenhower's disparaging name for the tight-knit relationship that emerged between some branches of industry and the Department of Defense in the 1950s.

millennialism   Belief in the imminent arrival of a thousand-year reign of Christ that will usher in the Last Judgment or more generally an anticipation of imminent apocalyptic change.

Millerites   Adherents of William Miller's millennialist prophecies in the 1840s.

mining frontier   Miners' eastward movement in the second half of the nineteenth century from California to newly discovered ore deposits in Nevada, Montana, Idaho, Colorado, and elsewhere.

Mississippi Plan   Southern Democrats' plan to suppress Black and Republican voters by means of militia violence and intimidation.

Mississippian civilization   Term used by archaeologists and historians to describe a shared culture and a network of political influence, centered in Cahokia near present-day St. Louis, linking a broad range of Native American groups in the Midwest and Southeast.

Missouri Compromise   1820 legislation that balanced free and slave states and determined the legal status of slavery in western territories by the geographical line 36°30′.

modern American Christmas   Indoor, family-centered festivity that emerged in the antebellum period.

modern corporation   Large, hierarchical business enterprise, staffed by salaried and waged employees and owned by stockholders, that came to play a dominant and sometimes controversial role in the American economy after 1865.

modern Republicanism   Approach to government, championed by Dwight D. Eisenhower in the 1950s, that followed a conciliatory middle path between New Deal liberalism and conservative Republicanism and promoted the interests of both corporations and middle-class Americans.

Monkey Trial   Sensational 1925 trial of John Scopes, who was tried and convicted for teaching Darwinian evolution in Tennessee.

monopoly   Term used by critics of big business in the nineteenth and early twentieth centuries to describe companies that were free to charge high prices because they had no or only a few competitors.

Monroe Doctrine   James Monroe's foreign policy principle that the United States would not tolerate European interference with the sovereignty of nations in the Americas.

Moore's Ford lynchings   1946 murders of four Black people in Georgia, which caused national outrage among civil rights organizations and prompted President Truman to propose anti-lynching and civil rights initiatives.

moral drama   Reform-minded theatrical entertainment, deemed respectable for women and children, introduced in American cities in the mid-nineteenth century.

Moral Majority   Conservative evangelical political organization founded by Jerry Falwell in 1979.

Mormon exodus   Mormon migration from Illinois to Utah in 1846, led by Brigham Young in an effort to isolate the Mormon community from other Americans.

moundbuilding   Massive earthworks construction used by numerous indigenous North American groups for ceremonial and political purposes many centuries before European contact.

muckrakers   Name that President Theodore Roosevelt gave journalists of the Progressive Era who investigated and publicized governmental corruption, dangerous living and working conditions, and the ruthlessness of certain leading businessmen.

Muslim ban   President Donald Trump's executive action disallowing people from majority-Muslim countries to enter the United States.

My Lai Massacre   Mass murder of over four hundred Vietnamese civilians by American G.I.s in 1968 during the Vietnam War.

N

Nation of Islam   Muslim organization and movement that encouraged Black nationalism and is known for its relationship with Malcolm X.

National Aeronautics and Space Administration   Federal U.S. agency, commonly referred to as NASA, formed in 1958 to develop research and technology for the space race.

National Association for the Advancement of Colored People   Black civil rights organization, formed by Black and white progressives, that would figure prominently in twentieth-century legal battles over racial discrimination and segregation.

National Consumers League   Women's reform organization that used consumer awareness and boycotts to support or protest women's labor.

National Industrial Recovery Act   Pillar of the First New Deal, which sought to strike a compromise between business and labor interests but which the Supreme Court struck down in 1935.

National Interstate and Defense Highways Act   1956 legislation authorizing development of the interstate highway system, which was seen as crucial to national defense.

National Liberation Front (Viet Cong) South Vietnamese communist political and military organization that rebelled against Ngo Dinh Diem's government and fought United States and South Vietnamese troops during the Vietnam War.

National Organization for Women Women's rights organization cofounded by Betty Friedan in 1966, which emphasized equal access to jobs and resources and decried sexism in mass culture.

National Recovery Administration New Deal agency that regulated the relations among government, businesses, and labor unions and established parameters for work hours and wages in hundreds of industries.

National Road Federally funded road linking the Eastern seaboard and Western waterways.

National Security Act 1947 act that created the Department of Defense, the National Security Council, and the Central Intelligence Agency.

National Security Council Report 68 1950 National Security Council report that warned of an apocalyptic Soviet threat and recommended policies of containment and military buildup.

National Union for Social Justice Populist organization, led by New Deal and FDR critic Father Charles Coughlin, that demanded the nationalization of banks, industries, and the railroads.

National Woman Suffrage Association Women's suffrage organization, founded by Susan B. Anthony and Elizabeth Cady Stanton, that advocated a constitutional amendment to enfranchise women.

National Woman's Party Suffragist organization that lobbied for women's political rights and staged public demonstrations outside Woodrow Wilson's White House.

nationalization Controversial strategy, popular among postcolonial peoples after World War II and frequently opposed by the U.S. government, of returning the ownership of national resources such as land and oil deposits to the people, usually through a government takeover.

nation-state Political unit claiming sovereignty over a distinct territory with a shared ethnic or historical identity, as distinguished from an individual city-state or an empire governing diverse lands.

nativists Advocates of the interests and privileges of native-born citizens and supporters of immigration restriction.

natural rights Basic individual rights that many eighteenth-century pamphleteers, orators, and theorists believed to emanate from nature or God rather than from tradition or government.

Naturalization Act 1870 legislation that extended naturalization rights to people of African descent or nativity but continued to deny Asian and other non-white immigrants the same rights.

naval blockade Military tactic utilizing seas, oceans, and waterways to isolate an enemy's territory, imposed by the North during the Civil War.

Navigation Acts Series of laws imposed by England's Parliament, beginning in 1651, regulating the commerce and shipping of its colonies.

Negro Fort British-built fort in Spanish Florida, destroyed by Andrew Jackson, that gave refuge to Seminoles, Redsticks, and fugitives from slavery.

New Amsterdam Central settlement of New Netherland on the southern tip of Manhattan on land purchased from the Lenape people.

New Deal President Franklin D. Roosevelt's collective name for the reforms he pushed through Congress during the Depression era and that historians later distinguished as the First New Deal (1933–1935) and Second New Deal (1935–1936).

New Economy Term coined in the 1990s to describe the changing economy, which was increasingly service-oriented and based on digital technologies.

New Federalism Conservative judicial philosophy, increasingly influential in the late twentieth century, holding that the courts should compel the federal government to devolve as much regulatory power as possible to the states.

New Jersey Plan Constitutional proposal countering the Virginia Plan and recommending that all states receive equal representation in Congress.

New Lights Acolytes of the Great Awakening's revivalist leaders, who emphasized individual conversion experiences.

New Look foreign policy Strategic shift under President Eisenhower's administration toward smaller peacetime military forces and a larger stockpile of nuclear arms.

New Mexico Spanish colony established by Juan de Oñate and run as a Franciscan theocracy.

New Netherland Dutch colony in North America (present-day New York) until 1664 with a multicultural population of diverse Europeans, Africans, and others.

New York Draft Riots Violent three-day riot that pit protesters of the Conscription Act, mostly anti-Black Democrats and immigrants, against police and Union soldiers.

New York Society for the Suppression of Vice Conservative lobby group, founded in 1873 and led by Anthony Comstock, that championed marriage and procreative marital sex.

New York State Constitution of 1821 State constitution that allowed white men without property to vote but imposed property restrictions on Black voters.

New York Sun First cheap daily newspaper, which introduced a new model of modern journalism.

New York World Democratic partisan newspaper that grew in popularity in the 1880s through sensationalism and coverage of national politics.

Nickelodeon Pittsburgh venue that exclusively showed moving pictures, which opened as Americans increasingly attended cinemas around the turn of the twentieth century.

Nineteenth Amendment Constitutional amendment, ratified in 1920, that gave women the right to vote.

nonconsumption Strategy of broad consumer boycotts of British-made goods by colonists opposed to Parliament's taxation and regulation.

nonimportation agreements Boycotts of British imports by colonial merchants seeking to reverse Parliament's taxation and regulation.

Non-Intercourse Act   1809 U.S. law barring trade with either France or Britain, intended to preserve American neutrality in the Napoleonic Wars.

North American Free Trade Agreement   Trilateral trade treaty in 1993 among Canada, Mexico, and the United States that established a common market within which goods would not be subject to tariffs.

North Atlantic Treaty Organization   Military and collective security alliance first formed in 1949 among the United States, Canada, and Western European states.

Northwest Ordinance   1787 ordinance specifying the processes by which new U.S. states would form and prohibiting slavery in the Northwest Territory.

Northwest Territory   Land west of the Appalachians that the United States organized through a series of eighteenth-century land ordinances.

nuclear brinksmanship   Negotiating tactic, adopted under President Dwight D. Eisenhower, by which the United States refused to back down in a Cold War crisis even if it meant taking the nation to the brink of nuclear war.

nullification crisis   1832–1833 political crisis wherein South Carolina, led by John C. Calhoun, attempted to nullify federal tariffs.

Nuremberg trials   Post–WWII series of trials to prosecute Nazi leaders for war crimes.

O

Ocala Demands   Farmers' Alliances' 1890 platform, which demanded numerous reforms including free silver and direct election of senators.

Occupational Safety and Health Act   1970 law regulating healthful conditions and safety in the workplace.

Occupy Wall Street   Leftist, populist protest movement that emerged in 2011 in response to corporate influence in American politics and that indirectly forced the Democratic Party to develop policies aimed at reducing economic inequality.

Office of War Information   Primary U.S. government propaganda organ during World War II, designed to drum up support for the war effort among American citizens.

omnibus   Horse-drawn, fixed-route urban public transit that first appeared along Broadway in 1829.

Open Door   Foreign affairs policy, first articulated in 1899, that all major powers should have trading rights with China and respect China's administrative and territorial integrity.

Operation Desert Storm   Codename for U.S. military operations in Iraq during the Gulf War of 1991, which were represented to the American public as high-tech and precise.

Operation Overlord   U.S. strategy in World War II to invade German-controlled Western Europe through the English Channel, which the Allies executed in Normandy in 1944.

Operation Wetback   Mass deportation program in 1954 that targeted Mexican immigrants and farmworkers in the West and Southwest and in which some Mexican American citizens were illegally deported.

Ordinances of Discovery   Model of Spanish colonization declared by King Phillip II that empowered missionaries and priests.

Oregon settlement   1849 diplomatic agreement of the northwestern border between Britain and the United States.

Organization of the Petroleum Exporting Countries   International organization formed in 1960 by oil-rich countries, notably Saudi Arabia and Venezuela, to control global oil prices.

Overland Trail   Land route across the Rocky Mountains, traversed by tens of thousands of Americans every year from the mid-1840s through the 1860s.

P

Pacific Railway Acts   1862 and 1864 acts that granted railroad companies 200 million acres of Western land and capital through government bonds.

Paleo-Indians   Ancient indigenous Americans who crossed Beringia and settled throughout present-day North and South America.

Panama Canal   Canal connecting the Atlantic and Pacific Oceans, whose construction involved a U.S.-facilitated coup in Colombia and thousands of workers' deaths from disease.

Panic of 1819   Economic crisis caused in part by rampant land speculation and bank failure in the South and West.

Panic of 1837   Complex and large-scale economic depression, which many Americans blamed on Democrats' mismanagement of the economy.

Panic of 1893   Economic crisis that caused widespread unemployment and workers' unrest and was largely blamed on silver and the Sherman Act.

pan-Indian   Outlook that minimized the differences among Native American villages and nations and asserted the common political interest and identity of all Native Americans.

paper ballots   Election ballots, which in the nineteenth century were not secret or neutral and clearly identified voters' party preference.

Paris Climate Agreement   International accord that committed signatory countries to fighting climate change.

Paris Commune   Revolutionary alliance between middle and working classes that briefly ruled Paris, France, in 1871 and was subsequently portrayed in the mainstream American press as proof that the world's laboring classes were organized and dangerous.

Paris Peace Conference   Negotiations that concluded World War I, which emphasized German reparations, self-determination (in Europe), and creation of the League of Nations.

paternalism   Form of labor discipline and ideology associated with slaveholders who knew their enslaved workers intimately, took an active and meddlesome interest in their lives, and regarded them as childlike inferiors who needed care and protection.

Patient Protection and Affordable Care Act   Signature and controversial law of Barack Obama's presidency devised to reform and expand affordable health care.

patriarch   Male head of household who wields broad authority over household members, including women, children, relatives, and other dependents.

Paxton Boys   Scots-Irish farmers in Pennsylvania who massacred the Conestoga people in 1763.

Pay As You Earn   Barack Obama's 2012 reform program designed to ease the burdens of student debt.

Peace Corps   Agency that sent students abroad to provide educational, health, and technical services as part of JFK's Cold War policy to extend diplomacy informally.

Peak TV   Popular twenty-first-century phenomenon in which people consume television programming asynchronously through streaming services such as Hulu and Netflix.

Peggy Eaton affair   Sex scandal involving Secretary of War John Eaton, resulting in the turnover of Andrew Jackson's cabinet.

Pennsylvania Dutch   Large group of German-speaking immigrants who settled in Pennsylvania between 1700 and 1750.

penny press   Cheap daily urban newspapers pitched to a mass readership.

Pentagon Papers   Department of Defense report leaked to *The New York Times* in 1971, which revealed that the Johnson administration had lied about the goals and progress of the Vietnam War.

Pequot War   1636–1637 military conflict, mainly involving the Pequot people and colonists of Massachusetts and Connecticut and their native allies.

personal computer   Computer for use by the general population; they first became commercially successful in 1984 with Apple's Macintosh.

Personal Responsibility and Work Opportunity Act   1996 welfare reform legislation, enacted by a Republican Congress and signed by a Democratic president, that limited and slashed welfare benefits and shifted welfare responsibilities to the states.

pietism   Religious movements that stress rigorous personal observance and intense prayer experience.

Pilgrims   Radical religious dissenters in seventeenth-century England who favored separating themselves from the corrupting influence of the Anglican Church and from English society.

Pinckney's Treaty   1795 treaty with Spain granting Americans the right to ship goods along the Mississippi and through the Gulf of Mexico.

Plains bison   Near-extinct species of bison common on the Great Plains before the 1870s and of great spiritual and economic importance to Plains Indians.

Plan of Union   1754 proposal by Benjamin Franklin to create a governing body for defense purposes among Britain's mainland colonies.

plantation   Large farm engaged in commercial agricultural production, typically worked by enslaved laborers.

Platt Amendment   U.S. stipulations for Cuban independence, including the right of the United States to intervene and the leasing of land for naval bases.

Plessy v. *Ferguson*   1896 Supreme Court ruling that affirmed the rights of cities and states to racially segregate public amenities.

pluralist nationalism   Belief, widely promoted by government and the culture industries during World War II, that the United States is made up of people from many ethnic and religious backgrounds who nevertheless constitute one unified people.

Plymouth   Pilgrim settlement that attracted hardline Protestants and established diplomatic ties with Massasoit.

polio epidemic   Deadly disease outbreak that was significantly mitigated after mass immunizations with Jonas Salk's vaccine in the 1950s.

political abolitionists   Historians' term for antislavery activists who favored participating in the political process in order to achieve their goals.

political machine   Hierarchical political organization, influential in the nineteenth and early twentieth centuries, that controlled enough votes through a system of rewards and incentives to maintain control over city, county, or state government.

political newspapers   Newspapers with clear allegiances to particular political parties during the period of the First Party System.

Pontiac's Rebellion   1763 military conflict between the British Empire and the native peoples of the Great Lakes region, the result of shifting European territorial claims after the French and Indian War.

Popular Front   Broad coalition of anti-fascist leftist groups, including American organizations, that fought the spread of fascism in Spain in the 1930s.

popular sovereignty   Principle that the legal status of slavery in a Western territory or a new state should be determined by a vote of that territory's inhabitants.

Populists   Political movement, made up mostly of rural and small-town Americans in the 1890s, that demanded that the supposed interests of the people be put first in politics and the economy.

Posse Comitatus Act   1878 legislation that prohibited the federal government from using the army to enforce the law.

Post Office Act of 1792   Law that established congressional authority over a national broadcast network and facilitated the cheap circulation of newspapers.

postage reform   Series of laws in the 1840s and 1850s that significantly lowered postage rates, making the mail a popular medium of social interaction.

potato famine   1845 natural disaster caused by a fungus on the Irish potato crop, resulting in 1 to 1.5 million deaths and massive immigration to America.

Potosí   Site of a major silver mine in present-day Bolivia where indigenous peoples were forced to labor under the Spanish encomienda.

Poverty Point   One of the earliest-known cities in North America, located in present-day Louisiana, with large earthwork mounds built for religious exhibitions.

praying towns   Special villages in New England where Native Americans who embraced Christianity were gathered in the mid-seventeenth century.

preparedness   Proposition, initially promoted by Theodore Roosevelt and eventually embraced by Woodrow Wilson during World War I, that the nation ought to mobilize its military and people in preparation for war.

President's Committee on Civil Rights Commission established by President Truman in the wake of the Moore's Ford lynchings to investigate and recommend actions to bolster civil rights.

prisons State and private institutions for criminals, which antebellum reformers innovated by emphasizing moral transformation during confinement.

Proclamation Line of 1763 George III's decree, meant to stem conflict between native groups and settlers, that forbade western land purchases without royal authorization.

producers Identity that many workers and farmers assumed in the Gilded Age as a way of distinguishing themselves from alleged nonproducers such as bankers, lawyers, and gamblers.

progressive idealism Historians' term for the view, popular among middle-class social reformers in the Progressive Era, that the United States has a special, even divine, mission to improve the world, chiefly by ending war and spreading American-style democracy.

Prohibition Period from 1920 to 1933, during which it was a federal crime to produce, sell, or transport alcohol.

Proposition 13 Successful 1978 California ballot proposition that limited property taxes in the state.

proprietary colony Type of English colony in the Americas entrusted to the control of an individual or a group to whom the monarch granted special authority.

proslavery ideology Beliefs and claims in the antebellum era that chattel slavery, at least for African Americans, was a blessing rather than a necessary evil.

protective tariffs Taxes on foreign imports, typically passed along to consumers, designed to make domestic goods more attractive.

Protestant Reformation Religious movement in sixteenth-century northern Europe that rejected the authority of the pope and ignited a revolution in Christian thought and practice.

Pueblo Revolt Successful multicultural and multilingual indigenous uprising against Spanish rule in the Rio Grande valley in 1680.

Pueblos Diverse group of indigenous peoples whom Spanish colonists encountered and attempted to convert and control (the word in lowercase refers to the villages they constructed).

Pullman strike Nationwide strike of railroad workers in 1894, which the mainstream press ultimately condemned as anarchistic and un-American.

Pure Food and Drug Act 1906 legislation, championed by progressives, that created the Food and Drug Administration.

Puritans Radical Protestants in seventeenth-century England who opposed the Anglican Church.

quadroon balls Formal social gatherings in New Orleans at which elite white men cultivated intimate relationships with free women of color.

Quaker migration Late-seventeenth- and early-eighteenth century immigration of Quakers to American colonies, mostly to Pennsylvania.

Quartering Act of 1765 Act that required American colonies to provide and pay for British soldiers' accommodations.

Québec First permanent French settlement in North America, established by Samuel Champlain.

Quebec Act Britain's effort to increase imperial loyalty and protect Catholics in Quebec colony.

Queen Anne's War North American theater of the War of Spanish Succession, which produced no clear power shifts there.

R

radical feminism Ideology, which emerged from the women's rights movement in the 1970s, that celebrates distinctively female worlds and values and stresses the paramount significance of sexism as a form of social oppression.

Radical Republicans Faction of the Republican Party during Reconstruction that pursued full rights for freed people and advocated against the rapid readmission of the Confederate states to the union.

Rainbow Coalition Inclusive political organization, tied to Jesse Jackson's 1984 presidential run, that advocated the political engagement of Americans of all ethno-racial and socio-economic backgrounds.

ranching frontier Movement of ranching north from Texas and west Louisiana to Colorado and the Great Plains after the Civil War.

ratification conventions Special state conventions for the purposes of ratifying the U.S. Constitution.

Reagan Democrats Democrats who supported Ronald Reagan in the 1980s, becoming a vital group of swing voters in elections.

Reagan Doctrine Ronald Reagan's foreign policy doctrine, which pledged to financially and militarily support anti-communist and anti-leftist governments and political movements.

Reaganomics Ronald Reagan's economic policy, which emphasized lower taxes, less federal spending, and fewer regulations for business and assumed that the accumulation of wealth among the richest Americans would eventually trickle down to the less affluent classes in the form of more employment and higher wages.

real estate covenant Written agreement, typical of the early and mid-twentieth century, by which a white home purchaser promised to sell or rent his or her property only to another white person, thereby excluding Black Americans and other minorities from the neighborhood or suburb.

Reconquista Crusades by Catholic powers on the Iberian Peninsula to oust Muslim rule and colonize Atlantic islands between the eighth and fifteenth centuries.

Reconstruction Political, social, and economic projects of reintegrating seceded states into the Union, in large part by stripping former slaveholders of power and protecting Black civil rights.

Reconstruction Act of 1867 Act by which Congress divided the South into military districts and revised the terms of secessionist states' readmission.

Reconstruction Finance Corporation Federal agency, established under Herbert Hoover, that provided stimulus loans to banks, insurers, and corporations in an unsuccessful effort to stem the Great Depression.

Reconstruction governments State governments elected by the multiracial electorates that Reconstruction made possible between 1866 and 1877.

Red Scare Originally the alleged spread of communism and worker radicalism in the United States after communists seized power in Russia in 1917 and subsequently episodes of intensive anti-communist scare-mongering that took place in 1919–1920 and 1947–1957.

Redeemers Southern Democrats, espousing white supremacy, who regained political power during Reconstruction and ousted Republican rule in the South.

redlining Institutional practice, common in mid-twentieth-century cities, of either withholding home mortgages, insurance, health care, and other resources from residents in minority-intensive neighborhoods or overcharging them for such services.

Redsticks Creek rebels inspired by Tecumseh, who clashed with their national council and U.S. forces.

referendum Progressive Era reform that enabled citizens in some states, provided they had gathered enough signatures for a petition, to invalidate a state or city law through a popular vote.

Regulars Full-time soldiers in a professional, hierarchical army.

Regulators Name adopted by various rural Revolutionary-era protest movements claiming the right to use violence against the government in order to redress wrongs and express broadly shared grievances.

repatriation Forcible return of persons presumed to be foreigners to their alleged homeland, most controversially carried out against almost half a million Mexican nationals and U.S. citizens of Mexican descent during the Great Depression.

Republican establishment Twenty-first-century term for entrenched, moderate, and elitist political leadership in the Republican Party, often subject to attacks from the Tea Party and other right-wing and conservative activists.

Republicans National political party in the early republic, led by Thomas Jefferson, that called for a restrained national government with modest expenditures and often called Jeffersonian Republicans to distinguish them from the later Republican Party.

Resistance to Civil Government Henry David Thoreau's 1849 essay inspired by his opposition to paying taxes to support the Mexican War.

Restoration Period in English history initiated by the return of the Stuart monarchy to power in 1660.

Revenue Act One of several 1916 laws championed by progressives, which raised income taxes and imposed an inheritance tax on the wealthy.

Revised Philadelphia Plan Richard Nixon's plan for minority hiring of federal building contractors in 1969, a milestone for affirmative action.

revolutions of 1848 Series of European political revolutions instigated by liberal nationalist movements.

rhythm and blues American music genre, mainly performed by Black musicians, that influenced rock 'n' roll.

rice Crop grown mainly in South Carolina that distinguished Lowcountry slavery from that of the Chesapeake.

Roanoke Island Failed English colony in present-day North Carolina, which Walter Raleigh attempted to establish between 1585 and 1590.

rock 'n' roll American popular music genre, characterized by amplified guitar riffs and suggestive lyrics, that first appeared in the 1950s and appealed to white teenagers.

Roe v. Wade 1973 court case in which the Supreme Court ruled that laws prohibiting abortion violated women's right to privacy.

Roosevelt Corollary Theodore Roosevelt's foreign policy interpretation of the Monroe Doctrine, authorizing the United States to act as a policing power in the Western Hemisphere.

Roosevelt recession 1937 economic recession that weakened the progress of the New Deal and exacerbated the divide between liberal Democrats and Southern and other conservative Democrats.

Roots Historical novel and popular 1977 television miniseries that followed several generations of an African American family through slavery and freedom.

Rough Riders Nickname for an American regiment led by Theodore Roosevelt in the Spanish-American War, whose exploits in Cuba were mythologized in American popular culture.

Royal African Company Slave-buying operation chartered by the English Crown in 1672 that transported thousands of enslaved Africans.

Rush-Bagot Treaty 1817 agreement between the United States and Britain, in which both sides agreed to disarmament in the Great Lakes.

Rwandan genocide Killing of hundreds of thousands of Rwanda's Tutsi minority ethnic group by Hutu militias over a few months in 1994 during the Rwandan Civil War, provoking international shock and outcry but no forceful intervention.

S

Sabbatarianism Movement to enforce Sabbath observance.

Sacco and Vanzetti Italian immigrants and anarchists whose 1921 murder conviction (on flimsy evidence) contributed to a wave of nativism and immigration restriction.

SALT 1 Agreement between Richard Nixon and Leonid Brezhnev to limit and reduce arms production in the United States and Soviet Union.

same-sex marriage Legal conjugal union between two individuals of the same gender, prohibited in U.S. law before the twenty-first century and the subject of intense political controversy during the years of George W. Bush's presidency.

San Francisco general strike 1934 workers' strike that was sparked by frustrated dockworkers but spread to numerous industries, paralyzing San Francisco.

San Patricio battalion   Mexican battalion composed of roughly three hundred Irish-Catholic immigrants who deserted from the U.S. Army in the Mexican War.

sanctuary movement   Social movement begun by a network of churches and synagogues in 1982 to aid Salvadorans and Guatemalans fleeing Contra violence.

Sand Creek Massacre   1864 murder of hundreds of Cheyenne in Colorado by the U.S. military after their peaceful surrender.

Santee Rebellion   1862 Sioux uprising in Minnesota sparked by inadequate federal aid to reservations.

São Tomé and Príncipe   Islands in the Gulf of Guinea colonized by Portugal in 1485, where Africans were transported and enslaved to work sugar plantations.

Saturday Night Massacre   The resignations and firings of Richard Nixon's attorney general and deputy attorney general, as well as an independent prosecutor related to the Watergate scandal.

savings and loan association   Financial institution, initially designed to offer affordable mortgages, that widely failed following deregulation in the 1980s, mostly at the expense of taxpayers.

scalawags   Derisive name for white Southern Republicans, used by Southern Democrats during Reconstruction.

scientific management   Approach to industrial production, popularized by Frederick Winslow Taylor in the Progressive Era, by which the physical motions of laborers were measured, analyzed, and optimized with the objective of accelerating production.

Scots-Irish immigrants   Large group of immigrants to eighteenth-century British America who settled parts of Virginia, the Carolina backcountry, and the Middle Colonies.

Scottsboro Boys   Nine Black teenagers who were falsely accused of the rape of two white women, ardently defended by the American Communist Party, and convicted by an all-white jury.

Second Confiscation Act   1862 U.S. law broadening the Union army's authorization to harbor fugitives from slavery.

Second Continental Congress   Colonial body formed in 1775 to mobilize for armed conflict with Britain.

Second Empire   Term used by historians of art and architecture to describe the blend of traditional and new styles that flourished in mid-nineteenth-century France under Emperor Napoleon III and that elite and middle-class Americans replicated in the Gilded Age.

Second Great Awakening   Historians' term for a series of religious revivals in different parts of the United States, climaxing between 1825 and 1835 in the Northeast.

second Ku Klux Klan   Reincarnation of the Klan organized around tenets of Protestant nativism, white supremacy, and immigration restriction and particularly strong in Midwestern cities.

Second Party System   Highly organized national political competition between Whigs and Democrats during the second quarter of the nineteenth century.

Second Seminole War   U.S. effort to remove the Seminole Nation, which also included escapees from slavery, from Florida between 1835 and 1842.

Sedition Act   Law enacted during the Adams administration, that criminalized political dissent.

Selective Service Act (1917)   Legislation that conscripted fit and healthy men aged eighteen to thirty (later forty-five) into military service during World War I.

Selective Service Act (1940)   Legislation that created the nation's first peacetime military draft.

self-determination   Term coined in the World War I era to describe the right of a people to form their own independent state.

Seneca Falls Convention   Most famous of a series of conventions in the 1840s devoted to women's rights, including woman suffrage.

separate spheres   Nineteenth-century doctrine that men and women, because of their allegedly different natures, ought to perform different social roles and occupy different kinds of social spaces.

settlement movement   Late-nineteenth-century social reform movement aimed at improving and uplifting poor communities.

Seventeenth Amendment   Constitutional amendment mandating the direct election of senators.

sexual revolution   Rejection of conventional sexual norms and practices, particularly the prohibition on extramarital sex, most strongly associated with the counterculture and radical political movements of the late 1960s and 1970s.

Share-Our-Wealth Plan   Huey Long's response to the First New Deal, which called for more radical redistribution of wealth.

Shawnee Prophet   Tenskwatawa, brother of Tecumseh, who preached a pan-Indian message of spiritual regeneration.

Shays's Rebellion   1786 regulator movement in rural Massachusetts that violently resisted the state's imposition of direct taxes.

Sherman Antitrust Act   1890 legislation that empowered the federal government to break up monopolies.

siege of Vicksburg   1863 Union siege in Mississippi, a key military victory led by Ulysses Grant.

Sioux Treaty of 1868   Treaty that established the Great Sioux Reservation, comprised of lands in and adjoining Dakota Territory.

sit-in   Protest tactic, popularized by the civil rights movement of the early 1960s, in which activists integrated lunch counters, bus terminals, and other public spaces by physically occupying them.

Sixteenth Amendment   Constitutional amendment allowing Congress to impose a graduated income tax.

skyscrapers   Tall, multi-floored commercial buildings, which first appeared in the late nineteenth and early twentieth centuries in Chicago and New York City.

Slaughterhouse Cases   1873 case heard by the Supreme Court, which ruled that the Fourteenth Amendment only protected rights of federal citizenship and that states could define and delimit other rights.

slave codes Special laws regulating the status and conduct of enslaved people, first instituted in the second half of the seventeenth century.

slave communities Results of the relationships and identities that Africans and their descendants formed in the American colonies, drawing upon various cultural practices and shared experiences.

slave mutinies Revolts of African captives aboard slave ships that were usually suppressed violently by armed crews.

slave narratives Examples of a literary genre in which formerly enslaved people recounted their lives in print as a means of dramatizing the horrors and injustice of slavery.

slave patrols Police forces staffed by white men and established by Southern states to enforce racial hierarchy and protect against slave rebellions.

Slave Power Term used by critics of slavery to suggest that slaveholders were rigging the political system for their own benefit and undermining the freedom of white Americans.

slave societies Societies that depend primarily or heavily on the labor of enslaved people (*see also* societies with slaves).

Sleepy Lagoon Trial 1942 murder trial in Los Angeles, the investigation and prosecution of which unfairly targeted young Mexican Americans.

Social Gospel Early-twentieth-century Protestant movement that was concerned with social justice and inequality and did not attribute poverty to individual moral failing.

social networking services Internet-based communication networks, such as Facebook, Twitter, and Reddit, that dominated everyday life in the early twenty-first century.

Social Security Act Second New Deal act that set up pensions for retirees and unemployment assistance through taxes.

social work Term that middle-class social reformers coined in the Progressive Era to describe their poor-relief activity and imbue it with professional status.

Socialist Party Political party, formed in 1900 whose platform espoused such aims as economic cooperation and the nationalization of railroads.

societies with slaves Societies in which slavery exists but other labor systems predominate.

Sons of Liberty Groups of American dissenters who organized to protest the Stamp Act, sometimes using tactics of intimidation.

Sons of Temperance One of several fraternal associations founded in the 1840s demanding pledges to abstain from alcohol.

South Carolina British colony with a distinctively large enslaved population, which mainly cultivated rice.

southern campaign British military campaign in the southern mainland colonies during the later stages of the Revolution.

Southern Christian Leadership Conference Black civil rights organization led by Martin Luther King, Jr., which emphasized nonviolent civil disobedience and Christian activism.

Southern Farmers' Alliance All-white farmers' organization that advocated cooperative action, promoted education, and lobbied for political reform to help farmers in the late nineteenth century.

Southern Manifesto Document, signed by 101 members of the House and Senate, that condemned and vowed resistance to racial desegregation.

Spanish Louisiana Territorial claim ceded to Spain by France after the French and Indian War.

Spanish-American War 1898 military conflict between the United States and Spain whose root cause was Cuban independence, and which resulted in U.S. control of Puerto Rico and several Pacific islands.

speakeasy Unlicensed saloon that illegally sold alcohol and became prominent in the 1920s under Prohibition.

spheres of influence Term referring to European trade monopolies in China, from which the United States was initially excluded despite territorial possession of the Philippines.

spirituals Sacred songs created by enslaved African American Christians.

spoils system Practice and policy of awarding government jobs and resources to one's partisan supporters.

Sputnik World's first satellite, launched by the USSR in 1957, which alarmed the United States and accelerated the Cold War space race.

St. Augustine Spanish settlement in Florida, established in 1565 by Pedro Menéndez de Avilés and the oldest continuously inhabited city in the present-day United States.

stagflation Economic term developed in the 1970s to describe the convergence of inflation, stagnation, and high unemployment.

Stamp Act 1765 act that levied a tax on all printed matter and legal documents in the British colonies.

Stamp Act Congress Colonial representatives who gathered to reject the British government's authority to impose taxes on colonists.

Standard Oil Company Corporate monopoly, owned by John D. Rockefeller, that dominated the U.S. petroleum market by 1879.

standardized regional time zones Four regional time zones first adopted by railroad corporations in 1883 to synchronize and simplify train scheduling.

Staple Act 1663 Navigation Act, stipulating that European goods imported to North America had to first pass through England.

states' rights Ideology and slogan advocating the right of individual states to resist intervention by the federal government.

steamboat travel Travel technology widely introduced in the United States after 1811, that greatly facilitated the development of the nineteenth-century West.

stem cells Cells from either embryonic or fully developed mammals that can be differentiated, reproduced, and used to develop new treatments for disorders and diseases; the use of embryonic stem cells was condemned by abortion opponents and initially restricted by the federal government.

Stonewall Riots 1969 clash between police and gay and transgender youth that helped grow the gay rights movement.

Stono Rebellion 1739 slave revolt in South Carolina that contributed to slaveholders' increased surveillance of people living in slavery and fear of potential insurrections.

streaming services Form of multimedia transmission that delivers content, such as music or video, to Internet users on demand.

strict construction Approach to constitutional interpretation that favors limiting the federal government to those powers explicitly enumerated in the Constitution.

Student Nonviolent Coordinating Committee Leading civil rights organization of the early 1960s, spearheaded by students and young activists who staged sit-ins and registered Black voters.

Student Volunteer Movement for Foreign Missions Protestant evangelical organization founded in 1886, that recruited young adults from around the country to participate in missionary endeavors.

Students for a Democratic Society Political organization founded in 1960 that became a leading group of the New Left by emphasizing participatory democracy.

Sugar Act Britain's tax on West Indian molasses after the French and Indian War, which caused significant colonial protest.

supply-side economics Theory, popular among conservatives from the 1980s onward but derided by most economists, that economic growth is best achieved by stimulating production through tax cuts and deregulation.

surveillance laws Series of three laws passed in 1917–1918 that enabled the federal government to suppress criticism of its policies.

T

Taft-Hartley Act Business-friendly legislation passed in 1947—despite President Truman's veto—that outlawed certain kinds of strikes and weakened unions and the labor movement.

Tainos Inhabitants of the Caribbean islands Columbus encountered, who became targets of Spanish violence and forced labor.

Tammany Hall New York City Democratic political machine that harnessed the support of immigrants and dominated the city's political affairs in the Gilded Age.

tariff Tax on imported goods, which often figures in debates about economic protectionism and the free market.

tarring and feathering Trademark ritual of colonial urban rioting wherein victims were stripped, covered with tar and feathers, and publicly paraded.

task system Method of labor management in which enslaved laborers are assigned quotas of work to complete in a certain time.

taverns Places for genteel sociability—and in some cases sites of political dissent—in eighteenth-century British America.

Tea Act 1773 British tax on tea imported to America by the East India Company, leading to boycotts and protests among colonists.

Tea Party Conservative populist movement, most active between 2009 and 2014, that chiefly sought to overturn Obamacare, restrict immigration, and replace moderate Republicans with conservatives.

Teapot Dome scandal 1922–1923 political scandal in which Secretary of the Interior Albert Fall illegally awarded leases to oil reserves.

teenager Young adult around whom distinctive cultures, trends, identities, and behaviors formed in the New Deal era.

teetotaler Term coined by antebellum temperance reformers for someone who had signed a pledge of total abstinence from alcohol.

Tehran Conference 1943 meeting of FDR, Joseph Stalin, and Winston Churchill to strategize about the course of World War II and plan for the postwar order.

temperance novels Genre of writing popular in the antebellum period, that dramatized the tragedies of alcohol consumption.

temps Temporary workers whose wages were generally lower than their unionized counterparts' and who were typically employed by agencies that sent them to different employers for short periods of time.

Ten Percent Plan Abraham Lincoln's 1863 plan to reintegrate secessionist states, so-called because it required a loyalty oath of at least 10 percent of each state's voters.

tenement Substandard and typically overcrowded form of urban rental housing that arose with industrialization in the nineteenth century and in which the poor, particularly immigrants, lived and sometimes worked.

ten-hour movement Workers' successful movement to cap the workday at ten hours, which had become the norm by the 1840s.

Tennessee Valley Authority Major New Deal project that brought electricity to rural Southerners by harnessing hydroelectric power.

Tenure of Office Act 1867 act prohibiting the president from removing officials whose appointment required Senate approval.

Tet Offensive 1968 military campaign by the Viet Cong and North Vietnamese against the United States, which negatively impacted the American public's and government's view of the Vietnam War.

Texas annexation The U.S. annexation of Texas in 1845, which was politically controversial and contributed to the outbreak of the Mexican War.

The Birth of a Nation D. W. Griffith's popular and cinematically pathbreaking 1915 film that celebrated the Reconstruction-era Ku Klux Klan and promoted anti-Black racism.

"the country" Name that prosperous Gilded Age urbanites gave rural areas in which resorts, spas, and inns were replacing working farms.

"the establishment" Critical term, popularized in the 1960s, for long-standing social conventions, entrenched elites, and political and cultural institutions.

The Federalist Collection of eighty-five newspaper pieces by James Madison, Alexander Hamilton, and John Jay that argued in favor of constitutional ratification.

The Holocaust Nazi Germany's systematic murder of 6 million Jews.

The Jungle 1906 muckraker novel by Upton Sinclair that exposed conditions in the meatpacking industry.

The Leatherstocking Tales James Fenimore Cooper's series of historical novels, which featured Native American characters and were commercially successful.

The Living Newspaper Theatrical series, supported by the Works Progress Administration, that nearly lost federal funding by engaging with overly political subject matter.

The Netherlands Coalition of provinces, led by Holland, that became a dominant maritime and commercial power in the seventeenth century.

the 1% Term popularized by Occupy Wall Street, referring to the richest minority of Americans who owned a historically disproportionate share of the nation's wealth.

the secret vice Nineteenth-century reformers' term for masturbation, which they feared would cause both moral ruin and bodily debility.

third wave feminism Social movement, emerging in the 1980s and 1990s, characterized by engagement in culture wars and debates within feminism over such issues as sex positivity.

Thirteenth Amendment Constitutional amendment, ratified in 1865, that outlawed slavery except as punishment for crime.

three-fifths clause 1787 constitutional compromise that counted 60 percent of a state's enslaved population for the purposes of apportioning representation.

Tontine Coffee House New York City coffeehouse that became a locus of social, political, and commercial interaction in the Early Republic.

Tories Name of a royalist political party in England, used by colonial Whigs to describe their local political opponents (those who remained loyal to Britain).

Townshend Duties 1767 bill that imposed import taxes on glass, lead, paint, paper, and tea in the British colonies.

Trail of Tears Historians' term for the forced migration of Cherokee people from their homeland to Oklahoma in the mid-1830s.

tramping Practice of hitching a ride on a train for free, usually in search of work, that was popular among laborers of the Gilded Age and Great Depression eras.

transcendentalists Group of New England intellectuals, philosophers, and critics who believed in human perfectibility and the divinity of nature.

Transcontinental Treaty of 1819 (Adams-Onis Treaty) Treaty between the United States and Spain, under which Spain ceded Florida and agreed to U.S. boundaries.

transported convicts British convicts sentenced to hard labor in America as punishment in the eighteenth century, usually for minor crimes.

Treaty of Burlingame 1868 treaty between the United States and China facilitating the immigration of Chinese citizens who provided cheap labor for railroad construction.

Treaty of Detroit 1950 auto industry agreement that provided autoworkers benefits for a guaranteed five-year period.

Treaty of Fort Stanwix 1784 treaty ceding a large amount of Native American land in the Ohio River valley to the United States, despite objections and challenges from the Iroquois.

Treaty of Guadalupe Hidalgo Treaty concluding the Mexican War, which in part ceded 500,000 square miles of Mexican territory to the United States.

Treaty of New Echota 1835 treaty facilitating Cherokee removal, negotiated by the Jackson administration and a faction of the Cherokee.

Treaty of Paris (1763) Treaty ending the Seven Years' War, which greatly altered the British, French, and Spanish Empires.

Treaty of Paris (1783) Treaty between Britain and the United States that recognized its political independence and nominally identified its borders.

Treaty of Portsmouth 1905 treaty, brokered in part by Theodore Roosevelt, that concluded the Russo-Japanese War.

Treaty of Versailles Treaty in 1919 resulting from the Paris Peace Conference, which the U.S. Senate did not ratify due to resistance to the League of Nations and Woodrow Wilson's multilateral approach to geopolitics.

trench warfare Warfare, used on a mass scale in World War I, in which troops created fighting lines in the form of trenches, that came to connote any kind of protracted conflict characterized by little progress.

Truman Doctrine President Truman's foreign policy principles of containing Soviet expansion and influence.

Tsenacommacah Native American name for the tidewater region of the Chesapeake, where settlers would establish the first lasting English colony in the Americas.

Tulsa race massacre Significant episode of anti-Black racial violence and murder in 1921, in which a white mob targeted a Black neighborhood and Black businesses.

Tuscarora War 1711–1713 conflict between native peoples and settlers in North and South Carolina, resulting in the Tuscarora joining the Haudenosaunee.

Twenty-sixth Amendment Constitutional amendment, ratified in 1971, that lowered the voting age from twenty-one to eighteen.

U

U.S. Steel Corporation Corporation formed in a merger between Carnegie Steel and other companies, which became a billion-dollar corporation.

Uncle Tom's Cabin 1852 antislavery novel by Harriet Beecher Stowe, that greatly influenced antebellum political and literary culture.

Underground Railroad Secret network of people, routes, and safe houses that aided fugitive enslaved people attempting to escape the South during the antebellum era.

Union Leagues Southern chapters of Republican clubs that attracted many Southern yeomen after the Civil War.

United Dutch East India Company Dutch commercial enterprise, founded in the seventeenth century, that facilitated trade and exploration.

United Farm Workers Labor union, founded by Cesar Chavez and Dolores Huerta, which lobbied for Mexican American and other agricultural workers.

United Nations   Major international organization created after World War II to facilitate international cooperation, provide collective security, and prevent future wars.

United States Information Agency   Government agency formed in 1953 to promote interest in American culture, politics, and capitalism among foreign populations.

United States Sanitary Commission   Organization that studied military hygiene, trained nurses, and provided women opportunities to contribute to the Union war effort.

universal manhood suffrage   Antebellum political ideal of granting all adult white men the right to vote.

urban crowd   Experience of an impersonal urban community, which first emerged in the United States in the large cities of the 1830s.

urban frontier   Network of cities established west of the Appalachian Mountains in the early national period that encouraged and facilitated westward migration and economic development.

urban gentrification   Migration, beginning in the 1980s, of wealthy people from the suburbs to the cities, which pushed rents up and poorer residents out.

urban renewal   Official name for a series of urban development schemes undertaken after World War II in which slums were bulldozed to make way for expressways, skyscrapers, civic centers, and middle-class apartment blocks at the expense of poor (typically Black) residents, who were compelled to relocate.

urban rioting   Established practice in eighteenth-century America, which notably escalated after the Stamp Act, typically involving destruction of symbolic properties or goods.

urbanization   Process by which increasing proportions of a population come to live in cities.

USA PATRIOT Act   Law, passed in 2001 in response to the September 11 terrorist attacks, authorizing domestic law enforcement agencies to conduct broad surveillance on U.S. citizens and to detain and deport immigrants suspected of ties to terrorism.

utopian communities   Idealistic ventures to form societies of like-minded people who would live harmoniously and according to novel theories of the good life.

V

vagrancy laws   State laws passed in the nineteenth century under which a person who could not show proof of a permanent abode (home) or, in some cases, steady employment could be fined or imprisoned.

Vermont constitution   State constitution drafted in 1777, that explicitly outlawed slavery.

Vietnam syndrome   Term for the American public's weariness and disapproval of war, which George H. W. Bush believed was resolved by victory in the Gulf War.

Vietnamization   Richard Nixon's policy during the Vietnam War of withdrawing American troops and shifting combat responsibilities to South Vietnam.

Virginia Plan   Constitutional proposal recommending that state representation in a bicameral legislature be proportional to state population.

Viva Kennedy clubs   Political organizations formed to shore up support for John F. Kennedy's presidential campaign among Mexican Americans.

Voice of America   International radio station, operated by the Office of War Information during World War II, that played swing and other classically American genres of music to boost morale among American troops.

voluntarism   Idea, championed by Herbert Hoover in the 1920s and Great Depression, that the federal government, rather than legislating solutions, should work collaboratively with big business, the states, and voluntary relief organizations to solve the nation's problems.

Voting Rights Act of 1965   Civil rights legislation that enforced prohibitions on racial discrimination in voting.

W

Wade-Davis Bill   Radical Republicans' 1864 plan for secessionist states' readmission, which Abraham Lincoln did not support.

wage slavery   Rhetorical metaphor that compares wage labor to chattel slavery for a variety of political purposes.

Wagner Act   Major reform of the Second New Deal that sought to equalize power between employers and workers by guaranteeing nonagricultural workers the right to unionize, engage in collective bargaining, and call strikes (under certain conditions).

Wall Street crash   1929 financial crisis in which investors, realizing that stocks listed on the New York Stock Exchange were vastly overvalued, rushed to sell, triggering a collapse of stock prices, bank runs, and a global financial panic.

Waltham-Lowell system   Innovative system of textile production in the early nineteenth century that employed single women and housed them in tightly regulated dormitories.

wampum   Shells from whelks or quahog clams, strung together in beads and used as currency in North America after 1600 in commercial exchanges between European colonists and Native Americans.

war collectivism   Action by which the federal government, during the two world wars, worked with industry, agriculture, labor unions, consumers, and the culture industries to channel all available resources into the war effort.

War Hawks   Republican proponents of invading British Canada in 1811–1812, mostly from Western states.

War Industries Board   Government agency established in 1917 to coordinate the war economy.

War of 1812   Military conflict between the United States and Great Britain that defeated Britain's Native American allies and paved the way for westward expansion of the United States.

War of Jenkins's Ear   Anglo-Spanish conflict named for Robert Jenkins's severed ear, one of many imperial wars spilling into North American colonies.

war on drugs   Term coined by President Ronald Reagan in the 1980s to promote what became a thirty-year process of stiffening drug sentences for some users and targeting the illegal drug trade at home and overseas.

war on terror   Ongoing conflict, which began in 2001, with al-Qaeda and its suspected affiliates.

War Powers Resolution   1973 resolution limiting the president's authority to wage war without congressional consent.

War Production Board   World War II government agency that incentivized U.S. industries, through subsidies and contracts, to convert to manufacturing for war production.

wartime slave rebellion   Armed revolt by enslaved Black people who took advantage of the Revolutionary crisis to seek their own freedom, typically by joining the British camps.

Washingtonians   One of several fraternal associations founded in the 1840s demanding pledges to abstain from alcohol.

Watergate   Political scandal in which burglars connected to Richard Nixon's presidential campaign broke into the Democratic National Committee's headquarters.

weapons of mass destruction   Nuclear, chemical, and other biological large-scale weaponry, the specter of which was invoked by George W. Bush to argue for the necessity of a preemptive attack on Iraq.

West India Company   Seventeenth-century Dutch corporation that targeted Spanish commerce and established trading settlements in the Atlantic world.

Western Front   Major theater of war during World War I, stretching from eastern France to Belgium.

Whigs   Name of an English political party, adopted by colonial critics of Britain's imperial policies in the 1760s and 1770s.

Whiskey Rebellion   Western Pennsylvanian farmers' resistance to the whiskey tax in 1794, which the Washington administration successfully suppressed.

white flight   Emigration of white urbanites to suburbs in the twentieth century, which depleted cities' tax base and hastened urban decline.

white man's burden   Originally the title of a poem by English poet Rudyard Kipling, a phrase that came to denote the controversial view that white peoples had an obligation to tutor and uplift supposedly more "backward" peoples of color and that this goal could best be achieved through colonization.

Wilderness Act   1964 law that defined *wilderness* and protected roughly 9 million acres of federal land.

Wilmot Proviso   U.S. Representative David Wilmot's unsuccessful proposition to prohibit slavery in any territories gained in the Mexican War.

witchcraft accusations   Seventeenth-century allegations of witchcraft, which occurred most frequently in Massachusetts Bay and Connecticut, often against property-owning women.

Woman's Christian Temperance Union   Women's reform organization that most notably lobbied for prohibition in the Progressive Era.

Woman's Peace Party   Organization, formed by suffragists in 1915 and led by Jane Addams, that lobbied against war.

women's liberation   Diverse movement arising out of the radical political movements and counterculture of the late 1960s and that variously demanded equal opportunity, rights, wages, respect, and sexual enjoyment for women.

women's rights   Political movement in the antebellum period designed to secure certain forms of legal and political equality for women.

woman suffrage   Women's legal right to vote.

Worcester* v. *Georgia   Supreme Court ruling, which Andrew Jackson refused to enforce, declaring that Georgia violated the sovereignty of the Cherokee Nation.

Works Progress Administration   Major New Deal initiative that provided employment and invested in a variety of small- and large-scale construction, art, and other projects.

World Trade Organization   Large intergovernmental organization, founded in Switzerland in 1995, that regulates international trade and pursues the goals of deregulation, free trade, and globalization.

World Wide Web   Internet-based information system introduced in the early 1990s for linking documents and making them available through a browser.

Wounded Knee Massacre   1890 massacre of Lakota Sioux and Ghost Dancers by the U.S. military, to which the American public mostly reacted favorably.

written constitutions   Genre of texts, which emerged in the late eighteenth century, invested with supreme authority to organize governments and protect citizens.

X

XYZ affair   1798 diplomatic crisis between France and the United States that contributed to an undeclared war.

Y

Yalta Conference   1945 meeting of FDR, Joseph Stalin, and Winston Churchill, during which the "Big Three" sought to advance, but were forced to compromise, their divergent interests in the postwar order.

yellow journalism   Critical term coined in the 1890s to describe sensationalist newspaper stories that had little or no factual basis and that were designed by rival publishers Joseph Pulitzer and William Randolph Hearst to boost sales.

yeoman farmer   Free agricultural landowner, typically without enslaved laborers or many dependents outside the family.

Yorktown   1781 American military victory against the British in Virginia, which effectively destroyed Britain's southern campaign.

Young America   Name adopted in the late 1840s by both the expansionist wing of the Democratic Party and a nationalist literary movement.

Z

Zenger case   1735 trial of New York newspaper publisher Peter Zenger, whom a jury acquitted of the charge of publishing seditious libel.

zoot suit sailor riots   Days-long attack on the Los Angeles Mexican American community in 1943, during which white sailors and police officers beat zoot suiters and destroyed their clothing.

INDEX

Page numbers with the *m* refers to map; *t* refers to table; *f* refers to figure

A

Abenaki Indians, 97, 110
abolitionists/abolitionism. *See also* Douglass, Frederick; Garrison, William Lloyd
anti-Catholicism and, 268, 284–285, 286, 331
charge of Slave Power as first developed by, 262
1844 presidential election and, 226, 290, 292–293, A-16
and evangelical circles, 275
feminist reform movement as emerging out of, 283
flow of tracts from, 261
Fugitive Slave Act (1850) and, 320–321
as fundamental critique of social order, 275
immediatism, 275–276
internal divisions among, 278–279
Jackson's view of, 261
John Brown's raid and, 337
mob violence against, 277–278
petition drives by, 261, 278
political abolitionists, 278
Radical Republicans and, 376, 381, 384
rhetoric of, 247
on role of women, 268
slave narratives and, 277
slave testimony, 276–277
states/regions abolishing slavery, 259
U.S.-Mexican War and (*See* U.S.-Mexican War)
view of colonization by, 260
abortion, 79
abstinence, of temperance movement, 271–274
Acadian diaspora, 110–111
Acoma, NM, 29
Act of Union (1707), 101–102
Act to Amend the Laws Relating to the Post-Office Department (1863), 367*t*

Act to Establish a Department of Agriculture (1862), 367*t*
Adams, Abigail, 136, 180
Adams, Charles Francis, 318
Adams, John
about, 143–144, 145, 161
Declaration of Independence and, 145
election and presidency of, 176, 177, 179, 180, A-15
Adams, John Quincy
about, 203, 218, 220, 221, 261, 265, 293
Adams-Onis Treaty and, 203, 206, 291
election and presidency of, 211, A-15
Adams, Samuel, 119, 121, 124
Adams-Onis Treaty (1819), 203, 206, 291
"An Address Delivered by Abraham Lincoln, Before the Springfield Washington Temperance Society," 272
adelantados, 10
Adena cultures, 4*m*
Adobe housing, 28
Affleck, Thomas, 256
Africa/Africans
contact between America and about, 8–13, 9*m*
Atlantic Ocean islands, 10, 12
Latin Christendom, 10, 11
nation-states, 9–10
Islam and, 11, 12–13
Liberia, 260
in Lower South, 81–83
in North America, 58–64
West African sources of slavery, 12–13, 59*m*
African Americans. *See also* Blacks; free Blacks; slavery
African diaspora and, 62–64
apprehension of by patrollers, 249, 250
Black Codes and, 381–383, 386
in California gold rush, 301
Christianity of, 64, 254, 257

Colored Troops in Civil War, 355, 356
as denied opportunity to serve in U.S.-Mexico War, 295
emancipation of, 259, 353–355
enslavement of, 225, 243, 245, 247, 251
folkways of, 257
gradual abolition, 169–170
limitations of universal manhood suffrage for, 219–220
as members of Seminole Nation, 263
New York Draft Riots and, 367–368
social surveillance of, 254
as sold across state lines, 245
in Union Army, 355
African diaspora, 62–64
African Methodist Episcopal (A.M.E.) Church, 172–173, 209
African slave trade. *See also* slavery
Amistad case, 243, 264–265
Muslims and, 12–13
West African sources of slavery, 12–13, 59*m*
agricultural economy, 85–86
agricultural revolution, 5–6
agriculture. *See also* cotton production; livestock; sugar; tobacco; wheat farms
agricultural revolution, 5–6
corn and maize, 3, 5, 18, 38
indigo production, 74–75
North America before 1600 and, 3–4
Northwestern Europe, 8–10
Panic of 1819 and, 204
sharecropping, 389
before slavery, 54
Alabama, 344
Alamo, Battle of the, 243, 263
Albany, NY, 134
Albany Convention, 104
alcohol
reform movement against, 271–274

temperance campaign, 268, 271–274
water as alternative to, 273
Alcott, Louisa May, 360
Alexander VI, Pope, 14
Alexandria, VA, 87
Algonquian Chief, 20
Algonquian people, 37, 48, 98–99
Alien Acts, 177, 178
Allen, Ethan, 116–117, 123, 129
Allen, Richard, 171–172
"Am I Not a Man and a Brother?," 277
amalgamationists, 336
A.M.E. (African Methodist Episcopal) Church, 172–173, 209
America, naming of, 14
American Anti-Slavery Society, 260, 261, 268, 277, 279
American Bible Society (ABS), 207, 208
American Board of Commissioners of Foreign Missions (ABCFM), 207, 212–213
American Colonization Society, 260
American Female Moral Reform Society, 374
American identity, 146
American Missionary Fellowship, 207
American Museum, 307
American novel, 163–164
American Party. *See* Know-Nothing Party
American Renaissance, 313
American Revolution. *See* Revolutionary War
American Society for the Promotion of Temperance, 271
American Temperance Society, 268
Amherst, Jeffrey, 107, 111–112
Amistad case, 243, 264–265
amputations, 359
Anasazi, 6. *See also* Hohokam people
Ancestral Puebloan, 6
Anderson, "Bloody Bill," 370